# THE NEW BOOK OF
# KNOWLEDGE

## *Home and School*
# READING
# AND
# STUDY
# GUIDES

### GROLIER
E D U C A T I O N A L

The editors of THE NEW BOOK OF KNOWLEDGE wish to acknowledge educational consultant Barbara Darga, whose experience as a teacher and whose research into current curriculum issues and trends guided the development and preparation of this edition of the HOME AND SCHOOL READING AND STUDY GUIDES.

The editors also wish to thank the teachers, librarians, and parents whose experiences, reviews, and suggestions help keep the information in these guides both useful and practical.

For the 2002 edition:
Editors: Donna M. Lusardi; Rosemarie Kent
Copy Editor: Sara A. Boak
Art Director: Elizabeth DeBella
Composition: Emilia Urra Smith; Linda Dillon; Stephanie Grant
Production Manager: Elizabeth Kovats Steger
Production Editor: Carolyn F. Reil

THE HOME AND SCHOOL READING GUIDE
THE HOME AND SCHOOL STUDY GUIDE

# CONTENTS

## PART I · THE READING GUIDE

## PART II · THE STUDY GUIDE

# PART III • ACTIVITIES

# APPENDIX

# PART I
# THE READING GUIDE

# INTRODUCTION

You have probably already discovered that THE NEW BOOK OF KNOWLEDGE is a valuable resource for finding information about a topic of special interest, beginning a school report or project, or answering a specific question. In pursuing your search for information, you may also have had the experience of wanting to know even more about a topic than what you found in its many articles. No single reference work—even one as comprehensive as THE NEW BOOK OF KNOWLEDGE—can contain everything known about a topic. It simply isn't possible to hold within the covers of 21 volumes the vast storehouse of knowledge that has been accumulated during thousands of years of discovery, experience, and research.

The HOME AND SCHOOL READING GUIDE has been compiled to help you expand the information in THE NEW BOOK OF KNOWLEDGE. The READING GUIDE is a unique listing of more than 6,000 quality books dealing with hundreds of different topics. Almost every title in the list has been recommended by parent groups, teachers, librarians, literature specialists, or by young people themselves. Many of the books have also been cited by textbook publishers as recommended supplements to their science, social studies, or language arts series. Where can you find the books that may be of interest to you? The titles in the READING GUIDE should be readily available through your local bookstores or in your school or public library.

You will find the READING GUIDE a handy resource for building collections of books about many different subject areas for users at different ability levels. Because the READING GUIDE is updated each year, it will also help you keep such collections current and relevant to young people's school needs and extracurricular interests.

THE NEW BOOK OF KNOWLEDGE provides additional book listings in two of its articles: "Caldecott and Newbery Medals" and "Children's Literature," both in Volume C.

Nancy Larrick, the Children's Literature Adviser for THE NEW BOOK OF KNOWLEDGE, helped establish the guidelines for the development of the READING GUIDE. The original READING GUIDE was prepared by John T. Gillespie and Christine B. Gilbert, co-editors of *Best Books for Children*, published by the R. R. Bowker Company.

To make it easy for you to use the READING GUIDE with THE NEW BOOK OF KNOWLEDGE, book titles are listed under alphabetically arranged topic headings that correspond directly to the titles of THE NEW BOOK OF KNOWLEDGE articles. Wherever possible, books on a topic cover a range of ability levels from primary to advanced.

Key to abbreviations used in the READING GUIDE:

| | | | |
|---|---|---|---|
| (P) | primary (through 4th grade) | ed. | editor; edited; edition |
| (I) | intermediate (5th through 8th grade) | illus. | illustrator; illustrated |
| | | retel. | reteller; retelling |
| (A) | advanced (9th grade and up) | sel. | selector; selected |
| ad. | adapter; adapted | trans. | translator; translation |
| comp. | compiler; compiled | | |

The following book lists are among the sources used in the preparation of the READING GUIDE:

**Adventuring with Books: A Booklist for Pre-K—Grade 6.** 10th ed., edited by Julie M. Jensen and Nancy L. Rosen, National Council of Teachers of English, 1993.

**Appraisal: Science Books for Young People.** Published three times a year by the Children's Science Book Review Committee, sponsored by the Science and Mathematics Program of Boston University School of Education and the New England Roundtable of Children's Librarians.

**Best Books for Children,** by John T. Gillespie and Corrine J. Naden, R. R. Bowker, 1994 (5th ed.).

**Best Books for Junior High Readers,** by John T. Gillespie, R. R. Bowker, 1991.

**Booklist.** American Library Association.

**Bulletin of the Center for Children's Books.** University of Chicago.

**Children's Books.** New York Public Library. Published annually.

**Children's Catalog.** 16th ed. H. W. Wilson, 1991.

**Children's Choices.** October issues of The Reading Teacher.

**The Elementary School Library Collection,** edited by Lauren K. Lee et al, 19th ed. Brodart, 1994.

**The Horn Book Magazine.** Horn Book, Inc.

**Notable Children's Books,** 1976–80. American Library Association, 1986.

**Notable Children's Trade Books in the Field of Social Studies.** April/May issues of Social Education, a professional journal of the National Council for the Social Studies.

**Outstanding Science Trade Books for Children.** March issues of Science and Children, a professional journal of the National Science Teachers Association.

## ABOLITION MOVEMENT

Altman, Linda Jacobs. *Slavery and Abolition: In American History.* Enslow, 1999. *(I; A)*

Rockwell, Anne F. *Only Passing Through: The Story of Sojourner Truth.* Knopf, 2000. *(P; I)*

## ABORIGINES, AUSTRALIAN

Browne, Rollo. *An Aboriginal Family.* Lerner, 1986. *(P)*

Reynolds, Jan. *Down Under: Vanishing Cultures.* HarBraceJ, 1992. *(P; I)*

## ABORTION

Herda, D. J. *Roe v. Wade: The Abortion Question.* Enslow, 1994. *(I; A)*

Lowenstein, Felicia. *The Abortion Battle: Looking at Both Sides.* Enslow, 1996. *(A)*

Roamine, Deborah S. *Roe vs. Wade: Abortion and the Supreme Court.* Lucent, 1998. *(I; A)*

## ACID RAIN

Baines, John. *Acid Rain.* Steck-Vaughn, 1990. *(I)*

Gay, Kathlyn. *Acid Rain.* Watts, 1983. *(I; A)*

Lucas, Eileen. *Acid Rain.* Children's, 1991. *(I)*

Pringle, Laurence. *Rain of Troubles: The Science and Politics of Acid Rain.* Macmillan, 1988. *(A)*

Turck, Mary. *Acid Rain.* Crestwood, 1990. *(I)*

## ADAMS, JOHN

Dwyer, Frank. *John Adams.* Chelsea House, 1989. *(I)*

Santrey, Laurence. *John Adams: Brave Patriot.* Troll, 1986. *(P; I)*

Stefoff, Rebecca. *John Adams: 2nd President of the United States.* Garrett Educational, 1988. *(A)*

## ADAMS, JOHN QUINCY

Coelho, Tony. *John Quincy Adams.* Chelsea House, 1990. *(I; A)*

Kent, Zachary. *John Quincy Adams: Sixth President of the United States.* Children's, 1987. *(I)*

## ADAMS, SAMUEL

Fritz, Jean. *Why Don't You Get a Horse, Sam Adams?* Putnam, 1974. *(I)*

## ADDAMS, JANE

Kittredge, Mary. *Jane Addams.* Chelsea House, 1988. *(I; A)*

Wheeler, Leslie A. *Jane Addams.* Silver Burdett, 1990. *(I)*

## ADOLESCENCE

Greenberg, Harvey R., M.D. *Hanging In: What You Should Know about Psychotherapy.* Scholastic, 1982. *(A)*

## ADOPTION

Banish, Roslyn, and Jordan-Wong, Jennifer. *A Forever Family.* HarperCollins, 1992. *(P)*

Cohen, Shari. *Coping with Being Adopted.* Rosen, 1988. *(A)*

D'Antonio, Nancy. *Our Baby from China: An Adoption Story.* Albert Whitman, 1997. *(P)*

DuPrau, Jeanne. *Adoption: The Facts, Feelings and Issues of a Double Heritage.* Messner, 1990. *(I; A)*

Gravelle, Karen, and Fischer, Susan. *Where Are My Birth Parents? A Guide for Teenage Adoptees.* Walker, 1993. *(A)*

Hyde, Margaret O. *Foster Care and Adoption.* Watts, 1982. *(I; A)*

Krementz, Jill. *How It Feels to Be Adopted.* Knopf, 1982. *(I)*

Nickman, Steven L. *The Adoption Experience.* Messner, 1985. *(A)*

Rogers, Fred. *Let's Talk about It: Adoption.* Putnam, 1995. *(P)*

Rosenberg, Maxine B. *Being Adopted.* Lothrop, 1984. *(P; I)*

Sobol, Harriet Langsam. *We Don't Look Like Our Mom and Dad.* Coward, 1984. *(P; I)*

Stewart, Gail B. *Adoption.* Crestwood, 1989. *(P; I)*

## ADVERTISING

Day, Nancy. *Advertising: Information or Manipulation?* Enslow, 1999. *(I; A)*

Dunn, John. *Advertising.* Lucent, 1997. *(I;A)*

Gourley, Catherine. *Media Wizards: A Behind-the-Scenes Look at Media Manipulations.* Twenty-First Century, 1999. *(I; A)*

Greenberg, Jan. *Advertising Careers.* Holt, 1987. *(A)*

Klein, Naomi. *No Logo: Taking Aim at the Brand Bullies.* St. Martin's Press, 2000. *(A)*

Mierau, Christina B. *Accept No Substitutes! The History of American Advertising.* Lerner, 2000. *(I; A)*

## AENEID

Church, Alfred J. *The Aeneid for Boys and Girls.* Macmillan, 1962. *(I)*

## AERODYNAMICS

Schultz, Ron. *Looking inside Sports Aerodynamics.* Avalon Travel, 1992. *(I)*

## AFGHANISTAN

*Afghanistan . . . in Pictures.* Lerner, 1989. *(I; A)*

Clifford, Mary Louise. *The Land and People of Afghanistan.* Lippincott, 1989. (rev. ed.) *(I; A)*

Howarth, Michael. *Afghanistan.* Chelsea House, 1988. *(P)*

## AFRICA

*Botswana . . . in Pictures.* Lerner, 1990. *(I; A)*

*Morocco . . . in Pictures.* Lerner, 1989. *(I; A) Tanzania . . . in Pictures.* Lerner, 1988. *(I) Tunisia . . . in Pictures.* Lerner, 1989. *(I)*

Anderson, Lydia. *Nigeria, Cameroon, and the Central African Republic.* Watts, 1981. *(I; A)*

Baynham, Simon. *Africa: From 1945.* Watts, 1987. *(I; A)*

Blumberg, Rhoda. *Southern Africa: South Africa, Namibia, Swaziland, Lesotho, and Botswana.* Watts, 1981. *(I; A)*

Boyd, Herb. *The Former Portuguese Colonies: Angola, Mozambique, Guinea-Bissau, Cape Verde, São Tomé, and Príncipe.* Watts, 1981. *(I; A)*

Chiasson, John. *African Journey.* Bradbury, 1987. *(I; A)*

Conway, Jessica. *Swaziland.* Chelsea House, 1989. *(P; I)*

Davidson, Basil. *The Story of Africa.* Mitchell Beazley, 1984. *(I)*

Ellis, Veronica Freeman. *Afro-Bets First Book About Africa: An Introduction for Young Readers.* Just Us Books, 1990. *(P)*

Fichter, George S. *The Bulge of Africa: Senegal, Guinea, Ivory Coast, Togo, Benin, and Equatorial Guinea.* Watts, 1981. *(I; A)*

Foster, F. Blanche. *East Central Africa: Kenya, Uganda, Tanzania, Rwanda, and Burundi.* Watts, 1981. *(I; A)*

Gilfond, Henry. *Gambia, Ghana, Liberia, and Sierra Leone.* Watts, 1981. *(I; A)*

Godbeer, Deardre. *Somalia.* Chelsea House, 1988. *(P; I)*

Gould, D. E. *Namibia.* Chelsea House, 1988. *(P; I)*

Hathaway, Jim. *Cameroon . . . in Pictures.* Lerner, 1989. *(I)*

Hintz, Martin. *Enchantment of the World Series.* Children's, 1985. *(P;I)*

Holmes, Timothy. *Zambia.* Chelsea House, 1988. *(P; I)*

Hornburger. *African Countries and Cultures: A Concise Illustrated Dictionary.* McKay, 1981. *(I; A)*

Lawson, Don. *South Africa.* Watts, 1986. *(I)*

Margolies, Barbara A. *Rehema's Journey: A Visit in Tanzania.* Scholastic, 1990. *(P)*

McCulla, Patricia E. *Tanzania.* Chelsea House, 1988. *(I)*

Milsome, John. *Sierra Leone.* Chelsea House, 1988. *(P; I)*

Newman, Gerald. *Zaïre, Gabon, and the Congo.* Watts, 1981. *(I; A)*

Pomeray, J. K. *Rwanda.* Chelsea House, 1988. *(I)*

Taylor, L. B., Jr. *South East Africa: Zimbabwe, Zambia, Malawi, Madagascar, Mauritius, and Réunion.* Watts, 1981. *(I; A)*

Tonsing-Carter, Betty. *Lesotho.* Chelsea House, 1988. *(P; I)*

Wolbers, Marian F. *Burundi.* Chelsea House, 1989. *(I)*

Woods, Harold, and Woods, Geraldine. *The Horn of Africa: Ethiopia, Sudan, Somalia, and Djibouti.* Watts, 1981. *(I; A)*

Zimmerman, Robert. *The Gambia.* Children's, 1994. *(A)*

## AFRICA, ART AND ARCHITECTURE OF

Kerina, Jane. *African Crafts.* Lion, 1970. *(P; I)*

Price, Christine. *Dancing Masks of Africa.* Scribner's, 1975. *(P; I)*

## AFRICA, LITERATURE OF

Aardema, Verna, comp. *Misoso: Once upon a Time Tales from Africa.* Knopf, 1994. *(P)*

Aardema, Verna. *Bringing the Rain to Kapiti Plain.* Dial, 1981; *Why Mosquitoes Buzz in People's Ears,* 1978. *(P)*

Abrahams, Roger. *African Folktales.* Pantheon, 1983. *(I)*

Courlander, Harold. *A Treasury of African Folktales.* Crown, 1975. *(P); The Crest and the Hide and Other African Stories.* Coward, 1982. *(I)*

Courlander, Harold, and Herzog, George, eds. *The Cow-Tail Switch and Other West African Stories.* Holt, 1975. *(I)*

Feelings, Muriel. *Jambo Means Hello: Swahili Alphabet Book.* Dial, 1981. *(P)*

Mathabane, Mark. *Kaffir Boy.* New American Library, 1987. *(I; A)*

Parrinder, Geoffrey. *African Mythology.* Harper, 1986 (rev. ed.). *(A)*

Sullivan, Charles, ed. *Children of Promise: African-American Literature and Art for Young People.* Abrams, 1991. *(I; A)*

## AFRICAN AMERICANS

Adams, Russell L. *Great Negroes Past and Present.* Afro-Am Publishing, 1984. *(I)*

Altman, Susan. *Extraordinary Black Americans: From Colonial to Contemporary Times.* Children's, 1989. *(I)*

Andrews, Bert. *In the Shadow of the Great White Way: Images from the Black Theatre.* Thunder's Mouth Press, 1989. *(I; A)*

Ashabranner, Brent. *The New African Americans.* Linnet, 1999. *(I; A)*

Brodie, James Michael. *Created Equal: The Lives and Ideas of Black American Innovators.* Morrow, 1993. *(A)*

Curtis, Christopher Paul. *The Watsons Go to Birmingham—1963.* Delacorte, 1995. *(I)*

De Angelis, Gina. *Black Cowboys.* Chelsea House, 1997. *(I)*

Everett, Gwen. *Li'l Sis and Uncle Willie.* Rizzoli, 1991. *(P; I)*

Evitts, William J. *Captive Bodies, Free Spirits: The Story of Southern Slavery.* Messner, 1985. *(I)*

Greene, Carol. *Thurgood Marshall: First African-American Supreme Court Justice.* Children's, 1991. *(P; I)*

Hacker, Carlotta. *Great African Americans in the Arts.* Crabtree, 1997. *(I)*

Hamilton, Virginia. *Anthony Burns: The Defeat and Triumph of a Fugitive Slave.* Knopf, 1988. *(I; A); Drylongso.* Harcourt, 1992. *(P; I); The People Could Fly: American Black Folktales.* Dillon, 1985. *(I)*

Hancock, Sibyl. *Famous Firsts of Black Americans.* Pelican, 1983. *(P; I)*

Haskins, Jim. *Outward Dreams: Black Inventors and Their Inventions.* Walker, 1991. *(I)*

Hoobler, Dorothy, and Hoobler, Thomas. *The African American Family Album.* Oxford University Press, 1995. *(I; A)*

Igus, Toyomi, ed. *Great Women in the Struggle.* Just Us Books, 1991. *(P; I)*

Johnson, James Weldon. *Lift Every Voice and Sing*. Walker, 1993. *(P; I; A)*

Klots, Steve. *Richard Allen: Religious Leader and Social Activist*. Chelsea House, 1991. *(I)*

Lawrence, Jacob. *The Great Migration: An American Story*. HarperCollins, 1994. *(I)*

Lester, Julius. *Long Journey Home: Stories from Black History*. Dial, 1972. *(I)*; *Tales of Uncle Remus and The Adventures of Brer Rabbit*. Dial, 1987. *(P; I)*; *This Strange New Feeling*. Dial, 1982. *(A)*

Lucas, Eileen. *Cracking the Wall: The Struggles of the Little Rock Nine*. Carolrhoda, 1998. *(P)*

McKissack, Patricia. *Mary McLeod Bethune: A Great American Educator*. Children's, 1985. *(P; I)*

McKissack, Patricia, and McKissack, Fredrick. *African-American Inventors*. Millbrook, 1994. *(I; A)*; *African-American Scientists*. Millbrook, 1994. *(I)*; *Black Diamond: The Story of the Negro Baseball Leagues*. Scholastic, 1994. *(I)*

Medearis, Angela Shelf. *Come This Far to Freedom: A History of African Americans*. Atheneum, 1993. *(I)*

Myers, Walter Dean. *Now Is Your Time: The African-American Struggle for Freedom*. HarperCollins, 1991. *(I; A)*

Parker, Janice. *Great African Americans in Film*. Crabtree, 1997. *(I)*

Parks, Rosa, with Haskins, Jim. *Rosa Parks: My Story*. Dial, 1992. *(I)*

Potter, Joan, and Clayton, Constance. *African-American Firsts*. Pinto Press, 1994; *(A) African Americans Who Were First*. Dutton/Cobblehill, 1997. *(I)*

Rediger, Pat. *Great African Americans in Business*. Crabtree, 1996. *(P; I)*; *Great African Americans in Civil Rights*. Crabtree, 1996. *(P; I)*; *Great African Americans in Literature*. Crabtree, 1996. *(P; I)*

Reef, Catherine. *Buffalo Soldiers*. 21st Century, 1993. *(I; A)*

Ringgold, Faith. *Tar Beach*. Crown, 1991. *(P; I)*

Roberts, Naurice. *Barbara Jordan: The Great Lady from Texas*. Children's, 1984. *(I; A)*

Rummel, Jack. *Malcolm X: Militant Black Leader*. Chelsea House, 1989. *(I; A)*

Silverman, Jerry. *Just Listen to This Song I'm Singing: African-American History Through Song*. Millbrook, 1996. *(I; A)*

Spangler, Earl. *Blacks in America*. Lerner, 1980 (rev. ed.). *(I; A)*

Tate, Eleanora E., and Haskins, James. *African American Musicians*. Wiley, John & Sons, Inc., 2000. *(I; A)*

Yannuzzi, Della A. *Madam C. J. Walker: Self-Made Businesswoman*. Enslow, 2000. *(I; A)*

## AGING

Dychtwald, Ken, and Flower, Joe. *Age Wave: The Challenges and Opportunities of an Aging America*. Tarcher, 1989. *(A)*

Helmer, Diana S. *Let's Talk About When Someone You Love Is in a Nursing Home*. Rosen, 1998. *(P)*

Landau, Elaine. *Growing Old in America*. Messner, 1985. *(I)*

Langone, John. *Growing Older: What Young People Should Know about Aging*. Little, 1990. *(I; A)*

LeShan, Eda. *Grandparents: A Special Kind of Love*. Macmillan, 1984. *(I)*

Sobol, Harriet. *Grandpa: A Young Man Grown Old*. Coward, 1980. *(I)*

Stewart, Gail B. *The Elderly*. Lucent Books, 1996. *(I; A)*

Worth, Richard. *You'll Be Old Someday, Too*. Watts, 1986. *(A)*

## AGRICULTURE

Bowman, Keith. *Agriculture*. Silver Burdett, 1987. *(I)*

Horwitz, Elinor L. *On the Land: The Evolution of American Agriculture*. Atheneum, 1980. *(I; A)*

Hughes, Meredith Sayles. *Spill the Beans and Pass the Peanuts: Legumes*. Lerner, 1999. *(P; I)*

Murphy, Wendy. *The Futureworld of Agriculture*. Watts, 1985. *(I; A)*

White, William, C., and Collins, Donald N. *Opportunities in Agriculture Careers*. VGM Career Books, 1987. *(A)*

Woods, Michael, and Woods, Mary B. *Ancient Agriculture: From Foraging to Farming*. Runestone, 2000. *(I)*

## AGRICULTURE, UNITED STATES DEPARTMENT OF

Hurt, Douglas R., and Schlesinger, Arthur M. *The Department of Agriculture*. Chelsea House, 1989. *(P; I)*

## AIDS

Cozic, Charles P., ed. *The AIDS Crisis*. Greenhaven, 1991. *(I; A)*

Eagles, Douglas A. *The Menace of AIDS: A Shadow on Our Land*. Watts, 1988. *(I)*

Ford, Michael Thomas. *The Voices of AIDS*. Morrow, 1995. *(I; A)*

Gonzales, Doreen. *AIDS: Ten Stories of Courage*. Enslow, 1996. *(I)*

Hawkes, Nigel. *AIDS*. Watts, 1987. *(I)*

Hyde, Margaret O., and Forsyth, Elizabeth H. *AIDS: What Does It Mean to You?* Walker, 1990. (rev. ed.) *(I; A)*; *Know about AIDS*. Walker, 1994. (rev. ed.) *(P; I)*

Jussim, Daniel. *AIDS & HIV: Risky Business*. Enslow, 1997. *(I;A)*

Kuklin, Susan. *Fighting Back: What Some People Are Doing about AIDS*. Putnam, 1989. *(A)*

Kurland, Morton L. *Coping with AIDS: Facts and Fears*. Rosen, 1988. *(A)*

Landau, Elaine. *We Have AIDS*. Watts, 1990. *(I; A)*

Madaras, Lynda. *Lynda Madaras Talks to Teens about AIDS: An Essential Guide for Parents, Teachers, and Young People*. Harper, 1988. *(A)*

Nash, Carol Rust. *AIDS: Choices for Life*. Enslow, 1997. *(I; A)*

Nourse, Alan E. *AIDS*. Watts, 1989. *(I; A)*

White, Ryan, and Cunningham, Ann Marie. *Ryan White: My Own Story.* Dial, 1991. *(I; A)*

Wilson, Jonnie. *AIDS.* Lucent Books, 1989. *(I; A)*

## AIRPLANE MODELS

Berliner, Don. *Flying-Model Airplanes.* Lerner, 1982; *Scale-Model Airplanes,* 1982. *(P; I)*

Herda, O. J. *Model Historical Aircraft.* Watts, 1982. *(I; A)*

Radlauer, Ed. *Model Fighter Planes.* Children's, 1983. *(P; I)*

## AIR POLLUTION

Dolan, Edward F. *Our Poisoned Sky.* Cobblehill, 1991. *(I; A)*

Kahl, Jonathan D.W. *Hazy Skies: Weather and the Environment.* Lerner, 1997. *(I)*

Miller, Christina G., and Berry, Louise A. *Air Alert: Rescuing the Earth's Atmosphere.* Simon & Schuster, 1996. *(I; A)*

Yount, Lisa, and Rodgers, Mary M. *Our Endangered Planet.* Lerner, 1995. *(I)*

## AIRPORTS

Davis, Meredith. *Up and Away!: Taking a Flight.* Mondo, 1997. *(P)*

Sullivan, George E. *How an Airport Really Works.* Dutton, 1993. *(I; A)*

## ALABAMA

Davis, Lucile. *Alabama.* Children's Press, 1999. *(I; A)*

Thompson, Kathleen. *Alabama.* Raintree, 1988. *(P; I)*

## ALASKA

*People of the Ice and Snow.* Time-Life, 1994. *(I; A)*

Cheney, Cora. *Alaska: Indians, Eskimos, Russians, and the Rest.* Dodd, 1980. *(I)*

Dubois, Muriel L. *Alaska: Facts and Symbols.* Capstone/Hilltop, 2000. *(P)*

Lewin, Ted. *World within a World— Pribilofs* Dodd, 1980. *(I)*

Murphy, Claire Rudolf. *A Child's Alaska.* Alaska Northwest Books, 1994. *(P; I)*

Stefansson, Evelyn, and Yahn, Linda. *Here Is Alaska.* Scribner's, 1983 (4th ed.). *(I; A)*

Thompson, Kathleen. *Alaska.* Raintree, 1988. *(P; I)*

## ALBANIA

Lear, Aaron E. *Albania.* Chelsea House, 1987. *(A)*

## ALBERTA

Yates, Sarah. *Alberta.* Lerner, 1998. *(P; I)*

## ALCOHOLISM

Barbour, Scott, ed. *Alcohol: Opposing Viewpoints.* Greenhaven, 1997. *(A)*

Claypool, Jane. *Alcohol and You.* Watts, 1988. (rev. ed.) *(I; A)*

Graeber, Laurel. *Are You Dying for a Drink?: Teenagers and Alcohol Abuse.* Messner, 1985. *(A)*

Hyde, Margaret O., and Setaro, John F. *Alcohol 101: An Overview for Teens.* Twenty-First Century, 1999. *(I; A)*

Monroe, Judy. *Alcohol.* Enslow, 1994. *(I; A)*

Nielsen, Nancy J. *Teen Alcoholism.* Lucent Books, 1990. *(I)*

O'Neill, Catherine. *Focus on Alcohol.* 21st Century Books, 1990. *(I)*

Rosenberg, Maxine B. *Not My Family: Sharing the Truth about Alcoholism.* Bradbury, 1988. *(I)*

Ryan, Elizabeth A. *Straight Talk about Drugs and Alcohol.* Facts on File, 1996. *(I; A)*

Silverstein, Herma. *Alcoholism.* Watts, 1990. *(I; A)*

Torr, James D., ed. *Alcoholism.* Greenhaven, 2000. *(I; A)*

Wijnberg, Ellen. *Alcohol.* Raintree Steck-Vaughn, 1993. *(I; A)*

## ALCOTT, LOUISA MAY

Burke, Kathleen. *Louisa May Alcott.* Chelsea House, 1987. *(I; A)*

Greene, Carol. *Louisa May Alcott: Author, Nurse, Suffragette.* Children's, 1984. *(I)*

Johnston, Norma. *Louisa May: The World and Works of Louisa May Alcott.* Four Winds, 1991. *(I; A)*

Meigs, Cornelia. *Invincible Louisa.* Little, 1968. *(A)*

Santrey, Laurence. *Louisa May Alcott: Young Writer.* Troll, 1986. *(P; I)*

## ALEXANDER

Van der Kiste, John. *The Romanovs 1818-1959: Alexander II of Russia and His Family.* Sutton, 1998. *(A)*

## ALEXANDER THE GREAT

Harris, Nathaniel. *Alexander the Great and the Greeks.* Bookwright, 1986. *(I)*

Krensky, Stephen. *Conqueror and Hero: The Search for Alexander.* Little, 1981. *(I)*

## ALGAE

Daegling, Mary. *Monster Seaweeds: The Story of Giant Kelp.* Dillon, 1986. *(I)*

Kavaler, Lucy. *Green Magic: Algae Rediscovered.* Harper, 1983. *(I; A)*

## ALGEBRA

Stallings, Pat. *Puzzling Your Way into Algebra.* Activity Resources, 1978 (new ed.). *(I; A)*

## ALGERIA

Kaqda, Falaq. *Algeria.* Marshall Cavendish, 1997. *(I)*

## ALLEN, ETHAN

Holbrook, Stewart. *America's Ethan Allen.* Houghton, n.d. *(I)*

Peck, Robert Newton. *Rabbits and Redcoats.* Walker, 1976. *(I)*

## ALPHABET

*Scrawl! Writing in Ancient Times.* Runestone Press, 1994. *(I)*

Berger, Terry. *Ben's ABC Day.* Lothrop, 1982. *(P)*

Boynton, Sandra. *A Is for Angry.* Workman, 1983. *(P)*

Brunhoff, Laurent de. *Babar's ABC.* Random House, 1983. *(P)*

Greenaway, Kate. *A— Apple Pie.* Warne, 1987 (rev. ed.). *(P)*

Isadora, Rachel. *City Seen from A to Z.* Greenwillow, 1983. *(P)*

Jewell, Nancy. *ABC Cat.* Harper, 1983. *(P)*

Kaye, Cathryn Berger. *Word works: Why the Alphabet Is a Kid's Best Friend.* Little, 1985. *(I)*

Lear, Edward. *An Edward Lear Alphabet.* Lothrop, 1983. *(P)*

Oxenbury, Helen. *Helen Oxenbury's ABC of Things.* Delacorte, 1983. *(P)*

Samoyault, Tiphaine. *Alphabetical Order: How the Alphabet Began.* Viking, 1998. *(P; I)*

Scarry, Richard. *Richard Scarry's Find Your ABC's.* Random House, 1973. *(P)*

Seuss, Dr. *Dr. Seuss' ABC.* Random House, 1963. *(P)*

Warburton, Lois. *The Beginning of Writing.* Lucent Books, 1990. *(I)*

## ALUMINUM

Heiserman, David L. *Exploring Chemical Elements and Their Compounds.* McGraw-Hill, 1991. *(A)*

## AMAZON RIVER

Cheney, Glenn Alan. *The Amazon.* Watts, 1984. *(I; A)*

Cousteau Society. *An Adventure in the Amazon.* Simon & Schuster, 1992. *(P; I)*

Pollard, Michael. *The Amazon.* Benchmark, 1997. *(P; I)*

Reynolds, Jan. *Amazon Basin: Vanishing Cultures.* Harcourt, 1993. *(P; I)*

## AMERICAN LITERATURE

Plotz, Helen, ed. *The Gift Outright: America to Her Poets.* Greenwillow, 1977. *(I; A)*

Thum, Marcella. *Exploring Literary America.* Atheneum, 1979. *(I; A)*

## AMPHIBIANS

Gove, Doris. *Red-Spotted Newt.* Atheneum, 1994. *(I)*

Kalman, Bobbie, and Langille, Jacqueline. *What Is an Amphibian?* Crabtree/A Bobbie Kalman Bk., 1999. *(P)*

## ANCIENT CIVILIZATIONS

Board, Tessa. *Ancient Greece.* Watts, 1984 (rev. ed.). *(P; I)*

Broida, Marian. *Ancient Egyptians and Their Neighbors: An Activity Guide.* Chicago Review, 1999. *(I)*

Burrell, Roy. *The Greeks.* Oxford University Press, 1990. *(I)*

Cohen, Daniel. *Ancient Egypt.* Doubleday, 1990. *(P; I)*

Connolly, Peter. *Pompeii.* Oxford University Press, 1990. *(I)*

Corbishley, Mike. *The Roman World.* Watts, 1987. *(I; A)*

Defrates, Joanna. *What Do We Know about the Egyptians?* Peter Bedrick, 1991. *(I)*

Goor, Ron, and Goor, Nancy. *Pompeii.* Crowell, 1987. *(I)*

Harris, Geraldine. *Ancient Egypt.* Facts on File, 1990. *(I)*

Hart, George. *Ancient Egypt.* Knopf, 1990. *(I)*

Hoobler, Dorothy, and Hoobler, Thomas. *Lost Civilizations.* Walker, 1992. *(P; I)*

Hull, Robert. *Greece.* Raintree/Steck-Vaughn, 1998. *(I; A)*

James, Simon. *Ancient Rome.* Knopf, 1990. *(I)*

Koenig, Viviane, and Ageorges, Veronique. *The Ancient Egyptians: Life in the Nile Valley.* Millbrook, 1992. *(I)*

Landau, Elaine. *The Assyrians; The Sumerians.* Millbrook Press, 1997. *(I)*

Macdonald, Fiona. *A Greek Temple.* Peter Bedrick, 1992. *(P; I)*

Millard, Anne. *Ancient Civilizations.* Watts, 1983. *(P; I)*

Pearson, Anne. *Ancient Greece.* Knopf, 1992. *(P; I; A)*

Perl, Lila. *Mummies, Tombs and Treasure: Secrets of Ancient Egypt.* Clarion, 1987. *(P)*

Reeves, Nicholas. *Into the Mummy's Tomb: The Real-Life Discovery of Tutankhamun's Treasures.* Scholastic, 1992. *(I)*

Robinson, Charles A., Jr. *First Book of Ancient Egypt; First Book of Ancient Greece.* Watts, 1984 (rev. by Lorna Greenberg). *(I; A)*

Rutland, Jonathan. *See Inside a Roman Town.* Kingfisher, 1986. *(I)*

Sheehan, Sean. *Great African Kingdoms.* Raintree/Steck-Vaughn, 1998. *(I; A) Ancient Rome.* Raintree/Steck-Vaughn, 1999. *(P; I)*

Sheehan, Sean, and Levy, Pat. *Rome.* Raintree/Steck-Vaughn, 1998. *(I; A)*

Stolz, Mary. *Zekmet, the Stone Carver: A Tale of Ancient Egypt.* Harcourt, 1988. *(P; I)*

Tubb, Jonathan. *Bible Lands.* Knopf, 1991. *(I; A)*

## ANDERSEN, HANS CHRISTIAN

Andersen, Hans Christian. *Hans Andersen's Fairy Tales.* Penguin, 1981; *Hans Christian Andersen's Favorite Fairy Tales.* Western, 1974; *Michael Hague's Favorite Hans Christian Andersen Fairy Tales.* Holt, 1981. *(I)*

## ANESTHESIA

Fradin, Dennis Brindell. *We Have Conquered Pain: The Discovery of Anesthesia.* Simon & Schuster, 1996. *(I)*

Galas, Judith C. *Anesthetics: Surgery without Pain.* Lucent, 1992. *(I; A)*

## ANGOLA

Boyd, Herb. *The Former Portuguese Colonies: Angola, Mozambique, Guinea-Bissau, Cape Verde, São Tomé, and Príncipe.* Watts, 1981. *(I; A)*

## ANIMALS

Arnold, Caroline. *South American Animals.* Morrow, 1999. *(P)*

Brooks, Bruce. *Making Sense: Animal Perception and Communication.* Farrar, 1993. *(I)*

Bruemmer, Fred. *Arctic Animals.* North Word, 1987. *(A)*

Cohen, Daniel. *Animal Rights: A Handbook for Young Adults.* Millbrook, 1993. *(I; A)*

Collard, Sneed B. *Making Animal Babies.* Houghton, 2000. *(P)*

Curtis, Patricia. *Animals You Never Even Heard Of.* Little, 1997. *(P); Aquatic Animals in the Wild and in Captivity.* Lodestar, 1992. *(I)*

Cutchins, Judy, and Johnston, Ginny. *Parenting Papas: Unusual Animal Fathers.* Morrow, 1994. *(I)*

Evans, Lisa Gollin. *An Elephant Never Forgets Its Snorkel: How Animals Survive without Tools and Gadgets.* Crown, 1992. *(I)*

Facklam, Margery. *Bees Dance and Whales Sing.* Sierra, 1992. *(I)*

Goble, Paul. *The Great Race of the Birds and Animals.* Bradbury, 1985. *(P)*

Gutfreund, Geraldine Marshall. *Animals Have Cousins Too: Five Surprising Relatives of Animals You Know.* Watts, 1990. *(P; I)*

Herbst, Judith. *Animal Amazing.* Atheneum, 1991. *(I)*

Hickman, Pamela. *Animals in Motion: How Animals Swim, Jump, Slither and Glide.* Kids Can, 2000. *(P; I)*

Hodgkins, Fran. *Animals Among Us: Living with Suburban Wildlife.* Shoe String/Linnet, 2000. *(I)*

Johnston, Ginny, and Cutchins, Judy. *Windows on Wildlife.* Morrow, 1990. *(P; I)*

Kaner, Etta. *Animal Defenses: How Animals Protect Themselves.* Kids Can, 1999. *(P; I)*

Kitchen, Bert. *And So They Build.* Candlewick, 1993. *(P; I)*

Lauber, Patricia. *Fur, Feathers, and Flippers: How Animals Live Where They Do.* Scholastic, 1994. *(P; I)*

Lesinski, Jeanne M. *Exotic Invaders: Killer Bees, Fire Ants, and Other Alien Species Are Infesting America!* Walker, 1996. *(P; I)*

Loewer, Peter. *The Inside-Out Stomach: An Introduction to Animals without Backbones.* Atheneum, 1990. *(P; I)*

Matthews, Rupert. *Ice Age Animals.* Bookwright, dist. by Watts, 1990. *(P; I)*

Paladino, Catherine. *Our Vanishing Farm Animals: Saving America's Rare Breeds.* Joy Street, 1991. *(P; I)*

Parsons, Alexandra. *Amazing Poisonous Animals.* Knopf, 1989. *(P)*

Presnall, Judith. *Animals That Glow.* Watts, 1993. *(I)*

Pringle, Laurence. *Feral: Tame Animals Gone Wild.* Macmillan, 1983. *(I; A)*

Riha, Suzanne. *Animal Journeys: Life Cycles and Migrations; Animals at Rest: Sleeping Patterns and Habitats.* Blackbirch, 1999. *(P; I)*

Shedd, Warner. *The Kids' Wildlife Book: Exploring Animal Worlds through Indoor/Outdoor Experiences.* Williamson, 1994. *(P; I)*

Simon, Seymour. *They Walk the Earth: The Extraordinary Travels of Animals on Land.* Harcourt/Browndeer, 2000. *(P; I)*

Sowler, Sandie. *Amazing Animal Disguises.* Knopf, 1992. *(P); Amazing Armored Animals.* Knopf, 1992. *(P)*

Staple, Michele, and Gamlin, Linda. *The Random House Book of 1001 Questions and Answers about Animals.* Random House, 1990. *(P; I; A)*

Taylor, Barbara. *The Animals Atlas.* Knopf, 1992. *(I; A)*

Taylor, David. *Nature's Creatures of the Dark.* Dial, 1993. *(P; I)*

Taylor, Kim. *Hidden by Darkness.* Delacorte, 1990. *(I); Hidden Inside.* Delacorte, 1990. *(I); Hidden Underneath.* Delacorte, 1990. *(I); Hidden under Water.* Delacorte, 1990. *(I)*

Thomas, Peggy. *Big Cat Conservation; Reptile Rescue.* Twenty-First Century, 2000. *(I)*

Van Der Meer, Atie and Ron. *Amazing Animal Senses.* Joy Street, 1990. *(P; I)*

Whyman, Kate. *The Animal Kingdom.* Raintree/Steck-Vaughn, 1999. *(I)*

Yabuuchi, Masayuki. *Animals Sleeping.* Putnam, 1983. *(P)*

Zoehfeld, Kathleen Weidner. *What Lives in a Shell?* HarperCollins, 1994. *(P)*

## ANIMATION

Hahn, Don. *Disney's Animation Magic: A Behind-the-Scenes Look at How an Animated Film Is Made.* Disney, 1996. *(P; I)*

Scott, Elaine. *Look Alive: Behind the Scenes of an Animated Film.* Morrow, 1992. *(P; I; A)*

Thomas, Bob. *Disney's Art of Animation: From Mickey Mouse to Beauty and the Beast.* Hyperion, 1991. *(P; I; A)*

## ANTARCTICA

Chester, Jonathan. *A for Antarctica.* Tricycle, 1995. *(P; I)*

Hackwell, W. John. *Desert of Ice: Life and Work in Antarctica.* Scribner's, 1991. *(I; A)*

Johnson, Rebecca L. *Science on the Ice: An Antarctic Journal.* Lerner, 1995. *(I;A)*

Lye, Keith. *Take a Trip to Antarctica.* Watts, 1984. *(P; I)*

McMillan, Bruce. *Summer Ice: Life along the Antarctic Peninsula.* Houghton, 1995. *(I)*

Pringle, Laurence. *Antarctica: Our Last Unspoiled Continent.* Simon & Schuster, 1992. *(I; A)*

Reader's Digest Press. *Antarctica.* Random House, 1985. *(A)*

Sayre, April Pulley. *Antarctica.* Twenty-First Century, 1998. *(I)*

Wheeler, Sara. *Greetings from Antarctica.* Peter Bedrick, 1999. *(P; I)*

Woods, Michael. *Science on Ice: Research in the Antarctic.* Millbrook, 1995. *(I; A)*

## ANTHONY, SUSAN B.

Archer, Jules. *Breaking Barriers: The Feminist Revolution from Susan B. Anthony to Margaret Sanger to Betty Friedan.* Penguin Putnam, 1996. *(A)*

Kendall, Martha E. *Susan B. Anthony: Voice for Women's Voting Rights.* Enslow, 1997. *(I)*

## ANTHROPOLOGY

Asimov, Isaac. *Our Human Roots.* Walker, 1979. *(I)*

Bell, Neill. *Only Human: Why We Are the Way We Are.* Little, 1983. *(P; I)*

Branigan, Keith. *Prehistory.* Watts, 1984. *(I; A)*

Corbishley, Mike. *What Do We Know about Prehistoric People?* Peter Bedrick, 1995. *(I)*

Coville, Bruce. *Prehistoric People.* Doubleday, 1990. *(I)*

Fisher, Maxine P. *Recent Revolutions in Anthropology.* Watts, 1986. *(A)*

Gallant, Roy A. *Early Humans.* Marshall Cavendish/ Benchmark, 1999. *(I; A)*

Jackson, Donna M. *The Bone Detectives: How Forensic Anthropologists Solve Crimes and Uncover Mysteries of the Dead.* Little, Brown, 1996. *(I; A)*

Jaspersohn, William. *How People First Lived.* Watts, 1985. *(P)*

Johanson, Donald C., and O'Farrell, Kevin. *Journey from the Dawn: Life with the World's First Family.* Villard, 1990. *(I; A)*

Lasky, Kathryn. *Traces of Life.* Morrow, 1989. *(I; A)*

Leakey, Richard E. *Human Origins.* Dutton, 1982. *(I; A)*

Leakey, Richard E., and Lewin, Roger. *People of the Lake.* Avon, 1983. *(I; A)*

Martell, Hazel Mary. *Over 6,000 Years Ago: in the Stone Age.* Macmillan, 1992. *(I)*

Merriman, Nick. *Early Humans.* Knopf, 1989. *(P; I; A)*

Milbauer, Barbara. *Suppose You Were a Netsilik: Teenagers in Other Societies.* Messner, 1981. *(A)*

Millard, Anne. *Early People.* Watts, 1982. *(I; A)*

Nance, John. *Lobo of the Tasaday: A Stone Age Boy Meets the Modern World.* Pantheon, 1982. *(A)*

Sattler, Helen Roney. *The Earliest Americans.* Clarion, 1993. *(I; A); Hominids: A Look Back at Our Ancestors.* Lothrop, 1988. *(I; A)*

## ANTS

Cook, David. *Small World of Ants.* Watts, 1981. *(P)*

Dorros, Arthur. *Ant Cities.* Crowell, 1987. *(P)*

Fischer-Nagel, Heiderose, and Fischer-Nagel, Andrea. *An Ant Colony.* Carolrhoda, 1989. *(P; I)*

Overbeck, Cynthia. *Ants.* Lerner, 1982. *(P)*

Pascoe, Elaine. *Ants.* Blackbirch, 1998. *(P; I)*

Patent, Dorothy. *Looking at Ants.* Holiday, 1989. *(P; I)*

## APES

Arnold, Caroline. *Orangutan.* Morrow, 1990. *(I)*

Bailey, Jill. *Gorilla Rescue.* Steck-Vaughn, 1990. *(P; I)*

Barrett, N. S. *Monkeys and Apes.* Watts, 1988. *(P; I)*

Fossey, Dian. *Gorillas in the Mist.* Houghton, 1983. *(A)*

Gallardo, Evelyn. *Among the Orangutans: The Birute Galdikas Story.* Chronicle, 1993. *(P)*

Gelman, Rita Golden. *Monkeys and Apes of the World.* Watts, 1990. *(P)*

Goodall, Jane. *The Chimpanzee Family Book.* Picture Book Studio, 1989. *(P; I)*

Hunt, Patricia. *Gibbons.* Dodd, 1983. *(P; I)*

McDearmon, Kay. *Orangutans.* Dodd, 1983. *(P; I)*

Schlein, Miriam. *Gorillas.* Atheneum, 1990. *(I)*

## APPLE

Bourgeois, Paulette. *The Amazing Apple Book.* Addison Wesley Longman, 1990. *(P; I)*

Gibbons, Gail. *Apples.* Holiday, 2000. *(P)*

## AQUARIUMS

Braemer, Helga, and Scheurmann, Ines. *Tropical Fish.* Barron, 1983. *(I; A)*

Broekel, Ray. *Aquariums and Terrariums.* Children's, 1982; *Tropical Fish,* 1983. *(P)*

Carrington, Neville. *A Fishkeeper's Guide to Maintaining a Healthy Aquarium.* Arco, 1986. *(A)*

Simon, Seymour. *Tropical Saltwater Aquariums: How to Set Them Up and Keep Them Going.* Viking, 1976. *(P; I)*

Watts, Barrie. *Keeping Minibeasts Series.* Watts, 1989. *(P)*

## AQUINO, CORAZON C.

Chua-Eoan, Howard. *Corazon Aquino.* Chelsea House, 1987. *(A)*

Haskins, James. *Corazon Aquino: Leader of the Philippines.* Enslow, 1988. *(A)*

Siegel, Beatrice. *Cory: Corazon Aquino and the Philippines.* Lodestar, 1988. *(I)*

## ARACHNIDS

Pipe, Jim. *The Giant Book of Bugs and Creepy Crawlies.* Millbrook Press, 1998. *(P)*

## ARCHAEOLOGY

Anderson, Joan. *From Map to Museum: Uncovering Mysteries of the Past.* Morrow, 1988. *(P)*

Arnold, Caroline. *Easter Island: Giant Stone Statues Tell of a Rich and Tragic Past.* Clarion, 2000. *(P; I); Dinosaurs Down Under: And Other Fossils from Australia.* Clarion, 1989. *(P; I)*

Bishop, Nic. *Digging for Bird-Dinosaurs: An Expedition to Madagascar.* Houghton Mifflin, 2000. *(I)*

Caselli, Giovanni. *In Search of Troy: One Man's Quest for Homer's Fabled City; In Search of Tutankhamun: The Discovery of a King's Tomb.* NTC, 1999. *(P; I)*

Ford, Barbara, and Switzer, David C. *The Underwater Dig: The Excavation of a Revolutionary War Privateer.* Morrow, 1982. *(P; I)*

Goor, Ron. *Pompeii: Exploring a Roman Ghost Town.* Crowell, 1986. *(P; I)*

Hackwell, W. John. *Digging to the Past: Excavations in Ancient Lands.* Scribner's, 1986. *(I; A)*

Kunhardt, Edith. *Pompeii: Buried Alive!* Random House, 1987. *(I)*

Lasky, Kathryn. *Traces of Life: The Origins of Humankind.* Morrow, 1989. *(I; A)*

Marston, Elsa. *Mysteries in American Archeology.* Walker, 1986. *(A)*

Patent, Dorothy Hinshaw. *The Incredible Story of China's Buried Warriors; Lost City of Pompeii.* Marshall Cavendish, 1999. *(I; A)*

Perl, Lila. *Mummies, Tombs, and Treasure.* Clarion, 1987. *(I)*

Rollin, Sue. *The Illustrated Atlas of Archaeology.* Watts, 1982. *(P; I)*

Sloan, Christopher. *Feathered Dinosaurs.* National Geographic, 2000. *(I)*

Snyder, Thomas F. *Archeology Search Book.* McGraw, 1982. *(P; I; A)*

Tantillo, Joe. *Amazing Ancient Treasures.* Pantheon, 1983. *(P; I)*

Ventura, Piero, and Ceserani, Gian Paolo. *In Search of Ancient Crete.* Silver Burdett, 1985. *(I; A); In Search of Troy,* 1985. *(I; A); In Search of Tutankhamun,* 1985. *(I; A)*

Williams, Barbara. *Breakthrough: Women in Archaeology.* Walker, 1981. *(I; A)*

## ARCHERY

Thomas, Art. *Archery Is for Me.* Lerner, 1981. *(P; I)*

## ARCHITECTURE

Carter, Katherine. *Houses.* Children's, 1982. *(P)*

Fagg, C. D. *How They Built Long Ago.* Watts, 1981. *(I; A)*

Gibbons, Gail. *Up Goes the Skyscraper.* Macmillan, 1986. *(P)*

Greenberg, Jan, and Jordan, Sandra. *Frank O. Gehry: Outside In.* DK, 2000. *(I)*

MacGregor, Anne, and MacGregor, Scott. *Domes: A Project Book.* Lothrop, 1982; *Skyscrapers: A Project Book,* 1981. *(I)*

Milo, Francesco. *The Story of Architecture.* Peter Bedrick, 2000. *(P; I)*

Morris, Ann. *Houses and Homes.* Lothrop, 1992. *(P)*

Van Zandt, Eleanor. *Architecture.* Steck-Vaughn, 1990. *(I; A)*

Weiss, Harvey. *Shelters: From Teepee to Igloo.* Crowell, 1988. *(I; A)*

## ARCTIC

Dekkers, Midas. *Arctic Adventure.* Watts, 1987. *(A)*

Hiscock, Bruce. *Tundra: The Arctic Land.* Atheneum, 1986. *(P; I)*

Lynch, Wayne. *Arctic Alphabet: Exploring the North from A to Z.* Firefly, 1999. *(P; I)*

Osborn, Kevin. *The Peoples of the Arctic.* Chelsea House, 1990. *(I; A)*

## ARGENTINA

Fox, Geoffrey. *The Land and People of Argentina.* Lippincott, 1990. *(I; A)*

Huber, Alex. *We Live in Argentina.* Watts, 1984. *(I; A)*

Liebowitz, Sol. *Argentina.* Chelsea House, 1990. *(I; A)*

Lye, Keith. *Take a Trip to Argentina.* Watts, 1986. *(P)*

Peterson, Marge, and Peterson, Rob. *Argentina: A Wild West Heritage.* Dillon, 1990. *(I)*

## ARITHMETIC

Allison, Linda, and Weston, Martha. *Eenie, Meenie, Miney Math! Math Play for You and Your Preschooler.* Little, 1993. *(P)*

Clement, Rod. *Counting on Frank.* Gareth Stevens, 1991. *(P; I)*

Hulme, Joy N. *Sea Squares.* Hyperion, 1991. *(P; I)*

## ARIZONA

Filbin, Dan. *Arizona.* Lerner, 1991. *(I)*

Fradin, Dennis. *Arizona: In Words and Pictures.* Children's, 1980. *(P; I)*

Tufts, Lorraine S. *Secrets in the Grand Canyon, Zion and Bryce Canyon National Parks.* National Photographic Collections, 1998. *(P; I)*

## ARKANSAS

Fradin, Dennis. *Arkansas: In Words and Pictures.* Children's, 1980. *(P; I)*

Heinrichs, Ann. *Arkansas.* Children's, 1989. *(P; I)*

## ARMOR

Gravett, Chris. *Arms and Armor.* Raintree, 1995. *(I)*

Mango, Karin. *Armor: Yesterday and Today.* Messner, 1980. *(I; A)*

Watts, Edith. *A Young Person's Guide to European Arms and Armor in the Metropolitan Museum of Art.* Metropolitan Museum of Art, 1982. *(I)*

Wilkinson, Frederick. *Arms and Armor.* Watts, 1984. *(P; I)*

Yue, Charlotte. *Armor.* Houghton, 1994. *(I)*

## ARMSTRONG, NEIL A.

Bredeson, Carmen. *Neil Armstrong: A Space Biography.* Enslow, 1998. *(I)*

Brown, Don. *One Giant Leap: The Story of Neil Armstrong.* Houghton, 1998. *(P)*

Kramer, Barbara. *Neil Armstrong: The First Man on the Moon.* Enslow, 1997. *(I)*

## ARNOLD, BENEDICT

Alderman, Clifford L. *The Dark Eagle: The Story of Benedict Arnold.* Macmillan, 1976. *(I; A)*

Fritz, Jean. *Traitor: The Case of Benedict Arnold.* Putnam, 1981. *(I; A)*

## ART

Aronson, Marc. *Art Attack: A Short Cultural History of the Avant-Garde.* Clarion, 1998. *(A)*

Connolly, Sean. *Henry Moore*. Heinemann, 1999. *(P; I)*

Cummings, Pat, ed. *Talking with Artists*. Bradbury, 1992. *(P; I); Talking with Artists, Volume Two*. Simon & Schuster, 1995. *(I; A)*

Giesecke, Ernestine. *Mary Cassatt*. Heinemann, 1999. *(P; I)*

Greenberg, Jan, and Jordan, Sandra. *The American Eye: Eleven Artists of the Twentieth Century*. Delacorte, 1995. *(I; A); The Painter's Eye: Learning to Look at Contemporary Art*. Delacorte, 1991. *(I; A)*

Greenfeld, Howard. *Marc Chagall*. Abrams, 1990. *(I; A)*

Henderson, Kathy. *Market Guide for Young Artists & Photographers*. Betterway, 1990. *(I; A)*

Isaacson, Philip M. *A Short Walk around the Pyramids & through the World of Art*. Knopf, 1993. *(I; A)*

Janson, H. W., and Janson, Anthony F. *History of Art for Young People*. Abrams, 1997. (rev. ed.) *(I; A)*

Micklethwait, Lucy. *A Child's Book of Art: Discover Great Paintings*. DK, 1999. *(P; I)*

Powell, Jillian. *Painting and Sculpture*. Steck-Vaughn, 1990. *(I; A)*

Sills, Leslie. *Visions: Stories about Women Artists*. Albert Whitman, 1993. *(I)*

Welton, Jude. *Drawing: A Young Artist's Guide*. Dorling Kindersley, 1994. *(I; A)*

Wolfe, Gillian. *Oxford First Book of Art*. Oxford, 1999. *(P)*

Woolf, Felicity. *Picture This: A First Introduction to Paintings*. Doubleday, 1990. *(I)*

Yenawine, Philip. *Colors*. Delacorte, 1991. *(P); Lines*. Delacorte, 1991. *(P); Shapes*. Delacorte, 1991. *(P)*

Zadrzynska, Ewa. *The Girl with a Watering Can*. Chameleon, 1990. *(P; I)*

## ARTHUR, CHESTER ALAN

Stevens, Rita. *Chester A. Arthur: 21st President of the United States*. Garrett Educational, 1989. *(I)*

## ARTHUR, KING

Hastings, Selina. *Sir Gawain and the Green Knight*. Lothrop, 1981. *(P; I)*

Malory, Thomas. *King Arthur and His Knights of the Round Table*, ed. by Sidney Lanier and Howard Pyle. Putnam, n.d. *(P; I)*

Pyle, Howard. *The Story of King Arthur and His Knights*. Scribner's, 1903. *(I; A)*

Riordan, James. *Tales of King Arthur*. Rand, 1982. *(I)*

Sutcliff, Rosemary. *The Light beyond the Forest*. Dutton, 1980; *The Road to Camlann: The Death of King Arthur*, 1982. *The Sword and the Circle: King Arthur and Knights of the Round Table*, 1981. *(I; A)*

## ASIA

Asian Cultural Center for UNESCO, ed. *Folk Tales from Asia for Children Everywhere: Bks. 1-6*. Weatherhill, 1975-1978. *(P; I)*

Franck, Irene M., and Brownstone, David M. *Across Asia by Land*. Facts on File, 1990. *(A)*

## ASTRONAUTS

Briggs, Carole S. *Women in Space*. Lerner, 1999. *(I)*

Cole, Michael D. *Astronauts: Training for Space*. Enslow, 1999. *(I)*

Burns, Khephra, and Miles, William. *Black Stars in Orbit: NASA's African American Astronauts*. Harcourt, 1995. *(I; A)*

Mullane, R. Mike. *Liftoff! An Astronaut's Dream*. Silver Burdett Press, 1994. *(I)*

## ASTRONOMY

Apfel, Necia H. *Astronomy Projects for Young Scientists*. Arco, 1984. *(A)*

Asimov, Isaac. *Astronomy Today*. Gareth Stevens, 1990. *(P; I); How Did We Find Out about the Universe?* Walker, 1983; *How Was the Universe Born?* Gareth Stevens, 1989. *(P; I)*

Berger, Melvin. *Bright Stars, Red Giants, and White Dwarfs*. Putnam, 1983; *Star Gazing, Comet Tracking and Sky Mapping*. Putnam, 1985. *(I; A)*

Branley, Franklyn M. *Venus: Magellan Explores Our Twin Planet*. Harper, 1994. *(I); Superstar: The Supernova of 1987*. HarperCollins, 1990. *(P; I); Journey into a Black Hole*. Harper, 1988. *(P); The Sky Is Full of Stars*. Harper, 1983. *(P); Space Telescope*. Crowell, 1985. *(P; I)*

Couper, Heather, and Henbest, Nigel. *How the Universe Works*. Reader's Digest, 1994. *(I)*

Fisher, David E. *The Origin and Evolution of Our Own Particular Universe*. Atheneum, 1988. *(A)*

Fradin, Dennis B. *Astronomy*. Children's, 1987. *(A)*

Gallant, Roy A. *Earth's Place in Space*. Marshall Cavendish/Benchmark, 1999. *I; A; The Macmillan Book of Astronomy*. Atheneum, 1986. *(P; I)*

Jastrow, Robert. *Red Giants and White Dwarfs*. Norton, 1990. *(I; A)*

Jespersen, James, and Fitz-Randolph, Jane. *Looking at the Invisible Universe*. Atheneum, 1990. *(A)*

Kelsey, Larry, and Hoff, Darrel. *Recent Revolutions in Astronomy*. Watts, 1987. *(I; A)*

Levinson, Riki. *Watch the Stars Come Out*. Dutton, 1985. *(P)*

Lippincott, Kristen. *Astronomy*. Dorling Kindersley, 1994. *(I; A)*

Moeschl, Richard. *Exploring the Sky: 100 Projects for Beginning Astronomers*. Chicago Review Press, 1988. *(I; A)*

Moore, Patrick, ed. *International Encyclopedia of Astronomy*. Orion Books, 1987. *(A)*

Simon, Seymour. *Galaxies*. Morrow, 1988. *(P)*

Vbrova, Zuza. *Space and Astronomy*. Gloucester Press, 1990. *(I)*

Vogt, Gregory. *Deep Space Astronomy*. Twenty-First Century, 1999. *(I)*

## ATLANTA

Pedersen, Anne. *Kidding Around Atlanta: A Young Person's Guide to the City*. John Muir, 1989. *(I; A)*

## ATMOSPHERE

Branley, Franklyn M. *Air Is All Around You.* Crowell, 1986. *(P)*

Gallant, Roy A. *Rainbows, Mirages, and Sun Dogs: The Sky As a Source of Wonder.* Macmillan, 1987. *(I)*

Jefferies, Lawrence. *Air, Air, Air.* Troll, 1983. *(P; I)*

Lloyd, David. *Air.* Dial, 1983. *(P)*

## ATOMS

Ardley, Neil. *The World of the Atom.* Gloucester Press, 1989. *(I)*

Asimov, Isaac. *How Did We Find Out about Atoms?* Walker, 1976. *(I; A)*

Mebane, Robert C., and Rybolt, Thomas R. *Adventures with Atoms and Molecules, Book II; Chemistry Experiments for Young People.* Enslow, 1987. *(I; A)*

## AUDUBON, JOHN JAMES

Brenner, Barbara. *On the Frontier with Mr. Audubon.* Putnam, 1977. *(I)*

## AUGUST

Updike, John. *A Child's Calendar.* Holiday House, 1999. *(P; I)*

Warner, Penny. *Kids' Holiday Fun: Great Family Activities Every Month of the Year.* Meadowbrook Press, 1997. *(P)*

## AUSTEN, JANE

LeFaye, Deirdre. *Jane Austen.* Oxford, 1999. *(A)*

## AUSTRALIA

Arnold, Caroline. *Australia Today.* Watts, 1987. *(P; I)* *Australia.* Gareth Stevens, 1988. *(P)*

Dolce, Laura. *Australia.* Chelsea House, 1990. *(I)*

Grupper, Jonathan. *Destination: Australia.* National Geographic, 2000. *(P; I)*

Kelly, Andrew. *Australia.* Bookwright, 1989. *(I)*

North, Peter, and McKay, Susan. *Welcome to Australia.* Gareth Stevens, 1999. *(P)*

Reynolds, Jan. *Down Under: Vanishing Cultures.* Harcourt, 1992. *(P; I)*

Schneck, S., ed. *Australian Animals.* Western, 1983. *(I; A)*

Stark, Al. *Australia: A Lucky Land.* Dillon, 1987. *(P; I)*

## AUSTRIA

Wohlrabe, Raymond, and Krusch, Werner. *The Land and People of Austria.* Lippincott, 1972. *(I; A)*

## AUTOMATION

Harrar, George. *Radical Robots: Can You Be Replaced?* Simon & Schuster, 1990. *(P)*

Lauber, Patricia. *Get Ready for Robots!* HarperCollins, 1987. *(P)*

Macaulay, David. *The New Way Things Work.* Houghton Mifflin, 1998. *(P; I; A)*

## AUTOMOBILE RACING

Harmer, Paul. *Racing Cars.* Rourke, 1988. *(P)*

Knudson, Richard L. *Land Speed Record Breakers.* Lerner, 1981. *Racing Yesterday's Cars,* 1984. *(I; A)*

Sheffer, H. R. *Race Cars.* Crestwood, 1982. *(I; A)*

Wilkinson, Sylvia. *Stock Cars.* Children's, 1981. *(I; A)*

## AUTOMOBILES

Bendick, Jeanne. *The First Book of Automobiles.* Watts, 1984 (rev. ed.). *(I)*

Cole, Joanna. *Cars and How They Go.* Harper, 1983. *(P)*

Florian, Douglas. *An Auto Mechanic.* Greenwillow, 1991. *(P)*

Ford, Barbara. *The Automobile.* Walker, 1987. *(I)*

Gunning, Thomas G. *Dream Cars.* Dillon, 1990. *(P; I)*

Lord, Harvey G. *Car Care for Kids and Former Kids.* Atheneum, 1983. *(I; A)*

Lord, Trevor. *Amazing Cars.* Knopf, 1992. *(P)*

Sullivan, George. *Cars.* Doubleday, 1991. *(I)*

Sutton, Richard. *Car.* Knopf, 1990. *(I)*

Taylor, John. *How Cars Are Made.* Facts on File, 1987. *(I)*

Tessendorf, K. C. *Look Out! Here Comes the Stanley Steamer.* Atheneum, 1984. *(P; I)*

## AVALANCHES AND LANDSLIDES

Goodwin, Peter H. *Landslides, Slumps, and Creep.* Franklin Watts, 1998. *(P; I)*

## AVIATION

Ardley, Neil. *Air and Flight.* Watts, 1984. *(I)*

Bellville, Cheryl Walsh. *The Airplane Book.* Carolrhoda, 1991. *(P; I)*

Berliner, Don. *Before the Wright Brothers.* Lerner, 1990. *(I); Personal Airplanes.* Lerner, 1982. *(I; A)*

Boyne, Walter J. *Flight.* Time-Life, 1990. *(A); The Smithsonian Book of Flight for Young People.* Aladdin, 1988. *(I; A)*

Burleigh, Robert. *Flight: The Journey of Charles Lindbergh.* Philomel, 1991. *(P; I)*

Cave, Joyce, and Cave, Ronald. *Aircraft.* Watts, 1982. *(P)*

Dwiggins, Don. *Flying the Frontiers of Space.* Dodd, 1982. *(I; A)*

Jaspersohn, William. *A Week in the Life of an Airline Pilot.* Little, 1991. *(I)*

Kerrod, Robin. *Amazing Flying Machines.* Knopf, 1992. *(P)*

Levinson, Nancy S. *Chuck Yeager: The Man Who Broke the Sound Barrier.* Walker, 1988. *(I; A)*

Lindblom, Steven. *Fly the Hot Ones.* Houghton, 1991. *(I; A)*

Maurer, Richard. *Airborne: The Search for the Secret of Flight.* Simon & Schuster, 1990. *(I)*

Maynard, Chris, and Paton, John. *The History of Aircraft.* Watts, 1982. *(I)*

Nahum, Andrew. *Flying Machine.* Knopf, 1990. *(I)*

Rosenblum, Richard. *The Golden Age of Aviation.* Atheneum, 1984. *(P; I)*

Stacey, Tom. *Airplanes: The Lure of Flight.* Lucent Books, 1990. *(I)*

Tessendorf, K. C. *Barnstormers and Daredevils.* Atheneum, 1988. *(I; A)*

Weiss, Harvey. *Strange and Wonderful Aircraft.* Houghton, 1995. *(I)*

## AZTECS

Chrisp, Peter. *The Aztecs.* Raintree/Steck-Vaughn, 1999. *(P; I)*

Hull, Robert. *The Aztecs.* Raintree/Steck-Vaughn, 1998. *(I; A)*

Kimmel, Eric A. *Montezuma and the Fall of the Aztecs.* Holiday, 2000. *(P; I)*

## BABY

Banish, Roslyn. *I Want to Tell You about My Baby.* Wingbow, 1982. *(P)*

Knight, Margy Burns. *Welcoming Babies.* Tilbury House, 1994. *(P)*

Ormerod, Jan. *101 Things to Do with a Baby.* Lothrop, 1984. *(P)*

Sandeman, Anna. *Babies.* Millbrook, 1996. *(P)*

Wilkes, Angela. *See How I Grow: A Photographic Record of a Baby's First Eighteen Months.* Dorling Kindersley, 1994. *(P)*

## BACTERIA

Berger, Melvin. *Germs Make Me Sick!* HarperCollins, 1995. *(P)*

Facklam, Howard, and Facklam, Margery. *Bacteria; Parasites; Viruses.* Twenty-First Century, 1995. *(I)*

Ricciuti, Edward. *Microorganisms.* Blackbirch Press, 1994. *(I)*

## BADMINTON

Wright, Len. *Your Book of Badminton.* Transatlantic, 1972. *(I; A)*

## BAHAMAS

Barlas, Robert. *Bahamas.* Marshall Cavendish, 2000. *(A)*

## BAHRAIN

Fox, Mary Virginia. *Bahrain.* Children's Press, 1995. *(I; A)*

## BALKANS

Lear, Aaron E. *Albania.* Chelsea House, 1987. *(A)*

Otfinoski, Steven. *Bulgaria.* Facts on File, 1998. *(I; A)*

## BALLADS

Cushman, Karen. *The Ballad of Lucy Whipple.* HarperCollins, 1998. *(I)*

Hooks, William H. *The Ballad of Belle Dorcas.* Knopf, 1995. *(P)*

Yolen, Jane. *The Ballad of the Pirate Queens.* Harcourt, 1998. *(P; I)*

## BALLET

Bussell, Darcey. *Ballet.* DK, 2000. *(P; I)*

Jessel, Camilla. *Ballet School.* Viking, 2000. *(P; I)*

Varriale, Jim. *Kids Dance: The Students of Ballet Tech.* Dutton, 1999. *(P; I)*

## BALLOONS AND BALLOONING

Briggs, Carole S. *Ballooning.* Lerner, 1986. *(P; I)*

Scarry, Huck. *Balloon Trip: A Sketchbook.* Prentice-Hall, 1983. *(I)*

## BALTIMORE

## BANANA

Farmer, Jacqueline. *Bananas!* Charlesbridge, 1999. *(P)*

Hughes, Meredith Sayles. *Yes, We Have Bananas: Fruits from Shrubs and Vines.* Lerner, 1999. *(P; I)*

## BANDS AND BAND MUSIC

Venezia, Mike. *John Philip Sousa.* Children's Press, 1999. *(P)*

## BANGKOK (KRUNG THEP)

McNair, Sylvia. *Bangkok.* Children's Press, 2000. *(P)*

## BANGLADESH

Laure, Jason. *Bangladesh.* Children's Press, 1992. *(I; A)*

Wright, R. E. *Bangladesh.* Chelsea House, 1988. *(P)*

## BANKS AND BANKING

Cantwell, Lois. *Money and Banking.* Watts, 1984. *(I; A)*

Godfrey, Neale S. *Neale S. Godfrey's Ultimate Kids' Money Book.* Simon & Schuster, 1998. *(P; I; A)*

Otfinoski, Steven. *The Kid's Guide to Money: Earning It, Saving It, Spending It, Growing It, Sharing It.* Scholastic, 1996. *(P; I)*

Scott, Elaine. *The Banking Book.* Warne, 1981. *(I; A)*

## BARBADOS

Elias, Marie Louise. *Barbados.* Marshall Cavendish, 2000. *(I)*

## BARNUM, PHINEAS TAYLOR

Andronik, Catherine M. *Prince of Humbugs: A Life of P.T. Barnum.* Atheneum, 1994. *(I; A)*

## BARRIE, SIR JAMES MATTHEW

Aller, Susan Bivin. *J. M. Barrie: The Magic behind Peter Pan.* Lerner, 1994. *(I)*

## BARRYMORE FAMILY

Horner, Matina S., and Thorliefson, Alex. *Ethel Barrymore.* Chelsea House, 1991. *(I; A)*

## BARTON, CLARA

Bains, Rae. *Clara Barton: Angel of the Battlefield.* Troll, 1982. *(P; I)*

Stevenson, Augusta. *Clara Barton: Founder of the American Red Cross.* Bobbs, 1983. *(P; I)*

Whitelaw, Nancy. *Clara Barton: Civil War Nurse.* Enslow, 1997. *(I)*

## BASEBALL

Arnow, Jan. *Louisville Slugger: The Making of a Baseball Bat.* Pantheon, 1984. *(P; I)*

Berler, Ron. *The Super Book of Baseball.* Sports Illustrated for Kids Books, 1991. *(I; A)*

Brundage, Buz. *Be a Better Hitter: Baseball Basics.* Sterling, 2000. *(I)*

Clark, Steve. *The Complete Book of Baseball Cards.* Putnam, 1982. *(P; I; A)*

Cluck, Bob. *The Winning Edge: Baserunning; The Winning Edge: Catching; The Winning Edge: Hitting; The Winning Edge: Shortstop.* Pantheon, 1987. *(I; A)*

Frommer, Harvey. *A Hundred and Fiftieth Anniversary Album of Baseball.* Watts, 1988. *(I; A); Baseball's Hall of Fame.* Watts, 1985. *(P; I)*

Jaspersohn, William. *Bat, Ball, Glove: The Making of Major League Baseball Gear.* Little, 1989. *(I; A)*

Kelley, James. *Baseball.* DK, 2000. *(P; I)*

Kisseloff, Jeff. *Who Is Baseball's Greatest Hitter?* Holt, 2000. *(I)*

Kreutzer, Peter, and Kerley, Ted. *Little League's Official How-to-Play Baseball Book.* Doubleday, 1990. *(I)*

Ritter, Lawrence S. *The Story of Baseball.* Morrow, 1983; 1990; 1999. *(I)*

Sandak, Cass R. *Baseball and Softball.* Watts, 1982. *(P)*

Savage, Jeff. *Home Run Kings.* Raintree/Steck-Vaughn, 1999. *(P; I)*

Solomon, Chuck. *Major-League Batboy.* Crown, 1992. *(P; I)*

Sullivan, George. *All about Baseball.* Putnam, 1989. *(P; I); The Art of Base-Stealing.* Dodd, 1982; *Better Baseball for Boys,* 1981 (rev. ed.). *(I); Baseball Backstage.* Holt, 1986. *(I)*

## BASKETBALL

Aaseng, Nate. *Basketball: You Are the Coach; Basketball's Playmakers; Basketball's Sharpshooters.* Lerner, 1983. *(I; A)*

Anderson, Dave. *The Story of Basketball.* Morrow, 1988. *(I; A)*

Beard, Butch, and others. *Butch Beard's Basic Basketball.* Michael Kesend, 1985. *(A)*

Finney, Shan. *Basketball.* Watts, 1982. *(P)*

Lerner, Mark. *Careers in Basketball.* Lerner, 1983. *(P; I)*

Liss, Howard. *Strange but True Basketball Stories.* Random House, 1983. *(I; A)*

Mullin, Chris. *Basketball.* DK, 2000. *(P; I)*

Rosenthal, Bert. *Basketball.* Children's, 1983. *(P)*

Stewart, Mark. *Basketball: A History of Hoops.* Watts, 1999. *(I; A)*

Young, Faye, and Coffey, Wayne. *Winning Basketball for Girls.* Facts on File, 1984. *(I; A)*

## BATS

Bash, Barbara. *Shadows of Night: The Hidden World of the Little Brown Bat.* Sierra Club Books, 1993. *(P)*

Cannon, Janell. *Stellaluna.* Harcourt, 1993. *(P)*

Earle, Ann. *Zipping, Zapping, Zooming Bats.* HarperCollins, 1995. *(P; I)*

Gibbons, Gail. *Bats.* Holiday, 1999. *(P)*

Greenaway, Frank. *Amazing Bats.* Knopf, 1991. *(P)*

Hopf, Alice L. *Bats.* Dodd, 1985. *(P; I)*

Johnson, Sylvia A. *Bats.* Lerner, 1985. *(P; I)*

McNulty, Faith. *When I Lived with Bats.* Scholastic/Cartwheel, 1999. *(P)*

Mulleneux, Jane. *Discovering Bats.* Bookwright, 1989. *(P)*

Pringle, Laurence. *Bats! Strange and Wonderful.* Boyds Mills, 2000. *(P; I); Batman: Exploring the World of Bats.* Scribner's, 1991. *(P; I)*

Selsam, Millicent E., and Hunt, Joyce. *A First Look at Bats.* Walker, 1991. *(P)*

## BATTERIES

Challoner, Jack. *My First Batteries and Magnets.* DK, 1992. *(P)*

Glover, David. *Batteries, Bulbs, and Wires.* Larousse Kingfisher Chambers, 1993. *(P; I)*

## BATTLES

Ferrie, Richard. *The World Turned Upside Down: George Washington and the Battle of Yorktown.* Holiday, 1999. *(I; A)*

Fraser, Mary Ann. *Vicksburg: The Battle That Won the Civil War.* Holt, 1999. *(I)*

## BEARS

Banks, Martin. *The Polar Bear on the Ice.* Gareth Stevens, 1990. *(I)*

Calabro, Marian. *Operation Grizzly Bear.* Four Winds, 1989. *(I)*

Harrison, Virginia. *The World of Polar Bears.* Gareth Stevens, 1990. *(P)*

Hoshino, Michio. *The Grizzly Bear Family Book.* North-South Books, 1994. *(P; I)*

Larsen, Thor. *The Polar Bear Family.* Picture Books Studio, 1990. *(P; I)*

Markle, Sandra. *Growing Up Wild: Bears.* Simon & Schuster/Atheneum, 2000. *(P)*

Weaver, John L. *Grizzly Bears.* Dodd, 1982. *(P; I)*

## BEATLES, THE

Evans, Mike. *The Art of the Beatles.* Beech Tree Books, 1985. *(A)*

Harry, Bill. *The Book of Beatle Lists.* Javelin Books, 1985. *(A)*

Hoffmann, Dezo. *The Beatles Conquer America.* Avon, 1985. *(A)*

## BEAVERS

Hodge, Deborah. *Beavers.* Kids Can, 1998. *(P; I)*
Lane, Margaret. *The Beaver.* Dial, 1982. *(P)*
Nentl, Jerolyn. *Beaver.* Crestwood, 1983. *(P; I)*
Rounds, Glen. *Beaver.* Holiday, 1999. *(P)*
Ryden, Hope. *The Beaver.* Putnam, 1987. *(I; A)*

## BEES

Cole, Joanna. *The Magic School Bus inside a Beehive.* Scholastic, 1996. *(P)*
Fischer-Nagel, Heiderose, and Fischer-Nagel, Andreas. *Life of the Honeybee.* Carolrhoda, 1985. *(P)*
Micucci, Charles. *The Life and Times of the Honeybee.* Houghton, 1995. *(P)*
Migutsch, Ali. *From Blossom to Honey.* Carolrhoda, 1981. *(P)*

## BEETHOVEN, LUDWIG VAN

Blackwood, Alan. *Beethoven.* Watts, 1987. *(I)*
Callahan, John F. *Ludwig Van Beethoven: Composer.* Chelsea House, 1997. *(I)*
Thompson, Wendy. *Ludwig van Beethoven.* Viking, 1991. *(I)*
Venezia, Mike. *Ludwig Van Beethoven.* Children's Press, 1996. *(P)*

## BEETLES

Still, John. *Amazing Beetles.* Knopf, 1991. *(P)*

## BEIJING

Kent, Deborah. *Beijing.* Children's, 1996. *(I)*

## BELGIUM

Hargrove, Jim. *Belgium.* Children's, 1988. *(P; I)*
Pateman, Robert. *Belgium.* Marshall Cavendish, 1995. *(I; A)*

## BELIZE

Maynard, Caitlin; Maynard, Thane; and Rullman, Stan. *Rain Forests and Reefs: A Kid's Eye-View of the Tropics.* Watts, 1996. *(I)*
Morrison, Marion. *Belize.* Children's Press, 1996. *(I; A)*
Staub, Frank J. *Children of Belize.* Lerner, 1997. *(P)*

## BELL, ALEXANDER GRAHAM

Fisher, Leonard Everett. *Alexander Graham Bell.* Simon & Schuster/Atheneum, 1999. *(P; I)*
Matthews, Tom L. *Always Inventing: A Photobiography of Alexander Graham Bell.* National Geographic, 1999. *(P; I)*
Shippen, Katherine B. *Alexander Graham Bell Invents the Telephone.* Random House, 1982. *(P; I)*

## BENIN

Fichter, George S. *The Bulge of Africa: Senegal, Guinea, Ivory Coast, Togo, Benin, and Equatorial Guinea.* Watts, 1981. *(I; A)*

Mama, Raouf, trans. *Why Goats Smell Bad: And Other Stories from Benin.* Shoe String, 1997. *(I; A)*

## BEOWULF

Crossley-Holland, Kevin, tr. *Beowulf.* Oxford University Press, 1984. *(I; A)*
Hieatt, Constance B., ed. *Beowolf and Other Old English Poems.* Bantam, 1982. *(A)*
Nye, Robert. *Beowulf.* Dell, 1982. *(I; A)*
Thompson, Stephen P., ed. *Readings on Beowulf.* Greenhaven Press, 1998. *(A)*

## BERLIN

Epler, Doris M. *The Berlin Wall: How It Rose and Why It Fell.* Millbrook, 1992. *(I; A)*

## BERLIN, IRVING

Streissguth, Tom. *Say It with Music: A Story about Irving Berlin.* Carolrhoda, 1994. *(I)*

## BHUTAN

Foster, Leila Merrell. *Bhutan.* Children's, 1989. *(I)*

## BHUTTO, BENAZIR

Hughes, Libby. *From Prison to Prime Minister: A Biography of Benazir Bhutto.* Dillon, 1990. *(I; A)*

## BIBLE

Holy Bible. *King James Version.Holy Bible. Rev. Standard Version (Catholic Edition).* Many publishers.
Daniel, Rebecca. *Women of the Old Testament.* Good Apple, 1983. *(I; A)*
De Paola, Tomie. *Noah and the Ark.* Winston, 1983. *(P)*
Gerstein, Mordicai, reteller. *Noah and the Great Flood.* Simon, 1999. *(P)*
Hutton, Warwick, ad. and illus. *Jonah and the Great Whale.* Atheneum, 1984. *(P)*
L'Engle, Madeleine. *The Glorious Impossible.* Simon & Schuster, 1990. *(I; A)*
Petersham, Maud, and Petersham, Miska. *The Christ Child.* Macmillan, 1931; 1980 (paper). *(P)*
Rock, Lois, ed. *Words of Gold: A Treasury of Bible Poetry and Wisdom.* Eerdmans, 2000. *(P; I)*
Stoddard, Sandol. *Doubleday Illustrated Children's Bible.* Doubleday, 1983. *(P; I); Five Who Found the Kingdom: New Testament Stories,* 1981. *(I)*
Turner, Philip. *The Bible Story.* Merrimack, 1982. *(P; I)*

## BIBLE, PEOPLE IN THE

Chaikin, Miriam. *Esther.* Jewish Publication Society, 1987. *(I)*

## BIBLE STORIES

McCaughrean, Geraldine, retel. *God's Kingdom: Stories from the New Testament.* Simon & Schuster/Margaret K. McElderry Bks., 2000. *(P; I)*

Pilling, Ann. *Before I Go to Sleep: Bible Stories, Poems, and Prayers for Children.* Crown, 1990. *(P)*

## BICYCLING

Berto, Frank J. *Bicycling Magazine's Complete Guide to Upgrading Your Bike.* Rodale, 1988. *(A)*

Coombs, Charles. *BMX: A Guide to Bicycle Motocross.* Morrow, 1983. *(I)*

Eds. of *Bicycling. Bicycling's Complete Guide to Bicycle Maintenance and Repair.* Rodale, 1986. *(A)*

LeMond, Greg, and Gordis, Kent. *Greg LeMond's Complete Book of Bicycling.* Putnam, 1987. *(A)*

Murphy, Jim. *Two Hundred Years of Bicycles.* Lippincott, 1983. *(I)*

Olney, Ross. *Riding High: Bicycling for Young People.* Lothrop, 1981. *(I; A)*

Roth, Harold. *Bike Factory.* Pantheon, 1985. *(I)*

Scioscia, Mary. *Bicycle Rider.* Harper, 1983. *(P; I)*

Stine, Megan. *Wheels!: The Kids' Bike Book.* Sports Illustrated for Kids Books, 1990. *(P; I)*

## BILL OF RIGHTS

Krull, Kathleen. *A Kid's Guide to America's Bill of Rights: Curfews, Censorship, and the 100-Pound Giant.* Avon/Camelot, 1999. *(I)*

## BIOGRAPHY, AUTOBIOGRAPHY, AND BIOGRAPHICAL NOVEL

Blackwood, Alan. *Captain Cook.* Bookwright, 1987. *(I)*

Carpenter, Angelica Shirley, and Shirley, Jean. *L. Frank Baum: Royal Historian of Oz.* Lerner, 1991. *(I; A)*

Chaney, J. R. *Aleksandr Pushkin: Poet for the People.* Lerner, 1991. *(I; A)*

Collins, David R. *Pioneer Plowmaker: A Story About John Deere.* Carolrhoda, 1991. *(I)*

Faber, Doris. *Calamity Jane.* Houghton, 1992. *(I)*

Ferris, Jeri. *Arctic Explorer: The Story of Matthew Henson.* Carolrhoda, 1989. *(I)*

Finkelstein, Norman H. *Theodor Herzl: Architect of a Nation.* Lerner, 1991. *(I; A)*

Fritz, Jean. *Surprising Myself.* Richard C. Owen, 1992. *(P; I)*

Green, Carl R., and Sanford, William R. *Belle Starr.* Enslow, 1992. *(I)*

Greenfield, Eloise. *Mary McLeod Bethune.* HarperCollins, 1994. *(P; I)*

Hamilton, Virginia. *Anthony Burns: The Defeat and Triumph of a Fugitive Slave.* Knopf, 1988. *(I; A)*

Haskins, James. *I Am Somebody! A Biography of Jesse Jackson.* Enslow, 1992. *(I)*

Haskins, Jim, and Benson, Kathleen. *Space Challenger: The Story of Guion Bluford.* Carolrhoda, 1984. *(I)*

Ipsen, D. C. *Archimedes: Greatest Scientist of the Ancient World.* Enslow, 1988. *(I; A)*

McKissack, Patricia, and McKissack, Fredrick. *Carter G. Woodson: The Father of Black History.* Enslow, 1991. *(P)*

McPherson, Stephanie S. *Ordinary Genius: The Story of Albert Einstein.* Carolrhoda, 1995. *(I); Rooftop Astronomer: A Story about Maria Mitchell.* Carolrhoda, 1990. *(I)*

Pinkney, Andrea Davis. *Alvin Ailey.* Hyperion, 1993. *(P; I)*

Roberts, Naurice. *Barbara Jordan: Great Lady from Texas.* Children's, 1990. *(I)*

Stanley, Diane, and Vennema, Peter. *Bard of Avon: The Story of William Shakespeare.* Morrow, 1992. *(I); Shaka, King of the Zulus.* Morrow, 1988. *(I)*

Stanley, Fay. *The Last Princess: The Story of Princess Ka'iulani of Hawaii.* Four Winds, 1991. *(I)*

Stevens, Bryna. *Handel and the Famous Sword Swallower of Halle.* Philomel, 1990. *(P)*

Tarnes, Richard. *Alexander Fleming.* Watts, 1990. *(I)*

Towle, Wendy. *The Real McCoy: The Life of an African-American Inventor.* Scholastic, 1993. *(P; I)*

Vare, Ethlie Ann. *Adventurous Spirit: A Story about Ellen Swallow Richards.* Carolrhoda, 1992. *(I)*

Wisniewski, David. *Sundiata, Lion King of Mali.* Clarion, 1992. *(P; I)*

## BIOLOGY

Evans, Ifor. *Biology.* Watts, 1984. *(I)*

Silver, Donald M. *Life on Earth: Biology Today.* Random House, 1983. *(A)*

Stewart, Melissa. *Life without Light: A Journey to Earth's Dark Ecosystems.* Watts, 1999. *(I; A)*

Tocci, Salvatore. *Biology Projects for Young Scientists.* Watts, 1987; 2000. *(A)*

## BIOLUMINESCENCE

Jacobs, Francine. *Nature's Light: The Story of Bioluminescence.* Morrow, 1974. *(P; I)*

## BIOMES

Sayre, April Pulley. *Lake and Pond.* Century Books, 1996. *(I); River and Stream.* Century Books, 1996. *(I); Wetland.* Century Books, 1996. *(I)*

## BIRDS

Arnosky, Jim. *Crinkleroot's 25 Birds Every Child Should Know.* Bradbury, 1993. *(P); Crinkleroot's Guide to Knowing the Birds.* Bradbury, 1992. *(P; I); Watching Water Birds.* National Geographic, 1997. *(P)*

Barrie, Anmarie. *A Step-by-Step Book about Canaries; A Step-by-Step Book about Cockatiels.* TFH Publications, 1988. *(I; A)*

Bash, Barbara. *Urban Roosts: Where Birds Nest in the City.* Sierra Club Books, 1990. *(P; I)*

Blassingame, Wyatt. *Wonders of Egrets, Bitterns, and Herons.* Dodd, 1982. *(I; A)*

Brown, Mary Barrett. *Wings along the Waterway.* Orchard, 1992. *(P; I)*

Burnie, David. *Bird.* Knopf, 1988. *(I)*

Burton, Maurice. *Birds.* Facts on File, 1985. *(I)*

Fischer-Nagel, Heiderose, and Fischer-Nagel, Andreas. *Season of the White Stork.* Carolrhoda, 1985. *(P; I)*

Fleischman, Paul. *Townsend's Warbler.* Harper, 1992. *(I)*

Goble, Paul. *The Great Race of the Birds and Animals.* Bradbury, 1985. *(P)*

Greenberg, Polly. *Birds of the World.* Putnam, 1983. *(P; I)*

Hume, Rob. *Birdwatching.* Random House, 1993. *(I)*

Klein, Tom. *Loon Magic for Kids.* Gareth Stevens, 1990. *(P)*

Matthews, Downs. *Skimmers.* Simon & Schuster, 1990. *(P; I)*

McCauley, Jane B. *Baby Birds and How They Grow.* National Geographic, 1984. *(P)*

McDonald, Mary Ann. *Doves.* Child's World, 1999. *(P)*

McMillan, Bruce. *Wild Flamingos.* Houghton/Lorraine, 1997. *(P;I)*

Merrick, Patrick. *Cardinals; Loons.* Child's World, 1999. *(P)*

Milkins, Colin S. *Discovering Songbirds.* Bookwright, 1990. *(P; I)*

Peters, Lisa Westberg. *This Way Home.* Holt, 1994. *(P; I)*

Sattler, Helen Roney. *The Book of Eagles.* Lothrop, 1989. *(I)*

Sill, Cathryn. *About Birds: A Guide for Children.* Peachtree, 1991. *(P)*

Singer, Marilyn. *Exotic Birds.* Doubleday, 1991. *(P; I)*

Stone, Lynn M. *Birds of Prey.* Children's, 1983. *(P)*

Taylor, Barbara. *The Bird Atlas.* Dorling Kindersley, 1993. *(P; I)*

Wharton, Anthony. *Discovering Ducks, Geese, and Swans.* Watts, 1987. *(P)*

Witmer, Lawrence M. *The Search for the Origin of Birds.* Watts, 1995. *(I;A)*

Yolen, Jane. *Bird Watch.* Philomel, 1990. *(P)*

## BIRDS AS PETS

Gutman, Bill. *Becoming Your Bird's Best Friend.* Millbrook Press, 1996. *(P; I)*

## BIRTH CONTROL

Nourse, Alan E. *Birth Control.* Watts, 1988. *(A)*

## BLACK HOLES

Couper, Heather, and Henbest, Nigel. *Black Holes.* Dorling Kindersley, 1996. *(I;A)*

## BLACKWELL, ELIZABETH

Kline, Nancy. *Elizabeth Blackwell: A Doctor's Triumph.* Conari Press, 1997. *(A)*

Schleichert, Elizabeth. *The Life of Elizabeth Blackwell.* 21st Century Books, 1992. *(P; I)*

## BLINDNESS

Arnold, Caroline. *A Guide Dog Puppy Grows Up.* Harcourt, 1991. *(P; I)*

Brighton, Catherine. *My Hands, My World.* Macmillan, 1984. *(P)*

Curtis, Patricia. *Greff, The Story of a Guide Dog.* Dutton, 1982. *(P; I; A)*

Weiss, Malcolm E. *Blindness.* Watts, 1980. *(P; I)*

## BLOOD

Sandeman, Anna. *Blood.* Millbrook, 1996. *(P)*

Ward, Brian R. *The Heart and Blood.* Watts, 1982. *(I)*

## BLY, NELLIE

Fredeen, Charles. *Nellie Bly: Daredevil Reporter.* Lerner, 2000. *(I; A)*

Quackenbush, Robert. *Stop the Presses, Nellie's Got a Scoop! A Story of Nellie.* Simon & Schuster, 1992. *(P)*

## BOARDSAILING

Coombs, Charles. *Be a Winner in Windsurfing.* Morrow, 1982. *(P; I)*

Evans, Jeremy. *The Complete Guide to Shortboard Sailing.* International Marine Publishing, 1987. *(A)*

## BOATS AND BOATING

Gelman, Rita G., and Buxbaum, Susan K. *Boats That Float.* Watts, 1981. *(P)*

Gibbons, Gail. *Boat Book.* Holiday, 1983. *(P)*

Kentley, Eric. *Boat.* Knopf, 1992. *(I; A)*

Rockwell, Anne. *Boats.* Dutton, 1982. *(I)*

## BOBSLEDDING

Brimmer, Larry Dane. *Bobsledding and the Luge.* Children's Press, 1997. *(P)*

## BODYBUILDING

Feder, R. F., and Taylor, G. J. *Junior Body Building.* Sterling, 1982. *(I; A)*

Savage, Jeff. *Fundamental Strength Training.* Lerner, 1998. *(I; A)*

## BODY CHEMISTRY

Wilcox, Frank H. *DNA: The Thread of Life.* Lerner, 1988. *(I; A)*

## BODY, HUMAN

*Reader's Digest ABC's of the Human Body.* Reader's Digest, 1987. *(I; A)*

Avraham, Regina. *The Circulatory System.* Chelsea House, 1989. *(I)*

Baldwin, Dorothy, and Lister, Claire. *How You Grow and Change.* Watts, 1984. *(P; I)*

Beckelman, Laurie. *The Fact about Transplants.* Crestwood, 1990. *(P; I)*

Berger, Gilda. *The Human Body.* Doubleday, 1989. *(P)*

Berger, Melvin, and Berger, Gilda. *Why Don't Haircuts Hurt?: Questions and Answers about the Human Body.* Scholastic, 1999. *(P)*

Branley, Franklyn M. *Shivers and Goose Bumps: How We Keep Warm.* Crowell, 1984. *(I; A)*

Brunn, Ruth Dowling, M.D., and Brunn, Bertel, M.D. *The Human Body: Your Body and How It Works.* Random House, 1982. *(I; A)*

Cole, Joanna. *Cuts, Breaks, Bruises, and Burns: How Your Body Heals.* Crowell, 1985. *(I); The Human Body: How We Evolved.* Morrow, 1987. *(P); The Magic School Bus Inside the Human Body.* Scholastic, 1989. *(P; I); Your Insides.* Putnam, 1992. *(P)*

Cosgrove, Margaret. *Your Muscles and Ways to Exercise Them.* Dodd, 1980. *(P; I)*

Day, Trevor. *The Random House Book of 1001 Questions and Answers about the Human Body.* Random House, 1994. *(I)*

Facklam, Margery, and Facklam, Howard. *Spare Parts for People.* Harcourt, 1987. *(I; A)*

Fekete, Irene, and Ward, Peter D. *Your Body.* Facts on File, 1984. *(I)*

Gamlin, Linda. *The Human Body.* Watts, 1988. *(I; A)*

Harris, Robie H. *It's Perfectly Normal: A Book about Changing Bodies, Growing Up, Sex, and Sexual Health.* Candlewick, 1994. *(I)*

Isberg, Emily. *Peak Performance: Sports, Science, and the Body in Action.* Simon & Schuster, 1989. *(P; I)*

Janulewicz, Mike, and Widdows, Richard. *Yikes! Your Body, Up Close!* Simon & Schuster, 1997. *(P; I)*

Jukes, Mavis. *It's a Girl Thing: How to Stay Healthy, Safe, and in Charge.* Knopf, 1996. *(I; A)*

Lauersen, Niles H., and Stukane, Eileen. *You're in Charge: A Teenage Girl's Guide to Sex and Her Body.* Fawcett, 1993. *(I; A)*

Leinwand, Gerald. *Transplants: Today's Medical Miracles.* Watts, 1985. *(I; A)*

Machotka, Hana. *Breathtaking Noses.* Morrow, 1992. *(P)*

Metos, Thomas H. *Artificial Humans: Transplants and Bionics.* Messner, 1985. *(I)*

Parker, Steve. *Eating a Meal: How You Eat, Drink, and Digest.* Watts, 1991. *(P); Food and Digestion.* Watts, 1990. *(I); Human Body.* Dorling Kindersley, 1994. *(P; I)*

Patterson, Claire. *It's OK to Be You: A Frank and Funny Guide to Growing Up.* Tricycle Press, 1994. *(I)*

Pringle, Laurence. *Hearing; Smell; Taste.* Marshall Cavendish/Benchmark, 1999. *(P; I)*

Rowan, Dr. Pete. *Some Body!* Knopf, 1995. *(P; I)*

Royston, Angela. *The Human Body and How It Works.* Random House, 1991. *(P; I)*

Settel, Joanne, and Baggett, Nancy. *Why Does My Nose Run?: (and Other Questions Kids Ask about Their Bodies).* Atheneum, 1985. *(I; A)*

Silverstein, Alvin, and Silverstein, Virginia B. *The Story of Your Mouth.* Coward, 1984. *(I; A); The Story of Your Foot.* Putnam, 1987. *(I; A)*

Sweeney, Joan. *Me and My Amazing Body.* Crown, 1999. *(P)*

Westheimer, Ruth. *Dr. Ruth Talks to Kids: Where You Came From, How Your Body Changes, and What Sex Is All About.* Macmillan, 1993. *(I; A)*

## BODY SIGNALS

Berger, Melvin. *Why I Cough, Sneeze, Shiver, Hiccup, and Yawn.* Harper, 1983. *(P)*

## BOLIVIA

*Bolivia . . . In Pictures.* Lerner, 1987. *(I; A)*

Blair, David Nelson. *The Land and People of Bolivia.* Lippincott, 1990. *(I)*

Hermes, Jules M. *The Children of Bolivia.* Carolrhoda, 1996. *(P; I)*

Morrison, Marion. *Bolivia.* Children's, 1988. *(I)*

Schimmel, Karen. *Bolivia.* Chelsea House, 1990. *(I)*

## BOOKS

Ahlstrom, Mark. *Books.* Crestwood, 1983. *(P; I)*

Aliki. *How a Book Is Made.* Crowell, 1986. *(P)*

Althea. *Making a Book.* Cambridge University Press, 1983. *(I; A)*

Kehoe, Michael. *The Puzzle of Books.* Carolrhoda, 1982. *(P)*

## BOONE, DANIEL

Brandt, Keith. *Daniel Boone: Frontier Adventures.* Troll, 1983. *(P; I)*

Lawlor, Laurie. *Daniel Boone.* Albert Whitman, 1989. *(I)*

Stevenson, Augusta. *Daniel Boone: Young Hunter and Tracker.* Bobbs, 1983. *(P; I)*

## BOSNIA AND HERZEGOVINA

Black, Eric. *Bosnia.* Lerner, 1999. *(I; A)*

Fireside, Harvey, and Fireside, Bryna J. *Young People from Bosnia Talk about War.* Enslow, 1996. *(I; A)*

Reger, James P. *The Rebuilding of Bosnia.* Lucent, 1997. *(I)*

## BOSTON

Kent, Deborah. *Boston.* Children's Press, 1998. *(P; I)*

Monke, Ingrid. *Boston.* Dillon, 1989. *(P; I)*

Vanderwarker, Peter. *Boston Then and Now: Sixty-Five Boston Sites Photographed in the Past and Present.* Dover, 1982. *(P; I)*

## BOTANY

Kalman, Bobbie, and Walker, Niki. *What Is a Plant?* Crabtree, 2000. *(P; I)*

Penny, Malcolm. *How Plants Grow.* Marshall Cavendish, 1996. *(P; I)*

Powledge, Fred. *Pharmacy in the Forest: How Medicines Are Found in the Natural World.* Simon & Schuster, 1998. *(I)*

Silverstein, Alvin; Silverstein, Virginia; and Nunn, Laura Silverstein. *Photosynthesis.* Millbrook Press, 1998. *(I; A)*

## BOTSWANA

*Botswana . . . in Pictures.* Lerner, 1990. *(I; A)*

Blumberg, Rhoda. *Southern Africa: South Africa, Namibia, Swaziland, Lesotho, and Botswana.* Watts, 1981. *(I; A)*

## BOWLING

Holman, Marshall, and Nelson, Roy G. *Marshall Holman's Bowling Tips and Techniques.* Contemporary Books, 1985. *(A)*

Lerner, Mark. *Bowling Is for Me.* Lerner, 1981. *(P; I)*

## BOXING

Riciutti, Edward R. *How to Box: Boxing for Beginners.* Harper, 1982. *(P; I)*

## BOY SCOUTS

Blassingame, Wyatt. *Story of the Boy Scouts.* Garrard, 1968. *(I)*

Boy Scouts of America. *Bear Cub Scoutbook.* Boy Scouts, 1973. *(I); Boy Scout Fieldbook.* Workman, 1967. *(A); Scout Handbook.* Boy Scouts, 1972. *(I); Wolf Cub Scoutbook.* 1986 (rev. ed.). *(I)*

## BRAHMS, JOHANNES

Venezia, Mike. *Johannes Brahms.* Children's Press, 1999. *(P; I)*

## BRAIN

Baldwin, Dorothy, and Lister, Claire. *Your Brain and Nervous System.* Watts, 1984. *(I; A)*

Berger, Melvin. *Exploring the Mind and Brain.* Harper, 1983. *(I; A)*

Funston, Sylvia, and Ingram, Jay. *It's All in Your Brain.* Grosset, 1995. *(I)*

Parker, Steve. *The Brain and Nervous System.* Watts, 1990. *(I)*

Silverstein, Alvin, and Silverstein, Virginia. *World of the Brain.* Morrow, 1986. *(P; I)*

Simon, Seymour. *The Brain: Our Nervous System.* Morrow, 1997. *(I)*

Stafford, Patricia. *Your Two Brains.* Macmillan, 1986. *(I)*

## BRAZIL

Bennett, Olivia. *A Family in Brazil.* Lerner, 1986. *(P; I)*

Carpenter, Mark L. *Brazil: An Awakening Giant.* Dillon, 1987. *(P; I)*

Cross, Wilbur, and Cross, Susanna. *Brazil.* Children's, 1984. *(I; A)*

Haverstock, Nathan A. *Brazil in Pictures.* Lerner, 1987. *(I)*

Lye, Keith. *Take a Trip to Brazil.* Watts, 1983. *(P; I)*

## BREAD AND BAKING

Lucas, Angela. *A Loaf of Bread.* Watts, 1983. *(I)*

Mitgutsch, Ali. *From Grain to Bread.* Carolrhoda, 1981. *(P; I)*

Ogren, Sylvia. *Shape It and Bake It: Quick and Simple Ideas for Children from Frozen Bread Dough.* Dillon, 1981. *(I)*

Sumption, Lois L., and Ashbrook, Marguerite L. *Breads from Many Lands.* Dover, 1982. *(I)*

## BRIDGES

Ardley, Neil. *Bridges.* Garrett Educational, 1990. *(P; I)*

Carlisle, Norman, and Carlisle, Madelyn. *Bridges.* Children's, 1983. *(P)*

Carter, Polly. *The Bridge Book.* Simon & Schuster, 1992. *(P; I)*

Johmann, Carol A., and Rieth, Elizabeth J. *Bridges! Amazing Structures to Design, Build and Test.* Williamson, 1999. *(P; I)*

Pelta, Kathy. *Bridging the Golden Gate.* Lerner, 1987. *(P)*

Robbins, Ken. *Bridges.* Dial, 1991. *(P; I)*

St. George, Judith. *The Brooklyn Bridge: They Said It Couldn't Be Built.* Putnam, 1982. *(I; A)*

Sandak, Cass R. *Bridges.* Watts, 1983. *(P)*

## BRONTË SISTERS

Brontë, Charlotte. *Jane Eyre,* ad. by Diana Stewart. Raintree, 1983. (Fiction) *(I)*

Brontë, Emily. *Wuthering Heights,* ad. by Betty K. Wright. Raintree, 1983. (Fiction) *(I; A)*

Martin, Christopher. *The Brontës.* Rourke, 1989. *(I; A)*

O'Neill, Jane. *The World of the Brontës.* Carlton, 1999. *(I; A)*

Sarnoff, Jane. *That's Not Fair.* Scribner's, 1980. *(P)*

## BRUNEI

Major, John S. *Land and People of Malaysia and Brunei.* HarperCollins, 1991. *(I; A)*

## BUCHANAN, JAMES

Brill, Marlene Targ. *James Buchanan.* Children's, 1988. *(I)*

## BUCK, PEARL

La Farge, Ann. *Pearl Buck.* Chelsea House, 1988. *(A)*

## BUDDHA

Snelling, John. *Buddhism.* Bookwright, 1987. *(I; A)*

## BUDDHISM

Snelling, John. *Buddhism.* Bookwright, 1987. *(I; A)*

## BUFFALO AND BISON

Freedman, Russell. *Buffalo Hunt.* Holiday, 1988. *(P; I)*

Patent, Dorothy Hinshaw. *Buffalo: The American Bison Today.* Clarion, 1986. *(I)*

## BUFFALO BILL (WILLIAM FREDERICK CODY)

D'Aulaire, Ingri, and D'Aulaire, Edgar Parin. *Buffalo Bill.* Doubleday, 1952. *(I)*

## BUILDING CONSTRUCTION

Darling, David. *Spiderwebs to Skyscrapers.* Dillon, 1991. *(I)*

Fagg, C. D. *How They Built Long Ago.* Watts, 1981. *(I)*

Florian, Douglas. *A Carpenter.* Greenwillow, 1991. *(P)*

Gibbons, Gail. *How a House Is Built.* Holiday, 1990. *(P)*

Robbins, Ken. *Building a House.* Four Winds, 1984. *(P; I)*
Severance, John B. *Skyscrapers: How America Grew Up.* Holiday, 2000. *(I)*

## BULGARIA

Otfinoski, Steven. *Bulgaria.* Facts on File, 1998. *(I; A)*

## BULLETIN BOARDS

Finton, Esther. *Bulletin Boards for Science and Health.* Good Apple, 1980; *Math Bulletin Boards,* 1981. *(P; I)*

## BURBANK, LUTHER

Quakenbush, Robert. *Here a Plant, There a Plant, Everywhere a Plant, Plant! A Story of Luther Burbank.* Prentice-Hall, 1982. *(P; I)*

## BURMA (MYANMAR)

Knowlton, MaryLee, and Sachner, Mark J. *Burma; Indonesia; Malaysia.* Gareth Stevens, 1987. *(P)*
Parenteau, John. *Prisoner for Peace: Aung San Suu Kyi and Burma's Struggle for Democracy.* Morgan Reynolds, 1994. *(I; A)*
Wright, David K. *Burma.* Children's Press, 1996. *(I)*
Wright, David K. *Malaysia.* Children's, 1988. *(P; I)*

## BURUNDI

Foster, F. Blanche. *East Central Africa: Kenya, Uganda, Tanzania, Rwanda, and Burundi.* Watts, 1981. *(I; A)*
Wolbers, Marian F. *Burundi.* Chelsea House, 1989. *(I)*

## BUSH, GEORGE

Schneiderman, Ron. *The Picture Life of George Bush.* Watts, 1989. *(I)*
Sufrin, Mark. *George Bush: The Story of the Forty-first President of the United States.* Dell, 1989. *(I)*

## BUSINESS

Mariotti, Steve. *The Young Entrepreneur's Guide to Starting and Running a Business.* Times, 2000. (2nd ed.) *(A)*
Otfinoski, Steven. *The Kid's Guide to Money: Earning It, Saving It, Spending It, Growing It, Sharing It.* Scholastic, 1996. *(P; I)*

## BUTTER

Wake, Susan. *Butter.* Lerner, 1990. *(P; I)*

## BUTTERFLIES AND MOTHS

Cook, David. *Small World of Butterflies and Moths.* Watts, 1981. *(P)*
Dallinger, Jane, and Overbeck, Cynthia. *Swallowtail Butterflies.* Lerner, 1983. *(P; I)*
Gibbons, Gail. *The Monarch Butterfly.* Holiday, 1989. *(P; I)*
Jourdan, Eveline. *Butterflies and Moths around the World.* Lerner, 1981. *(I; A)*

Norsgaard, E. Jaediker. *How to Raise Butterflies.* Putnam, 1988. *(P)*
Penn, Linda. *Young Scientists Explore Butterflies and Moths.* Good Apple, 1983. *(P)*
Reidel, Marlene. *From Egg to Butterfly.* Carolrhoda, 1981. *(P)*
Ryder, Joanne. *Where Butterflies Grow.* Dutton, 1989. *(P)*
Tarrant, Graham. *Butterflies.* Putnam, 1983. *(P)*
Whalley, Paul. *Butterfly & Moth.* Knopf, 1988. *(P; I)*

## CABOT, JOHN AND SEBASTIAN

Goodnough, David. *John Cabot and Son.* Troll, 1979 (new ed.). *(P; I)*
Maestro, Betsy C. *The Discovery of the Americas.* Lothrop, 1991. *(P)*

## CACTUS

Holmes, Anita. *Cactus: The All-American Plant.* Scholastic, 1982; *The 100-Year-Old Cactus,* 1983. *(P; I)*
Overbeck, Cynthia. *Cactus.* Lerner, 1982. *(I)*

## CAESAR, GAIUS JULIUS

Matthews, Rupert. *Julius Caesar.* Bookwright, 1989. *(P; I)*
Shakespeare, William. *Julius Caesar,* ad. by Diana Stewart. Raintree, 1983. *(I; A)*

## CAIRO

Rodenbeck, Max. *Cairo: The City Victorious.* Knopf, 1999. *(A)*
Stein, R. Conrad. *Cairo.* Children's, 1996. *(I)*

## CALCUTTA (KOLKATA)

Rice, Tanya. *Mother Teresa.* Chelsea House, 1997. *(I)*

## CALENDAR

Apfel, Necia H. *Calendars.* Watts, 1985. *(I; A)*
Bolton, Carole. *The Good-Bye Year.* Lodestar, 1982. *(I; A)*
Hughes, Paul. *The Days of the Week: Stories, Songs, Traditions, Festivals, and Surprising Facts About the Days of the Week from All Over the World.* Garrett Educational, 1989. *(P; I)*; *The Months of the Year: Stories, Songs, Traditions, Festivals, and Surprising Facts About the Months of the Year from All Over the World.* Garrett Educational, 1989. *(P; I)*
Maestro, Betsy. *The Story of Clocks and Calendars: Marking a Millenium.* Lothrop, 1999. *(P; I)*
Perry, Susan. *How Did We Get Clocks and Calendars?* Creative Education, 1981. *(P; I)*
Watkins, Peter, and Hughes, Erica. *Here's the Year.* Watts, 1982. *(I; A)*

## CALIFORNIA

Altman, Linda Jacobs. *California.* Benchmark, 1996. *(I)*
Heinrichs, Ann. *California.* Children's Press, 1998. *(I)*
Oliver, Rice D. *Student Atlas of California.* California Weekly, 1982. *(I; A)*
Pack, Janet. *California.* Watts, 1987. *(I; A)*

Stein, R. Conrad. *California.* Children's, 1988. *(P)*

## CAMBODIA

*Cambodia . . . in Pictures.* Lerner, 1996. *(I; A)*

Chandler, David P. *The Land and People of Cambodia.* Harper, 1991. *(I; A)*

Sheehan, Sean. *Cambodia.* Marshall Cavendish, 1996. *(I)*

## CAMELS

Cloudsley-Thompson, John. *Camels.* Raintree, 1980. *(I; A)*

Wexo, John Bonnett. *Camels.* Creative Education, 1988. *(P)*

## CAMEROON

Anderson, Lydia. *Nigeria, Cameroon, and the Central African Republic.* Watts, 1981. *(I; A)*

Hathaway, Jim. *Cameroon . . . in Pictures.* Lerner, 1989. *(I)*

## CAMPING

Carlson, Laurie, and Dammel, Judith. *Kids Camp! Activities for the Backyard or Wilderness.* Chicago Review Press, 1995. *(I)*

Dolan, Edward. *Bicycle Camping and Touring.* Wanderer Books, 1982. *(I; A)*

Jay, Michael. *Camping and Orienteering.* Warwick Press, 1990. *(I)*

National Geographic Society. *Wilderness Challenge.* National Geographic, 1980. *(I; A)*

Neimark, Paul. *Camping and Ecology.* Children's, 1981. *(I)*

Riviere, Bill. *Camper's Bible.* Doubleday, 1984 (3rd rev. ed.). *(I; A)*

Zeleznak, Shirley. *Camping.* Crestwood, 1980. *(P; I; A)*

## CANADA

Barlas, Bob; Tompsett, Norman; and McKay, Susan. *Welcome to Canada.* Gareth Stevens, 1999. *(P)*

Bowers, Vivien. *Wow Canada! Exploring This Land from Coast to Coast to Coast.* Firefly, 2000. *(P; I)*

Brickenden, Jack. *Canada.* Bookwright, 1989. *(I)*

Harrison, Ted. *O Canada.* Ticknor & Fields, 1993. *(I; A)*

Holbrook, Sabra. *Canada's Kids.* Atheneum, 1983. *(I)*

Lye, Keith. *Take a Trip to Canada.* Watts, 1983. *(P)*

Morton, Desmond. *New France and War.* Watts, 1984. *(I; A)*

Shepherd, Jennifer. *Canada.* Children's, 1988. *(P; I)*

Skeoch, Alan. *The United Empire Loyalists and the American Revolution.* Watts, 1983. *(I; A)*

Thompson, Wayne C. *Canada 1985.* Stryker-Post, 1985. *(A)*

## CANADA, HISTORY OF

Barlas, Robert, and Tompsett, Norm. *Canada.* Gareth Stevens Audio, 1998. *(I)*

Xydes, Georgia. *Alexander MacKenzie and the Explorers of Canada.* Chelsea House, 1992. *(I)*

## CANALS

Boyer, Edward. *River and Canal.* Holiday, 1986. *(I)*

Gaines, Ann Graham. *The Panama Canal in American History.* Enslow, 1999. *(I; A)*

Gold, Susan Dudley. *The Panama Canal Transfer: Controversy at the Crossroads.* Raintree/Steck-Vaughn, 1999. *(I; A)*

Markun, Patricia Maloney. *It's Panama's Canal!* Shoe String/Linnet, 1999. *(I; A)*

Sandak, Cass R. *Canals.* Watts, 1983. *(P)*

St. George, Judith. *Panama Canal: Gateway to the World.* Putnam, 1989. *(I; A)*

## CANCER

Burns, Sheila L. *Cancer: Understanding and Fighting It.* Messner, 1982. *(I; A)*

Fine, Judylaine. *Afraid to Ask: A Book about Cancer.* Kids Can Press, 1984. *(A)*

Gaes, Jason. *My Book for Kids with Cansur.* Melius & Peterson, 1988. *(P; I)*

Holleb, Arthur I., ed. *The American Cancer Society Cancer Book.* Doubleday, 1986. *(A)*

Hyde, Margaret Oldroyd, and Hyde, Lawrence E. *Cancer in the Young: A Sense of Hope.* Westminster, 1985. *(A)*

Krisher, Trudy. *Kathy's Hats: A Story of Hope.* Marianist Press, 1991. *(P)*

Landau, Elaine. *Cancer.* 21st Century Books, 1994. *(I; A)*

Rodgers, Joann Ellison. *Cancer.* Chelsea House, 1990. *(I; A)*

Silverstein, Alvin and Virginia B. *Cancer: Can It Be Stopped?* Lippincott, 1987. *(A)*

Swenson, Judy Harris, and Kunz, Roxanne Brown. *Cancer: The Whispered Word.* Dillon, 1986. *(P; I)*

Trull, Patti. *On with My Life.* Putnam, 1983. *(I; A)*

Vogel, Carole Garbuny. *Will I Get Breast Cancer? Questions & Answers For Teenage Girls.* Messner, 1995. *(I; A)*

## CANDLES

Yonck, Barbara. *Candle Crafts.* Lion, 1981. *(P; I)*

## CANDY AND CANDY MAKING

Burford, Betty M. *Chocolate by Hershey: A Story about Milton S. Hershey.* Lerner, 1994. *(P; I)*

Simon, Charnan. *Milton Hershey: Chocolate King, Town Builder.* Children's Press, 1998. *(P)*

## CANOEING

Boy Scouts of America. *Canoeing.* Boy Scouts, 1977. *(I; A)*

Koon, Celeste A. *Canoeing.* Harvey, 1981. *(I; A)*

Moran, Tom. *Canoeing Is for Me.* Lerner, 1983. *(P; I)*

## CAPE VERDE

Boyd, Herb. *The Former Portuguese Colonies: Angola, Mozambique, Guinea-Bissau, Cape Verde, São Tomé, and Príncipe.* Watts, 1981. *(I; A)*

## CAPITOL, UNITED STATES

Hoig, Stan. *Capitol for the United States.* Dutton, 1990. *(P; I)*

## CARBON

Sparrow, Giles. *Carbon.* Marshall Cavendish, 1999. *(P; I)*

## CARD GAMES

Perry, Susan. *How to Play Rummy Card Games.* Creative Education, 1980. *(P; I)*

Sackson, Sid. *Playing Cards around the World.* Prentice-Hall, 1981. *(I; A)*

## CARIBBEAN SEA AND ISLANDS

Carroll, Raymond. *The Caribbean: Issues in U.S. Relations.* Watts, 1984. *(I; A)*

Hubley, John, and Hubley, Penny. *A Family in Jamaica.* Lerner, 1986. *(P)*

Saunders, Dave. *Through the Year in the Caribbean.* David & Charles, 1981. *(I; A)*

Wolkstein, Diane, ed. *The Magic Orange Tree and Other Haitian Folktales.* Schocken, 1980. *(I)*

## CARNIVALS

Kindersley, Barnabas; with Kindersley, Anabel; and UNICEF. *Celebrations!: Festivals, Carnivals, and Feast Days from around the World.* DK, 1997. *(P; I)*

## CAROLS

Cope, Dawn, and Cope, Peter, eds. *Christmas Carols for Young Children.* Evergreen, 1981. *(P; I)*

Cusack, Margaret. *The Christmas Carol Sampler.* Harcourt, 1983. *(P; I; A)*

Mohr, Joseph. *Silent Night.* Dutton, 1984. *(P; I; A)*

Tennyson, Noel, illus. *Christmas Carols: A Treasury of Holiday Favorites with Words and Pictures.* Random House, 1983. *(I; A)*

## CARROLL, LEWIS

Carroll, Lewis. *Alice's Adventures in Wonderland* (many editions and publishers); *Through the Looking Glass and What Alice Found There,* illus. by Barry Moser. University of California Press, 1983. *(I; A)*

## CARSON, KIT

McCall, Edith. *Hunters Blaze the Trails.* Children's, 1980. *(P; I; A)*

## CARSON, RACHEL

Goldberg, Jake. *Rachel Carson.* Chelsea House, 1991. *(P; I)*

Jezer, Marty. *Rachel Carson.* Chelsea House, 1988. *(A)*

Lear, Linda, ed. *Lost Woods: The Discovered Writing of Rachel Carson.* Beacon, 1998. *(A)*

Reef, Catherine. *Rachel Carson: A Wonder of Nature.* 21st Century Books, 1991. *(P; I)*

Stwertka, Eve. *Rachel Carson.* Watts, 1991. *(P; I)*

## CARTER, JAMES EARL, JR.

Richman, Daniel A. *James E. Carter.* Garrett Educational, 1989. *(I)*

## CARTIER, JACQUES

Averill, Esther. *Cartier Sails the St. Lawrence.* Harper, 1956. *(I)*

Syme, Ronald. *Cartier: Finder of the St. Lawrence.* Morrow, 1958. *(I)*

## CARTOONS

Weiss, Harvey. *Cartoons and Cartooning.* Houghton, 1990. *(I; A)*

## CARVER, GEORGE WASHINGTON

Carey, Charles W. *George Washington Carver* Child's World, 1999. *(P; I)*

Coil, Suzanne M. *George Washington Carver.* Watts, 1990. *(P; I)*

## CASSATT, MARY

Meyer, Susan E. *Mary Cassatt.* Abrams, 1990. *(I)*

Muhlberger, Richard, and Metropolitan Museum of Art. *What Makes a Cassatt a Cassatt?* Viking, 1994. *(I)*

Turner, Robyn Montana. *Mary Cassatt.* Little, 1992. *(P; I)*

## CASTLES

Davison, Brian. *Explore a Castle.* David & Charles, 1983. *(I)*

Macaulay, David. *Castle.* Houghton, 1982. *(I)*

Macdonald, Fiona. *A Medieval Castle.* Peter Bedrick, 1990. *(I)*

Monks, John. *Castles.* Rourke, 1988. *(P)*

Shuter, Jane. *Carisbrooke Castle.* Heinemann, 1999. *(I)*

Smith, Beth. *Castles.* Watts, 1988. *(I; A)*

Vaughan, Jennifer. *Castles.* Watts, 1984. *(P)*

## CASTRO, FIDEL

Brown, Warren. *Fidel Castro: Cuban Revolutionary.* Millbrook Press, 1994. *(A)*

Madden, Paul. *Fidel Castro.* Rourke, 1993. *(I; A)*

## CATHEDRALS

Gallagher, Maureen. *The Cathedral Book.* Paulist Press, 1983. *(I; A)*

Macaulay, David. *Cathedral: The Story of Its Construction.* Houghton, 1973. *(A); Cathedral.* Houghton, 1981. *(I)*

## CATS

Fischer-Nagel, Heiderose, and Fischer-Nagel, Andreas. *A Kitten Is Born.* Putnam, 1983. *(P)*

George, Jean Craighead. *How to Talk to Your Cat.* Harper-Collins, 2000. *(P)*

Hess, Lilo. *A Cat's Nine Lives.* Scribner's, 1984; *Listen to Your Kitten Purr,* 1980. *(P; I)*

Selsam, Millicent E., and Hunt, Joyce. *A First Look at Cats.* Walker, 1981. *(P; I)*

Steneman, Shep. *Garfield: The Complete Cat Book.* Random House, 1981. *(I; A)*

Tildes, Phyllis Limbacher. *Calico's Cousins: Cats from Around the World.* Charlesbridge, 1999. *(P)*

## CATS, WILD

Barrett, N. S. *Big Cats.* Watts, 1988. *(P; I)*

Cajacob, Thomas. *Close to the Wild: Siberian Tigers in a Zoo.* Carolrhoda, 1985. *(P; I)*

Eaton, Randall L. *Cheetah: Nature's Fastest Racer.* Dodd, 1981. *(I; A)*

Hamer, Martyn. *Cats.* Watts, 1983. *(P)*

Levitin, Sonia. *All the Cats in the World.* HarBraceJ, 1982. *(P)*

Middleton, Don. *Jaguars; Tigers.* Rosen, 1998. *(P)*

Parsons, Alexandra. *Amazing Cats.* Knopf, 1989. *(P)*

Ryden, Hope. *Bobcat.* Putnam, 1983. *(I; A)*

Simon, Seymour. *Big Cats.* Harper, 1991. *(P; I)*

Winston, Peggy D. *Wild Cats.* National Geographic, 1981. *(P)*

## CATTLE

Older, Jules. *Cow.* Charlesbridge, 1997. *(P)*

Patent, Dorothy Hinshaw. *Cattle.* Carolrhoda, 1993. *(P; I)*

## CAVES AND CAVERNS

Dean, Anabel. *Going Underground: All about Caves and Caving.* Dillon, 1984. *(I)*

Kerbo, Ronal C. *Caves* Children's, 1981. *(P; I)*

## CELLS

Balkwill, Dr. Fran. *Cells Are Us.* Carolrhoda, 1993. *(P; I)*

Fichter, George S. *Cells.* Watts, 1986. *(I; A)*

Young, John K. *Cells: Amazing Forms and Functions.* Watts, 1990. *(I; A)*

## CELTS

Hinds, Kathryn. *The Celts of Northern Europe.* Marshall Cavendish, 1996. *(I; A)*

Martell, Hazel Mary. *The Celts.* Viking, 1995. *(I)*

Matthews, John. *Classic Celtic Fairy Tales.* Cassell, 1999. *(I)*

## CENSUS

Kassinger, Ruth. *U.S. Census: A Mirror of America.* Raintree/Steck-Vaughn, 1999. *(I)*

## CENTIPEDES AND MILLIPEDES

Preston-Mafham, Ken. *Discovering Centipedes & Millipedes.* Bookwright, 1990. *(I)*

## CENTRAL AFRICAN REPUBLIC

Anderson, Lydia. *Nigeria, Cameroon, and the Central African Republic.* Watts, 1981. *(I; A)*

Lyman, Francesca, and American Museum of Natural History. *Inside the Dzanga-Sangha Rain Forest.* Workman, 1998. *(P; I)*

## CENTRAL AMERICA

*Central America.* Greenhaven, 1990. *(A)*

Adams, Faith. *El Salvador: Beauty among the Ashes.* Dillon, 1986. *(P; I)*

Cheney, Glenn Alan. *El Salvador: Country in Crisis.* Watts, 1990. *(A)*

Foley, Erin. *El Salvador.* Marshall Cavendish, 1994. *(I; A)*

Hanmer, Trudy J. *Nicaragua.* Watts, 1986. *(I)*

Haverstock, Nathan A. *El Salvador in Pictures.* Lerner, 1987. *(I); Nicaragua . . . In Pictures,* 1987. *(I; A)*

Kott, Jennifer. *Nicaragua.* Marshall Cavendish, 1994. *(I; A)*

Markun, Patricia M. *Central America and Panama.* Watts, 1983 (rev. ed.). *(P; I)*

Perl, Lila. *Guatemala: Central America's Living Past.* Morrow, 1982. *(I; A)*

Visual Geography. *Costa Rica in Pictures.* Lerner, 1987. *(I); Guatemala in Pictures,* 1987. *(I)*

## CERAMICS

Weiss, Harvey. *Ceramics: From Clay to Kiln.* Addison-Wesley, 1982. *(I; A)*

## CHAMPLAIN, SAMUEL DE

Grant, Matthew G. *Champlain.* Creative Education, 1974. *(I)*

## CHAPLIN, CHARLIE

Schroeder, Alan. *Charlie Chaplin: The Beauty of Silence.* Watts, 1997. *(I; A)*

Turk, Ruth. *Charlie Chaplin: Genius of the Silent Screen.* Lerner, 2000. *(I; A)*

## CHARLEMAGNE

Biel, Timothy L. *The Charlemagne.* Lucent, 1997. *(I; A)*

MacDonald, Fiona. *The World in the Time of Charlemagne.* Silver Burdett Press, 1998. *(I)*

Pyle, Katharine. *Charlemagne and His Knights.* Lippincott, 1932. *(I)*

Winston, Richard. *Charlemagne.* Harper, 1968. *(I; A)*

## CHAUCER, GEOFFREY

Chaucer, Geoffrey. *Canterbury Tales.* Hyman, 1988. *(P; I; A); The Canterbury Tales,* adapt. by Geraldine McCaughrean. Rand, 1985. *(I; A)*

Cohen, Barbara. *Canterbury Tales.* Lothrop, 1988. *(P; I; A)*

## CHEKHOV, ANTON

Bloom, Harold, ed. *Anton Chekhov.* Chelsea House, 1998. *(A)*

## CHEMISTRY

Cobb, Vicki. *Chemically Active! Experiments You Can Do at Home.* Lippincott, 1985. *(A)*

Conway, Lorraine. *Chemistry Concepts.* Good Apple, 1983. *(I; A)*

Corrick, James A. *Recent Revolutions in Chemistry.* Watts, 1986. *(I)*

Gardner, Robert. *Science Projects about Kitchen Chemistry.* Enslow, 1999. *(I; A)*

Mebane, Robert C., and Rybolt, Thomas R. *Adventures with Atoms and Molecules, Book II: Chemistry Experiments for Young People.* Enslow, 1987. *(P; I)*

Pimentel, George C., and Coonrod, Janice A. *Opportunities in Chemistry, Today and Tomorrow.* National Academy Press, 1987. *(I; A)*

Walters, Derek. *Chemistry.* Watts, 1983. *(I; A)*

## CHESS

Berg, Barry. *Opening Moves: The Making of a Very Young Chess Champion.* Little, Brown, 2000. *(P; I)*

Kidder, Harvey. *The Kids' Book of Chess.* Workman, 1990. *(I)*

Marsh, Carole. *Go Queen Go! Chess for Kids.* Gallopade, 1983. *(P; I)*

## CHICAGO

Stein, Richard Conrad. *Chicago.* Grolier, 1997. *(I; A)*

## CHILD ABUSE

Benedict, Helen. *Safe, Strong and Streetwise.* Joy Street, 1987. *(A)*

Dolan, Edward F., Jr. *Child Abuse.* Watts, 1984. *(A)*

Hall, Lynn. *The Boy in the Off-White Hat.* Scribner's, 1984. *(I; A)*

Hong, Maria. *Family Abuse: A National Epidemic.* Enslow, 1997. *(I; A)*

Hyde, Margaret O. *Cry Softly! The Story of Child Abuse.* Westminster, 1986 (rev. ed.). *(I; A); Sexual Abuse: Let's Talk about It,* 1984. *(A)*

Irwin, Hadley. *Abby, My Love.* Atheneum, 1985. *(A)*

Landau, Elaine. *Child Abuse: An American Epidemic.* Messner, 1990 (rev. ed.). *(A)*

Morgan, Marcia. *My Feelings.* Equal Justice (Eugene, OR 97405), 1984. *(P; I)*

Mufson, Susan, and Kranz, Rachel. *Straight Talk about Child Abuse.* Facts on File, 1990. *(I; A)*

Newman, Susan. *Never Say Yes to a Stranger.* Putnam, 1985. *(I; A)*

Stanek, Muriel. *Don't Hurt Me, Mama.* Albert Whitman, 1983. *(P)*

Terkel, Susan N., and Rench, Janice E. *Feeling Safe, Feeling Strong: How to Avoid Sexual Abuse and What to Do if it Happens to You.* Lerner, 1984. *(P; I; A)*

Wachter, Oralee. *No More Secrets for Me.* Little, 1983. *(P)*

## CHILD LABOR

Bartoletti, Susan Campbell. *Growing up in Coal Country; Kids on Strike!* Houghton Mifflin, 1999. *(I; A)*

## CHILDREN'S LITERATURE

Byars, Betsy. *The Moon and I.* Simon & Schuster, 1992. *(I)*

Carpenter, Angelica. *L. Frank Baum: Royal Historian of Oz.* Lerner, 1992. *(I)*

Cleary, Beverly. *My Own Two Feet: A Memoir.* Morrow, 1995. *(P; I)*

German, Beverly. *E. B. White: Some Writer!* Atheneum, 1992. *(I)*

Lipson, Eden Ross. *The New York Times Parent's Guide to the Best Books for Children.* Times Books, 1991. *(A)*

Marcus, Leonard S. *A Caldecott Celebration: Six Artists and Their Paths to the Caldecott Medal.* Walker, 1998. *(P; I)*

Marcus, Leonard S., ed. *Author Talk.* Simon & Schuster, 2000. *(I)*

## CHILE

Galvin, Irene Flum. *Chile: Land of Poets and Patriots.* Dillon, 1990. *(I)*

Haverstock, Nathan A. *Chile in Pictures.* Lerner, 1988. *(I; A)*

Huber, Alex. *We Live in Chile.* Bookwright, 1986. *(P; I)*

## CHINA

Bradley, John. *China: A New Revolution?* Gloucester Press, 1990. *(I; A)*

Buck, Pearl. *Chinese Story Teller.* Harper, 1971. *(P)*

Dramer, Kim. *People's Republic of China.* Children's Press, 1999. *(I; A)*

Feinstein, Stephen C. *China . . . in Pictures.* Lerner, 1989. *(I)*

Fisher, Leonard. *The Great Wall of China.* Macmillan, 1986. *(P)*

Fritz, Jean. *China Homecoming.* Putnam, 1985. *(I); China's Long March: 6,000 Miles of Danger.* Putnam, 1988. *(I; A)*

Fyson, Nance Lui, and Greenhill, Richard. *A Family in China.* Lerner, 1986. *(P)*

Hacker, Jeffrey H. *The New China.* Watts, 1986. *(A)*

Keeler, Stephen. *Passport to China.* Watts, 1987. *(I; A)*

Major, John S. *The Land and People of China.* Lippincott, 1989. *(I; A)*

Mamdani, Shelby. *Traditions from China.* Raintree/Steck-Vaughn, 1999. *(P; I)*

McLenighan, Valjean. *China: A History to 1949.* Children's, 1983. *(I)*

Merton, Anna, and Kan, Shio-yun. *China: The Land and Its People.* Silver Burdett, 1987. *(P; I)*

Murphey, Rhoads, ed. *China.* Gateway Press, 1988. *(I; A)*

Ross, Stewart. *China Since 1945.* Bookwright, 1989. *(I; A)*

Sadler, Catherine. *Heaven's Reward: Fairy Tales from China.* Macmillan, 1985. *(I); Two Chinese Families.* Atheneum, 1981. *(P; I)*

Sherwood, Rhoda, with Sally Tolan. *China.* Gareth Stevens, 1988. *(P)*

Steele, Philip. *China.* Steck-Vaughn, 1989. *(I)*

Yee, Paul. *Tales from Gold Mountain.* Macmillan, 1989. *(I; A)*

Yep, Lawrence. *The Rainbow People.* Harper, 1989. *(I; A); The Serpent's Children.* Harper, 1984. *(I)*

Yin Lien C Chin et al, eds. *Traditional Chinese Folktales.* M.E. Sharpe, 1989. *(I)*

Young, Ed. *Lon Po Po: A Red-Riding Hood Story from China.* Philomel, 1989. *(P)*

## CHOCOLATE

Ammon, Richard. *The Kids' Book of Chocolate.* Atheneum, 1987. *(P; I)*

Burford, Betty M. *Chocolate by Hershey: A Story about Milton S. Hershey.* Lerner, 1994. *(P; I)*

Simon, Charnan. *Milton Hershey: Chocolate King, Town Builder.* Children's Press, 1998. *(P)*

## CHOPIN, FREDERIC

Cavelletti, Carlo. *Chopin and Romantic Music.* Barron's Educational Series, 2000. *(I; A)*

Tames, Richard. *Frederic Chopin.* Watts, 1991. *(I)*

Venezia, Mike. *Frederic Chopin.* Children's Press, 2000. *(P)*

## CHRISTMAS

Anderson, Joan. *Christmas on the Prairie.* Clarion, 1985. *(P)*

Daniel, Mark. *A Child's Christmas Treasury.* Dial, 1988. *(P)*

Hunt, Roderick. *The Oxford Christmas Book for Children.* Merrimack, 1983. *(P; I)*

Kelly, Emily. *Christmas around the World.* Carolrhoda, 1986. *(P)*

Patent, Dorothy Hinshaw. *Christmas Trees.* Dodd, 1987. *(P)*

Purdy, Susan. *Christmas Cooking around the World.* Watts, 1983. *(I; A)*

Ross, Kathy. *Christmas Decorations Kids Can Make.* Millbrook, 1999. *(P; I)*

Thomas, Dylan. *A Child's Christmas in Wales.* Holiday, 1985. *(P; I)*

## CHURCHILL, SIR WINSTON

Driemen, J. E. *Winston Churchill: An Unbreakable Spirit.* Dillon, 1990. *(I)*

## CIRCULATORY SYSTEM

Silverstein, Alvin; Silverstein, Virginia; and Silverstein, Robert. *The Circulatory System.* 21st Century Books, 1994. *(I)*

## CIRCUS

Cushman, Kathleen, and Miller, Montana. *Circus Dreams.* Joy Street, 1990. *(I)*

Fenton, Don, and Fenton, Barb. *Behind the Circus Scene.* Crestwood, 1980. *(P; I)*

Granfield, Linda. *Circus: An Album.* Dorling Kindersley, 1998. *(I)*

Harmer, Mabel. *Circus.* Children's, 1981. *(P)*

Machotka, Hana. *The Magic Ring: A Year with the Big Apple Circus.* Morrow, 1988. *(P; I; A)*

## CITIES

Carey, Helen. *How to Use Your Community as a Resource.* Watts, 1983. *(I; A)*

Florian, Douglas. *The City.* Crowell, 1982. *(P)*

Hanmer, Trudy. *The Growth of Cities.* Watts, 1985. *(A)*

Isadora, Rachael. *City Seen from A to Z.* Greenwillow, 1983. *(P)*

Maestro, Betsy. *Taxi: A Book of City Words.* Clarion, 1989. *(P)*

Provensen, Alice, and Provensen, Martin. *Town and Country.* Crown, 1985. *(P)*

Rice, Eve. *City Night.* Greenwillow, 1987. *(P)*

## CITIZENSHIP

Abel, Sally. *How to Become a U.S. Citizen.* Nolo Pr, 1983. *(I; A)*

## CIVIL RIGHTS

Adler, David A. *A Picture Book of Martin Luther King, Jr.* Holiday, 1989. *(P)*

Bach, Julie S., ed. *Civil Liberties.* Greenhaven Press, 1988. *(A)*

Bradley, John. *Human Rights.* Gloucester Press, 1987. *(I)*

Bridges, Ruby. *Through My Eyes.* Scholastic, 1999. *(P; I)*

Collier, Christopher, and Collier, James Lincoln. *Reconstruction and the Rise of Jim Crow: 1864-1896.* Marshall Cavendish/Benchmark, 1999. *(I)*

Fradin, Dennis Brindell, and Fradin, Judith Bloom. *Ida B. Wells: Mother of the Civil Rights Movement.* Clarion, 2000. *(I; A)*

George, Charles. *Life under the Jim Crow Laws.* Lucent, 1999. *(I; A)*

Hampton, Henry, and Fayer, Steve. *Voices of Freedom.* Bantam, 1990. *(I)*

Hanley, Sally A. *Philip Randolph.* Chelsea House, 1989. *(I)*

Lapping, Brian. *Apartheid: A History.* Braziller, 1987. *(A)*

Levy, Debbie. *Civil Liberties.* Lucent, 1999. *(I; A)*

Meltzer, Milton. *The Bill of Rights: How We Got It and What It Means.* Crowell, 1990. *(A)*

Parks, Rosa, and Haskins, Jim. *I Am Rosa Parks.* Dial, 1997. *(P)*

Pascoe, Elaine. *Racial Prejudice.* Watts, 1985. *(I; A)*

Price, Janet R., and others. *The Rights of Students: the Basic ACLU Guide to a Student's Rights.* Southern Illinois University, 1988. *(A)*

Rochelle, Belinda. *Witnesses to Freedom: Young People Who Fought for Civil Rights.* Lodestar, 1993. *(I; A)*

Selby, David. *Human Rights.* Cambridge University Press, 1987. *(I; A)*

Swain, Gwenyth. *Civil Rights Pioneer: A Story about Mary Church Terrell.* Lerner, 1999. *(P; I)*

Tilley, Glennette. *Take a Walk in Their Shoes.* Cobblehill, 1989. *(P; I)*

Vernell, Marjorie. *Leaders of Black Civil Rights.* Lucent, 1999. *(I; A)*

Wormser, Richard. *The Rise and Fall of Jim Crow: The African-American Struggle against Discrimination, 1865-1954.* Watts, 1999. *(I; A)*

## CIVIL RIGHTS MOVEMENT

Dudley, William, ed. *The Civil Rights Movement.* Greenhaven, 1996. *(A)*

King, Casey, and Osborne, Linda Barrett. *Oh, Freedom! Kids Talk about the Civil Rights Movement with the People Who Made it Happen.* Knopf/Borzoi, 1997. *(I;A)*

McKissack, Patricia, and McKissack, Fredrick. *The Civil Rights Movement in America from 1865 to the Present.* Children's, 1991. (Revised) *(I; A)*

Winters, Paul A., ed. *The Civil Rights Movement.* Greenhaven, 2000. *(A)*

## CIVIL WAR, UNITED STATES

Brooks, Victor. *African Americans in the Civil War; Civil War Forts; Secret Weapons in the Civil War.* Chelsea House, 2000. *(P; I)*

Chang, Ina. *A Separate Battle: Women and the Civil War.* Lodestar, 1991. *(I)*

Colbert, Nancy. *The Firing on Fort Sumter: A Splintered Nation Goes to War.* Morgan Reynolds, 2000. *(I; A)*

Collier, Christopher, and Collier, James Lincoln. *The Civil War: 1860-1865.* Marshall Cavendish/Benchmark, 1999. *(I)*

Corrick, James A. *Life among the Soldiers and Cavalry.* Lucent, 2000. *(I; A)*

Damon, Duane. *When This Cruel War Is Over: The Civil War Home Front.* Lerner, 1996. *(I; A)*

Haskins, Jim. *Black, Blue and Gray: African Americans in the Civil War.* Simon & Schuster, 1998. *(I)*

Kent, Zachary. *The Story of Sherman's March to the Sea.* Children's, 1987. *(I); The Story of the Surrender at Appomattox Courthouse.* Children's, 1987. *(I)*

Meltzer, Milton, ed. *Voices from the Civil War: A Documentary History of the Great American Conflict.* Crowell, 1989. *(I; A)*

Murphy, Jim. *The Boys' War: Confederate and Union Soldiers Talk about the Civil War.* Clarion, 1990. *(I; A)*

Ray, Delia. *Behind the Blue and the Gray: The Soldier's Life in the Civil War.* Lodestar, 1991. *(I; A)*

Reit, Seymour. *Behind Rebel Lines: The Incredible Story of Emma Edmonds, Civil War Spy.* Harcourt, 1988. *(P; I)*

Robertson, James I., Jr. *Civil War! America Becomes One Nation.* Knopf, 1992. *(I; A)*

Stein, R. Conrad. *The Story of the Monitor and the Merimack.* Children's, 1983. *(P; I)*

Werner, Emmy E. *Reluctant Witnesses: Children's Voices from the Civil War.* Westview, 1998. *(A)*

Windrow, Martin. *The Civil War Rifleman.* Watts, 1985. *(I)*

## CLAY, HENRY

Kelly, Regina Z. *Henry Clay: Statesman and Patriot.* Houghton, 1960. *(I)*

## CLEVELAND, STEPHEN GROVER

Collins, David R. *Grover Cleveland: 22nd and 24th President of the United States.* Garrett Educational, 1988. *(A)*

Kent, Zachary. *Grover Cleveland: Twenty-Second and Twenty-Fourth President of the United States.* Children's, 1988. *(P; I)*

## CLIMATE

Lye, Keith. *Weather and Climate.* Silver Burdett, 1984. *(P)*

Peters, Lisa. *The Sun, the Wind, and the Rain.* Holt, 1988. *(P)*

Updegraffe, Imelda, and Updegraffe, Robert. *Continents and Climates.* Penguin, 1983. *(I; A)*

## CLINTON, WILLIAM

Cwiklik, Robert. *Bill Clinton: President of the 90's.* Millbrook, 1997. *(I)*

Gallen, David. *Bill Clinton as They Know Him.* Gallen, 1994. *(A)*

Martin, Gene L., and Boyd, Aaron. *Bill Clinton: President from Arkansas.* Tudor, 1993. *(I; A)*

## CLOCKS

Dash, Joan. *The Longitude Prize.* Farrar, 2000. *(I; A)*

Duffy, Trent. *The Clock.* Simon & Schuster/Atheneum, 2000. *(I; A)*

Duffy, Trent. *The Turning Point Inventions: The Clock.* Simon & Schuster, 2000. *(I; A)*

Maestro, Betsy C. *The Story of Clocks and Calendars: Marking a Millennium.* Morrow, 1999. *(P; I)*

Older, Jules. *Telling Time: How to Tell Time on Digital and Analog Clocks!* Charlesbridge, 2000. *(P)*

## CLOTHING

Cooke, Jean. *Costumes and Clothes.* Watts, 1987. *(P)*

Moss, Miriam. *Fashion Designer.* Crestwood, 1991. *(I)*

Perl, Lila. *From Top Hats to Baseball Caps, From Bustles to Blue Jeans: Why We Dress the Way We Do.* Clarion, 1990. *(I)*

Rowland-Warne, L. *Costume.* Knopf, 1992. *(I; A)*

Weil, Lisl. *New Clothes: What People Wore— from Cavemen to Astronauts.* Atheneum, 1988. *(I)*

## CLOUDS

Branley, Franklyn Mansfield. *Down Comes the Rain: Stage 2.* HarperCollins, 1999. *(P)*
McMillan, Bruce. *The Weather Sky.* Farrar, 1991. *(I)*

## CLOWNS

Fife, Bruce, and others. *Creative Clowning.* Java Publishing, 1988. *(A)*

## COAL AND COAL MINING

Asimov, Isaac. *How Did We Find Out about Coal?* Walker, 1980. *(I; A)*
Davis, Bertha, and Whitfield, Susan. *The Coal Question.* Watts, 1982. *(I; A)*
Kraft, Betsy. *Coal.* Watts, 1982 (rev. ed.). *(P; I)*

## CODES AND CIPHERS

Brandreth, Gyles. *Writing Secret Codes and Sending Hidden Messages.* Sterling, 1984. *(I)*
Fletcher, Helen J. *Secret Codes.* Watts, 1980. *(P)*
Grant, E. A. *The Kids' Book of Secret Codes, Signals, and Ciphers.* Running Press, 1989. *(P; I)*
Janeczko, Paul B. *Loads of Codes and Secret Ciphers.* Macmillan, 1984. *(I)*
Mango, Karin N. *Codes, Ciphers and Other Secrets.* Watts, 1988. *(P; I)*

## COINS AND COIN COLLECTING

Hobson, Burton H. *Coin Collecting as a Hobby.* Sterling, 1982 (rev. ed.). *(I; A)*
Reisberg, Ken. *Coin Fun.* Watts, 1981. *(P)*

## COLD WAR

Grant, R.G. *The Berlin Wall.* Raintree/Steck-Vaughn, 1998. *(I; A)*
Sherrow, Victoria. *Joseph McCarthy and the Cold War.* Blackbirch, 1998. *(I; A)*

## COLLAGE

Beaney, Jan. *Fun with Collage.* Sportshelf, 1980. *(P; I)*

## COLOMBIA

Jacobsen, Peter O., and Kristensen, Preben S. *A Family in Colombia.* Bookwright, 1986. *(P)*
Visual Geography. *Colombia in Pictures.* Lerner, 1987. *(I; A)*

## COLONIAL LIFE IN AMERICA

Knight, James. *The Farm: Life in Colonial Pennsylvania; Sailing to America: Colonists at Sea; Salem Days: Life in a Colonial Seaport; The Village: Life in Colonial Times.* Troll, 1982. *(I; A)*
Waters, Kate. *Sarah Morton's Day: A Day in the Life of a Pilgrim Girl.* Scholastic, 1990. *(P)*

## COLOR

Ardley, Neil. *The Science Book of Color.* Gulliver Books, 1991. *(P; I)*

## COLORADO

Ayer, Eleanor H. *Colorado.* Benchmark, 1997. *(P;I)*
Kent, Deborah. *Colorado.* Children's, 1989. *(P; I)*

## COLUMBUS, CHRISTOPHER

Adler, David A. *A Picture Book of Christopher Columbus.* Holiday, 1991. *(P)*
Batherman, Muriel. *Before Columbus.* Houghton, 1981. *(P)*
Brenner, Barbara. *If You Were There in 1492.* Bradbury, 1991. *(I)*
Columbus, Christopher. *The Log of Christopher Columbus' First Voyage to America in the Year 1492: As Copied out in Brief by Bartholomew Las Casas.* Linnet Books, 1989. *(P; I)*
Dodge, Stephen C. *Christopher Columbus and the First Voyages to the New World.* Chelsea House, 1990. *(A)*
Levinson, Nancy Smiler. *Christopher Columbus.* Lodestar, 1990. *(I; A)*
Meltzer, Milton. *Columbus and the World around Him.* Watts, 1990. *(I; A)*
Roop, Peter, and Roop, Connie, eds. *I, Columbus: My Journal— 1492-3*Walker, 1990. *(I)*
Sis, Peter. *Follow the Dream: The Story of Christopher Columbus.* Knopf, 1991. *(P)*
Weil, Lisl. *I, Christopher Columbus.* Atheneum, 1983. *(A)*

## COMETS, METEORITES, AND ASTEROIDS

Asimov, Isaac. *Comets and Meteors.* Gareth Stevens, 1990. *(P; I); Asimov's Guide to Halley's Comet.* 1985. *(I; A)*
Berger, Melvin. *Comets, Meteors, and Asteroids.* Putnam, 1981. *(A)*
Bonar, Samantha. *Comets.* Watts, 1998. *(P; I)*
Branley, Franklyn M. *Comets.* Harper, 1984. *(P); Halley: Comet 1986.* Lodestar, 1983. *(I; A)*
Darling, David J. *Comets, Meteors, and Asteroids: Rocks in Space.* Dillon, 1984. *(P)*
Hamer, Martyn. *Comets.* Watts, 1984. *(P; I)*
Krupp, Edwin C. *The Comet and You.* Macmillan, 1985. *(P)*
Simon, Seymour. *Comets, Meteors, and Asteroids.* Morrow, 1994. *(P; I); The Long Journey from Space.* Crown, 1982. *(P)*
Vogt, Gregory. *Halley's Comet: What We've Learned.* Watts, 1987. *(I)*

## COMIC BOOKS

Rovin, Jeff. *The Encyclopedia of Superheroes.* Facts on File, 1985. *(A)*

## COMMERCE, UNITED STATES DEPARTMENT OF

Griffin, Robert J., Jr. *The Department of Commerce.* Chelsea House, 1989. *(P; I)*

## COMMONWEALTH OF INDEPENDENT STATES

Clark, Mary Jane Behrends. *The Commonwealth of Independent States.* Millbrook Press, 1992. *(I)*

## COMMONWEALTH OF NATIONS

Lace, William W. *The British Empire: The End of Colonialism.* Lucent, 2000. *(I; A)*

## COMMUNICATION

Fisher, Trevor. *Communications.* David & Charles, 1985. *(I; A)*

Graham, Ian. *Communications.* Watts, 1989. *(P; I)*

Herda, D. J. *Communication Satellites.* Watts, 1988. *(I; A)*

Schefter, James L. *Telecommunications Careers.* Watts, 1988. *(A)*

Storrs, Graham. *The Telecommunications Revolution.* Bookwright, 1985. *(I; A)*

Sullivan, George. *How Do We Communicate?* Watts, 1983. *(P)*

Wilson, Anthony. *Communications.* Kingfisher, 1999. *(I; A)*

Wolverton, Ruth, and Wolverton, Mike. *The News Media.* Watts, 1981. *(I; A)*

## COMMUNISM

Forman, James D. *Communism.* Watts, 1979 (2nd ed.). *(I; A)*

## COMPUTERS

Asimov, Isaac. *How Did We Find Out about Computers?* Walker, 1984. *(I)*

Berger, Melvin. *Computer Talk.* Messner, 1984. *(I)*; *Computers in Your Life.* Crowell, 1984. *(I; A)*

Henderson, Harry. *The Internet.* Lucent, 1998. *(I)*

Howard, Penny. *Looking at Computers; Looking at Computer Programming; Looking at LOGO.* Watts, 1984. *(P)*

Koehler, Lora. *Internet.* Children's, 1995. *(P; I)*

Lampton, Christopher. *Advanced BASIC for Beginners; BASIC for Beginners; COBOL for Beginners; FORTRAN for Beginners; The Micro Dictionary; PASCAL for Beginners; PILOT for Beginners.* Watts, 1984. *(I; A)*; *Super-Conductors.* Enslow, 1989. *(I; A)*

Lipson, Shelley. *It's BASIC: The ABC's of Computer Programming.* Holt, 1982. *(P; I)*

Norback, Judith. *The Complete Computer Career Guide.* TAB Books, 1987. *(A)*

Owen, Trevor, and Owston, Ron. *The Learning Highway: Smart Students and the Net.* Key Porter, 1998. *(A)*

Petty, Kate. *Computers.* Watts, 1984. *(P)*

Sullivan, George. *Computer Kids.* Dodd, 1984. *(I; A)*

Wolinsky, Art. *Communicating on the Internet; Creating and Publishing Web Pages on the Internet.* Enslow, 1999. *(I)*; *The History of the Internet and the World Wide Web; Locating and Evaluating Information on the Internet.* Enslow, 1999. *(I; A)*

## CONGO

Newman, Gerald. *Zaire, Gabon, and the Congo.* Watts, 1981. *(I; A)*

## CONGO RIVER

*Zaire . . . in Pictures.* Lerner, 1992. *(I; A)*

Lauber, Patricia. *The Congo: River into Central Africa.* Garrard, 1964. *(I)*

## CONNECTICUT

Fradin, Dennis. *Connecticut: In Words and Pictures.* Children's, 1980. *(P; I)*

## CONRAD, JOSEPH

Fletcher, Chris. *Joseph Conrad.* Oxford, 1999. *(I; A)*

Reilly, Jim. *Life and Works: Joseph Conrad.* Rourke, 1990. *(I)*

## CONSERVATION

Kessler, Christina, and Mswati III. *All the King's Animals: The Return of Endangered Wildlife to Swaziland.* Boyds Mills Press, 1995. *(P; I)*

Pringle, Laurence. *Restoring Our Earth.* Enslow, 1987. *(P)*; *What Shall We Do with the Land?* Harper, 1981. *(I)*

Whitman, Sylvia. *This Land is Your Land: The American Conservation Movement.* Lerner, 1994. *(I)*

## CONSUMERISM

Arnold, Caroline. *What Will We Buy?* Watts, 1983. *(P)*

Kelly, Brendan. *Consumer Math.* EDC Publishing, 1981. *(I)*

Walz, Michael K. *The Law and Economics: Your Rights as a Consumer.* Lerner, 1990. *(I; A)*

## COOKING

*Betty Crocker's Cookbook for Boys and Girls.* Western, 1984. *(P; I)*

Bjork, Christina. *Elliot's Extraordinary Cookbook.* R & S Books, 1991. *(P; I)*

Coronado, Rosa. *Cooking the Mexican Way.* Lerner, 1982. *(I; A)*

D'Amico, Joan, and Drummond, Karen Eich. *The United States Cookbook: Fabulous Foods and Fascinating Facts from All 50 States.* Wiley, 2000. *(I)*

Delmar, Charles. *The Essential Cook: Everything You Really Need to Know about Foods and Cooking Except the Recipes.* Hill House, 1989. *(I; A)*

Drew, Helen. *My First Baking Book.* Knopf, 1991. *(P; I)*

Goldstein, Helen H. *Kid's Cuisine.* News & Observer, 1983. *(P; I)*

Greene, Karen. *Once upon a Recipe: Delicious, Healthy Foods for Kids of All Ages.* New Hope Press, 1988. *(P; I)*

Johnson, Sylvia A. *Tomatoes, Potatoes, Corn, and Beans: How the Foods of the Americas Changed Cooking Around the World.* Atheneum, 1997. *(I; A)*

Moore, Carolyn E., and others. *Young Chef's Nutrition Guide and Cookbook.* Barron, 1990. *(I)*

Ralph, Judy. *The Peanut Butter Cookbook for Kids.* Hyperion, 1995. *(I)*

Sanderson, Marie C., and Schroeder, Rosella J. *It's Not Really Magic: Microwave Cooking for Young People.* Dillon, 1981. *(I; A)*

Zalben, Jane Breskin. *To Every Season: A Family Holiday Cookbook.* Simon & Schuster, 1999. *(P; I)*

## COOLIDGE, CALVIN

Kent, Zachary. *Calvin Coolidge: Thirtieth President of the United States.* Children's, 1988. *(P; I)*

## COPPER

Beatty, Richard. *Copper.* Marshall Cavendish, 2000. *(P; I)*

Fodor, R. V. *Gold, Copper, Iron: How Metals Are Formed, Found, and Used.* Enslow, 1989. *(A)*

Lambert, Mark. *Spotlight on Copper.* Rourke, 1988. *(P; I)*

## CORALS

Bender, Lionel. *Life on a Coral Reef.* Gloucester Press, 1989. *(P; I)*

Cousteau Society. *Corals: The Sea's Great Builders.* Simon & Schuster, 1992. *(P; I)*

Maynard, Caitlin; Maynard, Thane; and Rullman, Stan. *Rain Forests and Reefs: A Kid's-Eye View of the Tropics.* Watts, 1996. *(I)*

Reese, Bob. *Coral Reef.* Children's, 1983. *(P)*

Sargent, William. *Night Reef: Dusk to Dawn on a Coral Reef.* Watts, 1991. *(P; I)*

Segaloff, Nat, and Erickson, Paul. *A Reef Comes to Life: Creating an Undersea Exhibit.* Watts, 1991. *(I)*

## CORN

Aliki. *Corn Is Maize: The Gift of the Indians.* Harper, 1976. *(P)*

Selsam, Millicent E. *Popcorn.* Morrow, 1976. *(P; I)*

## CORONADO, FRANCISCO

Haley, Alex. *Coronado's Golden Quest.* Raintree Steck-Vaughn, 1993. *(P; I)*

## CORTÉS, HERNANDO

Marrin, Albert. *Aztecs and Spaniards: Cortes and the Conquest of Mexico.* Atheneum, 1986. *(A)*

## COSMIC RAYS

Branley, Franklyn Mansfield. *Superstar: The Supernova of 1987.* HarperCollins, 1990. *(P; I)*

## COSTA RICA

*Costa Rica . . . in Pictures.* Lerner, 1997. *(I)*

## COTTON

Miles, Lewis. *Cotton.* Rourke Enterprises, 1987. *(P; I)*

Mitgutsch, Ali. *From Cotton to Pants.* Carolrhoda, 1981. *(P)*

Selsam, Millicent E. *Cotton.* Morrow, 1982. *(P; I)*

## COUNTRY MUSIC

Lomax, John. *Nashville: Music City USA.* Abrams, 1985. *(A)*

## COURTS

DeVillers, David. *The John Brown Slavery Revolt Trial: A Headline Court Case* Enslow, 2000. *(A)*

Frost-Knappman, Elizabeth; Knappman, Edward W.; and Paddock, Lisa. *Courtroom Drama: 120 of the World's Most Notable Trials, Vol. 3.* Gale Group, 1997. *(I; A)*

Lawson, Don. *Landmark Supreme Court Cases.* Enslow, 1987. *(A)*

Ogawa, Brian K. *To Tell the Truth.* Volcano Press, 1997. *(I)*

Riley, Gail Blasser. *Miranda v. Arizona: Rights of the Accused.* Enslow, 1994. *(I; A)*

## COWBOYS

Traditional. *Cowboy Songs.* Macmillan, 1938. *(I)*

De Angelis, Gina. *Black Cowboys.* Chelsea House, 1997. *(I)*

Freedman, Russell. *Cowboys of the Wild West.* Clarion, 1985. *(A)*

Helberg, Kristin. *Cowboys.* Troubador, 1982. *(I; A)*

Klausmeier, Robert. *Cowboy.* Lerner, 1995. *(P; I)*

Ling, Mary. *Calf.* Dorling Kindersley, 1993. *(P)*

Malone, Margaret G. *Cowboys and Computers: Life on a Modern Ranch.* Messner, 1982. *(P; I)*

Patent, Dorothy Hinshaw. *The Sheep Book.* Dodd, 1985. *(I)*

Sandler, Martin W. *Cowboys: A Library of Congress Book.* HarperCollins, 2000. *(P; I)*

## CRABS

Bailey, Jill. *Discovering Crabs and Lobsters.* Watts, 1987. *(P)*

Johnson, Sylvia A. *Crabs.* Lerner, 1982. *(P; I; A)*

## CRANE, STEPHEN

Sufrin, Mark. *Stephen Crane.* Atheneum, 1992. *(I; A)*

## CREDIT CARDS

Godfrey, Neale S. *Neale S. Godfrey's Ultimate Kids' Money Book.* Simon & Schuster, 1998. *(P; I; A)*

## CRIMEAN WAR

Bachrach, Deborah. *The Crimean War.* Lucent, 1997. *(A)*

## CROCHETING

O'Reilly, Susan. *Knitting and Crocheting.* Raintree Steck-Vaughn, 1994. *(P; I)*

Cone, Ferne G. *Classy Knitting: A Guide to Creative Sweatering for Beginners.* Atheneum, 1984; *Crazy Crocheting.* Atheneum, 1981. *(I; A)*

## CROCKETT, DAVID (DAVY)

McCall, Edith. *Hunters Blaze the Trails.* Children's, 1980. *(P; I; A)*

Santrey, Laurence. *Davy Crockett: Young Pioneer.* Troll, 1983. *(P; I)*

Townsend, Tom. *Davy Crockett: An American Hero.* Eakin Press, 1987. *(I)*

## CROCODILES AND ALLIGATORS

*Alligators and Crocodiles.* Facts on File, 1990. *(I)*

Arnosky, Jim. *All about Alligators.* Scholastic, 1994. *(P)*

Bare, Colleen Stanley. *Never Kiss an Alligator!* Cobblehill, 1989. *(P)*

Bender, Lionel. *Crocodiles and Alligators.* Gloucester Press, 1988. *(I)*

Harris, Susan. *Crocodiles and Alligators.* Watts, 1980. *(P)*

Scott, Jack Denton. *Alligators.* Putnam, 1984. *(P; I; A)*

Simon, Seymour. *Crocodiles and Alligators.* HarperCollins, 1999. *(I)*

## CRUSADES

Williams, Ann. *The Crusades.* Longman, 1975. *(I; A)*

Williams, Jay. *Knights of the Crusades.* Harper, 1962. *(I; A)*

## CRYSTALS

Gans, Roma. *Millions and Millions of Crystals.* Crowell, 1973. *(P)*

## CUBA

Ancona, George. *Cuban Kids.* Marshall Cavendish, 2000. *(P; I)*

Crouch, Clifford W. *Cuba.* Chelsea House, 1997. *(I)*

Dolan, Edward D., and Scariano, Margaret M. *Cuba and the United States.* Watts, 1987. *(A)*

Haverstock, Nathan. *Cuba . . . In Pictures.* Lerner, 1987. *(I; A)*

Morrison, Marion. *Cuba.* Children's Press, 1999. *(I; A)*

Vazquez, Ana Maria, and Casas, Rosa E. *Cuba.* Children's, 1988. *(P; I)*

## CURIE, MARIE AND PIERRE

Birch, Beverley. *Marie Curie: The Polish Scientist Who Discovered Radium and Its Life-Saving Properties.* Gareth Stevens, 1988. *(I)*

Brandt, Keith. *Marie Curie: Brave Scientist.* Troll, 1983. *(I)*

Conner, Edwina. *Marie Curie.* Watts, 1987. *(I)*

Keller, Mollie. *Marie Curie.* Watts, 1982. *(I; A)*

Tarnes, Richard. *Marie Curie.* Watts, n.d. *(I)*

## CYPRUS

*Cyprus . . . in Pictures.* Lerner, 1992. *(I)*

## CZECH REPUBLIC

Ish-Kishor, S. *A Boy of Old Prague.* Scholastic, 1980. *(P; I)*

Lye, Keith. *Take a Trip to Czechoslovakia.* Watts, 1986. *(P)*

## DAIRYING AND DAIRY PRODUCTS

Dineen, Jacqueline. *Food from Dairy and Farming.* Enslow, 1988. *(P; I)*

Gibbons, Gail. *The Milk Makers.* Macmillan, 1985. *(P)*

Moon, Cliff. *Dairy Cows on the Farm; Pigs on the Farm; Poultry on the Farm; Sheep on the Farm.* Watts, 1983. *(P)*

Older, Jules. *Cow.* Charlesbridge, 1997. *(P)*

Patent, Dorothy Hinshaw. *Cattle.* Carolrhoda, 1993. *(P; I)*

Patterson, Geoffrey. *Dairy Farming.* Andre Deutsch, 1984. *(P)*

Scuro, Vincent. *Wonders of Dairy Cattle.* Dodd, 1986. *(P; I)*

Wake, Susan. *Butter.* Lerner, 1990. *(P; I)*

## DALI, SALVADOR

Carter, David. *Salvador Dali.* Chelsea, 1994. *(I; A)*

## DALLAS

McComb, David G. *Texas: An Illustrated History.* Oxford, 1995. *(I; A)*

## DAMS

Ardley, Neil. *Dams.* Garrett Educational, 1990. *(P; I)*

Doherty, Craig A., and Doherty, Katherine M. *Hoover Dam.* Blackbirch Press, 1995. *(I)*

Sandak, Cass R. *Dams.* Watts. 1983. *(P)*

## DANCE

Barboza, Steven. *I Feel Like Dancing: A Year with Jacques D'Amboise and the National Dance Institute.* Crown, 1992. *(P; I)*

Brown, LouLou, ed. *Ballet Class.* Arco, 1985. *(I)*

Collard, Alexandra. *Two Young Dancers: Their World of Ballet.* Messner, 1984. *(I; A)*

Finney, Shan. *Dance.* Watts, 1983. *(I; A)*

Glover, Savion, and Weber, Bruce. *Savion!: My Life in Tap.* Morrow, 2000. *(I; A)*

Haskins, James. *Black Dance in America: A History Through Its People.* Crowell, 1990. *(I; A)*

Isadora, Rachel. *Opening Night.* Greenwillow, 1984. *(P)*

Johnson, Anne E. *Jazz Tap: From African Drums to American Feet.* Rosen, 1999. *(P; I)*

Jones, Bill T., and Kuklin, Susan. *Dance.* Hyperion, 1998. *(P)*

Kuklin, Susan. *Reaching for Dreams: A Ballet From Rehearsal to Opening Night.* Lothrop, 1987. *(I; A)*

Rosenberg, Jane. *Dance Me a Story.* Norton, 1985. *(I; A)*

Royal Academy of Dancing. *Ballet Class.* Arco, 1985. *(P; I)*

Sorine, D. *Imagine That! It's Modern Dance; At Every Turn: It's Ballet.* Knopf, 1981. *(P)*

Switzer, Ellen E. *Dancers!* Atheneum, 1982. *(I; A)*

## DARWIN, CHARLES ROBERT

Nardo, Don, ed. *Charles Darwin.* Greenhaven, 1999. *(A)*

Parker, Steve. *Charles Darwin and Evolution.* Harper, 1992. *(I)*

Skelton, Renee. *Charles Darwin and the Theory of Natural Selection.* Barron, 1987. *(P; I)*

Ward, Peter. *The Adventures of Charles Darwin: A Story of the Beagle Voyage.* Cambridge University Press, 1982. *(A)*

## DEAFNESS

Aseltine, Lorraine, and others. *I'm Deaf and It's Okay.* Albert Whitman, 1986. *(P)*

Curtis, Patricia. *Cindy: A Hearing Ear Dog.* Dutton, 1981. *(P; I)*

Flodin, Mickey. *Signing for Kids.* Perigee, 1991. *(P; I)*

Hlibok, Bruce. *Silent Dancer.* Perigee, 1991. *(P; I)* Messner, 1981. *(I)*

LaMore, Gregory S. *Now I Understand: A Book about Hearing Impairment.* Gallaudet College Press, 1986. *(P; I)*

Neimark, Anne E. *A Deaf Child Listened: Thomas Gallaudet, Pioneer in American Education.* Morrow, 1983. *(I; A)*

Walker, Lou Ann. *Amy: The Story of a Deaf Child.* Lodestar, 1985. *(P; I)*

## DEATH

Alexander, Sue. *Nadia the Willful.* Pantheon, 1983. *(P)*

Altman, Linda Jacobs. *Death: An Introduction to Medical-Ethical Dilemmas.* Enslow, 2000. *(I; A)*

Anson, Robert Sam. *Best Intentions— The Education and Killing of Edmund Perry.* Vintage, 1987. *(I; A)*

Bode, Janet. *Death Is Hard to Live With: Teenagers and How They Cope With Death.* Delacorte, 1993. *(A)*

Clardy, Andrea Fleck. *Dusty Was My Friend: Coming to Terms with Loss.* Human Sciences Press, 1984. *(P; I)*

Donnelley, Elfie. *So Long, Grandpa;* tr. from the German by Anthea Bell. Crown, 1981. *(P; I)*

Fry, Virginia Lynn. *Part of Me Died, Too: Stories of Creative Survival among Bereaved Children and Teenagers.* Dutton, 1995. *(I; A)*

Heegaard, Marge Eaton. *Coping with Death and Grief.* Lerner, 1990. *(I)*

Hermes, Patricia. *Who Will Take Care of Me?* Harcourt, 1983. *(P; I)*

Hyde, Margaret O., and Setaro, John F. *When the Brain Dies First.* Watts, 2000. *(A)*

Krementz, Jill. *How It Feels When a Parent Dies.* Knopf, 1981. *(I)*

Rofes, Eric E., ed. *The Kids' Book about Death and Dying: By and for Kids.* Little, 1985. *(I; A)*

Rohr, Janelle. *Death and Dying.* Greenhaven Press, 1987. *(A)*

## DEBATES AND DISCUSSIONS

Dunbar, Robert E. *How to Debate.* Watts, 1994. *(A)*

## DECEMBER

Updike, John. *A Child's Calendar.* Holiday House, 1999. *(P; I)*

Warner, Penny. *Kids' Holiday Fun: Great Family Activities Every Month of the Year.* Meadowbrook Press, 1997. *(P)*

## DECLARATION OF INDEPENDENCE

Brenner, Barbara. *If You Were There in 1776.* Simon & Schuster, 1994. *(P; I)*

Commager, Henry Steele. *The Great Declaration.* Bobbs, 1958. *(I; A)*

Dalgliesh, Alice. *The Fourth of July Story.* Scribner's, 1956. *(P; I)*

Fradin, Dennis B. *The Declaration of Independence.* Children's, 1988. *(P)*

Freedman, Russell. *Give Me Liberty: The Story of the Declaration of Independence.* Holiday House, 2000. *(I)*

Giblin, James C. *Fireworks, Picnics, and Flags: The Story of the Fourth of July.* Houghton, 1983. *(I)*

## DÉCOUPAGE

Gilbreath, Alice Thompson. *Simple Decoupage: Having Fun with Cutouts.* Morrow, 1978. *(I)*

## DEER

Ahlstrom, Mark. *The Whitetail.* Crestwood, 1983. *(P; I)*

Arnosky, Jim. *All about Deer.* Scholastic, 1996. *(P)*

Bailey, Jill. *Discovering Deer.* Watts, 1988. *(P)*

Hodge, Deborah. *Deer, Moose, Elk & Caribou.* Kids Can, 1998. *(P; I)*

McClung, Robert M. *White Tail.* Morrow, 1987. *(P; I)*

Patent, Dorothy Hinshaw. *Deer and Elk.* Houghton Mifflin, 1994. *(I)*

## DEFENSE, UNITED STATES DEPARTMENT OF

Heinsohn, Beth, and Cohen, Andrew. *The Department of Defense.* Chelsea House, 1990. *(P; I)*

## DEGAS, EDGAR

Janson, H. W., and Janson, Anthony F. *History of Art for Young People.* Abrams, 1997. (rev. ed.) *(I; A)*

Meyer, Susan E. *Edgar Degas.* Abrams, 1994. *(I; A)*

Muhlberger, Richard, and Metropolitan Museum of Art. *What Makes a Degas a Degas?* Viking, 1993. *(I)*

Venezia, Mike. *Edgar Degas.* Children's Press, 2000. *(P; I)*

Welton, Jude. *Eyewitness: Impressionism.* DK, 2000. *(P; I; A)*

## DELAWARE

Fradin, Dennis. *Delaware: In Words and Pictures.* Children's, 1980. *(P; I)*

## DEMOCRACY

Chute, Marchette. *The Green Tree of Democracy.* Dutton, 1971. *(I)*

Crout, George. *The Seven Lives of Johnny B. Free.* Denison, n.d. *(P; I)*

## DENMARK

Andersen, Ulla. *We Live in Denmark.* Watts, 1984. *(P; I)*

Haugaard, Erik C. *Leif the Unlucky.* Houghton, 1982. *(I)*

Mussari, Mark. *The Danish Americans.* Chelsea House, 1988. *(I; A)*

## DENTISTRY

Keller, Laurie. *Open Wide: Tooth School Inside.* Holt, 2000. *(P)*

Marsoli, Lisa Ann. *Things to Know before Going to the Dentist.* Silver Burdett, 1985. *(I)*

McGinty, Alice B. *Staying Healthy: Dental Care.* Rosen, 1998. *(P)*

Silverstein, Alvin; Silverstein, Virginia; and Nunn, Laura Silverstein. *Tooth Decay and Cavities.* Watts, 2000. *(P; I)*

Ward, Brian R. *Dental Care.* Watts, 1986. *(I; A)*

## DENVER

Spies, Karen. *Denver.* Dillon, 1988. *(P)*

## DEPARTMENT STORES

Gibbons, Gail. *Department Stores.* Harper, 1984. *(P)*

## DEPRESSIONS AND RECESSIONS

Farrell, Jacqueline. *The Great Depression.* Lucent, 1996. *(I; A)*

Fremon, David K. *The Great Depression in American History.* Enslow, 1997. *(P; I)*

McElvaine, Robert S. *The Depression and the New Deal: A History in Documents.* Oxford, 2000. *(A)*

Meltzer, Milton. *Brother, Can You Spare a Dime?: The Great Depression of 1929-1933.* Facts on File, 1990. *(I; A)*

Nardo, Don, ed. *The Great Depression.* Greenhaven, 1999. *(A)*

Schraff, Anne E., and Feinberg, Barbara Silberdick. *Great Depression and the New Deal: America's Economic Collapse and Recovery.* Watts, 1990. *(I; A)*

Sherrow, Victoria. *Hardship and Hope.* Twenty-First Century, 1995. *(I; A)*

Wormser, Richard. *Growing Up in the Great Depression.* Atheneum, 1994. *(I)*

## DESERTS

Bramwell, Martyn. *Deserts.* Watts, 1988. *(I)*

Dewey, Jennifer Owings. *A Night and Day in the Desert.* Little, 1991. *(P; I)*

Dixon, Dougal. *Deserts and Wastelands.* Watts, 1985. *(I)*

George, Jean Craighead. *One Day in the Desert.* Harper, 1983. *(P; I)*

Lye, Keith. *Deserts.* Silver Burdett, 1987. *(P)*

Moore, Randy, and Vodopich, Darrell S. *The Living Desert.* Enslow, 1991. *(I)*

Simon, Seymour. *Deserts.* Morrow, 1990. *(P; I)*

Twist, Clint. *Deserts.* Dillon: Macmillan, 1991. *(P; I)*

Watson, Jane W. *Deserts of the World; Future Threat or Promise?* Putnam, 1981. *(A)*

Watts, Barie. *24 Hours in a Desert.* Watts, 1991. *(P; I)*

Wiewandt, Thomas. *The Hidden Life of the Desert.* Crown, 1990. *(I)*

Wright-Frierson, Virginia. *A Desert Scrapbook: Dawn to Dusk in the Sonoran Desert.* Simon & Schuster, 1996. *(P; I)*

Yolen, Jane. *Welcome to the Sea of Sand.* Putnam, 1996. *(P)*

## DESIGN

Branley, Franklyn M. *Color: From Rainbows to Lasers.* Harper, 1978. *(A)*

## DETROIT

Zimmerman, Chanda K. *Detroit.* Dillon, 1989. *(P; I)*

## DIAMONDS

Rickard, Graham. *Spotlight on Diamonds.* Rourke, 1988. *(P; I)*

## DICKENS, CHARLES

Collins, David R. *Tales for Hard Times: A Story About Charles Dickens.* Carolrhoda, 1990. *(I)*

Martin, Christopher. *Life and Works: Charles Dickens.* Rourke, 1990. *(A)*

## DICKINSON, EMILY

Dickinson, Emily. *Poems for Youth.* Little, 1934. *(I; A)*

Steffens, Bradley. *Emily Dickinson.* Lucent, 1997. *(I; A)*

## DICTIONARIES

Karske, Robert. *The Story of the Dictionary.* Harcourt, 1975. *(I; A)*

## DINOSAURS

Bates, Robin, and Simon, Cheryl. *The Dinosaurs and the Dark Star.* Macmillan, 1985. *(I)*

Berger, Melvin, and Berger, Gilda. *Did Dinosaurs Live in Your Backyard?: Questions and Answers about Dinosaurs.* Scholastic, 1999. *(P)*

Bishop, Nic. *Digging for Bird-Dinosaurs: An Expedition to Madagascar.* Houghton, 2000. *(I)*

Booth, Jerry. *The Big Beast Book: Dinosaurs and How They Got That Way.* Little, 1988. *(P; I)*

Cohen, Daniel. *Dinosaurs.* Doubleday, 1987. *(P; I)*

Cohen, Daniel, and Cohen, Susan. *Where to Find Dinosaurs Today.* Dutton/Cobblehill, 1992. *(I)*

Currie, Philip J., and Mastin, Colleayn O. *The Newest and Coolest Dinosaurs.* Grasshopper, 1998. *(I)*

Dingus, Lowell, and Chiappe, Luis. *The Tiniest Giants: Discovering Dinosaur Eggs.* Doubleday, 1999. *(I)*

Dixon, Dougal. *Be a Dinosaur Detective.* Lerner, 1988. *(I)*

Eldredge, Niles, and others. *The Fossil Factory: A Kid's Guide to Digging Up Dinosaurs, Exploring Evolution, and Finding Fossils.* Addison-Wesley, 1990. *(I)*

Farlow, James O. *On the Tracks of Dinosaurs: A Study of Dinosaur Footprints.* Watts, 1991. *(I)*

Funston, Sylvia. *The Dinosaur Question and Answer Book: Everything Kids Want to Know about Dinosaurs, Fossils and Paleontology.* Joy Street/Little, 1992. *(P; I)*

Gay, Tanner Ottley. *Dinosaurs and Their Relatives in Action.* Aladdin, 1990. *(P)*

Horner, John R., and Gorman, James. *Maia: A Dinosaur Grows Up.* Courage Books, 1987. *(P)*

Lasky, Kathryn. *Dinosaur Dig.* Morrow, 1990. *(P; I)*

Lauber, Patricia. *Dinosaurs Walked Here: and Other Stories Fossils Tell.* Bradbury, 1987. *(P); Living with Dinosaurs.* Bradbury, 1991. *(P; I); The News about Dinosaurs.* Bradbury, 1989. *(I)*

Lindsay, William. *DK Great Dinosaur Atlas.* DK, 1999. *(P; I)*

Moseley, Keith. *Dinosaurs: A Lost World.* Putnam, 1984. *(P; I)*

Murphy, Jim. *The Last Dinosaur.* Scholastic, 1988. (Fiction) *(P; I)*

Norell, Mark A., and Dingus, Lowell. *A Nest of Dinosaurs: The Story of Oviraptor.* Doubleday, 1999. *(I; A)*

Norman, David, and Milner, Angela. *Dinosaur.* Knopf, 1989. *(I)*

Parker, Steve. *Dinosaurs and Their World.* Grosset, 1988. *(P; I)*

Sattler, Helen Roney. *The Illustrated Dinosaur Dictionary,* 1983. *(P; I); Pterosaurs, the Flying Reptiles.* Lothrop, 1985. *(P; I)*

Simon, Seymour. *The Largest Dinosaurs.* Macmillan, 1986. *(P; I); New Questions and Answers about Dinosaurs.* Morrow, 1990. *(P; I)*

Sloan, Christopher. *Feathered Dinosaurs.* National Geographic, 2000. *(I)*

Wilford, John Noble. *The Riddle of the Dinosaur.* Knopf, 1986. *(I; A)*

Willis, Paul, ed. *Dinosaurs.* Reader's Digest, 1999. *(P; I)*

Zalinger, Peter. *Dinosaurs and Other Archosaurs.* Random House, 1986. *(P; I)*

Zimmerman, Howard. *Dinosaurs! The Biggest Baddest Strangest Fastest.* Simon & Schuster/Atheneum, 2000. *(P; I)*

## DISABLED PEOPLE

Aaseng, Nathan. *Cerebral Palsy.* Watts, 1991. *(I; A)*

Alexander, Sally Hobart. *Mom Can't See Me.* Macmillan, 1990. *(P)*

Allen, Anne. *Sports for the Handicapped.* Walker, 1981. *(I; A)*

Almonte, Paul, and Desmond, Theresa. *Learning Disabilities.* Crestwood House, 1992. *(P; I)*

Bergman, Thomas. *Going Places: Children Living with Cerebral Palsy.* Gareth Stevens, 1991. *(P; I)*

Bernstein, Joanne E., and Fireside, Bryna J. *Special Parents, Special Children.* Albert Whitman, 1991. *(P; I)*

Boy Scouts of America. *Handicapped Awareness.* Boy Scouts, 1981. *(I; A)*

Brown, Tricia. *Someone Special: Just Like You.* Holt, 1984. *(P)*

Cattoche, Robert J. *Computers for the Disabled.* Watts, 1987. *(I)*

Dunn, Kathryn Boesel, and Boesel, Allison. *Trouble with School: A Family Story about Learning Disabilities.* Woodbine, 1992. *(P)*

Heelan, Jamee Riggio. *The Making of My Special Hand: Madison's Story.* Peachtree, 2000. *(P)*

Landau, Elaine. *Dyslexia.* Watts, 1991. *(P; I)*

Levinson, Harold N., and Sanders, Addie. *The Upside-Down Kids: Helping Dyslexic Children Understand Themselves and Their Disorder.* Evans, 1991. *(P; I)*

Mitchell, Joyce S. *See Me More Clearly: Career and Life Planning for Teens with Physical Disabilities.* Harcourt, 1980. *(I; A)*

Nardo, Don. *The Physically Challenged.* Chelsea House, 1994. *(I; A)*

Porterfield, Kay Marie. *Straight Talk about Learning Disabilities.* Facts on File, 1999. *(I; A)*

Rogers, Fred. *Let's Talk about It: Extraordinary Friends.* Putnam, 2000. *(P)*

Rosenberg, Maxine B. *My Friend Leslie: The Story of a Handicapped Child.* Lothrop, 1983. *(P; I)*

Roy, Ron. *Move Over, Wheelchairs Coming Through!* Clarion, 1985. *(I)*

## DISARMAMENT

Gold, Susan Dudley. *Arms Control.* 21st Century, 1997. *(A)*

## DISEASES

Aaseng, Nathan. *Multiple Sclerosis.* Watts, 2000. *(I; A)*

Aldape, Virginia Totrica. *Nicole's Story: A Book about a Girl with Juvenile Rheumatoid Arthritis.* Lerner, 1996. *(P; I)*

Altman, Linda Jacobs. *Plague and Pestilence: A History of Infectious Disease.* Enslow, 1998. *(I; A)*

Anderson, Madelyn Klein. *Environmental Diseases.* Watts, 1987. *(A)*

Arnold, Caroline. *Heart Disease.* Watts, 1990. *(I; A)*

Bee, Peta. *Living with Asthma.* Raintree/Steck-Vaughn, 1999. *(P; I)*

Beshore, George. *Sickle Cell Anemia.* Watts, 1994. *(I; A)*

Bode, Janet. *Food Fight: A Guide to Eating Disorders for Preteens and Their Parents.* Simon & Schuster, 1997. *(I)*

Brown, Fern G. *Hereditary Diseases.* Watts, 1987. *(A)*

Bryan, Jenny. *Living with Diabetes.* Raintree/Steck-Vaughn, 1999. *(P; I)*

Byers, Ann. *Sexually Transmitted Diseases.* Enslow, 1999. *(I; A)*

Check, William A. *Alzheimer's Disease.* Chelsea House, 1989. *(A)*

Eagles, Douglas A. *Nutritional Diseases.* Watts, 1987. *(A)*

Edelson, Edward. *Allergies.* Chelsea House, 1989. *(I; A)*

Fekete, Irene, and Ward, Peter Dorrington. *Disease and Medicine.* World of Science Series, 1985. *(A)*

Frank, Julia. *Alzheimer's Disease: The Silent Epidemic.* Lerner, 1985. *(I; A)*

Friedlander, Mark P. *Outbreak: Disease Detectives at Work.* Lerner, 2000. *(I; A)*

Giblin, James Cross. *When Plague Strikes: The Black Death, Smallpox, and AIDS.* HarperCollins, 1995. *(I; A)*

Hoff, Brent H., and Smith, Carter. *Mapping Epidemics: A Historical Atlas of Disease.* Watts, 2000. *(A)*

Hughes, Barbara. *Drug Related Diseases.* Watts, 1987. *(A)*

Jacobs, Francine. *Breakthrough— the True Story of Penicillin.* Dodd, 1985. *(I)*

Kubersky, Rachel. *Everything You Need to Know about Eating Disorders.* Rosen, 1992. *(I; A)*

Landau, Elaine. *Allergies.* 21st Century Books, 1994. *(I; A); Alzheimer's Disease.* Watts, 1996. *(P; I); Epilepsy.* 21st Century Books, 1994. *(I; A); Parkinson's Disease.* Watts, 1999. *(I; A) Rabies.* Lodestar, 1993. *(I); Why Are They Starving Themselves? Understanding Anorexia Nervosa and Bulimia.* Messner, 1983. *(I; A); Weight: A Teenage Concern.* Lodestar, 1991. *(I; A)*

Metos, Thomas. *Communicable Diseases.* Watts, 1987. *(A)*

Moe, Barbara. *Coping with Tourette Syndrome and Tic Disorders.* Rosen, 2000. *(I; A)*

Morgane, Wendy. *Allergies.* Twenty-First Century, 1999. *(I)*

Murphy, Wendy. *Asthma.* Millbrook, 1998. *(I; A)*

Peacock, Carol Antoinette; Gregory, Adair; and Gregory, Kyle Carney. *Sugar Was My Best Food: Diabetes and Me.* Albert Whitman, 1998. *(P)*

Seixas, Judith S. *Allergies: What They Are, What They Do.* Greenwillow, 1991. *(P)*

Silverstein, Alvin; Silverstein, Virginia; and Nunn, Laura Silverstein. *Allergies.* Watts, 1999. *(P; I); Asthma.* Enslow, 1997. *(I); Sickle Cell Anemia.* Enslow, 1997. *(I)*

Silverstein, Alvin; Silverstein, Virginia; and Silverstein, Robert. *Cystic Fibrosis.* Watts, 1994. *(I; A); Hepatitis.* Enslow, 1995. *(I; A); Mononucleosis.* Enslow, 1995. *(I; A); Overcoming Acne: The How and Why of Healthy Skin Care.* Morrow, 1990. *(I; A); So You Think You're Fat?* Harper, 1991. *(I; A)*

Simpson, Carolyn. *Coping with Asthma.* Rosen, 1995. *(I; A)*

Tiger, Steven. *Diabetes.* Messner, 1987. *(P; I)*

Weitzman, Elizabeth. *Let's Talk about When Someone You Love Has Alzheimer's Disease.* Rosen, 1996. *(P)*

Yancey, Diane. *Eating Disorders.* Twenty-First Century, 1999. *(I; A)*

## DISNEY, WALT

Cole, Michael D. *Walt Disney: Creator of Mickey Mouse.* Enslow, 1996. *(I)*

Fisher, Maxine R. *Walt Disney.* Watts, 1988. *(I)*

Ford, Barbara. *Walt Disney.* Walker, 1989. *(I; A)*

Schroeder, Russell, ed. *Walt Disney: His Life in Pictures.* Disney, 1996. *(P; I)*

## DIVING

Briggs, Carole S. *Diving Is for Me.* Lerner, 1983. *(P; I)*

## DIVORCE

Bolick, Nancy O'Keefe. *How to Survive Your Parents' Divorce.* Watts, 1994. *(I; A)*

Coleman, William L. *What Children Need to Know When Parents Get Divorced.* Bethany, 1983. *(P; I)*

Goldentyer, Debra. *Parental Divorce.* Steck-Vaughn, 1995. *(I; A)*

Holyoke, Nancy. *Help! A Girl's Guide to Divorce and Stepfamilies.* Pleasant, 1999. *(P; I)*

Krementz, Jill. *How It Feels When Parents Divorce.* Knopf, 1984. *(I)*

Lazo, Caroline Evensen. *Divorce.* Crestwood, 1989. *(P; I)*

## DIX, DOROTHEA LYNDE

Schleichert, Elizabeth. *The Life of Dorothea Dix.* 21st Century Books, 1992. *(P; I)*

## DJIBOUTI

Woods, Harold, and Woods, Geraldine. *The Horn of Africa: Ethiopia, Sudan, Somalia, and Djibouti.* Watts, 1981. *(I; A)*

## DOCTORS

Bluestone, Naomi. *So You Want to Be a Doctor: The Realities of Pursuing Medicine as a Career.* Lothrop, 1981. *(I; A)*

Curtis, Robert H. . *Great Lives: Medicine.* Atheneum, 1992. *(P; I)*

Forsey, Chris. *At the Doctor.* Watts, 1984. *(P)*

Oxenbury, Helen. *The Checkup.* Dutton, 1983. *(P)*

Storring, Rod. *A Doctor's Life: A Visual History of Doctors and Nurses Through the Ages.* Dutton, 1998. *(P; I)*

## DOGS

Benjamin, Carol Lea. *Dog Training for Kids.* Howell, 1988. *(I)*

Casey, Brigid, and Haugh, Wendy. *Sled Dogs.* Dodd, 1983. *(I)*

George, Jean Craighead. *How to Talk to Your Dog.* HarperCollins, 2000. *(P)*

Hart, Angela. *Dogs.* Watts, 1982. *(P)*

Patent, Dorothy Hinshaw. *Hugger to the Rescue.* Cobblehill, 1994. *(P)*

Rinard, Judith E. *Puppies.* National Geographic, 1982. *(P)*

Ring, Elizabeth. *Performing Dogs: Stars of Stage, Screen, and Television.* Millbrook, 1994. *(P; I); Ranch and Farm Dogs: Herders and Guards.* Millbrook, 1994. *(P; I); Search and Rescue Dogs: Expert Trackers and Trailers.* Millbrook, 1994. *(P; I)*

Schoder, Judith. *Canine Careers: Dogs at Work.* Messner, 1981. *(P; I)*

Silverstein, Alvin, and Silverstein, Virginia. *Dogs: All about Them.* Lothrop, 1986. *(I; A)*

## DOLLHOUSES

Boulton, Vivienne. *The Dollhouse Decorator.* Dorling Kindersley, 1992. *(I; A)*

Glubok, Shirley. *Doll's Houses: Life in Miniature.* Harper, 1984. *(I; A)*

Horwitz, Joshua. *Doll Hospital.* Pantheon, 1983. *(I)*

## DOLLS

McGraw, Sheila. *Dolls Kids Can Make.* Firefly, 1995. *(I)*

Schnurnberger, Lynn Edelman. *A World of Dolls That You Can Make.* Harper, 1982. *(P; I)*

## DOLPHINS AND PORPOISES

*Dolphins and Porpoises.* Facts on File, 1990. *(I)*

Dudzinski, Kathleen. *Meeting Dolphins: My Adventures in the Sea.* National Geographic, 2000. *(P; I)*

Grover, Wayne. *Dolphin Adventure: A True Story.* Greenwillow, 1990. *(P)*

Jacka, Martin. *Waiting for Billy.* Orchard Books, 1991. *(P)*

Leatherwood, Stephen, and Reeves, Randall. *The Sea World Book of Dolphins.* Harcourt, 1987. *(P; I)*

Patent, Dorothy Hinshaw. *Dolphins and Porpoises.* Holiday, 1988. *(I); Looking at Dolphins and Porpoises.* Holiday, 1989. *(P; I)*

Read, Andrew. *Porpoises.* Voyageur, 1999. *(I)*

Reed, Don C. *The Dolphins and Me.* Sierra Club Books, 1989. *(I)*

Samuels, Amy. *Follow That Fin! Studying Dolphin Behavior.* Raintree/Steck-Vaughn, 1999. *(P; I)*

Smith, Elizabeth Simpson. *A Dolphin Goes to School: The Story of Squirt, a Trained Dolphin.* Morrow, 1986. *(P)*

Walker, Sally M. *Dolphins.* Carolrhoda, 1999. *(P; I)*

## DOMINICAN REPUBLIC

Creed, Alexander. *Dominican Republic.* Chelsea House, 1987. *(A)*

Haverstock, Nathan A. *Dominican Republic in Pictures.* Lerner, 1988. *(P; I)*

## DONATELLO

Janson, H. W., and Janson, Anthony F. *History of Art for Young People.* Abrams, 1997. (rev. ed.) *(I; A)*

## DOUGLASS, FREDERICK

Douglass, Frederick. *Narrative of the Life of Frederick Douglass, an American Slave.* New American Library, 1968. *(I; A)*

Meltzer, Milton, ed. *Frederick Douglass: In His Own Words.* Harcourt, 1995. *(I; A)*

Miller, Douglas T. *Frederick Douglass and the Fight For Freedom.* Facts on File, 1988. *(A)*

Russell, Sharman. *Frederick Douglass and the Fight for Freedom.* Chelsea House, 1989. *(I; A)*

## DOWN SYNDROME

Tocci, Salvatore. *Down Syndrome.* Watts, 2000. *(I; A)*

## DOYLE, SIR ARTHUR CONAN

Doyle, Arthur Conan. *The Adventures of Sherlock Holmes, Books One–Four.* Adapted by Catherine E. Sadler. Avon, 1981. *(P; I); Sherlock Holmes,* adapted by Diana Stewart. Raintree, 1983. *(P; I; A)*

Pascal, Janet B. *Arthur Conan Doyle: Beyond Baker Street.* Oxford, 2000. *(I; A)*

## DRAKE, SIR FRANCIS

Goodnough, Davis. *Francis Drake.* Troll, 1979 (new ed.). *(P; I)*

## DRAMA

Bany-Winters, Lisa. *Show Time!: Music, Dance, and Drama Activities for Kids.* Chicago Review Press, 2000. *(P; I)*

Nardo, Don, ed. *Greek Drama.* Greenhaven, 1999. *(A)*

## DRAWING

Arnosky, Jim. *Drawing Life in Motion.* Lothrop, 1984. *(I; A); Drawing from Nature.* Lothrop, 1982. *(P; I)*

Bolognese, Don. *Drawing Dinosaurs and Other Prehistoric Animals.* Watts, 1982; *Drawing Spaceships and Other Spacecraft,* 1982. *(P; I)*

Nicklaus, Carol. *Drawing Pets; Drawing Your Family and Friends.* Watts, 1980. *(P)*

Witty, Ken. *A Day in the Life of an Illustrator.* Troll, 1981. *(I; A)*

## DREAMING

Stafford, Patricia A. *Dreaming and Dreams.* Atheneum, 1992. *(I)*

## DRED SCOTT DECISION

Herda, D. J. *The Dred Scott Case: Slavery and Citizenship.* Enslow, 1994. *(I; A)*

## DREYFUS, ALFRED

Schechter, Betty. *The Dreyfus Affair: A National Scandal.* Houghton, 1965. *(I; A)*

## DRUG ABUSE

*Chemical Dependency.* Greenhaven, 1991. *(I; A)*

Berger, Gilda. *Addiction: Its Causes, Problems and Treatment.* Watts, 1982. *(I; A); Crack: The New Drug Epidemic!; Drug Abuse: The Impact on Society.* Watts, 1988. *(A); Drug Testing.* Watts, 1987. *(A); Meg's Story:*

*Straight Talk about Drugs.* Millbrook, 1992. *(I; A); Patty's Story: Straight Talk about Drugs.* Millbrook, 1991. *(I; A)*

Clayton, Lawrence. *Coping with a Drug Abusing Parent.* Rosen, 1991. *(I; A)*

DeStefano, Susan. *Drugs and the Family.* 21st Century Books, 1991. *(I)*

Friedman, David. *Focus on Drugs and the Brain.* 21st Century Books, 1990. *(P; I)*

Gottfried, Ted. *Should Drugs Be Legalized?* Twenty-First Century, 2000. *(I; A)*

Madison, Arnold. *Drugs and You.* Messner, 1990 (rev. ed.). *(I)*

Nardo, Don. *Drugs and Sports.* Lucent Books, 1990. *(I)*

Perry, Robert. *Focus on Nicotine and Caffeine.* 21st Century Books, 1990. *(P; I)*

Rosenberg, Maxine B. *On the Mend: Getting Away from Drugs.* Bradbury, 1991. *(I; A)*

Sherry, Clifford. *Inhalants.* Rosen, 1994. *(I; A)*

Shulman, Jeffrey. *The Drug-Alert Dictionary and Resource Guide; Drugs and Crime; Focus on Cocaine and Crack.* 21st Century Books, 1990. *(P; I) Focus on Hallucinogens.* 21st Century Books, 1991. *(I)*

Stewart, Gail B. *Drug Trafficking.* Lucent Books, 1990. *(I; A)*

Super, Gretchen. *Drugs and Our World; What Are Drugs?; You Can Say " No" to Drugs!*21st Century Books, 1990. *(P)*

Talmadge, Katherine S. *Drugs and Sports; Focus on Steroids.* 21st Century Books, 1991. *(I)*

Terkel, Susan Neiburg. *Should Drugs Be Legalized?* Watts, 1990. *(I; A)*

Washton, Arnold M., and Boundy, Donna. *Cocaine and Crack: What You Need to Know.* Enslow, 1989. *(I; A)*

Yoslow, Mark. *Drugs in the Body.* Watts, 1992. *(A)*

Zeller, Paul Klevan. *Focus on Marijuana.* 21st Century Books, 1990. *(P; I)*

## DRUM

Dearling, Robert, ed. *The Illustrated Encyclopedia of Musical Instruments.* Gale Research, 1996. *(I; A)*

## DU BOIS, W. E. B.

Cryan-Hicks, Kathryn T. *W. E. B. Du Bois: Crusader for Peace.* Discovery, 1991. *(I)*

Troy, Don. *W.E.B. Du Bois.* Child's World, 1999. *(P; I)*

## DUCKS, GEESE, AND SWANS

Burton, Jane. *Dabble the Duckling.* Gareth Stevens, 1989. *(P)*

Freschet, Berniece. *Wood Duck Baby.* Putnam, 1983. *(P)*

Wharton, Anthony. *Discovering Ducks, Geese, and Swans.* Watts, 1987. *(P)*

## DUNBAR, PAUL LAURENCE

McKissack, Patricia. *Paul Laurence Dunbar: A Poet to Remember.* Children's, 1984. *(I)*

## EAGLES

Grambo, Rebecca L. *Eagles.* Voyageur, 1999. *(I)*

Horton, Casey. *Eagles.* Benchmark, 1996. *(I)*

McConoughey, Jane. *Bald Eagle.* Crestwood, 1983. *(P; I)*

Patent, Dorothy Hinshaw. *Where the Bald Eagles Gather.* Houghton, 1984. *(P; I)*

Ryden, Hope. *America's Bald Eagle.* Putnam, 1985. *(I; A)*

Sattler, Helen Roney. *The Book of Eagles.* Lothrop, 1989. *(P; I)*

Van Wormer, Joe. *Eagles.* Lodestar, 1985. *(P; I)*

Wildlife Education Staff. *Eagles.* Wildlife Education, 1983. *(I; A)*

## EAR

Showers, Paul. *Ears Are for Hearing.* Crowell, 1990. *(P)*

## EARHART, AMELIA

Sloate, Susan. *Amelia Earhart: Challenging the Skies.* Fawcett, 1990. *(I)*

## EARTH

Asimov, Isaac. *Earth: Our Home Base.* Gareth Stevens, 1989. *(P; I)*

Bain, Iain. *Mountains and Earth Movements.* Bookwright, 1984. *(I)*

Ballard, Robert D. *Exploring Our Living Planet.* National Geographic, 1983. *(I; A)*

Bennett, David. *Earth.* Bantam, 1988. *(P)*

Berger, Melvin. *As Old as the Hills.* Watts, 1989. *(P; I)*

Cole, Joanna. *The Magic Schoolbus inside the Earth.* Scholastic, 1987. *(I)*

Darling, David. *Could You Ever Dig a Hole to China?* Dillon, 1990. *(I)*

Durell, Ann; Paterson, Katherine; and George, Jean Craighead, eds. *The Big Book for Our Planet.* Dutton, 1993. *(P; I)*

Farndon, John. *How the Earth Works.* Reader's Digest, 1992. *(I)*

Fradin, Dennis. *Continents.* Children's, 1986. *(P); Earth.* Children's, 1989. *(P)*

George, Jean C. *The Talking Earth.* Harper, 1983. *(I; A)*

Gibbons, Gail. *Planet Earth/Inside Out.* Morrow, 1995. *(P; I)*

Gowell, Elizabeth Tayntor. *Fountains of Life: The Story of Deep Sea Vents.* Watts, 1998. *(P; I)*

Knapp, Brian. *Earth Science: Discovering the Secrets of the Earth.* Grolier, 2000 (8 vols.). *(I; A)*

Lauber, Patricia. *Seeing Earth from Space.* Orchard Books, 1990. *(I)*

Livingston, Myra Cohn. *Earth Songs.* Holiday, 1986. *(P)*

Markle, Sandra. *Digging Deeper: Investigations into Rocks, Shocks, Quakes, and Other Earthly Matters.* Lothrop, 1987. *(I); Earth Alive!* Lothrop, 1990. *(I)*

Patent, Dorothy Hinshaw. *Shaping the Earth.* Clarion, 2000. *(P; I)*

Sattler, Helen Roney. *Our Patchwork Planet.* Lothrop, 1995. *(I;A)*

Scarry, Huck. *Our Earth.* Messner, 1984. *(I)*

Silver, Donald M. *Earth: The Ever-Changing Planet.* Random House, 1989. *(I)*

Simon, Seymour. *Earth: Our Planet in Space.* Scholastic, 1984. *(P)*

Van Rose, Susanna. *Earth.* Dorling Kindersley, 1994. *(I; A)*

Whitfield, Philip. *Why Do Volcanoes Erupt?* Viking, 1990. *(I)*

## EARTH-MOVING MACHINERY

Jennings, Terry J. *Cranes, Dumptrucks, Bulldozers, and Other Building Machines.* Kingfisher, 1993. *(I)*

Royston, Angela. *Diggers and Dump Trucks.* Aladdin, 1991. *(P)*

Stephen, R. J. *Cranes.* Watts, 1987. *(P); Earthmovers.* Watts, 1987. *(P)*

## EARTHQUAKES

Dudman, John. *The San Francisco Earthquake.* Bookwright, 1988. *(P; I)*

Fradin, Dennis Brindell. *Disaster! Earthquakes.* Children's, 1982. *(P; I)*

Golden, Frederic. *The Trembling Earth: Probing and Predicting Earthquakes.* Scribner's, 1983. *(I; A)*

Lambert, David. *Earthquakes.* Watts, 1982. *(P)*

Levine, Ellen. *If You Lived at the Time of the Great San Francisco Earthquake.* Scholastic, 1987. *(P)*

Meister, Cari. *Earthquakes.* ABDO, 1999. *(P; I)*

Paananen, Eloise. *Tremor! Earthquake Technology in the Space Age.* Messner, 1982. *(A)*

Rogers, Daniel. *Earthquakes.* Raintree/Steck-Vaughn, 1999. *(P)*

Sherrow, Victoria. *San Francisco Earthquake, 1989: Death and Destruction.* Enslow, 1998. *(P; I)*

Simon, Seymour. *Earthquakes.* Morrow, 1991. *(P; I)*

Vogel, Carole G. *Shock Waves through Los Angeles: The Northridge Earthquake.* Little, 1996. *(P; I)*

Vogt, Gregory. *Predicting Earthquakes.* Watts, 1989. *(I)*

## EASTER

Berger, Gilda. *Easter and Other Spring Holidays.* Watts, 1983. *(P; I; A)*

Kimmel, Eric A., reteller. *The Birds' Gift: A Ukrainian Easter Story.* Holiday House, 1999. *(P)*

Thompson, Lauren. *Love One Another: The Story of Easter.* Scholastic, 2000. *(P)*

## EASTMAN, GEORGE

Mitchell, Barbara. *Click! A Story about George Eastman.* Carolrhoda, 1987. *(I)*

## ECLIPSES

Aronson, Billy. *Eclipses: Nature's Blackouts.* Watts, 1997. *(I)*

Branley, Franklyn Mansfield. *Eclipse: Darkness in Daytime.* HarperCollins, 1988. *(P)*

## ECOLOGY

Gardner, Robert. *Science Projects about the Environment and Ecology.* Enslow, 1999. *(I; A)*

Hughey, Pat. *Scavengers and Decomposers: The Cleanup Crew.* Atheneum, 1984. *(I)*

Leuzzi, Linda. *Life Connections: Pioneers in Ecology.* Watts, 2000. *(I; A)*

Parnall, Peter. *Woodpile.* Macmillan, 1990. *(P)*

Patent, Dorothy Hinshaw. *Places of Refuge: Our National Wildlife Refuge System.* Clarion, 1992. *(I)*

Pringle, Laurence. *Living Treasures: Saving Earth's Threatened Biodiversity.* Morrow, 1991. *(I)*

Sabin, Francene. *Ecosystems and Food Chains.* Troll, 1985. *(I)*

Stewart, Melissa. *Life without Light: A Journey to Earth's Dark Ecosystems.* Watts, 1999. *(I; A)*

## ECONOMICS

Aaseng, Nathan. *You Are the Corporate Executive.* Oliver, 1997. *(A)*

Abels, Harriette S. *Future Business.* Crestwood, 1980. *(I; A)*

Adler, David A. *Prices Go Up, Prices Go Down: The Law of Supply and Demand.* Watts, 1984. *(P)*

Kalman, Bobbie. *Early Stores and Markets.* Crabtree, 1981. *(I)*

Killen, M. Barbara. *Economics and the Consumer.* Lerner, 1990. *(I; A)*

Klevin, Jill. *The Turtle Street Trading Company.* Delacorte, 1982. *(P)*

Marsh, Carole. *The Teddy Bear Company: Easy Economics for Kids; The Teddy Bear's Annual Report: Tomorrow's Books.* Gallopade, 1983. *(P; I)*

O'Toole, Thomas. *Global Economics.* Lerner, 1991. *(A)*

Schmitt, Lois. *Smart Spending: A Young Consumer's Guide.* Scribner's, 1989. *(I; A)*

Shanaman, Fred, and Malnig, Anita. *The First Official Money Making Book for Kids.* Bantam, 1983. *(I)*

## ECUADOR

Beirne, Barbara. *The Children of the Ecuadorean Highlands.* Lerner, 1996. *(P; I)*

Foley, Erin L. *Ecuador.* Marshall Cavendish, 1995. *(I)*

## EDISON, THOMAS ALVA

Adler, David. *Thomas Alva Edison: Great Inventor.* Holiday, 1990. *(P)*

Buranelli, Vincent. *Thomas Alva Edison.* Silver Burdett, 1989. *(I)*

Greene, Carol. *Thomas Alva Edison: Bringer of Light.* Children's, 1985. *(I)*

Guthridge, Sue. *Thomas A. Edison: Young Inventor.* Bobbs, 1983. *(P; I)*

Lampton, Christopher. *Thomas Alva Edison.* Watts, 1988. *(P; I)*

Mintz, Penny. *Thomas Edison: Inventing the Future.* Fawcett, 1990. *(I)*

Quackenbush, Robert. *What Has Wild Tom Done Now?* Prentice-Hall, 1981. *(P)*

## EDUCATION

Fisher, Leonard. *Schoolmasters.* Godine, 1986. *(I); The Schools.* Holiday, 1983. *(I)*

Hand, Phyllis. *The Name of the Game Is . . . Learning.* Good Apple, 1983. *(P; I)*

Kalman, Bobbie. *Early Schools.* Crabtree, 1981. *(I)*

Loeper, John J. *Going to School in 1776.* Atheneum, 1984. *(I)*

## EDUCATION, UNITED STATES DEPARTMENT OF

Sneigoski, Stephen J. *The Department of Education.* Chelsea House, 1987. *(P; I)*

## EELS

Halton, Cheryl Mays. *Those Amazing Eels.* Dillon, 1990. *(I)*

## EGGS AND EMBRYOS

Burton, Robert. *Eggs: Nature's Perfect Package.* Facts on File, 1987. *(I; A)*

Griffin, Margaret, and Seed, Deborah. *The Amazing Egg Book.* Addison Wesley Longman, 1990. *(P; I)*

Johnson, Sylvia A. *Inside an Egg.* Lerner, 1982. *(I)*

McClung, Robert M. *The Amazing Egg.* Dutton, 1980. *(I)*

## EGYPT

*Egypt . . . in Pictures.* Lerner, 1988. *(I)*

Bianchi, Robert S. *The Nubians: People of the Ancient Nile.* Millbrook, 1994. *(I)*

Cross, Wilbur. *Egypt.* Children's, 1982. *(I; A)*

Kristensen, Preben, and Cameron, Fiona. *We Live in Egypt.* Bookwright, 1987. *(P)*

Lye, Keith. *Take a Trip to Egypt.* Watts, 1983. *(P)*

Shuter, Jane. *Egypt.* Raintree/Steck-Vaughn, 1998. *(I; A)*

Sullivan, George. *Sadat: The Man Who Changed Mid-East History.* Walker, 1981. *(I; A)*

## EGYPTIAN ART AND ARCHITECTURE

Hodge, Susie. *Ancient Egyptian Art.* Heinemann, 1997. *(P; I)*

Tyldesley, Joyce. *The Mummy: Unwrap the Ancient Secrets of the Mummies' Tombs.* Carlton, 2000. *(A)*

## EINSTEIN, ALBERT

Apfel, Necia H. *It's All Relative: Einstein's Theory of Relativity.* Lothrop, 1981. *(I; A)*

Dank, Milton. *Albert Einstein.* Watts, 1983. *(I; A)*

Hunter, Nigel. *Einstein.* Bookwright, 1987. *(P; I)*

McPherson, Stephanie Sammartino. *Ordinary Genius: The Story of Albert Einstein.* Carolrhoda, 1995. *(I)*

Severance, John B. *Einstein: Visionary Scientist.* Clarion, 1999. *(I; A)*

## EISENHOWER, DWIGHT DAVID

Cannon, Marian G. *Dwight David Eisenhower: War Hero and President.* Watts, 1990. *(I; A)*

Ellis, Rafaela. *Dwight D. Eisenhower: 34th President of the United States.* Garrett Educational, 1989. *(I)*

Hargrove, Jim. *Dwight D. Eisenhower: Thirty-Fourth President of the United States.* Children's, 1987. *(P; I)*

## ELECTIONS

Aaseng, Nathan. *America's Third-Party Presidential Candidates.* Oliver Press, 1995. *(I; A)*

Archer, Jules. *Winners and Losers: How Elections Work in America.* HarBraceJ, 1984. *(I; A)*

Fradin, Dennis. *Voting and Elections.* Children's, 1985. *(P)*

Hargrove, Jim. *The Story of Presidential Elections.* Children's, 1988. *(I)*

Marx, Jeff. *How to Win a High School Election.* Jeff Marx, 1999. *(A)*

Modl, Thomas, ed. *America's Elections.* Greenhaven Press, 1988. *(A)*

Priestly, E. J. *Finding Out about Elections.* David & Charles, 1983. *(I; A)*

Samuels, Cynthia. *It's a Free Country: A Young Person's Guide to Politics and Elections.* Atheneum, 1988. *(I; A)*

Scher, Linda. *The Vote: Making Your Voice Heard.* Raintree, 1993. *(I)*

Sullivan, George. *Campaigns and Elections.* Silver Burdett, 1991. *(I; A)*

## ELECTRIC GENERATORS

Berger, Melvin. *Switch On, Switch Off.* HarperCollins, 1990. *(P)*

## ELECTRICITY

Ardley, Neil. *Electricity.* New Discovery, 1992. *(I)*

Berger, Melvin. *Switch On, Switch Off.* Crowell, 1989. *(P)*

Billings, Charlene W. *Superconductivity.* Dutton, 1991. *(I)*

Dispezio, Michael. *Awesome Experiments in Electricity and Magnetism.* Sterling, 1999. *(I; A)*

Good, Keith. *Zap It!: Exciting Electricity Activities.* Lerner, 1999. *(P; I)*

Markle, Sandra. *Power Up: Experiments, Puzzles, and Games Using Electricity.* Macmillan, 1989. *(I)*

Math, Irwin. *More Wires and Watts: Understanding and Using Electricity.* Scribner's, 1988. *(I; A); Wires and Watts: Understanding and Using Electricity.* Scribner's, 1981. *(I; A)*

Stwertka, Eve, and Stwertka, Albert. *Heat, Lights, and Action!* Messner, 1991. *(I)*

Vogt, Gregory. *Electricity and Magnetism.* Watts, 1985. *(I); Generating Electricity.* Watts, 1986. *(I)*

Zubrowski, Bernie. *Blinkers and Buzzers.* Morrow, 1991. *(I)*

## ELECTRONICS

Billings, Charlene W. *Microchip: Small Wonder.* Dodd, 1984. *(I)*

Gutnik, Martin J. *Simple Electrical Devices.* Watts, 1986. *(I)*

Laron, Carl. *Electronics Basics.* Prentice-Hall, 1984. *(I; A)*

Tatchess, J., and Cutter, N. *Practical Things to Do.* EDC, 1983. *(I; A)*

## ELECTRON MICROSCOPE

Tomb, Howard. *Microaliens: Dazzling Journeys with an Electron Microscope.* Farrar, 1993. *(I)*

## ELEMENTS, CHEMICAL

Asimov, Isaac. *Building Blocks of the Universe.* Abelard, 1974 (rev. ed.). *(I; A)*

Heiserman, David L. *Exploring Chemical Elements and Their Compounds.* McGraw-Hill, 1991. *(A)*

## ELEPHANTS

Aliki. *Wild and Wooly Mammoths.* Har-Row, 1983. *(P)*

Bare, Colleen Stanley. *Elephants on the Beach.* Cobblehill, 1989. *(P)*

Barrett, N. S. *Elephants.* Watts, 1988. *(P; I)*

Bright, Michael. *Elephants.* Gloucester Press, 1990. *(P; I)*

Douglas-Hamilton, Oria. *The Elephant Family Book.* Picture Book Studio, 1990. *(P; I)*

Hintz, Martin. *Tons of Fun: Training Elephants.* Messner, 1982. *(P; I)*

Patent, Dorothy Hinshaw. *African Elephants: Giants of the Land.* Holiday, 1991. *(P; I)*

Payne, Katharine. *Elephants Calling.* Crown, 1992. *(I)*

Petty, Kate. *Elephants.* Gloucester Press, 1990. *(P; I)*

Schlein, Miriam. *Elephants.* Atheneum, 1990. *(I)*

Stewart, John. *Elephant School.* Pantheon, 1982. *(I; A)*

Torgersen, Dan. *Elephant Herds and Rhino Horns.* Children's, 1982. *(I; A)*

Yoshida, Toshi. *Elephant Crossing.* Philomel, 1990. *(P)*

## ELIJAH

Goldin, Barbara Diamond. *Journeys with Elijah: Eight Tales of the Prophet.* Harcourt/Gulliver, 1999. *(P; I)*

## ELIZABETH I

Greene, Carol. *Elizabeth the First: Queen of England.* Children's, 1990. *(P)*

Meltzer, Milton. *Ten Queens: Portraits of Women of Power.* Dutton, 1997. *(I; A)*

Stanley, Diane, and Vennema, Peter. *Good Queen Bess: The Story of Elizabeth I of England.* Four Winds, 1990. *(I)*

Thomas, Jane Resh. *Behind the Mask: The Life of Queen Elizabeth I.* Clarion, 1998. *(I; A)*

Turner, Dorothy. *Queen Elizabeth I.* Watts, 1987. *(I)*

Weir, Alison. *The Life of Elizabeth I.* Ballantine, 1998. *(A)*

Zamoyska, Betka. *Queen Elizabeth I.* McGraw, 1981. *(I; A)*

## ELIZABETH II

Turner, Dorothy. *Queen Elizabeth II.* Bookwright, 1985. *(I)*

## EMANCIPATION PROCLAMATION

Henry, Christopher E. *Forever Free: From the Emancipation Proclamation to the Civil Rights Bill of 1875.* Chelsea House, 1993. *(I; A)*

Tackach, James. *The Emancipation Proclamation: Abolishing Slavery in the South.* Lucent, 1999. *(I; A)*

## EMOTIONS

Sherrow, Victoria. *Dropping Out.* Marshall Cavendish, 1995. *(I; A)*

## ENDANGERED SPECIES

Arnold, Caroline. *On the Brink of Extinction: The California Condor.* Harcourt, 1993. *(I); Saving the Peregrine Falcon.* Carolrhoda, 1985. *(I)*

Banks, Martin. *Endangered Wildlife.* Rourke, 1988. *(I)*

Bloyd, Sunni. *Endangered Species.* Lucent Books, 1989. *(I; A)*

Burton, John. *Close to Extinction.* Gloucester Press, 1988. *(I)*

Hendrich, Paula. *Saving America's Birds.* Lothrop, 1982. *(I; A)*

Maynard, Thane. *Endangered Animal Babies.* Watts, 1993. *(I)*

Pringle, Laurence. *Saving Our Wildlife.* Enslow, 1990. *(I; A)*

Ricciuti, Edward. *Wildlife Special Agent: Protecting Endangered Species.* Blackbirch, 1996. *(P;I)*

Schlein, Miriam. *Project Panda Watch.* Atheneum, 1984. *(I; A)*

Schorsch, Nancy T. *Saving the Condor.* Watts, 1991. *(P; I)*

Stone, Lynn. *Endangered Animals.* Children's, 1984. *(P)*

Vergoth, Karin, and Lampton, Christopher. *Endangered Species.* Watts, 1999. *(I)*

Wolkomir, Joyce Rogers, and Wolkomir, Richard. *Junkyard Bandicoots & Other Tales of the World's Endangered Species.* Wiley, 1992. *(P; I)*

## ENERGY

*Energy.* Raintree, 1988. *(I)*

Adler, David. *Wonders of Energy.* Troll, 1983. *(P; I)*

Asimov, Isaac. *How Did We Find Out about Energy?* Avon, 1981. *(I)*

Berger, Melvin. *Energy.* Watts, 1983. *(P; I)*

Carey, Helen H. *Producing Energy.* Watts, 1984. *(I; A)*

Fogel, Barbara R. *Energy Choices for the Future.* Watts, 1985. *(A)*

Gardiner, Brian. *Energy Demands.* Gloucester Press, 1990. *(I)*

Kaplan, Sheila. *Solar Energy.* Raintree, 1985. *(I)*

McKie, Robin. *Energy.* Watts, 1989. *(P; I)*

Millard, Reed, and Editors of Science Book Associates. *Energy: New Shapes/New Careers.* Messner, 1982. *(I; A)*

Pringle, Laurence. *Nuclear Energy: Troubled Past, Uncertain Future.* Macmillan, 1989. *(I)*

Silverstein, Alvin and others. *Energy.* Twenty-First Century, 1998. *(P; I)*

Tuggle, Catherine, and Weir, Gary E. *The Department of Energy.* Chelsea House, 1989. *(I)*

### ENGINEERING

Brown, David J. *The Random House Book of How Things Were Built.* Random House, 1992. *(I; A)*

Gaff, Jackie. *Buildings, Bridges & Tunnels.* Random House, 1992. *(P; I)*

### ENGINES

Moxon, Julian. *How Jet Engines Are Made.* Facts on File, 1985. *(I; A)*

Olney, Ross R. *The Internal Combustion Machine.* Harper, 1982. *(I; A)*

### ENGLAND

Fairclough, Chris. *Take a Trip to England.* Watts, 1982. *(P)*

Ferguson, Sheila. *Village and Town Life.* David & Charles, 1983. *(I; A)*

Greene, Carol. *England.* Children's, 1982. *(I; A)*

James, Ian. *Inside Great Britain.* Watts, 1988. *(P; I)*

Lister, Maree; Sevier, Marti; and NgCheong-Lum, Roseline. *Welcome to England.* Gareth Stevens, 1999. *(P)*

Mitsumasa, Anno. *Anno's Britain.* Philomel, 1986. *(I)*

Sproule, Anna. *Great Britain.* Bookwright, 1988. *(P); Living in London.* Silver Burdett, 1987. *(P)*

St. John, Jetty. *A Family in England.* Lerner, 1988. *(P)*

### ENGLAND, HISTORY OF

Brooks, Polly Schoyer. *Queen Eleanor: Independent Spirit of the Medieval World: A Biography of Eleanor of Aquitaine.* Lippincott, 1983. *(I; A)*

Corbishley, Mike. *The Romans.* Warwick, 1984. *(I)*

Fyson, Nance L. *Growing Up in Edwardian Britain.* David & Charles, 1980. *(I; A)*

Lane, Peter. *Elizabethan England,* David & Charles, 1981; *Norman England,* 1980. *(I; A)*

Swisher, Clarice. *Victorian England.* Greenhaven, 2000. *(A)*

Wilkins, Frances. *Growing Up during the Norman Conquest.* David & Charles, 1980. *(I; A)*

### ENGLISH LITERATURE

Ashby, Ruth. *Elizabethan England.* Marshall Cavendish, 1999. *(I)*

Dominic, Catherine C., ed. *Epics for Students.* Gale Group, 1997. *(A)*

Swisher, Clarice, ed. *Victorian Literature.* Greenhaven, 1999. *(A)*

Thompson, Stephen P., ed. *Readings on Beowulf.* Greenhaven Press, 1998. *(A)*

### ENVIRONMENT

Anderson, Madelyn Klein. *Oil Spills.* Watts, 1990. *(I)*

Bailey, Donna. *What We Can Do about Litter.* Watts, 1991. *(P)*

Banks, Martin. *Conserving Rain Forests.* Steck-Vaughn, 1990. *(I)*

Bash, Barbara. *Desert Giant.* Little, 1989. *(P; I)*

Bellamy, David. *How Green Are You?* Clarkson Potter, 1991. *(P)*

Cherry, Lynne. *A River Ran Wild.* HarBraceJ/Gulliver, 1992. *(P); The Great Kapok Tree: A Tale of the Amazon Rain Forest.* Harcourt, 1990. *(P; I)*

Elkington, John, and others. *Going Green: A Kid's Handbook to Saving the Planet.* Viking, 1990. *(I)*

Foster, Joanna. *Cartons, Cans and Orange Peels: Where Does Your Garbage Go?* Clarion, 1991. *(I)*

George, Jean Craighead. *One Day in the Tropical Rain Forest.* Crowell, 1990. *(P; I)*

Hadingham, Evan, and Hadingham, Janet. *Garbage! Where It Comes From, Where It Goes.* Simon & Schuster, 1990. *(I; A)*

Herda, D. J. *Environmental America: The North Central States; Environmental America: The Northeastern States; Environmental America: The Northwestern States; Environmental America: The South Central States.* Millbrook, 1991. *(I; A); Environmental America: The Southeastern States; Environmental America: The Southwestern States.* Millbrook, 1991. *(I; A)*

Johnson, Rebecca. *The Greenhouse Effect: Life on a Warmer Planet.* Lerner, 1990. *(I)*

Kouhoupt, Rudy, and Marti, Donald B. *How on Earth Do We Recycle Metal?* Millbrook, 1992. *(I)*

Landau, Elaine. *Tropical Rain Forests around the World.* Watts, 1990. *(P)*

Lauber, Patricia. *She's Wearing a Dead Bird on Her Head!* Hyperion, 1995. *(P); You're aboard Spaceship Earth.* HarperCollins, 1996. *(P)*

Lee, Sally. *The Throwaway Society.* Watts, 1990. *(I; A)*

Lowery, Linda. *Earth Day.* Lerner, 1991. *(P)*

Miles, Betty. *Save the Earth: An Action Handbook for Kids.* Knopf, 1991. *(I; A)*

Milne, Margery, and Milne, Lorus J. *Dreams of a Perfect Earth.* Atheneum, 1982. *(I; A)*

Nelson, Corinna. *Working in the Environment.* Lerner, 1999. *(I)*

Patent, Dorothy Hinshaw. *Children Save the Rain Forest.* Cobblehill, 1996. *(I; A)*

Pringle, Laurence. *The Environmental Movement: From Its Roots to the Challenges of a New Century.* HarperCollins, 2000. *(I); Global Warming: Assessing the Greenhouse Threat.* Arcade, 1990. *(I); Lives At Stake: The Science and Politics of Environmental Health.* Macmillan, 1980. *(I); Restoring Our Earth.* Enslow, 1987. *(P);*

Stanley, Phyllis M. *American Environmental Heroes.* Enslow, 1996. *(I;A)*

Walker, Jane. *The Ozone Hole.* Gloucester, 1993. *(I; A)*

Wild, Russell, ed. *The Earth Care Annual 1990.* National

Wildlife Federation: Rodale, 1990. *(I; A)*

## EQUATORIAL GUINEA

Fichter, George S. *The Bulge of Africa: Senegal, Guinea, Ivory Coast, Togo, Benin, and Equatorial Guinea.* Watts, 1981. *(I; A)*

## ERICSON, LEIF

Humble, Richard. *The Age of Leif Eriksson.* Watts, 1989. *(I)*

Simon, Charnan. *Leif Eriksson and the Vikings.* Children's, 1991. *(I)*

## ERIE CANAL

Doherty, Craig A., and Doherty, Katherine M. *The Erie Canal.* Blackbirch Press, 1996. *(P; I)*

Harness, Cheryl. *The Amazing Impossible Erie Canal.* Simon & Schuster, 1995. *(P; I)*

Lourie, Peter. *Erie Canal: Canoeing America's Great Waterway.* Boyds Mills Press, 1999. *(P; I)*

Nirgiotis, Nicholas. *Erie Canal: Gateway to the West.* Watts, 1993. *(I)*

## ETHICS

Dronenwetter, Michael. *Journalism Ethics.* Watts, 1988. *(A)*

Finn, Jeffrey, and Marshall, Eliot L. *Medical Ethics.* Chelsea House, 1990. *(I; A)*

Hyde, Margaret O., and Forsyth, Elizabeth H. *Medical Dilemmas.* Putnam, 1990. *(I; A)*

Jussim, Daniel. *Medical Ethics.* Silver Burdett, 1990. *(I; A)*

Terkel, Susan Neiburg. *Ethics.* Lodestar, 1992. *(I; A)*

## ETHIOPIA

Abebe, Daniel. *Ethiopia in Pictures.* Lerner, 1988. *(I)*

Fradin, Dennis Brindell. *Ethiopia.* Children's, 1988. *(I)*

Gish, Steven. *Ethiopia.* Marshall Cavendish, 1996. *(I; A)*

Kleeberg, Irene Cumming. *Ethiopia.* Watts, 1986. *(I; A)*

Laird, Elizabeth. *The Miracle Child: A Story from Ethiopia.* Holt, 1985. *(P)*

Lye, Keith. *Take a Trip to Ethiopia.* Watts, 1986. *(P)*

Woods, Harold, and Woods, Geraldine. *The Horn of Africa: Ethiopia, Sudan, Somalia, and Djibouti.* Watts, 1981. *(I; A)*

## ETHNIC GROUPS

Levinson, David H. *Ethnic Groups Worldwide: A Ready Reference Handbook.* Greenwood, 1998. *(I; A)*

## ETIQUETTE

Adamson, Elizabeth C. *Mind Your Manners.* Good Apple, 1981. *(P)*

Aliki. *Manners.* Greenwillow, 1990. *(P)*

Brown, Fern G. *Etiquette.* Watts, 1985. *(I)*

Brown, Marc, and Krensky, Stephen. *Perfect Pigs: An Introduction to Manners.* Atlantic, 1983. *(P)*

Howe, James. *The Muppet Guide to Magnificent Manners.* Random House, 1984. *(P)*

Zeldis, Yona. *Coping with Social Situations: A Handbook of Correct Behavior.* Rosen, 1988. *(A)*

## EUROPE

Bradley, John. *Eastern Europe: The Road to Democracy.* Gloucester Press, 1990. *(I; A)*

Cairns, Trevor. *Europe around the World.* Lerner, 1982. *(I; A)*

Kronenwetter, Michael. *The New Eastern Europe.* Watts, 1991. *(I; A)*

Roberts, Elizabeth. *Europe 1992: The United States of Europe?* Gloucester Press, 1990. *(I; A)*

## EVEREST, MOUNT

Gaffney, Timothy. *Edmund Hillary: First to Climb Mt. Everest.* Children's, 1990. *(I; A)*

Jenkins, Steve. *The Top of the World: Climbing Mount Everest.* Houghton, 1999. *(P; I)*

## EVOLUTION

Asimov, Isaac. *How Did We Find Out about the Beginning of Life?* Walker, 1982. *(I)*

Attenborough, David. *Life on Earth: A Natural History.* Little, 1981. *(I)*

British Museum of Natural History. *Origin of Species.* Cambridge University Press, 1982. *(A)*

Gallant, Roy A. *Before the Sun Dies: The Story of Evolution.* Macmillan, 1989. *(A)*

Gamlin, Linda. *Origins of Life.* Watts, 1988. *(I; A)*

Matthews, Rupert. *How Life Began.* Bookwright, 1989. *(P; I)*

Peters, David. *From the Beginning: The Story of Human Evolution.* Morrow, 1991. *(I; A)*

Savage, R., and Long, M. *Mammal Evolution: An Illustrated Guide.* Facts on File, 1986. *(I)*

Stein, Sara B. *The Evolution Book.* Workman, 1986. *(I)*

## EXPERIMENTS AND OTHER SCIENCE ACTIVITIES

*Food and the Kitchen: Step-by-Step Science Activity Projects from the Smithsonian Institution.* Gareth Stevens, 1993. *(I)*

Adams, Richard, and Gardner, Robert. *Ideas for Science Projects.* Watts, 1997; *More Ideas for Science Projects.* Watts, 1998. *(I; A)*Barrow, Lloyd H. *Science Fair Projects Investigating Earthworms.* Enslow, 2000. *(P; I)*

Cash, Terry, and Taylor, Barbara. *175 More Science Experiments to Amuse and Amaze Your Friends.* Random House, 1991. *(I)*

Dekkers, Midas. *The Nature Book.* Macmillan, 1988. *(I)*

Filson, Brent. *Famous Experiments and How to Repeat Them.* Messner, 1986. *(P; I)*

Gardner, Robert. *Science Projects about Methods of Measuring; Science Projects about Solids, Liquids, and Gases; Science Projects about Sound; Science Projects about the Physics of Sports; Science Projects about* the Physics of Toys and Games. Enslow, 2000; Science Projects about Kitchen Chemistry; Science Projects about Physics in the Home; Science Projects about Plants; Science Projects about the Environment and Ecology. Enslow, 1999; Science Projects about Light. Enslow, 1994. (I; A)

Gold, Carol. Science Express: 50 Scientific Stunts from the Ontario Science Centre. Addison-Wesley, 1991. (P; I)

Goodstein, Madeline. Sports Science Projects: The Physics of Balls in Motion. Enslow, 1999. (I; A)

Krieger, Melanie Jacobs. How to Excel in Science Competitions Enslow, 1999. (rev. ed.) (I; A)

Levine, Shar, and Johnstone, Leslie. Shocking Science: Fun and Fascinating Electrical Experiments. Sterling, 2000. (P; I)

Markle, Sandra. The Kids' Earth Handbook. Atheneum, 1991. (P; I)

Marks, Dian F. Glues, Brews, and Goos: Recipes and Formulas for Almost Any Classroom Project. Teacher Ideas, 1996. (I)

McLoughlin, Andrea. Simple Science Experiments. Scholastic/Cartwheel, 1996. (P)

Mebane, Robert C., and Rybolt, Thomas R. Adventures with Atoms and Molecules. Enslow, 1991. (I; A)

Orii, Eiji and Masako. Simple Science Experiments with Circles; Simple Science Experiments with Marbles; Simple Science Experiments with Ping-Pong Balls; Simple Science Experiments with Water. Gareth Stevens, 1989. (P)

Richards, Jon. Chemicals and Reactions. Millbrook/Cooper, 2000. (P; I)

Richards, Roy. 101 Science Surprises: Exciting Experiments with Everyday Materials. Sterling, 1993. (P; I); Scienceworks: An Ontario Science Centre Book of Experiments. Kids Can Press, 1984. (I)

VanCleave, Janice. Janice VanCleave's Guide to More of the Best Science Fair Projects; Janice VanCleave's Solar System: Mind Boggling Experiments You Can Turn into Science Fair Projects. Wiley, 2000; Janice VanCleave's 203 Icy, Freezing, Frosty, Cool and Wild Experiments. Wiley, 1999. (I); Janice VanCleave's Earth Science for Every Kid: 101 Easy Experiments That Really Work. John Wiley, 1991. (P; I); Janice VanCleave's The Human Body for Every Kid: Easy Activities That Make Learning Science Fun. John Wiley, 1995. (I); Janice VanCleave's Physics for Every Kid. John Wiley, 1991. (I); Janice VanCleave's Play and Find Out about the Human Body: Easy Experiments for Young Children. John Wiley, 1998. (P); Janice VanCleave's Play and Find Out about Nature: Easy Experiments for Young Children. John Wiley, 1997. (P); Janice VanCleave's Play and Find Out about Science: Easy Experiments for Young Children. John Wiley, 1996. (P)

Walpole, Brenda. 175 Science Experiments to Amuse and Amaze Your Friends. Random House, 1988. (P; I)

Wellnitz, William K. Be a Kid Physicist. TAB Books, 1993. (I)

White, Laurence B., and Broekel, Ray. Shazam! Simple Science Magic. Albert Whitman, 1991. (P; I)

Willow, Diane, and Curran, Emily. Science Sensations. Addison-Wesley, 1989. (P; I)

Wood, Robert W. Physics for Kids: 49 Easy Experiments with Electricity and Magnetism. TAB Books, 1990. (I)

Zubrowski, Bernie. Balloons: Building and Experimenting with Inflatable Toys. Morrow, 1990. (P; I);

## EXPLORATION AND DISCOVERY

Armstrong, Jennifer. Shipwreck at the Bottom of the World: The Extraordinary True Story of Shackleton and the Endurance. Crown, 1998. (I; A)

Barden, Renardo. The Discovery of America. Greenhaven, 1990. (I; A)

Beattie, Owen, and Geiger, John. Buried in Ice: The Mystery of a Lost Arctic Expedition. Scholastic, 1992. (I; A)

Blumberg, Rhoda. Remarkable Voyages of Captain Cook. Simon & Schuster, 1991. (I; A)

Brosse, Jacques. Great Voyages of Discovery. Facts on File, 1985. (A)

Ferris, Jeri. Arctic Explorer: The Story of Matthew Henson. Carolrhoda, 1989. (P; I)

Fisher, Leonard Everett. Prince Henry the Navigator. Macmillan, 1990. (P; I)

Fradin, Dennis B. Explorers. Children's, 1984. (P)

Kimmel, Elizabeth Cody. Ice Story: Shackleton's Lost Expedition. Clarion, 1999. (I)

Krensky, Stephen. Who Really Discovered America? Hastings House, 1991. (I)

Lomask, Milton. Great Lives: Exploration. Scribner's, 1988. (I; A)

Maestro, Betsy. The Discovery of the Americas. Lothrop, 1991. (P)

Matthews, Rupert. Explorer. Knopf, 1991. (I; A)

Maurer, Richard. The Wild Colorado: The True Adventures of Fred Dellenbaugh, Age 17, on the Second Powell Expedition into the Grand Canyon. Crown, 1999. (I; A)

Poole, Frederick. Early Exploration of North America. Watts, 1989. (P; I)

Sandak, Cass R. Explorers and Discovery. Watts, 1983. (I; A)

Worth, Richard. Pizarro and the Conquest of the Incan Empire in World History; Stanley and Livingstone and the Exploration of Africa in World History. Enslow, 2000. (I; A)

## EXPLOSIVES

Anderson, Norman D., and Brown, Walter R. Fireworks! Pyrotechnics on Display. Dodd, 1983. (P; I)

Gleasner, Diana C. Dynamite. Walker, 1982. (I; A)

Grady, Sean M. Explosives: Devices of Controlled Destruction. Lucent, 1995. (I; A)

Greenberg, Keith Elliot. *Bomb Squad Officer: Expert with Explosives.* Blackbirch Press, 1995. *(P)*

## EXTINCTION

Arnold, Caroline. *On the Brink of Extinction: The California Condor.* Harcourt, 1993. *(P; I)*

Facklam, Howard, and Facklam, Marjorie. *Plants: Extinction or Survival?* Enslow, 1990. *(I; A)*

Facklam, Marjorie. *And Then There Was One: The Mysteries of Extinction, Vol. 1.* Little, Brown, 1993. *(P; I)*

Hoff, Mary King, and Rodgers, Mary M. *Our Endangered Planet: Groundwater.* Lerner, 1991. *(I)*

Hoyt, Erich. *Extinction A-Z.* Enslow, 1991. *(A)*

Lessem, Don. *Dinosaurs to Dodos: An Encyclopedia of Extinct Animals.* Scholastic, 1999. *(P; I; A)*

McClung, Robert M., and Hines, Bob. *Last of the Wild: Vanished and Vanishing Giants of the Animal World.* Shoe String Press, 1997; *Lost Wild America: The Story of Our Extinct and Vanishing Wildlife.* Shoe String Press, 1993. *(I; A)*

Stefoff, Rebecca. *Extinction.* Chelsea House, 1992. *(I; A)*

## EXTRASENSORY PERCEPTION (ESP)

Akins, William R. *ESP: Your Psychic Powers and How to Test Them.* Watts, 1980. *(P; I; A)*

Cohen, Daniel. *How to Test Your ESP.* Dutton. 1982. *(A)*

Deem, James M. *How to Read Your Mother's Mind.* Houghton, 1994. *(P; I)*

## EYE

Parker, Steve. *The Eye and Seeing.* Watts, 1989. *(P; I)*

Savage, Stephen. *Eyes.* Thomson, 1995. *(I)*

Thomson, Ruth. *Eyes.* Watts, 1988. *(P)*

## FABLES

Aesop. *Aesop's Fables,* illus. by Heidi Holder. Viking, 1981. *(I)*

Caldecott, Randolph. *The Caldecott Aesop—Twenty Fables.* Doubleday, 1978. *(I)*

Michie, James. *LaFontaine: Selected Fables.* Viking, 1979. *(P; I)*

Winter, Milo. *The Aesop for Children.* Rand, 1984. *(P; I)*

## FAIRS AND EXPOSITIONS

Bial, Raymond. *County Fair.* Houghton, 1992. *(P; I)*

Lewin, Ted. *Fair!* Lothrop, 1997. *(P)*

Pierce, Jack. *The State Fair Book.* Carolrhoda, 1980. *(P)*

Marsh, Carole. *A Fun Book of World's Fairs.* Gallopade, 1982. *(P; I)*

## FAIRY TALES

Corrin, Sara, ed. *The Faber Book of Modern Fairy Tales.* Faber, 1981 *(I)*

Lang, Andrew. *Blue Fairy Book.* Viking, 1978; *Green Fairy Book.* Airmont, 1969 (and other Lang Fairy Books). *(I)*

Philip, Neil, ed. *Fairy Tales of Eastern Europe.* Clarion, 1991. *(I)*

Steig, Jeanne. *A Handful of Beans: Six Fairy Tales.* HarperCollins, 1998. *(P)*

## FAMILY

Brown, Laurene Krasny. *Dinosaurs Divorce: A Guide for Changing Families.* Atlantic, 1986, *(P)*

Erlbach, Arlene. *The Families Book: True Stories about Real Kids and the People They Live with and Love.* Free Spirit, 1996. *(P; I)*

Friedman, Ina. *How My Parents Learned to Eat.* Houghton, 1987. *(P)*

Jenness, Aylette. *Families: A Celebration of Diversity, Commitment, and Love.* Houghton, 1990. *(P; I)*

LeShan, Eda. *Grandparents: A Special Kind of Love.* Macmillan, 1984. *(P; I)*

Locker, Thomas. *Family Farm.* Dial, 1988. *(P; I)*

Rench, Janice. *Family Violence: How to Recognize and Survive It.* Lerner, 1992. *(I; A)*

Streich, Corrine. *Grandparents' Houses: Poems about Grandparents.* Greenwillow, 1984. *(I)*

Worth, Richard. *The American Family.* Watts, 1984. *(I; A)*

## FAMINE

Lampton, Christopher F. *Famine.* Millbrook, 1994. *(P; I)*

## FARMS AND FARMING

Ancona, George, and Anderson, Joan. *The American Family Farm.* Harcourt, 1989. *(I)*

Bellville, Charyl Walsh. *Farming Today Yesterday's Way.* Carolrhoda, 1984. *(P)*

Bial, Raymond. *Portrait of a Farm Family.* Houghton, 1995. *(P; I)*

Bushey, Jerry. *Farming the Land: Modern Farmers and Their Machines.* Carolrhoda, 1987. *(P; I)*

Gibbons, Gail. *Farming.* Holiday, 1988. *(P)*

Goldberg, Jacob. *The Disappearing American Farm.* Watts, 1996. *(A)*

Gorman, Carol. *America's Farm Crisis.* Watts, 1987. *(A)*

Graff, Nancy Price. *The Strength of the Hills: A Portrait of a Family Farm.* Little, 1989. *(P; I; A)*

Kushner, Jill Menkes. *The Farming Industry.* Watts, 1984. *(I; A)*

Lambert, Mark. *Farming Technology.* Bookwright, 1990. *(I)*

Murphy, Jim. *Tractors: From Yesterday's Steam Wagons to Today's Turbocharged Giants.* Lippincott, 1984. *(P; I)*

Paladino, Catherine. *One Good Apple: Growing Our Food for the Sake of the Earth.* Houghton, 1999. *(I)*

Patent, Dorothy Hinshaw. *Farm Animals.* Holiday, 1984. *(P; I)*

Provensen, Alice, and Provensen, Martin. *The Year at Maple Hill Farm.* Macmillan, 1988. *(P)*

Smith, E. Boyd. *The Farm Book.* Houghton, 1982. *(P)*

Stephen, R. J. *Farm Machinery.* Watts, 1987. *(P)*

## FARRAGUT, DAVID

Latham, Jean Lee. *Anchor's Aweigh: The Story of David Glasgow Farragut.* Harper, 1968. *(I)*

## FASCISM

Mulvihill, Margaret. *Mussolini and Italian Fascism.* Gloucester Press, 1990. *(A)*

## FASHION

Hoobler, Dorothy, and Hoobler, Thomas. *Vanity Rules: A History of American Fashion and Beauty.* Twenty-First Century, 2000. *(I; A)*
Meech, Sue. *1900-20: Linen and Lace.* Gareth Stevens, 1999. *(P; I)*

## FEET AND HANDS

Goor, Ron, and Goor, Nancy. *All Kinds of Feet.* Crowell, 1984. *(P)*
Pluckrose, Henry. *Feet.* Watts, 1988. *(P)*
Thomson, Ruth. *Hands.* Watts, 1988. *(P)*

## FERDINAND AND ISABELLA

Meltzer, Milton. *Ten Queens: Portraits of Women of Power.* Dutton, 1997. *(I; A)*

## FERNS

Wexler, Jerome. *From Spore to Spore: Ferns and How They Grow.* Dodd, 1985. *(I)*

## FIBERS

Keeler, Patricia, and McCall, Francis X., Jr. *Unraveling Fibers.* Atheneum, 1995. *(I)*

## FIELD HOCKEY

Preston-Mauks, Susan. *Field Hockey Is for Me.* Lerner, 1983. *(P; I)*
Sullivan, George. *Better Field Hockey for Girls.* Dodd, 1981. *(I; A)*

## FIJI

Ngcheong-Lum, Roseline, and Lum, R. *Fiji.* Marshall Cavendish, 2000. *(I; A)*

## FILLMORE, MILLARD

Casey, Jane Clark. *Millard Fillmore: Thirteenth President of the United States.* Children's, 1988. *(P; I)*

## FINGER PAINTING

Carreiro, Carolyn. *Hand-Print Animal Art.* Williamson, 1997. *(P; I)*

## FINGERPRINTING

Jones, Charlotte Foltz. *Fingerprints and Talking Bones: How Real-Life Crimes Are Solved.* Bantam Doubleday Dell, 1999. *(I)*

## FINLAND

Hentz, Martin. *Finland.* Children's, 1983. *(I; A)*
Lander, Patricia, and Charbonneau, Claudette. *The Land and People of Finland.* Lippincott, 1990. *(I; A)*

## FIRE

Fradin, Dennis B. *Disaster! Fires.* Children's, 1982. *(I)*
Gibbons, Gail. *Fire! Fire!* Crowell, 1982. *(P)*
Satchwell, John. *Fire.* Dial, 1983. *(P)*

## FIRE FIGHTING AND PREVENTION

Beil, Karen Magnuson. *Fire in Their Eyes: Wildfires and the People Who Fight Them.* Harcourt, 1999. *(I; A)*
Bingham, Caroline. *Fire Truck.* Dorling Kindersley, 1995. *(P)*
Bourgeois, Paulette. *Fire Fighters.* Kids Can, 1998. *(P)*
Bundt, Nancy. *The Fire Station Book.* Carolrhoda, 1981. *(P)*
Fichter, George. *Disastrous Fires.* Watts, 1981. *(I)*
Gorrell, Gena K. *Catching Fire: The Story of Firefighting.* Tundra, 1999. *(I)*
Lee, Mary Price, and Lee, Richard S. *Careers in Firefighting.* Rosen, 1993. *(I; A)*
Loeper, John. *By Hook and Ladder.* Atheneum, 1981. *(I)*
Poynter, Margaret. *Wildland Fire Fighting.* Atheneum, 1982. *(I; A)*
Stephen, R. J. *Fire Engines.* Watts, 1987. *(P)*
Winkleman, Katherine K. *Firehouse.* Walker, 1994. *(P)*
Wolf, Bernard. *Firehouses.* Morrow, 1983. *(I)*

## FIREWORKS

Anderson, Norman D., and Brown, Walter R. *Fireworks! Pyrotechnics on Display.* Dodd, 1983. *(P; I)*

## FIRST AID

Boelts, Maribeth, and Boelts, Darwin. *Kids to the Rescue! First Aid Techniques for Kids.* Parenting Press, 1992. *(P; I)*
Boy Scouts of America. *First Aid.* Boy Scouts, 1981. *(I; A)*
Freeman, Lory. *What Would You Do If? A Children's Guide to First Aid.* Parenting Press, 1983. *(P)*
Masoff, Joy. *Emergency!* Scholastic Reference, 1999. *(I)*

## FIRST AMENDMENT FREEDOMS

Barbour, Scott, ed. *Free Speech.* Greenhaven, 1999. *(A)*
Evans, J. Edward. *Freedom of Religion.* Lerner, 1990. *(I; A); Freedom of Speech.* Lerner, 1990. *(I; A)*
Herda, D. J. *New York Times v. United States: National Security and Censorship.* Enslow, 1994. *(I; A)*

## FIRST LADIES

Boller, Paul F. *Presidential Wives.* Oxford University Press, 1988. *(I; A)*
Butwin, Miriam, and Chaffin, Lillie. *America's First Ladies.* (2 volumes). Lerner, n.d. *(I; A)*

Caroli, Betty Boyd. *First Ladies.* Oxford University Press, 1987. *(A)*

Feinberg, Barbara Silberdick. *America's First Ladies: Changing Expectations.* Watts, 1998. *(I; A)*

Healy, Diana Dixon. *America's First Ladies.* Atheneum, 1988. *(I; A)*

Stacey, T. J. *Hillary Rodham Clinton: Activist First Lady.* Enslow, 1994. *(I; A)*

## FISH

Broekel, Ray. *Dangerous Fish.* Children's, 1982. *(P)*

Freedman, Russell. *Killer Fish.* Holiday, 1982. *(P)*

Graham-Barber, Lynda. *Round Fish, Flatfish, and Other Animal Changes.* Crown, 1982. *(I)*

Henrie, Fiona. *Fish.* Watts, 1981. *(P; I)*

Lane, Margaret. *The Fish: The Story of the Stickleback.* Dial, 1982. *(P)*

## FISH AS PETS

Harris, Jack C. *A Step-by-Step Book about Goldfish.* TFH Publications, 1988. *(I; A)*

## FISHING

Arnosky, Jim. *Flies in the Water, Fish in the Air: A Personal Introduction to Fly Fishing.* Lothrop, 1986. *(I; A); Freshwater Fish and Fishing.* Four Winds, 1982. *(P; I)*

Bailey, John. *The Young Fishing Enthusiast: A Practical Guide for Kids.* DK, 1999. *(I; A)*

Evanoff, Vlad. *A Complete Guide to Fishing.* Harper, 1981 (rev. ed.). *(I; A)*

Fabian, John. *Fishing for Beginners.* Atheneum, 1980. *(P; I)*

Randolph, John. *Fishing Basics.* Prentice-Hall, 1981. *(P; I)*

Roberts, Charles P., and Roberts, George F. *Fishing for Fun: A Freshwater Guide.* Dillon, 1984. *(I)*

## FISHING INDUSTRY

Ferrell, Nancy Warren. *The Fishing Industry.* Watts, 1984. *(I; A)*

Scarry, Huck. *Life on a Fishing Boat: A Sketchbook.* Prentice-Hall, 1983. *(I; A)*

## FISSION

Barron, Rachel Stiffler. *Lise Meitner: Discoverer of Nuclear Fission.* Morgan Reynolds, 2000. *(I; A)*

## FLAGS

Crampton, William. *Flag.* Knopf, 1989. *(I)*

Johnson, Linda Carlson. *Our National Symbols.* Millbrook Press, 1994. *(P)*

Langton, Jane. *Fragile Flag.* Harper, 1984. *(I)*

Swanson, June. *I Pledge Allegiance.* Carolrhoda, 1990. *(P)*

White, David. *Flags.* Rourke, 1988. *(P)*

## FLEMING, SIR ALEXANDER

Kaye, Judith. *The Life of Alexander Fleming* Twenty-First Century, 1993. *(I)*

## FLOATING AND BUOYANCY

Challoner, Jack. *Floating and Sinking.* Raintree Steck-Vaughn, 1997. *(P)*

## FLOODS

Hiscock, Bruce. *The Big Rivers: The Missouri, the Mississippi, and the Ohio.* Atheneum, 1997. *(P; I)*

Lauber, Patricia. *Flood: Wrestling with the Mississippi.* National Geographic, 1996. *(P; I)*

## FLORIDA

Coil, Suzanne M. *Florida.* Watts, 1987. *(P; I)*

Fradin, Dennis. *Florida: In Words and Pictures.* Children's, 1980. *(P; I)*

Heinrichs, Ann. *Florida.* Children's Press, 1998. *(I)*

Stone, Lynn M. *Florida.* Children's, 1988. *(P; I)*

## FLOWERS

Allen, Sarah, ed. *Wildflowers: Eastern Edition; Western Edition.* Little, 1981. *(I; A)*

Crowell, Robert L. *The Lore and Legend of Flowers.* Harper, 1982. *(I; A)*

Dowden, Anne Ophelia. *The Clover & the Bee: A Book of Pollination.* Crowell, 1990. *(I; A)*

Kuchalla, Susan. *All about Seeds.* Troll, 1982. *(P)*

Lauber, Patricia. *From Flower to Flower: Animals and Pollination.* Crown, 1987. *(I)*

Lerner, Carol. *Plant Families.* Morrow, 1989. *(P; I)*

Overbeck, Cynthia. *How Seeds Travel.* Lerner, 1982; *Sunflowers.* Lerner, 1981. *(I; A)*

Patent, Dorothy Hinshaw. *Flowers for Everyone.* Cobblehill, 1990. *(I)*

## FOLK ART

Fowler, Virginia. *Folk Arts around the World: And How to Make Them.* Prentice-Hall, 1981. *(I; A)*

Wilson, Sule Greg C. *African American Quilting: The Warmth of Tradition.* Rosen, 1999. *(P; I)*

## FOLKLORE

Climo, Shirley. *The Egyptian Cinderella.* Crowell, 1989. *(P; I); Magic and Mischief: Tales from Cornwall.* Clarion, 1999. *(P; I); The Persian Cinderella.* HarperCollins, 1999. *(P; I)*

Crouch, Marcus. *The Whole World Storybook.* Oxford University Press, 1983. *(I)*

Daly, Jude. *Fair, Brown and Trembling: An Irish Cinderella Story.* Farrar, 2000. *(P)*

Dixon, Ann. *How Raven Brought Light to People.* McElderry, 1993. *(P; I)*

Gollub, Matthew. *Uncle Snake.* Tambourine, 1996. *(P)*

Goode, Diane. *Book of American Folktales and Songs.* Dutton, 1989. *(P; I)*

Grifalconi, Ann. *The Village of Round and Square Houses.* Little, 1986. *(P)*

Hamilton, Virginia. *Her Stories: African American Folktales, Fairy Tales and True Tales.* Scholastic, 1995. *(P; I); The People Could Fly: American Black Folktales.* Knopf, 1985. *(I; A); When Birds Could Talk and Bats Could Sing: The Adventures of Bruh Sparrow, Sis Wren, and Their Friends.* Scholastic/Blue Sky, 1996. *(P; I)*

Hong, Lily Toy, retel. *How the Ox Star Fell from Heaven.* Albert Whitman, 1991. *(P; I)*

Kellogg, Steven. *Chicken Little.* Morrow, 1985. *(P)*

Kipling, Rudyard. *The Elephant's Child.* Harcourt, 1983. *(P; I)*

Kurtz, Jane. *Fire on the Mountain.* Simon & Schuster, 1994. *(P); Miro in the Kingdom of the Sun.* Houghton, 1996. *(P)*

Lester, Julius. *The Tales of Uncle Remus: The Adventure of Brer Rabbit.* Dial, 1987. *(I; A); When the Beginning Began: Stories about God, the Creatures, and Us.* Silver Whistle/Harcourt, 1999. *(I; A)*

Lewis, J. Patrick. *At the Wish of the Fish: A Russian Folktale.* Simon & Schuster/Atheneum, 1999. *(P)*

Luenn, Nancy. *Song for the Ancient Forest.* Atheneum, 1993. *(P; I)*

Lunge-Larsen, Lise. *The Troll with No Heart in His Body.* Houghton, 1999. *(P)*

Lurie, Alison, retel. *The Black Geese: A Baba Yaga Story from Russia.* DK, 1999. *(P)*

MacDonald, Margaret Read. *Earth Care: World Folktales to Talk About.* Shoe String/Linnet, 1999. *(I; A)*

Marshall, James. *Hansel and Gretel.* Dial, 1990. *(P)*

McDermott, Gerald. *Raven.* Harcourt, 1993. *(P)*

Mollel, Tololwa M., retel. *Subira Subira.* Clarion, 2000. *(P)*

Newton, Pam. *The Stonecutter: An Indian Folktale.* Putnam, 1990. *(P)*

Oughton, Jerrie. *How the Stars Fell into the Sky: A Navajo Legend.* Houghton, 1992. *(P; I)*

Perrault, Charles. *Perrault's Complete Fairy Tales,* tr. by A. E. Johnson. Dodd, 1982. *(P; I)*

Pyle, Howard. *The Wonder Clock: Of Four and Twenty Marvelous Tales.* Dover, n.d. *(P)*

Rackham, Arthur, ed. *The Arthur Rackham Fairy Book.* Harper, 1950. *(I)*

Sanfield, Steve. *The Adventures of High John the Conqueror.* Watts, 1989. *(I; A)*

San Souci, Robert D., retel. *Cendrillon: A Caribbean Cinderella.* Simon & Schuster, 1998. *(P)*

Schwartz, Howard, ed. *A Journey to Paradise: And Other Jewish Tales.* Pitspopany, 2000. *(P)*

Scieszka, Jon. *The Frog Prince Continued.* Viking, 1991. *(P)*

Shetterly, Susan Hand. *The Dwarf-Wizard of Uxmal.* Atheneum, 1990. *(I)*

Sierra, Judy. *Tasty Baby Belly Buttons: A Japanese Folktale.* Knopf, 1999. *(P)*

Steptoe, John. *Mufaro's Beautiful Daughters: An African Tale.* Lothrop, 1987. *(P)*

Stevens, Janet, ed. *Coyote Steals the Blanket: A Ute Tale.* Holiday, 1993. *(P)*

Wells, Ruth, retel. *The Farmer and the Poor God: A Folktale from Japan.* Simon & Schuster, 1996. *(P; I)*

Winthrop, Elizabeth. *Vasilissa the Beautiful.* Harper, 1991. *(P; I)*

Wolf, A. *The True Story of the Three Little Pigs.* Puffin, 1989. *(P)*

Wright, Blanche Fisher. *The Real Mother Goose.* Rand, 1916. *(P)*

Zelinsky, Paul O. *Rumpelstiltskin.* Greenwillow, 1988. *(P)*

## FOLK MUSIC

Fox, Dan, ed. *Go in and out the Window: An Illustrated Songbook for Young People.* Holt, 1987. *(P; I; A)*

Seeger, Ruth C. *American Folk Songs for Children.* Doubleday, 1980. *(P; I)*

Yolen, Jane, ed. *The Lullaby Songbook.* Harcourt, 1986. *(P; I)*

## FOOD AROUND THE WORLD

Cooper, Terry, and Ratner, Marilyn. *Many Friends Cookbook: An International Cookbook for Boys and Girls.* Putnam, 1980. *(P; I)*

Hayward, Ruth Ann, and Warner, Margaret Brink. *What's Cooking: Favorite Recipes from around the World.* Little, 1981. *(I; A)*

Johnson, Sylvia A. *Tomatoes, Potatoes, Corn, and Beans: How the Foods of the Americas Changed Cooking Around the World.* Atheneum, 1997. *(I; A)*

Meltzer, Milton. *Food.* Millbrook, 1998. *(P; I)*

Pizer, Vernon. *Eat the Grapes Downward: An Uninhibited Romp through the Surprising World of Food.* Dodd, 1983. *(I; A)*

Solheim, James. *It's Disgusting and We Ate It: True Food Facts from around the World and throughout History.* Simon & Schuster, 1998. *(P; I)*

Van der Linde, Polly, and Van der Linde, Tasha. *Around the World in Eighty Dishes.* Scroll, n.d. *(P; I)*

## FOOD SHOPPING

Milios, Rita. . *Shopping Savvy.* Rosen, 1992. *(I; A)*

Yardley, Thompson. *Buy Now, Pay Later/Smart Shopping Counts.* Millbrook Press, 1992. *(P; I)*

## FOOD SUPPLY

Bonner, James. *The World's People and the World's Food Supply.* Carolina Biological, 1980. *(A)*

McCoy, J. J. *How Safe Is Our Food Supply?* Watts, 1990. *(A)*

Patent, Dorothy Hinshaw. *Where Food Comes From.* Holiday, 1991. *(P)*

## FOOTBALL

Aaseng, Nate. *Football: You Are the Coach.* Lerner, 1983. *(I; A)*

Anderson, Dave. *The Story of Football.* Morrow, 1985. *(I; A)*

Barrett, Norman. *Football.* Watts, 1989. *(P)*

Berger, Melvin. *The Photo Dictionary of Football.* Methuen, 1980. *(P; I)*

Broekel, Ray. *Football.* Children's, 1982. *(P)*

Madden, John. *The First Book of Football.* Crown, 1988. *(I; A)*

Miller, J. David. *The Super Book of Football.* Sports Illustrated for Kids Books, 1990. *(I)*

Namath, Joe. *Football for Young Players and Parents.* Simon & Schuster, 1986. *(I)*

Potts, Steve. *San Francisco 49ers.* Creative Education, 1991. *(I)*

Rambeck, Richard. *Detroit Lions (I); New England Patriots.* Creative Education, 1991. *(I)*

Sandak, Cass R. *Football.* Watts, 1982. *(P)*

Stewart, Mark. *Football: A History of the Gridiron Game.* Watts, 1998. *(P; I)*

Sullivan, George. *All about Football.* Dodd, 1987. *(P)*

## FORCES

Dispezio, Michael. *Awesome Experiments in Force and Motion.* Sterling, 1999. *(I; A)*

Lafferty, Peter. *Force and Motion.* Dorling Kindersley, 1992. *(I)*

## FORD, GERALD R.

Randolph, Sallie G. *Gerald R. Ford, President.* Walker, 1987. *(I)*

## FOREIGN AID PROGRAMS

Egendorf, Laura, ed. *The Third World.* Greenhaven, 2000. *(A)*

## FORENSIC SCIENCE

Campbell, Andrea. *Forensic Science: Evidence, Clues, and Investigation.* Chelsea House, 1999. *(I; A)*

Fridell, Ron. *Solving Crimes: Pioneers of Forensic Science.* Watts, 2000. *(I; A)*

Jackson, Donna M. *The Bone Detectives: How Forensic Anthropologists Solve Crimes and Uncover Mysteries of the Dead.* Little, Brown, 1996. *(I; A)*

Jones, Charlotte Foltz. *Fingerprints and Talking Bones: How Real-Life Crimes Are Solved.* Bantam Doubleday Dell, 1999. *(I)*

Oxlade, Chris. *Crime Detection.* Heinemann, 1997. *(P; I)*

## FORESTS AND FORESTRY

Aldis, Rodney. *Rainforests.* Dillon: Macmillan, 1991. *(P; I)*

Bellamy, David. *The Forest.* Clarkson Potter, 1988. *(P)*

Challand, Helen J. *Vanishing Forests.* Children's, 1991. *(I)*

Cowcher, Helen. *Rain Forest.* Farrar, 1989. *(P)*

Dixon, Dougal. *Forests.* Watts, 1984. *(P; I)*(Atlas format)

George, Jean. *One Day in the Woods.* Crowell, 1988. *(P)*

Newton, James. *A Forest Is Reborn.* Harper, 1982. *(P)*

Simon, Seymour. *Wildfires.* Morrow, 1996. *(I)*

Staub, Frank. *America's Forests.* Carolrhoda, 1999. *(P; I)*

Vogt, Gregory. *Forests on Fire: The Fight to Save Our Trees.* Watts, 1990. *(A)*

## FORTS AND FORTIFICATION

Peterson, Harold L. *Forts in America.* Scribner's, 1964. *(I)*

Stiles, David. *The Kids' Fort Book.* Avon, 1982. *(P; I)*

## FOSSEY, DIAN

Jerome, Leah. *Dian Fossey.* Bantam, 1991. *(I)*

## FOSSILS

Aliki. *Fossils Tell of Long Ago.* Crowell, 1990 (rev. ed.). *(P)*

Arnold, Caroline. *Dinosaur Mountain.* Clarion, 1989. *(I); Trapped in Tar: Fossils from the Ice Age.* Clarion, 1987. *(P)*

Baylor, Byrd. *If You Are a Hunter of Fossils.* Scribner's, 1980. *(P)*

Bishop, Nic. *Digging for Bird-Dinosaurs: An Expedition to Madagascar.* Houghton Mifflin, 2000. *(I)*

Curtis, Neil. *Fossils.* Watts, 1984. *(P; I)*

Eldredge, Niles. *The Fossil Factory.* Addison-Wesley, 1989. *(I)*

Gallant, Roy A. *Fossils.* Watts, 1985. *(P)*

Lambert, David, and the Diagram Group. *The Field Guide to Prehistoric Life.* Facts on File, 1985. *(I; A)*

*Dinosaur Dig.* Morrow, 1990. *(P)*

Lauber, Patricia. *Dinosaurs Walked Here (And Other Stories Fossils Tell).* Bradbury, 1987. *(I; A)*

Sloan, Christopher. *Feathered Dinosaurs.* National Geographic, 2000. *(I)*

Tyldesley, Joyce. *The Mummy: Unwrap the Ancient Secrets of the Mummies' Tombs.* Carlton, 2000. *(A)*

Taylor, Paul D. *Fossil.* Knopf, 1990. *(I; A)*

## FOSTER CARE

Blomquist, Geraldine M., and Blomquist, Paul. *Coping as a Foster Child.* Rosen, 1991. *(A)*

Davies, Nancy Millichap. *Foster Care.* Watts, 1994. *(I; A)*

## FOUNDERS OF THE UNITED STATES

Benchley, Nathaniel. *Sam the Minuteman.* Harper, 1969. *(P)*

Bennett, Wayne, ed. *Founding Fathers.* Garrard, 1975. *(I; A)*

Bliven, Bruce, Jr. *The American Revolution, 1760-1783.* Random House, 1981. *(I)*

## FOXES

Ahlstrom, Mark. *The Foxes.* Crestwood, 1983. *(P; I)*

Burton, Jane. *Trill the Fox Cub.* Gareth Stevens, 1989. *(P)*

Mason, Cherie. *Wild Fox: A True Story.* Down East Books, 1993. *(P; I: A)*

## FRACTIONS AND DECIMALS

Adler, David A. *Fraction Fun.* Holiday House, 1997. *(P)*

King, Andrew. *Making Fractions.* Millbrook Press, 1998. *(P)*

Murphy, Stuart J. *Jump, Kangaroo, Jump!: Level 3: Fractions.* HarperCollins, 1999. *(P)*

Stienecker, David L., and Maccabe, Richard. *Fractions.* Marshall Cavendish, 1995. *(P; I)*

## FRANCE

Balderdi, Susan. *France: The Crossroads of Europe.* Dillon, 1983. *(I; A)*

Blackwood, Alan, and Chosson, Brigitte. *France.* Bookwright, 1988. *(P)*

Harris, Jonathan. *The Land and People of France.* Lippincott, 1989. *(I; A)*

Harvey, Miles. *Look What Comes from France.* Watts, 1999. *(P; I)*

Jacobsen, Peter O., and Kristensen, Preben S. *A Family in France.* Watts, 1984. *(P; I)*

James, Ian. *France.* Watts, 1989. *(P; I)*

Morrice, Polly. *The French Americans.* Chelsea House, 1988. *(I; A)*

Moss, Peter, and Palmer, Thelma. *France.* Children's, 1986. *(P)*

Tomlins, James. *We Live in France.* Watts, 1983. *(I; A)*

## FRANCE, LANGUAGE OF

Wright, Nicola. *Getting to Know: France and French.* Barron's, 1993. *(P; I)*

## FRANCE, MUSIC OF

Cavelletti, Carlo. *Chopin and Romantic Music.* Barron's Educational Series, 2000. *(I; A)*

## FRANCIS OF ASSISI, SAINT

Mayo, Margaret. *Brother Sun, Sister Moon: The Life and Stories of St. Francis.* Little, Brown, 2000. *(P)*

## FRANK, ANNE

Gold, Alison Leslie. *Memories of Anne Frank: Reflections of a Childhood Friend.* Scholastic, 1997. *(P; I)*

Muller, Melissa. *Anne Frank: The Biography.* Metropolitan, 1998. *(A)*

Pressler, Mirjam. *Anne Frank: A Hidden Life.* Dutton, 2000. *(A)*

Wukovits, John F. *Anne Frank.* Lucent, 1998. *(I; A)*

## FRANKLIN, BENJAMIN

Adler, David A. *A Picture Book of Benjamin Franklin.* Holiday, 1990. *(P)*

Franklin, Benjamin. *The Autobiography of Benjamin Franklin.* Airmont, n.d. *(A); Poor Richard.* Peter Pauper, n.d. *(I; A)*

Giblin, James Cross. *The Amazing Life of Benjamin Franklin.* Scholastic, 2000. *(P; I)*

Greene, Carol. *Benjamin Franklin: A Man with Many Jobs.* Children's, 1988. *(P)*

Heiligman, Deborah. *The Mysterious Ocean Highway: Benjamin Franklin and the Gulf Stream.* Raintree Steck-Vaughn, 1999. *(P; I)*

Looby, Chris. *Benjamin Franklin.* Chelsea House, 1990. *(I; A)*

Meltzer, Milton. *Benjamin Franklin: The New American.* Watts, 1988. *(I; A)*

Sandak, Cass R. *Benjamin Franklin.* Watts, 1986. *(P; I)*

Stevens, Bryna. *Ben Franklin's Glass Armonica.* Carolrhoda, 1983. *(P)*

## FRENCH AND INDIAN WAR

Collier, Christopher, and Collier, James Lincoln. *The French and Indian War, 1660-1763.* Marshall Cavendish, 1997. *(I)*

Maestro, Betsy C. *Struggle for a Continent: The French and Indian Wars 1689-1763.* Morrow, 2000. *(P; I)*

Minks, Benton, and Minks, Louise. *The French and Indian War.* Lucent, 1994. *(I; A)*

## FRENCH REVOLUTION

Banfield, Susan. *The Rights of Man, the Reign of Terror: The Story of the French Revolution.* HarperCollins, 1990. *(A)*

Otfinoski, Steven. *Triumph and Terror: The French Revolution.* Facts on File, 1993. *(A)*

Stewart, Gail B. *Life during the French Revolution.* Lucent, 1995. *(I; A)*

## FREUD, SIGMUND

Lager, Marilyn. *Sigmund Freud: Doctor of the Mind.* Enslow, 1986. *(A)*

## FROGS AND TOADS

Clarke, Barry. *Amazing Frogs and Toads.* Knopf, 1990. *(P; I)*

Dallinger, Jane, and Johnson, Sylvia A. *Frogs and Toads.* Lerner, 1982. *(I; A)*

Lacey, Elizabeth A. *The Complete Frog: A Guide for the Very Young Naturalist.* Lothrop, 1989. *(I)*

Lavies, Bianca. *Lily Pad Pond.* Dutton, 1989. *(P)*

Modiki, Masuda. *Tree Frogs.* Lerner, 1986. *(I)*

Pascoe, Elaine. *Tadpoles.* Blackbirch, 1996. *(P; I)*

Tagholm, Sally. *The Frog.* Kingfisher, 2000. *(P)*

Tarrant, Graham. *Frogs.* Putnam, 1983. *(P)*

## FROST, ROBERT

Bober, Natalie S. *A Restless Spirit: The Story of Robert Frost.* Holt, 1991 (rev. ed.). *(I; A)*

Frost, Robert. *The Road Not Taken: An Introduction to Robert Frost.* Holt, 1951. *(A)*

## FRUITGROWING

Jaspersohn, William. *Cranberries.* Houghton, 1991. *(P; I)*

Johnson, Sylvia A. *Apple Trees.* Lerner, 1983. *(P; I; A)*

Mitgutsch, Ali. *From Lemon to Lemonade.* Carolrhoda, 1986. *(P); From Seed to Pear.* Carolrhoda, 1981. *(P)*

Potter, Marian. *A Chance Wild Apple*. Morrow, 1982. *(P; I)*

## FUELS

Rice, Dale. *Energy from Fossil Fuels*. Raintree, 1983. *(P; I)*

## FULTON, ROBERT

Philip, Cynthia. *Robert Fulton: A Biography*. Watts, 1985. *(A)*

Quackenbush, Robert. *Watt Got You Started, Mr. Fulton?* Prentice-Hall, 1982. *(P; I)*

## FUNERAL CUSTOMS

Colman, Penny. *Corpses, Coffins, and Crypts: A History of Burial*. Holt, 1997. *(I; A)*

Johnston, Marianne. *Let's Talk about Going to a Funeral*. Rosen/Power Kids Press, 1998. *(P)*

## FUNGI

Pascoe, Elaine. *Slime, Molds, and Fungi*. Blackbirch, 1998. *(P; I)*

## FURNITURE

Giblin, James Cross. *Be Seated: A Book about Chairs*. HarperCollins, 1993. *(P; I)*

## FUR TRADE IN NORTH AMERICA

Siegel, Beatrice. *Fur Trappers and Traders; The Indians, the Pilgrims, and the Beaver*. Walker, 1981. *(P; I)*

## GABON

Newman, Gerald. *Zaïre, Gabon, and the Congo*. Watts, 1981. *(I; A)*

## GALILEO

Fisher, Leonard Everett. *Galileo*. Simon & Schuster, 1992. *(P; I)*

Sis, Peter. *Starry Messenger: Galileo Galilei*. Farrar/Foster, 1996. *(P; I)*

White, Michael. *Galileo Galilei: Inventor, Astronomer and Rebel*. Blackbirch Press, 1999. *(I)*

## GAMA, VASCO DA

Knight, David. *Vasco Da Gama*. Troll, 1979 (new ed.). *(P; I)*

## GAMBIA, THE

Gilfond, Henry. *Gambia, Ghana, Liberia, and Sierra Leone*. Watts, 1981. *(I; A)*

Zimmerman, Robert. *The Gambia*. Children's Press, 1994. *(A)*

## GAMES

Cline, Dallas, and Tornborg, Pat. *How to Play Almost Everything*. Putnam, 1982. *(P; I)*

D'Amato, Alex, and D'Amato, Janet. *Galaxy Games*. Doubleday, 1981. *(P; I)*

Hass, E. A. *Come Quick! I'm Sick*. Atheneum, 1982. *(P)*

Levine, Shar, and Scudamore, Vicki. *Marbles: A Player's Guide*. Sterling, 1999. *(P; I)*

McToots, Rudi. *Best-Ever Book of Indoor Games*. Arco, 1985. *(I; A)*

Vecchione, Glen. *The Jump Rope Book*. Sterling, 1995. *(I)*

## GANDHI, MOHANDAS KARAMCHAND

Cheney, Glenn A. *Mohandas Gandhi*. Watts, 1983. *(I; A)*

Rawding, F. W. *Gandhi*. Cambridge University Press, 1980. *(I); Gandhi and the Struggle for India's Independence*. Lerner, 1982. *(I; A)*

## GANGES RIVER

Cumming, David. *The Ganges*. Raintree Steck-Vaughn, 1993. *(I)*

## GARDENS AND GARDENING

Creasy, Rosalind. *Blue Potatoes, Orange Tomatoes: How to Grow a Rainbow Garden*. Sierra, 1994. *(P; I)*

Krementz, Jill. *A Very Young Gardener*. Dial, 1991. *(P)*

Lerner, Carol. *My Indoor Garden*. Morrow, 1999. *(P; I)*

Markmann, Erika. *Grow It! An Indoor/Outdoor Gardening Guide for Kids*. Random House, 1991. *(P; I)*

Murphy, Louise. *My Garden: A Journal for Gardening around the Year*. Scribner's, 1980. *(P; I)*

Rangecroft, Derek, and Rangecroft, Sandra. *Nasturtiums; Pumpkins; Sunflowers; Tomatoes*. Dell, 1993. *(P; I)*

Talmage, Ellen. *Container Gardening for Kids*. Sterling, 1996. *(P; I)*

Vogel, Antje, illus. *The Big Book for Little Gardeners*. Green Tiger, 1983. *(P)*

Waters, Marjorie. *The Victory Garden Kid's Book*. Houghton, 1988. *(P; I)*

Wilkes, Angela. *My First Garden Book*. Knopf, 1992. *(P; I)*

## GARFIELD, JAMES ABRAM

Lillegard, Dee. *James A. Garfield*. Children's, 1988. *(P; I)*

McElroy, Richard L. *James A. Garfield - His Life and Times: A Pictorial History*. Daring, 1986. *(A)*

## GARIBALDI, GIUSEPPE

Viola, Herman J., and Viola, Susan. *Giuseppe Garbaldi*. Chelsea House, 1987. *(I; A)*

## GASES

Berger, Melvin *Solids, Liquids, and Gases*. Putnam, 1989. *(I; A)*

Darling, David. *From Glasses to Gases: The Science of Matter*. Silver Burdett Press, 1992. *(P; I)*

Gardner, Robert. *Science Projects about Solids, Liquids, and Gases*. Enslow, 2000. *(I; A)*

Griffin, Frank. *Industrial Gases*. Sportshelf, n.d. *(I; A)*

Mebane, Robert C., and Rybolt, Thomas R. *Air and Other Gases*. Twenty-First Century, 1995. *(I)*

Pechey, Roger. *Gas.* Rourke, 1987. *(P; I)*

## GEMSTONES

O'Neil, Paul. *Gemstones.* Time-Life, 1983. *(I)*

Symes, R. F., and Harding, Roger. *Crystal & Gem.* Knopf, 1991. *(I)*

## GENEALOGY

Cooper, Kay. *Where Did You Get Those Eyes? A Guide to Discovering Your Family History.* Walker, 1988. *(I)*

Douglas, Ann. *The Family Tree Detective: Cracking the Case of Your Family's Story.* Owl, 1999. *(I)*

Sweeney, Joan. *Me and My Family Tree.* Crown, 1999. *(P)*

Taylor, Maureen. *Through the Eyes of Your Ancestors: A Step-by-Step Guide to Uncovering Your Family's History.* Houghton, 1999. *(I; A)*

Wubben, Pamela G. *Genealogy for Children.* One Percent, 1981. *(P; I)*

## GENETICS

Arnold, Caroline. *Genetics: From Mendel to Gene Splicing.* Watts, 1986. *(I; A)*

Asimov, Isaac. *How Did We Find Out about Our Genes?* Walker, 1983. *(I)*

Bornstein, Sandy, and Bornstein, Jerry. *New Frontiers in Genetics.* Simon & Schuster, 1984 *(A); What Makes You What You Are: A First Look at Genetics.* Messner, 1989. *(I)*

Bryan, Jenny. *Genetic Engineering.* Thomson, 1995. *(I;A)*

Edelson, Edward. *Genetics and Heredity.* Chelsea House, 1990. *(I; A)*

Gutnik, Martin J. *Genetics: Projects for Young Scientists.* Watts, 1985. *(I)*

Hyde, Margaret O., and Hyde, Lawrence E. *Cloning and the New Genetics.* Enslow, 1984. *(A)*

Patent, Dorothy H. *Grandfather's Nose: Why We Look Alike or Different.* Watts, 1989. *(P)*

Snyder, Gerald S. *Test Tube Life: Scientific Advance and Moral Dilemma.* Messner, 1982. *(I; A)*

Stwertka, Eve, and Stwertka, Albert. *Genetic Engineering.* Watts, 1982. *(I; A)*

Tagliaferro, Linda. *Genetic Engineering: Progress or Peril?* Lerner, 1997. *(A)*

## GENOCIDE

Altman, Linda Jacobs. *Genocide: The Systematic Killing of a People.* Enslow, 1995. *(I; A)*

Grant, R.G. *Genocide.* Raintree/Steck-Vaughn, 1999. *(I; A)*

Spangenburg, Ray, and Moser, Kit. *The Crime of Genocide: Terror against Humanity.* Enslow, 2000. *(A)*

## GEOGRAPHY

Bell, Neill. *The Book of Where or How to Be Naturally Geographic.* Little, 1982. *(I; A)*

Grolier Incorporated. *Lands and Peoples* (6 volumes). Grolier, 1997. *(I)*

Knowlton, Jack. *Geography From A to Z.* Crowell, 1988. *(P)*

National Geographic Society. *Nature's World of Wonders.* National Geographic, 1983. *(I; A)*

## GEOLOGY

Boy Scouts of America. *Geology.* BSA, 1981. *(I; A)*

Dixon, Dougal. *Geology.* Watts, 1983. *(I; A); The Practical Geologist.* Simon and Schuster, 1992. *(I; A)*

Gallant, Roy A. *Dance of the Continents.* Marshall Cavendish/Benchmark, 1999. *(I; A)*

Jacobs, Linda. *Letting Off Steam: The Story of Geothermal Energy.* Carolrhoda, 1989. *(I; A)*

Lambert, David, and the Diagram Group. *The Field Guide to Geology.* Facts on File, 1988. *(A)*

Markle, Sandra. *Digging Deeper: Investigations into Rocks, Shocks, Quakes, and Other Earthly Matters.* Lothrop, 1987. *(I)*

Rossbacher, Lisa A. *Recent Revolutions in Geology.* Watts, 1986. *(I; A)*

## GEOMETRY

Srivastava, Jane J. *Spaces, Shapes, and Sizes.* Harper, 1980. *(P)*

VanCleave, Janice. *Janice VanCleave's Geometry for Every Kid.* Wiley, 1994. *(I)*

## GEORGIA

Blackburn, Joyce. *James Edward Oglethorpe.* Dodd, 1983. *(I; A)*

Hepburn, Lawrence R. *The Georgia History Book.* University of Georgia, 1982. *(I; A)*

Kent, Zachary A. *Georgia.* Children's, 1988. *(P; I)*

LaDoux, Rita C. *Georgia.* Lerner, 1991. *(I)*

Pedersen, Anne. *Kidding around Atlanta: A Young Person's Guide to the City.* John Muir, 1989. *(I; A)*

Snow, Pegeen. *Atlanta.* Dillon, 1989. *(P; I)*

## GERMANY

Ayer, Eleanor H. *Germany: In the Heartland of Europe.* Benchmark, 1996. *(I)*

Bradley, Catherine, and Bradley, John. *Germany: The Reunification of a Nation.* Gloucester Press, dist. by Watts, 1991. *(I)*

Epler, Doris M. *The Berlin Wall: How It Rose and Why It Fell.* Millbrook, 1992. *(I; A)*

Flint, David. *Germany.* Steck-Vaughn, 1994. *(I)*

Goldston, Robert. *Sinister Touches: The Secret War against Hitler.* Dial, 1982. *(I; A)*

Spencer, William. *Germany Then and Now.* Watts, 1994. *(A)*

## GERONIMO

Wilson, Charles M. *Geronimo.* Dillon, 1973. *(I; A)*

## GERSHWIN, GEORGE

Kresh, Paul. *An American Rhapsody: The Story of George Gershwin.* Dutton, 1988. *(I; A)*

Mitchell, Barbara. *America, I Hear You: A Story about George Gershwin.* Lerner, 1987. *(P)*

Reef, Catherine. *George Gershwin: American Composer.* Morgan Reynolds, 2000. *(A)*

## GETTYSBURG ADDRESS

Lincoln, Abraham. *The Gettysburg Address.* Houghton Mifflin, 1998. *(I)*

## GEYSERS AND HOT SPRINGS

Lauber, Patricia. *Tapping Earth's Heat.* Garrard, 1978. *(P; I)*

## GHANA

*Ghana . . . in Pictures.* Lerner, 1988. *(P; I)*
Barnett, Jeanie M. *Ghana.* Chelsea House, 1988. *(I)*
Gilfond, Henry. *Gambia, Ghana, Liberia, and Sierra Leone.* Watts, 1981. *(I; A)*

## GHOSTS

Cohen, Daniel. *Great Ghosts.* Dutton, 1990. *(P; I)*
Matthews, John. *The Barefoot Book of Giants, Ghosts and Goblins: Traditional Tales from around the World.* Barefoot, 1999. *(P; I)*
Walker, Paul Robert. *Giants!: Stories from around the World.* Harcourt, 1995. *(P; I)*

## GIOTTO DI BONDONE

Corrain, Lucia. *Giotto and Medieval Art: The Lives and Works of the Medieval Artists.* NTC, 1995. *(I)*
Janson, H. W., and Janson, Anthony F. *History of Art for Young People.* Abrams, 1997. (rev. ed.) *(I; A)*

## GIRAFFES

Arnold, Caroline. *Giraffe.* Morrow, 1987. *(P; I)*
Bush, John. *This Is a Book about Giraffes.* Watts, 1983. *(P)*
Lavine, Sigmund A. *Wonders of Giraffes.* Dodd, 1986. *(I; A)*
Sattler, Helen Roney. *Giraffes, the Sentinels of the Savannahs.* Lothrop, 1990. *(I)*
Torgersen, Don. *Giraffe Hooves and Antelope Horns.* Children's, 1982. *(P; I)*

## GIRL SCOUTS

Girl Scouts of the United States of America. *Daisy Low of the Girl Scouts: The Story of Juliette Gordon Low, Founder of the Girl Scouts of America.* Girl Scouts, 1975 (rev. ed.). *(I; A)*; *Wide World of Girl Guiding and Girl Scouting,* 1980. *(P; I)*; *Worlds to Explore for Brownie and Junior Girl Scouts,* 1977. *(P; I)*
World Association of Girl Guides and Girl Scouts. *The Story of the Four World Centres: For Girls and Leaders.* Girl Scouts, 1982 (rev. ed.). *(P; I)*; *Trefoil Round the World,* 1978. *(P; I; A)*

## GLACIERS

Gallant, Roy. *Glaciers.* Watts, 1999. *(P; I)*

Nixon, Hershell H., and Nixon, Joan L. *Glaciers: Nature's Frozen Rivers.* Dodd, 1980. *(P; I)*
Robin, Gordon De Q. *Glaciers and Ice Sheets.* Watts, 1984. *(I)*
Simon, Seymour. *Icebergs and Glaciers.* Morrow, 1987. *(P; I)*
Walker, Sally M. *Glaciers: Ice on the Move.* Carolrhoda, 1990. *(I)*

## GLANDS

Young, John K. *Hormones: Molecular Messengers.* Watts, 1994. *(I; A)*

## GLASS

Cackett, Susan. *Glass.* Gloucester Press, 1988. *(P; I)*
Corning Museum of Glass. *Masterpieces of Glass from the Corning Museum.* Dover, 1983. *(I; A)*
Giblin, James Cross. *Let There Be Light.* Crowell, 1988. *(A)*
Kolb, Kenneth E. and Doris K. *Glass: Its Many Facets.* Enslow, 1988. *(I; A)*
Mitgutsch, Ali. *From Sand to Glass.* Carolrhoda, 1981. *(P)*
Paterson, Alan J. *How Glass Is Made.* Facts on File, 1985. *(P; I)*

## GLENN, JOHN H., JR.

Kramer, Barbara. *John Glenn: A Space Biography.* Enslow, 1998. *(I)*

## GLIDERS

Penzler, Otto. *Hang Gliding.* Troll, 1976. *(I; A)*
Schmetz, Dorothy C. *Hang Gliding.* Crestwood, 1978. *(P)*

## GOATS

Chiefari, Janet. *Kids Are Baby Goats.* Dodd, 1984. *(P; I)*
Levine, Sigmund A., and Scuro, Vincent. *Wonders of Goats.* Dodd, 1980. *(P; I)*

## GODDARD, ROBERT HUTCHINGS

Farley, Karin Clafford. *Robert H. Goddard.* Silver Burdett Press, 1991. *(I; A)*

## GOLD, DISCOVERIES OF

Blumberg, Rhoda. *The Great American Gold Rush.* Bradbury, 1989. *(I)*
Cooper, Michael. *Klondike Fever: The Famous Gold Rush of 1898.* Clarion, 1989. *(I; A)*
Gough, Barry. *Gold Rush!* Watts, 1983. *(I; A)*
Jones, Charlotte Foltz. *Yukon Gold: The Story of the Klondike Gold Rush.* Holiday, 1999. *(I)*
McCall, Edith. *Gold Rush Adventures.* Children's, 1980. *(P; I; A)*
Murphy, Claire Rudolph, and Haigh, Jane G. *Children of the Gold Rush.* Roberts Rinehart, 1999. *(I)*
Shepherd, Donna Walsh. *The Klondike Gold Rush.* Watts, 1998. *(P; I)*

Stein, R. Conrad. *The Story of the Gold at Sutter's Mill.* Children's, 1981. *(P; I)*

## GOLF

Golf Digest Editors. *Better Golf.* Sportshelf, n.d. *(I; A)*

Collins, David R. *Tiger Woods, Golfing Champion.* Pelican, 1999. *(I)*

Merrins, Eddie, and McTeigue, Michael. *Golf for the Young.* Atheneum, 1983. *(I; A)*

Wakeman, Nancy. *Babe Didrikson Zaharias: Driven to Win.* Lerner, 2000. *(P; I)*

## GOODALL, JANE

Lucas, Eileen. *Jane Goodall, Friend of the Chimps.* Millbrook, 1992. *(I)*

## GORBACHEV, MIKHAIL

Caulkins, Janet. *The Picture Life of Mikhail Gorbachev.* Watts, 1989 (rev. ed.). *(P)*

Oleksy, Walter. *Mikhail Gorbachev: A Leader for Soviet Change.* Children's, 1989. *(P; I)*

Sullivan, George. *Mikhail Gorbachev.* Messner, 1988. *(I)*

## GOTHIC ART AND ARCHITECTURE

Gallagher, Maureen. *The Cathedral Book.* Paulist Press, 1983. *(P; I)*

## GOYA, FRANCISCO

Janson, H. W., and Janson, Anthony F. *History of Art for Young People.* Abrams, 1997. (rev. ed.) *(I; A)*

Muhlberger, Richard, and Metropolitan Museum of Art. *What Makes a Goya a Goya?* Viking, 1994. *(I)*

Riboldi, Silvia; Schiaffino, Mariarosa; and Trojer, Thomas. *Goya.* NTC, 1999. *(I)*

Waldron, Ann. *Francisco Goya.* Abrams, 1992. *(I)*

## GRAIN AND GRAIN PRODUCTS

Blackwood, Alan. *Grain.* Rourke, 1987. *(P; I)*

Gelman, Rita Golden. *Rice Is Life.* Holt, 2000. *(P)*

Johnson, Sylvia A. *Wheat.* Lerner, 1990. *(P; I)*

Patent, Dorothy Hinshaw. *Wheat: The Golden Harvest.* Putnam, 1987. *(P; I)*

## GRANT, ULYSSES SIMPSON

Archer, Jules. *A House Divided: The Lives of Ulysses S. Grant and Robert E. Lee.* Scholastic, 1996. *(I)*

Falkof, Lucille. *Ulysses S. Grant: 18th President of the United States.* Garrett Educational, 1988. *(A)*

Kent, Zachary. *Ulysses S. Grant.* Children's, 1989. *(P; I)*

O'Brien, Steven. *Ulysses S. Grant.* Chelsea House, 1990. *(I; A)*

## GRAPES AND BERRIES

Burns, Diane L. *Berries, Nuts and Seeds.* Creative, 1997. *(I)*

Hughes, Meredith Sayles. *Yes, We Have Bananas: Fruits from Shrubs and Vines.* Lerner, 1999. *(P; I)*

## GRAPHS

Fry, Edward B. *Graphical Comprehension: How to Read and Make Graphs.* Jamestown, 1981. *(I; A)*

Stwertka, Eve, and Stwertka, Albert. *Make It Graphic!: Drawing Graphs for Science and Social Studies Projects.* Messner, 1985. *(A)*

## GRASSES

Catchpole, Clive. *Grasslands.* Dial, 1984. *(I)*

Horton, Casey. *Grasslands.* Watts, 1985. *(I)*

## GRAVITY AND GRAVITATION

Cobb, Vicki. *Why Doesn't the Earth Fall Up?* Dutton, 1988. *(I)*

Haines, Gail Kay. *Which Way Is Up?* Atheneum, 1987. *(I)*

Smith, Howard E., Jr. *Balance It!* Scholastic, 1982. *(I; A)*

## GREAT LAKES

Henderson, Kathy. *The Great Lakes.* Children's, 1989. *(P)*

## GREECE

Elliott, Drossoula V., and Elliott, Sloane. *We Live in Greece.* Watts, 1984. *(I; A)*

Lye, Keith. *Take a Trip to Greece.* Watts, 1983. *(P)*

Monos, Dimitris. *The Greek Americans.* Chelsea House, 1988. *(I; A)*

Stein, R. Conrad. *Greece.* Children's, 1988. *(P; I)*

## GREEK MYTHOLOGY

Billout, Guy. *Thunderbolt and Rainbow: A Look at Greek Mythology.* Prentice-Hall, 1981. *(P; I)*

Colum, Padraic. *The Children's Homer: Adventures of Odysseus and the Tale of Troy.* Macmillan, 1982. *(I); Golden Fleece and the Heroes Who Lived before Achilles.* Macmillan, 1983. *(I)*

Evslin, Bernard. *Greeks Bearing Gifts.* Four Winds, 1971. *(I)*

Fisher, Leonard Everett. *The Olympians: Great Gods and Goddesses of Ancient Greece.* Holiday, 1984. *(P; I)*

Homer. *The Odyssey.* Random House, 1990. *(I; A); The Voyage of Odysseus.* Troll, 1984. *(P; I)*

Low, Alice. *Greek Gods and Heroes.* Macmillan, 1985. *(P)*

Wise, William. *Monster Myths of Ancient Greece.* Putnam, 1981. *(I; A)*

## GREENAWAY, KATE

Greenaway, Kate. *A— Apple Pie.* Warne, 1987 (rev. ed.); *The Language of Flowers,* 1977; *Mother Goose: Or, the Old Nursery Rhymes,* 1882. *(P; I)*

## GREENLAND

Anderson, Madelyn Klein. *Greenland: Island at the Top of the World.* Dodd, 1983. *(I; A)*

Lepthien, Emilie U. *Greenland.* Children's, 1989. *(I)*

## GREENPEACE

Brown, Paul. *Greenpeace.* Silver Burdett, 1995. *(I; A)*

## GRENADA

Devonshire, Hilary. *Greeting Cards and Gift Wrap.* Watts, 1992. *(I; A)*

Cheng, Pang Guek. *Grenada.* Marshall Cavendish, 2000. *(I)*

## GRIMM, JACOB AND WILHELM

*Grimm's Fairy Tales.* Simon & Schuster, 1989. *(P; I)*

Grimm Brothers. *The Best of Grimms' Fairy Tales.* Larousse, 1980. *(P)*

## GUATEMALA

*Guatemala . . . in Pictures.* Lerner, 1997. *(I)*

Hermes, Jules M. *The Children of Guatemala.* Carolrhoda, 1997. *(P; I)*

Perl, Lila. *Guatemala: Central America's Living Past.* Morrow, 1982. *(I; A)*

## GUINEA

Fichter, George S. *The Bulge of Africa: Senegal, Guinea, Ivory Coast, Togo, Benin, and Equatorial Guinea.* Watts, 1981. *(I; A)*

## GUINEA PIGS, HAMSTERS, AND GERBILS

Barrie, Anmarie. *A Step-by-Step Book about Guinea Pigs; A Step-by-Step Book about Hamsters.* TFH Publications, 1988. *(I; A)*

Burton, Jane. *Dazy the Guinea Pig.* Gareth Stevens, 1989. *(P)*

Hess, Lilo. *Making Friends with Guinea Pigs.* Scribner's, 1983. *(P; I)*

Rubins, Harriett. *Guinea Pigs: An Owner's Guide to Choosing, Raising, Breeding, and Showing.* Lothrop, 1982. *(I; A)*

## GUITAR

Dearling, Robert, ed. *The Illustrated Encyclopedia of Musical Instruments.* Gale Research, 1996. *(I; A)*

Hooper, Nigel, and Hooper, Carolyn. *Learn to Play Electric Guitar.* EDC, 1997. *(I)*

Woods, Samuel G. *Guitars: From Start to Finish.* Blackbirch, 1999. *(P; I)*

## GUNS AND AMMUNITION

Schulson, Rachel Ellenberg. *Guns: What You Should Know.* Albert Whitman, 1997. *(P)*

## GUYANA

*Guyana in Pictures.* Lerner, 1988. *(P; I)*

Jermyn, Leslie. *Guyana.* Marshall Cavendish, 2000. *(I; A)*

## GYMNASTICS

Barrett, Norman. *Gymnastics.* Watts, 1989. *(P)*

Berke, Art. *Gymnastics.* Watts, 1988. *(P; I)*

Bragg, Linda Wallenberg. *Play-by-Play Gymnastics.* Lerner, 2000. *(P; I; A)*

Green, Septima. *Shannon Miller: American Gymnast—From Girlhood Dreams to Olympic Glory.* Avon, 1996. *(P; I)*

Gribble, McPhee. *Body Tricks: To Teach Yourself.* Penguin, 1982. *(I; A)*

Jackman, Joan. *The Young Gymnast.* Dorling Kindersley, 1995. *(P; I); Gymnastics.* DK, 2000. *(P; I)*

Kuklin, Susan. *Going to My Gymnastics Class.* Bradbury, 1991. *(P)*

Miller, Shannon, and Richardson, Nancy Ann. *Winning Every Day: Gold Medal Advice for a Happy, Healthy Life!* Bantam, 1998. *(I; A)*

Murdock, Tony, and Nik, Stuart. *Gymnastics.* Watts, 1985. *(I)*

Readhead, Lloyd. *The Fantastic Book of Gymnastics.* Millbrook Press, 1997. *(P; I)*

Rutledge, Rachel. *The Best of the Best in Gymnastics.* Millbrook Press, 1999. *(I)*

Whitlock, Steve. *Gymnastics for Girls.* Sports Illustrated for Kids, 1991. *(I; A)*

## HAIR AND HAIRSTYLING

Blakely, Pat. *Why Do We Have Hair?* Creative Education, 1982. *(P; I; A)*

Bozic, Patricia, and Lee, Polå. *Cutting Hair at Home.* New American Library, 1986. *(A)*

## HAITI

Cheong-Lum, Roseline Ng. *Haiti.* Marshall Cavendish, 1994. *(I; A)*

Goldish, Meish. *Crisis in Haiti.* Millbrook, 1995. *(I)*

Hanmer, Trudy J. *Haiti.* Watts, 1988. *(I; A)*

## HALE, NATHAN

Poole, Susan. *Nathan Hale.* Dandelion, 1979. *(P)*

## HALLOWEEN

Corwin, Judith Hoffman. *Halloween Fun.* Messner, 1983. *(I)*

Gibbons, Gail. *Halloween.* Holiday, 1984. *(P)*

Herda, D. J. *Halloween.* Watts, 1983. *(P; I)*

## HALS, FRANS

Janson, H. W., and Janson, Anthony F. *History of Art for Young People.* Abrams, 1997. (rev. ed.) *(I; A)*

## HAMILTON, ALEXANDER

Whitelaw, Nancy. *More Perfect Union: The Story of Alexander Hamilton.* Morgan Reynolds, 1997. *(I)*

## HANCOCK, JOHN

Fritz, Jean. *Will You Sign Here, John Hancock?* Putnam, 1997. (rev. ed.) *(I)*

## HANDBALL

Page, Jason. *Ball Games: Soccer, Table Tennis, Handball, Hockey, Badminton, and Lots, Lots More.* Lerner, 2000. *(P; I; A)*

## HANDWRITING

Gourdie, Tom. *Handwriting.* Merry Thoughts, n.d. *(P; I)*

Sassoon, Rosemary. *A Practical Guide to Children's Handwriting.* Thames & Hudson, 1983. *(P; I)*

## HANNIBAL

Green, Robert. *Hannibal.* Watts, 1996. *(I)*

Nardo, Don. *The Battle of Zama; The Punic Wars.* Lucent, 1996. *(I; A)*

## HANUKKAH

Behrens, June. *Hanukkah.* Children's, 1983. *(P; I)*

Drucker, Malka. *Hanukkah: Eight Nights, Eight Lights.* Holiday, 1980. *(I; A)*

Hirsh, Marilyn. *I Love Hanukkah,* Holiday, 1984. *(P)*

Levoy, Myron. *The Hanukkah of Great-Uncle Otto.* Jewish Publication Society, 1984. *(P)*

Singer, Isaac B. *The Power of Light: Eight Stories for Hanukkah.* Farrar, 1980. *(P; I; A)*

## HARDING, WARREN G.

Wade, Linda R. *Warren G. Harding.* Children's, 1989. *(P; I)*

## HARDY, THOMAS

Lefebure, Molly. *Thomas Hardy's World: The Life, Work and Times of the Great Novelist Poet.* Carlton, 1999. *(A)*

## HARMONICA

Dearling, Robert, ed. *The Illustrated Encyclopedia of Musical Instruments.* Gale Research, 1996. *(I; A)*

## HARP

Dearling, Robert, ed. *The Illustrated Encyclopedia of Musical Instruments.* Gale Research, 1996. *(I; A)*

## HARRISON, BENJAMIN

Barber, James G. *Eyewitness: Presidents.* DK, 2000. *(P; I)*

Krull, Kathleen. *Lives of the Presidents: Fame, Shame and What the Neighbors Thought.* Raintree Steck-Vaughn, 1998. *(I)*

Pascoe, Elaine. *First Facts about the Presidents.* Blackbirch, 1996. *(I)*

## HARRISON, WILLIAM HENRY

Fitz-Gerald, Christine Maloney. *William Henry Harrison.* Children's, 1988. *(P; I)*

## HARVEY, WILLIAM

Yount, Lisa. *William Harvey: Discoverer of How Blood Circulates.* Enslow, 1994. *(I)*

## HAWAII

Bauer, Helen. *Hawaii: The Aloha State.* Bess Press, 1982 (new ed.). *(I)*

Dunford, Elizabeth P. *The Hawaiians of Old.* Bess Press, 1980. *(P; I)*

Fradin, Dennis Brindell. *Hawaii.* Children's, 1994. *(P; I)*

Jacobsen, Peter O., and Kristensen, Preben S. *A Family in Hawaii.* Bookwright, 1987. *(P)*

Potter, Norris, and Kasdon, Lawrence. *The Hawaiian Monarchy.* Bess Press, 1982. *(I)*

Rizzuto, Shirley O. *Hawaii's Pathfinders.* Bess Press, 1983. *(I)*

Rublowsky, John. *Born in Fire: A Geological History of Hawaii.* Harper, 1981. *(I)*

Stanley, Fay. *The Last Princess: The Story of Princess Ka'iulani of Hawaii.* Four Winds, 1991. *(P; I)*

## HAWTHORNE, NATHANIEL

Gaeddert, LouAnn. *A New England Love Story: Nathaniel Hawthorne and Sophia Peabody.* Dial, 1980. *(I; A)*

## HAYES, RUTHERFORD B.

Kent, Zachary. *Rutherford B. Hayes.* Children's, 1989. *(P; I)*

## HAZARDOUS WASTES

Gay, Kathlyn. *Global Garbage: Exporting Trash and Toxic Waste.* Watts, 1992 *(I; A)*

Hawkes, Nigel. *Toxic Waste and Recycling.* Gloucester Press, dist. by Watts, 1991. *(P; I)*

Kowalski, Kathiann M. *Hazardous Waste Sites.* Lerner, 1996. *(P; I)*

Stenstrup, Allen. *Hazardous Waste.* Children's, 1991. *(I)*

Zipko, Stephen James. *Toxic Threat: How Hazardous Substances Poison Our Lives.* Silver Burdett Press, 1990. *(I; A)*

## HEALTH

Berger, Melvin. *Ouch! A Book about Cuts, Scratches, and Scrapes.* Lodestar, 1991. *(P)*

Heron, Jackie. *Careers in Health and Fitness.* Rosen, 1988. *(A)*

Lindquist, Marie. *Body Makeovers.* Pinnacle, 1985. *(A)*

Lyttle, Richard B. *The New Physical Fitness: Something for Everyone.* Watts, 1981. *(I; A)*

Schwager, Tina, and Schuerger, Michele. *The Right Moves: A Girl's Guide to Getting Fit and Feeling Good.* Free Spirit, 1998. *(I; A)*

Trier, Carola S. *Exercise: What It Is, What It Does.* Greenwillow, 1982. *(P)*

Ward, Brian. *Health and Hygiene.* Watts, 1988. *(I)*

## HEALTH AND HUMAN SERVICES, UNITED STATES DEPARTMENT OF

Broberg, Merle. *The Department of Health and Human Services.* Chelsea House, 1989. *(P; I)*

## HEALTH FOODS

Krizmanic, Judy. *The Teen's Vegetarian Cookbook.* Penguin, 1999; *A Teen's Guide to Going Vegetarian.* Penguin, 1994. *(I; A)*

## HEART

Ballard, Carol. *The Heart and Circulatory System.* Raintree Steck-Vaughn, 1997. *(I)*

Gaskin, John. *The Heart.* Watts, 1985. *(P; I)*

McGowan, Tom. *The Circulatory System: From Harvey to the Artificial Heart.* Watts, 1988. *(I)*

Silverstein, Alvin, and Silverstein, Virginia B. *Heartbeats: Your Body, Your Heart.* Harper, 1983. *(I); Heart Disease: America's #1 Killer.* Lippincott, 1985. *(A)*

Simon, Seymour. *The Heart: Our Circulatory System.* Morrow, 1996. *(I)*

Ward, Brian. *The Heart and Blood.* Watts, 1982. *(I)*

## HEAT

Ardley, Neil. *Hot and Cold.* Watts, 1983. *(P)*

Challoner, Jack. *Hot and Cold.* Raintree Steck-Vaughn, 1997. *(P)*

Darling, David. *Between Fire and Ice: The Science of Heat.* Dillon, 1992. *(I)*

Friedhoffer, Robert. *Molecules and Heat.* Watts, 1992. *(I)*

Lafferty, Peter. *Heat and Cold.* Marshall Cavendish, 1996. *(P; I)*

Santrey, Laurence. *Heat.* Troll, 1985. *(I)*

Whyman, Kathryn. *Heat and Energy.* Gloucester Press, 1986. *(I)*

## HELICOPTERS

Berliner, Don. *Helicopters.* Lerner, 1983. *(I; A)*

Delear, Frank J. *Airplanes and Helicopters of the U.S. Navy.* Dodd, 1982. *(I; A)*

Petersen, David. *Helicopters.* Children's, 1983. *(P)*

White, David. *Helicopters.* Rourke, 1988. *(P)*

## HELIUM

Heiserman, David L. *Exploring Chemical Elements and Their Compounds.* McGraw-Hill, 1991. *(A)*

Stwertka, Albert. *SuperConductors: The Irresistible Future.* Watts, 1991. *(I; A)*

## HEMINGWAY, ERNEST

Sandison, David. *Ernest Hemingway: An Illustrated Biography.* Chicago Review, 1999. *(A)*

## HENRY, PATRICK

Fritz, Jean. *Where Was Patrick Henry on the 29th of May?* Putnam, 1975. *(P; I)*

Reische, Diana. *Patrick Henry.* Watts, 1987. *(P)*

Sabin, Louis. *Patrick Henry: Voice of the American Revolution.* Troll, 1982. *(P; I)*

## HERALDRY

Fradon, Dana. *Harold the Herald: A Book about Heraldry.* Dutton, 1990. *(P; I)*

## HERBS, SPICES, AND CONDIMENTS

Barker, Albert. *The Spice Adventure.* Messner, 1980. *(P; I)*

## HIBERNATION

Brimner, Larry Dane. *Animals That Hibernate.* Watts, 1991. *(P; I)*

Busch, Phyllis. *The Seven Sleepers: The Story of Hibernation.* Macmillan, 1985. *(I)*

Facklam, Margery. *Do Not Disturb: The Mysteries of Animal Hibernation and Sleep.* Sierra Club Books, 1989. *(P; I)*

## HIKING AND BACKPACKING

Larson, Randy. *Illustrated Backpacking and Hiking Dictionary for Young People.* Prentice-Hall, 1981. *(P; I; A)*

Peterson, P. J. *Nobody Else Can Walk It for You.* Delacorte, 1982. *(I; A)*

Randolph, John. *Backpacking Basics.* Prentice-Hall, 1982. *(P; I)*

Thomas, Art. *Backpacking Is for Me.* Lerner, 1980. *(P; I)*

## HIMALAYAS

Reynolds, Jan. *Himalaya: Vanishing Cultures.* Harcourt, 1991. *(P; I)*

## HINDUISM

Bahree, Patricia. *The Hindu World.* Silver Burdett, 1983. *(I)*

Kanitkar, V. P. (Hemant). *Hinduism.* Bookwright, 1987. *(I; A)*

## HIPPOPOTAMUSES

Arnold, Caroline. *Hippo.* Morrow, 1989. *(P; I)*

## HISPANIC AMERICANS

Catalano, Julie. *The Mexican Americans.* Chelsea House, 1988. *(P; I)*

Gonzales, Doreen. *Cesar Chavez: Leader for Migrant Farm Workers.* Enslow, 1996. *(I; A)*

Goodnough, David. *Jose Marti: Cuban Patriot and Poet.* Enslow, 1996. *(I; A)*

King, Elizabeth. *Quinceañera: Celebrating Fifteen.* Dutton, 1998. *(I)*

Larsen, Ronald J. *The Puerto Ricans in America.* Lerner, 1989. *(I)*

Meltzer, Milton. *The Hispanic Americans.* Harper, 1982. *(I; A)*

Morey, Janet, and Dunn, Wendy. *Famous Mexican Americans.* Cobblehill, 1989. *(I)*

Pinchot, Jane. *The Mexicans in America.* Lerner, 1989. *(I)*

Raintree Hispanic Stories. (Written in both English and Spanish) *Simon Bolivar; Hernando De Soto; David Farragut; Miguel Hildago Y Costilla; Jose Marti; Luis*

*Munoz Marin; Diego Rivera; Junipero Serra; Luis W. Alvarez; Juana Ines De La Cruz; Carlos Finlay; Bernardo De Galvez; Queen Isabella I; Benito Juarez; Vilma Martinez; Pedro Menendez De Aviles.* Raintree, 1989-90. *(P; I)*

## HISTORY

Chisholm. *First Guide to History.* EDC Publishing, 1983. *(I; A)*

## HITLER, ADOLF

Gray, Ronald. *Hitler and the Germans.* Lerner, 1983. *(I; A)*

Stalcup, Brenda, ed. *Adolf Hitler.* Greenhaven, 2000. *(I; A)*

## HOBBIES

The Muppet Workshop, and St. Pierre, Stephanie. *The Muppets Big Book of Crafts: 100 Great Projects to Snip, Sculpt, Stitch, and Stuff.* Workman, 2000. *(P; I)*

Bottomly, Jim. *Paper Projects for Creative Kids of All Ages.* Little, 1983. *(P; I; A)*

Churchill, E. Richard. *Building with Paper.* Sterling, 1990. *(I)*

Greene, Peggy R. *Things to Make.* Random House, 1981. *(P)*

Jackson, Paul. *Festive Folding: Decorative Origami for Parties and Celebrations.* North Light Books, 1991. *(P; I)*

Lewis, Shari. *The Do-It-Better Book; Things Kids Collect.* Holt, 1981. *(P; I)*

Lohf, Sabine. *Nature Crafts.* Children's, 1990. *(P; I)*

McGill, Ormond. *Paper Magic: Creating Fantasies and Performing Tricks with Paper.* Millbrook, 1992. *(P; I)*

Supraner, Robyn. *Fun-to-Make Nature Crafts.* Troll, 1981. *(P; I)*

Volpe, Nancee. *Good Apple and Seasonal Arts and Crafts.* Good Apple, 1982. *(P; I)*

## HOISTING AND LOADING MACHINERY

Lampton, Christopher. *Sailboats, Flag Poles, Cranes: Using Pulleys as Simple Machines.* Millbrook Press, 1991. *(P)*

## HOLBEIN, HANS, THE YOUNGER

Janson, H. W., and Janson, Anthony F. *History of Art for Young People.* Abrams, 1997. (rev. ed.) *(I; A)*

## HOLIDAYS

Behrens, June. *Gung Hay Fat Choy: Happy New Year.* Children's, 1982. *(P)*

Berger, Gilda. *Easter and Other Spring Holidays.* Watts, 1983. *(I)*

Chocolate, Deborah M. Newton. *Kwanzaa.* Children's, 1990. *(P; I)*

Cone, Molly. *The Story of Shabbat.* HarperCollins, 2000. *(P; I)*

Grigoli, Valorie. *Patriotic Holidays and Celebrations.* Watts, 1985. *(P; I)*

Hautzig, Esther. *Make It Special: Cards, Decorations, and Party Favors for Holidays and Other Celebrations.* Macmillan, 1986. *(P)*

Livingston, Myra Cohn. *Celebrations.* Holiday, 1985. *(I; A)*

Perl, Lila, and Ada, Alma F. *Pinatas and Paper Flowers (Pinatas y Flores de Papel): Holidays of the Americas in English and Spanish.* Houghton, 1983. *(P; I)*

Pienkowski, Jan. *Christmas.* Knopf, 1991. *(P; I)*

Pinkney, Andrea Davis. *Seven Candles for Kwanzaa.* Dial, 1993. *(P)*

Rosen, Mike. *Autumn Festivals; Winter Festivals.* Bookwright, 1990. *(I)*

Scott, Geoffrey. *Memorial Day.* Carolrhoda, 1983. *(P)*

Van Straalen, Alice. *The Book of Holidays around the World.* Dutton, 1987. *(A)*

Viesti, Joe, and Hall, Diane. *Celebrate! In Central America.* Lothrop, 1997. *(P; I); Celebrate! In South Asia; Celebrate! In Southeast Asia.* Lothrop, 1996. *(P;I)*

## HOLOCAUST

Abells, Chana Byers. *The Childen We Remember.* Greenwillow, 1986. *(I)*

Altman, Linda Jacobs. *The Holocaust, Hitler, and Nazi Germany.* Enslow, 1999; *The Holocaust Ghettos.* Enslow, 1998. *(I; A)*

Ayer, Eleanor H. *The Survivors.* Lucent, 1997. *(I; A)*

Bernbaum, Israel. *My Brother's Keeper.* Putnam, 1985. *(I; A)*

Byers, Ann. *The Holocaust Camps.* Enslow, 1998. *(I; A)*

Chaikin, Miriam. *A Nightmare in History: The Holocaust.* Clarion, 1987. *(P; I)*

Finkelstein, Norman H. *Remember Not to Forget: A Memory of the Holocaust.* Watts, 1985. *(P)*

Frank, Anne. *Anne Frank: Diary of a Young Girl.* Doubleday, 1967. *(I; A)*

Friedman, Ina R. *The Other Victims: First Person Stories of Non-Jews Persecuted by the Nazis.* Houghton, 1990. *(I)*

Games, Sonia. *Escape into Darkness.* Shapolsky, 1991. *(A)*

Gold, Alison Leslie. *A Special Fate: Chiune Sugihara: Hero of the Holocaust.* Scholastic, 2000. *(I; A)*

Greenfield, Howard. *The Hidden Children.* Ticknor & Fields, 1993. *(I)*

Handler, Andrew, and Meschel, Susan V., comp. and ed. *Young People Speak: Surviving the Holocaust in Hungary.* Watts, 1993. *(A)*

Mandell, Sherri Lederman. *Writers of the Holocaust.* Facts on File, 1999. *(A)*

Nieuwsma, Milton J., ed. *Kinderlager: An Oral History of Young Holocaust Survivors.* Holiday, 1998. *(I; A)*

Oertelt, Henry A., and Samuels, Stephanie Oertelt. *An Unbroken Chain: My Journey through the Nazi Holocaust.* Lerner, 2000. *(A)*

Opdyke, Irene Gut, and Armstrong, Jennifer. *In My Hands:*

*Memories of a Holocaust Rescuer.* Knopf/Borzoi, 1999. *(I; A)*

Orlev, Uri. *The Island on Bird Street,* tr. by Hillel Halkin. Houghton, 1984. *(I)*

Patterson, Charles. *Anti-Semitism: The Road to the Holocaust and Beyond.* Walker, 1982. *(I; A)*

Rogasky, Barbara. *Smoke and Ashes: The Story of the Holocaust.* Holiday, 1988. *(A)*

Rossel, Seymour. *The Holocaust: The Fire That Raged.* Watts, 1989. *(I; A)*

Sherrow, Victoria. *The Righteous Gentiles.* Lucent, 1997. *(I; A)*

Spielberg, Steven, and Survivors of the Shoah Visual History Foundation. *The Last Days.* St. Martin's, 1999. *(A)*

Toll, Nelly S. *Behind the Secret Window: A Memoir of a Hidden Childhood During World War Two.* Dial, 1993. *(I; A)*

## HOMER, WINSLOW

Goldstein, Ernest. *Winslow Homer: The Gulf Stream.* New American Library, 1983. *(I; A)*

## HOMES AND HOUSING

Carter, Katherine. *Houses.* Children's, 1982. *(P)*

Gibbons, Gail. *How a House Is Built.* Holiday, 1990. *(P)*

Morris, Ann. *Houses and Homes.* Lothrop, 1992. *(P)*

## HOMING AND MIGRATION

Arnold, Caroline. *Hawk Highway in the Sky: Watching Raptor Migration.* Harcourt, 1997. *(I)*

Lasky, Kathryn. *Monarchs.* Harcourt, 1993. *(I)*

Simon, Seymour. *They Walk the Earth: The Extraordinary Travels of Animals on Land.* Harcourt, 2000; *They Swim the Seas: The Mystery of Animal Migration.* Harcourt, 1998; *Ride the Wind: Airborne Journeys of Animals and Plants.* Harcourt, 1997. *(P; I)*

## HONDURAS

McGaffey, Leta. *Honduras.* Marshall Cavendish, 1999. *(I; A)*

## HONEY

Chinery, Michael. *How Bees Make Honey.* Marshall Cavendish, 1996. *(P; I)*

Johnson, Sylvia A. *A Beekeeper's Year.* Little, Brown & Co., 1994. *(P; I)*

Micucci, Charles. *The Life and Times of the Honey Bee.* Houghton Mifflin, 1995. *(P)*

## HONG KONG

Fairclough, Chris. *We Live in Hong Kong.* Bookwright, 1986. *(P; I)*

Kaqda, Falaq. *Hong Kong.* Marshall Cavendish, 1998. *(I)*

Lye, Keith. *Take a Trip to Hong Kong.* Watts, 1984. *(P; I)*

McKenna, Nancy Durrell. *A Family in Hong Kong.* Lerner, 1987. *(P)*

## HOOFED MAMMALS

Bailey, Jill. *Mission Rhino: Earth's Endangered Creatures.* Raintree Steck-Vaughn, 1992. *(P; I)*

Clutton-Brock, Juliet. *Eyewitness: Horse.* DK, 2000. *(P; I)*

Patent, Dorothy Hinshaw. *Horses.* Lerner, 1996; *Deer and Elk.* Houghton Mifflin, 1994. *(P; I)*

Miller, Sara Swan. *Horses and Rhinos: What They Have in Common.* Watts, 2000. *(P; I)*

Swan, Erin Pembrey. *Camels and Pigs: What They Have in Common.* Watts, 2000. *(P; I)*

Walker, Sally M. *Hippos.* Lerner, 1997. *(P; I)*

## HOOVER, HERBERT CLARK

Clinton, Susan. *Herbert Hoover: Thirty-First President of the United States.* Children's, 1988. *(P; I)*

Holford, David M. *Herbert Hoover.* Enslow, 1999. *(I)*

## HORSEBACK RIDING

Binder, Sibylle Luise, and Wolf, Gefion. *Riding for Beginners.* Sterling, 1999. *(I; A)*

Cole, Joanna. *Riding Silver Star.* Morrow, 1996. *(P; I)*

Dumas, Philippe. *The Lippizaners: And the Spanish Riding School.* Prentice-Hall, 1981. *(P; I)*

Haney, Lynn. *Show Rider.* Putnam, 1982. *(I; A)*

Henderson, Carolyn. *Improve Your Riding Skills.* DK, 1999. *(P; I)*

Pritchard, Louise. *My Pony Book.* Dorling Kindersley, 1998. *(P; I)*

Rodenas, Paula. *The Random House Book of Horses and Horsemanship.* Random House, 1991. *(I; A)*

Van Steenwyck, Elizabeth. *Illustrated Riding Dictionary for Young People.* Harvey, 1981. *(I; A)*

Wheatley, George. *The Young Rider's Companion.* Lerner, 1981. *(P; I)*

## HORSE RACING

Gutman, Bill. *Overcoming the Odds: Julie Krone.* Raintree Steck-Vaughn, 1996. *(P; I)*

## HORSES AND THEIR RELATIVES

Budiansky, Stephen. *The World according to Horses: How They Run, See, and Think.* Holt, 2000. *(P; I)*

Clutton-Brock, Juliet. *Horse.* Knopf, 1992. *(I; A)*

Cole, Joanna. *A Horse's Body.* Morrow, 1981. *(P)*

Lauber, Patricia. *The True-or-False Book of Horses.* HarperCollins, 2000. *(P)*

Lavine, Sigmund A., and Casey, Brigid. *Wonders of Draft Horses.* Dodd, 1983. *(P; I)*

Patent, Dorothy. *Arabian Horses.* Holiday, 1982; *Horses and Their Wild Relatives,* 1981; *Horses of America,* 1981; *Picture Book of Ponies,* 1983. *(P; I); Thoroughbred Horses,* 1985. *(A)*

Philp, Candace T. *Rodeo Horses.* Crestwood, 1983. *(P; I)*

Popescu, Charlotte. *Horses at Work.* David & Charles, 1983. *(P)*

## HORSESHOE CRAB

Day, Nancy. *The Horseshoe Crab*. Silver Burdett Press, 1992. *(P)*

## HOSPITALS

Dooley, Virginia. *Tubes in My Ears: My Trip to the Hospital*. Mondo, 1996. *(P)*

Elliott, Ingrid G. *Hospital Roadmap: A Book to Help Explain the Hospital Experience to Young Children*. Resources for Children in Hospitals, 1982. *(P)*

Holmes, Burnham. *Early Morning Rounds: A Portrait of a Hospital*. Scholastic, 1981. *(I; A)*

Howe, James. *The Hospital Book*. Crown, 1995 (rev. ed.). *(P)*

Rockwell, Anne F. *Emergency Room*. Macmillan, 1985. *(P)*

Rogers, Fred. *Going to the Hospital*. Putnam, 1988. *(P)*

Wolfe, Bob, and Wolfe, Diane. *Emergency Room*. Carolrhoda, 1983. *(I)*

## HOTELS AND MOTELS

Dineen, Jacqueline. *Hotel*. Silver Burdett Press, 1988. *(P; I)*

## HOUSING AND URBAN DEVELOPMENT, UNITED STATES DEPARTMENT OF

Bernotas, Bob. *The Department of Housing and Urban Development*. Chelsea House, 1990. *(P; I)*

## HOUSTON

McComb, David G. *Texas: An Illustrated History*. Oxford, 1995. *(I; A)*

## HOUSTON, SAMUEL

Collier, Christopher, and Collier, James L. *Hispanic America, Texas, and the Mexican War 1835-1850*. Benchmark, 1998. *(I)*

Fritz, Jean, and Primavera, Elise. *Make Way for Sam Houston*. Putnam, 1998. *(I)*

McComb, David G. *Texas: An Illustrated History*. Oxford, 1995. *(I; A)*

Sorrels, Roy. *The Alamo in American History*. Enslow, 1996. *(I)*

## HUDSON, HENRY

Goodman, Joan Elizabeth, and Duke, Bette. *Beyond the Sea of Ice: The Voyages of Henry Hudson*. Firefly, 1999. *(P; I)*

## HUGHES, LANGSTON

Hughes, Langston. *Don't You Turn Back: Poems Selected by Lee Bennett Hopkins*. Knopf, 1969. *(P; I); Selected Poems of Langston Hughes*. Knopf, 1926, 1943. *(I; A)*

Larson, Norita D. *Langston Hughes, Poet of Harlem*. Creative Education, 1981. *(I; A)*

Meltzer, Milton. *Langston Hughes: An Illustrated Edition*. Millbrook Press, 1997. *(I; A)*

Walker, Alice. *Langston Hughes, American Poet*. Harper, 1974. *(P; I)*

## HUMAN RIGHTS

Gold, Susan Dudley. *Human Rights*. 21st Century, 1997. *(I;A)*

Lucas, Eileen. *Contemporary Human Rights Activists*. Facts on File, 1997. *(I;A)*

## HUMMINGBIRDS

Rauzon, Mark J. *Hummingbirds*. Watts, 1997. *(P; I)*

Tyrrell, Esther Quesada, and Tyrrell, Robert A. *Hummingbirds: Jewels in the Sky*. Random House, 1992. *(P; I)*

## HUMOR

Fleischman, Albert Sidney. *McBroom's Almanac*. Little, 1984. *(P; I)*

Lear, Edward. *Complete Nonsense Book*. Dodd, n. d. *(P; I)*

Prelutsky, Jack, sel. *For Laughing Out Loud: Poems to Tickle Your Funnybone*. Knopf, 1991. *(P; I)*

Schwartz, Alvin. *Flapdoodle: Pure Nonsense from American Folklore*. Harper, 1980. *(I; A)*

Truesdale, Susan G. *Unriddling: All Sorts of Riddles to Puzzle Your Guessery*. Lippincott— Raven, 1983. *(P; I)*

Walton, Rick, and Walton, Ann. *Fossil Follies! Jokes about Dinosaurs*. Lerner, 1989. *(P)*

## HUNDRED YEARS' WAR

Lace, William W. *Hundred Years' War*. Lucent, 1994. *(I; A)*

## HUNGARY

Esbenshade, Richard S. *Hungary*. Marshall Cavendish, 1994. *(I; A)*

Hintz, Martin. *Hungary*. Children's, 1988. *(I)*

Siegal, Aranka. *Upon the Head of a Goat: A Childhood in Hungary*. Farrar, 1981. *(I; A)*

Steins, Richard. *Hungary: Crossroads of Europe*. Benchmark, 1997. *(P; I)*

St. John, Jetty. *A Family in Hungary*. Lerner, 1988. *(P)*

Truesdale, Susan G. *Unriddling: All Sorts of Riddles to Puzzle Your Guessery*. Lippincott-Raven, 1983. *(P; I)*

## HUNTING

Newton, David E. *Hunting*. Watts, 1992. *(I; A)*

## HURRICANES

Alth, Max, and Alth, Charlotte. *Disastrous Hurricanes and Tornadoes*. Watts, 1981. *(P; I)*

Fradin, Dennis Brindel. *Disaster! Hurricanes*. Children's, 1982. *(I)*

Larson, Erik. *Isaac's Storm: A Man, a Time, and the Deadliest Hurricane in History*. Crown, 2000. *(A)*

Lauber, Patricia. *Hurricanes: Earth's Mightiest Storms.* Scholastic, 1996. *(I; A)*

McNulty, Faith. *Hurricane.* Harper, 1983. *(P; I)*

Meister, Cari. *Hurricanes.* ABDO, 1999. *(P; I)*

Sherrow, Victoria. *Hurricane Andrew: Nature's Rage.* Enslow, 1998. *(P; I)*

Simon, Seymour. *Storms.* Morrow, 1989. *(P)*

## HUSSEIN, SADDAM

Mausky, Gregory, and Hayes, John Philip. *Hussein.* Chelsea House, 1987. *(I; A)*

Stefoff, Rebecca. *Saddam Hussein: Absolute Ruler of Iraq.* Millbrook Press, 1995. *(I; A)*

## HYDROGEN

Farndon, John. *Hydrogen.* Marshall Cavendish/Benchmark, 1999. *(I)*

Heiserman, David L. *Exploring Chemical Elements and Their Compounds.* McGraw-Hill, 1991. *(A)*

## HYENAS AND THE AARDWOLF

Moser, Barry, illus., and Moser, Madeline, comp. *Ever Heard of an Aardwolf?: A Miscellany of Uncommon Animals.* Harcourt, 1996. *(P; I)*

## HYMNS

Bryan, Ashley. *I'm Going to Sing: Black American Spiritu- als, Vol II.* Atheneum, 1982; *Walk Together, Children,* 1974. *(P; I)*

Konkel, Wilbur. *Living Hymn Stories.* Bethany, 1982. *(P; I)*

Krull, Kathleen, collector and arranger. *Songs of Praise.* Harcourt, 1988. *(P)*

## HYPNOTISM

Kirby, Vivian. *Hypnotism: Hocus Pocus or Science?* Mess- ner, 1985. *(I; A)*

## IBSEN, HENRIK

Bloom, Harold, ed. *Henrik Ibsen.* Chelsea House, 1998. *(A)*

## ICE AGES

Cole, Joanna. *Saber-Toothed Tiger and Other Ice-Age Mammals.* Enslow, 1981. *(P; I)*

Fodor, R. V. *Frozen Earth: Explaining the Ice Ages.* Enslow, 1981. *(I; A)*

## ICEBERGS

Greenberg, Jan. *The Iceberg and Its Shadow.* Dell, 1982. *(I; A)*

Robin, Gordon De Q. *Glaciers and Ice Sheets.* Watts, 1984. *(I)*

Simon, Seymour. *Icebergs and Glaciers.* Morrow, 1999. (rev. ed.) *(P; I)*

## ICE CREAM

Jaspersohn, William. *Ice Cream.* Macmillan, 1988. *(P)*

## ICE HOCKEY

Aaseng, Nathan. *Hockey's Fearless Goalies; Hockey's Super Scores.* Lerner, 1983. *(P; I)*

Leonetti, Mike. *Hockey Now!* Firefly, 1999. *(I; A)*

MacLean, Norman. *Hockey Basics.* Prentice-Hall, 1983. *(P; I)*

Olney, Ross R. *Winners! Super-Champions of Ice Hockey.* Houghton, 1982. *(I; A)*

Sullivan, George. *All about Hockey.* Putnam, 1998. *(P; I)*

## ICELAND

Lepthien, Emilie U. *Iceland.* Children's, 1987. *(P; I)*

Wilcox, Jonathan. *Iceland.* Marshall Cavendish, 1996. *(I; A)*

## ICE-SKATING

Fox, Mary V. *The Skating Heidens.* Enslow, 1981. *(I; A)*

Haney, Lynn. *Skaters: Profile of a Pair.* Putnam, 1983. *(I; A)*

Kalb, Jonah, and Kalb, Laura. *The Easy Ice Skating Book.* Houghton, 1981. *(P; I)*

MacLean, Norman. *Ice Skating Basics.* Prentice-Hall, 1984. *(P; I)*

Morrissey, Peter. *Ice Skating.* DK, 2000. *(P; I)*

Ryan, Margaret. *Figure Skating.* Watts, 1987. *(P)*

U.S. Figure Skating Association. *The Official Book of Fig- ure Skating.* Simon & Schuster, 1998. *(A)*

Wood, Tim. *Ice Skating.* Watts, 1990. *(P; I)*

## IDAHO

Fradin, Dennis. *Idaho: In Words and Pictures.* Children's, 1980. *(P; I)*

Kent, Zachary. *Idaho.* Children's, 1990. *(I; A)*

## ILIAD

Homer. *The Iliad.* Raintree Steck-Vaughn, 1983. *(P; I)*

Picard, Barbara L., ed. *The Iliad of Homer.* Oxford Univer- sity Press, 1980. *(I)*

## ILLINOIS

Brill, Marlene Targ. *Illinois.* Benchmark, 1996. *(I)*

Carter, Alden R. *Illinois.* Watts, 1987. *(P; I)*

Pfeiffer, Christine. *Chicago.* Dillon, 1989. *(P; I)*

Sandburg, Carl. "Chicago" from *Chicago Poems.* Bucca- neer, 1986. *(I; A)*

Santella, Andrew. *Illinois.* Children's Press, 1998. *(I)*

## ILLUMINATED MANUSCRIPTS

Wilson, Elizabeth B. *Bibles and Bestiaries: A Guide to Illuminated Manuscripts.* Farrar, 1994. *(I; A)*

## ILLUSTRATION AND ILLUSTRATORS

Marcus, Leonard S. *A Caldecott Celebration: Six Artists and Their Paths to the Caldecott Medal.* Walker, 1998. *(P; I)*

## IMAGING, DIAGNOSTIC

Winkler, Kathy. *Radiology.* Benchmark, 1996. *(I; A)*

## IMMIGRATION

Ashabranner, Brent. *Our Beckoning Borders: Illegal Immigration to America.* Cobblehill, 1996. *(I; A); Still a Nation of Immigrants.* Cobblehill: Dutton, 1993. *(I; A); To Seek a Better World: The Haitian Minority in America.* Cobblehill, 1997. *(I)*

Berg, Lois Anne. *An Eritrean Family.* Lerner, 1996. *(I)*

Blumenthal, Shirley. *Coming to America: Immigrants from Eastern Europe.* Delacorte, 1981. *(I; A)*

Bode, Janet. *The Colors of Freedom: Immigrant Stories.* Watts, 1999. *(I)*

Bohner, Charles. *Bold Journey.* Houghton, 1985. *(I)*

Bouvier, Leon F. *Immigration: Diversity in the U.S.* Walker, 1988. *(A)*

Caroli, Betty Boyd. *Immigrants Who Returned Home.* Chelsea House, 1990. *(A)*

Collier, Christopher, and Collier, James Lincoln. *A Century of Immigration: 1820-1924.* Marshall Cavendish/Benchmark, 1999. *(I)*

Dixon, Edward H., and Galan, Mark A. *The Immigration and Naturalization Service.* Chelsea House, 1990. *(I; A)*

Dudley, William, ed. *Immigration.* Greenhaven, 1990. *(I; A)*

Fisher, Leonard. *Ellis Island: Gateway to the New World.* Holiday, 1986. *(I)*

Garver, Susan, and McGuire, Paula. *Coming to North America: From Mexico, Cuba, and Puerto Rico.* Delacorte, 1981. *(I; A)*

Hoobler, Dorothy, and Hoobler, Thomas. *The Chinese American Family Album.* Oxford University Press, 1994. *(I; A)*

Kurelek, William. *They Sought a New World: The Story of European Immigration to North America.* Tundra Books, 1985. *(I; A)*

Meltzer, Milton. *The Chinese Americans.* Crowell, 1980. *(I; A)*

Perrin, Linda. *Coming to America: Immigrants from the Far East.* Delacorte, 1980. *(A)*

Reimers, David M., and Stotsky, Sandra. *A Land of Immigrants.* Chelsea House, 1995. *(I; A)*

Rips, Gladys N. *Coming to America: Immigrants from Southern Europe.* Dell, 1981. *(A)*

Robbins, Albert. *Coming to America: Immigrants from Northern Europe.* Dell, 1982. *(A)*

## IMMUNE SYSTEM

Aaseng, Nathan. *Autoimmune Diseases.* Watts, 1995. *(I; A)*

## INCAS

Hinds, Kathryn. *The Incas.* Marshall Cavendish, 1998. *(I)*

Wood, Tim. *The Incas.* Viking, 1996. *(I; A)*

Worth, Richard. *Pizarro and the Conquest of the Incan Empire in World History.* Enslow, 2000. *(I; A)*

## INDEPENDENCE HALL

Steen, Sandra, and Steen, Susan. *Independence Hall.* Silver Burdett Press, 1994. *(P; I)*

## INDIA

*India . . . in Pictures.* Lerner, 1989. *(I)*

Hermes, Jules M. *The Children of India.* Carolrhoda, 1993. *(P; I)*

Jacobsen, Peter O., and Kristensen, Preben S. *A Family in India.* Watts, 1984. *(P; I)*

Karan, P. P., ed. *India.* Gateway Press, 1988. *(I; A)*

Lye, Keith. *Take a Trip to India.* Watts, 1982. *(P)*

Mamdani, Shelby. *Traditions from India.* Raintree/Steck-Vaughn, 1999. *(P; I)*

McNair, Sylvia. *India.* Children's, 1990. *(I)*

Ogle, Carol, and Ogle, John. *Through the Year in India.* David & Charles, 1983. *(I; A)*

Sandal, Veenu. *We Live in India.* Watts, 1984. *(I)*

Sarin, Amitra Vohra. *India: An Ancient Land, a New Nation.* Dillon, 1984. *(I)*

Tames, Richard. *India and Pakistan in the Twentieth Century.* David & Charles, 1981. *(I; A)*

Tigwell, Tony. *A Family in India.* Lerner, 1985. *(P)*

Traub, James. *India: The Challenge of Change.* Messner, 1985 (rev. ed.). *(I; A)*

## INDIAN OCEAN

Taylor, Leighton R. *The Indian Ocean.* Blackbirch Press, 1998. *(P; I)*

## INDIANA

Brill, Marlene Targ. *Indiana.* Benchmark, 1997. *(P;I)*

Fradin, Dennis. *Indiana: In Words and Pictures.* Children's, 1980. *(P; I)*

## INDIANS, AMERICAN

*The Indians of California.* Time-Life, 1994. *(A)*

Ancona, George. *Powwow.* Harcourt, 1993. *(P; I)*

Ashabranner, Brent. *A Strange and Distant Shore: Indians of the Great Plains in Exile.* Cobblehill, 1996. *(I; A); To Live in Two Worlds: American Indian Youth Today.* Dodd, 1984. *(I; A)*

Avery, Susan, and Skinner, Linda. *Extraordinary American Indians.* Children's, 1992. *(I; A)*

Ayer, Eleanor H. *The Anasazi.* Walker, 1993. *(I)*

Beck, Barbara L. *The Ancient Mayas; The Incas,* both books rev. by Lorna Greenberg. Watts, 1983. *(I; A); The Aztecs,* rev. by Lorna Greenberg. Watts, 1983. *(I)*

Bial, Raymond. *The Comanche; The Ojibwe; The Pueblo; The Seminole.* Marshall Cavendish/Benchmark, 1999. *(I)*

Bierhorst, John, ed. *The Mythology of Mexico and Central America.* Morrow, 1990. *(A)*

Blood, Charles. *American Indian Games and Crafts.* Watts, 1981. *(P)*

Brown, Tricia. *Children of the Midnight Sun: Young Native Voices of Alaska.* Alaska Northwest Books, 1998. *(I)*

Connolly, James. *Why the Possum's Tail is Bare and Other North American Indian Native Tales.* Stemmer House, 1985. *(P)*

Cwiklik, Robert. *Sequoyah and the Cherokee Alphabet.* Silver Burdett, 1989. *(I)*

DeArmond, Dale. *Berry Woman's Children.* Greenwillow, 1985. *(P)*

De Paola, Tomie. *The Legend of the Bluebonnet: An Old Tale of Texas.* Putnam, 1983. *(P); The Legend of the Indian Paintbrush.* Putnam, 1988. *(P)*

Fixico, Donald L. *Urban Indians.* Chelsea House, 1991. *(I; A)*

Flanagan, Alice K. *The Pueblos.* Children's, 1998. *(P); The Shawnee.* Children's, 1998. *(P); The Zunis.* Children's, 1998. *(P)*

Freedman, Russell. *An Indian Winter.* Holiday, 1992. *(A); Indian Chiefs.* Holiday, 1987. *(I; A)*

Garbarino, Merwyn S. *The Seminole.* Chelsea House, 1988. *(A)*

Glassman, Bruce. *Wilma Mankiller: Chief of the Cherokee Nation.* Blackbirch Press: Rosen, 1992. *(I)*

Goble, Paul. *Beyond the Ridge.* Bradbury, 1990. *(I; A); Buffalo Woman.* Bradbury, 1984. *(P); Her Seven Brothers.* Bradbury, 1988. *(P; I); Iktomi and the Boulder: A Plains Indian Story.* Orchard Press, 1988. *(P)*

Graymont, Barbara. *The Iroquois.* Chelsea House, 1988. *(A)*

Green, Rayna. *Women in American Indian Society.* Chelsea House, 1992. *(I; A)*

Griffin, Lana T. *The Navajo.* Raintree/Steck-Vaughn, 1999. *(P; I)*

Harvey, Karen, ed. *American Indian Voices.* Millbrook, 1995. *(I)*

Highwater, Jamake. *Eyes of Darkness.* Lothrop, 1985. *(I; A)*

Hirschfelder, Arlene. *Happily May I Walk: American Indians and Alaska Natives Today.* Scribner's, 1986. *(I; A)*

Hirschfelder, Arlene B., and Singer, Beverly R., eds. *Rising Voices: Writings of Young Native Americans.* Scribner's, 1992. *(I; A)*

Hoyt-Goldsmith, Diane. *Buffalo Days.* Holiday, 1997. *(P; I); Totem Pole.* Holiday, 1990. *(P)*

Jones, Jayne Clark. *The American Indians in America.* Lerner, 1991. *(I; A)*

Kallen, Stuart A. *Native Americans of the Northeast.* Lucent, 2000. *(A); Native American Chiefs and Warriors; Native Americans of the Great Lakes.* Lucent, 1999. *(I; A)*

Kavasch, E. Barrie. *The Seminoles.* Raintree/Steck-Vaughn, 1999. *(P; I)*

Keegan, Marcia. *Pueblo Boy: Growing Up in Two Worlds.* Cobblehill, 1991. *(P; I)*

Kelly, Lawrence C. *Federal Indian Policy.* Chelsea House, 1989. *(I; A)*

Koslow, Philip. *The Seminole Indians.* Chelsea, 1994. *(I)*

Marrin, Albert. *Sitting Bull and His World.* Dutton, 2000. *(A)*

McClard, Megan, and Ypsilantis, George. *Hiawatha and the Iroquois League.* Silver Burdett, 1989. *(I)*

Monroe, Jean Guard, and Williamson, Ray A. *First Houses: Native American Homes and Sacred Structures.* Houghton, 1993. *(I; A)*

Osinski, Alice. *The Sioux.* Children's, 1984. *(P)*

Pasqua, Sandra M. *The Navajo Nation.* Bridgestone, 2000. *(P)*

Paterson, E. Palmer. *Indian Peoples of Canada.* Watts, 1982. *(I; A)*

Press, Petra. *Indians of the Northwest: Traditions, History, Legends, and Life.* Gareth Stevens, 2000. *(P; I)*

Remington, Gwen. *The Sioux.* Lucent, 1999. *(I)*

Rodanas, Kristina, adapt. *Dance of the Sacred Circle: A Native American Tail.* Little, 1994. *(P)*

Sayer, Chloe. *The Incas.* Raintree/Steck-Vaughn, 1998. *(I; A)*

Sewall, Marcia. *People of the Breaking Day.* Atheneum, 1990. *(P)*

Seymour, Tryntje Van Ness. *The Gift of Changing Woman.* Holt, 1993. *(I; A)*

Sherrow, Victoria. *Political Leaders and Peacemakers.* Facts on File, 1994. *(I; A)*

Shorto, Russell. *Tecumseh and the Dream of an American Indian Nation.* Silver Burdett, 1989. *(I)*

Sita, Lisa. *Indians of the Great Plains: Traditions, History, Legends, and Life; Indians of the Southwest: Traditions, History, Legends, and Life.* Gareth Stevens, 2000. *(P; I)*

Sneve, Virginia Driving Hawk. *Dancing Teepees: Poems of American Indian Youth.* Holiday, 1989. *(P; I; A)*

Taylor, C. J. *Bones in the Basket: Native Stories of the Origin of People.* Tundra Books, 1994. *(P; I)*

Terry, Michael Bad Hand. *Daily Life in a Plains Indian Village: 1868.* Clarion, 1999. *(P; I)*

Trottier, Maxine. *Native Crafts: Inspired by North America's First Peoples.* Kids Can, 2000. *(P; I)*

Weinstein-Farson, Laurie. *The Wampanoag.* Chelsea House, 1988. *(A)*

Wilson, Terry P. *The Osage.* Chelsea House, 1988. *(A)*

Wood, Ted, and Wanbli Numpa Afraid of Hawk. *A Boy Becomes a Man at Wounded Knee.* Walker, 1992. *(P; I)*

Yue, Charlotte, and Yue, David. *The Wigwam and the Longhouse.* Houghton Mifflin, 2000. *(I)*

## INDIAN WARS OF NORTH AMERICA

Bachrach, Deborah. *Custer's Last Stand.* Greenhaven, 1990. *(I; A)*

Halliburton, Warren J. *The Tragedy of Little Bighorn.* Watts, 1989. *(P; I)*

Marrin, Albert. *War Clouds in the West: Indians & Cavalrymen 1860– 1890.* Atheneum, 1984. *(A)*

McGaw, Jessie B. *Chief Red Horse Tells about Custer.* Lodestar, 1981. *(P; I)*

Mitchell, Barbara. *Tomahawks and Trombones.* Carolrhoda, 1982. *(P)*

Morris, Richard B. *The Indian Wars.* Lerner, 1986 (rev. ed.). *(I; A)*

Nardo, Don, ed. *North American Indian Wars.* Greenhaven, 1999. *(A)*

Wills, Charles. *The Battle of the Little Bighorn.* Silver Burdett, 1990. *(I)*

## INDONESIA

Fairclough, Chris. *We Live in Indonesia.* Bookwright, 1986. *(P; I)*

Knowlton, MaryLee, and Sachner, Mark J. *Burma; Indonesia; Malaysia.* Gareth Stevens, 1987. *(P)*

Lye, Keith. *Indonesia.* Watts, 1985. *(P)*

Smith, Datus C., Jr. *The Land and People of Indonesia.* Harper, 1983 (rev. ed.). *(I)*

## INDUSTRIAL DESIGN

Rubin, Susan Goldman. *Toilets, Toasters and Telephones: The how and why of Everyday Objects.* Harcourt, 1998. *(I)*

## INDUSTRIAL REVOLUTION

Bland, Ceclia. *The Mechanical Age: The Industrial Revolution in England.* Facts on File, 1995. *(I; A)*

Collier, Christopher, and Collier, James Lincoln. *The Rise of Industry: 1860-1900.* Marshall Cavendish/Benchmark, 1999. *(I)*

Stanley, Jerry. *Big Annie of Calumet: A True Story of the Industrial Revolution.* Crown, 1996. *(I)*

## INDUSTRY

Allan, Mabel. *The Mills Down Below.* Dodd, 1981. *(I)*

Burne, Gordon. *Tools and Manufacturing.* Watts, 1984. *(I)*

Claypool, Jane. *Manufacturing.* Watts, 1984. *(I; A)*

Grant, Neil. *The Industrial Revolution.* Watts, 1983. *(I)*

Grigoli, Valorie. *Service Industries.* Watts, 1984. *(I)*

Macaulay, David. *Mill.* Houghton, 1983. *(I)*

Sherwood, Martin. *Industry.* Watts, 1984. *(I)*

Vialls, Christine. *The Industrial Revolution Begins.* Lerner, 1982. *(I; A)*

## INSECTS

*The World in Your Backyard: And Other Stories of Insects and Spiders.* Zaner-Bloser, 1989. *(P; I)*

Berger, Melvin, and Berger, Gilda. *How Do Flies Walk Upside Down?: Questions and Answers about Insects.* Scholastic, 1999. *(P)*

Brinckloe, Julie. *Fireflies!* Macmillan, 1985. *(P)*

Cole, Joanna. *An Insect's Body.* Morrow, 1984. *(P)*

dos Santos, Joyce A. *Giants of Smaller Worlds Drawn in Their Natural Sizes.* Dodd, 1983. *(P)*

Facklam, Howard, and Facklam, Margery. *Insects.* Twenty-First Century, 1995. *(I)*

Goor, Ron, and Goor, Nancy. *Insect Metamorphosis: From Egg to Adult.* Atheneum, 1990. *(P)*

Johnson, Sylvia. *Water Insects.* Lerner, 1989. *(P; I)*

Lavies, Bianca. *Backyard Hunter: The Praying Mantis.* Dutton, 1990. *(I)*

Parker, Janice. *The Science of Insects.* Gareth Stevens, 1999. *(P; I)*

Selsam, Millicent E. *Where Do They Go? Insects in Winter.* Scholastic, 1982. *(P)*

Selsam, Millicent E., and Goor, Ronald. *Backyard Insects.* Scholastic, 1983. *(P)*

Shepherd, Elizabeth. *No Bones: A Key to Bugs & Slugs, Worms & Ticks, Spiders & Centipedes, & Other Creepy Crawlies.* Collier, 1988. *(P; I)*

## INTERIOR DESIGN

Greer, Michael. *Your Future in Interior Design.* Rosen, 1980. *(I; A)*

James, Elizabeth, and Barkin, Carol. *A Place of Your Own.* Dutton, 1981. *(A)*

## INTERIOR, UNITED STATES DEPARTMENT OF THE

Clement, Fred. *The Department of the Interior.* Chelsea House, 1989. *(P; I)*

## INTERNATIONAL RELATIONS

Goode, Stephen. *The Foreign Policy Debate: Human Rights in American Foreign Policy.* Watts, 1984. *(I; A)*

Hart, William B. *The United States and World Trade.* Watts, 1985. *(A)*

Woody, D. W. *The Kids of Mischief Island.* Carlton, 1981. (Fiction) *(I; A)*

## INUIT

Alexander, Bryan, and Alexander, Cherry. *An Eskimo Family.* Lerner, 1985. *(P)*

Ekoomiak, Normee. *Arctic Memories.* Holt, 1988. *(P; I)*

Foa, Maryclare. *Songs Are Thought: Poems of the Inuit.* Orchard, 1995. *(I)*

Hughes, Jill. *Eskimos.* Watts, 1984 (rev. ed.). *(P; I)*

Kendall, Russ. *Eskimo Boy: Life in an Inupiaq Eskimo Village.* Scholastic, 1992. *(I; A)*

Lassieur, Allison. *The Inuit.* Bridgestone, 2000. *(P)*

Patterson, E. Palmer. *Inuit Peoples of Canada.* Watts, 1982. *(I; A)*

Reynolds, Jan. *Frozen Land: Vanishing Cultures* Harcourt, 1993. *(P; I)*

Stewart, Gail B. *Life in an Eskimo Village.* Lucent, 1995. *(I; A)*

## INVENTIONS

Aaseng, Nathan. *Better Mousetraps.* Lerner, 1990. *(I); The Unsung Heroes: Unheralded People Who Invented Famous Products.* Lerner, 1989. *(I)*

Baker, Christopher W. *Scientific Visualization: The New Eyes of Science.* Millbrook, 2000. *(I)*

Bender, Lionel. *Invention.* Knopf, 1991. *(I)*

Caney, Steven. *Steven Caney's Invention Book.* Workman, 1985. *(P; I)*

Dash, Joan. *The Longitude Prize.* Farrar, Straus & Giroux, 2000. *(I; A)*

Gates, Phil. *Nature Got There First: Inventions Inspired by Nature.* Kingfisher, 1995. *(I; A)*

Haskins, Jim. *Outward Dreams: Black Inventors and Their Inventions.* Walker, 1991. *(I; A)*

Jackson, Garnet. *Elijah McCoy: Inventor.* Modern Curriculum, 1993. *(P; I)*

Jones, Charlotte Foltz. *Accidents May Happen: Fifty Inventions Discovered by Mistake.* Delacorte, 1996. *(P; I)*

Karenes, Frances A., and Bean, Suzanne M. *Girls and Young Women Inventing.* Free Spirit, 1995. *(I)*

Klein, Aaron E., and Klein, Cynthia L. *The Better Mousetrap: A Miscellany of Gadgets, Labor-Saving Devices, and Inventions That Intrigue.* Beaufort Books NY, 1983. *(I; A)*

Provensen, Alice. *The Glorious Flight across the Channel with Louis Bleriot.* Viking, 1983. *(P; I)*

Richards, Norman. *Dreamers and Doers: Inventors Who Changed the World.* Atheneum, 1984. *(I; A)*

Tucker, Tom. *Brainstorm! The Stories of Twenty American Kid Inventors.* Farrar, 1995. *(I)*

Vare, Ethlie Ann, and Ptacek, Greg. *Mothers of Invention: From the Bra to the Bomb, Forgotten Women and Their Unforgettable Ideas.* Morrow, 1988. *(I; A)*

## IODINE

Heiserman, David L. *Exploring Chemical Elements and Their Compounds.* McGraw-Hill, 1991. *(A)*

## IONS AND IONIZATION

Shepherd, Donna Walsh. *Auroras.* Watts, 1995. *(I)*

## IOWA

Fradin, Dennis. *Iowa: In Words and Pictures.* Children's, 1980. *(P; I)*

## IRAN

*Iran . . . in Pictures.* Lerner, 1989. *(I; A)*

Mannetti, Lisa. *Iran and Iraq: Nations at War.* Watts, 1986. *(I; A)*

Sanders, Renfield. *Iran.* Chelsea House, 1990. *(I; A)*

Spencer, William. *The United States and Iran.* Twenty-First Century, 2000. *(I; A)*

## IRAN-CONTRA AFFAIR

Lawson, Don, and Feinberg, Barbara Silberdick. *America Held Hostage: The Iran Hostage Crisis and the Iran-Contra Affair.* Watts, 1991. *(I)*

## IRAQ

Docherty, J. P. *Iraq.* Chelsea House, 1988. *(P)*

Mannetti, Lisa. *Iran and Iraq: Nations at War.* Watts, 1986. *(I; A)*

Pimlott, John. *Middle East: A Background to the Conflicts.* Watts, 1991. *(I)*

## IRELAND

James, Ian. *Take a Trip to Ireland.* Watts, 1984. *(P)*

Meyer, Kathleen A. *Ireland: Land of Mist and Magic.* Dillon, 1983. *(I; A)*

Ryan, Joan, and Snell, Gordon, eds. *Land of Tales: Stories of Ireland for Children.* Dufour, 1983. *(P; I)*

## IRON AND STEEL

Cherry, Mike. *Steel Beams and Iron Men.* Scholastic, 1980. *(I; A)*

Fodor, R. V. *Gold, Copper, Iron: How Metals Are Formed, Found, and Used.* Enslow, 1989. *(A)*

Harter, Walter. *Steel: The Metal with Muscle.* Messner, 1981. *(P; I)*

Heiserman, David L. *Exploring Chemical Elements and Their Compounds.* McGraw-Hill, 1991. *(A)*

Lambert, Mark. *Spotlight on Iron and Steel.* Rourke, 1988. *(P; I)*

Sparrow, Giles. *Iron.* Marshall Cavendish, 1999. *(P; I)*

## IRVING, WASHINGTON

Collins, David R. *Washington Irving: Storyteller for a New Nation.* Morgan Reynolds, 2000. *(I)*

Irving, Washington. *The Complete Tales of Washington Irving.* Doubleday, 1975. (Fiction) *(I; A); Knickerbocker's History of New York.* Sleepy Hollow, 1981. *(I; A); Rip Van Winkle, the Legend of Sleepy Hollow, and Other Tales.* Putnam, n.d. (Fiction) *(I; A)*

## ISLAM

Moktefi, Mokhtar. *The Rise of Islam.* Silver Burdett, 1987. *(P; I)*

Tames, Richard. *Islam.* David & Charles, 1985. *(A)*

## ISLAMIC ART AND ARCHITECTURE

Wilson, Elizabeth B. *Bibles and Bestiaries: A Guide to Illuminated Manuscripts.* Farrar, Straus & Giroux, 1994. *(I; A)*

## ISLANDS

Rydell, Wendy. *All about Islands.* Troll, 1984. *(P; I)*

Steele, Philip. *Geography Detective: Islands.* Carolrhoda, 1996. *(I)*

## ISRAEL

Ashabranner, Brent. *Gavriel and Jemal: Two Boys of Jerusalem.* Dodd, 1984. *(I)*

Burstein, Chaya M. *A Kid's Catalog of Israel.* Jewish Publication Society, 1988. *(I; A)*

Feinstein, Steve. *Israel . . . in Pictures.* Lerner, 1988. *(P; I)*

Haskins, Jim. *Count Your Way through Israel.* Carolrhoda, 1990. *(P)*

Jones, Helen Hinckley. *Israel.* Children's, 1986. *(P)*

Lawton, Clive A. *Israel*. Watts, 1988. *(P; I)*
Levine, Gemma. *We Live in Israel*. Watts, 1984. *(I; A)*
Schroeter, Daniel J. *Israel: An Illustrated History*. Oxford, 1998. *(A)*
Taitz, Emily, and Henry, Sondra. *Israel: A Sacred Land*. Dillon, 1987. *(P; I)*
Taylor, Allegra. *A Kibbutz in Israel*. Lerner, 1987. *(P)*
Worth, Richard. *Israel and the Arab States*. Watts, 1983. *(I; A)*

## ITALY

de Zulueta, Tana. *We Live in Italy*. Watts, 1984. *(I; A)*
DiFranco, Anthony. *Italy: Balanced on the Edge of Time*. Dillon, 1983. *(I; A)*
Foster, Leila Merrell. *Italy*. Lucent, 1998. *(I)*
James, Ian. *Inside Italy*. Watts, 1988. *(P; I)*
Mariella, Cinzia. *Passport to Italy*. Watts, 1986. *(P)*
Powell. *Renaissance Italy*. Watts, 1980. *(I; A)*
Stein, R. Conrad. *Italy*. Children's, 1984. *(I; A)*

## ITALY, LANGUAGE AND LITERATURE OF

Wright, Nicola. *Getting to Know: Italy and Italian*. Barron's, 1993. *(P; I)*

## ITALY, MUSIC OF

Geras, Adele, and Beck, Ian. *The Random House Book of Opera Stories*. Random House, 1998. *(P; I)*

## IVES, CHARLES

Sive, Helen R. *Music's Connecticut Yankee: An Introduction to the Life and Music of Charles Ives*. Atheneum, 1977. *(I; A)*

## IVORY

Havill, Juanita. *Sato and the Elephants*. Lothrop, 1993. *(P; I; A)*

## IVORY COAST (CÔTE D'IVOIRE)

*Côte d'Ivoire . . . in Pictures*. Lerner, 1988. *(I; A)*
Fichter, George S. *The Bulge of Africa: Senegal, Guinea, Ivory Coast, Togo, Benin, and Equatorial Guinea*. Watts, 1981. *(I; A)*
Sheehan, Patricia. *Ivory Coast*. Marshall Cavendish, 2000. *(P; I)*

## JACKSON, ANDREW

Osinski, Alice. *Andrew Jackson: Seventh President of the United States*. Children's, 1987. *(I)*
Stefoff, Rebecca. *Andrew Jackson, 7th President of the United States*. Garrett Educational, 1988. *(A)*

## JACKSON, JESSE

Haskins, James. *I Am Somebody!: A Biography of Jesse Jackson*. Enslow, 1992. *(A)*
Otfinoski, Steven. *Jesse Jackson: A Voice for Change*. Fawcett, 1990. *(I)*
Wilkinson, Brenda. *Jesse Jackson: Still Fighting for the Dream*. Silver Burdett, 1990. *(I; A)*

## JACKSON, THOMAS JONATHAN ("STONEWALL")

Fritz, Jean. *Stonewall*. Putnam, 1997. *(P)*
Harrison, and others. *Stonewall Jackson*. Dormac, 1981. *(P; I; A)*

## JAMAICA

Gunning, Monica. *Under the Breadfruit Tree: Island Poems*. Boyds Mills Press, 1998. *(P; I)*
Sheehan, Sean. *Jamaica*. Benchmark, 1996. *(I)*

## JAMES, JESSE

Bruns, Roger A. *Jesse James: Legendary Outlaw*. Enslow, 1998. *(P; I)*
Wukovits, John F. *Jesse James*. Chelsea House, 1996. *(I)*

## JAMESTOWN

Collier, Christopher, and Collier, James L. *The Paradox of Jamestown, 1585-1700*. Marshall Cavendish, 1997. *(I; A)*

## JANUARY

Updike, John. *A Child's Calendar*. Holiday House, 1999. *(P; I)*
Warner, Penny. *Kids' Holiday Fun: Great Family Activities Every Month of the Year*. Meadowbrook Press, 1997. *(P)*

## JAPAN

*Japan . . . in Pictures*. Lerner, 1989. *(I)*
Blumberg, Rhoda. *Commodore Perry in the Land of the Shogun*. Lothrop, 1985. *(I)*
Cobb, Vicki. *This Place is Crowded: Japan*. Walker, 1992. *(P)*
Davidson, Judith. *Japan: Where East Meets West*. Dillon, 1983. *(I)*
Dolan, Edward F., Jr., and Finney, Shan. *The New Japan*. Harper, 1983. *(A)*
Greene, Carol. *Japan*. Children's, 1983. *(I)*
Harvey, Miles. *Look What Comes from Japan*. Watts, 1999. *(P; I)*
Hersey, John. *Hiroshima*. Bantam, 1986. *(I; A)*
Kawamata, Kazuhide. *We Live in Japan*. Watts, 1984. *(I; A)*
Meyer, Carolyn. *A Voice from Japan: An Outsider Looks In*. Gulliver Books, 1988. *(I; A)*
Pitts, Forrest R. *Japan*. Gateway Press, 1988. *(I; A)*
Roberson, John R. *Japan Meets the World: The Birth of a Super Power*. Millbrook, 1998. *(I; A)*
Spry-Leverton, Peter, and Kornicki, Peter. *Japan*. Facts on File, 1987. *(A)*
Stefoff, Rebecca. *Japan*. Chelsea House, 1988. *(P; I)*
Tames, Richard. *Passport to Japan*. Watts, 1988. *(I)*

## JAZZ

Gourse, Leslie. *Fancy Fretwork: The Great Jazz Guitarists; Timekeepers: The Great Jazz Drummers.* Watts, 1999. *(I; A)*

Griffin, Clive D. *Jazz.* Batsford, dist. by David & Charles, 1989. *(I; A)*

Hughes, Langston. *The First Book of Jazz.* Watts, 1982 (rev. ed.). *(I)*

Jones, Max. *Talking Jazz.* Norton, 1988. *(A)*

Kliment, Bud. *Ella Fitzgerald.* Chelsea House, 1988. *(A)*

Lee, Jeanne. *Jam! The Story of Jazz Music.* Rosen, 1999. *(P; I)*

Mour, Stanley L. *American Jazz Musicians.* Enslow, 1998. *(I; A)*

Tanenhaus, Sam. *Louis Armstrong.* Chelsea House, 1989. *(P; I)*

Weatherford, Carole Boston. *The Sound that Jazz Makes.* Walker, 2000. *(P)*

## JEFFERSON, THOMAS

Adler, David A. *A Picture Book of Thomas Jefferson.* Holiday, 1990. *(P)*; *Thomas Jefferson: Father of Our Democracy.* Holiday House, 1987. *(P)*

Bober, Natalie S. *Thomas Jefferson: Man on a Mountain.* Atheneum, 1988. *(A)*

Ferris, Jeri Chase. *Thomas Jefferson: Father of Liberty.* Carolrhoda, 1998. *(I)*

Fisher, Leonard Everett. *Monticello.* Holiday, 1988. *(I)*

Hargrove, Jim. *Thomas Jefferson: Third President of the United States.* Children's, 1986. *(P; I)*

Milton, Joyce. *The Story of Thomas Jefferson: Prophet of Liberty.* Dell, 1990. *(I; A)*

Sabin, Francene. *Young Thomas Jefferson.* Troll, 1986. *(P; I)*

## JELLYFISH AND OTHER COELENTERATES

Gowell, Elizabeth Tayntor. *Sea Jellies: Rainbows in the Sea.* Watts, 1993. *(I)*

MacQuitty, Miranda. *Discovering Jellyfish.* Bookwright, 1989. *(P)*

## JERUSALEM

Kuskin, Karla. *Jerusalem, Shining Still.* Harper, 1987. *(P)*

Pirotta, Saviour. *Jerusalem.* Silver Burdett Press, 1993. *(I)*

Waldman, Neil. *The Golden City: Jerusalem's 3,000 Years.* Boyds Mills Press, 2000. *(P)*

## JESUS CHRIST

Bierhorst, John. *Spirit Child: A Story of the Nativity.* Morrow, 1984. *(P)*

Collins, David R. *The Wonderful Story of Jesus.* Concordia Publishing, 1980. *(P; I)*

Mayer, Marianna. *Young Jesus of Nazareth.* Morrow, 1999. *(P; I)*

Nystrom, Carolyn. *Jesus Is No Secret.* Moody, 1983. *(P; I)*; *Who Is Jesus?* 1980. *(P)*

Sherlock, Connie. *Life of Jesus.* Standard, 1983. *(P; I)*

Storr, Catherine, and Lindvall, Ella K. *The Birth of Jesus.* Moody Press, 1983 (rev. ed.); *Jesus Begins His Work.* Raintree, 1983 (rev. ed.). *(P; I)*

## JET PROPULSION

Moxon, Julian. *How Jet Engines Are Made.* Facts on File, 1985. *(P; I)*

## JEWS

Brownstone, David M. *The Jewish-American Heritage.* Facts on File, 1988. *(I; A)*

Costabel, Eva D. *The Jews of New Amsterdam.* Atheneum, 1988. *(P; I)*

Mann, Kenny. *The Ancient Hebrews* Marshall Cavendish, 1998. *(I; A)*

Muggamin, Howard. *The Jewish Americans.* Chelsea House, 1988. *(I; A)*

## JOAN OF ARC, SAINT

Boutet de Monvel, Maurice. *Joan of Arc.* Viking, 1980. *(I)*

Brooks, Polly Schoyer. *Beyond the Myth: The Story of Joan of Arc.* Lippincott, 1990. *(A)*

## JOGGING AND RUNNING

Parker, Steve. *Running a Race: How You Walk, Run and Jump.* Watts, 1991. *(P)*

Savage, Jeff. *Running.* Silver Burdett Press, 1995. *(P; I)*

## JOHN PAUL II, POPE

Pope John Paul II. *For the Children: Words of Love and Inspiration from His Holiness Pope John Paul II.* Scholastic, 2000. *(P; I)*

Sullivan, George E. *Pope John Paul II: The People's Pope.* Walker, 1984. *(I)*

Wilson, Jay. *Pope John Paul II: Religious Leader.* Chelsea House, 1992. *(P; I)*

## JOHNSON, ANDREW

Kent, Zachary. *Andrew Johnson.* Children's, 1989. *(P; I)*

Stevens, Rita. *Andrew Johnson: 17th President of the United States.* Garrett Educational, 1989. *(I)*

## JOHNSON, JAMES WELDON

Johnson, James Weldon. *Lift Every Voice and Sing: The Negro National Anthem.* Hyperion, 2001. *(P; I)*

## JOHNSON, LYNDON BAINES

Devaney, John. *Lyndon Baines Johnson, President.* Walker, 1986. *(I; A)*

Falkof, Lucille. *Lyndon B. Johnson: 36th President of the United States.* Garrett Educational, 1989. *(I)*

Hargrove, Jim. *Lyndon B. Johnson.* Children's, 1988. *(P; I)*

Kaye, Tony. *Lyndon B. Johnson.* Chelsea House, 1988. *(I; A)*

Schuman, Michael A. *Lyndon B. Johnson.* Enslow, 1998. *(I; A)*

## JOKES AND RIDDLES

Corbett, Scott. *Jokes to Tell Your Worst Enemy.* Dutton, 1984. *(P; I)*

Jansen, John. *Playing Possum: Riddles about Kangaroos, Koalas, and Other Marsupials.* Lerner, 1995. *(P; I)*

Maestro, Giulio. *A Raft of Riddles.* Dutton, 1982. *(P; I); Riddle Romp.* Houghton, 1983. *(P)*

## JOLLIET, LOUIS AND MARQUETTE, JACQUES

Stein, R. Conrad. *The Story of Marquette and Jolliet.* Children's, 1981. *(P; I)*

## JONES, JOHN PAUL

Lutz, Norma Jean. *John Paul Jones: Father of the U. S. Navy.* Chelsea House, 2000. *(P; I)*

## JORDAN

*Jordan . . . in Pictures.* Lerner, 1988. *(I)*

Whitehead, Susan. *Jordan.* Chelsea House, 1988. *(P)*

## JOURNALISM

Cohen, Daniel. *Yellow Journalism: Scandal, Sensationalism, and Gossip in the Media.* Twenty-First Century, 2000. *(I; A)*

Jaspersohn, William. *A Day in the Life of a Television News Reporter.* Little, 1981. *(I; A)*

Seidman, David. *Exploring Careers in Journalism.* Rosen, 2000. *(I; A)*

## JUDAISM

Chaikin, Miriam. *Menorahs, Mezuzas, and Other Jewish Symbols.* Clarion, 1990. *(I); Sound the Shofar: The Story and Meaning of Rosh Hashanah and Yom Kippur.* Clarion, 1986. *(I; A)*

Domnitz, Myer. *Judaism.* Bookwright, 1987. *(I; A)*

Finkelstein, Norman A. *The Other 1492: Jewish Settlement in the New World.* Scribner's, 1989. *(I; A)*

Freeman, Joan G., and Freeman, Grace R. *Inside the Synagogue.* UAHC, 1984. *(P)*

Greenberg, Judith E., and Carey, Helen H. *Jewish Holidays.* Watts, 1985. *(P; I)*

Kimmel, Eric. *Bar Mitzvah: A Jewish Boy's Coming of Age.* Viking, 1995. *(I; A)*

Kolatch, Alfred J. *Let's Celebrate Our Jewish Holidays.* Jonathan David, 1997. *(P)*

Metter, Bert. *Bar Mitzvah, Bat Mitzvah: How Jewish Boys and Girls Come of Age.* Houghton, 1984. *(I)*

Shamir, Ilana, and Shavit, Shlomo. *The Young Reader's Encyclopedia of Jewish History.* Viking, 1987. *(P; I)*

Strom, Yale. *A Tree Still Stands: Jewish Youth in Eastern Europe Today.* Philomel, 1990. *(I; A)*

Swartz, Sarah Silberstein. *Bar Mitzvah.* Doubleday, 1985. *(I; A)*

Turner, Reuben. *Jewish Festivals.* Rourke, 1987. *(P; I)*

Weitzman, Elizabeth. *I Am Jewish American.* Rosen/Power Kids Press, 1998. *(P)* .

## JUDO

Parulski, George R., Jr. *Karate Power!: Learning the Art of the Empty Hand.* Contemporary Bks., 1985. *(P)*

Queen, J. Allen. *Karate to Win.* Sterling, 1988. *(I; A)*

Wood, Tim. *Judo.* Watts, 1990. *(P; I)*

## JUGGLING

Besmehn, Bobby. *Juggling Step-by-Step.* Sterling, 1995. *(I; A)*

## JULY

Updike, John. *A Child's Calendar.* Holiday House, 1999. *(P; I)*

Warner, Penny. *Kids' Holiday Fun: Great Family Activities Every Month of the Year.* Meadowbrook Press, 1997. *(P)*

## JUNGLES

Forsyth, Andrian. *Journey through a Tropical Jungle.* Simon & Schuster, 1989. *(P; I)*

Gibbons, Gail. *Nature's Green Umbrella: Tropical Rain Forests.* Morrow, 1994. *(P)*

Kipling, Rudyard. *The Jungle Book.* Viking, 1987. *(Fiction) (I; A)*

Mutel, Cornelia F., and Rodgers, Mary M. *Tropical Rain Forests.* Lerner, 1991. *(I)*

Rowland-Entwistle, Theodore. *Jungles and Rain Forests.* Silver Burdett, 1987. *(P)*

## JUPITER

Dunbar, Robert E. *Into Jupiter's World.* Watts, 1981. *(I; A)*

Petersen, Carolyn Collins. *Jupiter.* Facts on File, 1990. *(P; I)*

Simon, Seymour. *Jupiter.* Morrow, 1985. *(I; A)*

## JURY

Ehrenfreund, Norbert. *You're the Jury: Solve Twelve Real-Life Court Cases Along with the Juries Who Decided Them.* Holt, 1992. *(A)*

## JUSTICE, UNITED STATES DEPARTMENT OF

Dunn, Lynne. *The Department of Justice.* Chelsea House, 1989. *(I)*

## JUVENILE CRIME

Atkin, S. Beth. *Voices from the Streets: Young Former Gang Members Tell Their Stories.* Little, 1996. *(I;A)*

Bosch, Carl. *Schools under Siege: Guns, Gangs, and Hidden Dangers.* Enslow, 1997. *(I;A)*

Dolan, Edward F., Jr., and Finney, Shan. *Youth Gangs.* Messner, 1984. *(I; A)*

Hyde, Margaret O. *Juvenile Justice and Injustice.* Watts, 1983 (rev. ed.). *(I; A)*

LeVert, Marianne. *Crime in America.* Facts on File, 1991. *(I; A)*

Margolis, Jeffrey A. *Teen Crime Wave: A Growing Problem.* Enslow, 1997. *(I; A)*

Riekes, Linda, and Ackerly, Sally M. *Juvenile Problems and Law.* West Publishing, 1980 (2nd ed.). *(P; I)*

Sadler, Amy E., and Barbour, Scott, eds. *Juvenile Crime: Opposing Viewpoints.* Greenhaven, 1997. *(I; A)*

Shanks, Ann Z. *Busted Lives: Dialogues with Kids in Jail.* Delacorte, 1982. *(I; A)*

## KALEIDOSCOPE

Newlin, Gary. *Simple Kaleidoscopes: 24 Spectacular Scopes to Make.* Sterling, 1996. *(I; A)*

## KANGAROOS

Arnold, Caroline. *Kangaroo.* Morrow, 1987. *(P)*

Eugene, Toni. *Koalas and Kangaroos: Strange Animals of Australia.* National Geographic, 1981. *(P)*

Jansen, John. *Playing Possum: Riddles about Kangaroos, Koalas, and Other Marsupials.* Lerner, 1995. *(P; I)*

Markle, Sandra. *Outside and Inside Kangaroos.* Simon & Schuster/Atheneum, 1999. *(P; I)*

## KANSAS

Fradin, Dennis. *Kansas: In Words and Pictures.* Children's, 1980. *(P; I)*

## KARATE

Brimner, Larry Dane. *Karate.* Watts, 1988. *(P; I)*

## KARTING

Fichter, George S. *Karts and Karting.* Watts, 1982. *(P; I; A)*

Leonard, Jerry. *Kart Racing.* Messner, 1980. *(I; A)*

Radlauer, Ed. *Karting Winners.* Children's, 1982. *(P; I)*

## KELLER, HELEN

Adler, David A. *A Picture Book of Helen Keller.* Holiday, 1990. *(P)*

Keller, Helen. *The Story of My Life.* Scholastic, 1973. *(I; A)*

Sabin, Francene. *The Courage of Helen Keller.* Troll, 1982. *(P; I)*

Wepman, Dennis. *Helen Keller.* Chelsea House, 1987. *(I; A)*

Wilkie, Katherine E. *Helen Keller: From Tragedy to Triumph.* Bobbs, 1983. *(P; I)*

## KENNEDY, JOHN FITZGERALD

Adler, David A. *A Picture Book of John F. Kennedy.* Holiday, 1991. *(P)*

Anderson, Catherine Corley. *John F. Kennedy: Young People's President.* Lerner, 1991. *(I; A)*

Denenberg, Barry. *John Fitzgerald Kennedy: America's 35th President.* Scholastic, 1988. *(I)*

Donnelly, Judy. *Who Shot the President? The Death of John F. Kennedy.* Random House, 1988. *(P)*

Falkof, Lucille. *John F. Kennedy: 35th President of the United States.* Garrett Educational, 1988. *(A)*

Kent, Zachary. *John F. Kennedy: Thirty-Fifth President of the United States.* Children's, 1987. *(P; I)*

Mills, Judie. *John F. Kennedy.* Watts, 1988. *(A)*

Swisher, Clarice, ed. *John F. Kennedy.* Greenhaven, 1999. *(A)*

Waggoner, Jeffrey. *The Assassination of President Kennedy.* Greenhaven, 1990. *(I; A)*

## KENNEDY, ROBERT F. AND EDWARD M.

Mills, Judie. *Robert Kennedy.* Millbrook, 1998. *(A)*

## KENTUCKY

Fradin, Dennis. *Kentucky: In Words and Pictures.* Children's, 1981. *(P; I)*

McNair, Sylvia. *Kentucky.* Children's, 1988. *(P; I)*

Stuart, Jesse. *The Thread That Runs So True.* Scribner's, 1958. *(I; A)*

## KEYBOARD INSTRUMENTS

Dearling, Robert, ed. *The Illustrated Encyclopedia of Musical Instruments.* Gale Research, 1996. *(I; A)*

## KINGDOMS OF LIVING THINGS

Wu, Norbert. *Beneath the Waves: Exploring the Hidden World of the Kelp Forest.* Chronicle, 1997. *(P; I)*

## KING, MARTIN LUTHER, JR.

Adler, David A. *Martin Luther King, Jr.: Free at Last.* Holiday, 1987. *(P; I)*

Darby, Jean. *Martin Luther King, Jr.* Lerner, 1990. *(I; A)*

Faber, Doris, and Faber, Harold. *Martin Luther King, Jr.* Messner, 1986. *(P; I)*

Hakim, Rita. *Martin Luther King, Jr. and the March Toward Freedom.* Millbrook, 1991. *(P; I)*

Harris, Jacqueline. *Martin Luther King, Jr.* Watts, 1983. *(I; A)*

King, Martin Luther, Jr. *Why We Can't Wait.* Harper, 1964. *(A)*

Marzollo, Jean. *Happy Birthday, Martin Luther King.* Scholastic, 1993. *(P)*

McKissack, Patricia. *Martin Luther King, Jr.: A Man to Remember.* Children's, 1984. *(I)*

Patterson, Lillie. *Martin Luther King, Jr. and the Freedom Movement.* Facts on File, 1989. *(I; A)*

Quayle, Louise. *Martin Luther King, Jr.: Dreams for a Nation.* Fawcett, 1990. *(I)*

Richardson, Nigel. *Martin Luther King, Jr.* David & Charles, 1983. *(P; I)*

Rowland, Della. *Martin Luther King, Jr.* Silver Burdett, 1989. *(I)*

Schloredt, Valerie. *Martin Luther King, Jr.: America's Great Nonviolent Leader in the Struggle for Human Rights.* Gareth Stevens, 1988. *(I)*

Siebold, Thomas, ed. *Martin Luther King, Jr.* Greenhaven, 2000. *(I; A)*

Thompson, Marguerite. *Martin Luther King, Jr.: A Story for Children.* Theo Gaus, 1983. *(P; I)*

## KIPLING, RUDYARD

Kamen, Gloria. *Kipling: Storyteller of East and West.* Atheneum, 1985. *(P; I)*

Kipling, Rudyard. *The Jungle Book.* Doubleday, 1981. *(I); Just So Stories.* Rand, 1982. *(P; I)*

## KISSINGER, HENRY

Israel, Fred L. *Henry Kissinger.* Chelsea House, 1986. *(I; A)*

## KITES

Kingfisher Books, and Grisewood, Sara. *Step-by-Step Crafts for Children.* Larousse Kingfisher Chambers, 2000. *(P; I)*

Marks, Burton, and Marks, Rita. *Kites for Kids.* Lothrop, 1980. *(P; I)*

Moran, Tom. *Kite Flying Is for Me.* Lerner, 1983. *(P; I)*

Newnham, Jack. *Kites to Make and Fly.* Penguin, 1982. *(P; I)*

Nicklaus, Carol. *Flying, Gliding, and Whirling: Making Things That Fly.* Watts, 1981. *(P)*

## KLEE, PAUL

Janson, H. W., and Janson, Anthony F. *History of Art for Young People.* Abrams, 1997. (rev. ed.) *(I; A)*

## KNIGHTS, KNIGHTHOOD, AND CHIVALRY

Barber, Richard. *The Reign of Chivalry.* St. Martin's, 1980. *(I)*

Gibson, Michael, and Pike, Tricia. *All about Knights.* EMC Publishing, 1982. *(P; I; A)*

Gravett, Christopher. *The World of the Medieval Knight.* Peter Bedrick, 1996. *(I)*

Lasker, Joe. *A Tournament of Knights.* Crowell, 1986. *(I)*

## KNITTING

Cone, Ferne G. *Classy Knitting: A Guide to Creative Sweatering for Beginners.* Atheneum, 1984; *Crazy Crocheting.* Atheneum, 1981. *(I; A)*

O'Reilly, Susan. *Knitting and Crocheting.* Raintree Steck-Vaughn, 1994. *(P; I)*

## KNIVES, FORKS, AND SPOONS

Giblin, James Cross. *From Hand to Mouth: Or, How We Invented Knives, Forks, Spoons, and Chopsticks and the Table Manners To Go With Them.* HarperCollins, 1987. *(P; I)*

## KNOTS

Adkins, Jan. *String: Tying It Up, Tying It Down.* Simon & Schuster, 1992. *(I; A)*

## KOALAS

Burt, Denise. *Koalas.* Carolrhoda, 1999. *(P; I)*

Jansen, John. *Playing Possum: Riddles about Kangaroos, Koalas, and Other Marsupials.* Lerner, 1995. *(P; I)*

## KOREA

Ashby, Gwynneth. *A Family in South Korea.* Lerner, 1987. *(P)*

Farley, Carol. *Korea: A Land Divided.* Dillon, 1983. *(I; A)*

Shepheard, Patricia. *South Korea.* Chelsea House, 1988. *(P)*

Solberg, S. E. *The Land and People of Korea.* Harper, 1991. *(I)*

So-un, Kim. *The Story Bag: A Collection of Korean Folk Tales.* Tuttle, 1955. *(I)*

## KOREAN WAR

Fincher, E. B. *The War in Korea.* Watts, 1981. *(I; A)*

Smith, Carter. *The Korean War.* Silver Burdett, 1990. *(I)*

Sorensen, Virginia. *Miracles on Maple Hill.* Harcourt, 1988. *(P; I)*

## KURDS

King, John. *Kurds.* Thomson Learning, 1994. *(I; A)*

## KUWAIT

*Kuwait . . . in Pictures.* Lerner, 1989. *(I)*

Mulloy, Martin. *Kuwait.* Chelsea House, 1989. *(P; I); O'Shea, Maria. *Kuwait.* Marshall Cavendish, 1999. *(I)*

Pimlott, John. *Middle East: A Background to the Conflicts.* Watts, 1991. *(I)*

## LABOR, UNITED STATES DEPARTMENT OF

Cutrona, Cheryl. *The Department of Labor.* Chelsea House, 1988. *(P; I)*

## LABOR-MANAGEMENT RELATIONS

Claypool, Jane. *The Worker in America.* Watts, 1985. *(A)*

Fisher, Leonard. *The Unions.* Holiday, 1982. *(I)*

Lens, Sidney. *Strikemakers & Strikebreakers.* Lodestar, 1985. *(A)*

Meltzer, Milton. *Bread and Roses: The Struggle of American Labor, 1865-1915.* Facts on File, 1990. *(I; A)*

Morton, Desmond. *Labour in Canada.* Watts, 1982. *(I; A)*

Pelham, Molly. *People at Work.* Dillon, 1986. *(P)*

## LACE

Meech, Sue. *1900-20: Linen and Lace.* Gareth Stevens, 1999. *(P; I)*

## LAFAYETTE, MARQUIS DE

Fritz, Jean. *Why Not, Lafayette?* Putnam, 1999. *(I)*

## LAKES

Hoff, Mary, and Rodgers, Mary M. *Rivers and Lakes.* Lerner, 1991. *(I)*

Mulherin, Jenny. *Rivers and Lakes.* Watts, 1984. *(P; I)*(Atlas format)

Rowland-Entwistle, Theodore. *Rivers and Lakes.* Silver Burdett, 1987. *(P; I)*

Updegraffe, Imelda, and Updegraffe, Robert. *Rivers and Lakes.* Penguin, 1983. *(I; A)*

## LANGUAGES

Ashton, Christian. *Words Can Tell: A Book about Our Language*. Messner, 1989. *(P; I; A)*

Colyer, Penrose. *I Can Read French*. Watts, 1981; *I Can Read Italian*, 1983; *I Can Read Spanish,* 1981. *(P; I)*

Heller, Ruth. *Merry-Go-Round: A Book about Nouns*. Grosset, 1990. *(P)*

## LAOS

*Laos . . . in Pictures*. Lerner, 1996. *(I; A)*

Mansfield, Stephen. *Laos*. Marshall Cavendish, 1998. *(I)*

Zickgraf, Ralph, and Buckmaster, Margie. *Laos*. Chelsea House, 1997. *(I; A)*

## LAPLAND

Reynolds, Jan. *Far North: Vanishing Cultures*. Harcourt, 1992. *(P; I)*

## LASERS

Asimov, Isaac. *How Did We Find Out about Lasers?* Walker, 1990. *(I)*

Bender, Lionel. *Lasers in Action*. Bookwright, 1985. *(I; A)*

De Vere, Charles. *Lasers*. Watts, 1984. *(P; I)*

Filson, Brent. *Exploring with Lasers*. Messner, 1984. *(I; A)*

French, P. M. W., and Taylor, J. W. *How Lasers Are Made*. Facts on File, 1987. *(A)*

Nardo, Don. *Lasers: Humanity's Magic Light*. Lucent Books, 1990. *(I; A)*

## LATIN AMERICA

Pascoe, Elaine. *Neighbors at Odds: U.S. Policy in Latin America*. Watts, 1990. *(I; A)*

Tenenbaum, Barbara A. *Latin America: History and Culture*. Gale Group, 1999. *(I; A)*

## LATIN AMERICA, ART AND ARCHITECTURE OF

Merrill, Yvonne Y. *Hands-On Latin America: Art Activities For All Ages*. KITS, 1998. *(I)*

## LATITUDE AND LONGITUDE

Dash, Joan. *The Longitude Prize*. Farrar, Straus & Giroux, 2000. *(I; A)*

## LATVIA

Barlas, Robert. *Latvia*. Marshall Cavendish, 2000. *(I; A)*

## LAVOISIER, ANTOINE LAURENT

Grey, Vivian. *The Chemist Who Lost His Head: The Story of Antoine Laurent Lavoisier*. Putnam, 1982. *(I)*

## LAW AND LAW ENFORCEMENT

Arnold, Caroline. *Why Do We Have Rules?* Watts, 1983. *(P)*

Atkinson, Linda. *Your Legal Rights*. Watts, 1982. *(I; A)*

Davis, Mary L. *Working in Law and Justice*. Lerner, 1999. *(I)*

Ehrenfreund, Norbert, and Treat, Lawrence. *You're the Jury*. Holt, 1992. *(A)*

Epstein, Sam, and Epstein, Beryl. *Kids in Court*. Four Winds, 1982. *(I)*

Fincher, E. B. *The American Legal System*. Watts, 1980. *(I; A)*

Hyde, Margaret O. *The Rights of the Victim*. Watts, 1983. *(I; A)*

Smith, Elizabeth Simpson. *Breakthrough: Women in Law Enforcement*. Walker, 1982. *(I; A)*

Stern, Ron. *Law Enforcement Careers: A Complete Guide from Application to Employment*. Lawman Press, 1988. *(A)*

Weiss, Ann E. *The Supreme Court*. Enslow, 1986. *(A)*

Zerman, Melvyn B. *Beyond a Reasonable Doubt: Inside the American Jury System*. Harper, 1981. *(I; A)*

## LEAD

Heiserman, David L. *Exploring Chemical Elements and Their Compounds*. McGraw-Hill, 1991. *(A)*

## LEAKEY FAMILY

Heiligman, Deborah. *Mary Leakey: In Search of Human Beginnings*. Freeman, 1995. *(I)*

Willis, Delta. *The Leakey Family*. Facts on File, 1992. *(I; A)*

## LEAVES

Johnson, Sylvia A. *How Leaves Change*. Lerner, 1986. *(I)*

Testa, Fulvio. *Leaves*. Peter Bedrick, 1983. *(I)*

## LEBANON

*Lebanon . . . in Pictures*. Lerner, 1988. *(I)*

Shapiro, William. *Lebanon*. Watts, 1984. *(I; A)*

## LEE, ROBERT E.

Aaseng, Nathan. *Robert E. Lee*. Lerner, 1991. *(I)*

Adler, David A. *A Picture Book of Robert E. Lee*. Holiday House, 1998. *(P)*

Archer, Jules. *A House Divided: The Lives of Ulysses S. Grant and Robert E. Lee*. Scholastic, 1996. *(I)*

Commager, Henry Steele, and Ward, Lynd. *America's Robert E. Lee*. Houghton, n.d. *(I)*

Kerby, Mona. *Robert E. Lee: Southern Hero of the Civil War*. Enslow, 1997. *(I; A)*

Monsell, Helen A. *Robert E. Lee: Young Confederate*. Bobbs, 1983. *(P; I)*

Weidhorn, Manfred. *Robert E. Lee*. Atheneum, 1988. *(I; A)*

## LEGENDS

De Paola, Tomie. *The Legend of Old Befana*. Harcourt, 1980. *(P)*; *The Legend of the Indian Paintbrush*. Putnam, 1988. *(P)*

Rohmer, Harriet. *The Invisible Hunters: A Legend from the Miskito Indians of Nicaragua*. Children's, 1987. *(P; I)*; *Uncle Nacho's Hat*. Children's, 1989. *(P; I)*

San Souci, Robert. *Cut from the Same Cloth: American Women of Myth, Legend and Tall Tale.* Philomel, 1993. *(I; A); The Talking Eggs.* Dial, 1989. *(P; I)*

## LEGER, FERNAND

Janson, H. W., and Janson, Anthony F. *History of Art for Young People.* Abrams, 1997. (rev. ed.) *(I; A)*

## LENIN, VLADIMIR ILICH

Rawcliffe, Michael. *Lenin.* Batsford, 1989. *(I; A)*
Resnick, Abraham. *Lenin: Founder of the Soviet Union.* Children's, 1988. *(I)*
Topalian, Elyse. *V. I. Lenin.* Watts, 1983. *(I; A)*

## LENSES

Aust, Siegfried. *Lenses! Take a Closer Look.* Lerner, 1991. *(I)*

## LEONARDO DA VINCI

Herbert, Janis. *Leonardo da Vinci for Kids: His Life and Ideas: 21 Activities.* Chicago Review, 1998. *(I)*
Janson, H. W., and Janson, Anthony F. *History of Art for Young People.* Abrams, 1997. (rev. ed.) *(I; A)*
McLanathan, Richard. *Leonardo da Vinci.* Abrams, 1990. *(I; A)*
Muhlberger, Richard, and Metropolitan Museum of Art. *What Makes a Leonardo a Leonardo?* Viking, 1994. *(I)*
Raboff, Ernest. *Leonardo da Vinci.* Lippincott, 1987. *(P; I)*

## LESOTHO

Blumberg, Rhoda. *Southern Africa: South Africa, Namibia, Swaziland, Lesotho, and Botswana.* Watts, 1981. *(I; A)*
Tonsing-Carter, Betty. *Lesotho.* Chelsea House, 1988. *(P; I)*

## LETTER WRITING

Leedy, Loreen. *Messages in the Mailbox: How to Write a Letter.* Holiday, 1991. *(P)*
Mischel, Florence D. *How to Write a Letter.* Watts, 1988. *(I)*

## LEWIS AND CLARK EXPEDITION

Ambrose, Stephen. *Lewis & Clark: Voyage of Discovery.* National Geographic, 1998. *(A)*
Blumberg, Rhoda. *The Incredible Journey of Lewis & Clark.* Lothrop, 1987. *(P; I)*
Fitz-Gerald, Christine A. *Meriwether Lewis and William Clark.* Children's, 1991. *(I)*
Kroll, Steven. *Lewis and Clark: Explorers of the American West.* Holiday, 1994. *(P)*
McGrath, Patrick. *The Lewis and Clark Expedition.* Silver Burdett, 1985. *(I; A)*

## LIBERIA

Gilfond, Henry. *Gambia, Ghana, Liberia, and Sierra Leone.* Watts, 1981. *(I; A)*
Hope, Constance Morris. *Liberia.* Chelsea House, 1987. *(A)*
Sullivan, Jo M. *Liberia . . . in Pictures.* Lerner, 1988. *(P; I)*

## LIBERTY, STATUE OF

Burchard, Sue. *The Statue of Liberty: Birth to Rebirth.* Harcourt, 1985. *(I)*
Fisher, Leonard Everett. *The Statue of Liberty.* Holiday, 1985. *(P; I)*
Haskins, James. *The Statue of Liberty: America's Proud Lady.* Lerner, 1986. *(P)*
Maestro, Betty. *The Story of the Statue of Liberty.* Morrow, 1986. *(P)*
Shapiro, Mary J. *How They Built the Statue of Liberty.* Random House, 1985. *(I)*

## LIBERTY BELL

Johnson, Linda Carlson. *Our National Symbols.* Millbrook Press, 1994. *(P)*
Sakurai, Gail. *The Liberty Bell.* Children's Press, 1996. *(P; I)*

## LIBRARIES

Cummins, Julie. *The Inside-Outside Book of Libraries.* Dutton, 1996. *(P)*
McInerney, Claire Fleischman. *Find It! The Inside Story of Your Library.* Lerner, 1989. *(I)*
Schurr, Sandra. *Library Lingo.* Incentive Publications, 1981. *(P; I)*

## LIBYA

Brill, Marlene Targ. *Libya.* Children's, 1988. *(P; I)*
Sanders, Renfield. *Libya.* Chelsea House, 1987. *(A)*

## LIE DETECTION

Jussim, Daniel. *Drug Tests and Polygraphs: Essential Tools or Violations of Privacy?* Silver Burdett Press, 1988. *(I; A)*

## LIES

Bawden, Nina. *Kept in the Dark.* Lothrop, 1982. *(I)*
Elliot, Dan. *Ernie's Little Lie.* Random House, 1983. *(P)*
Moncure, Jane B. *Honesty.* Child's World, 1981 (rev. ed.); *John's Choice,* 1983. *(P; I)*
Ruby, Lois. *Two Truths in My Pocket.* Viking, 1982. *(I; A)*
Yep, Laurence. *Liar, Liar.* Morrow, 1983. *(I; A)*

## LIFE

Berger, Melvin. *How Life Began.* Doubleday, 1991. *(P; I)*
Burnie, David. *Life.* Dorling Kindersley, 1994. *(I; A)*
Facklam, Margery. *Partners for Life: The Mysteries of Animal Symbiosis, Vol. 1.* Little, Brown & Co., 1991. *(P; I)*

Hoagland, Mahlon B., and Dodson, Bert. *The Way Life Works*. Times Books, 1995. *(I; A)*

Silverstein, Alvin; Silverstein, Virginia; and Nunn, Laura Silverstein. *Symbiosis*. Millbrook Press, 1998. *(I; A)*

## LIGHT

Ardley, Neil. *The Science Book of Light*. Gulliver Books, 1991. *(P; I)*

Billings, Charlene W. *Fiber Optics: Bright New Way to Communicate*. Dodd, 1986. *(I)*

Burkig, Valerie. *Photonics: The New Science of Light*. Enslow, 1986. *(A)*

Burnie, David. *Light*. Dorling Kindersley, 1992. *(I;A)*

Crews, Donald. *Light*. Greenwillow, 1981. *(P; I)*

Darling, David. *Making Light Work: The Science of Optics*. Dillon, 1991. *(I)*

Doherty, Paul, and Rathjen, Don. *The Magic Wand and Other Bright Experiments on Light and Color*. Wiley, 1995. *(I)*

Friedhofer, Robert. *Light*. Watts, 1992. *(I)*

Goor, Ron, and Goor, Nancy. *Shadows: Here, There, and Everywhere*. Harper, 1981. *(I)*

Hecht, Jeff. *Optics: Light for a New Age*. Scribner's, 1988. *(A)*

Lafferty, Peter. *Light and Sound*. Marshall Cavendish, 1996. *(I)*

Lauber, Patricia. *What Do You See and How Do You See It?* Crown, 1994. *(P;I)*

Levine, Shar, and Johnstone, Leslie. *The Optics Book: Fun Experiments with Light, Vision and Color*. Sterling, 1999. *(I)*

Lloyd, Gill, and Jefferis, David. *The History of Optics*. Thomson, 1995. *(I)*

Skurzynski, Gloria. *Waves: The Electromagnetic Universe*. National Geographic, 1996. *(I)*

Stuart, Gene S. *Hidden Worlds*. National Geographic, 1981. *(P; I)*

Taylor, Barbara. *Bouncing and Bending Light*. Watts, 1990. *(P; I); Seeing Is Not Believing! The Science of Shadow and Light*. Random House, 1991. *(P; I)*

Tomecek, Steve. *Bouncing and Bending Light: Phantastic Physical Phenomena*. Freeman, 1995. *(P; I)*

Ward, Alan. *Experimenting with Light and Illusions*. Batsford, 1985. *(I)*

Watson, Philip. *Light Fantastic*. Lothrop, 1983. *(P; I)*

White, Jack R. *The Invisible World of the Infrared*. Dodd, 1984. *(I)*

## LIGHTING

Aust, Siegfried. *Light!: A Bright Idea*. Lerner, 1992. *(P; I)*

Gardner, Robert. *Science Projects about Light*. Enslow, 1994. *(I); Experimenting with Light*. Watts, 1991. *(I; A); Investigate and Discover Light*. Silver Burdett Press, 1991. *(P; I)*

Levine, Shar, and Johnstone, Leslie. *The Optics Book: Fun Experiments With Light, Vision and Color*. Sterling, 1999. *(I)*

## LINCOLN, ABRAHAM

Adler, David A. *A Picture Book of Abraham Lincoln*. Holiday, 1989. *(P)*

Brandt, Keith. *Abe Lincoln: The Young Years*. Troll, 1982. *(P; I)*

Burchard, Peter. *Lincoln and Slavery*. Simon, 1999. *(I; A)*

D'Aulaire, Ingri, and D'Aulaire, Edgar P. *Abraham Lincoln*. Doubleday, 1957 (rev. ed.). *(P)*

Freedman, Russell. *Lincoln, A Photobiography*. Clarion, 1987. *(P; I; A)*

Gross, Ruth Belov. *True Stories about Abraham Lincoln*. Lothrop, 1990. *(P)*

Hargrove, Jim. *Abraham Lincoln*. Children's, 1988. *(I)*

Holzer, Harold, comp. and ed. *Abraham Lincoln the Writer: A Treasury of His Greatest Speeches and Letters*. Boyds Mills, 2000. *(I; A)*

Shorto, Russell. *Abraham Lincoln and the End of Slavery*. Millbrook, 1991. *(P; I)*

Stevenson, Augusta. *Abraham Lincoln: The Great Emancipator*. Bobbs, 1983. *(P; I)*

Zeinert, Karen. *The Lincoln Murder Plot*. Shoe String/Linnet, 1999. *(I; A)*

## LINDBERGH, CHARLES

Burleigh, Robert. *Flight: The Journey of Charles Lindbergh*. Philomel, 1991. *(P; I)*

Lindbergh, Charles A. *The Spirit of St. Louis*. Scribner's, 1956. *(A)*

Randolph, Blythe. *Charles Lindbergh*. Watts, 1990. *(I; A)*

## LINNAEUS, CAROLUS

Anderson, Margaret Jean. *Carl Linnaeus: Father of Classification*. Enslow, 1997. *(I; A)*

## LIONS

Adamson, Joy. *Born Free*. Pantheon, 1960. *(A); Living Free*. Harcourt, 1961. *(A)*

Ashby, Ruth. *Tigers*. Atheneum, 1990. *(I)*

Dutemple, Lesley A. *Tigers*. Lerner, 1996. *(P)*

Lewin, Ted. *Tiger Trek*. Macmillan, 1990. *(P)*

McClung, Robert M. *Rajpur: Last of the Bengal Tigers*. Morrow, 1982. *(P; I)*

Overbeck, Cynthia. *Lions*. Lerner, 1981. *(P; I; A)*

Stonehouse, Bernard. *A Visual Introduction to Wild Cats*. Facts on File, 1999. *(P; I; A)*

Torgersen, Don. *Lion Prides and Tiger Marks*. Children's, 1982. *(P; I)*

Yoshida, Toshi. *Young Lions*. Philomel, 1989. *(P)*

## LIQUIDS

Berger, Melvin *Solids, Liquids, and Gases*. Putnam, 1989. *(I; A)*

Gardner, Robert. *Science Projects about Solids, Liquids, and Gases*. Enslow, 2000. *(I; A)*

Mebane, Robert C., and Rybolt, Thomas R. *Water and Other Liquids*. Twenty-First Century, 1995. *(I)*

## LISTER, JOSEPH

McTavish, Douglas. *Joseph Lister: Pioneers of Science.* Watts, 1992. *(I; A)*

## LITHUANIA

*Lithuania: Then and Now.* Lerner, 1992. *(I)*

Chicoine , Stephen, and Ashabranner, Brent. *Lithuania: The Nation That Would Be Free.* Cobblehill, 1995. *(I)*

Kaqda, Sakina. *Lithuania.* Marshall Cavendish, 1997. *(I; A)*

## LITTLE LEAGUE BASEBALL

Hale, Creighton H. *Official Little League Baseball Rules in Pictures.* Putnam, 1981. *(P; I)*

Remmers, Mary. *Ducks on the Pond: A Lexicon of Little League Lingo.* Shoal Creek, 1981. *(P; I)*

Sullivan, George. *Baseball Kids.* Dutton, 1990. *(P; I)*

## LIZARDS

Chace, G. Earl. *The World of Lizards.* Dodd, 1982. *(I; A)*

Smith, Trevor. *Amazing Lizards.* Knopf, 1990. *(P; I)*

## LLAMAS

Arnold, Caroline. *Llama.* Morrow, 1992. *(P)*

Lepthien, Emilie U. *Llamas.* Children's Press, 1997. *(P)*

## LOBSTERS

Bailey, Jill. *Discovering Crabs and Lobsters.* Watts, 1987. *(P)*

## LOCKS AND KEYS

Gibbons, Gail. *Locks and Keys.* Harper, 1980. *(P)*

Tchudi, Stephen. *Lock and Key: The Secrets of Locking Things up, in, and Out.* Simon & Schuster, 1993. *(I; A)*

## LOCOMOTIVES

Weitzman, David L. *Locomotive: Building an Eight-Wheeler.* Houghton Mifflin, 1999. *(I)*

## LONDON

Sproule, Anna. *Living in London.* Silver Burdett, 1987. *(P)*

## LONDON, JACK

Schroeder, Alan. *Jack London.* Chelsea House, 1991. *(I; A)*

## LONG FAMILY

LeVert, Suzanne. *Huey Long: The Kingfish of Louisiana.* Facts on File, 1995. *(I; A)*

## LONGFELLOW, HENRY WADSWORTH

Longfellow, Henry Wadsworth. *The Children's Own Longfellow.* Houghton, n.d. *(P; I)*; *Hiawatha.* Dial, 1983. *(P)*

Longfellow, Henry Wadsworth. *The Midnight Ride of Paul Revere.* National Geographic, 2000. *(P; I)*

## LOS ANGELES

Cash, Judy. *Kidding around Los Angeles: A Young Person's Guide to the City.* John Muir, 1989. *(I; A)*

Jaskol, Julie, and Lewis, Brian. *City of Angels: In and around Los Angeles.* Dutton, 1999. *(P; I)*

## LOUISIANA

Fradin, Dennis. *Louisiana: In Words and Pictures.* Children's, 1981. *(P; I)*

Hintz, Martin. *Louisiana.* Children's Press, 1998. *(I)*

Kent, Deborah. *Louisiana.* Children's, 1988. *(P; I)*

## LOUISIANA PURCHASE

Phelan, Mary K. *The Story of the Louisiana Purchase.* Harper, 1979. *(P; I)*

## LULLABIES

McKellar, Shona, comp. *A Child's Book of Lullabies.* DK, 1997. *(P)*

## LUMBER AND LUMBERING

Abrams, Kathleen, and Abrams, Lawrence. *Logging and Lumbering.* Messner, 1980. *(P; I)*

Langley, Andres. *Timber.* Rourke, 1987. *(P; I)*

## LUNGS

Parker, Steve. *The Lungs and Respiratory System.* Raintree Steck-Vaughn, 1997. *(I)*

## LUTHER, MARTIN

Fehlauer, Adolph. *The Life and Faith of Martin Luther.* Northwest, 1981. *(I; A)*

## MACARTHUR, DOUGLAS

Fox, Mary Virginia. *Douglas MacArthur.* Lucent, 1999. *(I; A)*

## MACKENZIE, SIR ALEXANDER

Xydes, Georgia. *Alexander MacKenzie and the Explorers of Canada.* Chelsea House, 1992. *(I)*

## MACRAMÉ

Bress, Helene. *The Craft of Macramé.* Scribner's, 1977. *(I; A)*

## MADAGASCAR

*Madagascar . . . in Pictures.* Lerner, 1988. *(I)*

Stevens, Rita. *Madagascar.* Chelsea House, 1987. *(P; I)*

Taylor, L. B., Jr. *South East Africa: Zimbabwe, Zambia, Malawi, Madagascar, Mauritius, and Reunion.* Watts, 1981. *(I; A)*

## MADISON, JAMES

Leavell, J. Perry. *James Madison.* Chelsea House, 1988. *(A)*

## MAGELLAN, FERDINAND

Hargrove, Jim. *Ferdinand Magellan.* Children's, 1990. *(I)*

## MAGIC

Bernstein, Bob. *Monday Morning Magic.* Good Apple, 1982. *(P; I)*

Cobb, Vicki, and Darling, Kathy. *Bet You Can!* Lothrop, 1983. *(P; I)*

Cohen, Daniel. *Real Magic.* Dodd, 1982. *(P; I)*

Lewis, Shari. *Abracadabra: Magic and Other Tricks.* Ballantine, 1984. *(P; I)*

Nesbit, E. *The Story of the Treasure Seekers.* Scholastic, 1988. *(I; A)*

Severin, Bill. *Magic with Rope, Ribbon, and String.* McKay, 1981. *(I; A)*

Stoddard, Edward. *Magic.* Watts, 1983 (rev. ed.). *(I; A)*

White, Laurence B., Jr., and Broekel, Ray. *Math-a-Magic: Number Tricks for Magicians.* Albert Whitman, 1990. *(P; I)*

## MAGNESIUM

Heiserman, David L. *Exploring Chemical Elements and Their Compounds.* McGraw-Hill, 1991. *(A)*

Uttley, Colin. *Magnesium.* Marshall Cavendish/Benchmark, 1999. *(I)*

## MAGNETS AND MAGNETISM

Adler, David. *Amazing Magnets.* Troll, 1983. *(P; I)*

Ardley, Neil. *Exploring Magnetism.* Watts, 1984. *(I)*

Catherall, Ed. *Exploring Magnets.* Steck-Vaughn, 1990. *(I)*

Lampton, Christopher. *Superconductors.* Enslow, 1989. *(I; A)*

Satrey, Laurence. *Magnets.* Troll, 1985. *(I)*

Tomecek, Steve. *Simple Attraction.* Scientific American, 1995. *(P; I)*

## MAINE

Engfer, LeeAnne. *Maine.* Lerner, 1991. *(I)*

Harrington, Ty. *Maine.* Children's, 1989. *(P; I)*

## MALAWI

*Malawi . . . in Pictures.* Lerner, 1988. *(I)*

Sanders, Renfield. *Malawi.* Chelsea House, 1987. *(P; I)*

Taylor, L. B., Jr. *South East Africa: Zimbabwe, Zambia, Malawi, Madagascar, Mauritius, and Reunion.* Watts, 1981. *(I; A)*

## MALAYSIA

*Malaysia . . . in Pictures.* Lerner, 1989. *(I)*

Elder, Bruce. *Malaysia. Singapore.* Watts, 1985. *(P)*

Knowlton, MaryLee, and Sachner, Mark J. *Burma; Indonesia; Malaysia.* Gareth Stevens, 1987. *(P)*

Major, John S. *Land and People of Malaysia and Brunei.* HarperCollins, 1991. *(I; A)*

Wright, David K. *Malaysia.* Children's, 1988. *(P; I)*

## MALCOLM X

Brown, Kevin. *Malcolm X: His Life and Legacy.* Millbrook, 1995. *(I; A)*

Myers, Walter Dean. *Malcolm X: A Fire Burning Brightly.* HarperCollins, 2000. *(I; A)*

Myers, Walter Dean. *Malcolm X: By Any Means Necessary.* Scholastic, 1993. *(A)*

Stine, Megan. *The Story of Malcolm X, Civil Rights Leader.* Dell, 1994. *(I)*

## MALI

Brooks, Larry. *Daily Life in Ancient and Modern Timbuktu.* Lerner, 1999. *(I)*

O'Toole, Thomas. *Mali in Pictures.* Lerner, 1990. *(I)*

## MALTA

Sheehan, Sean. *Malta.* Marshall Cavendish, 2000. *(I; A)*

## MAMMALS

Anderson, Lucia. *Mammals and Their Milk.* Dodd, 1986. *(I)*

Crump, Donald J., ed. *Giants from the Past.* National Geographic, 1983. *(P; I)*

Parker, Steve. *Mammal.* Knopf, 1989. *(I)*

Patent, Dorothy Hinshaw. *Why Mammals Have Fur.* Cobblehill, 1995. *(P; I)*

## MANATEES

Ripple, Jeff. *Manatees and Dugongs of the World.* Voyageur, 2000. *(A)*

Staub, Frank. *Manatees.* Lerner, 1998. *(P)*

Walker, Sally M. *Manatees.* Carolrhoda, 1999. *(P; I)*

## MANDELA, NELSON

Cooper, Floyd. *Mandela: From the Life of the South African Statesman.* Philomel, 1996. *(P)*

Denenberg, Barry. *Nelson Mandela: No Easy Walk to Freedom.* Scholastic, 1991. *(I)*

## MANET, EDOUARD

Janson, H. W., and Janson, Anthony F. *History of Art for Young People.* Abrams, 1997. (rev. ed.) *(I; A)*

Welton, Jude. *Eyewitness: Impressionism.* DK, 2000. *(P; I; A)*

Wright, Patricia. *Eyewitness Art: Manet.* DK, 1993. *(P; I)*

## MAO ZEDONG

Stefoff, Rebecca. *Mao Zedong: Founder of the People's Republic of China.* Millbrook, 1996. *(I; A)*

## MAPLE SYRUP AND MAPLE SUGAR

Gokay, Nancy H. *Sugarbush: Making Maple Syrup.* Hillsdale, 1980. *(P)*

Lasky, Kathryn. *Sugaring Time.* Macmillan, 1983. *(I)*

Metcalf, Rosamund S. *The Sugar Maple.* Phoenix Publishing, 1982. *(P; I)*

## MAPS AND GLOBES

Arnold, Caroline. *Maps and Globes: Fun, Facts, and Activities.* Watts, 1984. *(P)*

Baynes, John. *How Maps Are Made.* Facts on File, 1987. *(I)*

Bramwell, Martyn. *How Maps Are Made; Mapping Our World; Mapping the Seas and Airways; Maps in Everyday Life.* Lerner, 1998. *(I)*

Carey, Helen. *How to Use Maps and Globes.* Watts, 1983. *(I; A)*

Johnson, Sylvia A. *Mapping the World.* Simon & Schuster/Atheneum, 1999. *(P; I)*

Knowlton, Jack. *Geography from A to Z.* Crowell, 1988. *(P); Maps and Globes.* Crowell, 1985. *(P; I)*

Madden, James F. *The Wonderful World of Maps.* Hammond, 1982. *(I; A)*

Mango, Karin. *Mapmaking.* Messner, 1984. *(P)*

Sweeney, Joan. *Me on the Map.* Crown, 1995. *(P)*

Weiss, Harvey. *Maps: Getting from Here to There.* Houghton, 1991. *(I)*

## MARBLES

Levine, Shar, and Scudamore, Vicki. *Marbles: A Player's Guide.* Sterling, 1999. *(P; I)*

## MARCH

Updike, John. *A Child's Calendar.* Holiday House, 1999. *(P; I)*

Warner, Penny. *Kids' Holiday Fun: Great Family Activities Every Month of the Year.* Meadowbrook Press, 1997. *(P)*

## MARCO POLO

Ceserani, Gian Paolo. *Marco Polo.* Putnam, 1982. *(P; I)*

Walsh, Richard, ed. *The Adventures of Marco Polo.* John Day, 1948. *(I)*

## MARS

Berger, Melvin. *If You Lived on Mars.* Lodestar, 1988. *(P; I)*

Cattermole, Peter. *Mars.* Facts on File, 1990. *(P; I)*

Fradin, Dennis Brindell. *Is There Life on Mars?* Simon & Schuster/Margaret K. McElderry Bks., 1999. *(I; A)*

Getz, David. *Life on Mars.* Holt, 1997. *(P;I)*

Kelch, Joseph W. *Millions of Miles to Mars.* Messner, 1995. *(I)*

Raeburn, Paul. *Mars: Uncovering the Secrets of the Red Planet.* National Geographic, 1998. *(A)*

Ride, Sally, and O'Shaughnessy, Tam. *The Mystery of Mars.* Crown, 1999. *(P; I)*

Simon, Seymour. *Destination: Mars.* HarperCollins, 2000. *(P; I)*

Vogt, Gregory. *Mars and the Inner Planets.* Watts, 1982. *(I; A)*

## MARSHALL, GEORGE C.

Lubetkin, Wendy. *George Marshall.* Chelsea House, 1990. *(I)*

Saunders, Alan. *George C. Marshall: A General for Peace.* Facts on File, 1995. *(A)*

## MARSHALL, JOHN

Silberdick-Feinberg, Barbara. *John Marshall: The Great Chief Justice.* Enslow, 1995. *(I; A)*

## MARSUPIALS

Jansen, John. *Playing Possum: Riddles about Kangaroos, Koalas, and Other Marsupials.* Lerner, 1995. *(P; I)*

Lavine, Sigmund A. *Wonders of Marsupials.* Dodd, 1979. *(I)*

## MARX, KARL

Hunter, Nigel. *Karl Marx.* Watts, 1987. *(P; I)*

## MARYLAND

Dubois, Muriel L. *Maryland: Facts and Symbols.* Capstone/Hilltop, 2000. *(P)*

Rollo, Vera F. *A Geography of Maryland: Ask Me!* Maryland Historical Press, 1981. *(P; I)*

Schaun, George, and Schaun, Virginia. *Everyday Life in Colonial Maryland.* Maryland Historical Press, 1981. *(P; I; A)*

## MASON-DIXON LINE

St. George, Judith. *Mason and Dixon's Line of Fire.* Putnam, 1991. *(I; A)*

## MASSACHUSETTS

Fradin, Dennis. *Massachusetts: In Words and Pictures.* Children's, 1981. *(P; I)*

Kent, Deborah. *Massachusetts.* Children's, 1988. *(P; I)*

Lewis, Taylor Biggs, and Heard, Virginia Scott. *Nantucket: Gardens and Houses.* Little, Brown & Co., 1990. *(A)*

McNair, Sylvia. *Massachusetts.* Children's Press, 1998. *(I)*

## MATERIALS SCIENCE

Bortz, Fred. *Superstuff!: Materials That Have Changed Our Lives.* Watts, 1990. *(I; A)*

## MATHEMATICS

Adler, Irving. *Mathematics.* Doubleday, 1990. *(I; A)*

Anno, Mitsumasa. *All in a Day.* Putnam, 1990. *(P); Anno's Math Games II.* Philomel, 1989. *(P); Anno's Math Games III.* Philomel, 1991. *(P; I); Anno's Mysterious Multiplying Jar.* Philomel, 1983. *(P)*

Bendick, Jeanne. *Mathematics Illustrated Dictionary.* Watts, 1989. *(I; A)*

Blocksma, Mary. *Reading the Numbers: A Survival Guide to the Measurement, Numbers and Sizes Encountered in Everyday Life.* Viking, 1989. *(P; I)*

Burns, Marilyn. *Math for Smarty Pants: Or Who Says Mathematicians Have Little Pig Eyes.* Little, 1983. *(I; A)*

Cushman, Jean. *Do You Wanna Bet? Your Chance to Find Out About Probability.* Clarion, 1991. *(I)*

Ferrell, Edmund. *Mathopedia.* Omni Books, 1994. *(I; A)*

Flansburg, Scott. *Math Magic.* Morrow, 1993. *(A)*

Haskins, Jim. *Count Your Way through Italy.* Carolrhoda, 1990. *(P)*

Lampton, Christopher. *Science of Chaos.* Watts, 1992. *(I; A)*

Latham, Jean Lee. *Carry On Mr. Bowditch.* Houghton, 1955. *(P; I)*

McMillan, Bruce. *Jellybeans for Sale.* Scholastic, 1996. *(P)*

Pappas, Theoni. *Fractals, Googols, and Other Mathematical Tales.* Wide World, 1993. *(I; A)*

Schwartz, David M. *If You Made a Million.* Lothrop, 1989. *(P; I)*

Scieszka, Jon. *Math Curse.* Viking, 1995. *(P; I)*

Sharp, Richard M., and Metzner, Seymour. *The Squeaky Square and 113 Other Math Activities for Kids.* TAB Books, 1990. *(I)*

VanCleave, Janice. *Math for Every Kid: Activities That Make Learning Math Fun.* John Wiley, 1991. *(P; I)*

White, Laurence B., Jr., and Broekel, Ray. *Math-A-Magic: Number Tricks for Magicians.* Albert Whitman, 1990. *(I)*

## MATHEMATICS, HISTORY OF

Reimer, Luetta, and Reimer, Wilbert. *Mathematicians Are People, Too.* Dale Seymour, 1990. *(I)*

## MATISSE, HENRI

Janson, H. W., and Janson, Anthony F. *History of Art for Young People.* Abrams, 1997. (rev. ed.) *(I; A)*

## MATTER

Clark, John. *Matter and Energy: Physics in Action.* Oxford University Press, 1995. *(I;A)*

Cobb, Vicki. *Why Can't You Unscramble an Egg?: and Other Not Such Dumb Questions about Matter.* Lodestar, 1990. *(P; I)*

Gardner, Robert. *Science Projects about Solids, Liquids, and Gases.* Enslow, 2000. *(I; A)*

Mebane, Robert C., and Rybolt, Thomas R. *Air and Other Gases; Salts and Solids; Water and Other Liquids.* Twenty-First Century, 1995. *(I)*

## MAURITANIA

Goodsmith, Lauren. *The Children of Mauritania: Days in the Desert and by the River Shore.* Lerner, 1994. *(I)*

## MAYA

Fisher, Leonard Everett. *Gods and Goddesses of the Ancient Maya.* Holiday, 1999. *(P; I)*

Galvin, Irene Flum, and Stein, R.C. *The Ancient Maya.* Marshall Cavendish, 1997. *(I)*

## MAYFLOWER

DeLage, Ida. *The Pilgrim Children on the Mayflower.* Garrard, 1980. *(P; I)*

## McCLINTOCK, BARBARA

Fine, Edith Hope. *Barbara McClintock: Nobel Prize Geneticist.* Enslow, 1998. *(I)*

Kittredge, Mary. *Barbara McClintock: Biologist.* Chelsea House, 1991. *(I; A)*

## McKINLEY, WILLIAM

Kent, Zachary. *William McKinley: Twenty-Fifth President of the United States.* Children's, 1988. *(P; I)*

## MEAD, MARGARET

Castiglia, Julie. *Margaret Mead.* Silver Burdett, 1989. *(I; A)*

Frevert, Patricia. *Margaret Mead Herself.* Creative Education, 1981. *(I; A)*

Ludle, Jacqueline. *Margaret Mead.* Watts, 1983. *(I; A)*

Saunders, Susan. *Margaret Mead: The World Was Her Family.* Viking, 1987. *(P; I)*

## MEDICINE

Ardley, Neil. *Health and Medicine.* Watts, 1982. *(P; I)*

Berger, Melvin. *Sports Medicine.* Harper, 1982. *(I; A)*

DeStefano, Susan. *Focus on Medicines.* 21st Century Books, 1991. *(P)*

Jackson, Gordon. *Medicine: The Body and Healing.* Watts, 1984. *(P; I)*

Kidd, J.S., and Kidd, Renee A. *Mother Nature's Pharmacy: Potent Medicines from Plants.* Facts on File, 1998. *(I; A)*

Miller, Brandon Marie. *Just What the Doctor Ordered: The History of American Medicine.* Lerner, 1997. *(I)*

Oleksy, Walter G. *Paramedics.* Messner, 1983. *(I)*

Parker, Steve. *Medicine.* Dorling Kindersley, 1995. *(I;A)*

## MEDICINE, HISTORY OF

Wilbur, Keith C. *Revolutionary Medicine: 1700-1800.* Chelsea House, 1997. *(I; A)*

## MEIR, GOLDA

Hitzeroth, Deborah. *Golda Meir.* Lucent, 1998. *(I)*

## MELONS

Hughes, Meredith Sayles. *Yes, We Have Bananas: Fruits from Shrubs and Vines.* Lerner, 1999. *(P; I)*

## MELVILLE, HERMAN

Stefoff, Rebecca. *Herman Melville.* Simon & Schuster, 1994. *(A)*

Szumski, Bonnie, ed. *Readings on Herman Melville.* Greenhaven Press, 1996. *(A)*

## MENDEL, GREGOR JOHANN

Klare, Roger. *Gregor Mendel: Father of Genetics.* Enslow, 1997. *(I)*

## MENSTRUATION

Berger, Gilda. *PMS: Premenstrual Syndrome.* Watts, 1984. *(I; A)*

Gravelle, Karen, and Gravelle, Jennifer. *The Period Book: Everything You Don't Want to Ask (but Need to Know).* Walker, 1996. *(P; I)*

Marzollo, Jean. *Getting Your Period: A Book about Menstruation.* Dial, 1989. *(I; A)*

Nourse, Alan E., M.D. *Menstruation: Just Plain Talk.* Watts, 1987. *(I; A)*

## MENTAL ILLNESS

Gilbert, Sara. *What Happens in Therapy.* Lothrop, 1982. *(I; A)*

Hurley, Jennifer A., ed. *Mental Health.* Greenhaven, 1999. *(I; A)*

Leigh, Vanora. *Mental Illness.* Raintree/Steck-Vaughn, 1999. *(I)*

Myers, Irma, and Myers, Arthur. *Why You Feel Down and What You Can Do About It.* Scribner's, 1982. *(I; A)*

Olshan, Neal H. *Depression.* Watts, 1982. *(I; A)*

Packard, Gwen K. *Coping with Stress.* Rosen, 1997. *(I;A)*

## MERCURY (PLANET)

Simon, Seymour. *Mercury.* Morrow, 1992. *(P)*

## METALS AND METALLURGY

Coombs, Charles. *Gold and Other Precious Metals.* Morrow, 1981. *(P; I)*

Fodor, R. V. *Gold, Copper, Iron: How Metals Are Formed, Found, and Used.* Enslow, 1989. *(A)*

Lambert, Mark. *Spotlight on Copper.* Rourke, 1988. *(P; I)*

Lye, Keith. *Spotlight on Gold.* Rourke, 1988. *(P; I)*

Lyttle, Richard B. *The Golden Path: The Lure of Gold through History.* Atheneum, 1983. *(I; A)*

Mitgutsch, Ali. *From Ore to Spoon.* Carolrhoda, 1981. *(P)*

Rickard, Graham. *Spotlight on Silver.* Rourke, 1988. *(P; I)*

Whyman, Kathryn. *Metals and Alloys.* Gloucester Press, 1988. *(P; I)*

## METAMORPHOSIS

Bailey, Jill. *How Caterpillars Turn into Butterflies.* Marshall Cavendish, 1998. *(P; I)*

Goor, Nancy, and Goor, Ron. *Insect Metamorphosis: From Egg to Adult.* Simon & Schuster, 1998. *(P)*

Ruiz, Andres Llamas, and Arredondo, Francisco. *Metamorphosis.* Sterling, 1996. *(P; I)*

## MEXICAN WAR

*The Mexican War of Independence.* Lucent, 1997. *(A)*

Collier, Christopher, and Collier, James L. *Hispanic America, Texas, and the Mexican War 1835-1850.* Benchmark, 1998. *(I)*

Lawson, Don. *The United States in the Mexican War.* Harper, 1976. *(I; A)*

Murphy, Keith. *The Battle of the Alamo.* Raintree, 1979. *(P; I)*

Nardo, Don. *The Mexican-American War.* Lucent, 1991. *(I; A)*

Sorrels, Roy. *The Alamo in American History.* Enslow, 1996. *(I)*

## MEXICO

Casagrande, Louis B., and Johnson, Sylvia A. *Focus on Mexico: Modern Life in an Ancient Land.* Lerner, 1987. *(I)*

Epstein, Sam, and Epstein, Beryl. *Mexico.* Watts, 1983 (rev. ed.). *(I)*

Fincher, E. B. *Mexico and the United States: Their Linked Destinies.* Harper, 1983. *(I; A)*

Goodwin, William. *Mexico.* Lucent, 1998. *(I; A)*

Jacobsen, Peter O., and Kristensen, Preben S. *A Family in Mexico.* Watts, 1984. *(P; I)*

Jacobson, Karen. *Mexico.* Children's, 1982. *(P)*

Kent, Deborah. *Mexico: Rich in Spirit and Tradition.* Benchmark, 1995. *(I)*

Lye, Keith. *Take a Trip to Mexico.* Watts, 1982. *(P)*

Moran, Tom. *A Family in Mexico.* Lerner, 1987. *(P)*

Palacios, Argentina. *Viva Mexico! The Story of Benito Juarez and Cinco de Mayo.* Steck-Vaughn, 1993. *(I)*

Smith, Eileen L. *Mexico: Giant of the South.* Dillon, 1983. *(I; A)*

Visual Geography. *Mexico in Pictures.* Lerner, 1987. *(I)*

## MEXICO CITY

Stein, R. Conrad. *Mexico City.* Children's, 1996. *(P; I)*

## MICHELANGELO

Giudici, Vittorio, and Galante, L.R. *The Sistine Chapel: Its History and Masterpieces.* NTC, 2000. *(I)*

Janson, H. W., and Janson, Anthony F. *History of Art for Young People.* Abrams, 1997. (rev. ed.) *(I; A)*

McLanathan, Richard B. *Michelangelo.* Abrams, 1993. *(I; A)*

Stanley, Diane. *Michelangelo.* HarperCollins, 2000. *(I)*

Ventura, Piero. *Michelangelo's World.* Putnam, 1990. *(P; I)*

## MICHIGAN

Hintz, Martin. *Michigan.* Watts, 1987. *(P; I)*

Stein, R. Conrad. *Michigan.* Children's, 1988. *(P; I)*

## MICROBIOLOGY

Dashefsky, H. Steven. *Microbiology: High-School Science Fair Experiments.* McGraw-Hill, 1995. *(A)*

Giblin, James Cross. *Milk: The Fight for Purity.* Crowell, 1986. *(I)*

Patent, Dorothy Hinshaw. *Bacteria: How They Affect Other Living Things.* Holiday, 1980. *(I)*; *Germs!* Holiday, 1983. *(P; I)*

Snedden, Robert. *A World of Microorganisms; Scientists and Discoveries.* Heinemann, 2000. *(I; A)*

Taylor, Ron. *Through the Microscope.* Facts on File, 1986. *(I)*

## MICRONESIA, FEDERATED STATES OF

Hermes, Jules M. *The Children of Micronesia.* Carolrhoda, 1995. *(I)*

## MICROSCOPES

Bleifeld, Maurice. *Experimenting with a Microscope.* Watts, 1988. *(I)*

Johnson, Gaylord, and Bleifeld, Maurice. *Hunting with the Microscope.* Arco, 1980 (rev. ed.). *(I; A)*

Klein, Aaron E. *The Complete Beginner's Guide to Microscopes and Telescopes.* Doubleday, 1980. *(I; A)*

Levine, Shar, and Johnstone, Leslie. *The Microscope Book.* Sterling, 1997. *(I)*

Simon, Seymour. *Hidden Worlds.* Morrow, 1983. *(P; I)*

Stwertka, Eve, and Stwertka, Albert. *Microscope: How to Use It and Enjoy It.* Messner, 1989. *(I)*

Tomb, Howard, and Kunkel, Dennis. *Microaliens: Dazzling Journeys With an Electron Microscope.* Farrar, Straus & Giroux, 1993. *(I; A)*

Yount, Lisa. *Antoni Van Leeuwenhoek: First to See Microscopic Life.* Enslow, 1996. *(I)*

## MICROWAVES

Asimov, Isaac. *How Did We Find Out about Microwaves?* Walker, 1989. *(P; I)*

## MIDDLE AGES

Aliki. *A Medieval Feast.* Harper, 1983. *(P)*

Brooks, Polly S. *Queen Eleanor: Independent Spirit of the Medieval World.* Harper, 1983. *(I; A)*

Corbishley, Mike. *The Middle Ages.* Facts on File, 1991. *(I; A)*

Cosman, Madeleine P. *Medieval Holidays and Festivals: A Calendar of Celebrations.* Scribner's, 1982. *(I; A)*

Hanawalt, Barbara A. *The Middle Ages: An Illustrated History.* Oxford, 1998. *(I; A)*

Langley, Andrew. *Medieval Life.* Knopf, 1996. *(I; A)*

Oakes, Catherine. *Exploring the Past: The Middle Ages.* Gulliver Books, 1988. *(I; A)*

Rice, Earle. *Life during the Middle Ages.* Lucent, 1998. *(I; A)*

Sancha, Sheila. *The Luttrell Village: Country Life in the Middle Ages.* Harper, 1983. *(I; A); Walter Dragun's Town: Crafts and Trades in the Middle Ages.* Crowell, 1989. *(I; A)*

Wood, Audrey. *King Bidgood's in the Bathtub.* Harcourt, 1985. *(P)*

Wright, Sylvia. *The Age of Chivalry: English Society, 1200-1400.* Warwick Press, 1988. *(P; I)*

## MIDDLE EAST

*Kuwait . . . in Pictures.* Lerner, 1989. *(I)*

Beaton, Margaret. *Syria.* Children's, 1988. *(I)*

Collinson, Alan. *Mountains.* Dillon, 1992. *(I; A)*

Feinstein, Steve. *Turkey . . . in Pictures.* Lerner, 1988. *(P: I)*

Gell, Anthea, tr. *Stories of the Arabian Nights.* Peter Bedrick, 1982. *(I)*

Husain, Akbar. *The Revolution in Iran.* Rourke, 1988. *(A)*

King, John. *The Gulf War.* Dillon: Macmillan, 1991. *(I; A)*

Lawless, Richard, and Bleaney, Heather. *The Middle East Since 1945.* Batsford, 1990. *(A)*

Long, Cathryn J. *The Middle East in Search of Peace.* Millbrook, 1994. *(I)*

McCaughrean, Geraldine. *One Thousand and One Arabian Nights.* Oxford University Press, 1982. *(I)*

Mulloy, Martin. *Syria.* Chelsea House, 1988. *(P)*

Pimlott, John. *Middle East: A Background to the Conflicts.* Gloucester Press, dist. by Watts, 1991. *(I)*

Spencer, William. *The Islamic States in Conflict.* Watts, 1983. *(I, A); The Land and People of Turkey.* Harper, 1990. *(I; A)*

## MILK

Bourgeois, Paulette; Ross, Catherine; and Wallace, Susan. *The Amazing Milk Book.* General Distribution Services, 1997. *(P; I)*

King, Hazel. *Milk and Yogurt.* Heinemann, 1998. *(P; I)*

## MILKY WAY

Gustafson, John R. *Stars, Clusters and Galaxies.* Silver Burdett Press, 1993. *(I; A)*

## MINERALS

Cheney, Glenn Alan. *Mineral Resources.* Watts, 1985. *(I)*

Eckert, Allan W. *Earth Treasures: Where to Collect Minerals, Rocks, and Fossils in the United States.* Harper, 1987. *(I; A)*

Harris, Susan. *Gems and Minerals.* Watts, 1982. *(P)*

Marcus, Elizabeth. *Rocks and Minerals.* Troll, 1983. *(P; I)*

McGowen, Tom. *Album of Rocks and Minerals.* Rand, 1981. *(P; I)*

Podendorf, Illa. *Rocks and Minerals.* Children's, 1982. *(P)*

Srogi, Lee Ann. *Start Collecting Rocks and Minerals.* Running Press, 1989. *(I; A)*

Symes, R. F. and the staff of the Natural History Museum. *Rocks and Minerals.* Knopf, 1988. *(I)*

Whyman, Kathryn. *Rocks and Minerals.* Gloucester Press, 1989. *(P; I)*

## MINES AND MINING

Kalman, Bobbie, and Calder, Kate. *The Life of a Miner.* Crabtree/A Bobbie Kalman Bk., 1999. *(P; I)*

## MINNESOTA

Finsand, Mary J. *The Town That Moved.* Carolrhoda, 1983. *(P)*

Fradin, Dennis. *Minnesota: In Words and Pictures.* Children's, 1980. *(P; I)*

## MINT

Wolman, Paul. *U. S. Mint.* Chelsea House, 1987. *(I; A)*

## MISSISSIPPI

Carson, Robert. *Mississippi.* Children's, 1989. *(P; I)*

Fradin, Dennis. *Mississippi: In Words and Pictures.* Children's, 1980. *(P; I)*

Twain, Mark. *Life on the Mississippi.* Oxford University Press, 1962. *(I; A)*

## MISSISSIPPI RIVER

Cooper, Kay. *Journeys on the Mississippi.* Messner, 1981. *(P; I)*

Crisman, Ruth. *The Mississippi.* Watts, 1984. *(I; A)*

Hiscock, Bruce. *The Big Rivers: The Missouri, the Mississippi, and the Ohio.* Atheneum, 1997. *(P; I)*

Lauber, Patricia. *Flood: Wrestling with the Mississippi.* National Geographic, 1996. *(P; I)*

St. George, Judith. *The Amazing Voyage of the New Orleans.* Putnam, 1980. *(I; A)*

Zeck, Pam, and Zeck, Gerry. *Mississippi Sternwheelers.* Carolrhoda, 1982. *(P; I)*

## MISSOURI

Fradin, Dennis. *Missouri: In Words and Pictures.* Children's, 1980. *(P; I)*

Wilder, Laura Ingalls, and Lane, Rose Wilder. *On the Way Home: The Diary of a Trip from South Dakota to Mansfield, Missouri, in 1894.* Harper, 1962. *(I)*

## MODELING, FASHION

Cantwell, Lois. *Modeling.* Watts, 1986. *(I; A)*

Lasch, Judith. *The Teen Model Book.* Messner, 1986. *(A)*

Moss, Miriam. *Fashion Model.* Crestwood House, 1991. *(I)*

## MODERN MUSIC

Venezia, Mike. *Igor Stravinsky.* Children's Press, 1997. *(P)*

## MOLDOVA

Sheehan, Patricia. *Moldova.* Marshall Cavendish, 2000. *(I; A)*

## MOLLUSKS

Pascoe, Elaine. *Snails and Slugs.* Blackbirch Press, 1998. *(I)*

## MONET, CLAUDE

Janson, H. W., and Janson, Anthony F. *History of Art for Young People.* Abrams, 1997. (rev. ed.) *(I; A)*

Muhlberger, Richard, and Metropolitan Museum of Art. *What Makes a Monet a Monet?* Viking, 1993. *(I)*

Venezia, Mike. *Monet.* Children's, 1990. *(P)*

Waldron, Ann. *Claude Monet.* Abrams, 1991. *(I; A)*

Welton, Jude. *Eyewitness: Impressionism.* DK, 2000. *(P; I; A)*

## MONGOLIA

Cheng, Pang Guek. *Mongolia.* Marshall Cavendish, 1999. *(I)*

Reynolds, Jan. *Mongolia: Vanishing Cultures.* Harcourt, 1994. *(P; I)*

## MONKEYS

Anderson, Norman D., and Brown, Walter R. *Lemurs.* Dodd, 1984. *(P)*

Barrett, N. S. *Monkeys and Apes.* Watts, 1988. *(P; I)*

Gelman, Rita Golden. *Monkeys and Apes of the World.* Watts, 1990. *(P)*

Overbeck, Cynthia. *Monkeys.* Lerner, 1981. *(P; I; A)*

Stone, Lynn M. *Baboons; Chimpanzees; Snow Monkeys.* Rourke, 1990. *(P)*

Whitehead, Patricia. *Monkeys.* Troll, 1982. *(P)*

## MONROE, JAMES

Fitzgerald, Christine Maloney. *James Monroe: Fifth President of the United States.* Children's, 1987. *(I)*

Wetzel, Charles. *James Monroe.* Chelsea House, 1989. *(I; A)*

## MONTANA

Fradin, Dennis. *Montana: In Words and Pictures.* Children's, 1981. *(P; I)*

## MONTEZUMA II

Kimmel, Eric A. *Montezuma and the Fall of the Aztecs.* Holiday House, 2000. *(P)*

## MONTREAL

Hamilton, Janice. *Destination Montreal.* Lerner, 1997. *(P; I)*

## MOON

Adler, David. *All about the Moon.* Troll, 1983. *(P; I)*

Apfel, Necia H. *The Moon and Its Exploration.* Watts, 1982. *(I; A)*

Branley, Franklyn M. *What the Moon Is Like.* HarperCollins, 2000. *(P)*

Graham, Ian. *The Best Book of the Moon.* Kingfisher, 1999. *(P; I)*

Hughes, David. *The Moon.* Facts on File, 1990. *(P; I)*

Jay, Michael, and Henbest, Nigel. *The Moon.* Watts, 1982. *(P)*

Simon, Seymour. *The Moon.* Four Winds, 1984. *(P)*

Vaughan, Jenny. *On the Moon.* Watts, 1983. *(P)*

## MORMONS

Simon, Charnan. *Brigham Young: Mormon and Pioneer.* Children's Press, 1999. *(P; I)*

Smith, Gary. *Day of Great Healing in Nauvoo.* Deseret, 1980. *(I; A)*

## MOROCCO

*Morocco . . . in Pictures.* Lerner, 1989. *(I; A)*

Hermes, Jules M. *The Children of Morocco.* Carolrhoda, 1995. *(P; I)*

Seward, Pat. *Morocco.* Benchmark, 1995. *(I)*

## MORSE, SAMUEL F. B.

Kerby, Mona. *Samuel Morse.* Watts, 1991. *(P; I)*

## MOSCOW

Adelman, Deborah. *The "Children of Perestroika" Come of Age: Young People of Moscow Talk about Life in the New Russia.* Sharpe, 1994. *(A)*

Kent, Deborah. *Moscow.* Children's Press, 2000. *(I)*

## MOSES

Auld, Mary. *Moses in the Bulrushes.* Grolier, 1999. *(P)*

Wildsmith, Brian. *Exodus.* Eerdmans, William B., 1999. *(P)*

## MOSSES

Greenway, Theresa. *Mosses and Liverworts.* Raintree Steck-Vaughn, 1992. *(I)*

## MOSES, GRANDMA

Kallir, Jane Katherine. *Grandma Moses: The Artist behind the Myth.* Clarkson Potter, 1982. *(I; A)*

Oneal, Zibby. *Grandma Moses: Painter of Rural America.* Viking Kestrel, 1986. *(I; A)*

## MOSQUITOES

Bernard, George, and Cooke, John. *Mosquito.* Putnam, 1982. *(I; A)*

Patent, Dorothy Hinshaw. *Mosquitoes.* Holiday, 1987. *(I)*

## MOTION

Ardley, Neil. *Making Things Move.* Watts, 1984. *(P; I); The Science Book of Motion.* Harcourt, 1992. *(P; I)*

Doherty, Paul, and Rathjen, Don. *The Spinning Blackboard and Other Dynamic Experiments on Force and Motion.* Wiley, 1996. *(I; A)*

Laithwaite, Eric. *Force: The Power behind Movement.* Watts, 1986. *(I)*

Murphy, Bryan. *Experiment with Movement.* Lerner, 1991. *(P; I)*

Taylor, Barbara. *Get it in Gear!* Random House, 1991. *(I)*

Taylor, Kim. *Action.* John Wiley, 1992. *(I)*

Watson, Philip. *Super Motion.* Lothrop, 1982. *(I)*

Zubrowski, Bernard. *Raceways: Having Fun with Balls and Tracks.* Morrow, 1985. *(I)*

## MOTION PICTURES

Aylesworth, Thomas G. *Monsters from the Movies.* Bantam, 1981. *(P; I)*

Cherrell, Gwen. *How Movies Are Made.* Facts on File, 1989. *(I)*

Cohen, Daniel. *Horror in the Movies.* Houghton, 1982. *(P; I; A)*

Gibbons, Gail. *Lights! Camera! Action! How a Movie Is Made.* Crowell, 1985. *(P)*

Levine, Michael L. *Moviemaking: A Guide for Beginners.* Scribner's, 1980. *(I; A)*

Meachum, Virginia. *Steven Spielberg: Hollywood Filmmaker.* Enslow, 1996. *(P; I)*

Platt, Richard. *Film.* Knopf, 1992. *(I; A)*

## MOTORCYCLES

Baumann, Elwood D. *An Album of Motorcycles and Motorcycle Racing.* Watts, 1982. *(I; A)*

Cave, Joyce, and Cave, Ronald. *What About . . . Motorbikes.* Watts, 1982. *(P)*

Jefferis, David. *Trailbikes.* Watts, 1984. *(P; I)*

Kerrod, Robin. *Motorcycles.* Gloucester Press, 1989. *(I)*

Radlauer, Ed, and Radlauer, Ruth. *Minibike Mania; Minibike Winners.* Children's, 1982. *(P; I)*

## MOUNTAIN CLIMBING

Bramwell, Martin. *Mountains.* Watts, 1987. *(I)*

Catchpole, Clive. *Mountains.* Dial, 1984. *(P)*

Dixon, Dougal. *Mountains.* Watts, 1984. *(P; I; A)(Atlas format)*

Fraser, Mary Ann. *On Top of the World: The Conquest of Mount Everest.* Holt, 1991. *(P; I)*

George, Jean Craighead. *One Day in the Alpine Tundra.* Harper, 1984. *(P; I)*

Hargrove, Jim, and Johnson, S. A. *Mountain Climbing.* Lerner, 1983. *(P; I; A)*

Radlauer, Ed. *Some Basics about Rock Climbing.* Children's, 1983. *(P; I; A)*

## MOUNTAINS

Bain, Ian. *Mountains and Earth Movements.* Bookwright, 1984. *(I)*

Lye, Keith. *Mountains.* Silver Burdett, 1987. *(P)*

Marcus, Elizabeth. *All about Mountains and Volcanoes.* Troll, 1984. *(P; I)*

Miller, Luree. *The Black Hat Dances: Two Buddhist Boys in the Himalayas.* Dodd, 1987. *(I)*

Siebert, Diane. *Sierra.* Harper, 1991. *(P; I)*

Stronach, Neil. *Mountains.* Lerner, 1996. *(I)*

Updegraffe, Imelda, and Updegraffe, Robert. *Mountains and Valleys.* Penguin, 1983. *(I; A)*

## MOZAMBIQUE

Boyd, Herb. *The Former Portuguese Colonies: Angola, Mozambique, Guinea-Bissau, Cape Verde, São Tomé, and Príncipe.* Watts, 1981. *(I; A)*

James, R. S. *Mozambique.* Chelsea House, 1987. *(P; I)*

## MOZART, WOLFGANG AMADEUS

Downing, Julie. *Mozart Tonight.* Bradbury, 1991. *(P)*

Gay, Peter. *Mozart.* Viking, 1999. *(A)*

Geras, Adele, and Beck, Ian. *The Random House Book of Opera Stories.* Random House, 1998. *(P; I)*

Krull, Kathleen. *Lives of the Musicians: Good Times, Bad Times (And What the Neighbors Thought).* Raintree

Steck-Vaughn, 1998. *(I; A)*

Thompson, Wendy. *Wolfgang Amadeus Mozart*. Viking, 1991. *(I)*

Weil, Lisl. *Wolferl: The First Six Years in the Life of Wolfgang Amadeus Mozart*. Holiday, 1991. *(P)*

## MUIR, JOHN

Tolan, Sally. *John Muir: Naturalist, Writer and Guardian of the North American Wilderness*. Gareth Stevens, 1990. *(I)*

## MUNICIPAL GOVERNMENT

Eichner, James A., and Shields, Linda M. *The First Book of Local Government*. Watts, 1983 (rev. ed.). *(I)*

## MUSCULAR SYSTEM

Silverstein, Alvin; Silverstein, Virginia; and Silverstein, Robert. *The Muscular System*. 21st Century Books, 1994. *(I)*

## MUSEUMS

Althea. *Visiting a Museum*. Cambridge University Press, 1983. *(I; A)*

Cutchins, Judy, and Johnston, Ginny. *Are Those Animals Real? How Museums Prepare Wildlife Exhibits*. Morrow, 1984. *(I)*

Papajani, Janet. *Museums*. Children's, 1983. *(P)*

Sandak, Cass R. *Museums: What They Are and How They Work*. Watts, 1981. *(P; I; A)*

Stan, Susan. *Careers in an Art Museum*. Lerner, 1983. *(P; I)*

## MUSHROOMS

Johnson, Sylvia A. *Mushrooms*. Lerner, 1982. *(I; A)*

Pascoe, Elaine. *Slime, Molds, and Fungi*. Blackbirch, 1998. *(P; I)*

Selsam, Millicent E. *Mushrooms*. Morrow, 1986. *(I)*

## MUSIC

Ardley, Neil. *Music*. Knopf, 1989. *(P; I; A); Sound and Music*. Watts, 1984. *(P; I)*

Ayazi-Hashjin, Sherry. *Rap and Hip Hop: The Voice of a Generation*. Rosen, 1999. *(P; I)*

Bailey, Eva. *Music and Musicians*. David & Charles, 1983. *(I; A)*

Beirne, Barbara. *A Pianist's Debut: Preparing for the Concert*. Carolrhoda, 1990. *(I)*

Geras, Adele, and Beck, Ian. *The Random House Book of Opera Stories*. Random House, 1998. *(P; I)*

Glazer, Tom. *Music for Ones and Twos: Songs and Games for the Very Young Child*. Doubleday, 1983. *(P)*

Jones, Hettie. *Big Star Fallin' Mama: Five Women in Black Music*. Viking, 1995 (rev. ed.). *(I; A)*

Kendall, Catherine W. *Stories of Composers for Young Musicians*. Toadwood, 1982. *(P; I)*

Kogan, Judith. *Nothing but the Best: The Struggle for Perfection at the Juilliard School*. Random House, 1987. *(I; A)*

Krementz, Jill. *A Very Young Musician*. Simon & Schuster, 1991. *(P; I)*

Krull, Kathleen. *Lives of the Musicians: Good Times, Bad Times (And What the Neighbors Thought)*. Harcourt, 1993. *(I; A)*

Kuskin, Karla. *The Philharmonic Gets Dressed*. Harper, 1982. *(P; I)*

Meyer, Carolyn. *Music Is for Everyone*. Good Apple, 1980. *(P; I)*

Mitchell, Barbara. *Raggin': A Story about Scott Joplin*. Scholastic, 1986. *(P; I)*

Nichols, Janet. *Women Music Makers: An Introduction to Women Composers*. Walker, 1992. *(I; A)*

Reich, Susanna. *Clara Schumann: Piano Virtuoso*. Clarion, 1999. *(I)*

Spence, Keith. *The Young People's Book of Music*. Millbrook, 1995. *(I; A)*

Tanenhaus, Sam. *Louis Armstrong*. Chelsea House, 1989. *(P; I)*

## MUSICAL INSTRUMENTS

Anderson, David. *The Piano Makers*. Pantheon, 1982. *(I)*

Berger, Melvin. *The Science of Music*. HarperCollins, 1989. *(I; A)*

Blackwood, Alan. *Musical Instruments*. Watts, 1987. *(P)*

Dearling, Robert, ed. *The Illustrated Encyclopedia of Musical Instruments*. Gale Research, 1996. *(I; A)*

Kettelkamp, Larry. *Electronic Musical Instruments: What They Do, How They Work*. Morrow, 1984. *(A)*

Koscielniak, Bruce. *The Story of the Incredible Orchestra*. Houghton, 2000. *(P)*

Sabbeth, Alex. *Rubber-Band Banjos and a Java-Jive Bass: Projects and Activities on the Science of Music and Sound*. Wiley, John & Sons, 1997. *(P; I)*

Walther, Tom. *Make Mine Music*. Little, 1981. *(P; I)*

## MUSICAL THEATER

Bany-Winters, Lisa. *Show Time!: Music, Dance, and Drama Activities for Kids*. Chicago Review Press, 2000. *(P; I)*

Malam, John. *Song and Dance*. Grolier, 2000. *(I)*

Powers, Bill. *Behind the Scenes of a Broadway Musical*. Crown, 1982. *(P; I)*

## MUSSOLINI, BENITO

Hartenian, Larry. *Benito Mussolini*. Chelsea House, 1988. *(A)*

Lyttle, Richard B. *Il Duce: The Rise and Fall of Benito Mussolini*. Atheneum, 1987. *(I)*

Mulvihill, Margaret. *Mussolini and Italian Fascism*. Gloucester Press, 1990. *(A)*

## MYTHOLOGY

*Goddesses, Heroes, and Shamans: The Young People's Guide to World Mythology*. Kingfisher, 1994. *(I)*

Al-Saleh, Khairat. *Fabled Cities, Princes, and Jinn from Arab Myths*. Peter Bedrick, 1995. *(I)*

Benson, Sally. *Stories of the Gods and Heroes.* Dial, 1940. *(P; I)*

Branston, Brian. *Gods and Heroes from Viking Mythology.* Peter Bedrick, 1994. *(I)*

Bullfinch, Thomas. *A Book of Myths.* Macmillan, 1942. *(I; A)*

D'Aulaire, Ingri, and D'Aulaire, Edgar P. *D'Aulaire's Book of Greek Myths.* Doubleday, 1962. *(P; I); D'Aulaire's Book of Norse Gods and Giants.* Doubleday, 1962. *(P; I)*

Evslin, Bernard. *Hercules.* Morrow, 1984. *(I)*

Gifford, Douglas. *Warrior Gods and Spirits from Central and South American Mythology.* Peter Bedrick, 1993. *(I); Warriors, Gods and Spirits.* Eurobook, 1983. *(I)*

Keats, Ezra Jack. *John Henry: An American Legend.* Knopf, 1965. *(P)*

Kellogg, Steven. *Paul Bunyan.* Morrow, 1984. *(P; I)*

Kingsley, Charles. *The Heroes.* W. H. Smith, 1980. *(P; I)*

Knappert, Jan. *Kings, Gods, and Spirits from African Mythology.* Peter Bedrick, 1995. *(I)*

Lanier, Sidney, ed. *Boy's King Arthur: Sir Thomas Malory's History of King Arthur and His Knights of the Round Table.* Scribner's, 1917. *(I; A)*

McCaughrean, Geraldine. *The Bronze Cauldron: Myths and Legends of the World.* Simon & Schuster/McElderry, 1998. *(P; I); The Crystal Pool: Myths and Legends of the World.* McElderry, 1999. *(P; I)*

McDermott, Gerald. *Musicians of the Sun.* Simon & Schuster, 1997. *(P)*

Mollel, Tololwa M. *The Orphan Boy.* Clarion, 1991. *(P)*

Richardson, I. M. *Demeter and Persephone: The Seasons of Time; Prometheus and the Story of Fire.* Troll, 1983. *(P; I)*

Ross, Harriet, comp. *Myths and Legends of Many Lands.* Lion, 1982. *(I; A)*

Sutcliff, Rosemary. *Sword and the Circle: King Arthur and the Knights of the Round Table.* Dutton, 1981. *(I)*

Switzer, Ellen and Costas. *Greek Myths: Gods, Heroes and Monsters: Their Sources, Their Stories and Their Meanings.* Atheneum, 1988. *(A)*

Warner, Elizabeth. *Heroes, Monsters, and Other Worlds from Russian Mythology.* Peter Bedrick, 1995. *(I)*

## NAILS, SCREWS, AND RIVETS

Welsbacher, Anne. *Screws.* Capstone Press, 2001. *(P; I)*

## NAMES AND NICKNAMES

Hook, J. N. *The Book of Names.* Watts, 1984. *(A)*

Lee, Mary P. *Your Name: All about It.* Westminster, 1980. *(P; I; A)*

Lee, Mary Price, and Lee, Richard S. *Last Names First . . . And Some First Names, Too.* Westminster, 1985. *(I; A)*

## NAMIBIA

Blumberg, Rhoda. *Southern Africa: South Africa, Namibia, Swaziland, Lesotho, and Botswana.* Watts, 1981. *(I; A)*

Gould, D. E. *Namibia.* Chelsea House, 1988. *(P; I)*

## NAPOLEON I

Marrin, Albert. *Napoleon and the Napoleonic Wars.* Viking, 1991. *(A)*

Masters, Anthony. *Napoleon.* McGraw, 1981. *(I; A)*

## NARCOTICS

Hanan, Jessica. *When Someone You Love Is Addicted.* Rosen, 1999. *(I)*

McLaughlin, Miriam Smith, and Hazouri, Sandra Peyser. *Addiction: The High That Brings You Down.* Enslow, 1997. *(I; A)*

Oliver, Marilyn Tower. *Drugs: Should They Be Legalized?* Enslow, 1996. *(I; A)*

## NASSER, GAMAL ABDEL

DeChancie, John. *Gamal Abdel Nasser.* Chelsea House, 1987. *(I; A)*

## NAST, THOMAS

Pflueger, Lynda. *Thomas Nast: Political Cartoonist.* Enslow, 2000. *(I)*

Shirley, David. *Thomas Nast: Cartoonist and Illustrator.* Watts, 1998. *(I; A)*

## NATIONAL ANTHEMS AND PATRIOTIC SONGS

Bangs, Edward. *Yankee Doodle.* Scholastic, 1980. *(P)*

Lyons, John Henry. *Stories of Our American Patriotic Songs.* Vanguard, n.d. *(I; A)*

Quiri, Patricia Ryon. *The National Anthem.* Children's Press, 1998. *(P)*

St. Pierre, Stephanie. *Our National Anthem.* Millbrook Press, 1994. *(P)*

## NATIONAL ARCHIVES

Smith, Christina Rudy. *National Archives and Record Administration.* Chelsea House, 1989. *(I; A)*

## NATIONAL ASSOCIATION FOR THE ADVANCEMENT OF COLORED PEOPLE

Fradin, Dennis Brindell, and Fradin, Judith Bloom. *Ida B. Wells: Mother of the Civil Rights Movement.* Clarion, 2000. *(I; A)*

Harris, Jacqueline L. *History and Achievement of the NAACP.* Watts, 1992. *(A)*

Hauser, Pierre. *Great Ambitions: From the 'Separate but Equal' Doctrine to the Birth of the NAACP.* Chelsea House, 1995. *(A)*

Ovington, Mary White. Luker, Ralph E., ed. *Black and White Sat Down Together: The Reminiscences of an NAACP Founder.* Feminist Press at The City University of New York, 1996. *(A)*

## NATIONAL FOREST SYSTEM

Dolan, Edward F. *American Wilderness and Its Future: Conservation Versus Use.* Watts, 1992. *(I; A)*

Patent, Dorothy Hinshaw. *Yellowstone Fires: Flames and Rebirth.* Holiday House, 1990. *(P; I)*

Vogt, Gregory. *Forests on Fire: The Fight to Save Our Trees.* Watts, 1990. *(A)*

## NATIONAL GUARD

Collins, Robert F. *America at Its Best: Opportunities in the National Guard.* Rosen, 1989. *(A)*

## NATIONAL PARK SYSTEM

Annerino, John. *Hiking the Grand Canyon.* Sierra Club Books, 1986. *(A)*

Dolan, Edward F. *American Wilderness and Its Future: Conservation Versus Use.* Watts, 1992. *(I; A)*

Lovett, Sarah. *The National Parks of the Southwest: A Young Person's Guide.* John Muir, 1990. *(P; I)*

National Park Service, Department of the Interior, Washington. D.C. 20240— a source of printed materials about the National Park System and the individual units.

Patent, Dorothy Hinshaw. *Yellowstone Fires: Flames and Rebirth.* Holiday House, 1990. *(P; I)*

Radlauer, Ruth. Books describing individual U.S. national parks: *Acadia; Bryce Canyon; Denali; Glacier; Grand Canyon; Grand Teton; Haleakala, Mammoth Cave; Mesa Verde; Olympic; Shenandoah; Zion.* Children's, 1977-1982. *(P; I; A)*

## NATURE, STUDY OF

Burnie, David. *How Nature Works: 100 Ways Parents and Kids Can Share the Secrets of Nature.* Reader's Digest, 1991. *(I)*

Faber, Doris, and Faber, Harold. *Great Lives: Nature and the Environment.* Scribner's, 1991. *(I; A)*

Huber, Carey. *Nature Explorer: A Step-by-Step Guide.* Troll, 1990. *(I)*

Keene, Ann T. *Earthkeepers: Observers and Protectors of Nature.* Oxford, 1993. *(I; A)*

Parker, Steve. *The Random House Book of How Nature Works.* Random House, 1993. *(I)*

Potter, Jean. *Nature in a Nutshell for Kids: Over 100 Activities You Can Do in Ten Minutes or Less.* John Wiley, 1995. *(P)*

## NAVIGATION

Dash, Joan. *The Longitude Prize.* Farrar, Straus & Giroux, 2000. *(I; A)*

Wilkinson, Philip. *Ships: History, Battles, Discovery, Navigation.* Larousse Kingfisher Chambers, 2000. *(P; I)*

## NEBRASKA

Fradin, Dennis. *Nebraska: In Words and Pictures.* Children's, 1980. *(P; I)*

Hargrove, Jim. *Nebraska.* Children's, 1989. *(P; I)*

Manley, Robert N. *Nebraska: Our Pioneer Heritage.* Media Productions, 1981. *(I)*

Thompson, Kathleen. *Nebraska.* Raintree, 1988. *(P; I)*

## NEBULAS

Branley, Franklyn M. *Superstar: The Supernova of 1987.* HarperCollins, 1990. *(P; I)*

## NEEDLECRAFT

Cone, Ferne G. *Classy Knitting: A Guide to Creative Sweatering for Beginners.* Atheneum, 1984; *Crazy Crocheting.* Atheneum, 1981. *(I; A)*

Eaton, Jan. *The Encyclopedia of Sewing Techniques.* Barron, 1987. *(A)*

## NEON AND OTHER NOBLE GASES

Heiserman, David L. *Exploring Chemical Elements and Their Compounds.* McGraw-Hill, 1991. *(A)*

## NEPAL

*Nepal . . . in Pictures.* Lerner, 1989. *(I; A)*

Knowlton, MaryLee, and Sachner, Mark J. *Nepal.* Gareth Stevens, 1987. *(P)*

Margolies, Barbara A. *Kanu of Kathmandu: A Journey in Nepal.* Four Winds, 1992. *(P; I)*

Watanabe, Hitomi. *Nepal.* Gareth Stevens, 1987. *(P)*

## NEPTUNE

Asimov, Isaac. *How Did We Find Out about Neptune?* Walker, 1990. *(I; A)*

Branley, Franklyn M. *Neptune: Voyager's Final Target.* HarperCollins, 1992. *(P; I)*

Simon, Seymour. *Neptune.* Morrow, 1991. *(P; I)*

## NERVOUS SYSTEM

Silverstein, Alvin; Silverstein, Virginia; and Silverstein, Robert. *The Nervous System.* 21st Century Books, 1994. *(I)*

## NETHERLANDS

Fairclough, Chris. *Take a Trip to Holland.* Watts, 1984. *(P; I)*

Fradin, Dennis B. *The Netherlands.* Children's, 1983. *(I; A)*

Jacobsen, Peter O., and Kristensen, Preben S. *A Family in Holland.* Watts, 1984. *(P; I)*

## NEVADA

Fradin, Dennis. *Nevada: In Words and Pictures.* Children's, 1981.

## NEW BRUNSWICK

Levert, Suzanne. *New Brunswick.* Chelsea House, 2000. *(I)*

## NEWFOUNDLAND

Jackson, Lawrence. *Newfoundland and Labrador.* Lerner, 1995. *(P)*

## NEW HAMPSHIRE

Dubois, Muriel L. *New Hampshire: Facts and Symbols.* Capstone/Hilltop, 2000. *(P)*

Fradin, Dennis. *New Hampshire: In Words and Pictures.* Children's, 1981; *The New Hampshire Colony,* 1988. *(P; I)*

## NEW JERSEY

Homer, Larona. *The Shore Ghosts and Other Stories of New Jersey.* Middle Atlantic Press, 1981. *(P; I)*

Kent, Deborah. *New Jersey.* Children's, 1988. *(P; I)*

Murray, Thomas C., and Barnes, Valerie. *The Seven Wonders of New Jersey— And Then Some*Enslow, 1981. *(P; I)*

Rabold, Ted, and Fair, Phillip. *New Jersey: Yesterday and Today.* Penns Valley, 1982. *(P; I)*

Stein, R. Conrad. *New Jersey.* Children's Press, 1998. *(I)*

## NEW MEXICO

Kent, Deborah. *New Mexico.* Children's Press, 1999. *(I; A)*

Stein, R. Conrad. *New Mexico.* Children's Press, 1988. *(P)*

## NEW ORLEANS

Hintz, Martin. *Destination New Orleans.* Lerner, 1997. *(P; I)*

## NEWSPAPERS

Carey, Helen, and Greenberg, Judith H. *How to Read a Newspaper.* Watts, 1983. *(I; A)*

Crisman, Ruth. *Hot off the Press: Getting the News into Print.* Lerner, 1991. *(I; A)*

English, Betty Lou. *Behind the Headlines at a Big City Paper.* Lothrop, 1985. *(A)*

Leedy, Loreen. *The Furry News: How to Make a Newspaper.* Holiday, 1990. *(P)*

Lipson, Greta, and Greenberg, Bernice. *Extra! Extra! Read All about It.* Good Apple, 1981. *(P; I)*

Miller, Margaret. *Hot off the Press! A Day at the Daily News.* Crown, 1985. *(I)*

Tebbel, John. *Opportunities in Journalism.* VGM Career Horizons, 1982. *(I; A)*

Waters, Sarah. *How Newspapers Are Made.* Facts on File, 1989. *(I)*

## NEWTON, ISAAC

Hizeroth, Deborah, and Leon, Sharon. *The Importance of Sir Isaac Newton.* Lucent, 1994. *(I; A)*

Ipsen, D. C. *Isaac Newton: Reluctant Genius.* Enslow, 1986. *(I; A)*

White, Michael. *Sir Isaac Newton: Discovering Laws That Govern the Universe.* Blackbirch Press, 1999. *(I)*

## NEW YEAR CELEBRATIONS AROUND THE WORLD

Van Straalen, Alice. *The Book of Holidays around the World.* Dutton, 1987. *(A)*

## NEW YORK

Schomp, Virginia. *New York.* Benchmark, 1996. *(I)*

Stein, R. Conrad. *New York.* Children's, 1989. *(P; I)*

Thompson, Kathleen. *New York.* Raintree, 1988. *(P; I)*

## NEW YORK CITY

Adams, Barbara Johnston. *New York City.* Dillon, 1988. *(P)*

Krustrup, Erik V. *Gateway to America: New York City.* Creative Education, 1982. *(I; A)*

Lovett, Sarah. *Kidding around New York City: A Young Person's Guide to the City.* John Muir, 1989. *(I; A)*

Munro, Roxie. *The Inside-Outside Book of New York City.* Dodd, 1985. *(P)*

## NEW ZEALAND

Anderson, Margaret J. *Light in the Mountain.* Knopf, 1982. *(I)*

Armitage, Ronda. *New Zealand.* Bookwright, 1988. *(P)*

Ball, John. *We Live in New Zealand.* Watts, 1984. *(I; A)*

Keyworth, Valerie. *New Zealand: Land of the Long White Cloud.* Dillon, 1990. *(I)*

Knowlton, MaryLee, and Sachner, Mark J. *New Zealand.* Gareth Stevens, 1987. *(P)*

Yanagi, Akinobu. *New Zealand.* Gareth Stevens, 1987. *(P; I)*

## NICARAGUA

Hanmer, Trudy J. *Nicaragua.* Watts, 1986. *(I)*

Haverstock, Nathan A. *Nicaragua . . . in Pictures.* Lerner, 1987. *(I; A)*

Kott, Jennifer. *Nicaragua.* Marshall Cavendish, 1994. *(I; A)*

## NICHOLAS

Vogt, George. *Nicholas II.* Chelsea House, 1987. *(I; A)*

## NICKEL

Heiserman, David L. *Exploring Chemical Elements and Their Compounds.* McGraw-Hill, 1991. *(A)*

## NIGERIA

*Nigeria . . . in Pictures.* Lerner, 1988. *(P; I)*

Adeeb, Hassan, and Adeeb, Bonnetta. *Nigeria: One Nation, Many Cultures.* Benchmark, 1995. *(I)*

Anderson, Lydia. *Nigeria, Cameroon, and the Central African Republic.* Watts, 1981. *(I; A)*

Barker, Carol. *A Family in Nigeria.* Lerner, 1985. *(P)*

Millar, Heather. *The Kingdom of Benin in West Africa.* Marshall Cavendish, 1996. *(I)*

Peffer, John. *The Benin Kingdom of West Africa.* Rosen, 1996. *(P)*

## NIGHTINGALE, FLORENCE

Gorrell, Gena K. *Heart and Soul: The Story of Florence Nightingale.* Tundra Books, 2000. *(I)*

Koch, Charlotte. *Florence Nightingale.* Dandelion, 1979. *(P; I)*

## NILE RIVER

Percefull, Aaron W. *The Nile.* Watts, 1984. *(I; A)*

## NITROGEN

Farndon, John. *Nitrogen.* Marshall Cavendish, 1998. *(P; I)*

Heiserman, David L. *Exploring Chemical Elements and Their Compounds.* McGraw-Hill, 1991. *(A)*

## NIXON, RICHARD M.

Barron, Rachel. *Richard Nixon: American Politician.* Morgan Reynolds, 1998. *(I; A)*

Cook, Fred J. *The Crimes of Watergate.* Watts, 1981. *(A)*

Lillegard, Dee. *Richard Nixon: Thirty-Seventh President of the United States.* Children's, 1988. *(P; I)*

Ripley, C. Peter. *Richard Nixon.* Chelsea House, 1987. *(A)*

## NOBEL PRIZES

Abrams, Irwin. *The Nobel Peace Prize and the Laureates: An Illustrated Biographical History 1901-1987.* G. K. Hall, 1988. *(A)*

Asseng, Nathan. *The Disease Fighters: The Nobel Prize in Medicine.* Lerner, 1987. *(P; I); The Inventors: Nobel Prizes in Chemistry, Physics, and Medicine,* 1988. *(I); The Peace Seekers: The Nobel Peace Prize,* 1987. *(I)*

McGrayne, Sharon Bertsch. *Nobel Prize Women in Science.* Birch Lane Press, 1993. *(A)*

## NOISE

Finney, Shan. *Noise Pollution.* Watts, 1984. *(I; A)*

Wright, Lynne. *The Science of Noise.* Raintree Steck-Vaughn, 2000. *(I)*

## NOMADS

Halliburton, Warren J. *Nomads of the Sahara.* Burdett Press, 1992. *(I)*

Jenkins, Martin. *Deserts.* Lerner, 1996. *(I)*

## NORSE MYTHOLOGY

Colum, Padraic. *The Children of Odin.* Haverton Books, 1920. *(I; A)*

Coolidge, Olivia. *Legends of the North.* Houghton, 1951. *(I; A)*

D'Aulaire, Ingri, and D'Aulaire, Edgar P. *Norse Gods and Giants.* Doubleday, 1967. *(P; I)*

Osborne, Mary Pope. *Favorite Norse Myths.* Scholastic, 1996. *(P; I)*

## NORTH AMERICA

Petersen, David. *North America.* Children's Press, 1998. *(P)*

Simon, Seymour. *Winter across America.* Hyperion, 1994. *(P; I)*

## NORTH CAROLINA

Fradin, Dennis. *North Carolina: In Words and Pictures.* Children's, 1980. *(P; I)*

Hintz, Martin, and Hintz, Stephen. *North Carolina.* Children's Press, 1998. *(I)*

## NORTH DAKOTA

Fradin, Dennis. *North Dakota: In Words and Pictures.* Children's, 1981. *(P; I)*

Herguth, Margaret S. *North Dakota.* Children's, 1990. *(I)*

## NORTHERN IRELAND

Parker, Tony. *May the Lord in His Mercy Be Kind to Belfast.* Holt, 1994. *(A)*

## NORTHWEST PASSAGE

Chrisp, Peter. *The Search for a Northern Route.* Thomson Learning, 1993. *(P; I)*

Delgado, James P. *Across the Top of the World: The Quest for the Northwest Passage.* Facts on File, 1999. *(A)*

## NORTHWEST TERRITORIES

Levert, Suzanne. *Northwest Territories.* Chelsea House, 1992. *(I; A)*

## NORWAY

Kagda, Sakina. *Norway.* Marshall Cavendish, 1995. *(I; A)*

St. John, Jetty. *A Family in Norway.* Lerner, 1988. *(P)*

## NOVA SCOTIA

Sheppard, George, and Levert, Suzanne. *Nova Scotia.* Chelsea House, 2000. *(I)*

## NUCLEAR ENERGY

Andryszewski, Tricia. *What to Do about Nuclear Waste.* Millbrook, 1995. *(I; A)*

Barron, Rachel Stiffler. *Lise Meitner: Discoverer of Nuclear Fission.* Morgan Reynolds, 2000. *(I; A)*

Beyer, Don E. *The Manhattan Project: America Makes the First Atomic Bomb.* Watts, 1991. *(A)*

Cheney, Glenn Alan. *Nuclear Proliferation: The Problems and Possibilities.* Watts, 1999. *(I; A)*

Cohen, Daniel. *The Manhattan Project.* Millbrook, 1999. *(I; A)*

Dolan, Edward F., and Scariano, Margaret M. *Nuclear Waste: The 10,000-Year Challenge.* Watts, 1990. *(A)*

Feldbaum, Carl B., and Bee, Ronald J. *Looking the Tiger in the Eye: Confronting the Nuclear Threat.* Harper, 1988. *(A)*

Fox, Karen. *The Chain Reaction: Pioneers of Nuclear Science.* Watts, 1998. *(I; A)*

Fradin, Dennis B. *Nuclear Energy.* Children's, 1987. *(P)*

Gonzales, Doreen. *The Manhattan Project and the Atomic Bomb in American History.* Enslow, 2000. *(I; A)*

Hare, Tony. *Nuclear Waste Disposal.* Gloucester Press, dist. by Watts, 1991. *(I)*

Holland, Gini. *Nuclear Energy.* Benchmark, 1996. *(I; A)*

Kidd, J.S., and Kidd, Renee A. *Quarks and Sparks: The Story of Nuclear Power.* Facts on File, 1999. *(I; A)*

Lampton, Christopher. *Nuclear Accident.* Millbrook, 1992. *(I)*

Nardo, Don. *Chernobyl.* Lucent Books, 1990. *(I; A)*

Pringle, Laurence. *Nuclear Energy: Troubled Past, Uncertain Future.* Macmillan, 1989. *(I; A); Radiation: Waves and Particles, Benefits and Risks.* Enslow, 1983. *(I; A)*

Smoke, Richard. *Nuclear Arms Control: Understanding the Arms Race.* Walker, 1988. *(A)*

Wilcox, Charlotte. *Powerhouse: Inside a Nuclear Power Plant.* Carolrhoda, 1996. *(I; A)*

Williams, Gene B. *Nuclear War, Nuclear Winter.* Watts, 1987. *(I; A)*

## NUMERALS AND NUMERATION SYSTEMS

Schmandt-Besserat, Denise. *The History of Counting.* Morrow, 1999. *(P; I)*

## NUMBER PATTERNS

Smoothey, Marion. *Let's Investigate Number Patterns; Let's Investigate Shape Patterns.* Marshall Cavendish, 1993. *(I)*

## NUMBER PUZZLES AND GAMES

Buller, Laura, and Taylor, Ron. *Calculation and Chance.* Marshall Cavendish, 1990. *(I)*

Weaver, Charles. *Hidden Logic Puzzles.* Sterling, 1992. *(I; A)*

## NUMBERS AND NUMBER SYSTEMS

Challoner, Jack. *The Science Book of Numbers.* Harcourt, 1992. *(P; I)*

Giesert, Arthur. *Roman Numerals I to MM.* Houghton, 1995. *(P; I)*

Hartmann, Wendy. *One Sun Rises: An African Wildlife Counting Book.* Dutton, 1994. *(P)*

Heinst, Marie. *My First Number Book.* Dorling Kindersley, 1992. *(P)*

Schmandt-Besserat, Denise. *The History of Counting.* Morrow, 1999. *(P; I)*

Smoothey, Marion. *Let's Investigate Numbers.* Marshall Cavendish, 1993. *(I)*

Tallarico, Tony. *Numbers.* Tuffy Books, 1982. *(P; I)*

## NUNAVUT

Finley, Carol. *Art of the Far North: Inuit Sculpture, Drawing, and Printmaking.* Lerner, 1998. *(P; I)*

Oberman, Sheldon. *The Shaman's Nephew: A Life in the Far North.* Stoddart, 2000. *(P; I)*

Wallace, Mary. *The Inuksuk Book.* Firefly, 1999. *(P; I)*

## NURSERY RHYMES

De Angeli, Marguerite. *Book of Nursery and Mother Goose Rhymes.* Doubleday, 1954. *(P; I)*

De Paola, Tomie. *Tomie de Paola's Mother Goose.* Putnam, 1985. *(P)*

Greenaway, Kate, illus. *Mother Goose: Or, the Old Nursery Rhymes.* Warne, 1882. *(P)*

Greenberg, David T. *Whatever Happened to Humpty Dumpty?: And Other Surprising Sequels to Mother Goose Rhymes.* Little, Brown, 1999. *(P; I)*

Kroll, Virginia. *Jaha and Jamil Went down the Hill: An African Mother Goose.* Charsbridge, 1995. *(P)*

Lewis, Bobby, illus. *Mother Goose: Home before Midnight.* Lothrop, 1984. *(P)*

Lobel, Arnold. *The Random House Book of Mother Goose.* Random House, 1986. *(P; I)*

Opie, Iona, and Opie, Peter. *A Nursery Companion.* Oxford University Press, 1980; *Oxford Nursery Rhyme Book,* 1955. *(P)*

Potter, Beatrix. *Appley Dapply's Nursery Rhymes.* Warne, 1917; *Cecily Parsley's Nursery Rhymes,* 1922. *(P)*

Provensen, Alice, and Provensen, Martin, illus. *Old Mother Hubbard.* Random House, 1982. *(P)*

Rockwell, Anne. *Gray Goose and Gander and Other Mother Goose Rhymes.* Harper, 1980. *(P)*

Wyndham, Robert. *Chinese Mother Goose Rhymes.* Putnam, 1982. *(P)*

## NURSES AND NURSING

Donahue, M. Patricia. *Nursing, the Finest Art: An Illustrated History.* Abrams, 1986. *(A)*

Seide, Diane. *Nurse Power: New Vistas in Nursing.* Lodestar, 1985. *(A)*

Storring, Rod. *A Doctor's Life: A Visual History of Doctors and Nurses Through the Ages.* Dutton, 1998. *(P; I)*

Wandro, Mark, and Blank, Joani. *My Daddy Is a Nurse.* Addison-Wesley, 1981. *(P; I)*

Witty, Margot. *A Day in the Life of an Emergency Room Nurse.* Troll, 1981. *(P; I)*

## NUTRITION

Arnold, Caroline. *Too Fat? Too Thin? Do You Have a Choice?* Morrow, 1984. *(I)*

Baldwin, Dorothy, and Lister, Claire. *Your Body Fuel.* Watts, 1984. *(I; A)*

Fretz, Sada. *Going Vegetarian: A Guide for Teenagers.* Morrow, 1983. *(I; A)*

Hughes, Meredith Sayles. *Spill the Beans and Pass the Peanuts: Legumes.* Lerner, 1999. *(P; I)*

Krizmanic, Judy. *A Teen's Guide to Going Vegetarian.* Viking, 1994. *(A)*

Newton, Lesley. *Meatballs and Molecules: The Science Behind Food.* A. & C. Black, 1984. *(P; I)*

Nottridge, Rhoda. *Fats.* Carolrhoda, 1993. *(I)*

Patent, Dorothy Hinshaw. *Nutrition: What's in the Food We Eat.* Holiday, 1992. *(P; I)*

Peavy, Linda, and Smith, Ursula. *Food, Nutrition, and You.* Scribner's, 1982. *(I; A)*

Sanchez, Gail Jones, and Gerbino, Mary. *Overeating: Let's Talk about It.* Dillon, 1986. *(I; A)*

Sexias, Judith S. *Junk Food: What It Is, What It Does.* Greenwillow, 1984. *(P)*

Silverstein, Dr. Alvin. *Carbohydrates; Fats; Proteins; Vitamins and Minerals.* Millbrook, 1992. *(I)*

Smaridge, Norah. *What's on Your Plate?* Abingdon, 1982. *(P)*

Thompson, Paul. *Nutrition.* Watts, 1981. *(I; A)*

VanCleave, Janice. *Janice VanCleave's Food and Nutrition for Every Kid: Easy Activities That Make Learning Science Fun.* Wiley, 1999. *(I)*

## NYLON AND OTHER SYNTHETIC FIBERS

Keeler, Patricia A., and McCall, Francis X., Jr. *Unraveling Fibers.* Macmillan, 1995. *(I)*

## OAKLEY, ANNIE

Harrison, and others. *Annie Oakley.* Dormac, 1981. *(P; I; A)*

## OATS

Hughes, Meredith Sayles, and Hughes, E. Thomas. *Glorious Grasses: The Grains.* Lerner, 1998. *(I)*

## OCCUPATIONAL HEALTH AND SAFETY

Wax, Nina. *Occupational Health.* Chelsea House, 1994. *(A)*

## OCEAN

Carson, Rachel L. *The Sea around Us.* Oxford University Press, 1961. *(A)*

Carter, Katherine J. *Oceans.* Children's, 1982. *(P)*

Cole, Joanna. *The Magic School Bus on the Ocean Floor.* Scholastic, 1992. *(P)*

Doubilet, Anne. *Under the Sea from A to Z.* Crown, 1991. *(P)*

Elting, Mary. *Mysterious Seas.* Putnam, 1983. *(P; I)*

Fine, John Christopher. *Oceans in Peril.* Atheneum, 1987. *(A)*

Levinson, Riki. *Our Home Is the Sea.* Dutton, 1988. *(P)*

Mattson, Robert A. *The Living Ocean.* Enslow, 1991. *(I)*

Meyerson, A. Lee. *Seawater: A Delicate Balance.* Enslow, 1988. *(I; A)*

Rayner, Ralph. *Undersea Technology.* Bookwright, 1990. *(I)*

Sedge, Michael H. *Commercialization of the Oceans.* Watts, 1987. *(I; A)*

Simon, Anne W. *Neptune's Revenge: The Ocean of Tomorrow.* Watts, 1984. *(A)*

Simon, Seymour. *How to Be an Ocean Scientist in Your Own Home.* Lippincott, 1988. *(I; A); Oceans.* Morrow, 1990. *(P; I)*

VanCleave, Janice. *Janice VanCleave's Oceans for Every Kid: Easy Activities That Make Learning Science Fun.* Wiley, 1996. *(I; A)*

Wu, Norbert. *Life in the Oceans.* Little, 1991. *(I)*

## OCEAN LINERS

Huff, Barbara A. *Welcome Aboard!: Traveling on an Ocean Liner.* Houghton Mifflin, 1987. *(I)*

## OCEANOGRAPHY

Asimov, Isaac. *How Did We Find Out about Life in the Deep Sea?* Walker, 1981. *(I)*

Ballard, Robert D. *Exploring the Titanic.* Scholastic, 1988. *(P; I)*

Blair, Carvel Hall. *Exploring the Sea: Oceanography Today.* Random House, 1986. *(I)*

Blumberg, Rhoda. *The First Travel Guide to the Bottom of the Sea.* Lothrop, 1983. *(I)*

Bramwell, Martyn. *Oceanography.* Watts, 1989. *(P; I); Oceans.* Watts, 1984. *(P; I)* (Atlas format)

Gibbons, Gail. *Sunken Treasure.* Crowell, 1988. *(P); Exploring the Deep, Dark Sea.* Little, Brown, 1999. *(P; I)*

Kovacs, Deborah, and Madin, Kate. *Beneath Blue Waters: Meetings with Remarkable Deep-Sea Creatures.* Viking, 1996. *(I);*

Kovacs, Deborah. *Dive to the Deep Ocean: Voyages of Exploration and Discovery; Off to Sea: An Inside Look at a Research Cruise.* Raintree/Steck-Vaughn, 1999. *(P; I)*

Lampton, Christopher. *Undersea Archaeology.* Watts, 1988. *(I)*

Polking, Kirk. *Oceanographers and Explorers of the Sea.* Enslow, 1999. *(I; A)*

## OCEANS AND SEAS OF THE WORLD

Lambert, David. *The Oceans.* Watts, 1984. *(I; A)*

Polking, Kirk. *Oceans of the World: Our Essential Resource.* Putnam, 1983. *(I; A);*

## OCTOBER

Updike, John. *A Child's Calendar.* Holiday House, 1999. *(P; I)*

Warner, Penny. *Kids' Holiday Fun: Great Family Activities Every Month of the Year.* Meadowbrook Press, 1997. *(P)*

## ODYSSEY

Connoly, Peter, retel. *The Legend of Odysseus.* Oxford University Press, 1988. *(A)*

McLaren, Clemence, retel. *Waiting for Odysseus.* Simon & Schuster, 2000. *(I; A)*

Philip, Neil, retel. *The Adventures of Odysseus.* Orchard, 1997. *(P; I)*

Sutcliff, Rosemary, retel. *The Wanderings of Odysseus: The Story of the Odyssey.* Delacorte Press, 1996. *(I)*

## OGLETHORPE, JAMES

Blackburn, Joyce. *James Edward Oglethorpe.* Dodd, 1983. *(I; A)*

## OHIO

Fox, Mary Virginia. *Ohio.* Watts, 1987. *(P; I)*

Kent, Deborah. *Ohio.* Children's, 1989. *(P; I)*

## OILS AND FATS

Nottridge, Rhoda. *Fats.* Lerner, 1993. *(P)*

## O'KEEFFE, GEORGIA

Berry, Michael. *Georgia O'Keeffe.* Chelsea House, 1988. *(A)*

Gherman, Beverly. *Georgia O'Keeffe: The Wideness and Wonder of Her World.* Atheneum, 1986. *(I; A)*

Lowery, Linda. *Georgia O'Keefe.* Carolrhoda, 1996. *(P)*

Nicholson, Lois. P. *Georgia O'Keeffe.* Lucent, 1995. *(I; A)*

## OKLAHOMA

Heinrichs, Ann. *Oklahoma.* Children's, 1989. *(P; I)*

Newsom, D. Earl. *The Birth of Oklahoma.* Evans Publications, 1983. *(I; A)*

Reeds, Jerry. *Oklahoma.* Children's Press, 1998. *(I)*

Ross, Jim, and Meyers, Paul, eds. *Dear Oklahoma City, Get Well Soon.* Walker, 1996. *(I)*

## OLD AGE

Dychtwald, Ken, and Flower, Joe. *Age Wave: The Challenges and Opportunities of an Aging America.* Tarcher, 1989. *(A)*

Langone, John. *Growing Older: What Young People Should Know about Aging.* Little, 1990. *(I; A)*

## OLYMPIC GAMES

Aaseng, Nate. *Great Summer Olympic Moments; Great Winter Olympic Moments.* Lerner, 1990. *(I; A)*

Ditchfield, Christin. *Swimming and Diving.* Children's Press, 2000. *(P)*

Knight, Theodore. *The Olympic Games.* Lucent, 1991. *(P; I)*

Knotts, Bob. *The Summer Olympics.* Children's Press, 2000. *(P)*

Middleton, Haydn. *Crises at the Olympics; Modern Olympic Games.* Heinemann, 1999. *(P; I)*

Uschan, Michael V. *Male Olympic Champions.* Lucent, 1999. *(I; A)*

Wallechinsky, David. *The Complete Book of the Olympics.* Viking, 1987. *(A)*

Woff, Richard. *The Ancient Greek Olympics.* Oxford, 2000. *(I)*

## O'NEILL, EUGENE

Siebold, Thomas, ed. *Readings on Eugene O'Neill* Greenhaven Press, 1997. *(A)*

## ONTARIO

LeVert, Suzanne. *Ontario.* Chelsea House, 1990. *(I);*

## OPERA

Englander, Roger. *Opera! What's All the Screaming About?* Walker, 1983. *(I; A)*

Geras, Adele, and Beck, Ian. *The Random House Book of Opera Stories.* Random House, 1998. *(P; I)*

## OPOSSUMS

Rue, Leonard Lee, and Owen, William. *Meet the Opossum.* Dodd, 1983. *(P; I)*

## OPTICAL ILLUSIONS

Doherty, Paul, and Rathjen, Don. *The Cheshire Cat and Other Eye-Popping Experiments on How We See the World.* Wiley, 1995. *(I)*

O'Neill, Catherine. *You Won't Believe Your Eyes!* National Geographic, 1987. *(P; I)*

White, Laurence B., and Broekel, Ray. *Optical Illusions.* Watts, 1986. *(P; I)*

## OPTICAL INSTRUMENTS

Levine, Shar, and Johnstone, Leslie. *The Optics Book: Fun Experiments With Light, Vision and Color.* Sterling, 1999; *The Microscope Book.* Sterling, 1997. *(I)*

Tomb, Howard, and Kunkel, Dennis. *Microaliens: Dazzling Journeys With an Electron Microscope.* Farrar, Straus & Giroux, 1993. *(I; A)*

## ORCHESTRA

Blackwood, Alan. *The Orchestra: An Introduction to the World of Classical Music.* Millbrook, 1993. *(I; A)*

Hayes, Ann. *Meet the Orchestra.* Gulliver Books, 1991. *(P)*

Kuskin, Karla. *The Philharmonic Gets Dressed.* Harper, 1982. *(P)*

Rubin, Mark. *The Orchestra.* Douglas & McIntyre, 1984. *(P)*

Storms, Laura. *Careers with an Orchestra.* Lerner, 1983. *(P; I)*

## OREGON

Bratvold, Gretchen. *Oregon.* Lerner, 1991. *(I)*

Stein, R. Conrad. *Oregon.* Children's, 1989. *(P; I)*

## ORGAN

Dearling, Robert, ed. *The Illustrated Encyclopedia of Musical Instruments.* Gale Research, 1996. *(I; A)*

## ORIENTAL ART AND ARCHITECTURE

MacDonald, Fiona. *A Samurai Castle.* NTC, 1995. *(I)*

Zhensun, Zheng, and Low, Alice. *A Young Painter: The Life and Paintings of Wang Yani-China's Extraordinary Young Artist.* Scholastic, 1991. *(I; A)*

## ORIGAMI

Nakano, Dokuohtei. *Easy Origami.* Viking Kestrel, 1986. *(P)*

Takahama, Toshie. *Origami for Fun: Thirty-One Basic Models.* Tuttle, 1980. *(P; I)*

## ORTHODONTICS

Betancourt, Jeanne. *Smile: How to Cope with Braces.* Knopf, 1982. *(I; A)*

## ORWELL, GEORGE

Agathocleous, Tanya. *George Orwell: Battling Big Brother.* Oxford, 2000. *(I; A)*

Flynn, Nigel. *Life and Works: George Orwell.* Rourke, 1990. *(A)*

## OSCEOLA

Sanford, William Reynolds. *Osceola: Seminole Warrior.* Enslow, 1994. *(I)*

## OSTRICHES AND OTHER FLIGHTLESS BIRDS

Arnold, Carolyn. *Ostriches and Other Flightless Birds.* Carolrhoda, 1990. *(I)*

## OTHELLO

Lester, Julius, and Shakespeare, William. *Othello.* Scholastic, 1998. *(A)*

## OTTERS AND OTHER MUSTELIDS

Aronsky, Jim. *Otters Under Water.* Putnam, 1992. *(P)*
Ashby, Ruth. *Sea Otters.* Atheneum, 1990. *(I)*
Hurd, Edith T. *Song of the Sea Otter.* Pantheon, 1983. *(P; I)*
Lavine, Sigmund A. *Wonders of Badgers.* Dodd, 1985. *(I)*
Smith, Roland. *Sea Otter Rescue: The Aftermath of an Oil Spill.* Cobblehill, 1990. *(I)*

## OUTDOOR COOKING AND PICNICS

Haines, Gail K. *Baking in a Box, Cooking on a Can.* Morrow, 1981. *(I)*

## OVERLAND TRAILS

Blackwood, Gary L. *Life on the Oregon Trail.* Lucent, 1999. *(I)*
Calabro, Marian. *The Perilous Journey of the Donner Party.* Clarion, 1999. *(I)*

## OWLS

Arnosky, Jim. *All about Owls.* Scholastic, 1995. *(P)*
Burton, Jane. *Buffy the Barn Owl.* Gareth Stevens, 1989. *(P)*
Esbensen, Barbara Juster. *Tiger with Wings: The Great Horned Owl.* Orchard: Watts, 1991. *(P)*
George, Jean Craighead. *The Moon of the Owls.* HarperCollins, 1993. *(I)*
Guiberson, Brenda Z. *Spotted Owl: Bird of the Ancient Forest.* Holt, 1994. *(P; I)*
Hunt, Patricia. *Snowy Owls.* Dodd, 1982. *(P; I)*
Sadoway, Margaret W. *Owls: Hunters of the Night.* Lerner, 1981. *(P; I)*
Storms, Laura. *The Owl Book.* Lerner, 1983. *(P; I)*

## OXYGEN AND OXIDATION

Farndon, John. *Oxygen.* Marshall Cavendish, 1998. *(P; I)*
Fitzgerald, Karen. *The Story of Oxygen.* Watts, 1996. *(I; A)*

## OYSTERS, OCTOPUSES, AND OTHER MOLLUSKS

Bunting, Eve. *The Giant Squid.* Messner, 1981. *(I)*

Cerullo, Mary M. *The Octopus: Phantom of the Sea.* Cobblehill, 1997. *(I; A)*
Johnson, Sylvia A. *Snails.* Lerner, 1982. *(I)*
Martin, James. *Tentacles: The Amazing World of Octopus, Squid, and Their Relatives.* Crown, 1993. *(I)*

## PACIFIC OCEAN AND ISLANDS

Deverell, Gweneth. *Follow the Sun . . . to Tahiti, to Western Samoa, to Fiji, to Melanesia, to Micronesia.* Friends Press, 1982. *(P)*
Kamikamica, Esiteri, comp. by. *Come to My Place: Meet My Island Family.* Friends Press, 1982. *(P; I)*

## PAINE, THOMAS

Kaye, Harvey J. *Thomas Paine: Firebrand of the Revolution.* Oxford, 2000. *(I; A)*

## PAINTING

Couch, Tony. *Watercolor: You Can Do It!* North Light Books, 1987. *(A)*
Cumming, Robert. *Just Look: A Book about Paintings.* Scribner's, 1980. *(P; I)*

## PAKISTAN

Hughes, Libby. *From Prison to Prime Minister: A Biography of Benazir Bhutto.* Dillon, 1990. *(I; A)*
Rumalshah, Mano. *Pakistan.* Hamish Hamilton, 1992. *(P; I)*
Weston, Mark. *The Land and People of Pakistan.* HarperCollins, 1992. *(A)*
Yusufali, Jabeen. *Pakistan: An Islamic Treasure.* Dillon, 1990. *(I)*

## PALESTINE

Corzine, Phyllis. *The Palestinian-Israeli Accord.* Lucent, 1996. *(I; A)*

## PANAMA

Rau, Dana Meachen. *Panama.* Children's Press, 1999. *(I)*

## PANAMA CANAL

Gaines, Ann Graham. *The Panama Canal in American History.* Enslow, 1999. *(I; A)*
Gold, Susan Dudley. *The Panama Canal Transfer: Controversy at the Crossroads.* Raintree/Steck-Vaughn, 1999. *(I; A)*
Markun, Patricia Maloney. *It's Panama's Canal!* Linnet, 1999. *(I)*
St. George, Judith. *Panama Canal: Gateway to the World.* Putnam, 1989. *(I; A)*
Winkelman, Barbara Gaines. *The Panama Canal.* Children's Press, 1999. *(I)*

## PANDAS

Bailey, Jill. *Project Panda.* Steck-Vaughn, 1990. *(P; I)*
Barrett, N. S. *Pandas.* Watts, 1988. *(P; I)*

Dudley, Karen. *Giant Pandas*. Raintree/Steck-Vaughn, 1997. *(P; I)*

McClung, Robert M. *Lili: A Giant Panda of Sichuan*. Morrow, 1988. *(P; I)*

Wexo, John Bonnett. *Giant Pandas*. Creative Education, 1988. *(P)*

## PAPER

Perrins, Lesley. *How Paper Is Made*. Facts on File, 1985. *(P; I)*

## PAPIER-MÂCHÉ

McGraw, Sheila. *Papier-Mâché for Kids*. Firefly, 1991. *(P; I*

Schwartz, Renee F. *Papier-Mâché*. Kids Can Press, 2000. *(I)*

## PAPUA NEW GUINEA

Fox, Mary Virginia. *Papua New Guinea*. Children's Press, 1996. *(P; I)*

## PARAGUAY

Naverstock, Nathan A. *Paraguay in Pictures*. Lerner, 1988. *(P; I)*

## PARKS AND PLAYGROUNDS

Anderson, Norman D., and Brown, Walter R. *Ferris Wheels*. Pantheon, 1983. *(I)*

Silverstein, Herma. *Scream Machines: Roller Coasters, Past, Present, and Future*. Walker, 1986. *(I; A)*

Simon, Charnan. *Milton Hershey: Chocolate King, Town Builder*. Children's Press, 1998. *(P)*

Van Steenwyk, Elizabeth. *Behind the Scenes at the Amusement Park*. Albert Whitman, 1983. *(P; I)*

## PARLIAMENTARY PROCEDURE

Jones, O. Garfield. *Parliamentary Procedure at a Glance*. Viking, 1991. (rev. ed.) *(A)*

## PARROTS

Horton, Casey. *Parrots*. Benchmark Books, 1996. *(I)*

## PARTIES

Brinn, Ruth E., and Saypol, Judyth R. *101 Mix and Match Party Ideas for the Jewish Holidays*. Kar-Ben, 1981. *(P)*

Highlights editors. *Party Ideas with Crafts Kids Can Make*. Highlights, 1981. *(P; I)*

Pitcher, Caroline. *Party Time*. Watts, 1984. *(P)*

Wilkes, Angela. *My First Party Book*. Knopf, 1991. *(P; I)*

## PARTS OF SPEECH

Heller, Ruth. *Fantastic! Wow! And Unreal!: A Book About Interjections and Conjunctions*. Putnam, 2000; *Mine, All Mine: A Book about Pronouns*. Putnam, 1999; *Behind the Mask: A Book about Prepositions; Kites Sail High: A Book about Verbs; Many Luscious Lolli-pops: A Book about Adjectives; Merry-Go-Round: A Book about Nouns; Up, Up and Away: A Book about Adverbs*. Putnam, 1998. *(P; I)*

## PASSOVER

De Paola, Tomie. *My First Passover*. Putnam, 1991. *(P)*

Drucker, Malka. *Passover: A Season of Freedom*. Holiday, 1981. *(I; A)*

Fluek, Toby Knobel. *Passover As I Remember It*. Knopf, 1994. *(P; I; A)*

Hoyt-Goldsmith, Diane. *Celebrating Passover*. Holiday, 2000. *(P; I)*

Kimmelman, Leslie. *Hooray! It's Passover!* HarperCollins, 1996. *(P)*

Musleah, Rahel. *Why on This Night?: A Passover Haggadah for Family Celebration*. Simon & Schuster, 2000. *(I)*

## PASTEUR, LOUIS

Birch, Beverley. *Louis Pasteur*. Gareth Stevens, 1989. *(I)*

Sabin, Francene. *Louis Pasteur: Young Scientist*. Troll, 1983. *(P; I)*

Smith, Linda Wasmer. *Louis Pasteur: Disease Fighter*. Enslow, 1997. *(I)*

## PATRICK, SAINT

Corfe, Tom. *St. Patrick and Irish Christianity*. Lerner, 1978. *(I; A)*

## PAULING, LINUS

Newton, David E. *Linus Pauling: Scientist and Advocate*. Facts on File, 1994. *(A)*

## PEACE CORPS

Fitzgerald, Merni Ingrassia. *The Peace Corps Today*. Putnam, 1986. *(I)*

Weitsman, Madeline. *Peace Corps*. Chelsea House, 1989. *(I; A)*

## PEACE MOVEMENTS

Fitzgerald, Merni Ingrassia. *The Peace Corps Today*. Dodd, 1986. *(P; I)*

Meltzer, Milton. *Ain't Gonna Study War No More: The Story of America's Peace Seekers*. Harper, 1985. *(A)*

## PEARY, ROBERT E.

Anderson, Madelyn Klein. *Robert E. Peary and the Fight for the North Pole*. Watts, 1992. *(I)*

National Geographic Society. Israel, Fred L., ed. *Robert E. Peary and the Rush to the North Pole*. Chelsea House, 1999. *(A)*

## PELÉ

Krull, Kathleen. *Lives of the Athletes: Thrills, Spills (And What the Neighbors Thought)*. Raintree Steck-Vaughn, 1999. *(I; A)*

## PELICANS

Stone, Lynn. *The Pelican.* Dillon, 1990. *(I)*
Wildsmith, Brian. *Pelican.* Pantheon, 1983. *(P)*

## PENGUINS

Arnold, Caroline. *Penguin.* Morrow, 1988. *(P; I)*
Coldrey, Jennifer. *Penguins.* Andre Deutsch, 1983. *(P)*
Lepthien, Emilie U. *Penguins.* Children's, 1983. *(P)*
Paladino, Catherine. *Pomona: The Birth of a Penguin.* Watts, 1991. *(P)*
Sømme, Lauritz, and Kalas, Sybille. *The Penguin Family Book.* Picture Book Studio, 1988. *(P)*
Strange, Ian J. *Penguin World.* Dodd, 1981. *(I; A)*
Tenaza, Richard. *Penguins.* Watts, 1982. *(I; A)*
Vernon, Adele. *The Hoiho: New Zealand's Yellow-Eyed Penguin.* Putnam, 1991. *(I)*

## PENN, WILLIAM

Kroll-Smith, Steve. *William Penn: Founder of Pennsylvania.* Holiday House, 2000. *(I)*

## PENNSYLVANIA

Cornell, William A., and Altland, Millard. *Our Pennsylvania Heritage.* Penns Valley, 1978. *(I; A)*
Costabel, Eva D. *The Pennsylvania Dutch.* Atheneum, 1986. *(P; I)*
Faber, Doris. *The Amish.* Doubleday, 1991. *(P; I)*
Kent, Deborah. *Pennsylvania.* Children's, 1988. *(P)*
Knight, James E. *The Farm, Life in Colonial Pennsylvania.* Troll, 1982. *(I; A)*
Kroll-Smith, Steve. *William Penn: Founder of Pennsylvania.* Holiday House, 2000. *(I)*

## PERCUSSION INSTRUMENTS

Dearling, Robert, ed. *The Illustrated Encyclopedia of Musical Instruments.* Gale Research, 1996. *(I; A)*

## PERICLES

Poulton, Michael. *Pericles and the Ancient Greeks.* Raintree Steck-Vaughn, 1992. *(I)*

## PERRY, MATTHEW C.

Blumberg, Rhoda. *Commodore Perry in the Land of the Shogun.* Lothrop, 1985. *(I; A)*

## PERSIAN GULF WAR

Gay, Kathlyn, and Gay, Martin. *Persian Gulf War.* 21st Century Books, 1996. *(I)*

## PERU

Dewey, Ariane. *The Thunder God's Son: A Peruvian Folktale.* Greenwillow, 1981. *(P)*
Gemming, Elizabeth. *Lost City in the Clouds: The Discovery of Machu Picchu.* Putnam, 1980. *(P; I)*
Visual Geography. *Peru . . . In Pictures.* Lerner, 1987. *(I; A)*

Worth, Richard. *Pizarro and the Conquest of the Incan Empire in World History.* Enslow, 2000. *(I; A)*

## PETER THE GREAT

Stanley, Diane. *Peter the Great.* Four Winds, 1986. *(P; I)*

## PETROLEUM AND PETROLEUM REFINING

Alvarez, A. *Offshore: a North Sea Journey.* Houghton, 1986. *(A)*
Asimov, Isaac. *How Did We Find Out about Oil?* Walker, 1980. *(I)*
Pampe, William R. *Petroleum: How It Is Found and Used.* Enslow, 1984. *(A)*
Piper, Allan. *Oil.* Watts, 1980. *(I)*
Scott, Elaine. *Doodlebugging: The Treasure Hunt for Oil.* Warne, 1982. *(I)*
Stephen, R. J. *Oil Rigs.* Watts, 1987. *(P)*

## PETS

Arnold, Caroline. *Pets without Homes.* Houghton, 1983. *(P)*
Blumberg, Leda. *Pets.* Watts, 1983. *(P; I)*
Fields, Alice. *Pets.* Watts, 1981. *(P)*
Hess, Lilo. *Bird Companions.* Scribner's, 1981. *(I)*
Marrs, Texe, and Marrs, Wanda. *The Perfect Name for Your Pet.* Heian International, 1983. *(P; I; A)*
Peterson-Fleming, Judy, and Fleming, Bill. *Kitten Training and Critters, Too!; Puppy Training and Critters, Too!* Morrow/Tamborine, 1996. *(P)*

## PHILADELPHIA

Balcer, Bernadette and O'Byrne-Pelham, Fran. *Philadelphia.* Dillon, 1989. *(P; I)*
Clay, Rebecca. *Kidding around Philadelphia: A Young Person's Guide to the City.* John Muir, 1990. *(P; I)*
Knight, James E. *Seventh and Walnut, Life in Colonial Philadelphia.* Troll, 1982. *(I; A)*

## PHILIP

Nardo, Don. *Philip II and Alexander the Great Unify Greece in World History.* Enslow, 2000. *(I; A)*

## PHILIPPINES

Bjener, Tamiko. *Philippines.* Gareth Stevens, 1987. *(P)*
Cordero Fernando, Gilda. *We Live in the Philippines.* Bookwright, 1986. *(P; I)*
Kinkade, Sheila. *Children of the Philippines.* Lerner, 1996. *(P; I)*
Schraff, Anne E. *Philippines.* Lerner, 2000. *(P; I)*

## PHILOSOPHY

Allington, Richard L., and Krull, Kathleen. *Thinking.* Raintree, 1980. *(P)*
Magee, Bryan. *The Story of Philosophy.* DK, 1998. *(A)*
Plato. *The Republic.* Penguin, 1955. *(I; A)*

Post, Beverly, and Eads, Sandra. *Logic, Anyone? One Hundred Sixty-Five Brain-Stretching Problems.* Pitman, 1982. *(I; A)*

## PHOTOGRAPHY

Cumming, David. *Photography.* Steck-Vaughn, 1989. *(I)*

Henderson, Kathy. *Market Guide for Young Artists & Photographers.* Betterway, 1990. *(I; A)*

King, Dave. *My First Photography Book: A Life-Size Guide to Taking Creative Photographs and Making Exciting Projects with Your Prints.* Dorling Kindersley, 1994. *(P; I)*

Knudsen-Owens, Vic. *Photography Basics: An Introduction for Young People.* Prentice-Hall, 1983. *(P; I)*

Lasky, Kathryn. *Think like an Eagle: At Work with a Wildlife Photographer.* Joy Street: Little, 1992. *(I)*

Lawlor, Laurie. *Window on the West: The Frontier Photography of William Henry Jackson.* Holiday, 1999. *(I)*

Moss, Miriam. *Fashion Photographer.* Crestwood, 1991. *(I)*

Partridge, Elizabeth. *Restless Spirit: The Life and Work of Dorothea Lange.* Viking, 1998. *(I; A)*

Rubin, Susan Goldman. *Margaret Bourke-White: Her Pictures Were Her Life.* Abrams, 1999. *(I; A)*

Sullivan, George. *Black Artists in Photography.* Cobblehill, 1996. *(I; A)*

Varriale, Jim. *Take a Look Around: Photography Activities for Young People.* Millbrook, 1999. *(I)*

## PHOTOSYNTHESIS

Ross, Bill. *Straight from the Bear's Mouth: The Story of Photosynthesis.* Atheneum, 1995. *(I)*

Silverstein, Alvin; Silverstein, Virginia; and Nunn, Laura Silverstein. *Photosynthesis.* Millbrook Press, 1998. *(I; A)*

## PHYSICAL EDUCATION

Heron, Jackie. *Careers in Health and Fitness.* Rosen, 1990. *(A)*

## PHYSICAL FITNESS

Garell, Dale C., and Nardo, Don. *Exercise.* Chelsea House, 1992. *(I)*

Reef, Catherine. *Eat the Right Stuff: Food Facts; Stay Fit: Build a Strong Body; Think Positive: Cope with Stress.* Twenty-First Century, 1995. *(I)*

## PHYSICS

Adams, Richard C., and Goodwin, Peter H. *Physics Projects for Young Scientists: Rev. ed. 2000.* Watts, 2000. *(I; A)*

Ardley, Neil. *Exploring Magnetism.* Watts, 1984. *(I); Hot and Cold,* 1983. *(P; I; A); Making Things Move,* 1984. *(P; I; A)*

Berger, Melvin. *Our Atomic World.* Watts, 1989. *(P; I); Solids, Liquids, and Gases.* Putnam, 1989. *(I; A)*

Bortz, Fred. *Catastrophe! Great Engineering Failure— & Success.* Freeman, 1995. *(I; A); Mind Tools: The Science of Artificial Intelligence.* Watts, 1992. *(I: A)*

Clark, John. *Matter and Energy: Physics in Action.* Oxford University Press, 1995. *(I;A)*

Cobb, Vicki. *Why Can't You Unscramble an Egg?: and Other Not Such Dumb Questions about Matter.* Lodestar, 1990. *(P; I)*

Fleisher, Paul. *Secrets of the Universe: Discovering the Universal Laws of Science.* Atheneum, 1987. *(I; A)*

Gallant, Roy A. *The Ever-Changing Atom.* Marshall Cavendish/Benchmark, 1999. *(I; A)*

Gardner, Robert. *Science Projects about the Physics of Sports; Science Projects about the Physics of Toys and Games.* Enslow, 2000; *Science Projects about Physics in the Home.* Enslow, 1999. *(I; A)*

Gribbin, John, and Gribbin, Mary. *Time & Space: Explore the Changing Ideas about Our Universe— From the Flat Earth to the Latest Research into Black Holes.* Dorling Kindersley, 1994. *(I; A)*

Henbest, Nigel, and Couper, Heather. *Physics.* Watts, 1983. *(I; A)*

McGrath, Susan. *Fun with Physics.* National Geographic, 1986. *(I)*

Sherwood, Martin, and Sutton, Christine. *The Physical World.* Oxford University Press, 1988. *(A)*

Supplee, Curt. *Physics in the 20th Century.* Abrams, 1999. *(A)*

Watson, Philip. *Liquid Magic.* Lothrop, 1983. *(P; I)*

## PIANO

Dearling, Robert, ed. *The Illustrated Encyclopedia of Musical Instruments.* Gale Research, 1996. *(I; A)*

Krull, Kathleen. *Lives of the Musicians: Good Times, Bad Times (And What the Neighbors Thought).* Raintree Steck-Vaughn, 1998. *(I; A)*

## PICASSO, PABLO

Beardsley, John. *Pablo Picasso.* Abrams, 1991. *(I; A)*

Frevert, Patricia D. *Pablo Picasso: Twentieth Century Genius.* Creative Education, 1981. *(I; A)*

Janson, H. W., and Janson, Anthony F. *History of Art for Young People.* Abrams, 1997. (rev. ed.) *(I; A)*

Lowery, Linda. *Pablo Picasso.* Lerner, 1999. *(P)*

Muhlberger, Richard, and Metropolitan Museum of Art. *What Makes a Picasso a Picasso?* Viking, 1994. *(I)*

Raboff, Ernest. *Pablo Picasso.* Doubleday, 1982. *(P; I)*

Venezia, Mike. *Picasso.* Children's, 1988. *(P)*

## PIERCE, FRANKLIN

Brown, Fern G. *Franklin Pierce.* Garrett Educational, 1989. *(I)*

Simon, Charnan. *Franklin Pierce.* Children's, 1988. *(I)*

## PIGS

Ling, Mary. *Pig.* Dorling Kindersley, 1993. *(P)*

Scott, Jack Denton. *The Book of the Pig.* Putnam, 1981. *(I)*

## PINEAPPLE

Hughes, Meredith Sayles. *Yes, We Have Bananas: Fruits from Shrubs and Vines.* Lerner, 1999. *(P; I)*

## PIONEER LIFE

Anderson, Joan. *Pioneer Children of Appalachia.* Clarion, 1986. *(I)*

Fradin, Dennis B. *Pioneers.* Children's, 1984. *(P)*

Katz, William Loren. *Black Pioneers: An Untold Story.* Atheneum, 1999. *(I)*

## PIRATES

Lincoln, Margarette. *The Pirate's Handbook.* Cobblehill, 1995. *(P; I)*

Marrin, Albert. *Terror of the Spanish Main: Sir Henry Morgan and His Buccaneers.* Dutton, 1998. *(I; A)*

Stein, R. Conrad. *The Story of the Barbary Pirates.* Children's, 1982. *(P; I)*

## PIZARRO, FRANCISCO

Worth, Richard. *Pizarro and the Conquest of the Incan Empire in World History.* Enslow, 2000. *(I; A)*

## PLANETS

Asimov, Isaac. *Colonizing the Planets and Stars.* Gareth Stevens, 1990. *(P; I)*

Branley, Franklyn M. *The Planets in Our Solar System.* Crowell, 1998 (rev. ed.). *(P)*

Lampton, Christopher. *Stars and Planets.* Doubleday, 1988. *(P)*

Lauber, Patricia. *Journey to the Planets.* Crown, 1993 (rev. ed.). *(I; A)*

Levasseur-Regourd, Anny Chantal. *Our Sun and the Inner Planets.* Facts on File, 1990. *(P; I)*

Nourse, Alan E. *The Giant Planets.* Watts, 1982. *(I; A)*

Petty, Kate. *The Planets.* Watts, 1984. *(P)*

Vogt, Gregory. *Mars and the Inner Planets.* Watts, 1982. *(I; A)*

Yeomans, Don K. *The Distant Planets.* Facts on File, 1990. *(P; I)*

## PLANKTON

Cerullo, Mary M. *Sea Soup: Phytoplankton.* Tilbury, 1999. *(I)*

## PLANT PESTS

Lampton, Christopher. *Insect Attack.* Millbrook Press, 1994. *(I)*

Taylor, Ronald J. *Northwest Weeds: The Ugly and Beautiful Villains of Fields, Gardens, and Roadsides.* Mountain Press, 1990. *(I; A)*

## PLANTS

Batten, Mary. *Hungry Plants.* Golden, 2000. *(P)*

Bocknek, Jonathan. *The Science of Plants.* Gareth Stevens, 1999. *(P; I)*

Burnie, David. *Plant.* Knopf, 1989. *(I)*

Coil, Suzanne M. *Poisonous Plants.* Watts, 1991. *(P; I)*

Cross, Diana H. *Some Plants Have Funny Names.* Crown, 1983. *(P)*

Dowden, Anne O. *From Flower to Fruit.* Harper, 1995 (rev. ed.). *(I; A)*

Facklam, Howard, and Facklam, Margery. *Plants: Extinction or Survival?* Enslow, 1990. *(I; A)*

Gardner, Robert. *Science Projects about Plants.* Enslow, 1999. *(I; A)*

Greenaway, Theresa. *The Plant Kingdom.* Raintree/Steck-Vaughn, 1999. *(I)*

Janulewicz, Mike. *Plants.* Watts, 1984. *(I; A)*

Johnson, Sylvia A. *Mosses.* Lerner, 1983. *(I)*

Kerrod, Robin. *Plant Life.* Marshall Cavendish, 1994. *(P; I)*

Kite, L. Patricia. *Insect-Eating Plants.* Millbrook, 1995. *(P; I)*

Lambert, Mark. *Plant Life.* Watts, 1983. *(I; A)*

Lauber, Patricia. *Seeds: Pop, Stick, Glide.* Crown, 1981. *(P)*

Lerner, Carol. *Pitcher Plants: The Elegant Insect Traps.* Morrow, 1983. *(P; I)*; *Plant Families.* Morrow, 1989. *(P; I)*; *Dumb Cane and Daffodils: Poisonous Plants in the House and Garden.* Morrow, 1990. *(I; A)*

Marcus, Elizabeth. *Amazing World of Plants.* Troll, 1984. *(P; I)*

Podendorf, Illa. *Weeds and Wildflowers.* Children's, 1981. *(P)*

Pringle, Laurence P. *Being a Plant.* Crowell, 1983. *(I; A)*

Wexler, Jerome. *Jack-in-the-Pulpit.* Dutton, 1993. *(I)*; *Sundew Stranglers: Plants That Eat Insects.* Dutton/Penguin, 1995. *(P)*

## PLASTICS

Dineen, Jacqueline. *Plastics.* Enslow, 1988. *(I)*

Lambert, Mark. *Spotlight on Plastics.* Rourke, 1988. *(P; I)*

Whyman, Kathryn. *Plastics.* Gloucester Press, 1988. *(P; I)*

## PLATYPUS AND SPINY ANTEATERS

Short, Joan; Bird, Bettina; and Green, Jack. *Platypus.* Mondo, 1996. *(P; I)*

Squire, Ann O. *Anteaters, Sloths, and Armadillos.* Watts, 1999. *(I)*

## PLAYS

Bruchac, Joseph. *Pushing Up the Sky: Seven Native American Plays for Children.* Dial, 2000. *(P; I)*

McCullough, L.E. *Anyone Can Produce Plays with Kids: The Absolute Basics of Staging Your Own At-Home, In-School, Round-the-Neighborhood Plays.* Smith & Kraus, 1998. *(A)*

Winther, Barbara. *Plays from Hispanic Tales.* Plays, 1998. *(I)*

## PLUMBING

Colman, Penny. *Toilets, Bathtubs, Sinks, and Sewers.* Atheneum, 1994. *(I)*

## PLUTO

Asimov, Isaac. *How Did We Find Out about Pluto?* Walker, 1991. *(I; A); Pluto: A Double Planet?* Gareth Stevens, 1990. *(P; I)*

## PLYMOUTH COLONY

Doherty, Kieran. *William Bradford: Rock of Plymouth.* Twenty-First Century, 1999. *(I; A)*

Penner, Lucille Recht. *The Pilgrims at Plymouth.* Random, 1996. *(P)*

## POETRY

Booth, David, sel. *'Til All the Stars Have Fallen: A Collection of Poems for Children.* Viking, 1990. *(P; I)*

Brown, Marcia. *Sing a Song of Popcorn: Every Child's Book of Poems.* Scholastic, 1988. *(P; I)*

Bryan, Ashley, ed. *Beat the Story-Drum, Pum-Pum.* Atheneum, 1987. *(P; I)*

Cole, Joanna, comp. *A New Treasury of Children's Poetry: Old Favorites and New Discoveries.* Doubleday, 1984. *(P; I)*

Cummings, E. E. *Hist Whist and Other Poems for Children,* ed. by George J. Firmage. Liveright, 1983. *(P; I)*

Dunbar, Paul Laurence. *Jump Back, Honey: The Poems of Paul Laurence Dunbar.* Jump at the Sun/Hyperion, 1999. *(P)*

Fleischman, Paul. *Joyful Noise: Poems for Two Voices.* Harper, 1988. *(P; I)*

Fletcher, Ralph. *Relatively Speaking: Poems about Family.* Orchard, 1999. *(I)*

Florian, Douglas. *Mammalabilia.* Harcourt, 2000. *(P; I)*

Garlake, Teresa. *Poverty: Changing Attitudes 1900-2000.* Raintree/Steck-Vaughn, 1999. *(I)*

George, Kristine O'Connell. *Little Dog Poems.* Clarion, 1999. *(P)*

Hall, Donald, ed. *The Oxford Illustrated Book of American Children's Poems.* Oxford, 1999. *(P; I)*

Harrison, Michael, and Stuart-Clark, Christopher, comps. *One Hundred Years of Poetry for Children; The Oxford Treasury of Time Poems.* Oxford University, 1999. *(I; A)*

Harter, Penny. *Shadow Play: Night Haiku.* Simon & Schuster, 1994. *(P; I)*

Hodges, Margaret, ad. *Saint George and the Dragon,* ad. from Edmund Spenser's *Faerie Queene.* Little, 1984. *(P; I)*

Hopkins, Lee Bennett. *Side by Side: Poems to Read Together.* Simon & Schuster, 1988. *(P; I)*

Hughes, Ted. *The Mermaid's Purse.* Random, 2000. *(I; A)*

Janeczko, Paul. *The Place My Words Are Looking for: What Poets Say about and through Their Work.* Bradbury, 1990. *(I; A)*

Janeczko, Paul B., ed. *Strings: A Gathering of Family Poems.* Bradbury, 1984. *(I; A)*

Janeczko, Paul, sel. *Preposterous: Poems of Youth.* Orchard Books, 1991. *(I; A)*

Katz, Bobbi. *Puddle Wonderful: Poems to Welcome Spring.* Random House, 1992. *(P)*

Kellerman, Jonathan. *Daddy, Daddy, Can You Touch the Sky?* Bantam, 1994. *(P)*

Knudson, R. R., and Swenson, May, selector and ed. *American Sports Poems.* Orchard Books, 1988. *(I; A)*

Lear, Edward. *Of Pelicans and Pussycats: Poems and Limericks.* Dial, 1990. *(P)*

Millay, Edna St. Vincent. *Collected Poems.* Harper, 1981. *(P); Poems Selected for Young People.* Harper, 1979. *(I; A)*

Nicholls, Judith, ed. *Someone I Like: Poems about People.* Barefoot, 2000. *(P; I)*

Nye, Naomi Shihab. *What Have You Lost?* Greenwillow, 1999. *(I; A)*

Prelutsky, Jack. *It's Snowing! It's Snowing!* Greenwillow, 1984. *(P); Poems of A. Nonny Mouse.* Knopf, 1991. *(P); The Random House Book of Poetry for Children.* Random House, 1983. *(P; I)*

Prelutsky, Jack, sel. *The 20th Century Children's Poetry Treasury.* Knopf, 1999. *(P; I); When the Rain Sings: Poems by Young Native Americans.* Simon & Schuster, 1999. *(I; A);*

Ryder, Joanne. *Earthdance.* Holt, 1996. *(P; I)*

Schertle, Alice. *I Am the Cat.* Lothrop, 1999. *(P; I)*

Stevenson, James. *Candy Corn,* 1999; *Popcorn,* 1998; *Sweet Corn,* 1995; Greenwillow *(P; I);*

Stevenson, Robert Louis. *A Child's Garden of Verses.* Scribner's, n.d. (Other eds. and pubs.) *(P; I)*

Wildsmith, Brian, illus. *Oxford Book of Poetry for Children.* Merrimack, n.d. *(P; I)*

Wong, Janet S. *Behind the Wheel.* Simon & Schuster/ Margaret K. McElderry Bks., 1999. *(I; A); Night Garden: Poems from the World of Dreams.* Simon & Schuster/Margaret K. McElderry Bks., 2000. *(P; I)*

## POISONS AND ANTIDOTES

Dowden, Anne Ophelia. *Poisons in Our Path: Plants That Harm and Heal.* HarperCollins, 1994. *(P; I)*

Latta, Sara L. *Food Poisoning and Foodborne Diseases.* Enslow, 1999. *(I; A)*

Lerner, Carol. *Moonseed and Mistletoe: A Book of Poisonous Wild Plants.* Morrow, 1988. *(P)*

Zipko, Stephen James. *Toxic Threat: How Hazardous Substances Poison Our Lives.* Silver Burdett Press, 1990. *(I; A)*

## POLAND

Greene, Carol. *Poland.* Children's, 1983. *(I; A)*

Heale, Jay. *Poland.* Marshall Cavendish, 1994. *(I; A)*

Sandak, Cass R. *Poland.* Watts, 1986. *(I)*

Zyskind, Sara. *Stolen Years.* Lerner, 1981. *(I; A)*

## POLICE

Arnold, Caroline. *Who Keeps Us Safe?* Watts, 1982. *(P)*

Broekel, Ray. *Police.* Children's, 1981. *(P)*

Hewett, Joan. *Motorcycle on Patrol: The Story of a Highway Officer.* Clarion, 1986. *(P)*

Johnson, Jean. *Police Officers, A to Z.* Walker, 1986. *(P)*

Mathias, Catherine. *I Can Be a Police Officer.* Children's, 1984. *(P)*

Scott, Paul. *Police Divers.* Messner, 1982. *(I)*

## POLITICAL PARTIES

*The New World Order.* Greenhaven, 1991. *(A)*

Kronenwetter, Michael. *Are You a Liberal? Are You a Conservative?* Watts, 1984. *(I; A)*

Levenson, Dorothy. *Politics: How to Get Involved.* Watts, 1980. *(I; A)*

Raynor, Thomas. *Politics, Power, and People: Four Governments in Action.* Watts, 1983. *(I; A)*

Weiss, Ann E. *Party Politics, Party Problems.* Harper, 1980. *(I; A)*

## POLK, JAMES KNOX

Lillegard, Dee. *James K. Polk: Eleventh President of the United States.* Children's, 1988. *(P; I)*

## POLLOCK, JACKSON

Janson, H. W., and Janson, Anthony F. *History of Art for Young People.* Abrams, 1997. (rev. ed.) *(I; A)*

## POLLUTION

Blashfield, Jean F., and Black, Wallace B. *Oil Spills.* Children's, 1991. *(I)*

Bright, Michael. *The Dying Sea.* Gloucester Press, 1988. *(I)*

Duden, Jane. *The Ozone Layer.* Crestwood, 1990. *(I)*

Gay, Kathlyn. *Global Garbage: Exploring Trash and Toxic Waste.* Watts, 1992; *Ozone.* Watts, 1989; *Silent Killers: Radon and Other Hazards.* Watts, 1988. *(I; A)*

Harris, Jack C. *The Greenhouse Effect.* Crestwood, 1990. *(I)*

Kronenwetter, Michael. *Managing Toxic Wastes.* Messner, 1989. *(I; A)*

O'Connor, Karen. *Garbage.* Lucent Books, 1989. *(P; I)*

Phillips, Anne W. *The Ocean.* Crestwood, 1990. *(I)*

Snodgrass, Mary Ellen. *Air Pollution; Environmental Awareness: Solid Waste; Water Pollution.* Bancroft-Sage, 1991. *(P; I)*

Weiss, Malcolm E. *Toxic Waste: Clean Up or Cover Up?* Watts, 1984. *(I; A)*

Zipko, Stephen J. *Toxic Threat: How Hazardous Substances Poison Our Lives.* Messner, 1990 (rev. ed.). *(A)*

## POLO, MARCO

Stefoff, Rebecca. *Marco Polo and the Medieval Explorers.* Main Line, 1992. *(P: I)*

Twist, Clint. *Marco Polo: Overland to Medieval China.* Raintree Steck-Vaughn, 1994. *(P; I)*

## POMPEII

Connolly, Peter. *Pompeii.* Oxford University Press, 1990. *(I)*

Goor, Ron, and Goor, Nancy. *Pompeii.* Crowell, 1987. *(I)*

Kunhardt, Edith. *Pompeii: Buried Alive!* Random House, 1987. *(I)*

Patent, Dorothy Hinshaw. *Lost City of Pompeii.* Marshall Cavendish, 2000. *(I)*

## PONCE DE LÉON, JUAN

Dolan, Sean. *Juan Ponce De Léon.* Chelsea House, 1995. *(I)*

## PONTIAC

Bland, Celia. *Pontiac: Ottawa Rebel.* Chelsea House, 1994. *(I)*

## PONY EXPRESS

McCall, Edith. *Mail Riders.* Children's, 1980. *(P; I; A)*

Stein, R. Conrad. *The Story of the Pony Express.* Children's, 1981. *(P; I)*

## POPULATION

Becklake, John, and Becklake, Sue. *The Population Explosion.* Gloucester Press, 1990. *(I)*

McGraw, Eric. *Population Growth.* Rourke, 1987. *(I; A)*

Nam, Charles B. *Our Population: The Changing Face of America.* Walker, 1988. *(A)*

Winckler, Suzanne, and Rodgers, Mary M. *Population Growth.* Lerner, 1991. *(I)*

## PORTUGAL

Lye, Keith. *Take a Trip to Portugal.* Watts, 1986. *(P)*

Skalon, Ana de, and Stadtler, Christa. *We Live in Portugal.* Bookwright, 1987. *(P)*

## POSTAL SERVICE

Bolick, Nancy O'Keefe. *Mail Call: The History of the U.S. Postal Service.* Watts, 1995. *(I)*

Gibbons, Gail. *The Post Office Book: Mail and How It Moves.* Harper, 1982. *(P)*

McAfee, Cheryl Weant. *The United States Postal Service.* Chelsea House, 1987. *(I; A)*

Roth, Harold. *First Class! The Postal System in Action.* Pantheon, 1983. *(I)*

## POTATOES

Hughes, Meredith Sayles. *The Great Potato Book.* Macmillan, 1986. *(P)*

Johnson, Sylvia A. *Potatoes.* Lerner, 1986. *(I)*

Lobel, Anita. *Potatoes, Potatoes.* Harper, 1984. *(P)*

Meltzer, Milton. *The Amazing Potato: A Story in Which the Incas, Conquistadors, Marie Antoinette, Thomas Jefferson, Wars, Famines, Immigrants, and French Fries All Play a Part.* HarperCollins, 1992. *(I)*

## POTTER, HELEN BEATRIX

Collins, David R. *The Country Artist: A Story about Beatrix Potter.* Carolrhoda, 1989. *(I)*

Wallner, Alexandra. *Beatrix Potter.* Holiday, 1995. *(P)*

## POTTERY

Schwartz, Deborah; Sullivan, Missy; and the Brooklyn Museum. *The Native American Look Book: Art and Activities for Kids.* New Press, 2000. *(I)*

## POULTRY

Hopf, Alice L. *Chickens and Their Wild Relatives.* Dodd, 1982. *(I)*

## POVERTY

Berek, Judith. *No Place to Be: Voices of Homeless Children.* Houghton, 1992. *(I; A)*

Criswell, Sara Dixon. *Homelessness.* Lucent, 1998. *(I; A)*

Davis, Bertha. *Poverty in America: What We Do about It.* Watts, 1991. *(A)*

Dudley, William, ed. *Poverty.* Greenhaven Press, 1988. *(A)*

Gottfried, Ted. *Homelessness: Whose Problem Is It?* Millbrook, 1999. *(I; A)*

Greenberg, Keith Elliot. *Erik is Homeless.* Lerner, 1992. *(P; I)*

Hubbard, Jim, sel. *Shooting Back: A Photographic View of Life by Homeless Children.* Chronicle, 1991. *(P; I; A)*

Hyde, Margaret O. *The Homeless: Profiling the Problem.* Enslow, 1990. *(P; I)*

Kosof, Anna. *Homeless in America.* Watts, 1988. *(I; A)*

Meltzer, Milton. *Poverty in America.* Morrow, 1986. *(A)*

O'Connor, Karen. *Homeless Children.* Lucent Books, 1989. *(I; A)*

O'Neil, Terry. *The Homeless: Distinguishing Between Fact and Opinion.* Greenhaven, 1990. *(I)*

Stearman, Kaye. *Homelessness.* Raintree/Steck-Vaughn, 1999. *(I; A)*

Worth, Richard. *Poverty.* Lucent, 1997. *(A)*

## POWELL, COLIN

Banta, Melissa. *Colin Powell: A Complete Soldier.* Chelsea, 1994. *(I)*

Hughes, Libby. *Colin Powell: A Man of Quality.* Silver Burdett Press, 1996. *(I; A)*

Landau, Elaine. *Colin Powell: Four Star General.* Watts, 1991. *(I)*

## POWER PLANTS

Wilcox, Charlotte. *Powerhouse: Inside a Nuclear Power Plant.* Carolrhoda, 1996. *(I; A)*

## PRAIRIES

Brandenburg, Jim. *An American Safari: Adventures on the North American Prairie.* Walker, 1995. *(P; I)*

George, Jean Craighead. *One Day in the Prairie.* Crowell, 1986. *(I)*

## PRAYER

*Thanks Be to God: Prayers from around the World.* Macmillan, 1990. *(P; I)*

Brown, Susan Taylor. *Can I Pray with My Eyes Open?* Hyperion, 1999. *(P)*

Godwin, Laura. *Barnyard Prayers.* Hyperion, 2000. *(P)*

Hallinan, P. K. *I'm Thankful Each Day.* Children's, 1981. *(P)*

Nystrom, Carolyn. *What Is Prayer?* Moody, 1980. *(P; I)*

## PREHISTORIC ANIMALS

Cohen, Daniel. *Prehistoric Animals.* Doubleday, 1988. *(P; I)*

Dixon, Dougal. *A Closer Look at Prehistoric Reptiles.* Watts, 1984. *(I; A)*

Eldridge, David. *Flying Dragons: Ancient Reptiles That Ruled the Air; Sea Monsters: Ancient Reptiles That Ruled the Sea.* Troll, 1980. *(P; I)*

Giblin, James Cross. *The Mystery of the Mammoth Bones: And How It Was Solved.* HarperCollins, 1999. *(I)*

Hall, Derek. *Prehistoric Mammals.* Watts, 1984. *(P; I)*

Lampton, Christopher. *Prehistoric Animals.* Watts, 1983. *(I)*

Moody, Richard. *100 Prehistoric Animals.* Grosset, 1988. *(P; I)*

National Geographic editors. *Giants from the Past.* National Geographic, 1983. *(P; I; A)*

Zallinger, Peter. *Prehistoric Animals.* Random House, 1981. *(P)*

## PREHISTORIC ART

Hodge, Susie. *Prehistoric Art.* Heinemann, 1997. *(P; I)*

## PRESIDENCY OF THE UNITED STATES

Beard, Charles A. *The Presidents in American History.* Messner, 1985 (rev. ed.). *(A)*

Beckman, Beatrice. *I Can Be President.* Children's, 1984. *(P)*

Blassingame, Wyatt. *The Look-It-Up Book of Presidents.* Random House, 1990. *(I; A)*

Cooke, Donald E. *Atlas of the Presidents.* Hammond, 1981. *(I; A)*

Frank, Sid, and Melick, Arden. *Presidents: Tidbits and Trivia.* Hammond, 1980. *(P; I; A)*

Krull, Kathleen. *Lives of the Presidents: Fame, Shame (And What the Neighbors Thought).* Raintree Steck-Vaughn, 1998. *(I)*

Miers, Earl S. *America and Its Presidents.* Putnam, 1982. *(P; I; A)*

Morris, Juddi. *At Home with the Presidents.* Wiley, 1999. *(I)*

Parker, Nancy Winslow. *The President's Cabinet and How it Grew.* HarperCollins, 1991. *(P; I); The President's Car.* Harper, 1981. *(P; I)*

Pascoe, Elaine. *First Facts about the Presidents.* Blackbirch, 1996. *(I)*

Reische, Diana. *Electing a U.S. President.* Watts, 1992. *(I; A)*

Sullivan, George. *How the White House Really Works.* Dutton, 1989. *(P); Mr. President: A Book of U.S. Presidents.* Scholastic, 1989. *(P; I)*

## PRIMATES

Maynard, Thane. *Primates: Apes, Monkeys, Prosimians.* Watts, 1995. *(I)*

## PRINTING

Caselli, Giovanni. *A German Printer.* Peter Bedrick, 1986. *(I)*

Krensky, Stephen. *Breaking into Print: Before and after the Invention of the Printing Press.* Little, 1996. *(P)*

## PRISONS

Owens, Lois Smith, and Gordon, Vivian Verdell. *Think about Prisons and the Criminal Justice System.* Walker, 1991. *(I; A)*

Rickard, Graham. *Prisons and Punishments.* Watts, 1987. *(P)*

Warburton, Lois. *Prisons.* Lucent, 1993. *(I; A)*

Weiss, Anne E. *Prisons: A System in Trouble.* Enslow, 1988. *(A)*

Williams, Stanley "Tookie," and Becnel, Barbara Cottman. *Life in Prison.* Morrow, 1998. *(I; A)*

## PROKOFIEV, SERGEI

Krull, Kathleen. *Lives of the Musicians: Good Times, Bad Times (And What the Neighbors Thought).* Raintree Steck-Vaughn, 1998. *(I; A)*

## PROPAGANDA

Simon, Charnan. *Hollywood at War: The Motion Picture Industry and World War II.* Watts, 1993. *(I)*

Steffens, Bradley, and Buggey, Joanne. *Free Speech: Identifying Propaganda Techniques.* Greenhaven Press, 1992. *(I)*

## PROTESTANTISM

Kroll-Smith, Steve. *William Penn: Founder of Pennsylvania.* Holiday House, 2000. *(I)*

Williams, Jean Kinney. *The Amish.* Watts, 1996; *The Shakers.* Watts, 1997. *(I; A)*

## PSYCHOLOGY

Stwertka, Eve. *Psychoanalysis: From Freud to the Age of Therapy.* Watts, 1988 *(I; A)*

Weinstein, Grace W. *People Study People: The Story of Psychology.* Dutton, 1979. *(I; A)*

## PUBLIC HEALTH

Colman, Penny. *Toilets, Bathtubs, Sinks, and Sewers: A History of the Bathroom.* Simon & Schuster, 1994. *(I)*

Yount, Lisa. *Epidemics.* Lucent, 1999. *(I; A)*

## PUBLIC LANDS

Dolan, Edward F. *American Wilderness and Its Future: Conservation Versus Use.* Watts, 1992. *(I; A)*

## PUBLIC SPEAKING

Detz, Joan. *You Mean I Have To Stand Up and Say Something?* Atheneum, 1986. *(I; A)*

Gilbert, Sara. *You Can Speak Up in Class.* Morrow, 1991. *(I; A)*

Gilford, Henry. *How to Give a Speech.* Watts, 1980. *(I; A)*

## PUBLISHING

Greenfeld, Howard. *Books: From Writer to Reader.* Crown, 1989 (rev. ed.). *(A)*

## PUCCINI, GIACOMO

Geras, Adele, and Beck, Ian. *The Random House Book of Opera Stories.* Random House, 1998. *(P; I)*

## PUERTO RICO

Griffiths, John. *Take a Trip to Puerto Rico.* Watts, 1989. *(P; I)*

Harlan, Judith. *Puerto Rico: Deciding Its Future.* 21st Century Books, 1996. *(I;A)*

McKenley, Yvonne. *A Taste of the Caribbean.* Raintree Steck-Vaughn, 1995. *(P; I)*

Visual Geography. *Puerto Rico in Pictures.* Lerner, 1987. *(I)*

## PULITZER PRIZES

Whitelaw, Nancy. *Joseph Pulitzer and the New York World.* Morgan Reynolds, 1999. *(I; A)*

## PULSARS

Branley, Franklyn M. *Superstar: The Supernova of 1987.* HarperCollins, 1990. *(P; I)*

## PUMPS

Zubrowski, Bernie. *Messing around with Water Pumps and Siphons: A Children's Museum Activity Book.* Little, 1981. *(P; I)*

## PUNCTUATION

Forte, Imogene. *Punctuation Power.* Incentive Publications, 1981. *(P; I)*

Gregorich, Barbara. *Apostrophe, Colon, Hyphen; Comma; Period, Question Mark, Exclamation Mark.* EDC Publishing, 1980. *(P; I)*

Rigsby, Annelle. *Punctuation.* Enrich, 1980. *(P)*

Terban, Marvin. *Punctuation Power: Punctuation and How to Use It.* Scholastic, 2000. *(P; I; A)*

Tilkin, Sheldon L. *Quotation Marks and Underlining.* EDC, 1980. *(P; I)*

## PUNIC WARS

Green, Robert. *Hannibal.* Watts, 1996. *(I)*

Nardo, Don. *The Battle of Zama; The Punic Wars.* Lucent, 1996. *(I; A)*

## PUPPETS AND MARIONETTES

Griffith, Bonnie. *The Tree House Gang: Puppet Plays for Children*. Standard Publishing, 1983. *(P; I)*

Krisvoy, Juel. *The Good Apple Puppet Book*. Good Apple, 1981. *(P; I)*

Lade, Roger. *The Most Excellent Book of How to Be a Puppeteer*. Copper Beech, 1996. *(P;I)*

Lasky, Kathryn. *Puppeteer*. Macmillan, 1985. *(I)*

Marks, Burton, and Marks, Rita. *Puppets and Puppet-Making*. Plays, 1982. *(P; I)*

Supraner, Robyn, and Supraner, Lauren. *Plenty of Puppets to Make*. Troll, 1981. *(P; I)*

Venning, Sue, illus. *Jim Henson's Muppet Show Bill*. Random House, 1983. *(P; I)*

Wright, Lyndie. *Puppets*. Watts, 1989. *(P)*

## PURIM

Chaikin, Miriam. *Make Noise, Make Merry: The Story and Meaning of Purim*. Houghton, 1983. *(I)*

Cohen, Barbara. *Here Comes the Purim Players*. Lothrop, 1984. *(P)*

Greenfeld, Howard. *Purim*. Holt, 1983. *(P; I)*

## PURITANS

Collier, Christopher, and Collier, James L. *Pilgrims and Puritans, 1620-1676*. Marshall Cavendish, 1997. *(I; A)*

## PUZZLES

Anderson, Doug. *Picture Puzzles for Armchair Detectives*. Sterling, 1983. *(I; A)*

Churchill, Richard. *I Bet I Can— I Bet You Can'*Sterling, 1982. *(P; I)*

## PYRAMIDS

Mellett, Peter. *Pyramids*. Southwater, 2000. *(P; I)*

Morley, Jacqueline, and Bergin, Mark. *An Egyptian Pyramid*. NTC, 1993. *(P; I)*

Putnam, James. *Eyewitness: Pyramid*. DK, 2000. *(P; I)*

## QUAKERS

Kroll-Smith, Steve. *William Penn: Founder of Pennsylvania*. Holiday House, 2000. *(I)*

## QUASARS

Branley, Franklyn M. *Journey into a Black Hole*. Harper, 1988. *(P)*

## QUEBEC

LeVert, Suzanne. *Quebec*. Chelsea House, 1990. *(I)*

## RABBITS AND HARES

Bare, Colleen S. *Rabbits and Hares*. Dodd, 1983. *(P; I)*

Burton, Jane. *Freckles the Rabbit*. Gareth Stevens, 1989. *(P)*

Tagholm, Sally. *The Rabbit*. Kingfisher, 2000. *(P)*

## RACCOONS AND THEIR RELATIVES

Freschet, Berniece. *Raccoon Baby*. Putnam, 1984. *(P)*

MacClintock, Dorcas. *A Natural History of Raccoons*. Scribner's, 1981. *(I); A Raccoon's First Year*, 1982. *(P)*

## RACES, HUMAN

Gallant, Roy A. *Early Humans*. Benchmark, 2000. *(I)*

Glover, David M. *The Young Oxford Book of the Human Being*. Oxford University Press, 1997. *(I)*

## RACISM

Gay, Kathlyn. *Neo-Nazis: A Growing Threat*. Enslow, 1997. *(A)*

Green, Jen. *Dealing with Racism*. Copper Beech, 1998. *(P)*

Hamanaka, Sheila. *The Journey: Japanese Americans, Racism, and Renewal*. Orchard, 1990. *(I)*

Williams, Mary E. *Issues in Racism*. Lucent, 2000. *(I; A)*

## RACKET SPORTS

Hogan, Marty, and Wong, Ken. *High-Performance Racquetball*. HP Books, 1985. *(A)*

## RADIATION

McGowen, Tom. *Radioactivity: From the Curies to the Atomic Age*. Watts, 1986. *(I)*

Milne, Lorus, and Milne, Margery. *Understanding Radioactivity*. Atheneum, 1989. *(I)*

Pettigrew, Mark. *Radiation*. Gloucester Press, 1986. *(I)*

Pringle, Laurence. *Radiation: Waves and Particles, Benefits and Risks*. Enslow, 1983. *(I)*

## RADIO

Carter, Alden R. *Radio: From Marconi to the Space Age*. Watts, 1987. *(P; I)*

Gilmore, Susan. *What Goes On at a Radio Station?* Carolrhoda, 1983. *(P; I)*

Lerner, Mark. *Careers with a Radio Station*. Lerner, 1983. *(P; I)*

## RADIO, AMATEUR

Ferrell, Nancy Warren. *The New World of Amateur Radio*. Watts, 1986. *(I; A)*

Kuslan, Louis I., and Kuslan, Richard D. *Ham Radio*. Prentice-Hall, n.d. *(I; A)*

## RADIO AND RADAR ASTRONOMY

Fradin, Dennis Brindell. *Is There Life on Mars?* Simon & Schuster, 1999. *(I; A); Searching for Alien Life: Is Anyone Out There?* Twenty-First Century, 1997. *(I)*

## RAILROADS

Blumberg, Rhoda. *Full Steam Ahead: The Race to Build a Transcontinental Railroad*. National Geographic, 1996. *(P; I)*

Levinson, Nancy Smiler. *She's Been Working on the Railroad*. Lodestar, 1997. *(I; A)*

Macdonald, Fiona. *A 19th Century Railway Station.* Peter Bedrick, 1990. *(I)*

Marshall, Ray. *The Train: Watch It Work by Operating the Moving Diagrams!* Viking, 1986. *(P)*

Pollard, Michael. *Train Technology.* Bookwright, 1990. *(I)*

Smith, E. Boyd. *The Railroad Book.* Houghton, 1983. *(I)*

Streissguth, Thomas. *The Transcontinental Railroad.* Lucent, 1999. *(I)*

Wilson, Keith. *Railways in Canada: The Iron Link.* Watts, 1982. *(I; A)*

## RAIN, SNOW, SLEET, AND HAIL

Bennett, David. *Rain.* Bantam, 1988. *(P)*

Brandt, Keith. *What Makes It Rain?* Troll, 1981. *(P)*

Branley, Franklyn M. *Snow Is Falling.* HarperCollins, 2000. *Down Comes the Rain.* HarperCollins, 1997. *(P)*

Murphy, Jim. *Blizzard!* Scholastic, 2000. *(I; A)*

Williams, Terry T., and Major, Ted. *The Secret Language of Snow.* Pantheon, 1984. *(I; A)*

## RAINBOW

Kramer, Stephen. *Theodoric's Rainbow.* Scientific American, 1995. *(I)*

Krupp, E. C. *The Rainbow and You.* HarperCollins, 2000. *(P)*

## RAIN FORESTS

Aldis, Rodney. *Rainforests.* Dillon: Macmillan, 1991. *(P; I)*

Banks, Martin. *Conserving Rain Forests.* Steck-Vaughn, 1990. *(I)*

Cowcher, Helen. *Rain Forest.* Farrar, 1989. *(P)*

George, Jean Craighead. *One Day in the Tropical Rain Forest.* Crowell, 1990. *(P; I)*

Johnson, Linda Carlson. *Rain Forests: A Pro/Con Issue.* Enslow, 1999. *(I)*

Landau, Elaine. *Tropical Rain Forests around the World.* Watts, 1990. *(P)*

Lewington, Anna, and Parker, Edward. *People of the Rain Forests.* Raintree/Steck-Vaughn, 1998. *(P; I)*

Lyman, Francesca, and American Museum of Natural History. *Inside the Dzanga-Sangha Rain Forest.* Workman, 1998. *(P; I)*

Maynard, Caitlin; Maynard, Thane; and Rullman, Stan. *Rain Forests and Reefs: A Kid's-Eye View of the Tropics.* Watts, 1996. *(I)*

Mutel, Cornelia F., and Rodgers, Mary M. *Tropical Rain Forests.* Lerner, 1991. *(I)*

Patent, Dorothy Hinshaw. *Children Save the Rain Forest.* Cobblehill, 1996. *(I; A)*

Pirotta, Saviour. *People in the Rain Forest; Predators in the Rain Forest; Rivers in the Rain Forest; Trees and Plants in the Rain Forest.* Raintree/Steck-Vaughn, 1998. *(P)*

Rowland-Entwistle, Theodore. *Jungles and Rain Forests.* Silver Burdett, 1987. *(P)*

## RALEIGH, SIR WALTER

Aronson, Marc. *Sir Walter Ralegh and the Quest for El Dorado.* Clarion, 2000. *(I; A)*

## RANCH LIFE

De Angelis, Gina. *Black Cowboys.* Chelsea House, 1997. *(I)*

Klausmeier, Robert. *Cowboy.* Lerner, 1995. *(P; I)*

Sandler, Martin W. *Cowboys: A Library of Congress Book.* HarperCollins, 2000. *(P; I)*

## REAGAN, RONALD WILSON

Fox, Mary Virginia. *Mister President: The Story of Ronald Reagan.* Enslow, 1986 (rev. ed.). *(I; A)*

Sullivan, George. *Ronald Reagan.* Messner, 1985. *(A)*

Tax, Mary V. *Mister President: The Story of Ronald Reagan.* Enslow, 1982. *(I; A)*

## RECONSTRUCTION PERIOD

Hansen, Joyce. *"Bury Me Not in a Land of Slaves": African-Americans in the Time of Reconstruction.* Watts, 2000. *(I; A)*

Sterling, Dorothy, ed. *The Trouble They Seen: The Story of Reconstruction in the Words of African Americans.* Da Capo Press, 1994. *(I; A)*

## RED CROSS

Barton, Clara. *The Story of the Red Cross.* Airmont, 1968. *(P; I)*

Gilbo, Patrick. *The American Red Cross.* Chelsea House, 1987. *(I; A)*

## REFERENCE MATERIALS

Adams, Simon, et al. *Illustrated Atlas of World History.* Random House, 1992. *(I; A)*

Paton, John. *Picture Encyclopedia for Children.* Grosset, 1987. *(P; I)*

Reader's Digest. *The Reader's Digest Children's World Atlas.* Reader's Digest, 1991. *(I)*

## REFORMATION

Flowers, Sarah. *The Reformation.* Lucent, 1995. *(I; A)*

Stepanek, Sally. *John Calvin.* Chelsea House, 1986. *(I)*

## REFRIGERATION

Ford, Barbara. *Keeping Things Cool: The Story of Refrigeration and Air Conditioning.* Walker, 1986. *(I; A)*

## REFUGEES

Ashabranner, Brent, and Ashabranner, Melissa. *Into A Strange Land.* Dodd, 1987. *(I; A)*

Bentley, Judith. *Refugees: Search for a Haven.* Messner, 1986. *(P; I)*

Graff, Nancy Price. *Where the River Runs: A Portrait of a Refugee Family.* Little, 1993. *(I; A)*

Loescher, Gil, and Loescher, Ann D. *The World's Refugees: A Test of Humanity.* Harcourt, 1982. *(I; A)*

## REINDEER AND CARIBOU

Hodge, Deborah. *Deer, Moose, Elk & Caribou.* Kids Can Press, 1999. *(P)*

## RELATIVITY

Apfel, Necia H. *It's All Relative: Einstein's Theory of Relativity.* Lothrop, 1981. *(I)*
Fisher, David E. *The Ideas of Einstein.* Holt, 1980. *(P; I)*
Swisher, Clarice. *Relativity.* Greenhaven Press, 1990. *(I)*
Tauber, Gerald E. *Relativity: From Einstein to Black Holes.* Watts, 1988. *(I; A)*

## RELIGIONS OF THE WORLD

Ahsan, M. M. *Muslim Festivals.* Rourke, 1987. *(P; I)*
Bahree, Patricia. *The Hindu World.* Silver Burdett, 1983. *(I)*
Berger, Gilda. *Religions.* Watts, 1983. *(I; A)*
Butler, Jon. *Religion in Colonial America.* Oxford, 2000. *(I)*
Fisher, James T. *Catholics in America.* Oxford, 2000. *(I)*
Gellman, Rabbi Marc, and Hartman, Monsignor Thomas. *How Do You Spell God?: Answers to the Big Questions from around the World.* Morrow, 1997. *(I; A)*
Ghazi, Suhaib Hamid. *Ramadan.* Holiday, 1996. *(P)*
Kanitkar, V. P. (Hemant). *Hinduism.* Bookwright, 1987. *(I; A)*
Langley, Myrtle. *Religion.* Knopf, 1996. *(P; I ; A)*
Lugira, Aloysius. *African Religion.* Facts on File, 1999. *(I; A)*
Maestro, Betsy. *The Story of Religion.* Clarion, 1996. *(P; I)*
Martin, Nancy. *Christianity.* Bookwright, 1987. *(I; A)*
McNeer, May, and Ward, Lynd. *John Wesley.* Abingdon, 1957. *(I)*
Moktefi, Mokhtar. *The Rise of Islam.* Silver Burdett, 1987. *(P; I)*
Nardo, Don, ed. *The Rise of Christianity.* Greenhaven, 1998. *(A)*
Osborne, Mary Pope. *One World, Many Religions: The Ways We Worship.* Knopf, 1996. *(I)*
Peare, Catherine O. *John Woolman: Child of Light.* Vanguard, n.d. *(I; A)*
Raboteau, Albert J. *African-American Religion.* Oxford University, 1999. *(A)*
Snelling, John. *Buddhism.* Bookwright, 1987. *(I; A)*
Stepanek, Sally. *John Calvin.* Chelsea House, 1986. *(I)*
Tames, Richard. *Islam.* David & Charles, 1985. *(A)*
Wacker, Grant. *Religion in Nineteenth Century America.* Oxford, 2000. *(I)*

## REMBRANDT

Janson, H. W., and Janson, Anthony F. *History of Art for Young People.* Abrams, 1997. (rev. ed.) *(I; A)*
Muhlberger, Richard, and Metropolitan Museum of Art. *What Makes a Rembrandt a Rembrandt?* Viking, 1993. *(I)*
Schwartz, Gary D. *Rembrandt.* Abrams, 1992. *(A)*

## RENAISSANCE

Caselli, Giovanni. *The Renaissance and the New World.* NTC, 1998. *(I; A)*
Howarth, Sarah. *Renaissance People.* Millbrook, 1992. *(I); Renaissance Places.* Millbrook, 1992. *(I)*

## RENOIR, PIERRE AUGUSTE

Janson, H. W., and Janson, Anthony F. *History of Art for Young People.* Abrams, 1997. (rev. ed.) *(I; A)*
Parsons, Tom. *Pierre Auguste Renoir: Art for Young People.* Sterling, 1996. *(P; I)*
Rayfield, Susan. *Pierre-Auguste Renoir.* Abrams, 1998. *(I; A)*
Welton, Jude. *Eyewitness: Impressionism.* DK, 2000. *(P; I; A)*

## REPRODUCTION, HUMAN

Cole, Joanna. *How You Were Born.* Morrow, 1993 (rev. ed.). *(P)*
Girard, Linda W. *You Were Born on Your Very First Birthday.* Albert Whitman, 1983. *(P)*
Harris, Robie H. *It's So Amazing!: A Book about Eggs, Sperm, Birth, Babies, and Families.* Candlewick, 1999. *(P; I)*
Silverstein, Alvin; Silverstein, Virginia; and Silverstein, Robert. *The Reproductive System.* 21st Century Books, 1994. *(I)*

## REPTILES

Ballard, Lois. *Reptiles.* Children's, 1982. *(P; I)*
Cook, David. *Small World of Reptiles.* Watts, 1981. *(P)*
Daly, Kathleen N. *A Child's Book of Snakes, Lizards, and Other Reptiles.* Doubleday, 1980. *(P)*
DeTreville, Susan, and DeTreville, Stan. *Reptiles and Amphibians.* Troubador, 1981. *(P; I)*
Fichter, George S. *Reptiles and Amphibians of North America.* Random House, 1982. *(P; I)*
George, Lindsay Barrett, and George, William T. *Box Turtle at Long Pond.* Greenwillow, 1989. *(P)*
Johnston, Ginny, and Cutchins, Judy. *Scaly Babies: Reptiles Growing Up.* Morrow, 1988. *(I)*
Kuchalla, Susan. *What Is a Reptile?* Troll, 1982. *(P)*
Mattison, Chris. *The Care of Reptiles and Amphibians in Captivity.* Blandford Press, 1987. *(A)*
McCarthy, Colin, and Arnold, Nick. *Reptile.* Knopf, 1991. *(I)*
McNaughton, Lenor. *Turtles, Tadpoles, and Take-Me-Homes.* Good Apple, 1981. *(P; I)*
Snedden, Robert. *What Is a Reptile?* Sierra Club, 1995. *(I)*

## RESEARCH

Heiligman, Deborah. *The Kid's Guide to Research.* Scholastic, 1999. *(I)*
McInerney, Claire Fleischman. *Tracking the Facts: How to Develop Research Skills.* Lerner, 1990. *(I)*

Sullivan, Helen, and Sernoff, Linda. *Research Reports: A Guide for Middle and High School Students.* Millbrook Press, 1996. *(I; A)*

## RETAIL STORES

Gibbons, Gail. *Department Stores.* Harper, 1984. *(P)*

## RETARDATION, MENTAL

McNey, Martha. *Leslie's Story: A Book about a Girl with Mental Retardation.* Lerner, 1996. *(P; I)*

## REVERE, PAUL

Brandt, Keith. *Paul Revere: Son of Liberty.* Troll, 1982. *(P; I)*

Fritz, Jean. *And Then What Happened, Paul Revere?* Coward, 1982. *(P; I)*

Lee, Martin. *Paul Revere.* Watts, 1987. *(P)*

Longfellow, Henry Wadsworth. *" Paul Revere's Ride" from The Works of Henry Wadsworth Longfellow.* AMS Press, 1976. *(I)*

## REVOLUTIONARY WAR

Bliven, Bruce, Jr. *The American Revolution.* Random, 1996 (reissue). *(I; A)*

Carter, Alden R. *At the Forge of Liberty; Birth of the Republic; Colonies in Revolt; Darkest Hours.* Watts, 1988. *(P; I)*

Egger-Bovet, Howard, and Smith-Baranzini, Marlene. *Book of the American Revolution.* Little, 1994. *(I)*

Fritz, Jean. *And Then What Happened, Paul Revere?* Coward, 1982; *Why Can't You Make Them Behave, King George?* Putnam, 1982. *(P; I)*

Marrin, Albert. *The War for Independence: The Story of the American Revolution.* Atheneum, 1988. *(I)*

Meltzer, Milton. *The American Revolutionaries.* Crowell, 1987. *(A)*

Murphy, Jim. *A Young Patriot: The American Revolution As Experienced by One Boy.* Clarion, 1996. *(I; A)*

Smith, Carter, eds. *The Revolutionary War.* Millbrook, 1991. *(I)*

Stein, R. Conrad. *The Story of Lexington and Concord.* Children's, 1983. *(P; I)*

Zeinert, Karen. *Those Remarkable Women of the American Revolution.* Millbrook Press, 1996. *(I; A)*

## RHINOCEROSES

Bailey, Jill. *Mission Rhino.* Steck-Vaughn, 1990. *(P; I)*
Lavine, Sigmund A. *Wonders of Rhinos.* Dodd, 1982. *(I)*
Yoshida, Toshi. *Rhinoceros Mother.* Philomel, 1991. *(P)*

## RHODE ISLAND

Fradin, Dennis. *Rhode Island: In Words and Pictures.* Children's, 1981; *The Rhode Island Colony.* Children's, 1989. *(P; I)*

## RICE

Hughes, Meredith Sayles, and Hughes, E. Thomas. *Glorious Grasses: The Grains.* Lerner, 1998. *(I)*

## RIO DE JANEIRO

Kent, Deborah. *Rio de Janeiro.* Children's, 1996. *(P; I)*

## RIVERS

Bains, Rae. *Wonders of Rivers.* Troll, 1981. *(P)*

Bellamy, David. *The River.* Clarkson Potter, 1988. *(P)*

Carlisle, Norman, and Carlisle, Madelyn. *Rivers.* Children's, 1982. *(P)*

Crump, Donald. *Let's Explore a River.* National Geographic, 1988. *(P)*

Emil, Jane, and Veno, Joseph. *All about Rivers.* Troll, 1984. *(P; I)*

Hoff, Mary, and Rodgers, Mary M. *Rivers and Lakes.* Lerner, 1991. *(I)*

Lourie, Peter. *Hudson River: An Adventure from the Mountains to the Sea.* Boyds Mills Press, 1998. *(P; I)*

Martin, Patricia A. Fink. *Rivers and Streams.* Watts, 1999. *(I; A)*

Mulherin, Jenny. *Rivers and Lakes.* Watts, 1984. *(P; I)*(Atlas format)

Rawlins, Carol B. *The Orinoco River.* Watts, 1999. *(P; I)*

Rowland-Entwistle, Theodore. *Rivers and Lakes.* Silver Burdett, 1987. *(P; I)*

Updegraffe, Imelda, and Updegraffe, Robert. *Rivers and Lakes.* Penguin, 1983. *(I; A)*

Whitcraft, Melissa. *The Hudson River.* Watts, 1999. *(P; I)*

## ROADS AND HIGHWAYS

Crockett, Mary. *Roads and Traveling.* Sportshelf, n.d. *(P; I)*

Gibbons, Gail. *New Road!* Harper, 1983. *(P)*

Sauvain, Philip. *Roads.* Garrett Educational, 1990. *(P; I)*

Williams, Owen. *How Roads Are Made.* Facts on File, 1989. *(I)*

## ROBINSON, JACK ROOSEVELT (JACKIE)

Farr, Naunerle C. *Babe Ruth— Jackie Robinson* Pendulum Press, 1979. *(P; I; A)*

Frommer, Harvey. *Jackie Robinson.* Watts, 1984. *(I; A)*

Jacobs, William Jay. *They Shaped the Game.* Simon & Schuster, 1994. *(P; I)*

Krull, Kathleen. *Lives of the Athletes: Thrills, Spills (And What the Neighbors Thought).* Raintree Steck-Vaughn, 1999. *(I; A)*

Scott, Richard. *Jackie Robinson.* Chelsea House, 1987. *(I; A)*

## ROBOTS

Berger, Fredericka. *Robots: What They Are, What They Do.* Greenwillow, 1992. *(P)*

Chester, Michael. *Robots: Facts behind Fiction.* Macmillan, 1983. *(P; I)*

Hawkes, Nigel. *Robots and Computers.* Watts, 1984. *(I; A)*

Knight, David C. *Robotics: Past, Present and Future*. Morrow, 1983. *(I; A)*

Liptak, Karen. *Robotics Basics: An Introduction for Young People*. Prentice-Hall, 1984. *(I)*

Litterick, Ian. *Robots and Intelligent Machines*. Watts, 1984. *(I)*

Silverstein, Alvin, and Silverstein, Virginia. *The Robots Are Here*. Prentice-Hall, 1983. *(P; I)*

Skurzynski, Gloria. *Robots: Your High-Tech World*. Bradbury, 1990. *(I)*

Sonenklar, Carol. *Robots Rising*. Holt, 1999. *(P; I)*

## ROCKETS

Maurer, Richard. *Rocket! How a Toy Launched the Space Age*. Crown, 1995. *(I)*

## ROCK MUSIC

Fornatale, Pete. *The Story of Rock 'n' Roll*. Morrow, 1987. *(A)*

Hanmer, Trudy J. *An Album of Rock and Roll*. Watts, 1988. *(P; I)*

Tobler, John. *Thirty Years of Rock*. Exeter Books, 1985. *(A)*

## ROCKS

Cheney, Glenn Alan. *Mineral Resources*. Watts, 1985. *(I)*

Christian, Peggy. *If You Find a Rock*. Harcourt, 2000. *(P)*

Eckert, Allan W. *Earth Treasures: Where to Collect Minerals, Rocks, and Fossils in the United States*. Harper, 1987. *(I; A)*

Hiscock, Bruce. *The Big Rock*. Atheneum, 1988. *(P; I)*

Marcus, Elizabeth. *Rocks and Minerals*. Troll, 1983. *(P; I)*

Podendorf, Illa. *Rocks and Minerals*. Children's, 1982. *(P)*

Srogi, Lee Ann. *Start Collecting Rocks and Minerals*. Running Press, 1989. *(I; A)*

Symes, R. F. and the staff of the Natural History Museum. *Rocks and Minerals*. Knopf, 1988. *(I)*

Whyman, Kathryn. *Rocks and Minerals*. Gloucester Press, 1989. *(P; I)*

## ROCKWELL, NORMAN

Gherman, Beverly. *Norman Rockwell: Storyteller with a Brush*. Atheneum, 2000. *(I)*

## RODENTS

Bare, Colleen S. *Tree Squirrels*. Dodd, 1983. *(P; I)*

Gurnell, John. *The Natural History of Squirrels*. Facts on File, 1987. *(A)*

Kalman, Bobbie, and Langille, Jacqueline. *What Is a Rodent?* Crabtree/A Bobbie Kalman Bk., 1999. *(P)*

Lane, Margaret. *The Squirrel*. Dial, 1981. *(P)*

Lavine, Sigmund. *Wonders of Mice*. Dodd, 1980; *Wonders of Woodchucks*, 1984. *(I)*

McConoughey, Jana. *The Squirrels*. Crestwood, 1983. *(P; I)*

Schlein, Miriam. *Squirrel Watching*. Harper, 1992. *(P; I)*

## RODEOS

Fain, James W. *Rodeos*. Children's, 1983. *(P)*

Green, Carl R., and Sanford, William R. *Bill Pickett: African-American Rodeo Star*. Enslow, 1997. *(I)*

Munn, Vella. *Rodeo Riders*. Harvey, 1981. *(P; I; A)*

Tinkelman, Murray. *Rodeo: The Great American Sport*. Greenwillow, 1982. *(I; A)*

## ROLLER SKATING

Olney, Ross R., and Bush, Chan. *Roller Skating!* Lothrop, 1979. *(I)*

## ROMAN CATHOLIC CHURCH

Fisher, James T. *Catholics in America*. Oxford, 2000. *(I)*

## ROMANIA

Carran, Betty B. *Romania*. Children's, 1988. *(P; I)*

Diamond, Arthur. *The Romanian Americans*. Chelsea House, 1988. *(I; A)*

Sheehan, Sean. *Romania*. Marshall Cavendish, 1994. *(I; A)*

## ROMAN NUMERALS

Giesert, Arthur. *Roman Numerals I to MM*. Houghton, 1995. *(P; I)*

## ROME

Barghusen, Joan D. *Daily Life in Ancient and Modern Rome*. Lerner, 1999. *(P; I)*

## ROME, ANCIENT

Chisholm, Jan. *Roman Times*. EDC Publishing, 1982. *(I; A)*

Corbishley, Mike. *The Romans*. Watts, 1984. *(I; A)*

James, Simon. *Rome: 750 B.C.-500 A.D.* Watts, 1987. *(I)*

Lapper, Ivan. *Small World of Romans*. Watts, 1982. *(P)*

Lewis, Brenda R. *Growing Up in Ancient Rome*. David & Charles, 1980. *(I; A)*

Miguel, Pierre. *Life in Ancient Rome*. Silver Burdett, 1981. *(I)*

Mulvihill, Margaret. *Roman Forts*. Watts, 1990. *(I)*

Purdy, Susan, and Sandak, Cass R. *Ancient Rome*. (Civilization Project Book) Watts, 1982. *(I)*

Robinson, Charles A., Jr. *Ancient Rome*, rev. by Lorna Greenberg. Watts, 1984. *(I; A)*

Rutland, Jonathan. *See Inside a Roman Town*. Warwick Press, 1986. *(I)*

## ROOSEVELT, ELEANOR

Cooney, Barbara. *Eleanor*. Viking, 1996. *(P)*

Freedman, Russell. *Eleanor Roosevelt: A Life of Discovery*. Clarion, 1993. *(I; A)*

Jacobs, William J. *Eleanor Roosevelt: A Life of Happiness and Tears*. Putnam, 1983. *(I)*

Kulling, Monica. *Eleanor Everywhere: The Life of Eleanor Roosevelt*. Random, 1999. *(P)*

Roosevelt, Eleanor. *The Autobiography of Eleanor Roosevelt*. Harper, 1961. *(A)*

Roosevelt, Elliott. *Eleanor Roosevelt, with Love: A Centenary Remembrance.* Lodestar, 1984. *(A)*

Toor, Rachel. *Eleanor Roosevelt.* Chelsea House, 1989. *(I; A)*

Westervelt, Virginia Veeder. *Here Comes Eleanor: A New Biography of Eleanor Roosevelt for Young People.* Avisson, 1999. *(I)*

## ROOSEVELT, FRANKLIN D.

Devaney, John. *Franklin Delano Roosevelt, President.* Walker, 1987. *(I; A)*

Freedman, Russell. *Franklin Delano Roosevelt.* Clarion, 1990. *(I)*

Greenblatt, Miriam. *Franklin D. Roosevelt: 32nd President of the United States.* Garrett Educational, 1989. *(I)*

Hacker, Jeffrey H. *Franklin D. Roosevelt.* Watts, 1983. *(I; A)*

Osinski, Alice. *Franklin D. Roosevelt.* Children's, 1988. *(P; I)*

## ROOSEVELT, THEODORE

Fritz, Jean. *Bully for You, Teddy Roosevelt!* Putnam, 1991. *(I)*

Kent, Zachary. *Theodore Roosevelt: Twenty-Sixth President of the United States.* Children's, 1988. *(P; I)*

Sabin, Louis. *Teddy Roosevelt: Rough Rider.* Troll, 1986. *(P; I)*

Stefoff, Rebecca. *Theodore Roosevelt: 26th President of the United States.* Garrett Educational, 1988. *(A)*

## ROSS, BETSY

Miller, Susan Martins. *Betsy Ross: American Patriot.* Chelsea House, 2000. *(P; I)*

## ROWING

Page, Jason. *On the Water: Rowing, Yachting, Canoeing, and Lots, Lots, More.* Lerner, 2000. *(P; I; A)*

## RUBBER

Cosner, Sharon. *Rubber.* Walker, 1986. *(I)*

## RUSSIA

Adelman, Deborah. *The " Children of Perestroika" Come of Age: Young People of Moscow Talk about Life in the New Russia.* Sharpe, 1994. *(A)*

Harvey, Miles. *Look What Comes from Russia.* Watts, 1999. *(P; I)*

Kort, Michael. *Russia.* Facts on File, 1998. *(I; A)*

Murrell, Kathleen Berton. *Russia.* Knopf/Borzoi, 1998. *(I; A)*

## RUTH, GEORGE HERMAN (BABE)

Berke, Art. *Babe Ruth: The Best There Ever Was.* Watts, 1988. *(A)*

Burleigh, Robert. *Home Run: The Story of Babe Ruth.* Harcourt, 1998. *(P)*

Jacobs, William Jay. *They Shaped the Game.* Simon & Schuster, 1994. *(P; I)*

Krull, Kathleen. *Lives of the Athletes: Thrills, Spills (And What the Neighbors Thought).* Raintree Steck-Vaughn, 1999. *(I; A)*

## RWANDA

Aardema, Verna. *Sebgugugu the Glutton: A Bantu Tale from Rwanda.* Eerdmans, William B., 1993. *(P)*

Bodnarchuk, Kari. *Rwanda: Country Torn Apart.* Lerner, 1999. *(I; A)*

Foster, F. Blanche. *East Central Africa: Kenya, Uganda, Tanzania, Rwanda, and Burundi.* Watts, 1981. *(I; A)*

Greenberg, Keith. *Rwanda: Fierce Clashes in Central America.* Blackbirch, 1996. *(P;I)*

Pomeray, J. K. *Rwanda.* Chelsea House, 1988. *(I)*

## SAFETY

Brown, Marc, and Krensky, Stephen. *Dinosaurs, Beware! A Safety Guide.* Little, 1982. *(P)*

Chlad, Dorothy. *Matches and Fireworks Are Not Toys; Strangers; When I Cross the Street— By Myself.* Children's, 1982. *(P)*

Girard, Linda Walvoord. *Who Is a Stranger and What Should I Do?* Albert Whitman, 1985. *(P)*

Keller, Irene. *Thingumajig Book of Health and Safety.* Children's, 1982. *(P)*

Vogel, Carol G., and Goldner, Kathryn A. *The Danger of Strangers.* Dillon, 1983. *(I)*

## SAILING

Adkins, Jan. *The Craft of Sail: A Primer of Sailing.* Walker, 1983. *(I)*

Burchard, Peter. *Venturing: An Introduction to Sailing.* Little, 1986. *(I; A)*

Marshall Cavendish Corporation, ed. *Into the Wind: Sailboats Then and Now.* Marshall Cavendish, 1996. *(P; I)*

Slocombe, Lorna. *Sailing Basics.* Prentice-Hall, 1982. *(P; I)*

## SAINT KITTS AND NEVIS

McKenley, Yvonne. *A Taste of the Caribbean.* Raintree Steck-Vaughn, 1995. *(P; I)*

## SAINT LAWRENCE RIVER AND SEAWAY

Hanmer, Trudy J. *The St. Lawrence.* Watts, 1984. *(I; A)*

## SAINT LOUIS

Hintz, Martin. *Destination St. Louis.* Lerner, 1998. *(P; I)*

## SAINT LUCIA

McKenley, Yvonne. *A Taste of the Caribbean.* Raintree Steck-Vaughn, 1995. *(P; I)*

## SAINTS

Mayo, Margaret. *Brother Sun, Sister Moon: The Life and Stories of St. Francis.* Little, Brown, 2000. *(P; I)*

Morgan, Nina, and Wood, Richard. *Mother Teresa: Saint of the Poor.* Raintree Steck-Vaughn, 1998. *(P; I)*

Mulvihill, Margaret. *The Treasury of Saints and Martyrs.* Penguin, 1999. *(P; I)*

Schmidt, Gary D. *Saint Ciaran: The Tale of a Saint of Ireland.* Eerdmans, William B., 2000. *(P; I)*

## SAINT VINCENT AND THE GRENADINES

McKenley, Yvonne. *A Taste of the Caribbean.* Raintree Steck-Vaughn, 1995. *(P; I)*

## SALES AND MARKETING

Boy Scouts of America. *Salesmanship.* Boy Scouts, 1971. *(I; A)*

## SALT

Mebane, Robert C., and Rybolt, Thomas. *Salts and Solids.* Twenty-First Century, 1995. *(I)*

## SALT LAKE CITY

Doubleday, Veronica. *Salt Lake City.* Silver Burdett Press, 1994. *(I)*

## SALVATION ARMY

Green, Roger J. *Catherine Booth: A Biography of the Cofounder of the Salvation Army.* Baker Books, 1996. *(I; A)*

## SAN ANTONIO

McComb, David G. *Texas: An Illustrated History.* Oxford, 1995. *(I; A)*

Sorrels, Roy. *The Alamo in American History.* Enslow, 1996. *(I)*

## SANDBURG, CARL

Hacker, Jeffrey H. *Carl Sandburg.* Watts, 1984. *(I; A)*

Krull, Kathleen. *Lives of the Writers: Comedies, Tragedies (And What the Neighbors Thought).* Raintree Steck-Vaughn, 1998. *(I; A)*

Meltzer, Milton. *Carl Sandburg: A Biography.* Twenty-First Century, 1999. *(I; A)*

Sandburg, Carl. *Prairie-Town Boy.* Harcourt, 1977. *(A); Rootabaga Stories,* n.d. *(P; I)*

## SAN FRANCISCO

Haddock, Patricia. *San Francisco.* Dillon, 1988. *(P)*

## SANITATION

Colman, Penny. *Toilets, Bathtubs, Sinks, and Sewers: A History of the Bathroom.* Simon & Schuster, 1994. *(I)*

## SÃO TOMÉ AND PRÍNCIPE

Boyd, Herb. *The Former Portuguese Colonies: Angola, Mozambique, Guinea-Bissau, Cape Verde, São Tomé, and Príncipe.* Watts, 1981. *(I; A)*

## SASKATCHEWAN

Richardson, Gillian. *Saskatchewan.* Lerner, 1998. *(P; I)*

## SATELLITES

Barrett, Norman. *The Picture World of Rockets and Satellites; The Picture World of Space Shuttles.* Watts, 1990. *(P)*

Berger, Melvin. *Space Shots, Shuttles, and Satellites.* Putnam, 1983. *(I; A)*

Fox, Mary Virginia. *Satellites.* Benchmark, 1996. *(P; I)*

Furniss, Tim. *Space Rocket.* Gloucester Press, 1988. *(P; I)*

Irvine, Mat. *Satellites and Computers.* Watts, 1984. *(I; A)*

Petty, Kate. *Satellites.* Watts, 1984. *(P)*

Walker, Niki, and Kalman, Bobbie. *Satellites and Space Probes.* Crabtree, 1998. *(P)*

White, Jack R. *Satellites of Today and Tomorrow.* Dodd, 1985. *(I; A)*

## SATELLITES, ARTIFICIAL

Branley, Franklyn M. *The International Space Station.* HarperCollins, 2000. *(P); From Sputnik to Space Shuttles, into the New Space Age.* HarperCollins, 1989. *(P; I)*

## SATURN

Asimov, Isaac. *Saturn: The Ringed Beauty.* Gareth Stevens, 1989. *(P; I)*

Halliday, Ian. *Saturn.* Facts on File, 1990. *(P; I)*

Landau, Elaine. *Saturn.* Watts, 1991. *(P; I)*

Simon, Seymour. *Saturn.* Morrow, 1985. *(P)*

## SAUDI ARABIA

*Saudi Arabia . . . in Pictures.* Lerner, 1989. *(I)*

Lye, Keith. *Take a Trip to Saudi Arabia.* Watts, 1984. *(P; I)*

## SCANDINAVIA

Booss, Claire, ed. *Scandinavian Folk & Fairy Tales.* Crown, 1985. *(A)*

Franck, Irene M. *The Scandinavian-American Heritage.* Facts on File, 1988. *(I; A)*

## SCHLIEMANN, HEINRICH

Caselli, Giovanni. *In Search of Troy: One Man's Quest for Homer's Fabled City.* NTC, 1999. *(P; I)*

## SCHOOLS

Fisher, Leonard. *Schoolmasters.* Godine, 1986; *The Schools.* Holiday, 1983. *(I)*

Kalman, Bobbie. *Early Schools.* Crabtree, 1981. *(I)*

Loeper, John J. *Going to School in 1776.* Atheneum, 1984. *(I)*

## SCHWEITZER, ALBERT

Crawford, Gail, and Renna, Giani. *Albert Schweitzer.* Silver Burdett Press, 1990. *(I; A)*

Robles, Harold. *Albert Schweitzer: An Adventurer for Humanity.* Millbrook Press, 1994. *(I)*

## SCIENCE

Asimov, Isaac. *Great Ideas of Science.* Houghton, 1969. *(A)*

Folsom, Franklin. *Science and the Secret of Man's Past.* Harvey House, 1966. *(I)*

January, Brendan. *Science in the Renaissance.* Watts, 1999. *(P; I)*

Ross, Frank, Jr. *Oracle Bones, Stars, and Wheelbarrows: Ancient Chinese Science and Technology.* Houghton, 1982. *(I; A)*

Sayre, April Pulley. *Put on Some Antlers and Walk Like a Moose: How Scientists Find, Follow, and Study Wild Animals.* Twenty-First Century, 1997. *(I)*

Stille, Darlene R. *Extraordinary Women Scientists.* Children's, 1995. *(I)*

Tannenbaum, Beulah and Tannenbaum, Harold E. *Science of the Early American Indians.* Watts, 1988. *(I)*

Temple, Robert. *The Genius of China: 3000 Years of Science, Discovery and Invention.* Simon & Schuster, 1986. *(I; A)*

VanCleave, Janice. *Janice VanCleave's A + Projects in Earth Science: Winning Experiments for Science Fairs and Extra Credit.* Wiley, 1999. *(I; A)*

Woods, Geraldine. *Science of the Early Americas.* Watts, 1999. *(P; I)*

## SCIENCE FAIRS

Sobey, Ed. *How to Enter and Win an Invention Contest.* Enslow, 1999. *(I; A)*

Voth, Danna. *Kidsource: Science Fair Handbook.* Lowell House, 1998. *(P; I)*

## SCIENCE FICTION

*Science Fiction Hall of Fame,* 2 vols. Avon, 1983. *(I; A)*

Cohen, Daniel. *The Monsters of Star Trek.* Archway, 1980. *(P; I)*

Datnow, Claire L. *American Science Fiction and Fantasy Writers.* Enslow, 1999. *(I)*

Heinlein, Robert A., ed. *Tomorrow, the Stars.* Berkley, 1983. *(I; A)*

LeGuin, Ursula. *The Last Book of Earthsea.* Atheneum, 1990. *(I)*

Liebman, Arthur, ed. *Science Fiction: Creators and Pioneers.* Rosen, 1979. *(I; A)*

Reid, Suzanne Elizabeth. *Presenting Young Adult Science Fiction.* Twayne, 1998. *(I; A)*

Yolen, Jane, ed. *2041.* Delacorte, 1991. *(I)*

## SCOPES TRIAL

Blake, Arthur. *The Scopes Trial: Defending the Right to Teach.* Millbrook, 1994. *(P; I)*

## SCORPIONS

Hillyard, Paul. *Spiders and Scorpions: A Unique First Visual Reference.* Reader's Digest, 1995. *(P; I)*

Pringle, Laurence. *Scorpion Man: Exploring the World of Scorpions.* Simon & Schuster, 1994. *(I)*

## SCOTLAND

Lye, Kenneth. *Take a Trip to Scotland.* Watts, 1984. *(P; I)*

Meek, James. *The Land and People of Scotland.* Lippincott, 1990. *(I; A)*

Sutcliff, Rosemary. *Bonnie Dundee.* Dutton, 1984. *(I; A)*

## SCULPTURE

Fine, Joan. *I Carve Stone.* Harper, 1979. *(I)*

Haldane, Suzanne. *Faces on Places: About Gargoyles and Other Stone Creatures.* Viking, 1980. *(P; I)*

Janson, H. W., and Janson, Anthony F. *History of Art for Young People.* Abrams, 1997. (rev. ed.) *(I; A)*

## SEA LIONS

Patent, Dorothy Hinshaw. *Seals, Sea Lions and Walruses.* Holiday, 1990. *(P; I)*

Sherrow, Victoria. *Seals, Sea Lions & Walruses.* Watts, 1991. *(P)*

## SEALS

Fields, Alice. *Seals.* Watts, 1980. *(P)*

Grace, Eric S. *Seals.* Sierra Club Books/Little, 1991. *(I; A)*

Myers, Susan. *Pearson: A Harbor Seal Pup.* Dutton, 1981. *(P; I)*

Patent, Dorothy Hinshaw. *Seals, Sea Lions and Walruses.* Holiday, 1990. *(P; I)*

Sherrow, Victoria. *Seals, Sea Lions & Walruses.* Watts, 1991. *(P)*

## SEASONS

Bennett, David. *Seasons.* Bantam, 1988. *(P)*

Gibbons, Gail. *The Reasons for Seasons.* Holiday, 1995. *(P)*

Hirschi, Ron. *Spring; Winter.* Cobblehill, 1990. *(P)*

Lambert David. *The Seasons.* Watts, 1983. *(P)*

Markle, Sandra. *Exploring Autumn: A Season of Science Activities, Puzzlers, and Games.* Atheneum, 1991; *Exploring Winter.* Atheneum, 1984. *(I)*

McNaughton, Colin. *Autumn; Spring; Summer; Winter.* Dial, 1983. *(P)*

Penn, Linda. *Young Scientists Explore the Seasons.* Good Apple, 1983. *(P)*

Vaughan, Jenny. *The Four Seasons.* Watts, 1983. *(P)*

Zolotow, Charlotte. *Summer Is. . . .* Harper, 1983. *(P)*

## SEATTLE

Snelson, Karen. *Seattle: Downtown America.* Silver Burdett Press, 1992. *(P)*

Stein, R. Conrad. *Seattle.* Children's Press, 1999. *(P; I)*

## SEGREGATION

Bentley, Judith. *Busing: The Continuing Controversy.* Watts, 1982. *(I; A)*

Bullard, Pamela, and Stoia, Judith. *The Hardest Lesson: Personal Stories of a School Desegregation Crisis.* Little, 1980. *(I; A)*

## SENDAK, MAURICE

Marcus, Leonard S. *A Caldecott Celebration: Six Artists and Their Paths to the Caldecott Medal.* Walker, 1998. *(P; I)*

## SENEGAL

Fichter, George S. *The Bulge of Africa: Senegal, Guinea, Ivory Coast, Togo, Benin, and Equatorial Guinea.* Watts, 1981. *(I; A)*

Lutz, William. *Senegal.* Chelsea House, 1987. *(P; I)*

*Senegal . . . in Pictures.* Lerner, 1988. *(I; A)*

## SEPTEMBER

Updike, John. *A Child's Calendar.* Holiday House, 1999. *(P; I)*

Warner, Penny. *Kids' Holiday Fun: Great Family Activities Every Month of the Year.* Meadowbrook Press, 1997. *(P)*

## SERBIA

Milivojevic, Joann. *Serbia.* Children's Press, 1999. *(I; A)*

## SEUSS, DR.

Weidt, Maryann N. *Oh, the Places He Went: A Story About Dr. Seuss.* Carolrhoda, 1994. *(P; I)*

## SEWING

Cone, Ferne G. *Classy Knitting: A Guide to Creative Sweatering for Beginners.* Atheneum, 1984; *Crazy Crocheting.* Atheneum, 1981. *(I; A)*

Eaton, Jan. *The Encyclopedia of Sewing Techniques.* Barron, 1987. *(A)*

Wilson, Erica. *Erica Wilson's Children's World: Needlework Ideas from Childhood Classics,* 1983; *Erica Wilson's Christmas World,* 1982; *Erica Wilson's Embroidery Book; More Needleplay,* 1979; *Needleplay.* Scribner's, 1975; *Erica Wilson's Quilts of America.* Oxmoor House, 1979. *(I; A)*

## SHAKESPEARE, WILLIAM

Aliki. *William Shakespeare and the Globe.* HarperCollins, 1999. *(P; I)*

Bloom, Harold, ed. *Shakespeare's Histories.* Chelsea House, 1999. *(A)*

Brown, John Russell. *Shakespeare and His Theatre.* Lothrop, 1982. *(I)*

Ferris, Julie. *Shakespeare's London: A Guide to Elizabethan London.* Kingfisher, 2000. *(P; I)*

Hodges, C. Walter. *Shakespeare's Theatre.* Putnam, 1980. *(I)*

Krull, Kathleen. *Lives of the Writers: Comedies, Tragedies (And What the Neighbors Thought).* Raintree Steck-Vaughn, 1998. *(I; A)*

Lamb, Charles, and Lamb, Mary. *Tales from Shakespeare.* Puffin, 1988. *(I)*

Shellard, Dominic. *William Shakespeare.* Oxford, 1999. *(I; A)*

## SHARKS, SKATES, AND RAYS

*Sharks.* Facts on File, 1990. *(I)*

Albert, Burton. *Sharks and Whales.* Grosset, 1989. *(P)*

Batten, Mary. *Shark Attack Almanac.* Random, 1997. *(I)*

Blassingame, Wyatt. *Wonders of Sharks.* Dodd, 1984. *(P; I)*

Bunting, Eve. *The Great White Shark.* Messner, 1982. *(I)*

Cerullo, Mary M. *The Truth About Great White Sharks.* Chronicle, 2000. *(P; I)*

Dingerkus, Guido. *The Shark Watcher's Guide.* Messner, 1985. *(I)*

Gay, Tanner Ottley. *Sharks in Action.* Aladdin, 1990. *(P)*

Gibbons, Gail. *Sharks.* Holiday, 1992. *(P)*

Langley, Andrew. *The World of Sharks.* Bookwright, 1988. *(P)*

Markle, Sandra. *Outside and Inside Sharks.* Atheneum, 1996. *(I)*

Perrine, Doug. *Sharks and Rays of the World.* Voyageur, 2000. *(A)*

Zoehfeld, Kathleen Weidner. *Great White Shark: Ruler of the Sea.* Soundprints, 1995. *(P)*

## SHEEP

Levine, Sigmund A., and Scuro, Vincent. *Wonders of Sheep,* 1983. *(P; I)*

McDearmon, Kay. *Rocky Mountain Bighorns.* Dodd, 1983. *(P; I)*

Moon, Cliff. *Sheep on the Farm.* Watts, 1983. *(P; I)*

Paladino, Catherine. *Springfleece: A Day of Sheepshearing.* Little, 1990. *(P; I)*

## SHELLS

Arthur, Alex. *Shell.* Knopf, 1989. *(I)*

Selsam, Millicent E., and Hunt, Joyce A. *A First Look at Seashells.* Walker, 1983. *(P)*

## SHERMAN, WILLIAM TECUMSEH

Whitelaw, Nancy. *William Tecumseh Sherman: Defender and Destroyer.* Morgan Reynolds, 1996. *(I; A)*

## SHIPS AND SHIPPING

Bushey, Jerry. *The Barge Book.* Carolrhoda, 1984. *(P; I)*

Carter, Katherine. *Ships and Seaports.* Children's, 1982. *(P)*

Gibbons, Gail. *Boat Book.* Holiday, 1983. *(P)*

Graham, Ian. *Boats, Ships, Submarines, and Other Floating Machines.* Kingfisher, 1993. *(I)*

Lambert, Mark. *Ship Technology.* Bookwright, 1990. *(I)*

Maestro, Betsy, and DelVecchio, Ellen. *Big City Port.* Four Winds, 1983. *(P)*

Rutland, Jonathan. *Ships.* Watts, 1982 (updated ed.). *(I; A)*

Stephen, R. J. *The Picture World of Warships.* Watts, 1990. *(P)*

Thomas, David A. *How Ships Are Made.* Facts on File, 1989. *(I)*

Wilkinson, Philip. *Ships: History, Battles, Discovery, Navigation.* Larousse Kingfisher Chambers, 2000. *(P; I)*

Williams, Brian. *Ships and Other Seacraft.* Watts, 1984. *(P; I; A)*

## SHORT STORIES

Salem Press Staff, and May, Charles E., eds. *Short Story Writers.* Salem Press, 1997. *(A)*

## SIBERIA

Anderson, Madelyn Klein. *Siberia.* Putnam, 1988. *(I; A)*

Buell, Janet. *Ancient Horsemen of Siberia.* Millbrook Press, 1998. *(I; A)*

Hautzig, Esther. *The Endless Steppe: Growing up in Siberia.* HarperCollins, 1995. *(P; I; A)*

## SIERRA LEONE

Gilfond, Henry. *Gambia, Ghana, Liberia, and Sierra Leone.* Watts, 1981. *(I; A)*

Milsome, John. *Sierra Leone.* Chelsea House, 1988. *(P; I)*

## SILK

Johnson, Sylvia A. *Silkworms.* Lerner, 1982. *(P; I)*

## SILVER

Rickard, Graham. *Spotlight on Silver.* Rourke, 1988. *(P; I)*

## SINGAPORE

Elder, Bruce. *Malaysia. Singapore.* Watts, 1985. *(P)*

Layton, Lesley. *Singapore.* Marshall Cavendish, 1990. *(I)*

Stein, R. Conrad. *The Fall of Singapore.* Children's, 1982. *(P; I)*

## SKATEBOARDING

Cassorla, Albert. *The Ultimate Skateboard Book.* Running Press, 1989. *(I; A)*

Thatcher, Kevin J., and Brannon, Brian. *Thrasher: The Radical Skateboard Book.* Random House, 1992. *(I; A)*

## SKELETAL SYSTEM

Broekel, Ray. *Your Skeleton and Skin.* Children's, 1984. *(P)*

Llewellyn, Claire. *The Big Book of Bones: An Introduction to Skeletons.* Peter Bedrick, 1998. *(I)*

Sandeman, Anna. *Bones.* Millbrook, 1995. *(P)*

Silverstein, Alvin; Silverstein, Virginia; and Silverstein, Robert. *The Skeletal System.* 21st Century Books, 1994. *(I)*

Walker, Richard. *The Visual Dictionary of the Skeleton.* Dorling Kindersley, 1995. *(I; A)*

Ward, Brian T. *The Skeleton and Movement.* Watts, 1981. *(I)*

## SKIING

Berry, I. William. *The Great North American Ski Book.* Scribner's, 1982 (rev. ed.). *(I)*

Campbell, Stu, and others. *The Way to Ski!* HP Books, 1987. *(A)*

Krementz, Jill. *A Very Young Skier.* Dial, 1990. *(P; I)*

Marozzi, Alfred. *Skiing Basics.* Prentice-Hall, 1984. *(P; I)*

Sullivan, George. *Cross-Country Skiing: A Complete Beginner's Book.* Messner, 1980. *(P; I)*

Washington, Rosemary G. *Cross-Country Skiing Is for Me.* Lerner, 1982. *(I)*

## SKIN DIVING

Earle, Sylvia A. *Dive: My Adventures in the Deep Frontier.* National Geographic, 1999. *(P; I)*

## SKYDIVING

Benson, Rolf. *Skydiving.* Lerner, 1979. *(P; I; A)*

Nentl, Jerolyn. *Skydiving.* Crestwood, 1978. *(P)*

## SLAVERY

Bial, Raymond. *The Strength of These Arms: Life in the Slave Quarters.* Houghton, 1997. *(I)*

Collier, Christopher, and Collier, James Lincoln. *Slavery and the Coming of the Civil War: 1831-1861.* Marshall Cavendish/Benchmark, 1999. *(I)*

Cosner, Shaaron. *The Underground Railroad.* Watts, 1991. *(I; A)*

Currie, Stephen. *Life of a Slave on a Southern Plantation.* Lucent, 1999. *(I; A)*

Everett, Gwen. *John Brown: One Man Against Slavery.* Rizzoli, 1994. *(I; A)*

Haskins, James, and Benson, Kathleen. *Bound for America: The Forced Migration of Africans to the New World.* Lothrop, 1999. *(I; A)*

Haskins, Jim. *Get on Board: The Story of the Underground Railroad.* Scholastic, 1993. *(I; A)*

Johnson, Dolores. *Seminole Diary: Remembrances of a Slave.* Macmillan, 1994. *(P; I)*

Katz, William Loren. *Breaking the Chains: African-American Slave Resistance.* Atheneum, 1990. *(A)*

Lawrence, Jacob. *Harriet and the Promised Land.* Simon and Schuster, 1994. *(P; I)*

Lilley, Stephen R. *Fighters against American Slavery.* Lucent, 1998. *(I; A)*

Meltzer, Milton. *They Came in Chains: The Story of the Slave Ships.* Benchmark, 1999. *(I; A) All Times, All Peoples: A World History of Slavery.* Harper, 1980. *(A);*

Ofosu-Appiah, L. H. *People in Bondage: African Slavery Since the 15th Century.* Runestone Press, 1993. *(I; A)*

Winter, Jeanette. *Follow the Drinking Gourd.* Knopf, 1992. *(P)*

## SLEEP

Eldred, Patricia M. *What Do We Do When We're Asleep?* Creative Education, 1981. *(P)*

Silverstein, Alvin, and Silverstein, Virginia. *The Mystery of Sleep.* Little, 1987. *(P; I)*

Silverstein, Alvin, and others. *Sleep.* Watts, 2000. *(P; I)*

Simpson, Carolyn. *Coping with Sleep Disorders.* Rosen, 1995. *(I; A)*

## SLOVAKIA

Kinkade, Sheila. *Children of Slovakia.* Lerner, 2000. *(P; I)*

## SMITH, JOHN

Fritz, Jean. *The Double Life of Pocahontas.* Putnam, 1983. *(P; I)*

## SMITHSONIAN INSTITUTION

Collins, Mary. *The Smithsonian Institution.* Children's Press, 2000. *(P; I)*

## SMOKING

Berger, Gilda. *Smoking Not Allowed: The Debate.* Watts, 1987. *(A)*

Gano, Lila. *Smoking.* Lucent Books, 1989. *(I; A)*

Hirschfelder, Arlene. *Kick Butts! A Kid's Action Guide to a Tobacco-Free America.* Simon & Schuster/Messner, 1998. *(I; A)*

Kranz, Rachel. *Straight Talk about Smoking.* Facts on File, 1999. *(I; A)*

Lang, Susan, and Marks, Beth H. *Teens & Tobacco: A Fatal Attraction.* 21st Century Books, 1996. *(A)*

Pietrusza, David. *Smoking.* Lucent, 1997. *(I)*

Sonnett, Sherry. *Smoking.* Watts, 1988. *(I; A)*

Ward, Brian R. *Smoking and Health.* Watts, 1986. *(I; A)*

## SNAKES

Anderson, Robert. *A Step-by-Step Book about Snakes.* TFH Publications, 1988. *(I; A)*

Arnold, Caroline. *Snake.* Morrow, 1991. *(P; I)*

Broekel, Ray. *Snakes.* Children's, 1982. *(P)*

Chace, G. Earl. *Rattlesnakes.* Dodd, 1984. *(I)*

Freedman, Russell. *Rattlesnakes.* Holiday, 1984. *(P)*

Gove, Dors. *A Water Snake's Year.* Atheneum, 1991. *(P; I)*

Lauber, Patricia. *Snakes Are Hunters.* Crowell, 1988. *(P)*

Lavies, Bianca. *The Secretive Timber Rattlesnake.* Dutton, 1990. *(P)*

Maestro, Betsy. *Take a Look at Snakes.* Scholastic, 1992. *(P)*

Markle, Sandra. *Outside and inside Snakes.* Macmillan, 1995. *(I)*

McClung, Robert M. *Snakes: Their Place in the Sun.* Garrard, 1991 (rev. ed.). *(P; I)*

Montgomery, Sy. *The Snake Scientist.* Houghton, 1999. *(I)*

Rubio, Manny. *Rattlesnake: Portrait of a Predator.* Smithsonian, 1998. *(A)*

## SOAP BOX DERBY

Radlauer, Ed, and Radlauer, Ruth. *Soap Box Winners.* Children's, 1983. *(P; I)*

## SOCCER

Arnold, Caroline. *Soccer: From Neighborhood Play to the World Cup.* Watts, 1991. *(P; I)*

Butterfield, S. M. *The Wonderful World of Soccer.* Putnam, 1982. *(P; I; A)*

Cohen, Mervyn D. *Soccer for Children and Their Parents.* Brunswick, 1983. *(P; I)*

Delson, Paul. *Soccer Sense: Terms, Tips, and Techniques.* Bradson, 1983. *(I; A)*

Lineker, Gary. *Soccer.* DK, 2000. *(P; I)*

Longman, Jere. *The Girls of Summer: The U.S. Women's Soccer Team and How It Changed the World.* HarperCollins, 2000. *(A)*

Rosenthal, Bert. *Soccer.* Children's, 1983. *(P)*

Yannis, Alex. *Soccer Basics.* Prentice-Hall, 1982. *(P; I)*

## SOCIAL STUDIES

Jackson, Ellen B. *Turn of the Century.* Charlesbridge, 1998. *(P; I)*

## SOFTBALL

Sandak, Cass R. *Baseball and Softball.* Watts, 1982. *(P)*

Washington, Rosemary G. *Softball Is for Me.* Lerner, 1982. *(P; I)*

## SOILS

Bocknek, Jonathan. *The Science of Soil.* Gareth Stevens, 1999. *(P; I)*

Leutscher, Alfred. *Earth.* Dial, 1983. *(P; I)*

Prager, Ellen J. *Sand.* National Geographic, 2000. *(P)*

## SOLAR ENERGY

Asimov, Isaac. *How Did We Find Out about Solar Power?* Walker, 1981. *(P; I)*

Kaplan, Sheila. *Solar Energy.* Raintree, 1983. *(P; I)*

Spetgang, Tilly, and Wells, Malcolm. *The Children's Solar Energy Book.* Sterling, 1982. *(P; I)*

## SOLAR SYSTEM

Adams, Richard. *Our Wonderful Solar System.* Troll, 1983. *(P; I)*

Cole, Joanna. *The Magic Schoolbus: Lost in the Solar System.* Scholastic, 1990. *(I)*

Lambert, David. *The Solar System.* Watts, 1984. *(I; A)*

Roop, Peter, and Roop, Connie. *The Solar System.* Greenhaven Press, 1988. *(A)*

Smoluchowski, Roman. *The Solar System.* Freeman, 1983. *(I)*

## SOLIDS

Berger, Melvin *Solids, Liquids, and Gases.* Putnam, 1989. *(I; A)*

Gardner, Robert. *Science Projects about Solids, Liquids, and Gases.* Enslow, 2000. *(I; A)*

Mebane, Robert C., and Rybolt, Thomas R. *Salts and Solids.* Twenty-First Century, 1995. *(I)*

## SOMALIA

Godbeer, Deardre. *Somalia.* Chelsea House, 1988. *(P; I)*

Matthews, Jo, and Ganeri, Anita. *I Remember Somalia.* Raintree Steck-Vaughn, 1994. *(I)*

Woods, Harold, and Woods, Geraldine. *The Horn of Africa: Ethiopia, Sudan, Somalia, and Djibouti.* Watts, 1981. *(I; A)*

## SOUND AND ULTRASONICS

Broekel, Ray. *Sound Experiments.* Children's, 1983. *(P)*

Gardner, Robert. *Science Projects about Sound.* Enslow, 2000. *(I; A)*

Kettelkamp, Larry. *The Magic of Sound.* Morrow, 1982. *(I)*

Knight, David. *All about Sound.* Troll, 1983. *(P; I)*

Lampton, Christopher. *Sound: More Than What You Hear.* Enslow, 1992. *(I; A)*

Taylor, Barbara. *Hear! Hear! The Science of Sound.* Random House, 1991. *(P; I)*

Wicks, Keith. *Sound and Recording.* Watts, 1982. *(I; A)*

## SOUTH AFRICA

Blumberg, Rhoda. *Southern Africa: South Africa, Namibia, Swaziland, Lesotho, and Botswana.* Watts, 1981. *(I; A)*

Canesso, Claudia. *South Africa.* Chelsea House, 1999. *(I; A)*

Harris, Sarah. *Timeline: South Africa.* Dryad Press, 1988. *(I; A)*

Jacobsen, Karen. *South Africa.* Children's, 1989. *(P)*

Lawson, Don. *South Africa.* Watts, 1986. *(I)*

Meyer, Carolyn. *Voices of South Africa: Growing Up in a Troubled Land.* Gulliver Books, 1986. *(I; A)*

Pascoe, Elaine. *South Africa: Troubled Land.* Watts, 1992. (rev. ed.) *(A)*

Paton, Jonathan. *The Land and People of South Africa.* Lippincott, 1990. *(A)*

Stein, R. Conrad. *South Africa.* Children's, 1986. *(P)*

Watson, R. L. *South Africa . . . in Pictures.* Lerner, 1988. *(P; I)*

## SOUTH AMERICA

Carter, William E. *South America.* Watts, 1983 (rev. ed.). *(I; A)*

Petersen, David. *South America.* Children's Press, 1998. *(A)*

Reynolds, Jan. *Amazon Basin: Vanishing Cultures.* Harcourt, 1993. *(P; I)*

## SOUTH CAROLINA

Fradin, Dennis. *South Carolina: In Words and Pictures.* Children's, 1980. *(P; I)*

Osborne, Anne R. *A History of South Carolina.* Sandlapper Publishing, 1983. *(P; I)*

## SOUTH DAKOTA

Fradin, Dennis. *South Dakota: In Words and Pictures.* Children's, 1981. *(P; I)*

Santella, Andrew. *Mount Rushmore.* Children's Press, 1999. *(P; I)*

## SOUTHEAST ASIA

*Malaysia . . . in Pictures.* Lerner, 1989. *(I)*

*Thailand . . . in Pictures.* Lerner, 1989. *(I)*

Bjener, Tamiko. *Philippines.* Gareth Stevens, 1987. *(P)*

Chandler, David P. *The Land and People of Cambodia.* Harper, 1991. *(I; A)*

Cordero Fernando, Gilda. *We Live in the Philippines.* Bookwright, 1986. *(P; I)*

Elder, Bruce. *Malaysia. Singapore.* Watts, 1985. *(P)*

Fairclough, Chris. *We Live in Indonesia.* Bookwright, 1986. *(P; I)*

Fox, Mary Virginia. *Papua New Guinea.* Children's, 1994. *(I; A)*

Goldfarb, Mace. *Fighters, Refugees, Immigrants: A Story of the Hmong.* Carolrhoda, 1982. *(P; I)*

Huynh Quang Nhuong. *The Land I Lost: Adventures of a Boy in Vietnam.* Harper, 1982. *(I)*

Knowlton, MaryLee, and Sachner, Mark J. *Burma; Indonesia; Malaysia.* Gareth Stevens, 1987. *(P)*

Layton, Lesley. *Singapore.* Marshall Cavendish, 1990. *(I)*

Lee, Jeanne. *Toad Is the Uncle of Heaven: A Vietnamese Folk Tale.* Holt, 1985. *(P)*

Lye, Keith. *Indonesia.* Watts, 1985. *(P)*

Nickelson, Harry. *Vietnam.* Lucent Books, 1989. *(I; A)*

Smith, Datus C., Jr. *The Land and People of Indonesia.* Harper, 1983 (rev. ed.). *(I)*

Stein, R. Conrad. *The Fall of Singapore.* Children's, 1982. *(P; I)*

Thomson, Ruth, and Thomson, Neil. *A Family in Thailand.* Lerner, 1988. *(P)*

Withington, William A. *Southeast Asia.* Gateway Press, 1988. *(I; A)*

Wright, David K. *Burma.* Children's, 1996. *(I); Malaysia.* Children's, 1988. *(P; I)*

## SPACE EXPLORATION AND TRAVEL

Apfel, Necia H. *Voyager to the Planets.* Clarion, 1991. *(P; I)*

Asimov, Isaac. *Piloted Space Flights.* Gareth Stevens, 1990. *(P; I)*

Baird, Anne. *Space Camp: The Great Adventure for NASA Hopefuls.* Morrow, 1992. *(I)*

Becklake, Sue. *Space: Stars, Planets, and Spacecraft.* Dorling Kindersley, 1991. *(I; A)*

Berger, Melvin. *Space Shots, Shuttles, and Satellites.* Putnam, 1983. *(I; A)*

Bernards, Neal. *Living in Space.* Greenhaven Press, 1990. *(I; A)*

Bond, Peter. *DK Guide to Space: A Photographic Journey through the Universe.* DK, 1999. *(P; I)*

Branley, Franklyn M. *From Sputnik to Space Shuttles: Into the New Space Age.* Crowell, 1986. *(P; I)*

Burrows, William E. *Mission to Deep Space: Voyagers' Journey of Discovery.* Freeman, 1993. *(I; A)*

Darling, David. *Could You Ever Fly to the Stars?* Dillon, 1990. *(P; I)*

Dwiggins, Don. *Flying the Space Shuttles.* Dodd, 1985. *(I); Hello? Who's Out There?: The Search for Extraterrestrial Life,* 1987. *(P; I)*

Embury, Barbara. *The Dream Is Alive.* Harper, 1990. *(I)*

Ferguson, Kitty. *Black Holes in Spacetime.* Watts, 1991. *(I; A)*

Fox, Mary Virginia. *Women Astronauts aboard the Shuttle.* Messner, 1984. *(P; I)*

Harris, Alan, and Weissman, Paul. *The Great Voyager Adventure: A Guided Tour through the Solar System.* Messner, 1990. *(I)*

Kelch, Joseph W. *Small Worlds: Exploring the 60 Moons of Our Solar System.* Messner, 1989. *(I; A)*

Lampton, Christopher. *Rocketry: From Goddard to Space Travel.* Watts, 1988. *(P; I)*

Long, Kim. *The Astronaut Training Book for Kids.* Lodestar, 1990. *(I)*

Maurer, Richard. *Junk in Space.* Simon & Schuster, 1989. *(P; I); The Nova Space Explorer's Guide: Where to Go and What to See.* Crown, 1985. *(I; A)*

Moulton, Robert R. *First to Fly.* Lerner, 1983. *(P; I)*

O'Conner, Karen. *Sally Ride and the New Astronauts: Scientists in Space.* Watts, 1983. *(I; A)*

Sandak, Cass R. *The World of Space.* Watts, 1989. *(P; I)*

Schefter, James L. *Aerospace Careers.* Watts, 1987. *(A)*

Schick, Ron, and Van Haaften, Julia. *The View from Space.* Clarkson N. Potter, 1988. *(A)*

Solomon, Maury. *An Album of Voyager.* Watts, 1990. *(I)*

Spangenburg, Ray, and Moser, Diane. *Opening the Space Frontier.* Facts on File, 1989. *(I; A)*

Vogt, Gregory. *Space Laboratories.* Watts, 1990. *(P; I); Spaceships.* Watts, 1990. *(P; I)*

## SPACE PROBES

Ride, Sally, and O'Shaughnessy, Tam. *Voyager: An Adventure to the Edge of the Solar System.* Crown, 1992. *(P; I)*

## SPACE STATIONS

Dyson, Marianne J. *Space Station Science: Life in Free Fall.* Scholastic, 1999. *(I)*

Sipiera, Diane M., and Sipiera, Paul P. *Space Stations.* Grolier, 1998. *(P; I)*

## SPACE TELESCOPES

Cole, Michael D. *Hubble Space Telescope: Exploring the Universe.* Enslow, 1999. *(I)*

Scott, Elaine. *Adventure in Space: The Flight to Fix the Hubble.* Hyperion, 1995. *(I; A)*

## SPAIN

Hodges, Margaret. *Don Quixote and Sancho Panza.* Scribner's, 1992. *(I; A)*

Lye, Keith. *Passport to Spain.* Watts, 1987. *(P)*

Miller, Arthur. *Spain.* Chelsea House, 1989. *(P; I)*

Selby, Anna. *Spain.* Steck-Vaughn, 1994. *(I)*

Woods, Geraldine. *Spain: A Shining New Democracy.* Dillon, 1987. *(P; I)*

Yokoyama, Masami. *Spain.* Gareth Stevens, 1987. *(P; I)*

## SPANISH-AMERICAN WAR

Marrin, Albert. *The Spanish-American War.* Atheneum, 1991. *(I; A)*

## SPANISH ARMADA

Anderson, David. *The Spanish Armada.* Watts, 1988. *(I; A)*

## SPAIN, ART AND ARCHITECTURE OF

Carter, David. *Salvador Dali: Spanish Painter.* Chelsea House, 1994. *(I; A)*

Janson, H. W., and Janson, Anthony F. *History of Art for Young People.* Abrams, 1997. (rev. ed.) *(I; A)*

Muhlberger, Richard, and Metropolitan Museum of Art. *What Makes a Goya a Goya?* Viking, 1994. *(I)*

Riboldi, Silvia; Schiaffino, Mariarosa; and Trojer, Thomas. *Goya.* NTC, 1999. *(I)*

Venezia, Mike. *El Greco.* Children's Press, 1998. *(P)*

Waldron, Ann. *Francisco Goya.* Abrams, 1992. *(I)*

## SPAIN, LANGUAGE AND LITERATURE OF

De Saulles, Janet, and Wright, Nicola. *Getting to Know: Spain and Spanish.* Barron's, 1993. *(P; I)*

## SPECIAL OLYMPICS

Brown, Fern G., and Rich, Mary P., ed. *Special Olympics.* Watts, 1992. *(P; I)*

## SPEECH

Adams, Edith. *The Noisy Book Starring Yakety Yak.* Random House, 1983. *(P)*

Carlisle, Jock A. *Tangled Tongue.* University of Toronto Press, 1985. *(A)*

Minn, Loretta. *Teach Speech.* Good Apple, 1982. *(P; I)*

Showers, Paul. *How You Talk.* Harper, 1967; 1975; 1992 (paper). *(P)*

Silverstein, Alvin, and Silverstein, Virginia. *Wonders of Speech.* Morrow, 1988. *(A)*

## SPEECH DISORDERS

Berger, Gilda. *Speech and Language Disorders.* Watts, 1981. *(I; A)*

## SPELLING

Gordon, Sharon. *The Spelling Bee.* Troll, 1981. *(P)*

Wittels, Harriet, and Greisman, Joan. *How to Spell It: A Dictionary of Commonly Misspelled Words.* Putnam, 1982. *(P; I; A)*

## SPELUNKING

Dean, Anabel. *Going Underground: All about Caves and Caving.* Dillon, 1984. *(I)*

## SPIDERS

Dallinger, Jane. *Spiders.* Lerner, 1981. *(P; I; A)*

Fowler, Allan. *Spiders Are Not Insects.* Children's, 1996. *(P)*

Glaser, Linda. *Spectacular Spiders.* Millbrook, 1998. *(P)*

Hillyard, Paul. *Spiders and Scorpions: A Unique First Visual Reference.* Reader's Digest, 1995. *(P; I)*

Lane, Margaret. *The Spider.* Dial, 1982. *(P)*

Schnieper, Claudia. *Amazing Spiders.* Carolrhoda, 1989. *(P; I)*

Selsam, Millicent E., and Hunt, Joyce A. *A First Look at Spiders.* Walker, 1983. *(P)*

Webster, David. *Spider Watching.* Messner, 1984. *(I)*

## SPIES

Dann, Geoff. *Spy.* Knopf, 1996. *(P;I;A)*

Moss, Francis. *The Rosenberg Espionage Case.* Lucent, 1999. *(I; A)*

Ziff, John. *Espionage and Treason.* Chelsea House, 1999. *(I; A)*

## SRI LANKA

*Sri Lanka . . . in Pictures.* Lerner, 1989. *(I; A)*

Wilber, Donald N. *The Land and People of Ceylon.* Harper, 1972. *(I; A)*

## STALIN, JOSEPH

Caulkins, Janet. *Joseph Stalin.* Watts, 1990. *(I; A)*

Marrin, Albert. *Stalin: Russia's Man of Steel.* Viking, 1988. *(A)*

## STAMPS AND STAMP COLLECTING

Allen, Judy. *Guide to Stamps and Stamp Collecting.* EDC Publishing, 1981. *(P; I)*

Hobson, Burton. *Getting Started in Stamp Collecting.* Sterling. 1982 (rev. ed.) *(I; A)*

Lewis, Brenda Ralph. *Stamps!* Lodestar, 1991. *(I; A)*

## STANTON, ELIZABETH CADY

Fritz, Jean. *You Want Women to Vote, Lizzie Stanton?* Putnam, 1995. *(I)*

## STARFISH

Hurd, Edith Thacher. *Starfish.* HarperCollins, 2000. *(P)*

## STARS

Adler, Irving. *The Stars: Decoding Their Messages.* Crowell, 1980. *(I)*

Apfel, Necia H. *Nebulae: The Birth and Death of Stars.* Lothrop, 1988. *(P); Stars and Galaxies.* Watts, 1982. *(I; A)*

Berger, Melvin. *Bright Stars, Red Giants, and White Dwarfs.* Putnam, 1983. *(I; A); Star Gazing, Comet Tracking, and Sky Mapping.* Putnam, 1986. *(I)*

Berry, Richard. *Discover the Stars.* Harmony, 1987. *(P; I)*

Branley, Franklyn M. *Superstar: The Supernova of 1987.* HarperCollins, 1990. *(P; I); Star Guide.* Crowell, 1987. *(P; I); Journey into a Black Hole.* Crowell, 1986; *The Sky Is Full of Stars.* Crowell, 1981. *(P)*

Couper, Heather, and Henbest, Nigel. *Galaxies and Quasars.* Watts, 1986. *(I)*

Gibbons, Gail. *Stargazers.* Holiday, 1992. *(P)*

Gustafson, John R. *Stars, Clusters and Galaxies.* Silver Burdett Press, 1993.

Monroe, Jean. *They Dance in the Sky: Native American Star Myths.* Houghton, 1987. *(I)*

Rockwell, Anne. *Our Stars.* Harcourt/Silver Whistle, 1999. *(P)*

## STATE, UNITED STATES DEPARTMENT OF

Bartz, Carl. *The Department of the State.* Chelsea House, 1989. *(P; I)*

## STATE GOVERNMENTS

Goode, Stephen. *The New Federalism: States' Rights in American History.* Watts, 1983. *(I; A)*

## STATISTICS

Riedel, Manfred G. *Winning with Numbers: A Kid's Guide to Statistics.* Prentice-Hall, 1978. *(I; A)*

## STEAM ENGINES

Siegel, Beatrice. *The Steam Engine.* Walker, 1987. *(I)*

## STEINBECK, JOHN

Florence, Donne. *John Steinbeck: America's Author.* Enslow, 2000. *(I)*

Reef, Catherine. *John Steinbeck.* Clarion, 1996. *(A)*

## STOMACH

Ballard, Carol. *The Stomach and Digestive System.* Raintree/Steck-Vaughn, 1997. *(I)*

## STORYTELLING

Trelease, Jim, ed. *Hey! Listen to This: Stories to Read Aloud.* Viking Penguin, 1992. *(A)*

Trelease, Jim. *The New Read-Aloud Handbook.* Viking Penguin, 1989. *(A)*

## STOWE, HARRIET BEECHER

Jakoubek, Robert E. *Harriet Beecher Stowe: Author and Abolitionist.* Chelsea House, 1989. *(I; A)*

Scott, John A. *Woman against Slavery: The Story of Harriet Beecher Stowe.* Harper, 1978. *(I; A)*

## STRAVINSKY, IGOR

Venezia, Mike. *Igor Stravinsky.* Children's Press, 1997. *(P)*

## STRINGED INSTRUMENTS

Dearling, Robert, ed. *The Illustrated Encyclopedia of Musical Instruments.* Gale Research, 1996. *(I; A)*

## STUDY, HOW TO

Farnette, Cherrie. *The Study Skills Shop.* Incentive Publications, 1980. *(P; I)*

Fry, Ron. *" Ace" Any Test; How to Study.* Career, 1996. *(I; A)*

James, Elizabeth, and Barkin, Carol. *How to Be School Smart: Secrets of Successful Schoolwork.* Lothrop, 1988. *(I; A)*

Kesselman-Turkel, Judi, and Peterson, Franklynn. *Study Smarts: How to Learn More in Less Time.* Contemporary Books, 1981. *(I; A)*

## SUBMARINES

Graham, Ian. *Submarines.* Gloucester Press, 1989. *(I)*

Maas, Peter. *The Terrible Hours: The Man Behind the Greatest Submarine Rescue in History.* HarperCollins, 2000. *(A)*

Rossiter, Mike. *Nuclear Submarine.* Watts, 1983. *(I; A)*

Stephen, R. J. *The Picture World of Submarines.* Watts, 1990. *(P)*

Sullivan, George. *Inside Nuclear Submarines.* Dodd, 1982. *(I; A)*

Weiss, Harvey. *Submarines and Other Underwater Craft.* Crowell, 1990. *(P; I)*

White, David. *Submarines.* Rourke, 1988. *(P)*

## SUDAN

*Sudan . . . in Pictures.* Lerner, 1988. *(I)*

Stewart, Judy. *A Family in Sudan.* Lerner, 1988. *(P)*

Woods, Harold, and Woods, Geraldine. *The Horn of Africa: Ethiopia, Sudan, Somalia, and Djibouti.* Watts, 1981. *(I; A)*

## SUGAR

Cobb, Vicki. *Gobs of Goo.* Harper, 1983. *(P)*

Mitgutsch, Ali. *From Beet to Sugar.* Carolrhoda, 1981. *(P)*

Nottridge, Rhoda. *Sugars.* Lerner, 1993. *(P; I)*

## SUN

Adams, Richard. *Our Amazing Sun.* Troll, 1983. *(P; I)*

Ardley, Neil. *Sun and Light.* Watts, 1983. *(P; I)*

Asimov, Isaac. *How Did We Find Out about Sunshine?* Walker, 1987. *(P; I)*

Darling, David. *The Sun: Our Neighborhood Star.* Dillon, 1984. *(I)*

Fields, Alice. *The Sun.* Watts, 1980. *(P)*

Gibbons, Gail. *Sun Up, Sun Down.* Harcourt, 1983. *(P; I)*

Jaber, William. *Exploring the Sun.* Messner, 1980. *(P; I)*

Lampton, Christopher. *The Sun.* Watts, 1982. *(I; A)*

Palazzo, Janet. *Our Friend the Sun.* Troll, 1982. *(P)*

## SUPERSONIC FLIGHT

Aaseng, Nathan. *Breaking the Sound Barrier.* Silver Burdett Press, 1992. *(I; A)*

## SUPERSTITION

Nevins, Ann. *Super Stitches: A Book of Superstitions.* Holiday, 1983. *(P)*

Perl, Lila. *Don't Sing Before Breakfast, Don't Sleep in the Moonlight: Everyday Superstitions and How They Began.* Clarion, 1988. *(I)*

## SUPREME COURT OF THE UNITED STATES

Coy, Harold. *The Supreme Court,* rev. by Lorna Greenberg. Watts, 1981. *(I; A)*

Fox, Mary V. *Justice Sandra Day O'Connor.* Enslow, 1983. *(I; A)*

Goode, Stephen. *The Controversial Court: Supreme Court Influences on American Life.* Messner, 1982. *(I; A)*

Greene, Carol. *The Supreme Court.* Children's, 1985. *(P); Sandra Day O'Connor: First Woman of the Supreme Court.* Children's, 1982. *P*

Herda, D. J. *Furman v. Georgia: The Death Penalty Case; New York Times v. United States: National Security and Censorship; Roe v. Wade: The Abortion Question; The Dred Scott Case: Slavery and Citizenship.* Enslow, 1994. *(I; A)*

Lawson, Don. *Landmark Supreme Court Cases.* Enslow, 1987. *(A)*

McElroy, Lisa Tucker. *Meet My Grandmother: She's a Supreme Court Justice.* Millbrook, 1999. *(P)*

Rierden, Anne B. *Reshaping the Supreme Court: New Justices, New Directions.* Watts, 1988. *(A)*

Riley, Gail Blasser. *Miranda v. Arizona: Rights of the Accused.* Enslow, 1994. *(I; A)*

Stein, R. Conrad. *The Story of the Powers of the Supreme Court.* Children's, 1989. *(I)*

## SURFING

Freeman, Tony. *Beginning Surfing.* Children's, 1980. *(P; I)*

Wardlaw, Lee. *Cowabunga! The Complete Book of Surfing.* Avon, 1991. *(I; A)*

## SURGERY

Kittredge, Mary, and Thurman, Sandra. *Organ Transplants.* Chelsea House, 2000. *(I; A)*

Parker, Steve, and West, David. *Brain Surgery for Beginners and Other Major Operations for Minors.* Millbrook Press, 1995. *(I)*

Woods, Michael, and Woods, Mary B. *Ancient Medicine: From Sorcery to Surgery.* Lerner, 1999. *(I)*

## SURINAME

Beatty, Noelle B. *Suriname.* Chelsea House, 1987. *(P; I)*

## SURREALISM

Carter, David. *Salvador Dali: Spanish Painter.* Chelsea House, 1994. *(I; A)*

Gaff, Jackie, and Oliver, Clare. *1920-40: Realism and Surrealism.* Gareth Stevens, 2001. *(P; I)*

## SWAZILAND

Blumberg, Rhoda. *Southern Africa: South Africa, Namibia, Swaziland, Lesotho, and Botswana.* Watts, 1981. *(I; A)*

Conway, Jessica. *Swaziland.* Chelsea House, 1989. *(P; I)*

Kessler, Christina, and Mswati III. *All the King's Animals: The Return of Endangered Wildlife to Swaziland.* Boyds Mills Press, 1995. *(P; I)*

## SWEDEN

Bjener, Tamiko. *Sweden.* Gareth Stevens, 1987. *(P; I)*

Knowlton, MaryLee, and Sachner, Mark J. *Sweden.* Gareth Stevens, 1987. *(P)*

Lye, Keith. *Take a Trip to Sweden.* Watts, 1983. *(P)*

McGill, Allyson. *The Swedish Americans.* Chelsea House, 1988. *(I; A)*

Olsson, Kari. *Sweden: A Good Life for All.* Dillon, 1983. *(I; A)*

## SWIMMING

Adler, David A. *America's Champion Swimmer: Gertrude Ederle.* Harcourt, 2000. *(P)*

Chiefari, Jane, and Wightman, Nancy. *Better Synchronized Swimming for Girls.* Dodd, 1981. *(I)*

Cross, Rick. *Swimming.* DK, 2000. *(P; I)*

Gleasner, Diana C. *Illustrated Swimming, Diving, and Surfing Dictionary for Young People.* Harvey, 1980. *(P; I; A)*

Libby, Bill. *The Young Swimmer.* Lothrop, 1983. *(P; I)*

Orr, C. Rob, and Tyler, Jane B. *Swimming Basics.* Prentice-Hall, 1980. *(P; I; A)*

Sullivan, George. *Better Swimming for Boys and Girls.* Dodd, 1982. *(A)*

## SWITZERLAND

Cameron, Fiona, and Kristensen, Preben. *We Live in Switzerland.* Bookwright, 1987. *(P)*

Hintz, Martin. *Switzerland.* Children's, 1986. *(P)*

Levy, Patricia. *Switzerland.* Marshall Cavendish, 1994. *(P; I)*

Lye, Keith. *Take a Trip to Switzerland.* Watts, 1984. *(P; I)*

Schrepfer, Margaret. *Switzerland: The Summit of Europe.* Dillon, 1989. *(P; I)*

## SYRIA

*Syria.* Chelsea House, 1988. *(P)*

Beaton, Margaret. *Syria.* Children's, 1988. *(I)*

Mulloy, Martin. *Syria.* Chelsea House, 1988. *(P)*

## TABLE TENNIS

Sullivan, George. *Better Table Tennis for Boys and Girls.* Putnam, 1972. *(I)*

## TAFT, WILLIAM HOWARD

Casey, Jane Clark. *William Howard Taft.* Children's, 1989. *(P; I)*

## TAIWAN

Moiz, Azra. *Taiwan.* Marshall Cavendish, 1995. *(I; A)*

Yu, Ling. *A Family in Taiwan.* Lerner, 1990. *(P)*

## TAJIKISTAN

*Tajikistan.* Lerner, 1993. *(I)*

## TAJ MAHAL

Moorcroft, Christine. *The Taj Mahal.* Raintree Steck-Vaughn, 1997. *(P; I)*

## TANZANIA

*Tanzania . . . in Pictures.* Lerner, 1988. *(I)*

Foster, F. Blanche. *East Central Africa: Kenya, Uganda, Tanzania, Rwanda, and Burundi.* Watts, 1981. *(I; A)*

Margolies, Barbara A. *Rehema's Journey: A Visit in Tanzania.* Scholastic, 1990. *(P)*

McCulla, Patricia E. *Tanzania.* Chelsea House, 1988. *(I)*

## TAXATION

Taylor, Jack. *The Internal Revenue Service.* Chelsea House, 1987. *(A)*

## TAXIDERMY

Cutchins, Judy, and Johnston, Ginny. *Are Those Animals Real? How Museums Prepare Wildlife Exhibits.* Morrow, 1984. *(P; I)*

## TAXONOMY

Gutnik, Martin J. *The Science of Classification: Finding Order among Living and Non-Living Objects.* Watts, 1980. *(I; A)*

## TAYLOR, ZACHARY

Collins, David R. *Zachary Taylor: 12th President of the United States.* Garrett Educational, 1989. *(I)*

Kent, Zachary. *Zachary Taylor: Twelfth President of the United States.* Children's, 1988. *(P; I)*

## TCHAIKOVSKY, PETER ILYICH

Krull, Kathleen. *Lives of the Musicians: Good Times, Bad Times (And What the Neighbors Thought).* Raintree Steck-Vaughn, 1998. *(I; A)*

Thompson, Wendy. *Pyotr Ilyich Tchaikovsky.* Viking, 1993. *(I; A)*

Venezia, Mike. *Peter Tchaikovsky.* Children's Press, 1995. *(P)*

## TEACHERS AND TEACHING

Shockley, Robert J., and Cutlip, Glen W. *Careers in Teaching.* Rosen, 1988. *(A)*

## TECHNOLOGY

Adkins, Jan. *Moving Heavy Things.* Houghton, 1980. *(I; A)*

Ardley, Neil. *Fact or Fantasy.* Watts, 1982. *(I; A); Force and Strength.* Watts, 1985. *(P; I); Muscles to Machines.* Gloucester Press, 1990. *(I)*

Baker, Christopher W. *Virtual Reality: Experiencing Illusion.* Millbrook, 2000. *(I)*

Burnie, David. *Machines and How They Work.* Dorling Kindersley, 1991. *(I; A)*

Diagram Group. *Weapons: An International Encyclopedia from 5000 B.C. to 2000 A.D.* St. Martin's, 1990. *(I; A)*

Dunn, Andrew. *Wheels at Work; The Power of Pressure.* Thomson Learning, 1993. *(I)*

Gies, Frances, and Gies, Joseph. *Cathedral, Forge, and Waterwheel: Technology and Invention in the Middle Ages.* HarperCollins, 1994. *(A)*

Gross, Cynthia S. *The New Biotechnology: Putting Microbes to Work.* Lerner, 1988. *(I; A)*

Hodges, Henry. *Technology in the Ancient World.* Knopf, 1970. *(I)*

Horvatic, Anne. *Simple Machines.* Dutton, 1989. *(P)*

Lambert, David, and Insley, Jane. *Great Discoveries and Inventions.* Facts on File, 1985. *(I; A)*

Macaulay, David. *The Way Things Work.* Houghton, 1988. *(I; A)*

Math, Irwin. *Tomorrow's Technology: Experimenting With the Science of the Future.* Scribner's, 1992. *(I; A)*

McKie, Robin. *Technology: Science at Work.* Watts, 1984. *(I; A)*

Morgan, Kate. *The Story of Things.* Walker, 1991. *(P; I)*

National Geographic editors. *How Things Work.* National Geographic, 1983 *(P; I; A)*

Parker, Steve. *Everyday Things & How They Work.* Random House, 1991. *(P; I); The Random House Book of How Things Work.* Random House, 1991. *(I)*

Rockwell, Anne, and Rockwell, Harlow. *Machines.* Macmillan, 1985. *(P)*

Skurzynski, Gloria. *Almost the Real Thing: Simulation in Your High-Tech World.* Bradbury, 1991. *(I)*

Smith, Norman F., and Douglas W. *Simulators.* Watts, 1989. *(I; A)*

Stacy, Tom. *Wings, Wheel & Sails.* Random House, 1991. *(P; I)*

Weiss, Harvey. *Machines and How They Work.* Crowell, 1983. *(I)*

Wilson, Anthony. *Communications: How the Future Began.* Larousse Kingfisher Chambers, 1999. *(P; I)*

Zubrowski, Bernie. *Wheels at Work: Building and Experimenting with Models of Machines.* Morrow, 1986. *(I)*

## TEETH

Pluckrose, Henry. *Teeth.* Watts, 1988. *(P)*

Silverstein, Alvin; Silverstein, Virginia; and Nunn, Laura Silverstein. *Tooth Decay and Cavities.* Watts, 1999. *(P; I)*

## TELEGRAPH

Math, Irwin. *Morse, Marconi, and You: Understanding and Building Telegraph, Telephone, and Radio Sets.* Scribner's, 1979. *(I; A)*

## TELEPHONE

Cavanagh, Mary. *Telephone Power.* Enrich, 1980. *(P; I)*

Math, Irwin. *Morse, Marconi, and You: Understanding and Building Telegraph, Telephone, and Radio Sets.* Scribner's, 1979. *(I; A)*

Webb, Marcus. *Telephones: Words Over Wires.* Lucent Books, 1992. *(I)*

## TELESCOPES

Chaple, Glenn F. *Exploring with a Telescope.* Watts, 1988. *(I)*

## TELEVISION

Beale, Griffin. *TV and Video.* EDC Publishing, 1983. *(P; I)*

Borgenicht, David. *Sesame Street Unpaved: Scripts, Stories, Secrets, and Songs.* Hyperion, 1998. *(A)*

Calabro, Marian. *ZAP! A Brief History of Television.* Four Winds, 1992. *(I)*

Drucker, Malka, and James, Elizabeth. *Series TV: How a Television Show Is Made.* Houghton, 1983. *(I; A)*

Fields, Alice. *Television.* Watts, 1981. *(P)*

Jaspersohn, William. *A Day in the Life of a Television News Reporter.* Little, 1981. *(I)*

Riehecky, Janet. *Television.* Benchmark, 1996. *(P; I)*

Scott, Elaine. *Ramona: Behind the Scenes of a Television Show.* Morrow, 1988. *(P; I)*

Smith, Betsy. *Breakthrough: Women in Television.* Walker, 1981. *(A)*

## TENNESSEE

Feeney, Kathy. *Tennessee: Facts and Symbols.* Capstone/Hilltop, 2000. *(P)*

Fradin, Dennis. *Tennessee: In Words and Pictures.* Children's, 1980. *(P; I)*

## TENNIS

Braden, Vic, and Bruns, Bill. *Vic Braden's Quick Fixes.* Little, 1988. *(I; A)*

Knudson, R. R. *Martina Navratilova: Tennis Power.* Viking Kestrel, 1986. *(P; I)*

LaMarche, Bob. *Tennis Basics.* Prentice-Hall, 1983. *(P; I)*

Sullivan, George. *Better Tennis for Boys and Girls.* Dodd, 1987. *(I)*

Vicario, Arantxa Sanchez. *Tennis.* DK, 2000. *(P; I)*

Wright, David K. *Arthur Ashe: Breaking the Color Barrier in Tennis.* Enslow, 1996. *(I)*

## TERRARIUMS

Broekel, Ray. *Aquariums and Terrariums.* Children's, 1982. *(P)*

Mattison, Christopher. *The Care of Reptiles and Amphibians in Captivity.* Blandford Press, 1987. *(I; A)*

Steinberg, Phil. *You and Your Pet: Terrarium Pets.* Lerner, 1978. *(P; I)*

## TERRORISM

Arnold, Terrell E., and Kennedy, Moorhead. *Think about Terrorism: The New Warfare.* Walker, 1988. *(A)*

Coker, Chris. *Terrorism and Civil Strife.* Watts, 1987. *(I)*

Edwards, Richard. *International Terrorism.* Rourke, 1988. *(I)*

Greenberg, Keith Elliot. *Bomb Squad Officer: Expert with Explosives.* Blackbirch Press, 1995. *(P)*

Sherrow, Victoria. *The Oklahoma City Bombing: Terror in the Heartland; The World Trade Center Bombing: Terror in the Towers.* Enslow, 1998. *(P; I)*

## TESTS AND TEST TAKING

*How to Get Better Test Scores: Grades 3-4; How to Get Better Test Scores: Grades 5-6; How to Get Better Test Scores: Grades 7-8.* Random House, 1991. *(P; I)*

## TEXAS

Adams, Carolyn. *Stars over Texas.* Eakin Press, 1983. *(P; I)*

Collier, Christopher, and Collier, James L. *Hispanic America, Texas, and the Mexican War 1835-1850.* Benchmark, 1998. *(I)*

Fisher, Leonard. *The Alamo.* Holiday, 1987. *(I)*

Peacock, Howard. *The Big Thicket of Texas: America's Ecological Wonder.* Little, 1984. *(I; A)*

McComb, David G. *Texas: An Illustrated History.* Oxford, 1995. *(I; A)*

Phillips, Betty Lou and Bryce. *Texas.* Watts, 1987. *(P; I)*

Roderus, Frank. *Duster: The Story of a Texas Cattle Drive.* Texas Christian University Press, 1987. *(I)*

Sorrels, Roy. *The Alamo in American History.* Enslow, 1996. *(I)*

Stein, R. Conrad. *Texas.* Children's, 1989. *(P; I)*

Warren, Betsy. *Let's Remember When Texas Belonged to Spain.* Hendrick-Long, 1982; *Let's Remember When Texas Was a Republic,* 1983; *Texas in Historic Sites and Symbols,* 1982. *(I; A)*

Younger, Jassamine. *If These Walls Could Speak: A Story of Early Settlement in Texas.* Hendrick-Long, 1981. *(I)*

## TEXTILES

Cobb, Vicki. *Fuzz Does It!* Harper, 1982. *(P)*

Macaulay, David. *Mill.* Houghton, 1983. *(I; A)*

Whyman, Kathryn. *Textiles.* Gloucester Press, 1988. *(P; I)*

## THANKSGIVING DAY

Anderson, Joan. *The First Thanksgiving Feast.* Clarion, 1984. *(I)*

Baldwin, Margaret. *Thanksgiving.* Watts, 1983. *(I; A)*

Barkin, Carol, and James, Elizabeth. *Happy Thanksgiving!* Lothrop, 1987. *(P; I)*

Barth, Edna. *Turkey, Pilgrims, and Indian Corn: The Story of the Thanksgiving Symbols.* Houghton, 2000. *(P; I)*

Gibbons, Gail. *Thanksgiving Day.* Holiday, 1983. *(I)*

Kessel, Joyce K. *Squanto and the First Thanksgiving.* Carolrhoda, 1983. *(P)*

Penner, Ruth. *The Thanksgiving Book.* Hastings, 1983. *(I; A)*

## THATCHER, MARGARET

Faber, Doris. *Margaret Thatcher: Britain's "Iron Lady."* Viking Kestrel, 1985. *(I)*

Levin, Angela. *Margaret Thatcher.* David & Charles, 1981. *(P; I)*

Moskin, Marietta D. *Margaret Thatcher of Great Britain.* Silver Burdett, 1990. *(I; A)*

## THEATER

Cummings, Richard. *Simple Makeup for Young Actors.* Plays, 1990. *(A)*

Ellis, Roger, ed. *Audition Monologues for Student Actors: Selections from Contemporary Plays.* Meriwether, 1999. *(A)*

Gallo, Donald R. *Center Stage: One-Act Plays for Teenage Readers and Actors.* Harper, 1991. *(I; A)*

Gillette, J. Michael. *Theatrical Design and Production.* Mayfield, 1987. *(A)*

Greenberg, Jan. *Theater Careers.* Holt, 1983. *(I; A)*

Haskins, James S. *Black Theater in America.* Harper, 1982. *(I; A)*

Hewett, Joan. *On Camera: The Story of a Child Actor.* Clarion, 1987. *(P)*

Huberman, Caryn, and Wetzel, JoAnne. *Onstage/Backstage.* Carolrhoda, 1987. *(P)*

Judy, Susan, and Judy, Stephen. *Putting On a Play.* Scribner's, 1982. *(I)*

Krementz, Jill. *A Very Young Actress.* Knopf, 1991. *(P; I)*

Lowndes, Rosemary. *Make Your Own World of the Theater.* Little, 1982. *(I; A)*

Loxton, Howard. *Theater.* Steck-Vaughn, 1989. *(I)*

Surface, Mary Hall. *Short Scenes and Monologues for Middle School Actors.* Smith & Kraus, 2000. *(I; A)*

Williamson, Walter. *Behind the Scenes: The Unseen People Who Make Theater Work.* Walker, 1987. *(I; A)*

## THIRTEEN AMERICAN COLONIES

Anderson, Joan. *A Williamsburg Household.* Clarion, 1988. *(I)*

Blackburn, Joyce. *James Edward Oglethorpe.* Dodd, 1983. *(I; A)*

Daugherty, James. *The Landing of the Pilgrims.* Random, 1996. *(I)*

Doherty, Kieran. *Puritans, Pilgrims, and Merchants: Founders of the Northeastern Colonies; Soldiers, Cavaliers, and Planters: Settlers of the Southeastern Colonies.* Oliver, 1999. *(P; I)*

Fradin, Dennis B. *The Virginia Colony.* Children's, 1987. *(I)*

Fritz, Jean. *The Double Life of Pocahontas.* Putnam, 1983; *Who's That Stepping on Plymouth Rock?* 1975. *(P; I)*

Lukes, Bonnie L. *Colonial America.* Lucent, 1999. *(I; A)*

Reische, Diana. *Founding the American Colonies.* Watts, 1989. *(P; I)*

Scott, John Anthony. *Settlers on the Eastern Shore.* Facts on File, 1991. *(A)*

Sewall, Marcia. *The Pilgrims of Plimoth.* Atheneum, 1986. *(P)*

## THOREAU, HENRY DAVID

Burleigh, Robert. *A Man Named Thoreau.* Atheneum, 1985. *(P)*

Miller, Douglas T. *Henry David Thoreau: A Man for All Seasons.* Facts on File, 1991. *(I; A)*

Reef, Catherine. *Henry David Thoreau: A Neighbor to Nature.* 21st Century Books, 1991. *(P; I)*

## THORPE, JAMES FRANCIS (JIM)

Krull, Kathleen. *Lives of the Athletes: Thrills, Spills (And What the Neighbors Thought).* Raintree Steck-Vaughn, 1999. *(I; A)*

## THUNDER AND LIGHTNING

Branley, Franklyn M. *Flash, Crash, Rumble, and Roll.* HarperCollins, 1999. *(P)*

Hopping, Lorraine Jean. *Wild Weather: Lightning!* Scholastic, 1999. *(P)*

Simon, Seymour. *Lightning.* Morrow, 1997. *(P;I)*

## TIDES

Bowden, Joan. *Why the Tides Ebb and Flow.* Houghton, 1979. *(P)*

Stephens, William. *Life in the Tidepool.* McGraw, 1975. *(P; I)*

## TIGERS

Ashby, Ruth. *Tigers.* Atheneum, 1990. *(I)*

Dutemple, Lesley A. *Tigers.* Lerner, 1996. *(P)*

Harman, Amanda. *Tigers.* Marshall Cavendish, 1995. *(P; I)*

Lewin, Ted. *Tiger Trek.* Macmillan, 1990. *(P)*

McClung, Robert M. *Rajpur: Last of the Bengal Tigers.* Morrow, 1982. *(P; I)*

Stonehouse, Bernard. *A Visual Introduction to Wild Cats.* Facts on File, 1999. *(P; I; A)*

## TIME

Branley, Franklyn. *Keeping Time.* Houghton, 1993. *(I)*

Grey, Judith. *What Time Is It?* Troll, 1981. *(P)*

Humphrey, Henry, and Humphrey, Deirdre. *When Is Now: Experiments with Time and Timekeeping Devices.* Doubleday, 1981. *(I)*

Livoni, Cathy. *Elements of Time.* Harcourt, 1983. *(I; A)*

Llewellyn, Claire. *My First Book of Time.* Dorling Kindersley, 1992. *(P)*

Simon, Seymour. *The Secret Clocks: Time Senses of Living Things.* Penguin, 1981. *(I; A)*

Ziner, Feenie, and Thompson, Elizabeth. *Time.* Children's, 1982. *(P)*

## TIN

Heiserman, David L. *Exploring Chemical Elements and Their Compounds.* McGraw-Hill, 1991. *(A)*

## TINTORETTO

Janson, H. W., and Janson, Anthony F. *History of Art for Young People.* Abrams, 1997. (rev. ed.) *(I; A)*

## TITIAN

Janson, H. W., and Janson, Anthony F. *History of Art for Young People.* Abrams, 1997. (rev. ed.) *(I; A)*

## TITO

Schiffman, Ruth. *Josip Broz Tito.* Chelsea House, 1987. *(A)*

## TOBACCO

Heyes, Eileen. *Tobacco, USA: The Industry behind the Smoke Curtain.* Twenty-First Century, 1999. *(I; A)*

## TOGO

Fichter, George S. *The Bulge of Africa: Senegal, Guinea, Ivory Coast, Togo, Benin, and Equatorial Guinea.* Watts, 1981. *(I; A)*

Winslow, Zachery. *Togo.* Chelsea House, 1987. *(P; I)*

## TOLKIEN, J. R. R.

Collins, David R. *J.R.R. Tolkien: Master of Fantasy.* Lerner, 1991. *(I; A)*

Helms, Randel. *Tolkien's World.* Houghton, 1975. *(I; A)*

## TOMATOES

Watts, Barrie. *Tomato.* Silver Burdett Press, 1995. *(P)*

## TOOLS

Gibbons, Gail. *The Tool Book.* Holiday, 1982. *(P)*

Robbins, Ken. *Tools.* Scholastic, 1983. *(P)*

## TOPOLOGY

Froman, Robert. *Rubber Bands, Baseballs, and Doughnuts: A Book About Topology.* Harper, 1972. *(P)*

## TORNADOES

Alth, Max, and Alth, Charlotte. *Disastrous Hurricanes and Tornadoes.* Watts, 1981. *(P; I)*

Erlbach, Arlene. *Tornadoes.* Children's, 1994. *(P)*

Fradin, Dennis Brindel. *Disaster! Tornadoes.* Children's, 1982. *(I)*

Ruckman, Ivy. *Night of the Twisters.* Crowell, 1984. *(P)*

Sherrow, Victoria. *Plains Outbreak Tornadoes: Killer Twisters.* Enslow, 1998. *(P; I)*

Simon, Seymour. *Tornadoes.* Morrow, 1999. *(I)*

## TOULOUSE-LAUTREC, HENRI DE

Bryant, Jennifer Fisher. *Henri de Toulouse-Lautrec: Artist.* Chelsea House, 1995. *(P; I)*

Janson, H. W., and Janson, Anthony F. *History of Art for Young People.* Abrams, 1997. (rev. ed.) *(I; A)*

Venezia, Mike. *Henri de Toulouse-Lautrec.* Children's Press, 1995. *(P)*

## TOUSSAINT, L'OUVERTURE

Hoobler, Dorothy, and Hoobler, Thomas. *Toussaint L'Ouverture.* Chelsea House, 1990. *(I)*

Myers, Walter Dean. *Toussaint L'Ouverture: The Fight for Haiti's Freedom.* Simon & Schuster, 1996. *(P; I)*

## TOYS

Churchill, E. Richard. *Fast & Funny Paper Toys You Can Make.* Sterling, 1990. *(P; I; A)*

Gogniat, Maurice. *Indian and Wild West Toys You Can Make.* Sterling, 1980. *(P; I; A)*

Lerner, Mark. *Careers in Toy Making.* Lerner, 1980. *(P; I)*

Sibbett, Ed, Jr. *Easy-to-Make Articulated Wooden Toys: Patterns and Instructions for 18 Playthings That Move.* Dover, 1983. *(P; I; A)*

Wulffson, Don. *Toys! Amazing Stories behind Some Great Inventions.* Holt, 2000. *(P; I)*

## TRACK AND FIELD

Aaseng, Nathan. *Track's Magnificent Milers.* Lerner, 1981. *(P; I; A)*

Jackson, Colin. *The Young Track and Field Athlete: A Young Enthusiast's Guide to Track and Field Athletics.* Dorling Kindersley, 1996. *(P; I)*

Lyttle, Richard B. *Jogging and Running.* Watts, 1979. *(I; A)*

McMane, Fred. *Track and Field Basics.* Prentice-Hall, 1983. *(P; I)*

Owens, Jesse, and O'Connor, Dick. *Track and Field.* Atheneum, 1976. *(I; A)*

Ryan, Frank. *Jumping for Joy: The High Jump, the Pole Vault, the Long Jump, and the Triple Jump.* Scribner's, 1980. *(P; I)*

Sullivan, George. *Better Track for Boys, Better Cross-Country Running for Boys and Girls,* 1983; *Better Field Events for Girls,* 1982; 1985; *Better Track for Girls,* 1981; *Marathon: The Longest Race; Run, Run Fast; Track and Field: Secrets of the Champions,* 1980. Dodd. *(I; A)*

## TRADEMARKS

Arnold, Oren. *What's in a Name: Famous Brand Names.* Messner, 1979. *(I; A)*

## TRANSPORTATION

Arnold, Caroline. *How Do We Travel?* Watts, 1983. *(P)*

Graham, Ian. *Transportation.* Watts, 1989. *(P; I)*

Hamer, Mick. *Transport.* Watts, 1982. *(I)*

Taylor, Ron. *50 Facts about Speed and Power.* Watts, 1983. *(I)*

Woods, Michael, and Woods, Mary B. *Ancient Transportation: From Camels to Canals.* Runestone, 2000. *(I)*

## TREATIES

Corzine, Phyllis. *The Palestinian-Israeli Accord.* Lucent, 1996. *(I; A)*

Dunn, John M. *The Relocation of the North American Indian.* Lucent, 1994. *(I; A)*

Gold, Susan Dudley. *Land Pacts.* Twenty-First Century, 1997. *(I; A)*

## TREES

Arnold, Caroline. *The Biggest Living Thing.* Carolrhoda, 1983. *(P; I)*

Arnosky, Jim. *Crinkleroot's Guide to Knowing the Trees.* Bradbury, 1992. *(P)*

Boulton, Carolyn. *Trees.* Watts, 1984. *(P; I)*

Brandt, Keith. *Discovering Trees.* Troll, 1981. *(P)*

Burnie, David. *Tree.* Knopf, 1988. *(P; I)*

Dickinson, Jane. *All about Trees.* Troll, 1983. *(P; I)*

Mabley, Richard. *Oak and Company.* Greenwillow, 1983. *(P)*

Pine, Jonathan. *Trees.* HarperCollins, 1995. *(I)*

Podendorf, Illa. *Trees.* Children's, 1982. *(P)*

Selsam, Millicent E. *Tree Flowers.* Morrow, 1984. *(P; I)*

Wiggers, Ray. *Picture Guide to Tree Leaves.* Watts, 1991. *(I)*

## TRINIDAD AND TOBAGO

McKenley, Yvonne. *A Taste of the Caribbean.* Raintree Steck-Vaughn, 1995. *(P; I)*

## TROJAN WAR

Caselli, Giovanni. *In Search of Troy: One Man's Quest for Homer's Fabled City.* NTC, 1999. *(P; I)*

## TROPICS

Forsyth, Andrian. *Journey through a Tropical Jungle.* Simon & Schuster, 1989. *(P; I)*

Landau, Elaine. *Tropical Forest Mammals.* Children's Press, 1997. *(P; I); Tropical Rain Forests around the World.* Watts, 1990. *(P)*

Mutel, Cornelia F. *Tropical Rain Forests.* First Avenue, 1993. *(P; I)*

## TRUCKS AND TRUCKING

Abrams, Kathleen S., and Abrams, Lawrence F. *The Big Rigs: Trucks, Truckers, and Trucking.* Messner, 1981. *(P; I)*

Bushey, Jerry. *Monster Trucks and Other Giant Machines on Wheels.* Carolrhoda, 1985. *(P)*

Haddad, Helen R. *Truck and Loader.* Greenwillow, 1982. *(P)*

Herman, Gail. *Make Way for Trucks: Big Machines on Wheels.* Random House, 1990. *(P)*

Lines, Cliff. *Looking at Trucks.* Watts, 1984. *(P; I)*

Mitchell, Joyce Slayton. *Tractor-Trailer Trucker: A Powerful Truck Book.* Tricycle, 2000. *(P; I)*

Radlauer, Ed. *Some Basics about Minitrucks.* Children's, 1982; *Some Basics about Vans,* 1978; *Trucks,* 1980. *(P; I)*

Rockwell, Anne F. *Trucks.* Dutton, 1984. *(P)*

Siebert, Diane. *Truck Song.* Crowell, 1984. *(P)*

Wolverton, Ruth, and Wolverton, Mike. *Trucks and Trucking.* Watts, 1983. *(I; A)*

## TRUMAN, HARRY S.

Greenberg, Morrie. *The Buck Stops Here: A Biography of Harry Truman.* Dillon, 1989. *(I)*

Hargrove, Jim. *Harry S. Truman: Thirty-Third President of the United States.* Children's, 1987. *(P; I)*

Leavell, J. Perry, Jr. *Harry S. Truman.* Chelsea House, 1987. *(A)*

Melton, David. *Harry S Truman: The Man Who Walked with Giants.* Independence Press, MO, 1980. *(I; A)*

## TRUST FUND

## TUBMAN, HARRIET

Bentley, Judith. *Harriet Tubman.* Watts, 1990. *(A)*

McClard, Megan. *Harriet Tubman: Slavery and the Underground Railroad.* Silver Burdett, 1991. *(I; A)*

Taylor, M. W. *Harriet Tubman.* Chelsea House, 1990. *(I)*

## TUNDRA

Forman, Michael H. *Arctic Tundra.* Children's, 1997. *(P)*

Hiscock, Bruce. *Tundra: The Arctic Land.* Atheneum, 1986. *(P; I)*

## TUNISIA

*Tunisia . . . in Pictures.* Lerner, 1989. *(I)*

## TUNNELS

Dunn, Andrew. *Tunnels.* Thomson Learning, 1993. *(I)*

Epstein, Sam, and Epstein, Beryl. *Tunnels.* Little, 1985. *(I)*

Gibbons, Gail. *Tunnels.* Holiday, 1984. *(P)*

Rickard, Graham. *Tunnels.* Bookwright, 1988. *(P)*

Sauvain, Philip. *Tunnels.* Garrett Educational, 1990. *(P; I)*

## TURKEYS

Lavine, Sigmund A., and Scuro, Vincent. *Wonders of Turkeys.* Dodd, 1984. *(I)*

Patent, Dorothy Hinshaw. *Wild Turkey, Tame Turkey.* Clarion, 1989. *(I)*

## TURKS AND CAICOS ISLANDS

McKenley, Yvonne. *A Taste of the Caribbean.* Raintree Steck-Vaughn, 1995. *(P; I)*

## TURTLES

Arnosky, Jim. *All about Turtles.* Scholastic, 2000. *(P)*

Guiberson, Brenda Z. *Into the Sea.* Holt, 1996. *(P)*

Jahn, Johannes. *A Step-by-Step Book About Turtles.* TFH Publications, 1988. *(I; A)*

Staub, Frank. *Sea Turtles.* Lerner, 1995. *(P)*

## TWAIN, MARK

Frevert, Patricia D. *Mark Twain, an American Voice.* Creative Education, 1981. *(I; A)*

Krull, Kathleen. *Lives of the Writers: Comedies, Tragedies (And What the Neighbors Thought).* Raintree Steck-Vaughn, 1998. *(I; A)*

Meltzer, Milton. *Mark Twain: A Writer's Life.* Watts, 1985. *(I; A)*

Quackenbush, Robert. *Mark Twain? What Kind of Name Is That?* Prentice-Hall, 1984. *(P; I)*

## TYLER, JOHN

Lillegard, Dee. *John Tyler.* Children's, 1988. *(P; I)*

## UGANDA

Creed, Alexander. *Uganda.* Chelsea House, 1987. *(P; I)*

Foster, F. Blanche. *East Central Africa: Kenya, Uganda, Tanzania, Rwanda, and Burundi.* Watts, 1981. *(I; A)*

## UKRAINE

*Ukraine.* Lerner, 1992. *(I)*

Clay, Rebecca. *Ukraine: A New Independence.* Marshall Cavendish, 1997. *(I)*

Oparenko, Christina. *The Ukraine.* Chelsea House, 1988. *(P; I)*

## UNDERGROUND MOVEMENTS

Levine, Ellen. *Darkness over Denmark: The Danish Resistance and the Rescue of the Jews.* Holiday House, 1999. *(I)*

Meltzer, Milton. *Rescue: The Story of How Gentiles Saved Jews in the Holocaust.* HarperCollins, 1999. *(I; A)*

## UNDERGROUND RAILROAD

Fradin, Dennis Brindell. *Bound for the North Star: True Stories of Fugitive Slaves.* Houghton Mifflin, 2000. *(I; A)*

Gorrell, Gena Kinton; Oubrerie, Clement; and Cullen, Malcolm. *North Star to Freedom: The Story of the Underground Railroad.* Bantam Doubleday Dell, 1999. *(I)*

Haskins, Jim. *Get on Board: The Story of the Underground Railroad.* Scholastic, 1995. *(I)*

Kallen, Stuart A. *Life on the Underground Railroad.* Lucent, 2000. *(I)*

Swain, Gwenyth. *President of the Underground Railroad: A Story about Levi Coffin.* Lerner, 2001. *(P; I)*

## UNICORNS

Giblin, James Cross. *The Truth about Unicorns.* HarperCollins, 1996. *(I; A)*

## UNIDENTIFIED FLYING OBJECTS

Asimov, Isaac. *Unidentified Flying Objects.* Gareth Stevens, 1989. *(P; I)*

Berger, Melvin. *UFOs, ETs and Visitors From Space.* Putnam, 1988. *(I)*

Darling, David. *Could You Ever Meet an Alien?* Dillon, 1990. *(I)*

Rasmussen, Richard Michael. *The UFO Challenge.* Lucent Books, 1990. *(I; A)*

## UNION OF SOVIET SOCIALIST REPUBLICS

Andrews, William G. *The Land and People of the Soviet Union.* Harper, 1991. *(I; A)*

Bernards, Neal, ed. *The Soviet Union.* Greenhaven Press, 1987. *(A)*

Campling, Elizabeth. *The Russian Revolution.* David & Charles, 1985. *(I; A); How and Why: The Russian Revolution.* Batsford, 1987. *(A); The USSR Since 1945.* Batsford, 1990. *(I; A)*

Dolphin, Laurie. *Georgia to Georgia: Making Friends in the U.S.S.R.* Tambourine, 1991. *(P; I)*

Fannon, Cecilia. *Soviet Union.* Rourke, 1990. *(I)*

Harvey, Miles. *The Fall of the Soviet Union.* Children's Press, 1995. *(I)*

Jackson, W. A. Douglas. *Soviet Union.* Gateway Press, 1988. *(I; A)*

Keeler, Stephen. *Soviet Union.* Watts, 1988. *(P; I)*

Matthews, John R. *The Rise and Fall of the Soviet Union.* Lucent, 1999. *(I; A)*

Resnick, Abraham. *Russia: A History to 1917.* Children's, 1983. *(I)*

Riordan, James. *Soviet Union: The Land and Its People.* Silver Burdett, 1987. *(P; I)*

Ross, Stewart. *The Russian Revolution.* Bookwright, 1989. *(I; A)*

Smith, Samantha. *Journey to the Soviet Union.* Little, 1985. *(I)*

## UNITED KINGDOM

Lindop, Edmund. *Great Britain and the United States: Rivals and Partners.* Twenty-First Century, 1999. *(A)*

Lye, Keith. *Take a Trip to Wales.* Watts, 1986. *(P)*

Mitsumasa, Anno. *Anno's Britain.* Philomel, 1986. *(I)*

Sutherland, Dorothy B. *Wales.* Children's, 1987. *(P; I)*

## UNITED NATIONS

Brenner, Barbara. *The United Nations 30th Anniversary Book.* Atheneum, 1995. *(I)*

Carroll, Raymond. *The Future of the United Nations.* Watts, 1985. *(I; A)*

Jacobs, William Jay. *Search for Peace: The Story of the United Nations.* Simon & Schuster, 1994. *(I; A)*

Parker, Nancy Winslow. *The United Nations from A to Z.* Dodd, 1985. *(I)*

Ross, Stewart. *The United Nations.* Watts, 1990. *(I; A)*

Stein, Conrad. *The Story of the United Nations.* Children's, 1986. *(I)*

Woods, Harold, and Woods, Geraldine. *The United Nations.* Watts, 1985. *(I)*

## UNITED STATES

Berger, Gilda. *The Southeast States.* Watts, 1984. *(I)*

Brandt, Sue R. *Facts about the Fifty States.* Watts, 1979 (rev. ed.). *(I)*

Costabel, Eva. *A New England Village.* Atheneum, 1983. *(I); The Pennsylvania Dutch.* Atheneum, 1986. *(I)*

Gilfond, Henry. *The Northeast States.* Watts, 1984. *(I)*

Jacobson, Daniel. *The North Central States.* Watts, 1984. *(I)*

Johnson, Linda Carlson. *Our National Symbols.* Millbrook Press, 1994. *(P)*

Lawson, Don. *The Pacific States.* Watts, 1984. *(I)*

Leedy, Loreen. *Celebrate the 50 States!* Holiday, 1999. *(P)*

Mitsumasa, Anno. *Anno's U.S.A.* Philomel, 1983. *(I)*

Quiri, Patricia Ryon. *The National Anthem.* Children's Press, 1998. *(P)*

Ronan, Margaret. *All about Our Fifty States.* Random House, 1978 (rev. ed.). *(I; A)*

St. George, Judith. *The Mount Rushmore Story.* Putnam, 1985. *(I)*

St. Pierre, Stephanie. *Our National Anthem.* Millbrook Press, 1994. *(P)*

Taylor, L. B., and Taylor, C. *The Rocky Mountain States.* Watts, 1984. *(I)*

Woods, Harold, and Woods, Geraldine. *The South Central States.* Watts, 1984. *(I)*

## UNITED STATES, ARMED FORCES OF THE

Bradley, Jeff. *A Young Person's Guide to Military Service.* Kampmann, 1987. *(A)*

Cohen, Andrew, and Heinsohn, Beth. *The Department of Defense.* Chelsea House, 1990. *(I; A)*

Ferrell, Nancy Warren. *The U.S. Air Force.* Lerner, 1990. *(I); The U.S. Coast Guard.* Lerner, 1989. *(I; A)*

Fisch, Arnold G., Jr. *The Department of the Army.* Chelsea House, 1987. *(A)*

Kraus, Theresa L. *The Department of the Navy.* Chelsea House, 1989. *(P; I)*

Moran, Tom. *The U.S. Army.* Lerner, 1990. *(I)*

Pelta, Kathy. *The U.S. Navy.* Lerner, 1990. *(I)*

Petersen, Gwenn B. *Careers in the United States Merchant Marine.* Lodestar, 1983. *(I; A)*

Rhea, John. *The Department of the Air Force.* Chelsea House, 1990. *(P; I)*

Rummel, Jack. *The U.S. Marine Corps.* Chelsea House, 1990. *(I; A)*

Stefoff, Rebecca. *The U.S. Coast Guard.* Chelsea House, 1989. *(I; A)*

Warner, J. F. *The U.S. Marine Corps.* Lerner, 1991. *(I)*

## UNITED STATES, ART AND ARCHITECTURE OF THE

McLanathan, Richard. *Gilbert Stuart: The Father of American Portraiture.* Abrams, 1986. *(I; A)*

## UNITED STATES, CONGRESS OF THE

Aaseng, Nathan. *You Are the Senator.* Oliver, 1997. *(I;A)*

Coy, Harold. *Congress,* rev. by Barbara L. Dammann. Watts, 1981. *(I; A)*

Ragsdale, Bruce A. *The House of Representatives.* Chelsea House, 1988. *(A)*

## UNITED STATES, CONSTITUTION OF THE

Feinberg, Barbara Silberdick. *The Dictionary of the U.S. Constitution.* Watts, 1999. *(I; A)*

Fritz, Jean. *Shh! We're Writing the Constitution.* Putnam, 1987. *(I)*

Levy, Elizabeth. *If You Were There When They Signed the Constitution.* Scholastic, 1987. *(I)*

Lindrop, Edmund. *Birth of the Constitution.* Enslow, 1986. *(I)*

Lomask, Milton. *The Spirit of 1787: The Making of Our Constitution.* Farrar, 1980. *(P; I; A)*

Maestro, Betsy. *A More Perfect Union: The Story of Our Constitution.* Lothrop, 1987. *(P; I)*

Ritchie, Donald A. *The U.S. Constitution.* Chelsea House, 1988. *(A)*

Sgroi, Peter. *This Constitution.* Watts, 1986. *(I)*

Spier, Peter. *We The People: The Constitution of the United States of America.* Doubleday, 1987. *(P)*

## UNITED STATES, GOVERNMENT OF THE

Bartz, Carl F. *The Department of State.* Chelsea House, 1988. *(A)*

Bender, David L., ed. *American Government.* Greenhaven Press, 1987. *(A)*

Ellis, Rafaela. *The Central Intelligence Agency.* Chelsea House, 1987. *(A)*

Fisher, Leonard Everett. *The White House.* Holiday, 1990. *(P; I)*

Nardo, Don. *The Declaration of Independence: A Model for Individual Rights.* Lucent, 1998. *(A)*

Paine, Thomas. *Common Sense.* Penguin, 1982. *(I; A)*

Parker, Nancy Winslow. *The President's Cabinet and How It Grew.* Harper, 1991. *(P; I)*

Quiri, Patricia Ryon. *The Bill of Rights; The Declaration of Independence.* Children's Press, 1998. *(P)*

## UNITED STATES, HISTORY OF THE

Faber, Doris, and Faber, Harold. *The Birth of a Nation: The Early Years of the United States.* Scribner's, 1989. *(I; A)*

Goode, Stephen. *The New Federalism: States' Rights in American History.* Watts, 1983. *(A)*

Steins, Richard. *Exploration and Settlement.* Raintree/Steck-Vaughn, 2000. *(I)*

Weber, Michael. *The Young Republic.* Raintree Steck-Vaughn, 2000. *(I)*

## UNITED STATES, MUSIC OF THE

Krull, Kathleen. *Lives of the Musicians: Good Times, Bad Times (And What the Neighbors Thought).* Raintree Steck-Vaughn, 1998. *(I; A)*

## UNIVERSE

Asimov, Isaac. *How Did We Find Out about the Universe?* Walker, 1982. *(I)*

Couper, Heather, and Henbest, Nigel. *Big Bang: The Story of the Universe.* Dorling Kindersley, 1997. *(A)*

Gallant, Roy. *101 Questions and Answers about the Universe.* Macmillan, 1984. *(I); Our Universe.* National Geographic, 1986. *(I; A)*

Hirst, Robin, and Hirst, Sally. *My Place in Space.* Orchard Books, 1988. *(P)*

Lampton, Christopher. *New Theories on the Birth of the Universe.* Watts, 1989. *(I)*

## UNIVERSITIES AND COLLEGES

The Yale Daily News Staff, eds. *The Insider's Guide to the Colleges, 1992.* St. Martin's, 18th ed., 1986. *(A)*

Buckalew, M. W., and Hall, L. M. *Coping with Choosing a College.* Rosen, 1990. *(A)*

## URANIUM

Heiserman, David L. *Exploring Chemical Elements and Their Compounds.* McGraw-Hill, 1991. *(A)*

## URANUS

Asimov, Isaac. *Uranus: The Sideways Planet.* Gareth Stevens, 1988. *(P; I)*

Branley, Franklyn M. *Uranus: The Seventh Planet.* Crowell, 1988. *(I; A)*

Simon, Seymour. *Uranus.* Morrow, 1987. *(P)*

## URBAN PLANNING

Hinds, Kathryn. *The City.* Marshall Cavendish, 2000. *(I; A)*

Parker, Philip. *Global Cities.* Raintree Steck-Vaughn, 1995. *(P: I)*

Royston, Robert. *Cities, 2000.* Facts on File, 1985. *(I; A)*

## URUGUAY

*Uruguay . . . in Pictures.* Lerner, 1987. *(I; A)*

## UTAH

Feeney, Kathy. *Utah: Facts and Symbols.* Capstone/Hilltop, 2000. *(P)*

Fradin, Dennis. *Utah: In Words and Pictures.* Children's, 1980. *(P; I)*

Tufts, Lorraine S. *Secrets in the Grand Canyon, Zion and Bryce Canyon National Parks.* National Photographic Collections, 1998. *(P; I)*

## VALENTINES

Barth, Edna. *Hearts, Cupids, and Red Roses: The Story of the Valentine Symbols.* Houghton, 1982. *(P; I)*

Brown, Fern G. *Valentine's Day.* Watts, 1983. *(I; A)*

Bulla, Clyde Robert. *The Story of Valentine's Day.* HarperCollins, 1999. *(P)*

Fradin, Dennis Brindell. *Valentine's Day.* Enslow, 1990. *(P)*

Graham-Barber, Lynda. *Mushy!: The Complete Book of Valentine Words.* Bradbury, 1990. *(I)*

Prelutsky, Jack. *It's Valentine's Day.* Greenwillow, 1983. *(P)*

Sandak, Cass R. *Valentine's Day.* Watts, 1980. *(P)*

Supraner, Robyn. *Valentine's Day: Things to Make and Do.* Troll, 1981. *(P; I)*

## VAN BUREN, MARTIN

Ellis, Rafaela. *Martin Van Buren.* Garrett Educational, 1989. *(I)*

Hargrove, Jim. *Martin Van Buren.* Children's, 1988. *(P; I)*

## VAN GOGH, VINCENT

Janson, H. W., and Janson, Anthony F. *History of Art for Young People.* Abrams, 1997. (rev. ed.) *(I; A)*

Lucas, Eileen. *Vincent Van Gogh.* Watts, 1991. *(I)*

Muhlberger, Richard, and Metropolitan Museum of Art. *What Makes a Van Gogh a Van Gogh?* Viking, 1993. *(I)*

Venezia, Mike. *Van Gogh.* Children's, 1988. *(P; I)*

## VEGETABLES

Back, Christine. *Bean and Plant.* Silver Burdett, 1986. *(P)*

Blanchet, Francoise, and Doornekamp, Rinke. *What to Do with . . . Vegetables.* Barron, 1981. *(P; I)*

Brown, Elizabeth B. *Vegetables: An Illustrated History with Recipes.* Prentice-Hall, 1981. *(I; A)*

Johnson, Sylvia. *Potatoes.* Lerner, 1984. *(I)*

Sobol, Harriet L. *A Book of Vegetables.* Dodd, 1984. *(P)*

Wake, Susan. *Vegetables.* Lerner, 1990. *(P)*

## VENEZUELA

*Venezuela . . . in Pictures.* Lerner, 1987. *(I; A)*

Morrison, Marion. *Venezuela.* Children's, 1989. *(I)*

## VENICE

Ventura, Piero. *Venice: Birth of a City.* Putnam, 1988. *(I; A)*

## VENTRILOQUISM

Bergen, Edgar. *How to Become a Ventriloquist.* Presto Books, 1983. *(P; I; A)*

Hutton, Darryl. *Ventriloquism: How to Put On an Act, Use the Power of Suggestion, Write a Clever Accompanying Patter, and Make Your Own Dummy.* Sterling, 1982. *(I; A)*

Ritchard, Dan, and Moloney, Kathleen. *Ventriloquism for the Total Dummy.* Villard, 1988. *(A)*

## VENUS

Schloss, Muriel. *Venus.* Watts, 1991. *(P; I)*

Simon, Seymour. *Venus.* Morrow, 1992. *(P; I)*

## VERMEER, JAN

Janson, H. W., and Janson, Anthony F. *History of Art for Young People.* Abrams, 1997. (rev. ed.) *(I; A)*

## VERMONT

Cheney, Cora. *Vermont: The State with the Storybook Past.* New England Press, 1981. *(P; I)*

Fradin, Dennis. *Vermont: In Words and Pictures.* Children's, 1980. *(P; I)*

## VERNE, JULES

Streissguth, Thomas. *Science Fiction Pioneer: A Story about Jules Verne.* Lerner, 2000. *(P; I)*

Teeters, Peggy. *Jules Verne: The Man Who Invented Tomorrow.* Walker, 1993. *(I; A)*

## VETERINARIANS

Bellville, Rod, and Bellville, Cheryl W. *Large Animal Veterinarians.* Carolrhoda, 1983. *(P)*

Carris, Joan Davenport. *Pets, Vets, and Marty Howard.* Lippincott, 1984. *(I)*

Gibbons, Gail. *Say Woof! The Day of a Country Veterinarian.* Macmillan, 1992. *(P)*

Maze, Stephanie. *I Want to Be a Veterinarian.* Harcourt, 1997. *(P;I)*

Riser, Wayne H. *Your Future in Veterinary Medicine.* Rosen, 1982. *(I; A)*

Sobol, Harriet Langsam. *Pet Doctor.* Putnam, 1988. *(I)*

## VICE PRESIDENCY OF THE UNITED STATES

Alotta, Robert I. *Number Two: A Look at the Vice Presidency.* Messner, 1981. *(I; A)*

Feerick, John D., and Feerick, Amalie P. *Vice-Presidents.* Watts, 1981 (updated ed.). *(I)*

Hoopes, Roy. *The Changing Vice-Presidency.* Harper, 1981. *(I; A)*

## VICTORIA, QUEEN

Green, Robert. *Queen Victoria.* Watts, 1998. *(I)*

Shearman, Deirdre. *Queen Victoria.* Chelsea House, 1987. *(I)*

## VIDEO GAMES

Erlbach, Arlene. *Video Games.* Lerner, 1995. *(I)*

## VIDEO RECORDING

Andersen, Yvonne. *Make Your Own Animated Movies and Videotapes.* Little, 1991. *(I; A)*

Biel, Jackie. *Video.* Benchmark, 1996. *(P; I)*

Cooper, Carolyn E. *VCRs.* Watts, 1987. *(P)*

Frantz, John Parris. *Video Cinema: Techniques and Projects for Beginning Filmmakers.* Chicago Review Press, 1994. *(I; A)*

Irvine, Mat. *TV & Video.* Watts, 1984. *(I)*

Meigs, James B., and Stern, Jennifer. *Make Your Own Music Video.* Watts, 1986. *(I; A)*

Shachtman, Tom and Harriet. *Video Power: A Complete Guide to Writing, Planning, and Shooting Videos.* Holt, 1988. *(I; A)*

Yurko, John. *Video Basics.* Prentice-Hall, 1983. *(P; I)*

## VIENNA

Stein, R. Conrad. *Vienna.* Children's Press, 1999. *(P; I)*

## VIETNAM

*Vietnam . . . in Pictures.* Lerner, 1998 *(I; A).*
Huynh Quang Nhuong. *The Land I Lost: Adventures of a Boy in Vietnam.* Harper, 1982. *(I)*
Lee, Jeanne. *Toad Is the Uncle of Heaven: A Vietnamese Folk Tale.* Holt, 1985. *(P)*
Nickelson, Harry. *Vietnam.* Lucent Books, 1989. *(I; A)*
Wright, David K. *Vietnam.* Children's Press, 1989. *(I)*

## VIETNAM WAR

Bender, David L., ed. *The Vietnam War.* Greenhaven Press, 1984. *(A)*
Bunting, Eve. *The Wall.* Clarion, 1990. *(I; A)*
Dolan, Edward F. *America after Vietnam: Legacies of a Hated War.* Watts, 1989. *(I; A)*
Hauptly, Denis J. *In Vietnam.* Atheneum, 1985. *(A)*
Hoobler, Dorothy, and Hoobler, Thomas. *Vietnam: Why We Fought.* Knopf, 1990. *(I; A)*
Lawson, Don. *The War in Vietnam.* Watts, 1981. *(I); An Album of the Vietnam War,* 1986. *(A)*
McCormick, Anita Louise. *The Vietnam Antiwar Movement in American History.* Enslow, 2000. *(I; A)*
Palmer, Laura. *Shrapnel in the Heart—Letters and Remembrances from the Vietnam Memorial.* Random House, 1987. *(I; A)*
Warren, James A. *Portrait of a Tragedy: America and the Vietnam War.* Lothrop, 1990. *(A)*
Wright, David K. *A Multicultural Portrait of the War in Vietnam.* Benchmark, 1995. *(I)*
Zeinert, Karen. *The Valiant Women of the Vietnam War.* Millbrook, 2000. *(I; A)*

## VIKINGS

Atkinson, Ian. *The Viking Ships.* Lerner, 1980. *(I; A)*
Clare, John D., ed. *The Vikings.* Gulliver, 1992. *(I; A)*
Ferguson, Sheila. *Growing Up in Viking Times.* David & Charles, 1981. *(I)*
Hughes, Jill. *Vikings.* Watts, 1984 (rev. ed.). *(P; I; A)*
Janeway, Elizabeth. *The Vikings.* Random House, 1981. *(I; A)*
Jones, Terry. *The Saga of Erik the Viking.* Schocken, 1983. *(P; I)*
Martell, Hazel. *The Vikings.* Warwick Press, 1986. *(I)*
Pluckrose, Henry, ed. *Small World of Vikings.* Watts, 1982. *(P)*

## VIOLENCE AND SOCIETY

Schwartz, Ted. *Kids and Guns: The History, the Present, the Dangers, and the Remedies.* Watts, 1999. *(I; A)*
Torr, James D., and Swisher, Karin L., eds. *Violence against Women.* Greenhaven, 1998. *(A)*

## VIRGINIA

McNair, Sylvia. *Virginia.* Children's, 1989. *(P; I)*
Sirvaitis, Karen. *Virginia.* Lerner, 1991. *(I)*

## VIRUSES

Berger, Melvin. *Germs Make Me Sick!* HarperCollins, 1995. *(P)*
Facklam, Howard, and Facklam, Margery. *Bacteria; Parasites; Viruses.* Twenty-First Century, 1995. *(I)*
Knight, David C. *Viruses: Life's Smallest Enemies.* Morrow, 1981. *(I)*
Nourse, Alan E. *Viruses.* Watts, 1983 (rev. ed.). *(I; A)*

## VOCATIONS

Black, Judy. *Fashion.* Silver Burdett, 1994. *(A)*
Blumenthal, Howard J. *Careers in Television.* Little, 1992. *(I; A)*
Claypool, Jane. *How to Get a Good Job.* Watts, 1982. *(I; A)*
Clayton, Lawrence. *Careers in Psychology.* Rosen, 1992. *(I; A)*
Collins, Robert F. *America at Its Best: Opportunities in the National Guard.* Rosen, 1989. *(A)*
DeGalan, Julie, and Lambert, Stephen. *Great Jobs for Foreign Language Majors.* VGM Career Horizons, 1994. *(A)*
Epstein, Lawrence. *Careers in Computer Sales.* Rosen, 1990. *(A)*
Epstein, Rachel. *Careers in Health Care.* Chelsea House, 1989. *(A)*
Fulton, Michael. *Exploring Careers in Cyberspace.* Rosen, 1998. *(I; A)*
Haddock, Patricia. *Careers in Banking and Finance.* Rosen, 1989. *(A)*
Johnson, Neil. *All in a Day's Work: Twelve Americans Talk about Their Jobs.* Little, 1989. *(I)*
Johnston, Tony. *Odd Jobs.* Putnam, 1982. *(P)*
Lobb, Charlotte. *Exploring Apprenticeship Careers.* Rosen, 1982; *Exploring Vocational School Careers,* 1982 (2nd rev. ed.). *(I; A)*
Maynard, Thane. *Working with Wildlife: A Guide to Careers in the Animal World.* Watts, 1999. *(I; A)*
Maze, Stephanie. *I Want to Be a Chef; I Want to Be a Firefighter.* Harcourt/A Maze Productions Bk., 1999; *I Want to Be a Fashion Designer.* Harcourt/A Maze Productions Bk., 2000. *(P; I)*
McGuire-Lytle, Erin. *Careers in Graphic Arts and Computer Graphics.* Rosen, 1999. *(I; A)*
Pitz, Mary Elizabeth. *Careers in Government.* VGM Career Horizons, 1994. *(A)*
Reeves, Diane Lindsey. *Career Ideas for Kids Who Like Science; Career Ideas for Kids Who Like Writing.* Facts on File, 1998. *(I; A)*
Schulz, Marjorie Rittenberg. *Hospitality and Recreation; Transportation; Travel and Tourism.* Watts, 1990. *(I; A)*
Sipiera, Paul. *I Can Be an Oceanographer.* Children's, 1989. *(P)*

Vitkus-Weeks, Jessica. *Television*. Crestwood, 1994. *(I)*

Weigant, Chris. *Careers as a Disc Jockey*. Rosen, 1997. *(I; A)*

## VOLCANOES

Asimov, Isaac. *How Did We Find Out about Volcanoes?* Walker, 1981. *(P; I)*

Aylesworth, Thomas G., and Aylesworth, Virginia L. *The Mount St. Helens Disaster: What We've Learned*. Watts, 1983. *(I; A)*

Branley, Franklyn M. *Volcanoes*. Crowell, 1985. *(P)*

Carson, James. *Volcanoes*. Watts, 1984. *(I)*

Fradin, Dennis. *Disaster! Volcanoes*. Children's, 1982. *(I)*

Lauber, Patricia. *Volcano: The Eruption and Healing of Mount St. Helens*. Bradbury, 1986. *(I)*

Marcus, Elizabeth. *All about Mountains and Volcanoes*. Troll, 1984. *(P; I)*

Meister, Cari. *Volcanoes*. ABDO, 1999. *(P; I)*

Rogers, Daniel. *Volcanoes*. Raintree/Steck-Vaughn, 1999. *(P)*

Simon, Seymour. *Volcanoes*. Morrow, 1988. *(P; I)*

Taylor, G. Jeffrey. *Volcanoes in Our Solar System*. Dodd, 1983. *(I; A)*

Tilling, Robert I. *Born of Fire: Volcanoes and Igneous Rocks*. Enslow, 1991. *(I; A)*

## VOLLEYBALL

Crossingham, John, and Dann, Sarah. *Volleyball in Action*. Crabtree/A Bobbie Kalman Bk., 1999. *(P; I)*

Sullivan, George. *Better Volleyball for Girls*. Lerner, 1980. *(P; I)*

Thomas, Art. *Volleyball Is for Me*. Lerner, 1980. *(P; I)*

## WALES

*Wales . . . in Pictures*. Lerner, 1994. *(I)*

Lye, Keith. *Take a Trip to Wales*. Watts, 1986. *(P)*

Sutherland, Dorothy B. *Wales*. Children's, 1987. *(P; I)*

## WALESA, LECH

Craig, Mary. *Lech Walesa*. Gareth Stevens, 1990. *(I; A)*

Kaye, Tony. *Lech Walesa: Polish Labor Leader*. Chelsea House, 1991. *(I; A)*

## WALLENBERG, RAOUL

Streissguth, Thomas. *Raoul Wallenberg: Swedish Diplomat and Humanitarian*. Rosen, 2000. *(I; A)*

## WALRUSES

Darling, Kathy. *Walrus*. Lothrop, 1991. *(P; I)*

Patent, Dorothy Hinshaw. *Seals, Sea Lions and Walruses*. Holiday, 1990. *(P; I)*

Scott, Jack Denton. *The Fur Seals of Pribilof*. Putnam, 1983. *(I; A)*

Sherrow, Victoria. *Seals, Sea Lions & Walruses*. Watts, 1991. *(P)*

## WAR OF 1812

Bosco, Peter I. *The War of 1812*. Millbrook Press, 1991. *(I)*

Greenblatt, Miriam. *The War of 1812*. Facts on File, 1994. *(I; A)*

Marrin, Albert. *Eighteen Twelve: The War Nobody Won*. Simon & Schuster, 1985. *(I)*

Morris, Richard Brandon. *The War of 1812*. Lerner, 1985. *(I)*

Stefoff, Rebecca. *The War of 1812*. Marshall Cavendish, 2000. *(I)*

## WARSAW

Landau, Elaine. *The Warsaw Ghetto Uprising*. Simon & Schuster, 1992. *(I; A)*

## WASHINGTON

Field, Nancy, and Machlis, Sally. *Discovering Mount Rainier*. Dog-Eared Publications, 1980. *(P; I)*

Fradin, Dennis. *Washington: In Words and Pictures*. Children's, 1980. *(P; I)*

Olson, Joan, and Olson, Gene. *Washington Times and Trails*. Windyridge Press, 1983. *(I; A)*

## WASHINGTON, BOOKER T.

Hauser, Pierre. *Great Ambitions: From the 'Separate but Equal' Doctrine to the Birth of the NAACP*. Chelsea House, 1995. *(A)*

Troy, Don. *Booker T. Washington*. Child's World, 1999. *(P; I)*

Washington, Booker T. *Up from Slavery*. Airmont, n.d. *(I; A)*

## WASHINGTON, D.C.

Feeney, Kathy. *Washington, D.C. Facts and Symbols*. Capstone/Hilltop, 2000. *(P)*

Kent, Deborah. *Washington, D.C.* Children's, 1990. *(I)*

Krementz, Jill. *A Visit to Washington, D.C.* Scholastic, 1987. *(P)*

Munro, Roxie. *The Inside-Outside Book of Washington, D.C.* Dutton, 1987. *(P)*

## WASHINGTON, GEORGE

Adler, David A. *A Picture Book of George Washington*. Holiday, 1989. *(P)*; *George Washington, Father of Our Country: A First Biography*. Holiday, 1988. *(P)*

D'Aulaire, Ingri, and D'Aulaire, Edgar P. *George Washington*. Doubleday, n.d. *(P)*

Falkof, Lucille. *George Washington: 1st President of the United States*. Garrett Educational, 1989. *(I)*

Ferrie, Richard. *The World Turned Upside Down: George Washington and the Battle of Yorktown*. Holiday, 1999. *(I; A)*

Giblin, James Cross. *George Washington: A Picture Book Biography*. Scholastic, 1992. *(P)*

Harness, Cheryl. *George Washington*. National Geographic, 2000. *(P; I)*

Kent, Zachary. *George Washington: First President of the United States.* Children's, 1986. *(P; I)*

Meltzer, Milton. *George Washington and the Birth of Our Nation.* Watts, 1986. *(I; A)*

Santrey, Laurence. *George Washington: Young Leader.* Troll, 1982. *(P; I)*

Seigal, Beatrice. *George and Martha Washington Home in New York.* Four Winds, 1989. *(I)*

## WATCHES

Dash, Joan. *The Longitude Prize.* Farrar, Straus & Giroux, 2000. *(I; A)*

Duffy, Trent. *The Clock.* Simon & Schuster/Atheneum, 2000. *(I; A)*

Maestro, Betsy .C. *The Story of Clocks and Calendars: Marking a Millennium.* Morrow, 1999. *(P; I)*

Older, Jules. *Telling Time: How to Tell Time on Digital and Analog Clocks!* Charlesbridge, 2000. *(P)*

Perry, Susan. *How Did We Get Clocks and Calendars?* Creative Education, 1981. *(P)*

## WATER

Ardley, Neil. *The Science Book of Water.* Gulliver Books, 1991. *(P; I); Working with Water.* Watts, 1983. *(P)*

Bain, Iain. *Water on the Land.* Watts, 1984. *(I)*

Beck, Gregor Gilpin. *Watersheds: A Practical Handbook for Healthy Water.* Firefly, 1999. *(I; A)*

Branley, Franklyn M. *Water for the World.* Harper, 1982. *(I)*

Dickinson, Jane. *Wonders of Water.* Troll, 1983. *(P; I)*

Dorros, Arthus. *Follow the Water from Brook to Ocean.* HarperCollins, 1991. *(P)*

Gardner, Robert. *Water, the Life Sustaining Resource.* Messner, 1982. *(A)*

Ginsburg, Mirra. *Across the Stream.* Morrow, 1982. *(P)*

Hoff, Mary, and Rodgers, Mary M. *Groundwater.* Lerner, 1991. *(I)*

Leutscher, Alfred. *Water.* Dutton, 1983. *(P)*

Pringle, Laurence. *Water: The Next Great Resource Battle.* Macmillan, 1982. *(I; A)*

Sexias, Judith. *Water— What It Is, What It Does*Greenwillow, 1987. *(P)*

Smeltzer, Patricia, and Smeltzer, Victor. *Thank You for a Drink of Water.* Winston, 1983. *(P; I)*

Taylor, Barbara. *Sink or Swim? The Science of Water.* Random House, 1991. *(I)*

Walker, Sally M. *Water up, Water down: The Hydrologic Cycle.* Carolrhoda, 1992. *(I)*

## WATERCOLOR

Couch, Tony. *Watercolor: You Can Do It!* North Light Books, 1987. *(A)*

## WATERGATE

Genovese, Michael A. *The Watergate Crisis.* Greenwood, 1999. *(A)*

## WATERSKIING

Radlauer, Ed. *Some Basics about Water Skiing.* Children's, 1980. *(I)*

## WEATHER

Adler, David. *The World of Weather.* Troll, 1983. *(P; I)*

Baker, Thomas Richard. *Weather in the Lab.* TAB Books, 1993. *(I)*

Bramwell, Martyn. *Weather.* Watts, 1988. *(I)*

Cosgrove, Brian. *Weather.* Knopf, 1991. *(I)*

DeBruin, Jerry. *Young Scientists Explore the Weather.* Good Apple, 1983. *(P; I)*

Dickinson, Terence. *Exploring the Sky by Day: The Equinox Guide to Weather and the Atmosphere.* Camden House, 1988. *(P; I)*

Fishman, Jack, and Kalish, Robert. *The Weather Revolution.* Plenum Press, 1994. *(A)*

Gardner, Robert, and Webster, David. *Science Projects about Weather.* Enslow, 1994. *(I; A)*

Gibbons, Gail. *Weather Forecasting.* Four Winds, 1987. *(P); Weather Words and What They Mean.* Holiday, 1990. *(P)*

Hopping, Lorraine Jean. *Wild Weather: Blizzards!; Wild Weather: Lightning!* Scholastic/Cartwheel, 1999. *(P)*

Kahl, Jonathan D. *Weather Watch: Forecasting the Weather; Weatherwise: Learning about the Weather.* Lerner, 1992. *(I); Wet Weather: Rain Showers and Snowfall.* Lerner, 1992. *(I)*

Lambert, David. *Weather.* Watts, 1983. *(P)*

Lye, Keith. *Weather and Climate.* Silver Burdett, 1984. *(P)*

Mandell, Muriel. *Simple Weather Experiments with Everyday Materials.* Sterling, 1990. *(I)*

Mason, John. *Weather and Climate.* Silver Burdett, 1991. *(I)*

McMillan, Bruce. *The Weather Sky.* Farrar, 1991. *(I)*

Murphy, Jim. *Blizzard!* Scholastic, 2000. *(I; A)*

Peters, Lisa. *The Sun, the Wind, and the Rain.* Holt, 1988. *(P)*

Purvis, George, and Purvis, Anne. *Weather and Climate.* Watts, 1984. *(I; A)*

Silverstein, Alvin, and others. *Weather and Climate.* Twenty-First Century, 1998. *(P; I)*

Simon, Seymour. *Weather.* Morrow, 1993. *(I)*

Singer, Marilyn. *On the Same Day in March: A Tour of the World's Weather.* HarperCollins, 2000. *(P)*

Tannenbaum, Beulah, and Tannenbaum, Harold. *Making and Using Your Own Weather Station.* Watts, 1989. *(I)*

VanCleave, Janice. *Janice VanCleave's Weather.* Wiley, 1995. *(I)*

Yvart, Jacques, and Forgeot, Claire. *The Rising of the Wind: Adventures along the Beaufort Scale.* Green Tiger, 1986. *(I)*

## WEAVING

Alexander, Marthann. *Simple Weaving.* Taplinger, n.d. *(P; I)*

Hobden, Eileen. *Fun with Weaving.* Sportshelf, n.d. *(I)*

## WEBSTER, NOAH

Ferris, Jeri Chase. *What Do You Mean?: A Story about Noah Webster.* Lerner, 1988. *(P; I)*

## WEDDING CUSTOMS AROUND THE WORLD

Gelber, Carol. *Love and Marriage around the World.* Millbrook Press, 1997. *(I)*

Rosenblum, Richard. *My Sister's Wedding.* Morrow, 1987. *(P)*

## WEEDS

Collins, Pat L. *Tumble, Tumble, Tumbleweed.* Albert Whitman, 1981. *(P)*

Podendorf, Illa. *Weeds and Wild Flowers.* Children's, 1981. *(P)*

## WEIGHT LIFTING

Smith, Tim. *Junior Weight Training and Strength Training.* Sterling, 1985. *(I; A)*

## WEIGHTS AND MEASURES

Ardley, Neil. *Making Metric Measurements.* Watts, 1984. *(I)*

Arnold, Caroline. *Measurements: Fun, Facts, and Figures.* Watts, 1984. *(P)*

Bendick, Jeanne. *How Much and How Many? The Story of Weights and Measures.* Watts, 1989. *(P; I)*

## WELFARE, PUBLIC

Cozic, Charles P. *Welfare Reform.* Greenhaven, 1996. *(A)*

## WELLS

Lynch, Michael. *How Oil Rigs Are Made.* Facts on File, 1985. *(I)*

Olney, Ross R. *Offshore!* Dutton, 1981. *(I)*

## WELLS, H. G.

Boerst, William J. *Time Machine: The Story of H. G. Wells.* Morgan Reynolds, 1999. *(I)*

## WEST VIRGINIA

Feeney, Kathy. *West Virginia: Facts and Symbols.* Capstone/Hilltop, 2000. *(P)*

Fradin, Dennis. *West Virginia: In Words and Pictures.* Children's, 1980. *(P; I)*

## WESTWARD MOVEMENT

Bentley, Judith. *Brides, Midwives, and Widows.* 21st Century Books, 1995. *(I)*

Bercuson, David, and Palmer, Howard. *Pioneer Life in the West.* Watts, 1984. *(I; A)*(Canadian West)

Collins, James L. *Exploring the American West.* Watts, 1989. *(P; I)*

Dalgliesh, Alice. *The Courage of Sarah Noble.* Scribner's, 1954. *(P; I)*

Doherty, Kieran. *Explorers, Missionaries, and Trappers: Trailblazers of the West.* Oliver, 2000. *(I)*

Dolan, Edward F. *Beyond the Frontier: The Story of the Trails West.* Benchmark, 1999. *(I; A)*

Flatley, Dennis R. *The Railroads: Opening the West.* Watts, 1989. *(P; I)*

Freedman, Russell. *Children of the Wild West.* Houghton, 1983. *(I)*

Fritz, Jean. *Make Way for Sam Houston.* Putnam, 1986. *(P; I)*

Hilton, Suzanne. *Getting There: Frontier Travel without Power.* Westminster, 1980. *(I; A)*

Holling, Holling C. *Tree in the Trail.* Houghton, 1978 (1942). *(P; I)*

Johnston, Tony. *The Quilt Story.* Putnam, 1985. *(P)*

Katz, William Loren. *Black Women of the Old West.* Atheneum, 1995. *(I)*

Laycock, George. *How the Settlers Lived.* McKay, 1980. *(I; A)*

Lyons, Grant. *Mustangs, Six-Shooters, and Barbed Wire: How the West Was Really Won.* Messner, 1981. *(P; I)*

McCall, Edith. *Cumberland Gap and Trails West; Hunters Blaze the Trails; Pioneering on the Plains; Wagons over the Mountains.* Children's, 1980. *(P; I; A)*

Miller, Brandon Marie. *Buffalo Gals: Women of the Old West.* Lerner, 1995. *(I)*

Poole, Frederick King. *Early Exploration of North America.* Watts, 1989. *(P; I)*

Schlissel, Lillian, et al. *Far from Home: Families of the Westward Journey.* Schocken, 1989. *(I)*

Scott, Lynn H. *The Covered Wagon and Other Adventures.* University of Nebraska Press, 1987. *(I; A)*

Takaki, Ronald. *Journey to Gold Mountain: The Chinese in 19th-Century America.* Chelsea House, 1994. *(I)*

## WETLANDS

Amsel, Sheri. *A Wetland Walk.* Millbrook, 1993. *(P; I)*

Cone, Molly. *Squishy, Misty, Damp & Muddy: The In-Between World of Wetlands.* Sierra Club, 1996. *(P;I)*

Matthews, Downs. *Wetlands.* Simon & Schuster, 1994. *(P)*

Rood, Ronald. *Wetlands.* HarperCollins, 1994. *(P)*

Staub, Frank. *America's Wetlands.* Carolrhoda, 1995. *(I; A)*

## WHALES

*Whales.* Facts on File, 1990. *(I)*

Berger, Melvin, and Berger, Gilda. *Do Whales Have Belly Buttons?: Questions and Answers about Whales and Dolphins.* Scholastic, 1999. *(P)*

Darling, Jim. *Gray Whales.* Voyageur, 1999. *(I; A)*

Gardner, Robert. *The Whale Watchers' Guide.* Messner, 1984. *(P; I)*

Gibbons, Gail. *Whales.* Holiday, 1991. *(P)*

Kelsey, Elin. *Finding Out about Whales.* Owl, 1998. *(P; I)*

Kraus, Scott, and Mallory, Kenneth. *The Search for the Right Whale: How Scientists Rediscovered the Most Endangered Whale in the Sea.* Crown, 1993. *(I)*

Lauber, Patricia. *Great Whales: The Gentle Giants.* Holt, 1991. *(P; I)*

Mallory, Kenneth, and Conley, Andrea. *Rescue of the Stranded Whales.* Simon & Schuster, 1989. *(I)*

McNulty, Faith. *How Whales Walked into the Sea.* Scholastic, 1999. *(P)*
Patent, Dorothy Hinshaw. *Killer Whales.* Holiday, 1993. *(P); Whales: Giants of the Deep.* Holiday, 1984. *(P; I)*
Sattler, Roney Helen. *Whales, the Nomads of the Sea.* Lothrop, 1987. *(P; I)*
Selsam, Millicent E., and Hunt, Joyce. *A First Look at Whales.* Walker, 1980. *(P)*
Simon, Seymour. *Whales.* Crowell, 1989. *(P; I)*
Torgersen, Don. *Killer Whales and Dolphin Play.* Children's, 1982. *(P; I)*

## WHEAT

Hughes, Meredith Sayles, and Hughes, E. Thomas. *Glorious Grasses: The Grains.* Lerner, 1998. *(I)*
Johnson, Sylvia A. *Wheat.* Lerner, 1990. *(P; I)*
Patent, Dorothy Hinshaw. *Wheat: The Golden Harvest.* Putnam, 1987. *(P; I)*

## WHEELS

Scarry, Huck. *On Wheels.* Putnam, 1980. *(P)*
Tunis, Edwin. *Wheels: A Pictorial History.* Harper, 1977. *(I)*

## WHITE, E. B.

Krull, Kathleen. *Lives of the Writers: Comedies, Tragedies (And What the Neighbors Thought).* Raintree Steck-Vaughn, 1998. *(I; A)*

## WHITE HOUSE

Quiri, Patricia Ryon. *The White House.* Watts, 1996. *(P; I)*

## WHITMAN, WALT

Reef, Catherine. *Walt Whitman.* Clarion, 1995. *(I; A)*

## WILLIAMS, ROGER

Gaustad, Edwin S. *Roger Williams.* Oxford University Press, 2001. *(A)*

## WILSON, WOODROW

Collins, David R. *Woodrow Wilson: 28th President of the United States.* Garrett Educational, 1989. *(I)*
Jacobs, David. *An American Conscience: Woodrow Wilson's Search for World Peace.* Harper, n.d. *(I; A)*
Osinski, Alice. *Woodrow Wilson.* Children's, 1989. *(P; I)*

## WIND INSTRUMENTS

Dearling, Robert, ed. *The Illustrated Encyclopedia of Musical Instruments.* Gale Research, 1996. *(I; A)*

## WINDS

Cross, Mike. *Wind Power.* Watts, 1985. *(I)*

## WISCONSIN

Blashfield, Jean F. *Wisconsin.* Children's Press, 1998. *(I)*
Stein, R. Conrad. *Wisconsin.* Children's, 1988. *(P; I)*

Wilder, Laura Ingalls. *Little House in the Big Woods.* Harper, 1953. *(Fiction) (I)*

## WITCHCRAFT

Jack, Adrienne. *Witches and Witchcraft.* Watts, 1981. *(P; I)*
Jackson, Shirley. *The Witchcraft of Salem Village.* Random House, 1956. *(I)*
Petry, Ann. *Tituba of Salem Village.* Harper, 1964. *(I)*
Rinaldi, Ann. *A Break with Charity.* HarBraceJ, 1992. *(Fiction) (I; A)*
Zeinert, Karen. *The Salem Witchcraft Trials.* Watts, 1989. *(I; A)*

## WOLVES

George, Jean Craighead. *The Moon of the Gray Wolves.* Harper, 1991. *(I)*
Gibbons, Gail. *Wolves.* Holiday, 1994. *(P)*
Hansen, Rosanna. *Wolves and Coyotes.* Putnam, 1981. *(P; I)*
Johnson, Sylvia A., and Aamodt, Alice. *Wolf Pack: Tracking Wolves in the Wild.* Lerner, 1985. *(I)*
Lawrence, R. D. *Wolves.* Sierra Club Books, 1989. *(P; I)*
Milton, Joyce. *Wild, Wild Wolves.* Random House, 1992. *(P)*
Murphy, Jim. *The Call of the Wolves.* Scholastic, 1989. *(P; I)*
Patent, Dorothy H. *Gray Wolf, Red Wolf.* Clarion, 1990. *(I)*
Pringle, Laurence. *Wolfman: Exploring the World of Wolves.* Scribner's, 1983. *(I; A)*
Smith, Roland. *Journey of the Red Wolf.* Cobblehill, 1996. *(I)*
Swinburne, Stephen R. *Once a Wolf: How Wildlife Biologists Fought to Bring Back the Gray Wolf.* Houghton, 1999. *(I)*

## WOMEN'S RIGHTS MOVEMENT

Archer, Jules. *Breaking Barriers: The Feminist Movement from Susan B. Anthony to Margaret Sanger to Betty Friedan.* Viking, 1991. *(A)*
Berger, Gilda. *Women, Work and Wages.* Watts, 1986. *(A)*
Briggs, Carole S. *At the Controls: Women in Aviation.* Lerner, 1991. *(I)*
Fisher, Maxine P. *Women in the Third World.* Watts, 1989. *(I; A)*
Gay, Kathlyn. *The New Power of Women in Politics.* Enslow, 1994. *(A)*
Gulotta, Charles. *Extraordinary Women in Politics.* Children's Press, 1998. *(I; A)*
Gutman, Bill. *Women Who Work with Animals.* Dodd, 1982. *(I)*
Hodgman, Ann, and Djabbaroff, Ruby. *Skystars: The History of Women in Aviation.* Atheneum, 1981. *(I)*
Ingraham, Gloria D., and Ingraham, Leonard W. *An Album of American Women: Their Changing Role.* Watts, 1987. *(P; I)*
Johnston, Norma. *Remember the Ladies.* Scholastic, 1995. *(I)*

Levinson, Nancy S. *The First Women Who Spoke Out.* Dillon, 1983. *(I; A)*

McPherson, Stephanie Sammartino. *I Speak for the Women: A Story about Lucy Stone.* Carolrhoda, 1992. *(I)*

Peavy, Linda, and Smith, Ursula. *Women Who Changed Things.* Scribner's, 1983. *(I; A)*

Rappaport, Doreen, ed. *American Women: Their Lives in Their Words.* Crowell, 1990. *(I; A)*

Saxby, Maurice, and Ingpen, Robert. *The Great Deeds of Heroic Women.* Peter Bedrick, 1990. *(I)*

Scheader, Catherine. *Contributions of Women: Music.* Dillon, 1985. *(I; A)*

Stalcup, Brenda. *The Women's Rights Movement.* Greenhaven, 1996. *(A)*

Stein, R. Conrad. *The Story of the Nineteenth Amendment.* Children's, 1982. *(P; I)*

Wekesser, Carol, and Polesetsky, Matthew, eds. *Women in the Military.* Greenhaven, 1991. *(I; A)*

Whitney, Sharon. *The Equal Rights Amendment: The History of the Movement.* Watts, 1984. *(I; A); Women in Politics,* 1986. *(A)*

## WOOD, GRANT

Duggleby, John. *Artist in Overalls: The Life of Grant Wood.* Chronicle, 1996. *(I)*

Goldstein, Ernest. *Grant Wood: American Gothic.* New American Library, 1984. *(I; A)*

## WOOD AND WOOD PRODUCTS

Brown, William F. *Wood Works: Experiments with Common Wood and Tools.* Atheneum, 1984. *(I)*

Jaspersohn, William. *Timber: From Trees to Wood Products, Vol. 1.* Little, Brown & Co., 1996. *(P)*

Martin, Patricia A. Fink. *Woods and Forests.* Watts, 2000. *(I; A)*

## WOOD CARVING

Jensen, Vicki. *Carving a Totem Pole.* Henry Holt & Co., 1996. *(I)*

## WOODWORKING

McGuire, Kevin. *Woodworking for Kids: Forty Fabulous, Fun, and Useful Things for Kids to Make.* Sterling, 1993. *(P; I)*

Wilbur, C. Keith. *Homebuilding and Woodworking in Colonial America.* Chelsea House, 1997 *(A).*

## WOOL

Mitgutsch, Ali. *From Sheep to Scarf.* Carolrhoda, 1981. *(P)*

## WORK, POWER, AND MACHINES

Lampton, Christopher. *Sailboats, Flag Poles, Cranes: Using Pulleys as Simple Machines.* Millbrook Press, 1991. *(P)*

Woods, Michael, and Woods, Mary B. *Ancient Machines: From Wedges to Waterwheels.* Runestone, 2000. *(I)*

## WORLD, HISTORY OF THE

Fry, Plantagenet Somerset. *The DK History of the World.* DK, 1994. *(I)*

## WORLD WAR I

Clare, John D., ed. *First World War.* Harcourt Brace, 1995. *(P; I)*

Cooper, Michael L. *Hell Fighters: African American Soldiers in World War I.* Lodestar, 1997. *(I; A)*

Dolan, Edward F. *America in World War I.* Millbrook, 1996. *(I; A)*

Pimlott, John. *The First World War.* Watts, 1986. *(I)*

Ross, Stewart. *The Origins of World War I.* Bookwright, 1989. *(I; A)*

Stewart, Gail B. *World War I.* Lucent, 1991 *(I; A)*

## WORLD WAR II

Bunting, Eve. *Terrible Things: An Allegory of the Holocaust.* Jewish Publication Society, 1990. *(P; I)*

Carter, Hodding. *The Commandos of World War II.* Random House, 1981. *(I; A)*

Dank, Milton. *D-Day.* Watts, 1984. *(I; A)*

Davis, Daniel S. *Behind Barbed Wire: The Imprisonment of Japanese Americans During World War II.* Dutton, 1982. *(I; A)*

Dunnahoo, Terry. *Pearl Harbor: America Enters the War.* Watts, 1991. *(I; A)*

Foreman, Michael. *War Boy: A Country Childhood.* Arcade, 1990. *(I)*

Frank, Anne. *Anne Frank: The Diary of a Young Girl.* Doubleday, 1967 (rev. ed.). *(I); The Diary of Anne Frank.* Random House, 1956. *(I)*

Gordon, Sheila. *3rd September 1939.* Batsford, 1988. *(I; A)*

Jones, Madeline. *Find Out about Life in the Second World War.* David & Charles, 1983. *(I; A)*

Knapp, Ron, and Green, Carl R. *American Generals of World War II.* Enslow, 1998. *(I)*

Lawson, Ted. *Thirty Seconds over Tokyo.* Random House, 1981. *(I)*

Markl, Julia. *The Battle of Britain.* Watts, 1984. *(I; A)*

Marrin, Albert. *The Airman's War: World War II in the Sky.* Atheneum, 1982; *Victory in the Pacific,* 1983. *(I; A)*

Maruki, Toshi. *Hiroshima No Pika.* Lothrop, 1982. *(I; A)*

McGowen, Tom. *Midway and Guadalcanal.* Watts, 1984. *(I; A)*

Messenger, Charles. *The Second World War.* (Conflict in the Twentieth Century) Watts, 1987. *(A)*

Miner, Jane C. *Hiroshima and Nagasaki.* Watts, 1984. *(I; A)*

Mitcham, Samuel W. *Rommel's Greatest Victory: The Desert Fox and the Fall of Tobruk, Spring 1942.* Presidio Press, 1998. *(A)*

Morimoto, Junko. *My Hiroshima.* Viking, 1990. *(I)*

Richardson, Nigel. *How and Why: The Third Reich.* Batsford, 1988. *(I; A)*

Saunders, Alan. *The Invasion of Poland.* Watts, 1984. *(I; A)*

Siegal, Aranka. *Upon the Head of a Goat.* New American Library, 1981. *(I; A)*

Snyder, Louis L. *World War II.* Watts, 1981 (rev. ed.). *(I; A)*

Sullivan, George. *The Day Pearl Harbor Was Bombed: A Photo History of World War II.* Scholastic, 1991. *(P; I); Strange but True Stories of World War II.* Walker, 1983. *(I; A)*

Sweeney, James. *Army Leaders of World War II.* Watts, 1984. *(I)*

Tunnell, Michael O., and Chilcoat, George W. *The Children of Topaz: The Story of a Japanese American Internment Camp: Based on a Classroom Diary.* Holiday, 1996. *(I)*

Zeinert, Karen. *Those Incredible Women of World War II.* Millbrook Press, 1994. *(I; A)*

## WORMS

O'Hagan, Caroline, ed. *It's Easy to Have a Worm Visit You.* Lothrop, 1980. *(P)*

## WRESTLING

Hellickson, Russ, and Baggott, Andrew. *An Instructional Guide to Amateur Wrestling.* Perigee Books, 1987. *(A)*

Lewin, Ted. *I Was a Teenage Professional Wrestler.* Orchard, 1993. *(I; A)*

## WRIGHT, FRANK LLOYD

Boulton, Alexander O. *Frank Lloyd Wright, Architect: An Illustrated Biography.* Rizzoli, 1993. *(I; A)*

McDonough, Yona Z. *Frank Lloyd Wright.* Chelsea House, 1992. *(I; A)*

## WRIGHT, WILBUR AND ORVILLE

Freedman, Russell. *The Wright Brothers: How They Invented the Airplane.* Holiday, 1991. *(I)*

Krensky, Stephen. *Taking Flight: The Story of the Wright Brothers.* Simon & Schuster, 2000. *(P)*

Reynolds, Quentin. *The Wright Brothers: Pioneers of American Aviation.* Random House, 1981. *(I; A)*

Sabin, Louis. *Wilbur and Orville Wright: The Flight to Adventure.* Troll, 1983. *(I)*

Stein, R. Conrad. *The Story of the Flight at Kitty Hawk.* Children's, 1981. *(I)*

## WRITING

Bauer, Marion Dane. *What's Your Story?: A Young Person's Guide to Writing Fiction.* Houghton Mifflin, 1992. *(I; A)*

Carpenter, Angelica S., and Shirley, Jean. *Frances Hodgson Burnett: Beyond the Secret Garden.* Lerner, 1990. *(I; A)*

Cleary, Beverly. *A Girl from Yamhill: A Memoir.* Morrow, 1988. *(I; A)*

Dubrovin, Vivian. *Write Your Own Story.* Watts, 1984. *(I; A)*

Duncan, Lois. *Chapters: My Growth as a Writer.* Little, 1982. *(I)*

Fleischman, Sid. *The Abracadabra Kid: A Writer's Life.* Greenwillow, 1996. *(I; A)*

Fritz, Jean. *China Homecoming.* Putnam, 1985. *(P; I); Homesick: My Own Story.* Putnam, 1982. *(P; I)*

Henderson, Kathy. *Market Guide for Young Writers.* Shoe Tree Press, 1988. *(I; A)*

James, Elizabeth, and Barkin, Carol. *How to Write Your Best Book Report; How to Write a Great School Report; How to Write a Term Paper.* Lothrop, 1988. *(I; A)*

Lester, Helen. *Author: A True Story.* Houghton/Lorraine, 1997. *(P)*

Livingston, Myra Cohn. *Poem-Making: Ways to Begin Writing Poetry.* Harper, 1991. *(I)*

Peet, Bill. *Bill Peet: An Autobiography.* Houghton, 1989. *(P; I)*

Sears, Peter. *Gonna Bake Me a Rainbow Poem: A Student Guide to Writing Poetry.* Scholastic, 1990. *(I; A)*

Tchudi, Susan. *The Young Writer's Handbook.* Scribner's, 1984. *(I; A)*

Zindel, Paul. *The Pigman and Me.* Harper, 1992. *(I; A)*

## WYOMING

Dubois, Muriel L. *Wyoming: Facts and Symbols.* Capstone/Hilltop, 2000. *(P)*

Fradin, Dennis. *Wyoming: In Words and Pictures.* Children's, 1980. *(P; I)*

Tufts, Lorraine S. *Secrets in Yellowstone and Grand Teton National Parks.* National Photographic Collections, 1997. *(P; I)*

Willems, Arnold, and Hendrickson, Gordon. *Living Wyoming's Past.* Pruett, 1983. *(P; I)*

## X RAYS

McClafferty, Carla Killough. *The Head Bone's Connected to the Neck Bone: The Weird, Wacky, and Wonderful X-Ray.* Farrar Straus & Giroux, 2001. *(I)*

Parker, Janice. *Engines, Elevators, and X-Rays (Science at Work).* Raintree/Steck Vaughn, 2000. *(I)*

## YANGTZE (CHANG) RIVER

Pollard, Michael. *The Yangtze.* Marshall Cavendish, 1997. *(I)*

## YELTSIN, BORIS

Otfinoski, Steven. *Boris Yeltsin: And the Rebirth of Russia.* Millbrook, 1995. *(I; A)*

## YEMEN

Rodgers, Mary M., ed. *Yemen . . . in Pictures.* Lerner, 1993. *(I)*

## YUGOSLAVIA

Andryszewski, Tricia. *Kosovo: The Splintering of Yugoslavia.* Millbrook, 2000. *(I; A)*

Kronenwetter, Michael. *The New Eastern Europe.* Watts, 1991. *(I; A)*

Popescu, Julian. *Yugoslavia.* Chelsea House, 1988. *(I; A)*

## YUKON TERRITORY

Levert, Suzanne. *Yukon.* Chelsea House, 1992. *(I; A)*

## ZAÏRE (DEMOCRATIC REPUBLIC OF CONGO)

*Zaïre . . . in Pictures.* Lerner, 1992. *(I; A)*

Newman, Gerald. *Zaïre, Gabon, and the Congo.* Watts, 1981. *(I; A)*

Stefoff, Rebecca. *Republic of Zaïre.* Chelsea House, 1987. *(A)*

## ZAMBIA

Holmes, Timothy. *Zambia.* Benchmark, 1998. *(P; I)*

Taylor, L. B., Jr. *South East Africa: Zimbabwe, Zambia, Malawi, Madagascar, Mauritius, and Reunion.* Watts, 1981. *(I; A)*

## ZIMBABWE

*Zimbabwe . . . in Pictures.* Lerner, 1988. *(A)*

Barnes-Svarney, Patricia. *Zimbabwe.* Chelsea House, 1989. *(I)*

Cheney, Patricia. *The Land and People of Zimbabwe.* Lippincott, 1990. *(I; A)*

Lauré, Jason. *Zimbabwe.* Children's, 1988. *(P; I)*

Stark, Al. *Zimbabwe: A Treasure of Africa.* Dillon, 1986. *(I)*

Taylor, L. B., Jr. *South East Africa: Zimbabwe, Zambia, Malawi, Madagascar, Mauritius, and Reunion.* Watts, 1981. *(I; A)*

## ZINC

Heiserman, David L. *Exploring Chemical Elements and Their Compounds.* McGraw-Hill, 1991. *(A)*

## ZOOS

Altman, Joyce, and Goldberg, Sue. *Dear Bronx Zoo.* Macmillan, 1990. *(I)*

Anderson, Madelyn Klein. *New Zoos.* Watts, 1987. *(P; I)*

Barton, Miles. *Zoos and Game Reserves.* Gloucester Press, 1988. *(P; I)*

Curtis, Patricia. *Animals and the New Zoos.* Lodestar, 1991. *(I)*

Jacobson, Karen. *Zoos.* Children's, 1982. *(P)*

Moss, Miriam. *Zoos.* Watts, 1987. *(P)*

Rinard, Judith E. *Zoos without Cages.* National Geographic, 1981. *(P; I)*

Thomson, Peggy. *Keepers and Creatures at the National Zoo.* Crowell, 1988. *(P; I)*

## ZOROASTRIANISM

Hartz, Paula R. *Zoroastrianism.* Facts on File, 1999. *(I; A)*

# PART II
# THE STUDY GUIDE

# INTRODUCTION

THE NEW BOOK OF KNOWLEDGE is a valuable source of information. Whether you are searching for the answer to a question that made a conversation with a child memorable or investigating a topic for a young student's school assignment, this encyclopedia will help you find the information you need.

THE NEW BOOK OF KNOWLEDGE can be used in a variety of settings—home, school, and library. It is written in a clear, direct style and organized so that information can be located quickly and easily. Precise and colorful photographs, illustrations, maps, charts, and diagrams assist understanding and encourage further reading and browsing. Articles are written by experts in their fields and cover topics of general interest as well as every important area of the school curriculum. Among the many categories covered are literature, language arts, history, government, geography, mathematics, social, natural, and physical sciences, technology, health and safety, art, music, and sports and physical education.

The HOME AND SCHOOL STUDY GUIDE was prepared to help teachers, librarians, and especially parents make optimal use of THE NEW BOOK OF KNOWLEDGE. The first part of the Study Guide offers suggestions about how the home-school partnership can assist the education of children. This is followed by an overview of school curriculum areas. The Study Guide then discusses the school years in three separate sections: Kindergarten through Grade 3; Grades 4 through 6; and Grades 7 through 9. Each section briefly describes what children will be learning in the classroom at those grade levels and then lists some of the articles in the set that are important to each curriculum area at those grade levels. These lists of curriculum-related articles can be used in several ways with young people. For example:

- To identify and skim through articles about a topic before it is actually covered in the classroom. This can provide important background knowledge for youngsters that will help them understand and remember information about the topic presented in class. This activity can also make the topic more interesting.
- The lists can be used to locate articles in which answers to specific questions raised in the classroom or information needed for homework assignments, research projects, or writing reports can be found. As they seek out the information they need, students will also find in the set cross-references to additional articles that will help them complete their assignments.
- Some students want to know more about subjects of particular interest to them, and they will find their interests satisfied and their learning enhanced by reading the variety of articles listed about that subject.

Learning the habit of turning to reference books for information is invaluable, as is the close association of parents and children searching for knowledge together. One of the goals of THE NEW BOOK OF

KNOWLEDGE is to help parents share in their children's learning and growing experiences.

Parents of elementary-school children will be particularly interested in the Home Activities in the STUDY GUIDE for the subject areas of Reading, Language, and Literature; Mathematics; Social Studies; and Science and Technology. These simple activities require no special materials or preparation and can be incorporated easily into a busy schedule. An estimation activity in mathematics, for example, asks the child to estimate how many puffs or flakes are in a bowl of cereal. These activities can be used to stimulate and encourage a child's interest and creativity or to help a child achieve a better understanding and increased skill in a difficult subject. There are activities for the four core subject areas in the section Kindergarten and Grades 1 through 3 and in the section Grades 4 through 6. Each set of activities for a subject area immediately follows the curriculum discussion for it. In addition, a set of twelve activities for youngsters in grades 4 through 9 is provided on pages 217–44 in the section How to Do Research for Reports and Projects. These activities may be duplicated using any copying machine. As students work through the activities, they will learn how to best use THE NEW BOOK OF KNOWLEDGE to locate and organize information and to prepare reports and projects.

Other unique features to be found in THE NEW BOOK OF KNOWLEDGE include the Wonder Questions that cover a broad range of unusual topics young people always find interesting. There are also the many activities, projects, and experiments they can do on their own, along with a complete listing of the variety of literary selections found in the set. Lists of the articles in which all of these can be found are provided in the Appendix at the end of the STUDY GUIDE. A separate listing of literary selections is organized by grade level. Each grouping is included in the lists of curriculum-related articles printed in the appropriate sections of the STUDY GUIDE: K through 3; 4 through 6; and 7 through 9.

Preschool children will also have enjoyable learning experiences with THE NEW BOOK OF KNOWLEDGE. They can wander through the set with its many illustrations and photographs of the people, places, and objects, past and present, that represent the wide range of knowledge they will acquire as they grow older. They will be delighted to listen to someone read them the nursery rhymes, poems, and stories in the set. When they ask those questions that defy immediate answers, they will observe how answers and explanations are found in its pages and thereby learn a valuable lesson and skill.

Much of the appeal of THE NEW BOOK OF KNOWLEDGE springs from the articles about subjects that may not be covered in the typical school curriculum but which will broaden a young person's overall education. Just a few of the topics that are covered include those in the cultural arts, popular entertainment, food and cooking, games, clothing and fashions, and hobbies and crafts. The Study Guide lists some of these articles in the section Hobbies and Other Leisure-Time Activities in the Appendix.

Today's educators realize that, because the world's body of knowledge is constantly and quickly changing and expanding, one of their most important missions is to teach children how to become independent discoverers, researchers, and learners. The innate curiosity of children turns them into eager questioners. In the classroom, discussions often produce dozens of questions about events, people, and places. Knowing how to find the answers to their questions is not always easy for young people. Out of the mass of resources readily available— books and textbooks, newspapers and magazines, picture files, recordings, videos, films, and electronic data bases— we often direct students to begin their search for a first answer or basic understanding in an encyclopedia.

THE NEW BOOK OF KNOWLEDGE was planned to be an early, authoritative, and efficient resource for school-age children. Many of its editors and advisers have been educators or librarians or have worked in other important ways with young people. Its contributors are experts in their fields and are able to write for young audiences. You can direct students to THE NEW BOOK OF KNOWLEDGE confident that its articles are accurate, up-to-date, and set within the contexts needed to help readers understand and use the information in them. Sometimes an article will tell students as much as they want or need to know about a particular subject. Often the encyclopedia will be only a first resource, providing an overview of basic information and stimulating the student to seek out additional resources.

Educators today are often required to fit new topics such as global studies, environmental education, multicultural studies, and substance-abuse education into their regular programs. These and similar topics have been integrated into the STUDY GUIDE'S lists of articles for traditional curriculum areas. Many educators are also concerned about helping children make connections across the curriculum. An encyclopedia is an invaluable tool for implementing such activities, and the lists of curriculum articles will be helpful in making such connections in the classroom or library, as well as in planning and helping students achieve classroom and homework assignments. As the HOME AND SCHOOL STUDY GUIDE is used with THE NEW BOOK OF KNOWLEDGE, you will discover numerous other ways in which the encyclopedia can be used to help young people become better learners.

# ARTICLES OF PARTICULAR INTEREST TO PARENTS

▶**SCHOOLS, EDUCATION, AND THE FAMILY**

As your children progress from infancy through childhood and adolescence into young adulthood, you will have many questions about their growth, development, and education. Questions like these:

- Is each of us born with a certain level of intelligence that will never change throughout our lives? What does an intelligence test score really mean?
- What important questions should I ask in choosing a good day-care facility? What can I do to help my children improve their learning abilities?
- Am I free to provide schooling for my children at home? Are there specific federal or state laws that regulate home schooling?
- Does my adolescent youngster really want me to say "No" to certain requests or demands?

THE NEW BOOK OF KNOWLEDGE contains dozens of informative articles about child development, the family, schools, curriculum subjects, and various other aspects of education that will help you find answers to these questions. You will find helpful information about these topics, for example, in the articles INTELLIGENCE, DAY CARE, LEARNING, EDUCATION, and ADOLESCENCE. If you are the parent of a preschool or school-age child, you will find the following list of a few of the key articles in the set that will be of special interest to you.

## FAMILY AND CHILD DEVELOPMENT

| Volume | Articles |
|---|---|
| A | Adolescence<br>Adoption |
| B | Baby |
| C | Child Abuse<br>Child Development |
| D | Divorce |
| E | Ethnic Groups<br>Etiquette |
| F | Family<br>Foster Care |
| G | Genealogy |
| I | Intelligence |
| J-K | Juvenile Crime |
| L | Learning |
| P | Psychology |
| Q-R | Reproduction |
| S | Speech Disorders |

## EDUCATION AND SCHOOLS

| Volumes | Articles |
|---|---|
| C | Children's Literature |
| D | Day Care |
| E | Education |
| G | Guidance Counseling |
| J-K | Kindergarten and Nursery Schools |
| L | Libraries |
| P | Parent-Teacher Associations<br>Preparatory Schools |
| Q-R | Reading<br>Reference Materials<br>Research |
| S | Schools<br>Storytelling<br>Study, How to |
| T | Teachers and Teaching<br>Tests and Test Taking<br>Toys |
| U-V | Universities and Colleges |

## CURRICULUM SUBJECTS

| Volume | Articles |
|---|---|
| A | Arithmetic<br>Art |
| G | Geography |
| H | Handwriting<br>Health<br>History<br>Home Economics |
| I | Industrial Arts |
| M | Mathematics<br>Music |
| P | Phonics<br>Physical Fitness |
| Q-R | Reading |
| S | Science |

Social Studies
Spelling

**W-X-Y-Z** Writing An extended list of curriculum-
related articles appears after each
main section: Kindergarten and
Grades 1 through 3, Grades 4
through 6, and Grades 7 through 9.

▶ **HOME, HEALTH, RECREATION, AND FINANCE**

Does someone among your family or friends
have a health problem that you would like to
know more about? Are you looking for help
in decorating your home or balancing the family budget? Or are you, perhaps, searching for
ideas about where to go for a vacation? THE
NEW BOOK OF KNOWLEDGE contains a
wealth of articles relating to the home, health,
finance, recreation, and other nonacademic
topics. The article INTERIOR DESIGN, for
example, reveals the secret of good interior
design— how to choose the style, balance and
scale, color, light, pattern, and texture that will
work well together in a room. In the article
BUDGETS, FAMILY, you can learn how a simple
six-step plan will help you get the most from
your money. The article DISEASE provides
information about more than 60 specific diseases, ranging from acne and bulimia to heart
disease and sickle-cell anemia. THE NEW
BOOK OF KNOWLEDGE is also a wonderful resource for vacation planning. There are
articles filled with important and fascinating
facts about each of the 50 states in the United
States, every country in the world, from
Afghanistan to Zimbabwe, and many of the
world's major cities. There are also many special articles such as NATIONAL PARK SYSTEM,
which provides listings of more than 300 of
our nation's scenic, historical, and scientific
treasures, including parks, monuments, historic
sites, recreational areas, nature preserves, and
military parks and battlefield sites. The following is just a small representative selection of
the various nonacademic topics included in
THE NEW BOOK OF KNOWLEDGE. As
you browse through the list, you will undoubt-
edly find many articles of special interest to
you, and those articles will lead you to many
more.

**THE HOME**

| Volume | Articles |
|---|---|
| **A** | Air Conditioning<br>Antiques and Antique Collecting |
| **B** | Bread and Baking<br>Building Construction |
| **C** | Clothing<br>Computers<br>Cooking |
| **D** | Decorative Arts<br>Detergents and Soap<br>Dry Cleaning |
| **E** | Electric Lights<br>Electronics |
| **F** | Fashion<br>Food Around the World<br>Food Preservation<br>Food Regulations and Laws<br>Food Shopping<br>Furniture |
| **G** | Gardens and Gardening |
| **H** | Heating Systems<br>Homelessness<br>Homes and Housing<br>Homeschooling<br>Household Pests<br>Houseplants |
| **I** | Interior Design |
| **P** | Parties<br>Pets<br>Plant Pests<br>Plumbing |
| **Q-R** | Recipes<br>Refrigeration |
| **T** | Time Management |
| **W-X-Y-Z** | Weeds |

**HEALTH**

| Volume | Articles |
|---|---|
| **A** | Abortion<br>ADHD<br>AIDS<br>Alcoholism<br>Autism |
| **D** | Dentistry<br>Diseases<br>Doctors<br>Drug Abuse<br>Drugs |

| | | | | |
|---|---|---|---|---|
| **E** | Emotions | **N** | National Forest System |
| **F** | First Aid | | National Park System |
| **H** | Hepatitis | **O** | Opera |
| | Homosexuality | | Operetta |
| | Hormones | **P** | Parks and Playgrounds |
| **L** | Learning Disorders | **Q-R** | Radio |
| **M** | Medicine, Tools and Techniques of | **S** | Sound Recording |
| | Mental Illness | | Space Agencies and Centers |
| **N** | Narcotics | **T** | Television |
| | Nutrition | | Theater |
| **P** | Poisons and Antidotes | **U-V** | Video Games |
| **S** | Safety | | Video Recording |
| | Smoking | **W-X-Y-Z** | Zoos An extensive list of the articles |
| | Surgery | | about hobbies and other leisure-time |
| **U-V** | Vaccination and Immunization | | activities appears in the Appendix of |
| | Vegetarianism | | this STUDY GUIDE. |

**RECREATION**

| Volume | Articles |
|---|---|
| **B** | Ballet |
| | Books |
| | Botanical Gardens |
| **D** | Dance |
| | Drama |
| **F** | Flower Arranging |
| | Folk Art |
| | Folk Music |
| **G** | Games |
| **H** | High-Fidelity Systems |
| | Holidays |
| | Hotels and Motels |
| **M** | Magazines |
| | Motion Pictures |
| | Museums |
| | Musical Theater |

**FINANCE**

| Volume | Articles |
|---|---|
| **B** | Banks and Banking |
| | Budgets, Family |
| | Business |
| **C** | Consumerism |
| | Credit Cards |
| **D** | Dollar |
| **E** | Economics |
| **I** | Income Tax |
| | Insurance |
| **M** | Money |
| **S** | Stocks and Bonds |
| **T** | Taxation |
| **U-V** | Unemployment and Unemployment Insurance |
| **W-X-Y-Z** | Wills |

# THE HOME-SCHOOL PARTNERSHIP

From the moment of birth, a child begins to learn. Parents or other primary care givers are not only a child's first teachers, they may be the most important teachers a child will ever have. Children learn much in their first few years of life, and once they begin school, their home life strongly affects their school performance. A recent study found that parents make a significant difference in a child's school achievement.

Most adults feel that it is harder to be a parent today, and they consider it particularly difficult to find sufficient time to spend with their children. Nevertheless, parents want the best for their youngsters. They are concerned about preparing them for their school years, and they want to share in their day-to-day school experiences by providing support in the home for schoolwork.

▶ **THE HOME ENVIRONMENT**

When teachers across the nation were asked in a recent survey about what would help improve American education, their overwhelming response was that they could do their best job educating children who were sent to school in good physical condition and with positive mental attitudes toward learning.

Children need adequate food, clothing, and shelter to be physically fit to learn. It is equally important for children to develop a sense of self-worth. Children who feel good about themselves are better able to learn. Their self-esteem comes from knowing that they are valued members of the family and that they have the loving support and understanding of family members. Allowing children freedom and independence within consistent limits; providing just enough supervision and guidance for their protection; and rewarding their efforts with praise and encouragement are all ways by which children learn that they are loved and respected for who they are.

Given this kind of atmosphere in which to grow, children also need a few key learning experiences. There are at least two things par-ents can do that will help children be successful in school—reading to them, daily if possible, and talking with them as you share time together.

Educational studies have shown that children who are read to on a regular basis come to school ready to learn to read and that they experience fewer difficulties mastering the art of reading. Fortunately, children's books are readily available. Inexpensive books for young children can be purchased at bookstore sales and in supermarket and discount stores. They can be picked up for a few coins at tag sales. Local public libraries contain shelves full of wonderful fiction and nonfiction books for children of all ages, free to anyone with a library card. School-age children are able to buy books at discounted prices at school book fairs, and teachers often encourage book sharing by providing time for youngsters to trade favorite books with their classmates. Children of any age love to be read to, and they should be encouraged to participate actively in the reading experience.

Talk with children about what they are reading. Ask them about what is taking place in the story and what they think will happen next. Have them find things in the illustrations that are named in the story. Encourage them to ask questions. Praise them when they "read" to you from a favorite book they have heard many, many times. Demonstrate to children that you enjoy reading, too. Let them see you enjoying a book, magazine, or newspaper in your leisure moments. A few minutes a day spent with children and a book can make a substantial difference to their success in school.

Talking with children is another essential learning experience. Telling stories, explaining the steps you use in preparing a meal or fixing a faucet, playing word games, posing riddles, and singing songs are just a few meaningful ways to communicate with youngsters. Encourage your children to talk to you. Show your interest in the questions they raise. Help them work out solutions to problems verbally.

Take the time to listen when they are eager to share an experience or a feeling. By learning how to use language to communicate with others, children build a speaking and listening vocabulary that will form the foundation for learning to read and write.

In addition to reading to and talking with children, parents should try to provide, as much as they are able, a wide variety of experiences for their children. Taking them for walks around the neighborhood and stopping in at local businesses, parks, playgrounds, and libraries are free activities that offer fruitful opportunities for talking and learning. Trips to museums, zoos, athletic events, and concerts have obvious benefits in broadening children's interests and knowledge.

By participating actively in your children's learning experiences, you will learn their preferences, interests, strengths, and weaknesses. You will then be better prepared to provide the successful experiences at home that will give them the confidence they need to meet the challenges of school.

### ▶ PARENT INVOLVEMENT IN SCHOOL

Once children are in school, they find that their learning becomes more regimented. Parents and care givers often discover that schools today are very different from the schools they attended. They are not sure about what the school expects or what actually goes on in the classroom. Some parents come to believe that their children's education is now out of their hands and should be left to the professionals.

Research, however, documents that children do best in school when parents view themselves as being in charge of their children's education. Parental involvement has proven to be more important to children's success in school than family income or level of education. Most educators realize that well-informed parents can be strong supporters and allies in the work they do. They are reaching out more frequently to involve parents in the school and its activities.

Parents demonstrate that they think educa-tion is valuable when they continually share their children's school experiences. Getting to know your youngster's teachers is of primary importance. What do they expect of their students? Do children in their classrooms spend some of their time at their desks listening and completing teacher-directed activities? Are students expected to take responsibility for their own learning for part of the day, moving around the room, choosing from a variety of activities to work on individually or cooperatively with other children? Are students required to learn facts for tests as well as solve problems requiring critical thinking? Do their teachers evaluate the progress of students by keeping a portfolio of their work? Knowing what is required of your children will enable you to offer the most effective support.

Schools recognize the need for good home-school communication and most schools use parent-teacher conferences and written reports as a means of reporting on children's progress. Because of working hours and other responsibilities, parents or other care givers sometimes find it difficult to keep in touch with teachers or to attend school functions. When that is the case, it is important that some other key family member make the contact or attend the meeting. When you miss teacher conferences or school functions, you are sending your children the message that school matters may not be important enough to take some of your time and concern. When the effort is made to be in regular contact with teachers and administrators, you signal your children that school and schoolwork are important and serious business for both of you. Increasingly, schools welcome parents' participation in other school activities. Many moms and dads, and grandparents, too, perform valuable services as classroom assistants and volunteer tutors or become active in parent-advisory or PTO groups.

### ▶ HOW IMPORTANT IS HOMEWORK?

Teachers typically assign homework to their students. But without guidance from their parents, children may find it difficult to organize their after-school time in order to complete the assignments. How important is homework? What can parents do to help children get over the homework hurdle?

Studies show that doing homework regularly and conscientiously helps raise student achievement. Teachers recognize the importance of homework in helping students become independent learners. Talk to teachers early in the school year to find out what, in general, the homework requirements will be for your children.

Work together with your children to set up ground rules that will promote good study habits. First, agree on a regular time and place for study, one that accommodates the needs of each child and the availability of a family helper, and be firm in sticking to it. Be ready to handle distractions—telephone calls, a turned-on TV set, interference from brothers and sisters. Help your children get started each day by making sure they understand what they are supposed to do for their assignments and that they have the materials they need. Do not do the homework for your children, but be ready to assist when they ask for help. Many parents, especially when younger children are involved, check completed assignments to make sure a child has not misunderstood the work. This can prevent embarrassment for youngsters and will enable you to alert the teacher to possible problems they may be having in learning the material. The articles LEARNING and STUDY, HOW TO, in THE NEW BOOK OF KNOWLEDGE include other useful homework and study tips.

Homework can help your children become better students with good study habits and keep you informed about their work in classes.

# OVERVIEW OF MAJOR CURRICULUM AREAS

### ▶ WHO DECIDES WHAT CHILDREN WILL LEARN?

There is no national curriculum for American schools. In recent years, however, the federal government has supported the establishment of national education goals, including specific goals in major curriculum areas, but these goals have not yet been adopted and put into common practice. There is a body of knowledge, though, that is taught in most school systems in kindergarten through grade 12 across the entire United States. Most state departments of education develop curriculum guidelines that recommend and sometimes mandate how this knowledge should be organized and sequenced through the grades in their state. It is usually the local school district, however, that makes the final decisions about what children in their schools will learn. These decisions, to some extent, reflect the values, attitudes, concerns, and cultures of the community in which the school district is located. Although regional influences may result in differences in emphasis or in the choice of specific topics to be covered, the curriculum requirements for the major subject areas are essentially the same for almost every school district in America.

### ▶ WHAT ARE CHILDREN EXPECTED TO LEARN?

Reading, writing, and arithmetic have been the focus of education in America ever since the first public schools were established by law in Massachusetts in 1647. More time is still spent on reading, language arts, and mathematics in today's elementary, middle, and junior-high schools than on any other subjects. Four subject areas—the language arts, mathematics, science, and social studies—do make up the core curriculum for all students from kindergarten through the ninth grade. However, because most educators agree that it is essential to build a strong foundation for reading and mathematics literacy in the primary grades, other subjects are often given much less attention at the primary levels. Although children in the primary grades are exposed in

various ways to science and social studies topics, in reality, these subjects do not generally become part of the regular curriculum until the fourth grade.

Depending on budget and time constraints, the core curriculum will be rounded out with art, music, physical education, and health. Most elementary schools in the United States do not provide the opportunity for children to learn a foreign language, and the percentage of middle school and junior high school students taking a foreign language is low. In addition, students in grades 6 through 9 generally take a semester or a year of a home economics or industrial arts or technology course. Computer technology is not usually offered as a separate subject until high school, but most youngsters are exposed to computers at various grades before they reach senior high school.

### ▶ READING, LANGUAGE, AND LITERATURE—THE LANGUAGE ARTS

Reading and writing are the keystones of the school learning experience. Everything else that children learn in school depends on their success in learning to read and write. Together with listening and speaking, they are the means by which one person communicates with another, and they are essential skills for living and working in our society.

Two quite different approaches to teaching these important skills predominate in today's elementary and middle schools. The one familiar to most parents is the traditional model in which grammar and usage, reading, writing, spelling, penmanship, and oral language are treated as separate subjects, each given its own time and emphasis in the school day. A number of schools use a newer method in which listening, speaking, and the various reading, writing, and grammar and usage skills are taught together as an integrated whole. This method, usually referred to as the whole language or integrated language arts method, tends to use literature as the unifying element around which language arts activities are woven.

In the traditional reading program, teachers use a series of graded textbooks as their instructional base. The readers contain relatively short selections that may be excerpts from classic children's literature or may be selections written specifically for the textbook. Vocabulary and sentence length and structure are tightly controlled to conform to the reading level of the book. In the primary grades, the reading process is broken down into a number of decoding or phonics skills and comprehension skills that children learn in a sequenced pattern. At the end of the third grade, it is expected that the student has acquired a sizable sight vocabulary, is also able to sound out or decode new words, and can use the various subskills of reading in an integrated way to construct meaning from the text. The student should be well on the way to becoming an independent reader.

In the whole language or integrated language arts classroom, the student is more likely to learn to read from an assortment of fiction and nonfiction books, student-authored books, and other reading materials than from a traditional reader. At times the teacher may select a title for the whole class or a group within the class to read together. At other times, students make their own choices about what they will read. Reading and grammar and usage subskills are not taught in isolation or in a set sequence. Their presentation is based on the contents and the styles of the books students are reading. Listening, speaking, and writing activities also tend to be assigned to stimulate and produce student responses to what is being read. Many whole language teachers plan their instruction around theme-based units focusing on topics that touch on many of the curriculum areas.

In the middle grades, it is assumed that students have learned the basics of reading and are now ready to read to learn. They are taught more complex comprehension skills such as inferential and critical-thinking skills, and they increase their reading vocabulary. They should be ready to read content-area textbooks and reference materials for information.

Reading is not usually taught as a separate subject in grades 7 through 9, except for those students who have exhibited reading difficulties. Middle and junior high school students are, however, given opportunities to develop and apply more sophisticated and complex reading abilities in literature courses. Some curriculum specialists recommend that at these grade levels, reading instruction be incorporated into every subject, especially English, social studies, science, and mathematics.

Regardless of the type of reading program employed, students are asked to do more writing in today's classroom than in earlier times, and to spend less time practicing formal rules of English grammar and usage. Beginning in the primary grades, youngsters generally learn to write using a technique called the writing process rather than by concentrating on the mechanics of writing. They learn that there are several stages in the writing process:

- Prewriting—gathering ideas, planning, and deciding on content, purpose, audience, and style
- Drafting—focusing on content and writing style rather than on the mechanics of grammar and usage
- Revising—making changes and improvements in content and style
- Editing—making corrections in spelling, capitalization and punctuation, grammar, and usage
- Publishing—producing, either by writing down or typing, a final draft of the finished work, and sharing it with an audience

Teachers sometimes ask youngsters to spend some time every day writing in a journal on any topic they choose and often to write a longer story, report, or essay. Attempts are also made to be sure students transfer what they learn about the writing process to their assignments in each of the other curriculum areas. A goal of every school's reading, language, and literature program is to make students effective communicators so that they can read, understand, and appreciate what others have written and be able to express their own ideas and feelings effectively in writing and speaking.

### ▶ MATHEMATICS

Mathematics is, more than ever before, a fundamental and basic curriculum area. As advances in different technologies cause our world to change, today's students will find it important to understand how to use mathematics to cope with these changes. The mathematics curriculum has recently undergone comprehensive analysis, reorganization, and modification to ensure that this instructional area reflects these changes as much as possible.

Mathematics is generally taught in a sequential and cumulative manner. Understanding certain math concepts is often necessary before one can understand higher-order, more abstract concepts. The scope of mathematics for grades K through 9 incorporates a number of strands, including:

- numbers and number patterns
- arithmetic operations involving addition, subtraction, multiplication, and division of whole numbers, fractions, and decimals
- measurement, using both standard and metric units
- geometry
- estimation and mental arithmetic
- statistics
- probability
- integers
- pre-algebra concepts and algebra

Today more emphasis than ever before is put on teaching mathematics in the context of problem solving and its applications to real-world situations. There is also less emphasis on isolated computational proficiency. Many educators believe that, while it is necessary to learn computational skills, the use of hand-held calculators should be accepted as a legitimate method of computation. Many middle school and junior high school students, therefore, are using calculators to do basic operations, allowing them more time to concentrate on the important aspects of problem solving

and mathematical reasoning.

Today's mathematics classroom is not always a place where children sit at their desks quietly doing only pencil-and-paper activities. It is also frequently a place containing diverse materials that young learners can take in their hands, manipulate, and explore. Especially in the early grades, math is becoming a hands-on subject. Younger children are not yet capable of understanding abstract mathematical concepts; they learn best by playing and experimenting with concrete materials that may include pattern blocks, an abacus, Cuisenaire rods, geoboards, counting and sorting materials, and measuring tools. Computers are often available to children of all ages to help them develop data bases of statistics, create geometric displays, construct graphs, or simulate real-life situations.

Throughout the grades, students are sometimes given experiences in which problems are solved using a group approach. This process brings individuals together to work as a problem-solving team that develops strategies and achieves solutions. Students also learn in these situations that there is often more than one way to solve mathematical problems and that sometimes such problems may have more than one right answer.

The goal of mathematics instruction is to help students achieve sufficient success in mathematics to have confidence in their ability to use it both in school and in the everyday world.

### ▶ SOCIAL STUDIES

The social studies program is an area of the school curriculum that focuses on people. Students in every grade, K through 9, study the diverse ways in which people work together to form societies and interact with one another in different environments and situations. In addition to history, government, civics, and geography, the social studies curriculum draws on some of the social sciences—anthropology, economics, political science, psychology, and sociology. Until junior high school, however, topics from these subject areas are not studied in any depth as separate disciplines.

Key goals for the social studies curriculum include:

- preparing young people to be informed citizens capable of fulfilling their responsibilities in a democratic society
- developing an understanding of the United States and the diversity of its political and social institutions, traditions, and values
- helping students understand and appreciate the history, diversity, and interdependence of world cultures
- involving students in identifying and analyzing local, national, and global problems and developing strategies needed to respond to them

The tremendous scope of the social studies curriculum has led to different views about how this important subject area should be taught. Some schools focus on traditional history and geography, sometimes teaching them as separate core subjects. Other schools believe that the world has become so complex and full of critical social issues that history and geography alone are not enough to provide a basis for preparing young people for their adult roles in society. In these schools, additional subjects are integrated into the social studies curriculum. State curriculum guidelines generally reflect one or the other of these views.

There is a basic or core social studies curriculum covered in most American classrooms, however. The typical framework is sometimes called the "expanding environments" or "widening horizons" organization. Children first learn about how people live together in families, neighborhoods, and communities, and in their own towns, cities, and states. At grades 5 through 9 the curriculum broadens to include separate courses on the history of the United States and on the regions and nations of the world.

Young people cannot understand the past or the present without acquiring skills that enable them to do much more than memorize names, dates, and places. Students must understand historical events and their relationship to current events and issues. In the social studies classroom students are often encouraged to go beyond their textbooks and to use a variety of print and nonprint materials as resources for information that will advance their ability to understand historical events.

To do this they are taught the research and reference skills they need to become successful gatherers of information. They are also taught how to be good critical thinkers who can analyze and evaluate information and make sound judgments about how to use it. Students are asked to read biographies and primary sources such as letters, diaries, journals, memoirs, and eyewitness accounts. They also read secondary sources ranging from encyclopedias and historical essays to novels, magazines, and newspapers that offer a variety of interpretations and points of view. Maps and globes enable students to locate places and learn about the different physical features of world regions and how such differences influence historical events. An appreciation and understanding of the world's diversity is gained also through their experiences with the literature, art, and music of different cultures, and through field trips to historical sites and museums.

Students also use various media and technology to gain insights into places and events they cannot get from print materials alone. These may include films, videotapes, videodiscs, CD-ROM's, and computer databases and simulations. Some schools also have telecommunications capabilities providing access to the Internet and other on-line systems.

Social studies homework frequently includes doing the research needed to write reports and essays, to prepare for debates, to conduct interviews or surveys, or to work on other special projects.

THE NEW BOOK OF KNOWLEDGE can be especially helpful to the social studies curriculum. It provides accurate and objective information about the people, places, and events associated with important periods in history. It provides youngsters with an excellent first source of information for each area of this curriculum they will study.

## ►SCIENCE AND TECHNOLOGY

Most children have a lively curiosity. Almost as soon as they can speak, youngsters start asking questions. The school science curriculum is committed to nurturing children's curiosity about the natural world in which they live.

In the elementary grades the science curriculum is usually broken into small units of study, each devoted to a topic from one of the scientific disciplines of life, earth, and physical science. The life science units in the early grades focus on plants, animals, human biology, and ecology. Life science expands in the middle grades to include studies of the cell, genetics, and evolution. Topics in astronomy, geology, the oceans, and weather make up the earth science units. Physical science concentrates on matter, on energy in its variety of forms (heat, light, sound, electricity, and magnetism), on physical forces and motion, on work and machines, and on chemistry. The study of technology, the science concerned with the ways in which we adapt our natural world to meet our needs, is included as it relates to specific units of study in each area.

Most students in grades 7 through 9 take separate year-long courses in life science, physical science, and earth science, although in some schools ninth graders take either a general science or a biology course.

Throughout the grades, scientific knowledge is sometimes taught within the context of major concepts and themes that help students understand connections and relationships across the different branches of science and technology. These concepts and themes may include energy and matter, scale and structure, cause and effect, patterns of change, systems and interaction, models and theories, and others.

The primary aim of the K through 9 science curriculum is to ensure that students will achieve scientific literacy. Goals often cited as important for scientific literacy include:

- knowledge of the facts, concepts, principles, laws, and theories that are used to explain the natural world
- development of a scientific habit of mind,

i.e., the ability to think scientifically when answering questions, solving problems, and making decisions
- understanding the possibilities and the limitations of science and technology in explaining the natural world and in solving human problems
- understanding how science, technology, and society influence one another and having the ability to use this knowledge in everyday decision making

In addition to textbooks, many schools use an open-ended, hands-on approach to teach science that calls for the active participation of students in conducting scientific inquiries and becoming familiar with the scientific process. The classroom becomes a laboratory containing plants, small animals, and a selection of scientific equipment. Small groups of children working together use these materials to learn the steps in the scientific method through their own explorations and investigations and by thinking and acting like real scientists:

- posing a question or a problem
- developing a hypothesis or a likely explanation
- designing and conducting an experiment to test the hypothesis
- making observations
- collecting, analyzing, and organizing data
- drawing conclusions

When it is not feasible for children to carry out their own experiments, teachers often conduct demonstrations. Classroom science experiences are extended through field trips to nature centers, parks, zoos, and science museums. Some schools have their own nature trails on school grounds with interesting signs and labels to stimulate children's learning. Some states and school districts have also invested in interactive multimedia programs produced on CD-ROM and other electronic technologies to take the place of traditional textbooks.

The middle school and junior high school are transitions between the elementary program, in which concepts from each of the scientific disciplines are taught each year, and the separate subject-area departments of high school. The science teachers for grades 7 through 9 are also more likely to be science specialists or to have had training in science. At these grade levels there is instructional emphasis on laboratory and field activities.

The science highlight of the year in many schools is the annual science fair, at which individuals or teams of students plan, construct, and explain original science projects. To assist students, information and tips for preparing outstanding science fair projects can be found in the articles SCIENCE FAIRS and EXPERIMENTS AND OTHER SCIENCE ACTIVITIES in THE NEW BOOK OF KNOWLEDGE.

Students of all ages are also encouraged by their teachers to apply their interests in science to activities outside of school. Many simple experiments can be done using materials readily available in the home. Children enjoy collecting things and are often asked to make leaf, insect, shell, seed, rock, or other types of natural science collections as homework assignments. The article EXPERIMENTS AND OTHER SCIENCE ACTIVITIES describes the scientific process and gives directions for simple experiments from each of the scientific disciplines that youngsters can do at home. The many different science articles and biographies in THE NEW BOOK OF KNOWLEDGE include many other science activities and projects that can be done in or out of school. It is an excellent resource for school reports and science projects as well as for continuing one's interest in an area of science outside the classroom.

As they conduct their scientific studies throughout their school years, young people discover that reading and learning about science can be a rich and enjoyable lifelong experience.

▶ HEALTH AND SAFETY
Children's health and safety is an important concern of the school. Every school gives evidence of this concern by offering numerous health services, including providing a

school nurse on the premises, maintaining cumulative health records for each student, and conducting screening tests to identify health and learning problems. There are also school district policies on emergency care, communicable disease control, and the administration of medication. Above all, schools attempt to provide safe and sanitary facilities for all students.

Although school personnel demonstrate their concern about students' health and safety in all these ways, not all children receive systematic, sequential instruction in health and safety as part of the standard K through 9 curriculum. Health education is usually cited as part of the curriculum in every school district. In some elementary schools, however, it may only be covered in one period a week or incidentally within the science or physical education curriculum. Many middle school and junior high school students, however, usually receive a one-semester health course that may be taught by the school nurse or by the physical education, science, or home economics teacher.

A comprehensive, up-to-date health program motivates and promotes the development of good, lifelong health habits and teaches the skills and strategies necessary to avoid risky behaviors. It encompasses physical, mental, emotional, and social health. These are usually integrated into the study of ten major health topics:

- human body systems
- prevention and control of disease
- substance use and abuse (drugs, alcohol, and tobacco)
- nutrition
- mental and emotional health
- accident prevention, safety, and first aid
- family life
- physical fitness and personal care
- consumer health
- community health, environmental health, and health care resources

In some school districts, sex education is considered part of the health program. It usually covers issues involving sexual development, as well as interpersonal relationships and gender roles. It tries to educate students about how to make responsible choices. In other school systems, special classes or one- or two-week sex education courses are offered at the middle school or junior high school level with parental permission required.

Health educators generally agree that, given today's social problems, students also need to learn and acquire decision-making and refusal skills. In many classrooms, the consequences of risky behavior are presented through role-playing, open discussion, and modeling strategies. Activities included in decision-making models, for example, help students make intelligent judgments about the course of action to take when confronted with a risky question, problem, or situation. Other models demonstrate how to resist negative peer pressure without losing good friends.

Health education is important. Good health programs produce knowledgeable students who possess the skills and motivation to become responsible individuals within families and communities.

▶ **MUSIC**

Music is not one of the core subjects in the school curriculum, but it is a significant element in the lives of students. All young people seem to have a natural affinity for music. Younger children sing, hum, and dance spontaneously. They enthusiastically repeat the recorded music they hear on audio systems and on radio and television. As children approach adolescence, they spend more time listening to music, often while doing some other activity, than they do watching television or reading.

Although it may not get the attention devoted to core subjects, music is, nevertheless, an integral factor in turning out well-rounded students. At the elementary level, some instruction in music is typically required for all students. In many elementary schools a music program is taught by a music specialist, who meets with each class or grade once or twice a week. The specialist strives for a balance between general musical knowledge and performance skills. If music instruction is the responsibility of the classroom teacher, it often consists primarily of listening activities.

Children in a music program in the primary grades sing, listen to different types of music, engage in rhythmic exercises and dramatic play, and play simple rhythm instruments. They begin to learn some of the basic musical elements, including tempo, pitch, melody, and rhythm.

Students in a music program in the middle grades learn musical symbols and notation and how to read music. They apply their knowledge as they perform vocally or on a simple instrument, such as a recorder, and as they improvise or compose music. By listening to live or recorded musical performances, youngsters learn to recognize different instruments and to appreciate various musical forms, styles, and periods. The history of music and the biographies of great composers and performers are often coordinated with listening experiences. There may be exposure to classical and contemporary masterworks as well as to the folk music of different cultures. Popular musical forms such as jazz, the blues, rock, and rap are often included in such courses.

Some schools offer instrumental lessons for middle grade students, who must usually be able to rent or purchase their own instrument. Instrumental lessons generally culminate in group performances.

In grades 7 through 9, students are usually offered as an elective one semester or one year of music taught by a music specialist. They also have opportunities to join a performing group, becoming active members of the school band, orchestra, or chorus or of an ensemble group for jazz, rock, or some other form of popular music. Even though rehearsals and performances occur outside regular class time, students are eager participants in these groups. They allow young people with special musical interests or talents to develop their full potential.

New technologies are appearing more frequently in general music classes. These may include computers, synthesizers, and electronic keyboards for composing and producing music.

Students who have gone through a music education program can be expected to:

- develop basic music skills that will enable them to establish a lifelong relationship to music
- understand music elements, vocabulary, and notation
- enjoy a wide variety of musical forms and styles that are part of our historical and cultural heritage
- perform and create music and respond to music through movement and dance

Youngsters who enjoy music will take pleasure in THE NEW BOOK OF KNOWLEDGE articles on musical instruments, the history and forms of classical and popular music, the biographies of famous composers and performers, and the music of other countries around the world.

## ▶ ART

Not every child has artistic talent, but most children enjoy and can benefit from art activities and experiences. Students are provided with opportunities to study art in most elementary schools, even though some states do not require that art be taught at this level. Tightened budgets and crowded school days have resulted in less frequent art instruction by specialists. When there is no art specialist available, art may be taught by the classroom teacher or may be incorporated into other subject areas. Children may illustrate stories they have listened to in reading periods or written in language arts classes, make posters with science or health themes, or construct models of historically significant structures for social studies projects.

Most schools, at the minimum, encourage youngsters to express themselves creatively, using a wide variety of art media and techniques. Children commonly have experiences in drawing, painting, printmaking, collage, sculpture, constructions, and an assortment of crafts. In well-equipped schools, students even become involved with photography, video production, and computer art.

When an art specialist is on hand, students will also learn something about the elements and principles of art and design, such as color, line, texture, and perspective. They will become familiar with all the forms art can take, ranging from architecture to painting, sculpture, and the graphic and decorative arts. A specialist may also introduce students to basics of art history and art criticism and help them begin to develop an appreciation for artworks produced by different cultures around the world.

Art fairs are popular events at many schools. Students proudly display examples of their best efforts for parents and others from the school and surrounding communities.

Art education provides a means of personal satisfaction for young people. It should also enable them to:

- perceive and understand basic elements of art and design
- use art as a means of communicating their ideas and feelings
- express themselves creatively in a variety of media
- appreciate and evaluate artworks
- enjoy art as part of our historical and cultural heritage

For students with special abilities or interests in art, THE NEW BOOK OF KNOWLEDGE offers a wealth of art information. There are biographies of famous artists; articles presenting the history of art from prehistoric to modern times; articles describing different art forms, processes, and media, many of which include special "how to" sections; and articles about the art and architecture of major countries around the world. Beautiful full-color art reproductions illustrate most of these articles.

## ▶ PHYSICAL EDUCATION AND SPORTS

Largely because of new technologies and an increase in labor-saving devices, many Americans lead sedentary life-styles at home, in the workplace, and in their leisure activities. Consequently, many Americans are not physically fit. Although our children seem to be constantly on the move, they too have been influenced by our changing life-styles, and numerous studies show that too many of our youngsters are out of shape and lack basic physical and athletic skills. One of the key aims of the school physical education program is to help students develop healthy patterns of activity and preferences for athletic pursuits that they will carry into their adult lives.

Only a handful of states include physical education as part of their curriculum requirements. Most elementary, middle, and junior-high schools, however, do have gym and playground facilities, even if they may not have trained physical education instructors. Much learning does take place in these facilities under the direction of the classroom teacher.

In schools with physical education specialists and regularly scheduled gym classes, the physical education program is often thorough. These schools recognize that many of their students have little opportunity for vigorous exercise and that a number of them have neither the ability nor the motivation to participate or excel in competitive team sports. The well-balanced physical education program, therefore, offers a variety of activities involving:

• physical fitness and conditioning
• movement skills, rhythmic activities, and dance
• stunts, tumbling, and gymnastics
• game skills
• individual and two-person sports
• team sports

In gym classes for younger children, the emphasis is on the coordination of large and small muscles and on the development and coordination of general motor skills through play, game, and dance experiences. Many primary-grade students also learn simple tumbling, stunt, and conditioning activities, as well as basic athletic skills they will apply in later grades to more sophisticated games and sports.

Youngsters in the middle and junior-high grades are offered activities that will help them develop agility, strength, endurance, power, flexibility, and speed. Although competitive team sports become important for many students at this level, there is equal emphasis on fitness training, individual and two-person games and sports, track and field, gymnastics, dance, and self-testing. In the middle grades, softball, basketball, soccer, and volleyball are commonly taught team sports. Football, wrestling, field hockey, racket and paddle games, and swimming, if a pool is available, are added to the program for grades 7 through 9.

Since the passage of Title IX as federal law, girls and young women must be given equal opportunity and equal treatment in all school physical education activities and programs.

In the physical education curriculum, students can experience the joy, exhilaration, and satisfaction that accompany successful physical performance. They can also develop:

• an acceptable level of fitness with a lasting desire to maintain it
• the physical and movement skills needed to participate successfully in leisure activities of their choice
• a positive self-concept
• appropriate social and emotional behaviors including sportsmanship, cooperation, self-control, and leadership
• an appreciation and understanding of specific sports

In THE NEW BOOK OF KNOWLEDGE, most team sports and games are discussed in articles written by notable athletes or other sports experts. Accurate rules, directions, and diagrams accompany these articles. In addition, enthusiasts will find information on individual sports such as skiing, golf, running, ice-skating, and many, many more.

# KINDERGARTEN AND GRADES 1 THROUGH 3

▶ **MEET THE EARLY SCHOOL CHILD**

Even though each child grows and learns at an individual pace, nearly all children go through similar stages of development. Teachers in kindergarten and the early grades recognize these growth characteristics and take them into account when they plan a program for early childhood education.

Rapid growth and development is the primary characteristic of the child from ages 5 through 8. Most 5-year-olds are extremely active, physically and mentally. They seem to be in a state of perpetual motion and they are curious about everything. Large muscles develop more rapidly than small muscles and younger children need outdoor play with space to run, jump, and climb. Small muscle growth is aided by activities such as cutting, coloring, pasting, and drawing. Although 5-year-olds have fairly short attention spans, their eyes, ears, and other senses all come into play as they explore the world and the people around them. These youngsters are friendly, eager to please, and need interaction and secure relationships with family members, friends, and teachers. Thinking is stimulated by experiences with concrete objects and a need to relate their learning to their own personal experiences.

Kindergarten classrooms reflect the nature of the 5-year-old. Kindergarten rooms are usually large and open with movable tables and chairs and a variety of learning areas. Children select many of their own activities as they move from one corner to another. Among the activities may be building a block bridge; observing how plants grow from seeds they have planted; measuring and mixing in the cooking area; examining picture books; singing and listening to music; and fingerpainting or making clay animals. What seems like play to the casual observer is really young children's work. It is how they learn. The kindergarten teacher moves among groups and individuals, guiding, leading, facilitating their activities, and helping them develop social skills. Outdoor activity is also an important part of the typical kindergarten day.

Children from ages 6 through 8 exhibit many of the same traits as 5-year-olds, but as they grow physically and as their experiences expand, changes take place. Although they are still active, hands-on learners, primary-grade youngsters develop considerable verbal ability, are increasingly able to reason, and begin to acquire problem-solving skills. They are able to concentrate on tasks for longer periods of time. As they grow less self-centered, they become more tolerant and open-minded and they take more interest in other people. Eagerly seeking new experiences, these youngsters are constantly expanding their horizons and exploring the world beyond home, family, and school. Developing 8-year-olds become increasingly independent and they need guidance and clear limits. With many positive learning experiences behind them, as third graders they can be self-confident, enthusiastic learners.

Youngsters must make a big adjustment between kindergarten and the elementary classroom. In grades 1 through 3 learning takes place in a more serious and structured, less playful environment. Children are usually required to spend a large part of the day in quiet, small-group or whole-class activities. Teachers realize, however, that youngsters in these grade-level classrooms are still literal learners and thinkers, and they still need numerous opportunities for hands-on learning experiences.

The K through 3 years are wonderful years during which children are reaching out to a wide and exciting world. These students are still very young, however, and much is expected of them. They need support, understanding, and friendship. Above all they need to feel accepted and appreciated by family members and teachers. Enjoyable activities you and your youngsters can do together to reinforce what they are learning in the core curriculum areas—Reading, Language, and Literature; Mathematics; Social Studies; and Science—are listed after each of those sections.

The lists of articles at the very end of this

section for Kindergarten and grades 1 through 3 include many, but certainly not all, of the articles about each subject area that appear in THE NEW BOOK OF KNOWLEDGE. It is important that students look up the names of topics they want to read about in the Index or in the set itself to locate all of the information they may need or want.

▶ **READING, LANGUAGE, AND LITERATURE**

The overall objectives of the reading, language, and literature programs that begin in the primary grades are: mastering the mechanics of reading and writing; acquiring the ability to read with comprehension and to write with proficiency; and developing good, life-long reading and writing habits.

In kindergarten the focus of the reading program is on readiness skills that prepare the child for reading and writing. These include auditory and visual discrimination skills and those motor and coordination skills that will enable the young child to hold a crayon or pencil, to color and draw, and eventually to print and write. Kindergarten youngsters are also given repeated opportunities to develop and practice listening and speaking skills. They learn to follow simple rules and directions, deliver messages, ask and answer questions about their various activities, and share their ideas, feelings, and experiences with others. Inviting picture books, with and without words, are readily available to look at and use for imagining and creating stories. Their teachers tell them stories, read books and poems aloud, and lead them in word games and songs. In kindergartens using a more academic approach, youngsters will also begin to learn the relationships between alphabet letters and the sounds they represent.

In grades 1 through 3, as much as half the day may be devoted to reading instruction. Children begin to read by learning word recognition and word-attack skills. There are simple words that they may learn to recognize on sight. Children learn how to decode other words by being shown how to associate phonetic sounds with a letter or group of letters. Later, children also learn to identify words by dividing them into their structural parts. Dividing words into syllables, finding common prefixes and word endings, and breaking compound words into smaller words are all techniques for unlocking longer, more difficult words encountered for the first time. Children also learn how to identify a new word and its meaning by its context in a sentence.

By the end of the third grade, young readers will usually have acquired a literal level of comprehension. They should be able to locate details, identify main ideas, arrange events in a logical sequence, predict outcomes, and draw conclusions. In addition, many children will be able to demonstrate some appreciation of literature and a grasp of several literary elements including character, author's purpose, figurative language, and the difference between realism and fantasy.

In a traditional reading program, the class is usually divided according to reading ability into three relatively homogeneous reading groups. While the teacher works on direct instruction with one group, the rest of the class completes reading-related assignments or participates in self-directed individual or group activities. In a whole language or integrated language arts program, grouping tends to be more flexible and informal.

Primary-grade teachers are particularly alert to signs of reading difficulties, and they try to take steps to eliminate problems before they block a child's progress. Most schools also provide special reading teachers who are trained to make diagnoses and provide corrective help for children with reading problems. If you feel that your child requires special help, it is important that you approach the teacher or principal who can recommend appropriate action.

At the same time that they are learning to read what others have written, primary-grade youngsters begin to express their own ideas and feelings in written language. Kindergarten children can usually print their own names and perhaps a few other well-known names and words. In first grade, children typically learn manuscript writing because it is easier to read and write and resembles the printed words in books. Toward the end of second grade or at the beginning of third grade, children are taught how to change over to connected cursive writing.

As they are taught the steps in the writing process— drafting, composing, revising, editing, and publishing— primary-grade students also learn about proper word usage, spelling, capitalization, and punctuation, as these skills are needed. Many teachers allow youngsters to use "invented spelling" at first, writing words as they would sound when spoken, so that spelling issues do not slow down the youngsters' learning how to write down their ideas. Lessons on spelling and language mechanics are offered at a time when they will not interfere with the natural flow of ideas onto paper. By the time they enter fourth grade, students usually have developed some proficiency in writing sentences, paragraphs, and short reports, and they should enjoy expressing themselves creatively in writing.

**Home Activities for Reading, Language, and Literature**

- Read aloud to your children, every day if you can. Discuss the people, places, and events you read about.
- Take your children to the local library and let them share with you choosing books to bring home.
- Make up and tell stories to one another. One of you might begin a story and the other finish it. Help your children make their own books by writing and illustrating stories.
- Encourage your children to read to you from school or library books. Help them pronounce difficult words. Praise their efforts. Make this an enjoyable shared experience.
- Teach your children to observe the world around them and provide opportunities for them to talk about their experiences.
- Encourage your children to speak clearly and to listen carefully.

- Listen to your children retell favorite stories they have heard or read.
- Play simple word games. "Give a word that means the same as...." "Give a word that means the opposite of...." "Give a word that rhymes with...."
- As your children get older, urge them to do simple crossword puzzles.
- Help your children write letters, invitations, and thank-you notes to relatives and friends.
- Encourage your children to make a "New Words" dictionary, and try to add a special word to it at least once a week.
- Help your children enjoy educational television programs so that they have many opportunities to listen to how standard English is used and spoken.

### ▶ MATHEMATICS

Children in kindergarten and the primary grades work with a variety of materials to develop concepts, understandings, and skills in mathematics. Kindergarten youngsters often come to school knowing something about counting and numbers, but they must acquire math readiness skills before they will be able to work with numbers in meaningful ways.

In the kindergarten classroom, youngsters learn to sort by using simple objects such as buttons, and by comparing how objects are alike and different. They compare groups of objects to determine which group has less or more objects than another. They learn the concept of one-to-one correspondence by discovering that three oranges have the same number as three apples. They learn the concept of conservation by recognizing that three boxes are three boxes no matter how they are spread out or pulled together. Kindergarten children learn to count using cardinal (1, 2, 3) and ordinal (first, second, third) numbers. Simple geometry, measurement, money, time, and spatial relationships also have a place in the readiness curriculum. Students receive extensive practice using manipulative materials to solve math problems presented as stories that are based on real-life experiences.

Students in the primary grades are not yet abstract thinkers. They continue to use concrete objects as they learn the basic facts and techniques of computation with whole numbers. Frequent work with number lines and hands-on experiences to determine and understand place values are important activities for them. From the beginning, youngsters are also taught to estimate before making calculations as a way of judging the reasonableness of an answer. Primary students enjoy measuring length, volume, weight, time, and temperature using an assortment of measuring tools and expressing answers in both standard and metric units. They learn to identify common geometric shapes, to create and interpret simple pictorial, bar, and line graphs, and to predict outcomes and carry out simple activities involving probability. They conduct simple surveys and experiments and begin to learn how to organize and interpret statistical data. Seeing and understanding mathematical relationships and patterns is another important skill that may be introduced to them in the early grades. Helping students acquire skill in solving problems is an ongoing activity and is usually based on situations appropriate to the students' level of understanding, and experience. Students are given opportunities to try solutions using a variety of problem-solving strategies.

By the end of the third grade most youngsters will possess confidence in their ability to compute and to solve math problems in school and in their everyday lives. Many respond to the fascination of math and it becomes their favorite subject. A few will have difficulties with mathematics' abstract concepts and more complicated methods. These students may need special coaching at home as well as in school.

### Home Activities for Mathematics

- Encourage your children to find and read numbers on common objects—cereal boxes, jar and can labels, calendars, newspaper ads, store signs, traffic signs.

- Ask your children to count common objects. "How many clouds are in the sky today?" "How many people are in the checkout line?"
- Ask your children to estimate quantities. "How many puffs are in your bowl of cereal?" "How much milk will this container hold?"
- Encourage your children to read the time from analog and digital clocks. Ask time questions. "How long will it take before the cookies are done?" "What time do you have to leave to get to school on time?"
- Help your children follow simple cooking recipes. Let them measure the ingredients with appropriate measuring utensils.
- Plan a party or special event with your children. Let them work out how many invitations are needed, how many favors, how much food, and how much these things will cost.
- Help your children find books in the library that contain number puzzles and math games.
- Encourage your children to look for geometric shapes such as circles, squares, rectangles, triangles, and cones in common household objects.
- Discuss with your children how you use math at home or in your job. Help them understand how math is involved in many day-to-day activities.
- Play games together that use math and probability. "How many times will the coin come up heads in 10 tries? In 15 tries? In 20 tries?"

### ▶ SOCIAL STUDIES

One of the first social studies lessons children will have is learning that they belong to a family. Youngsters also learn that belonging to a family brings with it responsibility and that the people in family groups depend upon one another. Gradually youngsters learn that each family is part of a larger group, a community, and that there are many different kinds of communities. During the kindergarten and primary school years, the social studies curriculum concentrates initially on children's families, neighborhood, and community. Youngsters learn that there are basic needs families share and that there are many different kinds of family groups in our own country and in other nations. They examine how different families live, work, and play together. They soon discover that everyone must follow rules if people are to live and work together successfully. What youngsters know about family units is then applied to the school community.

In the second and third grades, the social studies curriculum expands to include the neighborhood, local village, town, or city. Short class trips to the local post office, bank, supermarket, or police station demonstrate in a very real way how social and business institutions work in a community. Classroom visits by community workers teach youngsters about the many services needed to keep a community running smoothly. Police officers may talk about traffic rules and the reasons for them. A mail carrier may explain how letters are delivered.

Through these firsthand experiences, children also discover basic economic principles about how goods and services are produced and used and how earning money allows people to buy the things they need and want.

Classroom teachers use books, posters, films, newspapers, postcards, and photographs to help children understand that all neighborhoods and cities have many similarities but also many differences, and each has its own special needs and problems.

Primary-grade youngsters are also introduced to some key facts about our country's history and cultural heritage. Many schools focus on Native Americans, the voyages of Columbus, and the early American colonies. Facts about our history and the people who played important roles in our development as a nation are taught along with the study of national symbols, such as the American flag and the Statue of Liberty, and the celebration of national holidays.

Learning about geography grows out of the

study of communities and United States history. Students begin to work with simple maps and globes. Often they make maps of their neighborhoods, pinpointing the location of their own homes and schools. Later they might also work with map puzzles and trace, draw, and color maps of the United States and of the world.

As their social studies knowledge expands and as they become more adept readers and writers, students learn and use the research skills they need to gather information and to write reports. Among the commonly taught skills for this age-group are: locating information; using library resources; using tables of contents and glossaries in books; making and interpreting diagrams and graphs; and selecting and organizing information.

### Home Activities for Social Studies

- Get your children started on a stamp, coin, or postcard collection. Help them find out more about the people and places shown.
- If you can, start bank accounts for your children. Help them fill out the necessary forms.
- Give your children opportunities to earn money for work done, and help them plan how to use it.
- Talk with your children about the significance of the different holidays. Include them in activities you pursue to make and do things to celebrate each holiday.
- Read together the folklore, legends, and myths of different cultures and communities. Libraries have excellent collections of these stories.
- Watch television programs about different regions and cultures of the world. Discuss the similarities and differences between these groups and our own culture.
- When you take trips outside your community, help your children locate the destination on a map. Share with them how you have decided what direction you will take and calculate the distance. As time goes on they may be able to make such deci-

sions, too. When you arrive, discuss any special geographical features.

### ▶ SCIENCE AND TECHNOLOGY

The chief task of the K through 3 science program is to nurture the natural curiosity young children have about themselves, about the living and nonliving things around them, and about the forces of nature. A good primary science program provides a balanced curriculum that includes the life, earth, and physical sciences. Throughout the science program, children are introduced to basic concepts about scientific facts and principles. They begin to learn how to ask questions, make observations and predictions, plan and do simple experiments, and come to conclusions—all aspects of the scientific method.

Beginning in kindergarten, students begin to learn about the needs, habits, and relationships of living things. Youngsters might plant seeds and observe growth patterns. They might learn the special traits of mammals, birds, reptiles, amphibians, and fish and observe the life cycles of butterflies and frogs. Dinosaur studies offer a favorite way to learn about things that lived long ago. Classroom terrariums and aquariums provide an authentic means of observing the interrelationships within an aquatic, desert, or woodlands habitat. Youngsters are eager to care for the plant and animal specimens these miniature environments contain.

Young children are fascinated by space and space exploration, and they enjoy accumulating information about the sun, moon, planets, and other objects such as stars and the constellations.

Changing weather patterns are often observed and charted with youngsters measuring temperature, wind, rainfall, and humidity, describing cloud formations, and competing with the weather forecaster in making predictions about future weather.

Rock, mineral, soil, and water samples are collected to learn about the earth and its resources. The dynamics of our planet are made understandable as youngsters make mod-els and diagrams of volcanoes and earthquakes.

By manipulating levers, inclined planes, pulleys, gears, and other simple machines that may be in their classroom, children learn about how things move and how they work. The importance of energy in their everyday lives is shown with investigations into magnetism, electricity, light, and sound.

The K through 3 years are the years when children's natural curiosity is at its peak. They are the ideal years during which to start a child on the exciting path of scientific discovery.

### Home Activities for Science and Technology

- Take your children into your yard or a neighborhood park on a spring day and see how many different forms of life can be found. Include flowers, trees, grasses, large and small land animals, insects, and birds. Repeat the activity in the summer, fall, and winter.
- If you can, encourage your children to keep and care for a small pet. Ask your children to help tend houseplants or plant a garden. Let them have a special plot of their own.
- Get your children started on collections of objects from nature—small rocks, tree leaves, weeds, seeds. Borrow field guides from the library and help them identify and label the specimens.
- Help your children become sky watchers. Ask them to keep a record of the changing shape of the moon over the period of a month. Find out together what causes this phenomenon. Locate easily identifiable constellations like the Big Dipper.
- Watch science and nature programs on television together. Talk about the interesting things you learn.
- Let your children help take responsibility for household recycling of items such as paper and plastics or for plans you have made to conserve water and gas or electricity.

### ▶ HEALTH AND SAFETY

The early grades are a good time to help children begin to learn good health habits and attitudes that will last throughout their lives. The primary-grade curriculum introduces young children to the major body systems and organs. They also learn about some of the causes of disease and how to prevent some infections. Caring for the body so that it functions smoothly is often taught through simple units on nutrition, physical fitness, and personal care.

Like adults, children are not always happy. They, too, experience sadness, loneliness, anger, shame, jealousy, and other feelings that can be frightening. They learn that everyone has these feelings sometimes, and they begin to learn how to handle these emotions and how to get along well with others.

Primary-grade youngsters are vulnerable to many types of danger. They need to be taught safety rules that will help them avoid accidents at home, at school, and in other places. It is also important to stress that youngsters remember such safety rules when they are around strangers or in areas unfamiliar to them.

In today's society, even very young children are exposed to the dangers of drugs. A good health program teaches youngsters how to use medicines safely and encourages them to make healthy choices about alcohol, tobacco, and illegal drugs.

Young children have frequent contact with doctors, dentists, and nurses in health clinics or hospitals. The school health program helps them become familiar with the work of these people and institutions.

### ▶ MUSIC

Young children respond to music spontaneously. Even when music specialists are not available, kindergarten and primary-grade youngsters are offered a variety of musical activities. They sing, clap, listen to music, dance, and play simple rhythm and percussion instruments. The primary-grade teacher often knows how to play the piano or guitar and how to accompany and direct children's singing and dancing.

In a structured music program, students can learn to keep time to a beat, match pitch, identify high and low musical sounds, and sing a melody. By grades 2 and 3 they can begin to learn the basic elements of musical notation.

Youngsters are also sometimes taught how to identify different singing voices and musical instruments as they listen to recorded music. They listen and respond to marches, lullabies, American folk songs, and songs from other cultures.

The main goal of the primary music curriculum is to help and encourage youngsters to enjoy and appreciate music of all kinds and to feel comfortable expressing themselves musically.

### ▶ ART

The primary-grade art program provides opportunities for children to express themselves creatively with freedom and satisfaction. In the primary grades children have access to a wide variety of art materials and tools. They use poster and finger paints, sand, clay, colored paper, string, papier-mâché, and fabrics of different textures. Even common objects such as buttons, pipe cleaners, and egg cartons are used in the collages, drawings, and paintings they create. Because it is known that large muscles develop first, children are encouraged to work with large sheets of paper, large brushes, and thick crayons. By experimenting and exploring freely, youngsters discover on their own how these tools and materials work.

Teachers understand that young children are not yet ready to represent the things they see in a realistic style and that adult standards should not yet be imposed on the youngsters' creations.

Reproductions and posters of the works of great artists are sometimes examined and discussed during the art period. Students can learn something about color, line, and design as they are encouraged to talk about a master painting or sculpture.

## ▶ PHYSICAL EDUCATION AND SPORTS

The physical education program is designed to help children acquire physical and athletic skills, habits, and attitudes that will last beyond their school years. In many schools the regular classroom teacher is responsible for gym or physical education instruction. In others, there is a special physical education teacher.

The emphasis of the primary physical education program is often on fitness, rhythmic movement, some gymnastic activities, games, and sports.

Fitness and conditioning activities often begin with running, walking, jumping rope, or dancing. They continue with muscle stretching and strengthening exercises including bending, toe touches, crab walks, rope climbing, push-ups, and sit-ups. By the second and third grades youngsters are ready for activities that improve muscle coordination, such as the standing broad jump.

Young children enjoy discovering all the different ways in which their bodies can move. In gymnastics they run, skip, slide, hop, and gallop. They move arms and legs, manipulate objects to a rhythmic beat, and learn simple dances. Gymnastic activities sometimes include walking a balance beam and doing forward and backward rolls.

Primary-grade youngsters are taught a number of game skills basic to sports they will play when they are older. By third grade girls and boys can bounce a ball with one hand, dribble soccer balls and basketballs, strike a ball off a stationary object, and pass a ball in various ways to a partner. They use these skills in chasing games, relays, and team games.

In a good physical education program it is recognized that children will have varying levels of physical and athletic ability, but every child is included and involved in every activity. Every child also learns the importance of cooperation and sportsmanship in games and sports.

# CURRICULUM-RELATED ARTICLES

Some of the important articles in THE NEW BOOK OF KNOWLEDGE that relate to the K through 3 school curriculum are listed here. Many other articles you or your youngsters may want to read while they are studying topics in these curriculum areas can be found by looking them up in the Index or in the set itself.

## READING, LANGUAGE, AND LITERATURE

| Vol. | Reading, Writing, and Language |
|---|---|
| B | Book Reports and Reviews |
| D | Diaries and Journals |
| E | Encyclopedias |
| H | Handwriting |
| J-K | Jokes and Riddles |
| L | Language Arts<br>Letter Writing<br>Libraries |
| M | Magazines |
| P | Phonics |
| R | Reading |
| S | Spelling<br>Storytelling<br>Study, How to |
| T | Tests and Test Taking |
| U-V | Vocabulary |
| W-X-Y-Z | Writing |

| Vol. | Literature |
|---|---|
| A | Arabian Nights |
| C | Caldecott, Randolph<br>Caldecott and Newbery Medals<br>Children's Literature |
| F | Fables<br>Fairy Tales<br>Folklore<br>Folklore, American |
| I | Illustration and Illustrators |
| J-K | Jokes and Riddles |
| N | Newbery, John<br>Nonsense Rhymes<br>Nursery Rhymes |

| Vol. | Author Biographies |
|---|---|
| A | Andersen, Hans Christian |
| B | Barrie, Sir James Matthew |
| F | Field, Eugene<br>Frost, Robert |
| G | Grahame, Kenneth<br>Greenaway, Kate<br>Grimm, Jacob and Wilhelm |
| H | Hughes, Langston |
| J-K | Kipling, Rudyard |
| M | Milne, A. A. |
| P | Potter, Beatrix |
| S | Sandburg, Carl<br>Sendak, Maurice<br>Seuss, Dr.<br>Stevenson, Robert Louis |
| T | Thurber, James |
| W-X-Y-Z | White, E. B.<br>Wilder, Laura Ingalls<br>(See also the article CHILDREN'S LITERATURE for profiles of additional authors and illustrators.) |

| Vol. | Selections from Literature |
|---|---|
| A | Andersen, Hans Christian—The Emperor's New Clothes<br>Arabian Nights<br>  Aladdin and the Wonderful Lamp (excerpt)<br>  The Forty Thieves (excerpt) |
| B | Barrie, Sir James Matthew—Peter Pan (excerpt)<br>Bible Stories<br>  Noah's Ark<br>  David and Goliath<br>  Jonah<br>  Daniel in the Lions' Den<br>  The Boy Jesus |
| C | Christmas Story (Gospel according to Luke) |
| F | Fables<br>  The Lion and the Mouse (Aesop)<br>  The Ant and the Grasshopper (Aesop)<br>  The Four Oxen and the Lion (Aesop)<br>  The Tyrant Who Became a Just Ruler (Bidpai)<br>  The Blind Men and the Elephant (Saxe)<br>  The Moth and the Star (Thurber)<br>Fairy Tales<br>  The Enchanted Princess (German)<br>  The Princess on the Pea (Andersen)<br>  The Sleeping Beauty (Perrault)<br>  Little Red Riding-Hood (de la Mare)<br>Field, Eugene—A Dutch Lullaby<br>Figures of Speech |

Silver (de la Mare)
The Toaster (Smith, W. J.)
Dandelions (Frost, F. M.)
The Little Rose Tree (Field, Rachel)
Everyone Sang (Sassoon)
The Night Will Never Stay (Farjeon)
Brooms (Aldis, D.)
No Shop Does the Bird Use (Coatsworth, E.)
Folklore—Cinderella (Korean)
Folklore, American
  Coyote Places the Stars
  Wiley and the Hairy Man
Frost, Robert
  The Last Word of a Bluebird
  The Pasture
  Stopping by Woods on a Snowy
   Evening
  The Road Not Taken

**G**    Grahame, Kenneth—The Wind in the
    Willows (excerpt)
    Grimm, Jacob and Wilhelm
     The Shoemaker and the Elves
     Rapunzel
     Hansel and Gretel

**J-K**    Kipling, Rudyard—The Elephant's
    Child

**M**    Milne, A. A.—Missing

**N**    Nonsense Rhymes
    Jabberwocky (Carroll)
    Jellyfish Stew (Prelutsky)
    Habits of the Hippopotamus
     (Guiterman)
    Eletelephony (Richards)
    The Reason for the Pelican (Ciardi)
    Antigonish (Mearns)
    I Wish That My Room Had a Floor
     (Burgess)
    There Was a Young Lady of Woosester
     (Anonymous)
    There Was an Old Man with a Beard
     (Lear)
    There Was an Old Man of Peru
     (Anonymous)
    Nursery Rhymes
     The Old Woman in a Shoe
     Jack and Jill
     Hey Diddle, Diddle
     Miss Muffet
     Mary's Lamb
     Humpty Dumpty

**P**    Potter, Beatrix—The Tale of Jemima
    Puddle-Duck

**S**    Sandburg, Carl
    Fog
    The Skyscraper to the Moon and How

    the Green Rat with the Rheumatism
    Ran a Thousand Miles Twice
  Stevenson, Robert Louis
    Requiem
    My Shadow
    Looking-Glass River
    The Swing
    The Gardener
    Bed in Summer
    Kidnapped (excerpt)

**W-X-Y-Z**    White, E. B.—Charlotte's Web
    (excerpt)
    Wilder, Laura Ingalls—Little House on
    the Prairie (excerpt)

## MATHEMATICS

| Vol. | Article |
| --- | --- |
| **A** | Abacus |
| | Arithmetic |
| **C** | Calendar |
| **D** | Decimal System |
| **F** | Fractions and Decimals |
| **M** | Mathematics |
| | Money |
| **N** | Number Puzzles and Games |
| **T** | Time |
| **W-X-Y-Z** | Weights and Measures |

## SOCIAL STUDIES

| Vol. | Family, School, and Community |
| --- | --- |
| **A** | African Americans |
| **C** | Cities |
| | Colonial Life in America |
| **D** | Dentistry |
| | Doctors |
| **E** | Ethnic Groups |
| **F** | Family |
| | Farms and Farming |
| | Fire Fighting and Prevention |
| **H** | Hispanic Americans |
| | Homes and Housing |
| **J-K** | Kindergarten and Nursery Schools |
| **L** | Learning |
| | Learning Disorders |
| | Libraries |
| **M** | Money |
| **N** | Nurses and Nursing |

| | | | | |
|---|---|---|---|---|
| **P** | Parks and Playgrounds |  | | Friedan, Betty |
| | Police | | | Fulton, Robert |
| | Postal Service | | **H** | Henry, Patrick |
| **Q-R** | Restaurants | | | Hobby, Oveta Culp |
| | Retail Stores | | **J-K** | Jackson, Andrew |
| **S** | Schools | | | Jackson, Jesse |
| | Supermarkets | | | Jefferson, Thomas |
| **T** | Teachers and Teaching | | | Keller, Helen |
| | Traffic Control | | | Kennedy, John F. |
| **U-V** | Veterinarians | | | King, Martin Luther, Jr. |

**L** Lee, Robert E.
Lincoln, Abraham

**M** Madison, James

| **Vol.** | **The United States** |
|---|---|
| **C** | Capitol, United States |
| | Colonial Life in America |
| | Colonial Sites You Can Visit Today |
| | Columbus, Christopher |
| **D** | Democracy |
| **E** | Elections |
| **F** | Flags |
| **I** | Indians, American |
| **L** | Law and Law Enforcement |
| | Liberty, Statue of |
| | Liberty Bell |
| **M** | Mayflower |
| | Municipal Government |
| **P** | Plymouth Colony |
| | Presidency of the United States |
| | Puritans |
| **S** | State Governments |
| | Supreme Court of the United States |
| **T** | Thanksgiving Day |
| **U-V** | United Nations |
| | United States, Congress of |
| **W-X-Y-Z** | White House |

**Q-R** Revere, Paul
Roosevelt, Eleanor
Roosevelt, Franklin D.
Roosevelt, Theodore

**S** Sequoya
Stowe, Harriet Beecher
Stuyvesant, Peter

**T** Tecumseh
Tubman, Harriet

**W-X-Y-Z** Washington, George
Whitney, Eli
Wright, Orville and Wilbur

| **Vol.** | **Geography** |
|---|---|
| **A** | Agriculture |
| | Atlantic Ocean |
| **B** | Biomes |
| **C** | Cities |
| | Climate |
| | Continents |
| **D** | Deserts |
| **E** | Earth |
| | Equator |
| **F** | Forests and Forestry |
| **I** | Indian Ocean |
| | Islands |
| **L** | Lakes |
| **M** | Maps and Globes |
| **N** | National Park System |
| | Natural Resources |
| | North America |
| **O** | Oceans and Seas of the World |
| **P** | Pacific Ocean and Islands |
| **Q-R** | Rivers |
| **S** | Seasons |
| **U-V** | United States |
| **W-X-Y-Z** | Weather |

| **Vol.** | **Important People in American History** |
|---|---|
| **A** | Adams, John |
| | Anthony, Susan B. |
| **B** | Barton, Clara |
| | Bell, Alexander Graham |
| | Blackwell, Elizabeth |
| | Boone, Daniel |
| | Bush, George |
| | Bush, George W. |
| **C** | Carson, Rachel |
| | Carver, George Washington |
| | Clinton, William |
| **D** | Douglass, Frederick |
| **E** | Edison, Thomas Alva |
| | Ericson, Leif |
| **F** | Franklin, Benjamin |

Wetlands
World
THE NEW BOOK OF KNOWLEDGE
contains articles on individual cities,
states, countries, regions, and
continents. Young readers will find
information in these articles about the
land, people, history, and government
of places in which they are interested.

| Vol. | Holidays |
|------|----------|
| C | Christmas |
| E | Easter |
| H | Hanukkah<br>Holidays |
| I | Independence Day |
| N | New Year Celebrations Around the<br>World |
| P | Passover<br>Purim |
| Q-R | Religious Holidays |
| T | Thanksgiving Day |
| U-V | Valentines |

## SCIENCE AND TECHNOLOGY

| Vol. | Plants, Animals, and the Human Body |
|------|-------------------------------------|
| A | Animals<br>Apes |
| B | Bats<br>Birds<br>Body, Human<br>Butterflies and Moths |
| C | Cats |
| D | Dinosaurs<br>Dogs |
| E | Endangered Species |
| F | Flowers<br>Frogs and Toads |
| H | Hibernation<br>Horses and Their Relatives |
| I | Insects |
| L | Leaves<br>Life |
| M | Medicine, Tools and Techniques of<br>Monkeys |
| N | Nature, Study of |
| P | Plants |
| Q-R | Rabbits and Hares<br>Reindeer and Caribou |

| | |
|------|----------|
| T | Trees |
| W-X-Y-Z | Zebras |

| Vol. | Earth and Space |
|------|-----------------|
| A | Armstrong, Neil A.<br>Astronauts |
| C | Climate<br>Clouds<br>Constellations |
| E | Earth-Moving Machinery<br>Earthquakes<br>Electricity |
| F | Floating and Buoyancy |
| I | Ice |
| J-K | Jupiter |
| M | Magnets and Magnetism<br>Matter<br>Milky Way<br>Minerals<br>Moon |
| O | Ores |
| Q-R | Rainbow<br>Reindeer and Caribou<br>Rocks |
| S | Space Exploration and Travel<br>Sun |
| T | Telescopes<br>Thunder and Lightning |
| U-V | Venus |
| W-X-Y-Z | Water<br>Weather |

## HEALTH AND SAFETY

| Vol. | Article |
|------|---------|
| B | Baby |
| D | Digestive System<br>Doctors |
| E | Ear<br>Eggs and Embryos<br>Eye |
| H | Health<br>Hospitals |
| M | Mental Illness |
| N | Nurses and Nursing |
| P | Physical Fitness |
| S | Safety<br>Skeletal System |
| T | Teeth |

## MUSIC

| Vol. | Article |
| --- | --- |
| A | Anderson, Marian |
| B | Ballet |
| C | Carols<br>Country Music |
| D | Drum |
| F | Folk Dancing<br>Folk Music |
| H | Handel, George Frederick |
| L | Lullabies |
| M | Mozart, Wolfgang Amadeus<br>Musical Instruments |
| N | National Anthems and Patriotic Songs |
| O | Opera<br>Orchestra |
| P | Piano |
| Q-R | Recorder |
| S | Schubert, Franz |
| T | Tchaikovsky, Peter Ilyich |
| U-V | United States, Music of the |

## ART

| Vol. | Art and Artists |
| --- | --- |
| B | Bruegel, Pieter, the Elder |
| C | Cassatt, Mary<br>Chagall, Marc<br>Color |
| D | Drawing<br>Dürer, Albrecht |
| G | Gainsborough, Thomas |
| H | Homer, Winslow |
| I | Illustration and Illustrators |
| J-K | Kandinsky, Wassily<br>Klee, Paul<br>Klimt, Gustav |
| L | Leonardo da Vinci |
| M | Matisse, Henri<br>Miró, Joan<br>Moses, Grandma<br>Museums |
| O | O'Keeffe, Georgia |
| P | Picasso, Pablo |
| Q-R | Reynolds, Sir Joshua<br>Rockwell, Norman<br>Sendak, Maurice |

| Vol. | |
| --- | --- |
| U-V | Van Gogh, Vincent<br>Vermeer, Jan |
| W-X-Y-Z | Whistler, James Abbott McNeill |

| Vol. | Arts and Crafts |
| --- | --- |
| C | Clay Modeling |
| D | Decoupage |
| F | Finger Painting |
| L | Linoleum-Block Printing |
| N | Needlecraft |
| O | Origami |
| P | Papier-mâché<br>Posters<br>Puppets and Marionettes |
| Q-R | Rubbings |

## PHYSICAL EDUCATION AND SPORTS

| Vol. | Article |
| --- | --- |
| B | Badminton<br>Ball<br>Baseball<br>Basketball<br>Bicycling<br>Bowling |
| C | Croquet |
| D | Darts |
| F | Field Hockey<br>Fishing<br>Football |
| G | Gymnastics |
| H | Hiking and Backpacking<br>Horseshoe Pitching |
| I | Ice Hockey<br>Ice-Skating |
| J-K | Jogging and Running<br>Judo<br>Juggling |
| J-K | Karate |
| L | Little League Baseball |
| O | Olympic Games<br>Owens, Jesse |
| P | Paddle Tennis<br>Pelé<br>Physical Education<br>Physical Fitness |
| Q-R | Racing<br>Robinson, Jack Roosevelt (Jackie)<br>Roller-Skating |

S Shuffleboard
Skiing
Soccer and Youth Soccer
Softball
Swimming

T Table Tennis
Thorpe, James Francis (Jim)
Track and Field

# GRADES 4 THROUGH 6

▶ **THE STUDENT IN THE MIDDLE GRADES**

In grades 4 through 6, young students experience an interval of relative balance, calm, and stability compared with their earlier period of transition from home to school during the primary years, or compared with the coming years of confusion and stress that usually characterize adolescence. Physical growth continues, but the body changes in less striking ways. The mind and emotions steadily mature, and young learners are expected to have more control over their feelings and to accept more responsibility for how and what they learn.

These youngsters cherish their sense of growing independence, yet they want and accept limits. They are eager to find their place in their own age-group and to develop close relationships with friends. Peers begin to have more influence over their behavior and thinking, but family ties are still strong. This is the age of belonging—to a team, a group, a club, or a clique. It is also an age when youngsters enjoy family togetherness. They love to help plan family projects, trips, hobbies, and outings.

Middle grade students are eager to know what things are, how they work, how they were discovered, and how they are used. Children of this age have a great need to understand meanings behind facts and to see connections. Although their ability to comprehend at an abstract level is growing, these youngsters still need to learn by doing. However, attention spans are longer and interests are more intense. Children of 9 or 10 can spend hours with a favorite activity. Nevertheless, they may pass from interest to interest as they go through the grades, always ready to open doors to new experiences and understandings.

Depending on the community in which they live, students in grades 4 through 6 may attend one of three different types of school configurations. Most middle graders attend an elementary school, although it may not be the same building they attended in the primary grades. Many sixth graders and some fifth

graders go to a middle school. Some sixth graders move on to a junior high school.

Those students still in elementary schools will find their learning taking place in a familiar environment. They spend most of the day in a self-contained classroom, with one teacher for all the core curriculum subjects. In some middle schools, a team-teaching approach is used. Teams of two or more teachers will share teaching responsibilities for their classes. One may teach science and math; another may teach English and social studies. In other middle schools and most junior high schools, instruction is completely departmentalized, with a different teacher for each subject.

Whatever the type of school they attend, these youngsters continue to need parental or adult guidance and support during the middle grade years. Let them know you expect them to do well. Motivate them with encouragement and praise. Help them to feel good about themselves and their abilities. Provide assistance, as needed, with homework and other school activities. Keep the communication lines with your children and your children's teachers open and active. These are important years—years in which young people must acquire the confidence, the knowledge, and the skills they will need to do well in high school and in their adult years.

Enjoyable activities you and your youngsters can do together to reinforce what they are learning in the core curriculum areas—Reading, Language, and Literature; Mathematics; Social Studies; and Science—are listed after each of those sections.

The lists of articles at the very end of this section for grades 4 through 6 include many, but certainly not all, of the articles about each subject area that appear in THE NEW BOOK OF KNOWLEDGE. It is important that students look up the names of topics they want to read about in the Index or in the set itself to locate all of the information they may need or want. For example, in the Social Studies area, articles about each of the countries of the world are not listed in this section but can easily be located by looking each one up under its own name.

## ▶ READING, LANGUAGE, AND LITERATURE

The foundations of reading are taught in the primary grades. Students entering the middle grades should have sound word-attack and word-recognition skills, be able to comprehend what they read at least at a literal level, and begin to understand the elements of good literature. All these skills must be applied and expanded if students are to grow in ability. The reading curriculum in grades 4 through 6 is composed of a mix of developmental reading, content-area reading, and recreational reading.

Developmental reading instruction continues at grades 4, 5, and 6 so that middle grade students learn more advanced reading skills and strategies. Emphasis is on word analysis and higher-level comprehension and critical-thinking skills. Learning prefixes, suffixes, inflected endings, and root words teaches youngsters how to decipher most words, even difficult multisyllabic words. Vocabulary and dictionary skills are taught, usually also including the study of context clues, synonyms, antonyms, and words with multiple meanings, to give students the ability to learn how to unlock the meanings of words.

Reading is primarily a process of constructing meaning from written words, and students are also taught how to apply a variety of comprehension and critical-thinking skills and strategies to do it well. These skills range from making inferences, understanding cause and effect relationships, and summarizing main ideas and key facts to understanding a writer's point of view, recognizing various persuasive devices, and being able to distinguish between fact and opinion.

In the primary grades, youngsters learned the mechanics of reading and began to read simple essays, stories, and poems. In the middle grades, students need to know how to read to learn. They must use reading to get information from many different types of books, including content-area textbooks, reference books, nonfiction books such as biographies, and many other types of resources. Reading these many different texts for information requires the use of good study skills as well as advanced reading skills, so study skills are also emphasized at these levels. Students must also know how to use the various parts of a book—the table of contents, preface, copyright page, index, glossary—to find out where the information one needs in it may be located. They also learn how to skim or scan through a book to locate information quickly; how and when to use encyclopedias, atlases, almanacs, and other reference materials; how to locate resources by referring to a library card or electronic catalog; and how to use graphic sources of information, such as tables, lists, charts, graphs, time lines, pictures, diagrams, and maps and globes. In addition, youngsters are taught to adjust their method and rate of reading depending on the type of material and their purpose in reading it. As they read their social studies, science, and math textbooks, and as they consult the variety of other print materials they need to use, students are, in effect, applying their reading knowledge as well as their thinking, comprehension, and study skills throughout the school day.

Teachers in the middle grades also recognize the importance of nurturing their students' recreational reading interests and activities, and some classroom time is provided for reading for pure pleasure. Youngsters are motivated to explore many literary genres: traditional folktales, myths, fables, and epics; realistic fiction; fantasy and science fiction; suspense and mystery; historical fiction; poetry; biographies; and books about personal experiences and adventures. Class or group discussions revolve around students' reactions to and interpretations of what they have read and include discussions of the setting, plot, characters, mood, and the author's use of language. Knowing about the elements of good literature helps children make worthwhile reading choices and enhances their reading enjoyment.

Reading growth is a complex process. Middle grade teachers remember that each child is an individual with different needs and abilities. Whether they use a traditional or whole-language approach, they try to ensure that every child's needs are met.

Children are introduced to the basics of writing in the primary grades. In grades 4 through 6 more frequent writing opportunities help students hone their skills. Introducing them to the elements of writing as a craft during these years helps them become better users of written language.

Aware that most youngsters sometimes have difficulty selecting a topic to write about, many teachers conduct prewriting brainstorming sessions. Students and teacher join in discussion of a general theme, sharing ideas and suggestions for writing topics and approaches. Once topics have been selected, students are encouraged to write a first draft quickly, concentrating on key ideas and details. Many teachers ask students to review each other's drafts, either as partners or in small groups. Youngsters learn to make thoughtful, supportive comments and recommendations during this peer review, helping each other revise and improve their writing. Once revised drafts are completed, the editing process takes over. Teachers may conduct mini-lessons at this point, focusing on an aspect of spelling, grammar, usage, or capitalization and punctuation. Other teachers hold student-teacher conferences during the revising and editing steps. When all revisions and corrections have been made, students "publish" their final versions. This may mean simply writing their pieces in their best handwriting or typing them in a computer word processing program, or turning them into booklets or books with illustrations and covers.

During the writing process, students are often encouraged to think of themselves as authors and to find a personal writing voice, incorporating humor, colorful language, or other characteristics that are natural to their own personality or use of words.

Middle grade writing assignments will usually include stories, poetry, reports, and essays. Some youngsters write articles for class or school newspapers. Direct connection to the reading curriculum is made by encouraging youngsters to use the literature they read in the classroom or at home as models for their own writing.

In schools with computers, middle graders may use simple word-processing programs. Many children find this a less cumbersome way of writing. They can edit and make changes, substitutions, and deletions quickly and easily without having to produce several handwritten copies.

English and spelling textbooks are used to provide the basic instruction children need in the conventions and mechanics of written language, and students also learn how to use a dictionary and a thesaurus. The proof of their learning, however, is their growing ability to communicate effectively in writing.

Children acquire their basic speech patterns from their parents and families, from their neighborhood friends, and from the speech of the region in which they live. Their speech patterns are largely formed by the time they start school. The school can do much, however, to improve and polish them as necessary by providing instruction in oral expression. Teachers offer many opportunities for youngsters to practice oral expression. These range from making simple announcements to taking part in group discussions. In the middle grades, students report on individual and group projects, tell about personal experiences, give and explain information and directions, tell stories, recite poetry, take part in dramatics and choral speaking, make introductions, conduct interviews, read aloud, and dramatize telephone conversations.

Students are also taught that good listening habits are important. They are shown how to be attentive and courteous while others are speaking and responsive to the thoughts and questions expressed by a speaker. Above all, students learn that listening is an important avenue for learning.

**Home Activities for Reading, Language, and Literature**
Continue to read aloud to your youngsters

as often as possible. Listen to your youngsters read to you from books, magazines, or from stories and reports they have written themselves. Discuss authors and types of books you enjoy reading together. Find more books by the same author in your local library. Ask the librarian to recommend other authors and types of books similar to your current favorites. Help your youngsters develop the habit of looking up information in encyclopedias and other reference books. Encourage their enthusiasm and interests. Start a letter diary together. Each day, or once or twice a week, one of you write a letter to the other and ask the other person to write a response. As your youngsters come upon interesting new words in their reading or in other activities, encourage them to look up the meanings and usage of these words in a dictionary. Urge them to use these words in their own writing and conversation. Make dinner table conversation an enjoyable experience for the entire family. Tell riddles, jokes, and stories, and share with each other the day's special events and activities. This is a good age level for your youngsters to find regular pen pals. They may be friends or relatives who live some distance away. Many magazines for young people publish the names and addresses of Pen Pal Clubs or of youngsters who want to correspond with others having similar interests.

### ▶ MATHEMATICS

In grades 4 through 6, students consolidate and build on the mathematical skills they acquired in earlier grades. They are also taught how to develop their reasoning abilities further and use them to learn new, more complex and more advanced math concepts and strategies.

Middle grade youngsters apply their knowledge of addition, subtraction, multiplication, and division to larger numbers and to fractions and decimals. Their understanding of how to work with numbers is enhanced as they learn about the different properties of numbers. Concepts of prime and composite numbers, ratio, proportion, and percent are also intro-

duced at this level. Their work is not always done as paper-and-pencil activities. Students also learn estimation, mental arithmetic, and the use of calculators and computers.

Mathematical patterns and relationships are discovered as youngsters learn about equations, inequalities, ordered pairs, and coordinate graphs. Visual and concrete experiences help students also understand geometric concepts. Students create models and use rulers, compasses, and protractors as they explore two- and three-dimensional geometric figures, measure angles, and determine symmetry, congruency, and similarity in geometric forms.

Hands-on measuring tools, including yardsticks, meter sticks, gallon and liter containers, balance scales, and others, are often used to help students learn how to determine length and distance, weight and mass, volume and capacity, and area and perimeter. Youngsters learn to use both standard and metric units and to make conversions within both systems.

Experiences in collecting and interpreting numerical data are provided, and students present the results in the form of tables, charts, or graphs, or by calculating the mean, median, and mode of the statistical data they have collected. Experiments with coins, dice, playing cards, and other objects are often used as the basis for helping students learn the strategies they need to make probability predictions.

A key element in the middle grade mathematics curriculum is the problem-solving strand. All of the concepts and skills students learn in mathematics are applied in problem-solving situations. Students at this level learn how to use a logical sequence of steps and a variety of strategies for solving problems. Finding a pattern; using a picture, chart, or model; working backwards; making an organized list; and breaking a complex problem into two or more simple problems are among the strategies they learn to use in working out solutions to the problems they must solve.

By the time they finish the sixth grade, most students will have formed a lifelong attitude toward mathematics. Unfortunately, many youngsters lose interest in, and enjoyment of, math during the middle grade years. Many lack confidence in their ability to understand and use math in school and in everyday life. Parents also find that it becomes more difficult to help their youngsters in math as time goes on. It is important for parents to communicate with the teacher or principal if their children start to show negative attitudes toward the subject or seem to be having difficulty doing the work. Concerned parents and teachers will want to have every opportunity to ensure that math is a positive and pleasurable experience for every child.

**Home Activities for Mathematics**

- Help your youngsters become aware of how large numbers are used in news articles, books, and on television programs. Ask them to read a number and talk about how big a quantity it represents. Do the same with fractions and decimals.
- If your youngsters have a special interest in a sport, encourage them to collect statistics for the sport and its players. In baseball, for example, youngsters love to rattle off batting averages, runs batted in (RBI's), home runs, base hits, stolen bases, strikeouts, and many other statistics.
- Help your youngsters use mathematics in everyday activities. Encourage them to set up budgets that include money earned, an allowance, savings, and purchases. Help them figure out best buys when shopping together.
- Ask your youngsters to estimate measurements when you are on an excursion or trip. "How high do you think that building is?" "How far is it across the lake?" "How many people will fit in the elevator?" Follow up by trying to find the answer when you can.
- Encourage your youngsters to collect interesting number facts that appear in the media or in their reading. This activity may include the sales figures for the latest recording of a favorite entertainer or the distance between the Earth and the nearest star.

- Play games involving numbers with your youngster. Card and dice games call for computation and memory skills, and many board games call for the use of play money.
- Help your youngsters interpret and use the information in everyday schedules, graphs, and tables. You can use many items to do this, including television and movie schedules, arena and theater seating diagrams, train and bus timetables, and pie and line charts and graphs you find in newspaper and magazine articles.

▶ **SOCIAL STUDIES**

Social studies in the middle grades includes history, geography, political science, economics, current affairs, and topics from the social science subjects such as anthropology, sociology, and psychology. Although the social studies curriculum varies from school to school, in general, students in grades 4 through 6 learn about their own city and state; the history and geography of the United States and other nations in the Western Hemisphere; North and South America's historical and cultural roots; and the diverse regions and nations of the world.

The study of the history of the United States usually concentrates on Native Americans, the age of the discovery and exploration of the North American continent, the colonial and revolutionary periods, and the Civil War. Major events from the late 1800's to the present may be covered, but not in depth. Emphasis on modern and contemporary history is usually given in grades 7 through 9 and in high school. Middle grade teachers try to help students understand the traditions and the political and cultural institutions of the United States and to appreciate the events and the people that most influenced our history and the development of our society.

Students learn about the geography of the United States by reading a variety of information sources and comparing and contrasting information about the different regions of the country. Physical and political maps, population tables, product maps, travel brochures, and other tools are also examined to determine how the land, the economy, the people, and the cultural traditions of one region vary from those of another. During the study of the United States, many schools include a companion study of one or more neighbors—Canada and Central and South America.

The study of world history and geography in the middle grades focuses on prehistoric, ancient, and medieval civilizations and on the cultural and social characteristics of other countries and regions. Students also learn to identify the geographic influences that affect the way people live.

Because the future of our nation and of the world depends upon intelligent and informed citizens, students also begin to study current events. Some classes subscribe to a daily local newspaper or to professionally prepared school newspapers designed for particular grade levels. Many schools use educational television or radio programs to present and stimulate interest in current events.

An important outcome of current-events studies is that youngsters become able to identify national and world issues. They enthusiastically take part in discussions and debates about such topics as the environment and conflicts between nations, as well as issues such as hunger, homelessness, and racism. Middle grade students sometimes debate serious matters that touch directly on their own lives and futures. Their increasing ability to empathize with others leads many youngsters at these age levels to begin to take seriously their rights and responsibilities as citizens in a democracy.

Teachers and school administrators commonly encourage activities that promote the development of citizenship skills. Many schools have student councils made up of elected class representatives. Parliamentary procedure is followed as students work on the council or on school committees. Youngsters also learn that there are many ways in which one person or group can be effective in bringing about change and resolving problems. They learn how to write letters and interview people. They collect and raise money for worthy causes. They campaign to save a local landmark, a stream, or an endangered species in their community and bring these issues to the attention of local, state, or federal government officials.

In the pursuit of social studies information, students also use research and problem-solving techniques. They discover that the study, research, and problem-solving skills they are acquiring in their reading, writing, and mathematics classes can be applied to their social studies projects. Working alone or in groups, youngsters use these skills when they consult an assortment of resources to locate, gather, interpret, evaluate, and organize information and then to prepare and deliver oral and written reports.

By the end of the sixth grade, youngsters will have made giant strides toward acquiring the abilities they will need to understand the complexities and the development of human societies around the world.

### Home Activities for Social Studies

- Plan a trip with your youngsters. Show them how the scale and legends on a road map help you determine your route. As they develop an understanding of this kind of information, let them take charge of the road map and be responsible for directions to the driver.
- Discuss important news events at the family table. Help your youngsters distinguish between sensational gossip, unfounded rumor, and relevant facts that can be proven.
- Plan family outings or trips to include visits to museums and historical sites.
- Take your youngsters with you when you vote. Show them the ballot and voting machine. Talk about how you decide on the candidate you choose to vote for.
- Investigate and construct your family tree with your youngsters. Let them interview family members and fill in as many branches of the tree as possible. Talk about the family's origins.

- If you have a personal computer in your home, encourage your youngsters to use educational games, data bases, and simulations with social studies themes. Let them discover how much fun this can be.
- Help your youngsters find ways of taking action on local and national matters of concern to them. They may want to write a letter to the local newspaper or to a public official, or they may want to join a special interest youth club or other organization.
- Encourage and help your youngsters locate places in the news on a map or globe.

## ▶ SCIENCE AND TECHNOLOGY

The middle grade science program continues the balanced approach of the primary grades in which concepts from each of the scientific disciplines—life science, earth science, and physical science—are taught each year. The scope is much broader, however. Students are introduced to a wider range of topics—from atoms to the universe, from bacteria to elephants, from light bulbs to space telescopes. They study only a limited number of concepts and principles in depth, however, as they develop an appreciation of and the habit of scientific thinking.

Youngsters in grades 4 through 6 become familiar with plant and animal life. They learn the similarities and differences in the traits of the simplest living things, such as bacteria and protozoans, and in the traits of animals with and without backbones. They trace the growth and development of flowering plants and plants with seeds or spores. As they examine the many different forms that life takes, students arrive at several key understandings: what an ecosystem is; how plants and animals make adaptations to their environments and how they change or evolve over time; how living things interact; and how the relationships among all the members of an ecosystem are intertwined.

Studies about space expand to include not only our solar system but also the other stars, galaxies, and objects that make up the universe. The wonders and riches of our own planet are presented so that students can learn about rocks, minerals, soil, water, and natural forces. They learn how weather, plate tectonics, volcanoes, and earthquakes constantly build up and wear away the surface of the planet. Students weigh the benefits of advancements in science and technology against the costs and trade-offs to human society and to the environment as they investigate air, water, land, and energy resources.

Several of the most fundamental principles and laws of physical science are first taught in grades 4 through 6. In the study of matter and its properties, students learn about the laws of the conservation of matter, and about atoms, elements, the periodic table, and how substances interact with each other physically and chemically. Isaac Newton's three laws of motion are demonstrated as students acquire knowledge about work, energy, and forces. Experiments with heat, light, sound, electricity, and magnetism lead young scientists to the understanding that although energy can be transferred from one system to another, the total amount of energy remains constant.

Middle grade students are usually ready to understand quite sophisticated scientific and technological concepts. They do this best when they are given opportunities to experiment, to draw conclusions, and to work through problem-solving activities.

### Home Activities for Science and Technology

- Encourage your youngsters to find books in the library that give instructions for easy-to-do science experiments and activities. Help them do some of these activities and talk about the results.
- Youngsters at this age level have an exceptional empathy with animals. If it is possible, this is a good time to encourage them to have a pet, such as a puppy, kitten, or fish, and learn how to be responsible and care for it.
- Help your youngsters keep track of weather forecasts in the newspaper or from a radio or television newscast for a three-

to four-week period. Consider together how often the forecast was correct. Was there a difference in how often short-range forecasts (one to two days) were correct compared to longer-range forecasts (four to five days)? Decide whether or not you can draw any conclusions about the accuracy of weather forecasting.

• Young people at this age are curious about how things work. Help your youngsters find instruction booklets, articles, and books written for their age level that explain how some of the electronic devices in your home work. These might include telephones, VCR's, microwave ovens, and calculators.

• Try some roadside or curbside geology investigations. Whenever you and your youngsters pass a building or park, visit a beach, or spot a fresh roadcut, examine the rocks you find. How many different samples can you find? Can you identify any? Can you find fossils in any? Examine together some books about rocks written for the age levels of your youngsters.

• Encourage your youngsters to keep a science diary or logbook. They may write about any interesting science observations or experiences they have, or they may focus their diary on one science topic such as bird-watching or stargazing.

▶ **HEALTH AND SAFETY**

The school health program for grades 4 through 6 continues to develop many of the topics begun in the primary grades, including the human body, nutrition, physical fitness, personal care, diseases, mental health, safety, and drug, alcohol, and tobacco use and abuse. Students now study these subjects in more depth.

When studying the human body, students examine its important systems in more detail. For example, as they study the structure of the circulatory system, they also learn how each of its components—heart, blood, and blood vessels—functions; how the circulatory system and the respiratory system work together; and how diet and exercise affect both

systems. In addition, youngsters go beyond body systems to study simple aspects of more complex concepts such as heredity and genetics.

First aid is added to the concept of safety, and students learn the proper procedures to follow in various types of emergencies. Investigations into communicable and noncommunicable diseases expand to include heart disease, cancer, and other serious illnesses. In the area of mental health, youngsters continue to talk about effective ways of handling their feelings, and they also learn about how to improve their self-image and how to deal with stress. All children are encouraged to commit themselves to a regular exercise and fitness program and to maintain healthy attitudes toward the use of drugs, alcohol, and tobacco.

Students at this stage are ready to move beyond personal health and examine issues involved in consumer health and in community and environmental health. They learn how to use label and pricing information to make wise choices when shopping for food and health products, and they learn how to evaluate advertisements for these products. They become familiar with the various health services provided in their neighborhood: health departments, hospitals, health clinics, and emergency services.

Middle grade students often develop a keen sensitivity to environmental problems, and many youngsters become enthusiastic volunteers in environmental causes, working to reduce air, water, and garbage pollution in their homes and in their community.

Through the school health program, youngsters are provided with information and experiences that will help them maintain health-promoting attitudes and habits that are intended to last into adulthood.

▶ **MUSIC**

Music begins to become an important part of life for many children in the middle grades. At home they listen to music while working on hobbies, doing chores, or completing homework assignments. They enjoy watching music videos and often mimic popular entertainers. Many 10- and 11-year-olds eagerly pick up popular dance steps and dance at home or at parties with their friends.

In school most youngsters participate in singing activities, frequently learning songs related to themes in the curriculum, such as songs of pioneers and cowboys and folk songs from around the world. Music teachers encourage students to read music and to experiment with part singing and harmony.

As they are asked to listen to recorded or live music, youngsters become familiar with a variety of musical styles, periods, and forms, ranging from classical and baroque to jazz and rock. In a thorough curriculum, they examine the elements a composer uses to communicate a musical message, including tempo, rhythm, melody, timbre, and harmonics. Students also learn how to pay attention to the contributions of different types of instruments and voices in a musical work.

Many children of this age learn to play a musical instrument through private lessons or at school, where they often can play in a band or orchestra. Some take voice lessons or participate in a school choral group.

Through a variety of musical activities, students can expand their appreciation and enjoyment of music.

### ▶ ART

Art is a very enjoyable school experience for middle grade children. They paint, draw, model in clay, design posters, construct with wood, make puppets and models, and work with paper, fabric, and many other materials and tools. They are usually allowed to base much of their creative work on personal experiences, and they are also asked to create pieces for projects in other subject areas. For example, students learning about the Middle Ages in social studies may create their own stained-glass windows using colored cellophane and black construction paper. A science unit on the ecology of a wetland may prompt the painting of a classroom mural depicting the many life-forms found in a wetland habitat.

Youngsters in grades 4 through 6 increase their knowledge of the elements of design and are encouraged to experiment with color, line, shape, space, and texture in their own works. In some programs they learn how to compare the styles of different artists and different cultures or historical periods by viewing and discussing print reproductions, slides, or videotapes of a broad range of artworks.

The school art program for the middle grades motivates youngsters to express their own ideas and feelings through art activities and to appreciate art in many of its forms.

### ▶ PHYSICAL EDUCATION AND SPORTS

Physical fitness, rhythmic activities, gymnastics, and game skills constitute the core of the physical education program for grades 4 through 6. A wide variety of indoor and outdoor activities including walking, running, muscle stretching and strengthening, push-ups, pull-ups, and sit-ups help youngsters gain proficiency in agility, strength, endurance, power, flexibility, and speed.

The rhythmic and gymnastic part of the program calls for folk dancing, forward- and backward-roll variations, and various skills performed on the balance beam.

There is more emphasis for this age-group on games and sports skills. Students leaving the sixth grade usually have a basic knowledge of popular games and their rules including softball, soccer, volleyball, and basketball. Most students should be able to throw, hit, and field a softball; kick, pass, and dribble a soccer ball; shoot, pass, catch, and dribble a basketball; serve and volley a volleyball; and catch, pass, and kick a football.

At this age, students are not pressured to become star performers. They are encouraged to participate in activities and games for their own well-being and enjoyment and to develop skills and abilities they can use all of their lives. The physical education program in grades 4 through 6 tries to promote a positive self-image in each child. The program helps middle school children acquire appropriate social and emotional behaviors toward others.

# CURRICULUM-RELATED ARTICLES

Some of the important articles in THE NEW BOOK OF KNOWLEDGE that relate to the 4 through 6 school curriculum are listed here. Many other articles you or your youngsters may want to read while they are studying topics in these curriculum areas can be found by looking them up in the Index or in the set itself.

## READING, LANGUAGE, AND LITERATURE

| Vol. | Reading and Language |
|---|---|
| A | Alphabet |
| E | English Language |
| G | Grammar |
| L | Language Arts |
| P | Parts of Speech<br>Phonics |
| Q-R | Reading |
| S | Slang<br>Synonyms and Antonyms |
| W-X-Y-Z | Word Games<br>Word Origins |

| Vol. | Writing |
|---|---|
| A | Abbreviations<br>Address, Forms of |
| C | Compositions |
| D | Diaries and Journals |
| F | Figures of Speech |
| H | Handwriting<br>Homonyms |
| L | Letter Writing |
| O | Outlines |
| P | Proofreading<br>Punctuation |
| S | Spelling |
| U-V | Vocabulary |
| W-X-Y-Z | Writing |

| Vol. | Oral Language/Speech |
|---|---|
| D | Debates and Discussions |
| J-K | Jokes and Riddles |
| P | Plays<br>Pronunciation<br>Public Speaking |
| S | Speech<br>Speech Disorders<br>Storytelling |
| T | Tongue Twisters |

| Vol. | Reference, Research, and Study Skills |
|---|---|
| B | Book Reports and Reviews<br>Books: From Author to Reader |
| D | Dictionaries |
| E | Encyclopedias |
| I | Indexes and Indexing |
| L | Libraries |
| M | Magazines<br>Maps and Globes |
| N | Newspapers |
| P | Paperback Books |
| Q-R | Reference Materials<br>Research |
| S | Study, How to |
| T | Tests and Test Taking<br>Time Management |

| Vol. | Literature |
|---|---|
| A | Africa, Literature of<br>American Literature<br>Arabian Nights<br>Arabic Literature<br>Arthur, King |
| B | Ballads<br>Biography, Autobiography, and Biographical Novel |
| C | Caldecott, Randolph<br>Caldecott and Newbery Medals<br>Canada, Literature of<br>Children's Literature |
| D | Diaries and Journals<br>Drama |
| E | English Literature<br>Essays |
| F | Fables<br>Fairy Tales<br>Fiction<br>Figures of Speech<br>Folklore<br>Folklore, American |
| G | Greek Mythology |
| H | Humor |
| I | Iliad<br>Illustration and Illustrators |
| J-K | Jokes and Riddles |

| | |
|---|---|
| **L** | Legends |
| | Literature |
| **M** | Mystery and Detective Stories |
| | Mythology |
| **N** | Newbery, John |
| | Nonsense Rhymes |
| | Norse Mythology |
| **O** | Odyssey |
| **P** | Poetry |
| **Q-R** | Robin Hood |
| **S** | Science Fiction |
| | Short Stories |

**Vol.**   **Author Biographies**

| | |
|---|---|
| **A** | Alcott, Louisa May |
| | Andersen, Hans Christian |
| **B** | Barrie, Sir James Matthew |
| | Blume, Judy |
| | Browning, Elizabeth Barrett and Robert |
| | Burns, Robert |
| **C** | Carroll, Lewis |
| **D** | Dickens, Charles |
| | Dickinson, Emily |
| | Doyle, Sir Arthur Conan |
| | Dunbar, Paul Laurence |
| **E** | Eliot, T. S. |
| **F** | Frost, Robert |
| **G** | Grahame, Kenneth |
| | Grimm, Jacob and Wilhelm |
| **H** | Hawthorne, Nathaniel |
| | Hemingway, Ernest |
| | Henry, O. |
| | Homer |
| | Hughes, Langston |
| **I** | Irving, Washington |
| **J-K** | Kipling, Rudyard |
| **L** | London, Jack |
| | Longfellow, Henry Wadsworth |
| **P** | Poe, Edgar Allan |
| **Q-R** | Rossetti Family |
| **S** | Sandburg, Carl |
| | Sendak, Maurice |
| | Shakespeare, William |
| | Steinbeck, John |
| | Stevenson, Robert Louis |
| | Swift, Jonathan |
| **T** | Thurber, James |
| | Tolkien, J. R. R. |
| | Twain, Mark |
| **V** | Verne, Jules |

| | |
|---|---|
| **W-X-Y-Z** | White, E. B. |
| | Whittier, John Greenleaf |
| | Wilde, Oscar |
| | Wilder, Laura Ingalls |
| | Williams, William Carlos |
| | (See also the article CHILDREN'S LITERATURE for profiles of additional authors and illustrators.) |

**Vol.**   **Selections from Literature**

| | |
|---|---|
| **A** | Alcott, Louisa May—Little Women (excerpt) |
| | Andersen, Hans Christian—The Emperor's New Clothes |
| | Arabian Nights |
| |    Aladdin and the Wonderful Lamp (excerpt) |
| |    The Forty Thieves (excerpt) |
| **B** | Barrie, Sir James Matthew—Peter Pan (excerpt) |
| | Bible Stories |
| |    Noah's Ark |
| |    David and Goliath |
| |    Jonah |
| |    Daniel in the Lions' Den |
| |    The Boy Jesus |
| | Browning, Robert—Pied Piper of Hamelin (excerpt) |
| | Burns, Robert—A Red, Red Rose |
| **C** | Carroll, Lewis—Alice's Adventures in Wonderland (excerpt) |
| | Christmas Story (Gospel according to Luke) |
| **D** | Diaries and Journals—The Diary of Anne Frank (excerpt) |
| | Dickinson, Emily |
| |    A Bird Came Down the Walk |
| |    I'll Tell You How the Sun Rose |
| | Doyle, Sir Arthur Conan—The Red-Headed League (excerpt) |
| | Dunbar, Paul Laurence |
| |    Promise |
| |    Fulfilment |
| **F** | Fables |
| |    The Lion and the Mouse (Aesop) |
| |    The Ant and the Grasshopper (Aesop) |
| |    The Four Oxen and the Lion (Aesop) |
| |    The Tyrant Who Became a Just Ruler (Bidpai) |
| |    The Blind Men and the Elephant (Saxe) |
| |    The Moth and the Star (Thurber) |
| | Fairy Tales |
| |    The Enchanted Princess (German) |
| |    The Princess on the Pea (Andersen) |
| |    The Sleeping Beauty (Perrault) |

Little Red Riding-Hood (de la Mare)
Field, Eugene—A Dutch Lullaby
Figures of Speech
  Silver (de la Mare)
  The Toaster (Smith, W. J.)
  Dandelions (Frost, F. M.)
  The Little Rose Tree (Field, Rachel)
  Everyone Sang (Sassoon)
  The Night Will Never Stay (Farjeon)
  Brooms (Aldis, D.)
  No Shop Does the Bird Use (Coatsworth, E.)
Folklore—Cinderella (Korean)
Folklore, American
  Coyote Places the Stars
  Wiley and the Hairy Man
Frost, Robert
  The Last Word of a Bluebird
  The Pasture
  Stopping by Woods on a Snowy Evening
  The Road Not Taken

**G**  Gettysburg Address
Grahame, Kenneth—The Wind in the Willows (excerpt)
Grimm, Jacob and Wilhelm
  The Shoemaker and the Elves
  Rapunzel
  Hansel and Gretel

**H**  Hawthorne, Nathaniel—Young Goodman Brown

**I**  Irving, Washington—Rip Van Winkle (excerpt)

**L**  Legends
  The Vanishing Hitchhiker (United States)
  Roland and Oliver (France)
  The Legend of Robin Hood (England)
London, Jack—The Call of the Wild (excerpt)
Longfellow, Henry Wadsworth—The Arrow and the Song

**N**  Nonsense Rhymes
  Jabberwocky (Carroll)
  Jellyfish Stew (Prelutsky)
  Habits of the Hippopotamus (Guiterman)
  Eletelephony (Richards)
  The Reason for the Pelican (Ciardi)
  Antigonish (Mearns)
  I Wish That My Room Had a Floor (Burgess)
  There Was a Young Lady of Wooester (Anonymous)
  There Was an Old Man with a Beard (Lear)

There Was an Old Man of Peru (Anonymous)
**P**  Poe—Eldorado
**Q-R**  Rossetti—Who Has Seen the Wind
**S**  Sandburg, Carl
  Fog
  The Skyscraper to the Moon and How the Green Rat with the Rheumatism Ran a Thousand Miles Twice (Rootabaga Stories)
Stevenson, Robert Louis—Kidnapped (excerpt)
Swift, Jonathan—Gulliver's Travels (excerpt)
**T**  Thurber, James—The Great Quillow (excerpt)
Tolkien, J. R. R.—The Hobbit (excerpt)
Twain, Mark
  The Adventures of Tom Sawyer (excerpt)
  The Celebrated Jumping Frog of Calaveras County (excerpt)
**W-X-Y-Z**  White, E. B.—Charlotte's Web (excerpt)
Wilder, Laura Ingalls—Little House on the Prairie (excerpt)
Williams, Carlos William—The Red Wheelbarrow

## MATHEMATICS

| Vol. | Article |
| --- | --- |
| **A** | Abacus |
| | Algebra |
| | Arithmetic |
| **B** | Budgets, Family |
| **C** | Calendar |
| | Computers |
| **D** | Decimal System |
| **E** | Einstein, Albert |
| **F** | Fractions and Decimals |
| **G** | Gauss, Carl Friedrich |
| | Geometry |
| | Graphs |
| **I** | Interest |
| **M** | Mathematics |
| | Mathematics, History of |
| | Money |
| **N** | Newton, Isaac |
| | Number Patterns |
| | Number Puzzles and Games |

Mecca
Middle Ages
Middle Ages, Music of the
Mohammed

**Q-R** Romanesque Art and Architecture

**S** Stained-Glass Windows

**W-X-Y-Z** William the Conqueror
(See also the history section of articles on England, France, Portugal, and Spain.)

**Vol.** **United States History**
**(Note: You will find additional listings for U.S. History in Grades 7 Through 9—Social Studies: United States History.)**

### Age of Discovery and Exploration

**A** Aztecs

**B** Balboa, Vasco Núñez de

**C** Cabot, John
Cartier, Jacques
Champlain, Samuel de
Columbus, Christopher
Coronado, Francisco
Cortés, Hernando

**D** Drake, Sir Francis

**E** Eric the Red
Ericson, Leif
Exploration and Discovery

**F** Ferdinand and Isabella

**G** Gama, Vasco da

**H** Henson, Matthew
Herbs and Spices
Heyerdahl, Thor
Hillary, Sir Edmund
Hudson, Henry

**I** Incas
Indians, American

**J-K** Jolliet, Louis, and Jacques Marquette

**L** La Salle, Robert Cavelier, Sieur de

**M** Magellan, Ferdinand
Maya

**N** Navigation
Northwest Passage

**P** Pizarro, Francisco
Ponce De León

**U-V** Verrazano, Giovanni da
Vespucci, Amerigo
Vikings

### Colonial and Revolutionary Periods

**A** Adams, John
Adams, Samuel
African Americans
Allen, Ethan
Arnold, Benedict

**B** Bill of Rights
Boone, Daniel
Brant, Joseph

**C** Colonial Life in America
Colonial Sites You Can Visit Today

**D** Declaration of Independence

**F** Federalist, The
Founders of the United States
Franklin, Benjamin
French and Indian War

**H** Hale, Nathan
Hamilton, Alexander
Hancock, John
Henry, Patrick
Hutchinson, Anne

**I** Independence Hall

**J-K** Jamestown
Jay, John
Jefferson, Thomas
Jones, John Paul

**L** Lafayette, Marquis de
Lewis and Clark Expedition
Liberty Bell
Louisiana Purchase

**M** Madison, James

**O** Oglethorpe, James
Overland Trails

**P** Paine, Thomas
Penn, William
Perry, Oliver Hazard
Plymouth Colony
Puritans

**Q-R** Quakers

**Q-R** Raleigh, Sir Walter
Revere, Paul
Revolutionary War

**S** Samoset
Smith, John
Stuyvesant, Peter

**T** Tecumseh
Thirteen American Colonies

**U-V** United States, Constitution of the

**W-X-Y-Z** War of 1812
Washington, George
Westward Movement
Williams, Roger

### Civil War and an Expanding America

**A**
Abolition Movement
Addams, Jane
African Americans
Anthony, Susan B.

**B**
Barton, Clara
Boone, Daniel
Booth, John Wilkes
Bowie, James
Brown, John

**C**
Carson, Kit
Carver, George Washington
Child Labor
Civil War, United States
Clay, Henry
Compromise of 1850
Confederate States of America
Cowboys
Crockett, David (Davy)

**D**
Davis, Jefferson
Dix, Dorothea
Douglass, Frederick
Dred Scott Decision
Du Bois, W. E. B.

**E**
Emancipation Proclamation
Erie Canal
Ethnic Groups

**F**
Farragut, David
Frémont, John Charles
Fulton, Robert
Fur Trade in North America

**G**
Gettysburg Address
Gold, Discoveries of
Grant, Ulysses S.

**H**
Hickok, James Butler (Wild Bill)
Houston, Samuel

**I**
Immigration
Indians, American
Industrial Revolution

**J-K**
Jackson, Andrew
Jackson, Thomas Jonathan ("Stone-wall")

**J-K**
Kansas-Nebraska Act

**L**
Labor Movement
Lee, Robert E.
Liberty, Statue of
Lincoln, Abraham

**M**
Mexican War
Monroe Doctrine
Monroe, James
Mormons

**P**
Pioneer Life
Pony Express

**Q-R**
Ranch Life

Reconstruction Period

**S**
Scott, Winfield
Sherman, William Tecumseh
Slavery
Stowe, Harriet Beecher

**T**
Territorial Expansion of the United States
Tubman, Harriet

**U-V**
Underground Railroad

**W-X-Y-Z**
Washington, Booker T.
Whitney, Eli
Women's Rights Movement

**W-X-Y-Z**
Young, Brigham

### The Modern Era

**B**
Bush, George
Bush, George W.

**C**
Civil Rights
Clinton, William
Cold War
Communism
Cuban Missile Crisis

**D**
Depressions and Recessions
Disarmament

**F**
Famine
Fascism

**H**
Hijacking
Holocaust
Hoover, J. Edgar
Human Rights

**I**
Iran-Contra Affair

**J-K**
Kennedy, John F.
King, Martin Luther, Jr.
Korean War

**L**
League of Nations

**M**
Malcolm X

**N**
Nazism
Nixon, Richard M.

**P**
Panama Canal
Powell, Colin

**Q-R**
Racism
Reagan, Ronald W.

**S**
Spanish-American War

**T**
Terrorism

**U-V**
Un-American Activities Committee, House
United Nations

**U-V**
Vietnam War

**W-X-Y-Z**
Watergate
Women's Rights Movement
World War I
World War II

| Vol. | The Fifty States of the United States |
|---|---|
| A | Alabama |
| | Alaska |
| | Arizona |
| | Arkansas |
| C | California |
| | Colorado |
| | Connecticut |
| D | Delaware |
| F | Florida |
| G | Georgia |
| H | Hawaii |
| I | Idaho |
| | Illinois |
| | Indiana |
| | Iowa |
| J-K | Kansas |
| | Kentucky |
| L | Louisiana |
| M | Maine |
| | Maryland |
| | Massachusetts |
| | Michigan |
| | Minnesota |
| | Mississippi |
| | Missouri |
| | Montana |
| N | Nebraska |
| | Nevada |
| | New Hampshire |
| | New Jersey |
| | New Mexico |
| | New York |
| | North Carolina |
| | North Dakota |
| O | Ohio |
| | Oklahoma |
| | Oregon |
| P | Pennsylvania |
| Q-R | Rhode Island |
| S | South Carolina |
| | South Dakota |
| T | Tennessee |
| | Texas |
| U-V | Utah |
| U-V | Vermont |
| | Virginia |
| W-X-Y-Z | Washington |
| | West Virginia |
| | Wisconsin |
| | Wyoming |

| Vol. | Government |
|---|---|
| B | Bill of Rights |
| C | Cabinet of the United States |
| | Capitol, United States |
| | Citizenship |
| | Civil Rights |
| D | Declaration of Independence |
| | Democracy |
| E | Elections |
| F | First Amendment Freedoms |
| | First Ladies |
| G | Government, Forms of |
| | Greece, Ancient |
| L | Law and Law Enforcement |
| | Locke, John |
| M | Magna Carta |
| | Municipal Government |
| N | Naturalization |
| P | Presidency of the United States |
| Q-R | Rome, Ancient |
| S | State Governments |
| | Supreme Court of the United States |
| U-V | United Nations |
| | United States, Congress of |
| | United States, Constitution of the |
| | United States, Government of the |
| W-X-Y-Z | Washington, D.C. |
| | White House |
| | (See also names of presidents and individual departments of the United States government.) |

| Vol. | Geography |
|---|---|
| A | Atlantic Ocean |
| B | Biomes |
| C | Cities |
| | Climate |
| | Continents |
| D | Deserts |
| E | Earth |
| | Earthquakes |
| | Equator |
| | Erosion |
| F | Forests and Forestry |
| G | Geography |
| | Glaciers |
| | Greenwich Observatory |
| I | Indian Ocean |

## SCIENCE

| B | Baby |
| | Barnard, Christiaan |
| | Blindness |
| | Blood |
| | Body, Human |
| | Brain |
| C | Cancer |
| | Circulatory System |
| | Consumerism |
| D | Deafness |
| | Digestive System |
| | Diseases |
| | Doctors |
| | Drew, Charles Richard |
| | Drug Abuse |
| | Drugs |
| E | Ear |
| | Eggs and Embryos |
| | Emotions |
| | Eye |
| F | First Aid |
| | Fleming, Sir Alexander |
| | Food Preservation |
| | Food Regulations and Laws |
| | Food Shopping |
| G | Genealogy |
| | Glands |
| H | Hair and Hairstyling |
| | Health |
| | Heart |
| | Hepatitis |
| | Hijacking |
| | Homosexuality |
| | Hormones |
| | Hospitals |
| I | Immune System |
| J-K | Jenner, Edward |
| L | Learning Disorders |
| | Lymphatic System |
| M | Mental Illness |
| | Muscular System |
| N | Nurses and Nursing |
| | Nutrition |
| P | Pasteur, Louis |
| | Physical Fitness |
| | Poisons and Antidotes |
| Q-R | Reproduction |
| S | Safety |
| | Skeletal System |
| | Sleep |
| | Smoking |
| T | Taussig, Helen |
| | Teeth |

| U-V | Vaccination and Immunization |
| | Vectors of Disease |
| | Vegetarianism |
| | Vitamins and Minerals |

## MUSIC

| Vol. | **Music and Musical Instruments** |
| B | Ballads |
| | Ballet |
| | Bands and Band Music |
| | Bells and Carillons |
| C | Carols |
| | Choral Music |
| | Clarinet |
| | Country Music |
| D | Dance |
| | Dance Music |
| | Drum |
| G | Guitar |
| H | Harmonica |
| | Hymns |
| J-K | Jazz |
| J-K | Keyboard Instruments |
| L | Lullabies |
| M | Music |
| | Musical Instruments |
| | Musical Theater |
| N | National Anthems and Patriotic Songs |
| O | Opera |
| | Operetta |
| | Orchestra |
| | Orchestra Conducting |
| P | Percussion Instruments |
| | Piano |
| Q-R | Recorder |
| | Records and Record Collecting |
| | Rock Music |
| S | Stringed Instruments |
| U-V | Violin |
| | Voice Training and Singing |
| W-X-Y-Z | Wind Instruments |

| Vol. | **Music History and Biographies** |
| A | Ancient World, Music of the |
| | Anderson, Marian |
| B | Bach, Johann Sebastian |
| | Beethoven, Ludwig Van |
| C | Chopin, Frederic |

Classical Age in Music
Copland, Aaron

**D** Debussy, Claude

**F** Foster, Stephen

**G** Gershwin, George
Gilbert and Sullivan Operettas
Grieg, Edvard

**H** Handel, George Frederick

**M** Mendelssohn, Felix
Middle Ages, Music of the
Mozart, Wolfgang Amadeus

**O** Offenbach, Jacques

**P** Prokofiev, Sergei

**Q-R** Renaissance Music

**S** Schubert, Franz
Strauss, Johann, Jr.

**T** Tchaikovsky, Peter Ilyich

**U-V** Verdi, Giuseppe

| **Vol.** | **Music Around the World** |
|---|---|
| **A** | Africa, Music of |
| **E** | English Music |
| **F** | Folk Dance<br>Folk Music |
| **L** | Latin America, Music of |
| **O** | Oriental Music |
| **U-V** | United States, Music of the |

# ART

| **Vol.** | **Art** |
|---|---|
| **A** | Architecture<br>Art |
| **C** | Cathedrals<br>Color |
| **D** | Design<br>Drawing |
| **I** | Illuminated Manuscripts<br>Illustration and Illustrators |
| **L** | Louvre |
| **M** | Metropolitan Museum of Art<br>Museums |
| **N** | National Gallery (London)<br>National Gallery of Art (Washington, D.C.)<br>National Gallery of Canada |
| **O** | Obelisks |
| **P** | Painting |

Photography
Prado

**S** Sculpture

**U-V** Uffizi Gallery

**W-X-Y-Z** Watercolor

| **Vol.** | **Art History and Biographies** |
|---|---|
| **A** | Ancient World, Art of the |
| **B** | Benton, Thomas Hart<br>Botticelli, Sandro<br>Bruegel, Pieter, the Elder |
| **C** | Cassatt, Mary<br>Cezanne, Paul<br>Chagall, Marc |
| **D** | Dali, Salvador<br>Degas, Edgar<br>Drawing, History of<br>Dürer, Albrecht |
| **E** | Egyptian Art and Architecture<br>Escher, M. C. |
| **F** | Folk Art |
| **G** | Gainsborough, Thomas<br>Gothic Art and Architecture<br>Greece, Art and Architecture of |
| **H** | Hockney, David<br>Hogarth, William<br>Hokusai<br>Homer, Winslow |
| **J-K** | Klee, Paul<br>Klimt, Gustav |
| **L** | Léger, Fernand<br>Leonardo da Vinci |
| **M** | Michelangelo<br>Miró, Joan<br>Moses, Grandma |
| **O** | O'Keeffe, Georgia<br>Oriental Art and Architecture |
| **P** | Peale Family<br>Picasso, Pablo<br>Prehistoric Art |
| **Q-R** | Raphael<br>Rembrandt<br>Renaissance Art and Architecture<br>Renoir, Pierre Auguste<br>Reynolds, Sir Joshua<br>Rockwell, Norman<br>Roman Art and Architecture<br>Romanesque Art and Architecture |
| **U-V** | Van Gogh, Vincent<br>Vermeer, Jan |
| **W-X-Y-Z** | Whistler, James Abbott McNeill |

Wood, Grant
Wyeth Family

# PHYSICAL EDUCATION AND SPORTS

| T | Table Tennis | **W-X-Y-Z** | Water Polo |
| | Tennis | | Waterskiing |
| | Thorpe, James Francis (Jim) | | Wrestling |
| | Track and Field | | |
| **U-V** | Volleyball | | |

# GRADES 7 THROUGH 9

▶ **THE YOUNG ADOLESCENT**

There are moments when the parents of an early teen feel that, without warning, their child has become a stranger. The son or daughter they have known since birth suddenly looks very different and behaves in unaccustomed ways. Their youngster is caring and responsible one minute and sullen and uncooperative the next. These changes are all part of the normal pattern of transition and turmoil that characterize the young adolescent.

It is a time of considerable and often abrupt physical, emotional, social, and intellectual growth and development. No longer a child but not yet an adult, the teenager may exhibit the behavior and characteristics of both. It is a stage that is often as difficult for parents and teachers as it is for the teenager.

The young adolescent's problems usually start with bodily changes. They make rapid gains in height and weight. Their arms and legs, hands and feet, seem to outgrow the rest of their body, frequently resulting in clumsy, uncoordinated actions. There are wide variations in the size and maturity of individuals of the same age or grade level, and girls often become heavier and taller and mature earlier than boys their age. Along with rapid growth may come new problems with skin conditions or body odor. Sexual development and the onset of puberty are embarrassing for some, mystifying or exciting for others.

Many youngsters accept these startling changes gracefully. Others are made anxious and worry excessively about their health and their bodies. They may translate their worries into aggressive or withdrawn behavior and may experience many mood swings. Adults can help young adolescents accept their new growth by helping them understand that what is happening to them is a perfectly natural part of growing up.

Physical and hormonal changes have an impact on the emotional and social behaviors of early teens. Strong, often conflicting, needs dominate their personalities. They are redefining their relationships with adults and are fre-quently inconsistent in their need for independence from adult authority and their desire for guidance and regulation. They want respect and they want to be treated fairly and reasonably. They need to be able to place their trust in adult family members and teachers.

The need to conform to the code of their peers is all-important to the young adolescent. Because they are very afraid of being ridiculed, their friends' values and beliefs about right and wrong behavior, religion, drugs, sexuality, and education may conflict or seem to take precedence over the values of their family. Many inner-city youngsters face the additional pressures caused by youth gangs. Finding a place in a group takes on urgent importance at this stage, and adults should help channel this urge by helping their teenagers find appropriate clubs and other organizations to join.

Young teens are in the process of learning how to form friendships with members of their own sex and how to behave with persons of the opposite sex. At the same time they are struggling to develop a unique personal identity, and they may experiment with many roles before they find the personality that is their own. Craving success and recognition, they look to parents and teachers for guidance, understanding, and acceptance.

Along with their changing bodies, feelings, and social behaviors, early adolescents are developing intellectual sophistication. They are capable of abstract reasoning and reflective thinking. They are fascinated by concepts such as justice, democracy, friendship, and the obligations of freedom. A natural curiosity motivates their learning, and they are always ready to question and challenge the ideas and actions of others. Topics related to their own personal concerns and goals are more apt to arouse their enthusiasm and active involvement as learners.

Most students in grades 7 and 8 attend a middle school or junior high school. Ninth graders may already be in a senior high school. Most young teens will experience a more structured, departmentalized school program and will have to deal with many more teachers than they did in their earlier school years. Their school day usually consists of six periods, and each subject is given paramount importance by the instructor who teaches it.

All students study English, mathematics, social studies, and science each year in grades 7 through 9. Many begin a foreign language, usually French or Spanish. Depending on the school's facilities, physical education may be offered each year as well. In addition, students generally take at least one course in music, art, health, and home economics or industrial arts (technology education in some schools).

There is homework assigned for most subjects, and the work requires substantial time and effort on the part of the student. Tests and grades are taken very seriously and school can become yet another anxiety-producing factor in the young adolescent's life. On the other hand, many of the young person's social activities center on the school's extracurricular groups, clubs, and teams, and the school can serve as a conduit for social and emotional development as well as for intellectual growth.

For most teenagers the years of young adolescence are as scary, thrilling, and invigorating as a rollercoaster ride. Parents of young teens experience their own highs and lows, too. You can help make it a smoother ride by listening carefully to your teenagers. Pay close attention to what they tell you verbally and by their actions. Try to be patient and understanding. Let them know you are ready to take their concerns seriously, and try to help them find satisfactory solutions to their problems. They may not always admit it, but young adolescents need caring, supportive parents and adults more than ever to guide them on their quest for adulthood.

▶ **SUCCESS IN SCHOOL**

Young adolescents are very busy people. They spend most of their weekdays going to school, participating in after-school activities, doing homework, visiting with friends, and doing things on their own. For some teenag-

ers the only interaction with family members takes place around the table at mealtimes. Even on weekends, young teens often want to follow their own recreational agendas and can be drawn into family activities only with reluctance. Parents and teens can lose touch at this turning point in young people's lives.

Concerned parents and caregivers need to penetrate these barriers and continue to provide the support, direction, and encouragement that will help their youngsters achieve success in middle school or junior high school. The teenager who drops out of high school is often the youngster who falls behind scholastically in grades 7 through 9. It is also a fact that youngsters who do not perform to their full potential in these important years will not be sufficiently prepared to tackle the high school courses that make entry into a college or a job after graduation easier.

Parents can continue to exercise influence on their teenager's school performance in a number of direct, and sometimes subtle, ways:

- With the exception of real illness, make sure your teenagers attend classes every day. If it is absolutely necessary for them to be absent, make sure the schoolwork for all subjects is made up. If the absence has been longer than one or two days, talk to teachers yourself to get their help in making up what was missed in lectures or classroom activities

- Young teens may lack organization skills and have difficulty setting up a homework or study plan. Refer to pages 139–41 of this STUDY GUIDE for helpful homework suggestions. Make sure each student has a quiet, private spot for study

- Keep a regular household routine that accommodates the needs and schedules of all family members. There should be definite times set for meals, study periods, household chores, and family recreation

- Set aside time each day for a one-on-one conversation with your teenagers. If your youngsters are reluctant to talk about school, try asking questions that require more than a simple "yes" or "no" answer

"What's your favorite subject this semester?" "What do you like about it?" "Why do you think you did so well (or so poorly) on that last test?" "How can you do even better next time?" Talk about out-of-school interests and activities, too. Listen objectively. Try to be helpful and reassuring rather than judgmental

- Create a home atmosphere that encourages learning. Books and newspapers should be visible—library books are fine. Try to have a good dictionary, thesaurus, and other reference books on hand—inexpensive paperbacks or second-hand books will do the job. Let young people see adults reading for pleasure as well as for information. Make a habit of watching some educational documentaries and cultural programs on television. Try to talk about current events and local issues with your teenagers
- Include books as gifts on birthdays and holidays. Find out who the teenager's favorite authors are and what type of books are preferred. Historical? Mystery? Fantasy? Sports? Realistic? Good nonfiction books can start new interests and can support learning taking place in the classroom
- Continue to do things as a family group. Play games together. Have a picnic. Go to athletic events, concerts, museums, plays, or art shows. In many communities there are many free cultural and sporting events. High school and local college performances and sports events can be particularly enjoyable because you will probably know some of the players or performers in them
- Try to carry on the family reading-aloud activities that were part of your teenager's everyday life during his or her preschool and elementary school years. You probably will not get a young teen to sit still for this on a regular basis. When you have come across an especially good book, or magazine or newspaper article, however, capture a few minutes to read a particularly interesting passage and you may hook the youngster into wanting to read

it, too
- Many middle schools and junior high schools use a tracking system in which students are assigned to classes and subjects on the basis of test scores and past performance. If any of your youngsters are in a low-track group, speak with teachers, the guidance counselor, and the principal to find ways of helping them to do well and, if it seems possible, improve enough to be moved into a higher track
- If your teenagers have problems in school, try to pinpoint specific reasons and work with your youngsters and school personnel to create an action plan that will lead to a successful turnaround

Above all, know your youngsters, keep informed about the expectations and requirements of their school and teachers, and provide the guidance and support they need.

The lists of articles at the very end of this section for grades 7 through 9 include many, but certainly not all, of the articles about each subject area that appear in THE NEW BOOK OF KNOWLEDGE. It is important that students look up the names of topics they want to read about in the Index or in the set itself to locate all of the information they may need or want. For example, in the Social Studies area, articles about each of the countries of the world are not listed in this section but can easily be located by looking each one up under its own name.

▶ LANGUAGE AND LITERATURE

The emphasis of the English curriculum for grades 7 through 9 is on reading, understanding, and appreciating literature; writing in a grammatical, well-organized, and coherent manner; and speaking effectively in a variety of situations. Unless a youngster exhibits major deficiencies in reading, most students in middle school or junior high school do not have a period in which reading skills are taught. Students will take several semesters of literature and grammar and composition courses and sometimes a course in speech or communication.

Literature courses are usually organized so that students learn the distinguishing characteristics of short stories, novels, poetry, drama, and nonfiction. Students are exposed to a broad spectrum of classic and contemporary works by well-known American authors and by writers from other countries and cultures. Students learn how to analyze literary works and to become knowledgeable about the elements writers use to communicate their ideas and feelings: plot, character, setting, theme, mood, tone, language, symbolism, and imagery. Students are asked to think, write, and talk about their reading. By learning how to communicate their interpretations and evaluations, young people also learn how to read with greater insight and deeper understanding.

In their grammar and composition course, students learn how to apply the writing process to four main types of composition: narration, description, exposition, and persuasion. They study the intricacies of grammar, mechanics, and usage and learn how to construct coherent and effective sentences, paragraphs, and themes. In their compositions students are expected to demonstrate clear and logical thinking in the support and development of a central idea. Writing assignments are often assigned for homework and may include writing a character sketch, explaining a process, writing an essay to answer a question, or writing a poem, an editorial, or an autobiography. By ninth grade most youngsters have also learned how to do a research report.

Vocabulary study is an important component of both the literature and the grammar and composition course. Youngsters encounter many new and exciting words as they read, and they are encouraged to use the dictionary and word analysis techniques to learn the meanings of words not made clear by the text. Reviewing what they know or need to learn about affixes, common roots, synonyms, antonyms, and analogies also helps them determine word meanings.

The speech course promotes self-confidence in oral communication and involves students in public speaking, group discussion, debate, and dramatic reading activities. The importance of responding courteously and appropriately to a presenter is also stressed.

▶ **MATHEMATICS**

There is variation from school to school in the types of math courses offered in grades 7 through 9. Not all students in the same grade in a particular school will take the same courses. Students with more background and ability will usually take more advanced courses than the average or weaker student. For some youngsters, middle school or junior high mathematics will consist primarily of the review, extension, and application of familiar math skills and concepts. For others, the math curriculum will consist of preparation for the more rigorous courses in algebra, geometry, and trigonometry of high school.

All students will be offered at least one course in which previously taught skills—those involving numbers, measurement, geometry, patterns and functions, statistics, probability, and logical reasoning—are strengthened and taught in greater depth. Some youngsters will take a pre-algebra class. Some will take a transition course that combines applied mathematics with pre-algebra and pre-geometry topics and concepts. Others will undertake a course made up of a combination of consumer and business applications for a variety of real-life topics and situations: earning and spending money, budgeting, banking, taxes, insurance, housing, and transportation. The more able eighth graders will be offered an algebra course.

The college-bound ninth grade student studies high school level algebra or occasionally formal geometry. Algebra is also an option for non-college-bound students, or they may study general mathematics or business math.

Some students may end their experience with school mathematics in the ninth grade. More and more states and school districts are adopting more rigorous mathematics standards, however. All students in these districts must pass high-level mathematics courses to meet graduation requirements.

## SOCIAL STUDIES

American and world history and geography constitute the core of the social studies curriculum for grades 7 through 9. There are wide variations, however, in the specific courses offered at each of the grade levels by different school districts.

The study of American history may be a one-year or two-year course. It usually consists of a chronological presentation of political, cultural, social, economic, and geographic influences on the development of the United States as a nation, spanning the years from pre-colonial times to the present. More time and emphasis are assigned to the post–Civil War and contemporary eras than in earlier grades. As they survey and study important events and assess the contributions of key figures, students also learn about many of the major ideas and movements that influenced our country's past and present history. These will include abstract concepts such as democracy, freedom, responsibility, equality, and parity, as well as specific movements and processes such as the evolution of political and social institutions, slavery, immigration, the rise of industry, the impact of technology, the spread of cities and urban areas, and the role of women and diverse racial and ethnic groups.

The vast scope of world history and geography is presented in a number of different courses in different schools. These courses vary widely in their structure and emphasis. Some students study the history of Europe, Asia, Africa, and the Americas chronologically from ancient civilizations to early modern times. Other students will make in-depth investigations into selected world regions or world cultures. Still others will focus on key historical and contemporary trends, problems, and issues in a Global Studies course.

Along with their studies of America and the world, many youngsters have the opportunity to take separate courses in state history, civics, economics, or geography.

As they gather information on social studies topics, middle school and junior high school students are urged to use original primary and secondary sources; to apply critical and creative thinking to the analysis and evaluation of research data and its source; and to synthesize this information in order to make rational decisions about local, national, and international problems and issues.

## SCIENCE AND TECHNOLOGY

When they enter the seventh grade, most students have their first experience with science courses taught according to specific disciplines. In grades 7 through 9 science is offered in a three-year sequence by discipline: life science, physical science, and earth science, not necessarily in that order. All three courses incorporate information about technology, emphasizing its applications and its impact on society.

The life science course provides a survey of the five kingdoms into which living things are classified, according to their characteristics and relationships: the Prokaryotes (bacteria); the Protists (single-celled organisms); Fungi; Plants; and Animals. Students also conduct in-depth investigations into the structure and function of cells; genetics and the role of DNA; the evolutionary process; the structure and functions of the organ systems of humans and other animals; and the major ecosystems of the world. In many classrooms students use a microscope and do simple dissections for the first time.

In the physical science course, many topics introduced in earlier grades are extended. These include motion, forces, energy in all its forms, the properties of matter, atomic structure, and the periodic table. Students are usually ready at this age to begin new studies into the principles of chemistry. They learn about compounds, mixtures, chemical bonding, chemical interactions and reactions, and acids, bases, and salts. Demonstrations and experiments help them understand the more complex concepts of basic physics and chemistry.

Most ninth graders are offered the earth science course or a high school biology course. In earth science classes, students delve into the geology of the earth, its history, and the forces that shape it, emphasizing the role of plate tectonics. They also study the oceans of the earth, the earth's atmosphere, meteorology, and astronomy. The biology course covers the traditional life-science topics mentioned above, but with heavier concentration on the cell, microbiology, genetics, evolution, reproduction, and body chemistry.

Some ninth graders complete their science education with a general science course.

At present there is a need for people to understand the growing number of important problems in our society that require scientific and technological solutions and an equally important need for more young people to embark on science-based careers. For these reasons educators are urging students to continue their science studies through high school, and many states are mandating additional science courses as requirements for graduation. It is also important for youngsters in the middle school or junior high school to be better prepared for the more rigorous requirements of high school science.

▶ **HEALTH EDUCATION**

The study of health is especially important for the young adolescent who is experiencing physical, emotional, social, and intellectual changes. The comprehensive health program for grades 7 through 9 usually provides information about ten major health topics: human body systems; prevention and control of disease; substance use and abuse; nutrition; mental and emotional health; accident prevention, safety, and first aid; family life; physical fitness and personal care; consumer health; and community and environmental health and health care resources. It is important for students to take this opportunity to use the knowledge presented in the course they take to learn how to make healthy choices in their daily lives and to adopt positive behaviors and attitudes that will last a lifetime.

Important subtopics of particular interest to the young teen usually include: grooming and skin care; fitness programs; stress management; eating disorders and weight control; alcohol and drugs; the human life cycle; human repro-

duction; safe and effective cosmetic and health care products; emergency care; and sexually transmitted diseases. Understanding how to cope with these concerns helps adolescent youngsters become more comfortable with the changes they are experiencing in their own lives. It also gives them confidence in their ability to deal with the day-to-day problems and situations that may affect their well-being.

▶ **FOREIGN LANGUAGE**

Most elementary schools do not provide instruction in a foreign language. Many youngsters have their first contact with another language in the seventh, eighth, or ninth grades. French and Spanish are the languages most frequently offered and students are usually given their choice between the two. Ninth graders often have more of a selection from which to choose. Depending upon the composition and interests of the local community, students may have the opportunity to learn German, Italian, Japanese, or Latin as well as French or Spanish.

Foreign language courses for grades 7 through 9 usually employ a cultural and conversational approach. Students learn to listen, speak, read, and write the language. Emphasis is on modeling the dialogue of everyday situations—visiting friends, going to school, shopping, attending sports and cultural events, or taking a bus or train ride. These dialogue situations are used as a basis for learning about the culture, geography, customs, and traditions of the country or the countries in which the language predominates.

Although students learn the basic elements of the grammar of the language, more structured grammar study is reserved for high school.

▶ **MUSIC**

In grades 7 through 9 music is usually taught by a music specialist, and students have many opportunities to participate in a variety of musical experiences and activities.

A one-semester or one-year course in music

appreciation is generally offered to all students as an elective. Youngsters are introduced to the major periods and developments in classical and popular music history and to the biographies of major composers and performers. They study musical elements such as rhythm, melody, harmony, and counterpoint and learn to recognize a variety of musical forms, including the symphony, sonata, opera, and operetta. These topics are coordinated with experiences in listening to recorded or live performances.

Some youngsters may participate in school choral or dance groups or may play an instrument in the school band or in the orchestra.

All young adolescents enjoy listening to music. Many take private voice, instrument, or dance lessons; some even begin to form their own musical groups outside of school. Certain youngsters exhibit exceptional talent in music at this age, and they should be challenged to develop it to their full potential. All students, regardless of their musical ability, should be encouraged to develop a thoughtful response to music and to continue to participate in musical activities.

### ▶ ART

Art instruction in grades 7 through 9 provides young teenagers with a variety of art experiences in a one-semester or one-year art course often offered as an elective.

Students experiment with an assortment of art media, tools, processes, and techniques. They may delve into poster making, lettering, painting, drawing and illustration, clay modeling, costume design, advertising design, and interior and stage decoration. They explore the use of color, perspective, proportion, dimension, line, and other elements and principles of visual composition and design.

Students become familiar with the history of art as they examine and analyze major works from different historical periods. They learn how to identify and compare stylistic differences in the works of significant artists. The role of artists in the media is also probed as students investigate the work of photographers, illustrators, costume and set designers, cartoonists, computer-graphics artists, and artists in television, video, and film production.

In some schools, students with a special ability or interest in art may be able to take additional art courses or may participate in an after-school art club.

For young adolescents, activities in art and music can provide a positive and productive avenue for releasing emotions and for expressing thoughts and ideas.

### ▶ PHYSICAL EDUCATION AND SPORTS

Almost all youngsters enjoy participating in sports and physical activities during their elementary school years. Enthusiasm for these activities begins to decline at about age 10. Some early teens lose all interest in keeping their bodies fit and no longer take part in games and sports on their own. The school physical education program for grades 7 through 9 plays an important role in keeping all young adolescents involved in fitness and sports activities during this crucial period of physical change and growth.

As in the earlier grades, the physical education curriculum is a combination of fitness, gymnastic activities, and games and sports. There is more emphasis on team sports at this level, although individual sports are preferred by many youngsters, and some schools add table tennis, wrestling, badminton, and paddle and racket games to their sports program. In team sports, football, basketball, baseball, and track and field are popular with boys; basketball, track and field, softball, and volleyball are generally favored by girls.

Students are usually asked to demonstrate proficiency in skills involving balance, endurance, strength, flexibility, and agility. Social attitudes and skills such as responsibility, leadership, tolerance, and a positive self-image are also stressed.

Recognizing that not all youngsters are athletes, the school physical education program is geared to helping teenagers acquire attitudes and skills that will help them maintain physical fitness in later years and remain actively involved in worthwhile recreational activities.

## ▶ HOME ECONOMICS AND INDUSTRIAL ARTS

Students in middle school or junior high school usually have the opportunity to study home economics or industrial arts. In some schools, industrial arts is called technology education. These courses emphasize the learning and use of practical skills.

The home economics course focuses on the skills of day-to-day living. Topics studied usually include family life and home management; food and nutrition; clothing; home furnishings; and how to be a smart consumer. During the course, students are required to complete a number of hands-on projects, which may include planning a menu and preparing a meal, planning a room and making a three-dimensional model, or sewing a simple garment. Role playing and dramatization are used to clarify the complexities of home and community relationships and family living.

In the industrial arts or technology education course, students are introduced to hand and power tools and their applications to the basic elements of mechanical drawing or drafting. They also learn about common industrial materials such as metal, plastics, and ceramics and about the tools and processes used in electricity, electronics, printing and graphic arts, photography, and other general crafts. Students are required to complete several projects that demonstrate what they have learned about materials and processes and what level of skill they have reached with basic tools, techniques, and procedures.

# CURRICULUM-RELATED ARTICLES

Some of the important articles in THE NEW BOOK OF KNOWLEDGE that relate to the 7 through 9 school curriculum are listed here. Many other articles you or your youngsters may want to read while they are studying topics in these curriculum areas can be found by looking them up in the Index or in the set itself.

## LANGUAGE AND LITERATURE

| Vol. | Language |
|------|----------|
| A | Alphabet |
| E | English Language |
| G | Grammar |
| L | Language Arts |
| P | Parts of Speech |
| Q-R | Reading |
| S | Semantics |
| | Slang |
| | Synonyms and Antonyms |
| W-X-Y-Z | Word Games |
| | Word Origins |

| Vol. | Writing |
|------|---------|
| A | Abbreviations |
| | Address, Forms of |
| C | Compositions |
| D | Diaries and Journals |
| E | Essays |
| F | Figures of Speech |
| H | Handwriting |
| | Humor |
| J-K | Journalism |
| L | Letter Writing |
| O | Outlines |
| P | Proofreading |
| | Punctuation |
| S | Spelling |
| U-V | Vocabulary |
| W-X-Y-Z | Writing |

| Vol. | Oral Language/Speech |
|------|----------------------|
| D | Debates and Discussions |
| J | Jokes and Riddles |
| O | Oratory |
| P | Parliamentary Procedure |
| | Plays |
| | Pronunciation |
| | Public Speaking |
| S | Speech |
| | Speech Disorders |
| | Storytelling |
| T | Tongue Twisters |

| Vol. | Reference, Research, and Study Skills |
|------|---------------------------------------|
| B | Book Reports and Reviews |
| | Books: From Author to Reader |
| D | Dictionaries |
| E | Encyclopedias |
| I | Indexes and Indexing |
| L | Libraries |
| M | Magazines |
| N | Newspapers |
| P | Paperback Books |
| Q-R | Reference Materials |
| | Research |
| S | Study, How to |
| T | Tests and Test Taking |
| | Time Management |

| Vol. | Literature |
|------|------------|
| A | Aeneid |
| | Africa, Literature of |
| | American Literature |
| | Arabic Literature |
| | Arthur, King |
| B | Ballads |
| | Beowulf |
| | Biography, Autobiography, and Biographical Novel |
| C | Canada, Literature of |
| | Chinese Literature |
| D | Diaries and Journals |
| | Drama |
| E | English Literature |
| | Essays |
| F | Faust Legends |
| | Fiction |
| | Figures of Speech |
| | Folklore |
| | Folklore, American |
| G | Germany, Literature of |
| | Greece, Language and Literature of |

| | |
|---|---|
| **H** | Hebrew Language and Literature |
| | Humor |
| **I** | Iliad |
| | Illustration and Illustrators |
| | India, Literature of |
| | Ireland, Literature of |
| | Italy, Language and Literature of |
| **J-K** | Japanese Literature |
| **L** | Latin America, Literature of |
| | Latin Language and Literature |
| | Legends |
| | Literature |
| **M** | Mystery and Detective Stories |
| | Mythology |
| **N** | Newbery, John |
| | Nobel Prizes: Literature |
| | Nonsense Rhymes |
| | Norse Mythology |
| | Novels |
| **O** | Odes |
| | Odyssey |
| **P** | Poetry |
| | Pulitzer Prizes |
| **R** | Russia, Language and Literature of |
| **S** | Scandinavian Literature |
| | Science Fiction |
| | Short Stories |
| | Spain, Language and Literature of |

| **Vol.** | **Author Biographies** |
|---|---|
| **A** | Adams, Henry |
| | Austen, Jane |
| **B** | Baldwin, James |
| | Balzac, Honoré de |
| | Bellow, Saul |
| | Blake, William |
| | Brontë Sisters |
| | Browning, Elizabeth Barrett and Robert |
| | Bryant, William Cullen |
| | Buck, Pearl |
| | Burns, Robert |
| | Byron, George Gordon, Lord |
| **C** | Cervantes Saavedra, Miguel de |
| | Chaucer, Geoffrey |
| | Chekov, Anton |
| | Conrad, Joseph |
| | Cooper, James Fenimore |
| | Crane, Stephen |
| **D** | Dante Alighieri |
| | Defoe, Daniel |
| | Dickens, Charles |
| | Dickinson, Emily |
| | Donne, John |

| | |
|---|---|
| | Dos Passos, John |
| | Dostoevski, Fëdor |
| | Doyle, Sir Arthur Conan |
| | Dreiser, Theodore |
| | Dryden, John |
| | Dumas, Alexandre *Père* and Alexandre *Fils* |
| | Dunbar, Paul Laurence |
| **E** | Eliot, George |
| | Eliot, T. S. |
| | Emerson, Ralph Waldo |
| **F** | Faulkner, William |
| | Fitzgerald, F. Scott |
| | Frost, Robert |
| **G** | Goethe, Johann Wolfgang von |
| | Greene, Graham |
| **H** | Hardy, Thomas |
| | Hawthorne, Nathaniel |
| | Heine, Heinrich |
| | Hemingway, Ernest |
| | Henry, O. |
| | Hesse, Hermann |
| | Homer |
| | Horace |
| | Hughes, Langston |
| | Hugo, Victor |
| **I** | Ibsen, Henrik |
| | Irving, Washington |
| **J-K** | James, Henry |
| | Johnson, James Weldon |
| | Johnson, Samuel |
| **J-K** | Keats, John |
| | Kipling, Rudyard |
| **L** | Lewis, Sinclair |
| | London, Jack |
| | Longfellow, Henry Wadsworth |
| | Lowell, Robert |
| **M** | Marlowe, Christopher |
| | Melville, Herman |
| | Milton, John |
| | Moliére |
| | Morrison, Toni |
| **P** | Poe, Edgar Allan |
| | Pope, Alexander |
| **Q-R** | Racine, Jean Baptiste |
| | Rossetti Family |
| **S** | Sandburg, Carl |
| | Schiller, Johann |
| | Scott, Sir Walter |
| | Shakespeare, William |
| | Shaw, George Bernard |
| | Shelley, Percy Bysshe |
| | Spenser, Edmund |
| | Stein, Gertrude |

(excerpt)
Tolkien, J. R. R.—The Hobbit (excerpt)
Twain, Mark
  The Adventures of Tom Sawyer
  (excerpt)
  The Celebrated Jumping Frog of
  Calaveras County (excerpt)

**W-X-Y-Z** Whitman, Walt—When Lilacs Last in
  the Dooryard Bloom'd
Wilder, Laura Ingalls—Little House on
  the Prairie (excerpt)
Williams, William Carlos—The Red
  Wheelbarrow
Wordsworth, William
  Daffodils
  My Heart Leaps up When I Behold
World War I—In Flanders Fields
  (McCrae)

# MATHEMATICS

| Vol. | Article |
|---|---|
| **A** | Algebra |
| | Arithmetic |
| **B** | Bernoulli Family |
| | Budgets, Family |
| **C** | Calendar |
| | Computer Graphics |
| | Computer Programming |
| | Computers |
| **D** | Decimal System |
| | Descartes, René |
| **E** | Einstein, Albert |
| **F** | Fractions |
| **G** | Gauss, Carl Friedrich |
| | Geometry |
| | Graphs |
| **I** | Interest |
| **L** | Leibniz, Gottfried Wilhelm von |
| **M** | Mathematics |
| | Mathematics, History of |
| | Money |
| **N** | Newton, Isaac |
| | Number Patterns |
| | Number Puzzles and Games |
| | Numbers and Number Systems |
| | Numerals and Numeration Systems |
| **P** | Percentage |
| | Pythagoras |
| **Q-R** | Ratio and Proportion |
| | Roman Numerals |

| Vol. | |
|---|---|
| **S** | Sets |
| | Statistics |
| **T** | Time |
| | Topology |
| | Trigonometry |
| **W-X-Y-Z** | Weights and Measures |

# SOCIAL STUDIES

| Vol. | United States History |
|---|---|

*From the Colonies to Civil War*

| | |
|---|---|
| **A** | Abolition Movement |
| | Adams, John |
| | African Americans |
| | Anthony, Susan B. |
| **B** | Bill of Rights |
| | Burr, Aaron |
| **C** | Calhoun, John C. |
| | Civil War, United States |
| | Clay, Henry |
| | Colonial Life in America |
| | Colonial Sites You Can Visit Today |
| | Columbus, Christopher |
| | Compromise of 1850 |
| | Confederate States of America |
| | Cooper, Peter |
| **D** | Declaration of Independence |
| | Douglas, Stephen A. |
| | Douglass, Frederick |
| | Dred Scott Decision |
| **E** | Emancipation Proclamation |
| | Exploration and Discovery |
| **F** | Federalist, The |
| | Fillmore, Millard |
| | Founders of the United States |
| | French and Indian War |
| **G** | Grant, Ulysses S. |
| **H** | Harrison, William Henry |
| **I** | Immigration |
| | Impeachment |
| | Indians, American |
| | Industrial Revolution |
| **J-K** | Jackson, Andrew |
| | Jamestown |
| | Jay, John |
| | Jefferson, Thomas |
| | Johnson, Andrew |
| **J-K** | Kansas-Nebraska Act |
| **L** | Latin America |
| | Lee, Robert E. |

Lewis and Clark Expedition
Lincoln, Abraham
Louisiana Purchase

**M** Mann, Horace
Marion, Francis
Marshall, John
Mexican War
Missouri Compromise
Monroe, James
Monroe Doctrine
Morris, Gouverneur

**N** Navigation
Northwest Passage

**P** Pirates
Plymouth Colony
Pontiac
Public Lands

**Q-R** Reconstruction Period
Revolutionary War

**S** Scott, Winfield
Slavery

**T** Territorial Expansion of the United
States
Thirteen American Colonies
Tyler, John

**U-V** Underground Railroad
United States, Constitution of the

**U-V** Vikings

**W-X-Y-Z** War of 1812
Washington, George
Webster, Daniel
Westward Movement
Women's Rights Movement

**W-X-Y-Z** Zenger, John Peter


*Modern America Takes Shape (1865–1900)*

**A** Addams, Jane
African Americans

**B** Barton, Clara
Blackwell, Elizabeth
Bryan, William Jennings
Buffalo Bill (William F. Cody)

**C** Carnegie, Andrew
Child Labor
Civil Rights
Civil Service
Cowboys

**D** Department Stores
DuBois, W. E. B.

**E** Ethnic Groups

**F** Field, Cyrus

**G** Geronimo

Gold, Discoveries of
Gompers, Samuel

**H** Hayes, Rutherford B.
Hickok, James Butler (Wild Bill)

**I** Immigration
Indian Wars of North America

**L** Labor Movement
Liberty, Statue of

**M** Manufacturing
Morgan, John Pierpont

**P** Petroleum and Petroleum Refining
Pioneer Life

**Q-R** Ranch Life
Red Cross
Rockefeller, John D.

**W-X-Y-Z** Washington, Booker T.
Westinghouse, George
Women's Rights Movement


*Modern America (1900–present)*

**A** Automobiles

**B** Bethune, Mary McLeod
Bunche, Ralph
Bush, George
Bush, George W.

**C** Civil Rights
Civil Rights Movement
Clinton, William
Cold War
Commonwealth of Independent States
Coolidge, Calvin
Cuban Missile Crisis

**D** Depressions and Recessions
Disarmament
Douglas, William O.
Draft, or Conscription

**E** Eisenhower, Dwight D.
Extinction

**F** Famine
Ferraro, Geraldine
Ford, Henry
Foreign Aid Programs
Freidan, Betty

**H** Hijacking
Hispanic Americans
Hobby, Oveta Culp
Homelessness
Homeschooling
Homosexuality
Hooks, Benjamin L.
Hoover, Herbert
Hoover, J. Edgar
Hughes, Charles Evans
Human Rights

| | | | |
|---|---|---|---|
| **I** | Imperialism | | Underground Movements |
| | International Relations | | United Nations |
| | International Trade | | Unknown Soldier |
| | Iran-Contra Affair | **U-V** | Vietnam War |
| **J-K** | Jackson, Jesse | | Violence and Society |
| | Johnson, Lyndon Baines | **W-X-Y-Z** | Warren Report |

**I**
- Imperialism
- International Relations
- International Trade
- Iran-Contra Affair

**J-K**
- Jackson, Jesse
- Johnson, Lyndon Baines

**J-K**
- Kennedy, John F.
- King, Martin Luther, Jr.
- Kissinger, Henry
- Korean War

**L**
- Labor-Management Relations
- League of Nations
- Lindbergh, Charles

**M**
- MacArthur, Douglas
- Malcolm X
- Marshall, George C.
- McKinley, William
- Missiles

**N**
- New Deal
- Nixon, Richard M.
- North Atlantic Treaty Organization (NATO)
- Nuclear Weapons

**O**
- Organization of American States (OAS)
- Organization of Petroleum Exporting Countries (OPEC)

**P**
- Panama Canal
- Paul, Alice
- Peace Corps
- Peace Movements
- Perry, Matthew C.
- Pershing, John J.
- Persian Gulf War
- Powell, Colin
- Prohibition

**Q-R**
- Racism
- Reagan, Ronald W.
- Reed, Walter
- Refugees
- Roosevelt, Eleanor
- Roosevelt, Franklin D.
- Roosevelt, Theodore

**S**
- Scopes Trial
- Segregation
- Social Security
- Spanish-American War
- Steinem, Gloria
- Stevenson, Adlai E.

**T**
- Taft, William H.
- Tanks
- Terrorism
- Treaties
- Truman, Harry S.

**U-V**
- Un-American Activities Committee, House

- Underground Movements
- United Nations
- Unknown Soldier

**U-V**
- Vietnam War
- Violence and Society

**W-X-Y-Z**
- Warren Report
- Watergate
- Wilson, Woodrow
- Women's Rights Movement
- World War I
- World War II

**Vol.    World History and Geography**

*Ancient Civilizations and the Middle Ages*

**A**
- Ancient Civilizations
- Aztecs

**B**
- Byzantine Empire

**C**
- Christianity
- Crusades

**G**
- Greece, Ancient

**H**
- Hittites
- Holy Roman Empire
- Hundred Years' War

**I**
- Incas
- Islam

**M**
- Magna Carta
- Maya
- Middle Ages
- Montezuma

**P**
- Peloponnesian War
- Persia, Ancient

**Q-R**
- Rome, Ancient
  (See also the list in Grades 4 Through 6—Social Studies: Early and Medieval History and Culture.)

*Renaissance and Reformation (1400's and 1500's)*

**B**
- Bacon, Francis
- Bellini Family
- Botticelli, Sandro

**C**
- Calvin, John
- Chaucer, Geoffrey

**D**
- Dante Alighieri
- Donatello
- Dürer, Albrecht
- Dutch and Flemish Art
- Dutch and Flemish Music

**E**
- Erasmus
- Exploration and Discovery

**F**
- Florence

**G**
- Galileo
- Gutenberg, Johann

| | | | | |
|---|---|---|---|
| **H** | Huguenots<br>Humanism<br>Hus, Jan | | Mary I (Tudor)<br>Mary, Queen of Scots<br>Mozart, Wolfgang Amadeus |
| **I** | Italy, Art and Architecture of<br>Italy, Language and Literature of | **N** | Napoleon I<br>Newton, Isaac |
| **L** | Leonardo da Vinci<br>Luther, Martin | **P** | Paris<br>Peter the Great |
| **M** | Medici<br>Michelangelo<br>More, Sir Thomas | **Q-R** | Rembrandt<br>Revolutionary War (United States)<br>Richelieu, Cardinal<br>Rousseau, Jean Jacques |
| **P** | Protestantism | **S** | San Martín, José de<br>Shakespeare, William<br>Socialism |
| **Q-R** | Raphael<br>Reformation<br>Renaissance<br>Renaissance Art and Architecture<br>Renaissance Music | **U-V** | Voltaire |
| | | **W-X-Y-Z** | Wellington, Duke of<br>Wren, Christopher |
| **S** | Spanish Armada | | |
| **T** | Thirty Years' War<br>Titian | | |
| **U-V** | Venice | | |
| **W-X-Y-Z** | Wesley, John | | |

### Absolutism, Enlightenment, and Revolution (1600's through 1800's)

| | |
|---|---|
| **B** | Bach, Johann Sebastian<br>Bolívar, Simón |
| **C** | Charles<br>Communism<br>Cromwell, Oliver |
| **D** | Darwin, Charles<br>Descartes, René |
| **E** | Elizabeth I<br>England, History of<br>Enlightenment, Age of |
| **F** | Frederick<br>French Revolution |
| **G** | Goethe, Johann Wolfgang Von |
| **H** | Habsburgs<br>Handel, George Frederick<br>Harvey, William<br>Henry VIII<br>Hume, David |
| **I** | Impressionism<br>Industrial Revolution |
| **J-K** | Kepler, Johannes |
| **L** | Labor Movement<br>Leeuwenhoek, Anton Van<br>Locke, John<br>Louis<br>Louis XIV |
| **M** | Marie Antoinette<br>Marx, Karl |

### Nationalism, Imperialism, and the Modern Age (1800's through 1900's)

| | |
|---|---|
| **A** | Africa<br>Arabs<br>Asia<br>Australia |
| **B** | Begin, Menahem<br>Ben-Gurion, David<br>Bismarck, Otto Van<br>Boer War<br>Bush, George<br>Bush, George W. |
| **C** | Castro, Fidel<br>Central America<br>Chiang Kai-Shek<br>China<br>Churchill, Sir Winston<br>Civil Rights<br>Clinton, William<br>Cold War<br>Commonwealth of Independent States<br>Communism<br>Conservation<br>Crimean War<br>Cuba<br>Cuban Missile Crisis |
| **D** | De Gaulle, Charles<br>Dewey, John<br>Disarmament<br>Disraeli, Benjamin<br>Dreyfus, Alfred |
| **E** | East India Company<br>Einstein, Albert<br>Enlightenment, Age of<br>Environment<br>Europe |

European Community
Expressionism

**F** Famine
Fascism
Foreign Aid Programs
Franco, Francisco
Frank, Anne
Friedan, Betty

**G** Gandhi, Mohandas
Garibaldi, Giuseppe
Geneva Accords
Geneva Conventions
Genocide
Germany
Gladstone, William
Gorbachev, Mikhail

**H** Haiti
Hijacking
Hitler, Adolf
Ho Chi Minh
Holocaust
Homelessness
Homosexuality
Honecker, Erich
Hoover, J. Edgar
Human Rights
Hussein, Saddam

**I** Imperialism
International Relations
International Trade
Iran-Contra Affair
Islam

**J-K** Kennedy, John F.
Khruschev, Nikita
King, Martin Luther, Jr.
Korean War

**L** League of Nations
Lenin, Vladimir Ilich
Lloyd George, David

**M** Mandela, Nelson
Mao Zedong
Mazzini, Giuseppe
Meir, Golda
Mexico
Middle East
Missiles
Modern Art
Modern Music
Mussolini, Benito

**N** Napoleon III
Nasser, Gamal Abdel
Nazism
Nehru, Jawaharlal
Nixon, Richard M.
North America

North Atlantic Treaty Organization
 (NATO)
Novels
Nuclear Weapons

**O** Organization of American States (OAS)
Ottoman Empire

**P** Palestine
Peace Movements
Population
Poverty
Putin, Vladimir

**Q-R** Reagan, Ronald W.
Refugees
Rhodes, Cecil
Roosevelt, Franklin D.

**S** Sadat, Anwar El-
Schindler, Oskar
Schmidt, Helmut
Schröder, Gerhard
Schweitzer, Albert
South Africa
South America
Southeast Asia
Spanish Civil War
Stalin, Joseph
Suez Canal
Sun Yat-Sen

**T** Terrorism
Thatcher, Margaret
Tito

**U-V** Union of Soviet Socialist Republics
United Nations
United States

**U-V** Vatican City
Victor Emmanuel
Victoria, Queen
Vietnam War

**W-X-Y-Z** Walesa, Lech
Watergate
Wilson, Woodrow
Women's Rights Movement
World War I
World War II

**W-X-Y-Z** Yeltsin, Boris

**W-X-Y-Z** Zionism

**Vol.** **Government**
**B** Bill of Rights
**C** Cabinet of the United States
Capital Punishment
Capitol, United States
Census
Central Intelligence Agency
Citizenship
Civil Rights

| | |
|---|---|
| O | Optical Instruments |
| P | Printing |
| Q-R | Radio |
| | Refrigeration |
| | Robots |
| | Rockets |
| S | Satellites, Artificial |
| | Ships and Shipping |
| | Sound Recording |
| | Space Exploration and Travel |
| | Space Probes |
| | Space Research and Technology |
| | Space Shuttles |
| | Space Stations |
| | Space Telescopes |
| | Submarines |
| | Supersonic Flight |
| T | Technology |
| | Telecommunications |
| | Telephone |
| | Telescopes |
| | Tools |
| | Transistors, Diodes, and Integrated Circuits |
| | Transportation |
| U-V | Video Recording |
| W-X-Y-Z | Westinghouse, George |
| W-X-Y-Z | X rays |

## HEALTH AND SAFETY

| Vol. | Article |
|---|---|
| A | ADHD |
| | Adolescence |
| | Aging |
| | AIDS |
| | Alcoholism |
| | Antibiotics |
| | Antibodies and Antigens |
| | Autism |
| B | Banting, Sir Frederick Grant |
| | Barnard, Christiaan |
| | Beaumont, William |
| | Birth Control |
| | Blindness |
| | Blood |
| | Body, Human |
| | Body Chemistry |
| | Brain |
| C | Cancer |
| | Child Abuse |
| | Child Development |
| | Circulatory System |
| | Consumerism |

| | |
|---|---|
| D | Deafness |
| | Death |
| | Dentistry |
| | Diagnosis and Treatment of Disease |
| | Digestive System |
| | Diseases |
| | Disinfectants and Antiseptics |
| | Divorce |
| | Dix, Dorothea Lynde |
| | Doctors |
| | Down Syndrome |
| | Dreaming |
| | Drug Abuse |
| | Drugs |
| E | Ear |
| | Ehrlich, Paul |
| | Emotions |
| | Eye |
| F | Family |
| | First Aid |
| | Food Preservation |
| | Food Regulations and Laws |
| | Food Shopping |
| | Freud, Sigmund |
| G | Glands |
| | Guidance Counseling |
| H | Hair and Hairstyling |
| | Harvey, William |
| | Health |
| | Health Foods |
| | Heart |
| | Hepatitis |
| | Homosexuality |
| | Hormones |
| | Hospitals |
| I | Immune System |
| J-K | Kidneys |
| L | Learning Disorders |
| | Lenses |
| | Lister, Joseph |
| | Lungs |
| | Lymphatic System |
| M | Medicine, History of |
| | Menstruation |
| | Mental Illness |
| | Muscular System |
| N | Narcotics |
| | Nervous System |
| | Nurses and Nursing |
| | Nutrition |
| O | Occupational Health and Safety |
| | Old Age |
| | Orthodontics |
| | Osler, Sir William |

| P | Physical Fitness |
| | Poisons and Antidotes |
| | Psychology |
| | Public Health |
| Q-R | Reed, Walter |
| | Reproduction |
| S | Safety |
| | Skeletal System |
| | Sleep |
| | Smoking |
| | Stomach |
| T | Taussig, Helen |
| | Teeth |
| | Transfusion, Blood |
| U-V | Vaccination and Immunization |
| | Vectors of Disease |
| | Vegetarianism |
| | Vitamins and Minerals |

## FOREIGN LANGUAGE

| Vol. | Article |
|---|---|
| F | France, Language of |
| G | Germany, Language of |
| | Greece, Language and Literature of |
| H | Hebrew Language and Literature |
| I | Italy, Language and Literature of |
| L | Languages |
| | Latin Language and Literature |
| Q-R | Russia, Language and Literature of |
| S | Spain, Language and Literature of |

## MUSIC

| Vol. | Music and Musical Instruments |
|---|---|
| B | Ballads |
| | Ballet |
| | Bands and Band Music |
| | Bells and Carillons |
| C | Carols |
| | Chamber Music |
| | Choral Music |
| | Clarinet |
| | Country Music |
| D | Dance |
| | Dance Music |
| | Drum |
| E | Electronic Music |
| G | Guitar |
| H | Harmonica |

| | Harp |
| | Hymns |
| J-K | Jazz |
| J-K | Keyboard Instruments |
| L | Lincoln Center for the Performing Arts |
| M | Music |
| | Musical Instruments |
| | Musical Theater |
| | Music Festivals |
| N | National Anthems and Patriotic Songs |
| O | Opera |
| | Operetta |
| | Orchestra |
| | Orchestra Conducting |
| | Organ |
| P | Percussion Instruments |
| | Piano |
| Q-R | Recorder |
| | Records and Record Collecting |
| | Rock Music |
| S | Stringed Instruments |
| U-V | Violin |
| | Voice Training and Singing |
| W-X-Y-Z | Wind Instruments |

| Vol. | Music History and Biographies |
|---|---|
| A | Ancient World, Music of the |
| | Anderson, Marian |
| B | Bach, Johann Sebastian |
| | Baroque Music |
| | Bartók, Béla |
| | Beatles, The |
| | Beethoven, Ludwig Van |
| | Berg, Alban |
| | Berlin, Irving |
| | Berlioz, Hector |
| | Brahms, Johannes |
| C | Chopin, Frederic |
| | Classical Age in Music |
| | Copland, Aaron |
| D | Dance Music |
| | Debussy, Claude |
| | Donizetti, Gaetano |
| | Dvořák, Antonin |
| E | Elgar, Sir Edward |
| F | Foster, Stephen |
| | Franck, César |
| G | Gershwin, George |
| | Gilbert and Sullivan Operettas |
| | Gluck, Christoph Willibald |
| | Grieg, Edvard |

| | |
|---|---|
| **H** | Handel, George Frederick |
| | Haydn, Joseph |
| **I** | Ives, Charles |
| **L** | Liszt, Franz |
| **M** | Macdowell, Edward |
| | Mahler, Gustav |
| | Mendelssohn, Felix |
| | Middle Ages, Music of the |
| | Modern Music |
| | Mozart, Wolfgang Amadeus |
| **O** | Offenbach, Jacques |
| **P** | Palestrina |
| | Prokofiev, Sergei |
| | Puccini, Giacomo |
| **Q-R** | Renaissance Music |
| | Romanticism |
| **S** | Schoenberg, Arnold |
| | Schubert, Franz |
| | Schumann, Robert |
| | Sibelius, Jean |
| | Strauss, Johann, Jr. |
| | Strauss, Richard |
| | Stravinsky, Igo |
| **T** | Tchaikovsky, Peter Ilyich |
| | Toscanini, Arturo |
| **U-V** | Verdi, Giuseppe |
| **W-X-Y-Z** | Wind Instruments |

| Vol. | **Music Around the World** |
|---|---|
| **A** | Africa, Music of |
| | The Mbira |
| | The Talking Drum |
| **D** | Dutch and Flemish Music |
| **E** | English Music |
| **F** | Folk Dancing |
| | Folk Music |
| | France, Music of |
| **G** | Germany, Music of |
| **I** | India, Music of |
| | Italy, Music of |
| **L** | Latin America, Music of |
| **O** | Oriental Music |
| **R** | Russia, Music of |
| **S** | Spain, Music of |
| **U-V** | United States, Music of the |

# ART

| Vol. | **Article** |
|---|---|
| **A** | Architecture |

| | |
|---|---|
| | Art |
| **C** | Cathedrals |
| | Color |
| **D** | Design |
| | Drawing |
| **E** | Engraving |
| | Etching |
| **G** | Graphic Arts |
| **H** | Hermitage Museum |
| **I** | Illuminated Manuscripts |
| | Illustration and Illustrators |
| **L** | Louvre |
| **M** | Metropolitan Museum of Art |
| | Museums |
| **N** | National Gallery (London) |
| | National Gallery of Art (Washington, D.C.) |
| **O** | Obelisks |
| **P** | Painting |
| | Photography |
| | Prado |
| **S** | Sculpture |
| **U-V** | Uffizi Gallery |
| **W-X-Y-Z** | Watercolor |

| Vol. | **Art History and Biographies** |
|---|---|
| **A** | Ancient World, Art of the |
| | Angelico, Fra |
| **B** | Baroque Art and Architecture |
| | Bellini Family |
| | Benton, Thomas Hart |
| | Bernini, Giovanni Lorenzo |
| | Botticelli, Sandro |
| | Brancusi, Constantin |
| | Braque, Georges |
| | Bruegel, Pieter, the Elder |
| | Byzantine Art and Architecture |
| **C** | Caravaggio, Michelangelo Merisi da |
| | Cassatt, Mary |
| | Cézanne, Paul |
| | Chagall, Marc |
| **D** | Dali, Salvador |
| | Daumier, Honoré |
| | Degas, Edgar |
| | Delacroix, Eugène |
| | Donatello |
| | Doré, Gustave |
| | Drawing, History of |
| | Dürer, Albrecht |
| **E** | Eakins, Thomas |
| | Egyptian Art and Architecture |

Escher, M. C.
Expressionism

F    Folk Art
Fragonard, Jean Honoré
Francesca, Piero della

G    Gainsborough, Thomas
Gauguin, Paul
Giorgione
Giotto di Bondone
Gothic Art and Architecture
Goya, Francisco
Greco, El
Greece, Art and Architecture of

H    Hals, Frans
Hockney, David
Hogarth, William
Hokusai
Holbein, Hans the Younger
Homer, Winslow

J-K    Kandinsky, Wassily
Klee, Paul
Klimt, Gustav

L    Le Corbusier
Léger, Fernand
Leonardo da Vinci

M    Manet, Édouard
Matisse, Henri
Michelangelo
Mies Van Der Rohe, Ludwig
Miró, Joan
Modern Art
Modigliani, Amedeo
Mondrian, Piet
Monet, Claude
Moses, Grandma

N    Nevelson, Louise

O    O'Keeffe, Georgia
Oriental Art and Architecture

P    Peale Family
Pei, I. M.
Picasso, Pablo
Pollock, Jackson
Prehistoric Art

Q-R    Raphael
Rembrandt
Renaissance Art and Architecture
Renoir, Pierre Auguste
Reynolds, Sir Joshua
Rockwell, Norman
Rodin, Auguste
Roman Art and Architecture
Romanesque Art and Architecture
Romanticism
Rubens, Peter Paul

S    Sargent, John Singer

Sullivan, Louis
Surrealism

T    Tintoretto
Titian
Toulouse-Lautrec, Henri de
Turner, Joseph Mallord William

U-V    Utrillo, Maurice

U-V    Van Dyck, Anthony
Van Gogh, Vincent
Velázquez, Diego
Vermeer, Jan

W-X-Y-Z    Warhol, Andy
Whistler, James Abbott McNeill
Wood, Grant
Wren, Christopher
Wright, Frank Lloyd
Wyeth Family

| Vol. | **Art Around the World** |
|------|------|
| A | Africa, Art and Architecture of |
| C | Canada, Art and Architecture of<br>Chinese Art |
| D | Dutch and Flemish Art |
| E | English Art and Architecture |
| F | France, Art and Architecture of |
| G | Germany, Art and Architecture of |
| I | India, Art and Architecture of<br>Islamic Art and Architecture<br>Italy, Art and Architecture of |
| J-K | Japanese Art and Architecture |
| L | Latin America, Art and Architecture of |
| Q-R | Russia, Art and Architecture of |
| S | Spain, Art and Architecture of |
| U-V | United States, Art and Architecture of |

| Vol. | **Decorative Arts and Crafts** |
|------|------|
| C | Ceramics<br>Collage |
| D | Decorative Arts<br>Decoupage |
| E | Enameling |
| J-K | Jewelry |
| L | Linoleum-Block Printing |
| M | Macramé<br>Mosaic |
| N | Needlecraft |
| O | Origami |
| P | Papier-mâché<br>Posters<br>Pottery |

| Q-R | Rubbings |
| S | Silk-Screen Printing |
| | Stained-Glass Windows |
| T | Tapestry |
| W-X-Y-Z | Weaving |
| | Wood Carving |
| | Woodcut Printing |

## PHYSICAL EDUCATION AND SPORTS

| Vol. | Article |
|------|---------|
| A | Archery |
| | Automobile Racing |
| B | Badminton |
| | Ball |
| | Baseball |
| | Basketball |
| | Bicycling |
| | Billiards |
| | Boardsailing |
| | Boats and Boating |
| | Bobsledding |
| | Bodybuilding |
| | Bowling |
| | Boxing |
| C | Canoeing |
| | Cheerleading |
| | Cricket |
| | Croquet |
| | Curling |
| D | Darts |
| | Diving |
| F | Fencing |
| | Field Hockey |
| | Fishing |
| | Football |
| G | Gehrig, Lou |
| | Gibson, Althea |
| | Golf |
| | Gymnastics |
| H | Handball |
| | Hiking and Backpacking |
| | Horseback Riding |
| | Horse Racing |
| | Horseshoe Pitching |
| | Hunting |
| I | Iceboating |
| | Ice Hockey |
| | Ice-Skating |
| J-K | Jai Alai |
| | Jogging and Running |
| | Jones, Robert Tyre (Bobby), Jr. |

| | Judo |
| | Juggling |
| J-K | Karate |
| | Karting |
| L | Lacrosse |
| | Little League Baseball |
| M | Mountain Climbing |
| O | Olympic Games |
| | Owens, Jesse |
| P | Paddle Tennis |
| | Pelé |
| | Physical Education |
| | Physical Fitness |
| | Polo |
| Q-R | Racing |
| | Racket Sports |
| | Rifle Marksmanship |
| | Robinson, Jack Roosevelt (Jackie) |
| | Roller-Skating |
| | Rugby |
| | Ruth, George Herman (Babe) |
| S | Sailing |
| | Shuffleboard |
| | Skateboarding |
| | Skiing |
| | Skin Diving |
| | Soap Box Derby |
| | Soccer and Youth Soccer |
| | Softball |
| | Special Olympics |
| | Surfing |
| | Swimming |
| T | Table Tennis |
| | Tennis |
| | Thorpe, James Francis (Jim) |
| | Track and Field |
| U-V | Volleyball |
| W-X-Y-Z | Water Polo |
| | Waterskiing |
| | Wrestling |

## HOME ECONOMICS AND INDUSTRIAL ARTS (TECHNOLOGY EDUCATION)

| Vol. | Article |
|------|---------|
| A | Adolescence |
| | Air Conditioning |
| B | Bread and Baking |
| | Budgets, Family |
| C | Candy and Candy Making |
| | Child Development |

Clothing
Consumerism
Cooking
Cotton
Crocheting

**D** Dairying and Dairy Products
Decorative Arts
Design
Detergents and Soap
Dry Cleaning
Dyes and Dyeing

**F** Family
Fashion
Fibers
First Aid
Fish Farming
Fishing Industry
Food Around the World
Food Preservation
Food Regulations and Laws
Food Shopping
Fruitgrowing
Furniture

**G** Grain and Grain Products

**H** Health
Health Foods
Heating Systems
Herbs and Spices
Home Economics
Homes and Housing

**I** Interior Design

**J-K** Knitting

**L** Laundry
Leather
Lighting

**M** Macramé
Meat and Meat Packing

**N** Needlecraft
Nutrition
Nylon and Other Synthetic Fibers

**O** Outdoor Cooking and Picnics
**P** Poultry
**Q-R** Recipes
Refrigeration
Rugs and Carpets
**S** Safety
Sewing
Silk
**T** Textiles
**U-V** Vegetables
Vitamins and Minerals
**W-X-Y-Z** Weaving
Wool

**Vol.** **Industrial Arts (Technology Education)**
**C** Ceramics
**D** Dies and Molds
**E** Electricity
Electric Motors
Electronics
Electroplating
Engraving
**G** Graphic Arts
Grinding and Polishing
**I** Industrial Arts
Industrial Design
**L** Locks and Keys
**M** Materials Science
Mechanical Drawing
Metals and Metallurgy
**N** Nails, Screws, and Rivets
**P** Photography
Plastics
Printing
**T** Tools
**W-X-Y-Z** Wood and Wood Products
Woodworking

# PART III
# ACTIVITIES

# HOW TO DO RESEARCH FOR REPORTS AND PROJECTS

## INTRODUCTION

THE NEW BOOK OF KNOWLEDGE is a valuable information resource. The twelve activities in this section are designed to help students learn how to find, organize, and use the information in the set and build good research skills in the process. The activities in Locating Information show them how to use the set's Index to find precisely the information they need. The Organizing Information activities demonstrate different ways information can be organized so that it is easy to understand and use. In Doing Research, the activities guide students through the process of researching and preparing a written or oral report and a project. Finally, in Fun with Facts, the activities show students how the set can be a useful resource in solving puzzles or playing word games. All of these activity sheets can be copied and used often.

## TABLE OF CONTENTS

NAME _____ DATE _____

## Locating Information by Finding Key Words

You can find the answers to specific questions in THE NEW BOOK OF KNOWLEDGE. To locate the information you need, it is a good idea to write down your question first. Then decide which word or words tell what person, place, event, or object the question is about. Called **key words**, they identify the topic. Look at the questions below and underline the key word or words in each question.

1. How many stars are in the Milky Way?

2. What was Dr. Seuss's real name?

3. Which mammal can truly fly?

4. Did the first bicycles have pedals?

5. How much did the original Liberty Bell cost?

6. Why is Alaska called the Land of the Midnight Sun?

7. What famous children's book did Sir James M. Barrie write?

8. What is the largest, deepest ocean?

Next you need to locate the article where the answer to your question will be found. Look at the list of articles below. Then look back at the key words you underlined. After each article, write the number of the question it will most likely answer.

Seuss, Dr. _____          Barrie, Sir James Matthew _____

Mammals _____             Alaska _____

Milky Way _____           Liberty Bell _____

Bicycling _____           Oceans and Seas of the World _____

Now choose one of the questions above. Go to the appropriate article in THE NEW BOOK OF KNOWLEDGE and skim through it until you find the information you need. Write the answer here.

_____

_____

_____

**NAME** _____ **DATE** _____

## Locating Information by Using Index Entries, Part 1

When you want to locate information in THE NEW BOOK OF KNOWLEDGE, it is best to look in the Index first. The Index is an alphabetical list of all the topics that are covered in the set. Each of volumes 1 through 20 has its own index, but Volume 21 is the Index for the entire encyclopedia. Use it for this activity. Suppose the topic you are looking up is Vikings. The following example from THE NEW BOOK OF KNOWLEDGE Index is called an **entry**. Use it to answer the questions below.

**Vikings V:339–43**

1. Is there an article about Vikings in THE NEW BOOK OF

KNOWLEDGE?_____

_____

2. In which volume will you find the article? _____

3. On what pages is the article located? _____

Here is another entry for a different topic, Rosa Parks.

**Parks, Rosa** (American civil rights leader) **A:**79m, 130, 143; **C:**328; **N:**28; **S:**115

4. Who was Rosa Parks? _____

5. Is there a separate article about Rosa Parks?_____

How do you know?_____

6. In which volumes can you read something about Rosa Parks?_____

_____

7. In which volume will you find information on more than one page?

_____

**NAME** _____ **DATE** _____

## Locating Information by Using Index Entries, Part 2

Many topics are too big to be covered in a single article. When you look up these topics in the Index, you find a list of related topics below the main entry. These are called **subentries**. Look at this example and answer the questions below.

**Whaling W:154–55**

    early Massachusetts industry **M:**150

    lighting by whale oil **L:**231

    overfishing **O:**28

    protecting whales **O:**25; **W:**153

8.  There is a separate article on whaling in Volume _____.

9.  How many subentries are there? _____

10.  If you want to know about the early whaling industry in

Massachusetts, which volume will you go to? _____

11.  To prepare a report on saving the whales, which subentries would

you refer to?_____.

Now choose a topic of your own. Find the Index entry for your topic in THE NEW BOOK OF KNOWLEDGE.

12.  Is there a separate article for your topic? _____

13.  If not, where can you find related information? _____

14.  List two subentries that you would choose as additional references:

_____ Volume _____ Pages _____

_____ Volume _____ Pages _____

**NAME** _____ **DATE** _____

## Locating Information by Using Cross-References, Part 1

When you look up a topic in THE NEW BOOK OF KNOWLEDGE Index, you will sometimes find the words *see also* in the entry. The *see also* listings are called **cross-references**. They refer you to another entry in the Index where you will find more information about your topic. Look at the following entry and answer the questions.

> **Bees** (insects) **B:116–21** *see also* Honey
>
> > biological classification **L:**207
> >
> > clock-compass **H:**200
> >
> > color vision **C:**428
> >
> > flower pollination **F:**285; **P:**308
> >
> > homing, example of **H:**195
> >
> > How do honeybees make honey? **H:**208
> >
> > strength of **I:**241
> >
> > vectors of disease **V:**284
> >
> > *picture(s)*
> >
> > > eggs in the hive **E:**100
> > >
> > > mouthparts **I:**238
> > >
> > > nests **B:**121

1. Where will you find the main article about bees? Volume _____

Pages_____

2. According to the *see also* cross-reference, which related topic can

you refer to in the Index? _____

3. How many of the subentries refer you to Volume H? _____

4. Where will you find a picture of the parts of the bee's mouth?_____

_____

**NAME** _____ **DATE** _____

## Locating Information by Using Cross-References, Part 2

Some persons, countries, and other subjects are known by more than one name. In such cases, the Index entries are usually listed by the best-known names. If you look up the alternate name, you will find the word *see* in the entry. This is another type of cross-reference. It leads you to the Index entry where you will find information on your topic. Look at the following examples, and answer the questions below.

**Bonaparte, Napoleon** *see* Napoleon I

**Bonney, William H.** (American outlaw) *see* Billy the Kid

**Mounties** *see* Royal Canadian Mounted Police

**Nyasaland** *see* Malawi

**Pyridoxine** *see* Vitamin B$_6$

**PVC** *see* Polyvinylchloride

5. Do any of these cross-references include a volume number or page numbers? _____

6. Where in the Index will you look for information about Napoleon Bonaparte? _____

7. What was Billy the Kid's full name?_____

8. PVC is a shortened form of the word _____

9. Pyridoxine is another name for _____

10. Malawi is the modern name for the part of Africa formerly known as_____

11. The Royal Canadian Mounted Police are often simply called the

_____

**NAME** _____ **DATE** _____

## Organizing Information by Making a Chart, Part 1

A chart is a method of organizing information. It allows you to group facts into categories and to compare what is alike or different about the items in each category. The chart below is based on information from the article BIRDS in THE NEW BOOK OF KNOWLEDGE. It is divided into three columns and nine rows. Read the headings at the top of each column. The column at the far left contains the names of different birds. The next two columns contain certain information about each bird. Use the facts in the chart to answer the questions below.

| Bird | Type of Bill | Type of Food |
|------|-------------|--------------|
| Bald eagle | tearing | fish, frogs, birds |
| Blue jay | cracking | seeds, nuts |
| Heron | spearing | fish, frogs |
| Woodpecker | hammering | insects |
| Redpoll | cracking | seeds, nuts |
| Snipe | probing | small freshwater creatures |
| Seagull | tearing | fish, frogs, shellfish |
| Flamingo | filtering | small seawater creatures |

1. What category is used as the heading for the middle column? _____

_____

2. Which bird has a hammering bill? _____

3. Which bird eats small sea creatures? _____

4. Name two birds that have tearing bills. _____

5. If you were to sort birds by the type of bill they have, how many

groups would there be? _____

**NAME** _____ **DATE** _____

## Organizing Information by Making a Chart, Part 2

Practice making a chart to organize information. Choose an article of special interest to you, or use one of those listed below. Draw your chart in the space below. Decide on your headings and choose appropriate facts. You may need more columns or rows for some charts and fewer for other charts.

Butterflies and Moths          Leaves

Dinosaurs                      Musical Instruments

Holidays                       Planets

Indians, American              Whales

NAME _____ DATE _____

## Organizing Information by Making a Web, Part 1

A web is a visual way of recording and organizing important information in an article you are reading. To make a web, start by writing the main topic of the article, or the portion of the article you are using, in the center of your paper. You will record information about the topic by working outward from the center of the web. Use boxes joined by connecting lines to jot down subtopics and specific facts that you think are important.

The sample web below is based on information from the article APES in THE NEW BOOK OF KNOWLEDGE. Use information from the web to answer these questions.

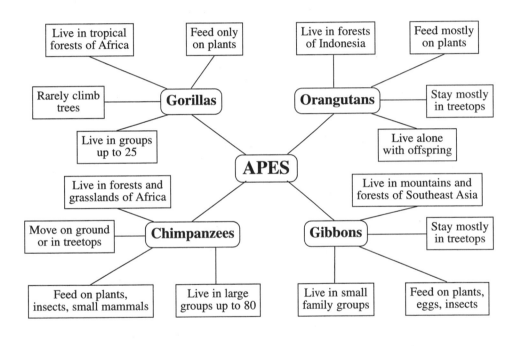

1. What are the four major groups of apes? _____

   _____

2. Which groups of apes live in Africa? _____

3. Do gorillas eat other animals? _____

4. Which type of ape does not live in a group? _____

5. Which groups rarely move about on the ground? _____

NAME _____ DATE _____

## Organizing Information by Making a Web, Part 2

You can make your own web organizer for any article or part of an article using the blank model on this page. Choose a topic in which you are particularly interested, or try one of these:

Africa, Music of          Eclipses

Aztecs                    Folk Dance

Cats                      Leaves

Colonial Life in America  Thunder and Lightning

You may not need all the boxes in this web, or you may find it necessary to add more boxes.

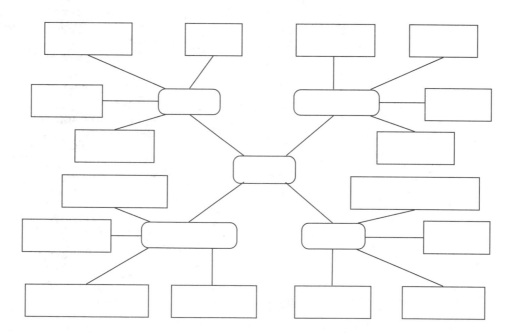

NAME _____ DATE _____

## Organizing Information by Making a Time Line, Part 1

A time line is a useful way of organizing events in the order in which they happened. This time line is based on data in the article ABOLITION MOVEMENT in THE NEW BOOK OF KNOWLEDGE. The "abolition movement" is the name given to the campaign to abolish slavery in the United States. The time line is divided into 25-year periods. Key events are entered at appropriate places along the line. Use dates from the time line to answer the questions below.

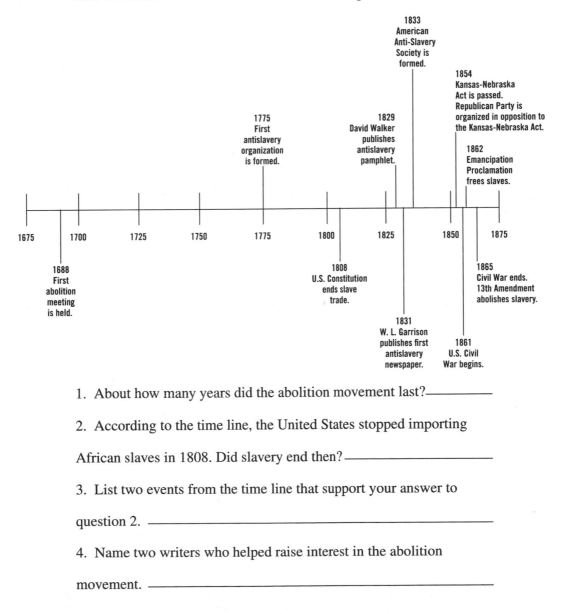

1833
American
Anti-Slavery
Society is
formed.

1854
Kansas-Nebraska
Act is passed.
Republican Party is
organized in opposition to
the Kansas-Nebraska Act.

1775
First
antislavery
organization
is formed.

1829
David Walker
publishes
antislavery
pamphlet.

1862
Emancipation
Proclamation
frees slaves.

1675    1700    1725    1750    1775    1800    1825    1850    1875

1688
First
abolition
meeting
is held.

1808
U.S. Constitution
ends slave
trade.

1865
Civil War ends.
13th Amendment
abolishes slavery.

1831
W. L. Garrison
publishes first
antislavery
newspaper.

1861
U.S. Civil
War begins.

1. About how many years did the abolition movement last? _____

2. According to the time line, the United States stopped importing

African slaves in 1808. Did slavery end then? _____

3. List two events from the time line that support your answer to

question 2. _____

4. Name two writers who helped raise interest in the abolition

movement. _____

**NAME** _____ **DATE** _____

## Organizing Information by Making a Time Line, Part 2

You may wish to make a time line of your own for one of the following articles, or a portion of one, from THE NEW BOOK OF KNOWLEDGE. To construct your time line, use the steps described below.

| | |
|---|---|
| Balloons and Ballooning | Poe, Edgar Allan |
| Crusades | Rock Music |
| French and Indian Wars | United Nations |
| Nightingale, Florence | Women's Rights Movement |

1. Draw a straight line across the middle of a sheet of blank paper. If your time line is to be put on a wall or bulletin board, you may wish to tape several sheets of paper together or use paper that comes in a roll.

2. Decide how you want to divide your time line. If you are making a time line to show important events in a person's life, you may want to divide it into 10-year periods. If you are showing key events in the history of a country, a movement, or an era, you may decide on intervals of 25 years, 50 years, or 100 years.

3. Think about the dates of the first event and last event that will be included in your time line. Then write a date on the left end of the line. It should be at an interval just before the date of the first event. Now write a date on the right end of the line. It should be at an interval just after the date of the last event.

4. Using short vertical lines, divide the time line into the intervals you have chosen. Write the appropriate date at each interval.

5. Using longer vertical lines above or below the line, record the dates of each key event at the appropriate spots along the line. Then, at each date, write out as briefly as possible what happened in each event.

6. If your time line is to be displayed, you may wish to add drawings, magazine illustrations, or photographs to the events.

**NAME** _____ **DATE** _____

## Doing Research to Prepare a Biography, Part 1

A biography is a true account of a person's life. It covers the important facts about the person and describes key events and accomplishments in the individual's life. When you are doing research for a biography, THE NEW BOOK OF KNOWLEDGE is a good starting point. The Index will direct you to a biographical article, to a profile, or to other articles about the person's life or work. Read the following and answer the questions that follow it.

> Sequoya was a Cherokee Indian who developed the first written Native American language. He was born in Loudon County, Tennessee, about 1770. His mother was the daughter of a chief; his father was a fur trader, a white man named either Gist or Guess.
> After he suffered a crippling hunting accident, Sequoya became an expert silversmith and mechanic. He later realized the value of communication through reading and writing. Sequoya began to think his people could advance further if they had a written language of their own. He began experimenting, carving symbols on birch bark, and continued even though his family and friends ridiculed his efforts. When he tested his system on his 6-year-old daughter, he saw that children could learn the language easily.
> In 1821, Sequoya completed his work. Within a few months, thousands of Cherokee learned to read and write using his system. In 1828 the *Cherokee Phoenix*, a weekly newspaper printed in English and Cherokee, first appeared. For his work Sequoya was honored by his tribe, and the Cherokee National Council rewarded him with a yearly allowance.
> Sequoya died in Mexico in 1843. The giant redwood trees of California have been named sequoias in his memory.

1. What was Sequoya's major accomplishment? _____

2. Find the facts:

Date and place of birth _____

Parents _____

Main occupation_____

Honors and awards _____

Date and place of death _____

3. Why did Sequoya develop a written Cherokee language? _____

_____

4. What hardships did Sequoya have to overcome? _____

_____

NAME _____ DATE _____

## Doing Research to Prepare a Biography, Part 2

Choose a person you would like to research for a biography. You may want to select someone from this list. Use the Biography Fact Sheet below to start your search for information for your biography.

Susan B. Anthony (American suffragist)

Simón Bolívar (South American patriot)

Elizabeth I (former queen of England)

Robert H. Goddard (American rocket scientist)

Martin Luther King, Jr. (American civil rights leader)

Wolfgang Amadeus Mozart (Austrian composer)

Jesse Owens (American track athlete)

Beatrix Potter (English writer)

### Biography Fact Sheet

Name of person ————————————————————

Birthdate and birthplace ————————————————

Parents and important family members ————————————

Important childhood events ————————————————

Education ——————————————————————

Main occupation——————————————————————

Key events in adult life————————————————————

Major accomplishment————————————————————

Honors and awards ————————————————————

Main character traits————————————————————

Date and place of death ————————————————————

Remember, when you prepare a biography, use several different resources in addition to THE NEW BOOK OF KNOWLEDGE. These may include biographies and autobiographies, diaries, history books, magazines, newspapers, films, and videos.

NAME _____ DATE _____

## Doing Research to Prepare a Report on a Country, Part 1

When you are preparing a report on a country, you will find much information in THE NEW BOOK OF KNOWLEDGE. Each country has its own article, and for some there are also separate articles about the country under the headings Language and Literature, Art and Architecture, and Music. The Index may have a listing of other articles related to your topic. Choose a country to report on. Then find the article about your country in the set and answer the questions below.

1. What is pictured next to the article's title? _____

2. The article is divided into sections. The headings for major sections are called **major headings**. They are printed in heavy type in capital letters. What is the first major heading? _____

3. List the other major headings in the article. _____

_____

4. **Subheadings** mark off smaller sections within major sections. Here are the subheadings under    THE LAND in the article on Mexico:

**The Central Plateau**          **Climate**

**Mountain Ranges**          **Natural Resources**

**Coastal Plains and Lowlands**

Under which subheading would you learn

a. the name of Mexico's highest peak? _____

b. that Mexico is a leading producer of silver? _____

c. about the range of temperature in Mexico? _____

5. Find the "Facts and figures" box in your article. List the major headings in the box. _____

## ACTIVITY 8

NAME _____ DATE _____

## Doing Research to Prepare a Report on a Country, Part 2

Use the Fact Sheet below to record the data you collect for your report on a country.

### Fact Sheet for a Report on a Country

Name of Country _____

The Land

    Location _____

    Major rivers, lakes, seas _____

    Major mountains and mountain ranges _____

The People

    Family life _____

    Education _____

    Language _____

    Art, music, recreation_____

    Holidays, customs, and foods _____

Industry and Agriculture

    Major industries _____

    Major agricultural products _____

    Natural resources _____

History

    Important events_____

    Type of government _____

    Major rulers or leaders_____

    Other important people _____

NAME _____ DATE _____

## Doing Research to Prepare a Science Project

When you are preparing a project for your science class at school, for an after-school organization, or for a science fair, THE NEW BOOK OF KNOWLEDGE can be useful at each step of the process. Use the activities below to guide you as you plan your project.

**A. Choosing a topic.**

Because you will be spending a lot of time on your project, make sure you are really interested in the topic you select.

1. Here is a list of some of the major areas of science. Check the one that is of most interest to you.

Plants _____          Environment _____

Animals _____          Health _____

Earth _____          Computers _____

Weather _____          Chemistry _____

Astronomy _____          Physics _____

2. In the Index of THE NEW BOOK OF KNOWLEDGE, look up the area of interest you checked above. Skim through the list of subtopics under the heading. List two or three references for subjects of interest to you. Include the volume and page numbers.

_____

**B. Choosing the purpose for your project.**

1. Locate each of the references you listed above. As you skim through an article, think of questions that can be answered, problems that can be solved, or ideas that can be demonstrated by a science project. Write these down.

_____

2. Decide which one of these project ideas you really want to work on. Write your idea down in the form of a question, or use a sentence that states the purpose of the activity.

_____

## C. Doing background research.

Before proceeding with your project, you should gather as much background information as you can. Check off in the list below the resources that you plan on using to research your topic.

Encyclopedia articles ———         Books ———

Magazines ———                     Videos ———

CD-ROM or computer software ———

Interview with an expert on the topic ———

Visit to a park, museum, recycling station, or some other facility ———

You are now ready to consult your resources. Keep a record of the information you collect.

## D. Planning an experiment.

Very often your science project will consist of an experiment. The article EXPERIMENTS AND OTHER SCIENCE ACTIVITIES in Volume E has many useful ideas for planning your experiment. The following passage is taken from this article. Read it and follow the steps below.

### What Is an Experiment?

An experiment is one method a scientist may use to solve a **problem**. First, the problem must be recognized and clearly stated. Next, the experimenter makes an educated guess about a possible solution to the problem. This guess, based on knowledge of the subject, is called a **hypothesis**. The experimenter tests the hypothesis by following a **procedure** that can show whether the hypothesis is true or false. Certain **materials** will be needed for the procedure. During the procedure, the experimenter makes **observations** and keeps careful records of the results that are observed. Then the experimenter draws a **conclusion** about whether the hypothesis is true or false.

1. Write a hypothesis for your experiment. ————————————

2. List the steps that you will use to test your hypothesis. ————————

   ————————————————————————————————————

3. List the materials you will need. ————————————————

4. What method will you use to record your observations and results?

   ————————————————————————————————————

Once you have completed these steps, you are ready to collect the materials you need, set up the experiment or demonstration, conduct your test, and draw your conclusions.

**NAME** _____ **DATE** _____

## Fun with Facts: A Guggenheim Game

A Guggenheim (GOOG-un-hime) is a game in which you must make up a list of words or objects that fit into particular categories, for example, cities, sports, or occupations. What makes the game challenging is the "Guggenheim word," a word that determines the beginning letters of the words in your list. You may play Guggenheim alone, against a partner, or as part of a team competition. Here is a Guggenheim for you to play. Before you start, look carefully at the Guggenheim framework and read the directions below.

|   | Animals | Foods | States |
|---|---------|-------|--------|
| **S** |  |  |  |
| **C** |  |  |  |
| **H** |  |  |  |
| **O** |  |  |  |
| **L** |  |  |  |
| **A** |  |  |  |
| **R** |  |  |  |

1. Find the Guggenheim word that is spelled out along the left side of the framework. The word is SCHOLAR.

2. To play, you must think of words that fit into each of the three categories: animals, foods, and states. The first letter of the word must match up with one of the letters in the Guggenheim word. For example, in the first row, the names of the animal, the food, and the state you write down must all begin with the letter *s*.

3. If you get stuck and cannot come up with a name, refer to related articles in THE NEW BOOK OF KNOWLEDGE.

4. To make the game more interesting, you may wish to set a time limit for yourself. If you are playing with other people, you may use a point system as well as a time limit. Extra points can be given for less common choices. "Lemur" would probably be a less common choice than "lion," for instance, and would get extra points.

If you enjoy this game, you can make your own version of Guggenheim. Simply choose a different Guggenheim word and at least three different categories. Set up your framework and you are ready to play.

NAME _____ DATE _____

## Fun with Facts: A Matching Game and a Wordsearch Game, Part 1

There are 16 countries of the world listed in the column on the left. Match each country to the river that flows through it. The rivers are listed in the column on the right. Use THE NEW BOOK OF KNOWLEDGE if you need help.

1. Australia _____          a. Amazon

2. Austria _____            b. Limpopo

3. Brazil _____             c. Danube

4. Burma (Myanmar) _____    d. Don

5. Canada _____             e. Ebro

6. China _____              f. Euphrates

7. India _____              g. Ganges

8. Mozambique _____         h. Huang He (Yellow)

9. Nicaragua _____          i. Irrawaddy

10. Poland _____            j. Mackenzie

11. Russia _____            k. Murray

12. Spain _____             l. Oder

13. Syria _____             m. Orinoco

14. United States _____     n. Santee

15. Venezuela _____         o. Tipitapa

16. Zimbabwe _____          p. Zambezi

NAME _____ DATE _____

## Fun with Facts: A Matching Game and a Wordsearch Game, Part 2

Now you can go exploring. The names of the 16 rivers are hidden in this puzzle. Read forward, backward, up, down, and diagonally. Circle the name of each river as you find it.

```
O  E  U  P  H  R  A  T  E  S  X  I  E
I  A  C  E  K  N  N  I  V  Q  G  B  I
E  R  Y  P  T  O  E  P  M  T  R  H  Z
H  X  R  L  D  Z  F  I  D  O  J  W  E
G  O  F  A  G  A  V  T  A  G  M  L  B
N  R  G  B  W  M  G  A  N  G  E  S  M
A  I  Q  N  Z  A  Q  P  U  H  I  A  A
U  N  B  J  O  E  D  A  B  O  K  N  Z
H  O  D  X  L  C  I  D  E  R  D  T  O
U  C  S  M  U  R  R  A  Y  W  L  E  H
Q  O  E  I  Z  N  E  K  C  A  M  E  R
```

NAME _____ DATE _____

## Fun with Facts: A Crossword Puzzle

Did you know that the first crossword puzzle was created by Arthur Wynne, a newspaperman, in 1913? Crossword puzzles are enjoyable and educational. The puzzle below is built around a theme, and most of the clues are related. If you need help with any of the answers, use THE NEW BOOK OF KNOWLEDGE. Have fun!

**ACROSS**

1. He invented the wireless telegraph.

5. Thomas Edison's middle name.

10. Country where paper was invented.

12. A colonial American inventor and statesman.

13. A period of history.

15. A young, furry animal.

17. He developed the Polaroid camera.

19. _ _ _ _ lite, an early plastic invented by Baekeland.

20. It was discovered by Roentgen in 1895.

22. Turn _ _ the engine.

23. The American who developed modern rockets.

27. Radio waves were aimed _ _ the target star.

29. Marie Curie won _ _ _ second Nobel Prize in 1911.

31. To be sorry for.

32. The gas that makes colored lights glow.

34. What this puzzle is mostly about.

37. Vermont, abbreviated.

38. A man's nickname.

39. One of Jupiter's moons.

41. Invention of Maiman in 1960.

43. The first space telescope.

46. A precious stone.

47. A code named for the American who invented it.

48. The short name for the Environmental Protection Agency.

50. To make a mistake.

51. It was invented by 5 across.

52. Nickname for the machine that explored the moon.

**DOWN**

2. It was invented by 24 down.

3. A container made of aluminum or tin.

4. The first synthetic fiber, invented by Carothers.

6. You use it to watch and record movies at home.

7. Open your mouth and say _ _.

8. James _ _ _ _, a Scottish inventor of the late 1700's.

9. The chemical in living cells used in genetic engineering.

11. It was invented by ancient Egyptians to use in writing.

14. A wheel with teeth used in automobiles and other devices with moving parts.

16. Freezing rain causes _ _ _ conditions.

17. One of four on a chair.

18. It was invented by Bardeen, Brattain, and Shockley.

19. The Danish physicist who won a Nobel Prize for his atomic theory.

21. Eat, _ _ _, eaten.

24. Wilbur Wright's brother.

25. The space flight was canceled _ _ _ to the bad weather.

26. Heavy cotton cloth used in blue jeans.

28. A powerful explosive.

30. To free from.

33. In 1785 two balloonists flew _ _ _ _ the English Channel.

35. Satellites send TV signals _ _ Earth.

36. An important liquid fuel.

40. A very early invention in transportation.

42. What 8 down used to run his engine.

44. What you can do when you complete this puzzle.

45. Inventor of the telephone.

47. Abbreviation for magnetic resonance imaging.

49. A special number used in measuring circles.

## Activities Answer Key

**Activity 1.** Key words: 1. Milky Way; 2. Dr. Seuss; 3. mammal; 4. bicycles; 5. Liberty Bell; 6. Alaska; 7. Sir James M. Barrie; 8. ocean.

Matching:

Seuss, Dr. 2

Mammals 3

Milky Way 1

Bicycling 4

Barrie, Sir James Matthew 7

Alaska 6

Liberty Bell 5

Oceans and Seas of the World 8

Answers to questions: 1. more than 300 billion; 2. Theodor Seuss Geisel; 3. bat; 4. No, they were pushed by the feet; 5. $300; 6. For three months the sun never sets; 7. *Peter Pan*; 8. Pacific.

**Activity 2.** 1. Yes; 2. Volume V; 3. pages 339–43; 4. an American civil rights leader; 5. No, there is no reference for Volume P; 6. Volumes A, C, N, and S; 7. Volume A; 8. Volume W, pages 154–55; 9. five; 10. Volume M, Massachusetts; 11. overfishing; protecting whales. Answers to the last three activities will vary depending on the topic chosen by the student.

**Activity 3.** 1. Volume B, pages 116–21; 2. honey; 3. three; 4. Volume I, page 238; 5. No; 6. under Napoleon I; 7. William H. Bonney; 8. polyvinylchloride; 9. Vitamin $B_6$; 10. Nyasaland; 11. Mounties.

**Activity 4.** 1. Type of Bill; 2. woodpecker; 3. flamingo; 4. bald eagle, seagull; 5. six. For the final activity, students create their own chart, so answers will vary.

**Activity 5.** 1. gorillas, orangutans, chimpanzees, gibbons; 2. gorillas, chimpanzees; 3. No, they feed only on plants; 4. orangutans; 5. gibbons. For the final activity, students create their own web, so answers will vary.

**Activity 6.** 1. almost 200 years; 2. No; 3. Students may select any two of the events from 1829 on; 4. David Walker and W. L. Garrison. For the final activity, students create their own time line, so answers will vary.

**Activity 7.** 1. He developed the first written Native American language; 2. 1770, Loudon County, Tennessee; his mother was the daughter of a chief and his father was a white fur trader named Gist or Guess; silversmith and mechanic; tribal honors, yearly allowance from the Cherokee National Council, and the giant redwoods of California were named after him; 1843 in Mexico; 3. Because he thought it would help his people advance; 4. As a Native American he had many disadvantages. He also had to overcome a crippling disability and he was ridiculed by his own people. For Part 2's activity, students research information for a biography and record it on a fact sheet, so answers will vary.

**Activity 8.** 1. the country's flag; 2. The People; 3. Answers may vary but will probably include Way of Life, The Land, Major Cities, The Economy, Government, and History. 4. a. Mountain Ranges; b. Natural Resources; c. Climate; 5. Answers may vary but will probably include Official Name, Location, Area, Population, Capital and Largest City, Major Languages, Major Religious Groups, Government, Chief Products, and Monetary Unit. For Part 2's activity, students research information about a country of their choice and record it on a fact sheet, so answers will vary.

**Activity 9.** Answers to all activities will vary.

**Activity 10.** Answers to the game categories in the Guggenheim Game will vary, but all answers must begin with the letters at the beginning of the row in which they are written.

**Activity 11.** Answers to Matching Game: **1.** k; **2.** c; **3.** a; **4.** i; **5.** j; **6.** h; **7.** g; **8.** p; **9.** o; **10.** l; **11.** d; **12.** e; **13.** f; **14.** n; **15.** m; **16.** b.

**Activity 11.** Answers to Wordsearch Game.

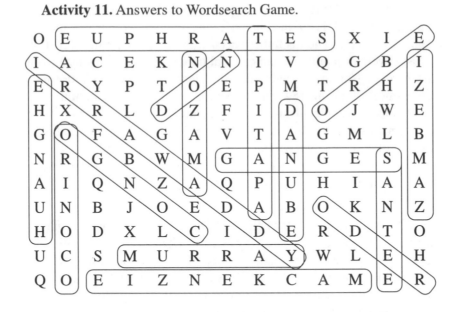

**Activity 12.** Answers to Crossword Puzzle.

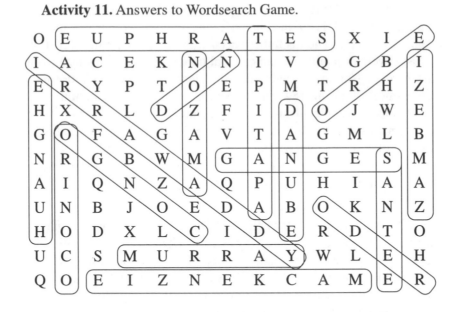

# APPENDIX

## HOBBIES AND OTHER LEISURE-TIME ACTIVITIES

The favorite leisure-time activities of American families include hobbies, arts and crafts, sports, and games. Your youngsters may share their hobbies and other recreational activities with family members or with their friends, or they may choose to pursue an interest by themselves.

THE NEW BOOK OF KNOWLEDGE is an especially valuable resource for the hobbyist or the arts and crafts, sports, or games enthusiast. It contains numerous articles that describe and provide simple directions for a variety of leisure-time pursuits.

|       | Basketball | S | Sailing |
|-------|------------|---|---------|
|       | Bicycling |   | Shuffleboard |
|       | Boardsailing |   | Skateboarding |
|       | Boats and Boating |   | Skiing |
|       | Bobsledding |   | Skin Diving |
|       | Bowling |   | Skydiving |
|       | Boxing |   | Soapbox Derby |
| **C** | Camping |   | Soccer |
|       | Canoeing |   | Softball |
|       | Cheerleading |   | Spelunking |
|       | Croquet |   | Surfing |
| **D** | Diving |   | Swimming |
| **F** | Fencing | **T** | Tennis |
|       | Field Hockey |   | Track and Field |
|       | Fishing | **U-V** | Volleyball |
|       | Football | **W-X-Y-Z** | Water Polo |
| **G** | Golf |   | Waterskiing |
|       | Gymnastics |   | Wrestling |
| **H** | Handball |   |   |
|       | Hiking and Backpacking | **Vol.** | **Indoor Activities and Games** |
|       | Horseback Riding | **B** | Backgammon |
|       | Horse Racing |   | Billiards |
|       | Horseshoe Pitching | **C** | Card Games |
|       | Hostels and Hosteling |   | Charades |
|       | Hunting |   | Checkers |
| **I** | Iceboating |   | Chess |
|       | Ice Hockey |   | Crossword Puzzles |
|       | Ice-Skating | **D** | Darts |
| **J-K** | Jogging and Running |   | Dominoes |
|       | Juggling (Learning the Cascade) | **F** | Folk Dance |
| **J-K** | Karting | **J-K** | Jacks |
|       | Kites | **M** | Magic |
| **L** | Lacrosse | **N** | Number Puzzles and Games |
|       | Little League Baseball | **P** | Plays |
| **M** | Marbles |   | Puzzles |
|       | Mountain Climbing | **Q-R** | Radio, Amateur |
| **P** | Paddle Tennis | **T** | Table Tennis |
|       | Polo | **U-V** | Ventriloquism |
| **Q-R** | Racing |   | Video Production at Home |
|       | Racket Sports | **W-X-Y-Z** | Word Games |
|       | Rifle Marksmanship |   |   |
|       | Roller-Skating |   |   |
|       | Roping |   |   |
|       | Rowing |   |   |
|       | Rugby |   |   |

# LITERATURE

As children browse through THE NEW BOOK OF KNOWLEDGE, they are often captivated by the many literary selections they come upon, sometimes returning to their favorites again and again. Parents, too, spend many pleasurable moments reading selections to youngsters not yet able to read to themselves.

The literary selections in the set include fiction, nonfiction, and poetry—classics, short stories, legends, fairy tales, fables, myths, essays, poems, and excerpts from novels and poems. Some selections accompany the biography of a famous writer. Others appear in articles that discuss a particular type of literature.

Below is a list of the literary selections contained in the encyclopedia. You will find information about selections that are particularly appropriate for your youngster's age-group in the grade-level sections of this STUDY GUIDE.

| Vol. | Article | Literary Selections |
|---|---|---|
| A | Africa, Literature of | African proverbs and riddles |
| | Alcott, Louisa May | Little Women (excerpt) |
| | Andersen, Hans Christian | The Emperor's New Clothes |
| | Arabian Nights | Aladdin and the Wonderful Lamp (excerpt) |
| | | The Forty Thieves (excerpt) |
| | Arthur, King | The Story of Arthur (excerpt, Mallory) |
| B | Barrie, Sir James Matthew | Peter Pan (excerpt) |
| | Bible Stories | Noah's Ark |
| | | David and Goliath |
| | | Jonah |
| | | Daniel in the Lions' Den |
| | | The Boy Jesus |
| | Browning, Elizabeth Barrett and Robert | How Do I Love Thee (from Sonnets from the Portuguese) |
| | | Pied Piper of Hamelin (excerpt) |
| | Buck, Pearl | The Good Earth (excerpt) |
| | Burns, Robert | A Red, Red Rose |
| | Byron, George Gordon, Lord | Childe Harold's Pilgrimage (excerpt) |
| | | The Prisoner of Chillon (excerpt) |
| C | Carroll, Lewis | Alice's Adventures in Wonderland (excerpt) |
| | Christmas Story | Gospel according to Luke |
| | Civil Rights Movement | I Have a Dream (excerpts) |

| Vol. | Article | Literary Selections |
|---|---|---|
| | Columbus, Christopher | The Log of Christopher Columbus' First Voyage to America in the Year 1492, As Copied Out in Brief by Bartholomew Las Casas (excerpt) |
| | Cooper, James Fenimore | The Last of the Mohicans (excerpt) |
| D | Defoe, Daniel | Robinson Crusoe (excerpt) |
| | Diaries and Journals | Anne Frank's Diary (excerpt) |
| | Dickens, Charles | David Copperfield (excerpt) |
| | | Oliver Twist (excerpt) |
| | Dickinson, Emily | A Bird Came Down the Walk |
| | | I'll Tell You How the Sun Rose |
| | Donne, John | Devotions upon Emergent Occasions (excerpt) |
| | Doyle, Sir Arthur Conan | The Red-Headed League (excerpt) |
| | Dumas, Alexandre *Père* and Alexandre *Fils* | The Three Musketeers (excerpt) |
| | Dunbar, Paul Laurence | Promise Fulfilment |
| E | Emerson, Ralph Waldo | The Concord Hymn |
| | Essays | Essay (excerpt, Franklin) |
| F | Fables | The Lion and the Mouse (Aesop) |
| | | The Ant and the Grasshopper (Aesop) |

| Vol. | Article | Literary Selections | Vol. | Article | Literary Selections |
|---|---|---|---|---|---|
| | | The Four Oxen and the Lion (Aesop) | | Grimm, Jacob and Wilhelm | The Shoemaker and the Elves |
| | | The Tyrant Who Became a Just Ruler (Bidpai) | | | Rapunzel |
| | | The Blind Men and the Elephant (Saxe) | | | Hansel and Gretel |
| | | | H | Hawthorne, Nathaniel | Young Goodman Brown |
| | | The Moth and the Star (Thurber) | | Hugo, Victor | Les Miserables (excerpt) |
| | Fairy Tales | The Enchanted Princess (German) | I | Irving, Washington | Rip Van Winkle (excerpt) |
| | | The Princess on the Pea (Andersen) | J-K | Keats, John | I Had a Dove |
| | | | | | Endymion (excerpt) |
| | | The Sleeping Beauty (Perrault) | | | When I Have Fears... |
| | | | | Kipling, Rudyard | The Elephant's Child |
| | | Little Red Riding-Hood (de la Mare) | L | Latin America, Literature of | The Heights of Machu Picchu (excerpt, Neruda) |
| | Field, Eugene | A Dutch Lullaby | | Legends | The Vanishing Hitch-hiker (United States) |
| | Figures of Speech | Silver (de la Mare) | | | Roland and Oliver (France) |
| | | The Toaster (Smith, W. J.) | | | The Legend of Robin Hood (England) |
| | | Dandelions (Frost, F. M.) | | Liberty, Statue of | The New Colossus (excerpt, Lazarus) |
| | | The Little Rose Tree (Field) | | Lincoln, Abraham | Excerpts from Lincoln's speeches, letters, and other writings |
| | | Everyone Sang (Sassoon) | | | |
| | | The Night Will Never Stay (Farjeon) | | London, Jack | The Call of the Wild (excerpt) |
| | | Brooms (Aldis) | | Longfellow, Henry Wadsworth | The Arrow and the Song |
| | | No Shop Does the Bird Use (Coatsworth) | | | |
| | Folklore | Cinderella (Korean) | M | Melville, Herman | Moby Dick (excerpt) |
| | Folklore, American | Coyote Places the Stars | | Milne, A. A. | Missing |
| | | | | Milton, John | L'Allegro (excerpt) |
| | | Wiley and the Hairy Man | N | Nonsense Rhymes | Jabberwocky (Carroll) |
| | Franklin, Benjamin | Quotations from Poor Richard's Almanack (attributed to Benjamin Franklin) | | | Jellyfish Stew (Prelutsky) |
| | | | | | Habits of the Hippopotamus (Guiterman) |
| | French Revolution | The Execution of Marie Antoinette (excerpt, Williams) | | | Eletelephony (Richards) |
| | | | | | The Reason for the Pelican (Ciardi) |
| | Frost, Robert | The Last Word of a Bluebird | | | Antigonish (Mearns) |
| | | The Pasture | | | I Wish That My Room Had a Floor (Burgess) |
| | | Stopping by Woods on a Snowy Evening | | | There Was a Young Lady of Woosester (Anonymous) |
| | | The Road Not Taken | | | There Was an Old Man with a Beard (Lear) |
| G | Gettysburg Address | Gettysburg Address | | | |
| | Grahame, Kenneth | The Wind in the Willows (excerpt) | | | There Was an Old Man of Peru (Anonymous) |

| Vol. | Article | Literary Selections | Vol. | Article | Literary Selections |
|------|---------|---------------------|------|---------|---------------------|
| | Nursery Rhymes | The Old Woman in a Shoe | | | My Shadow |
| | | Jack and Jill | | | Looking-Glass River |
| | | Hey Diddle, Diddle | | | The Swing |
| | | Miss Muffet | | | The Gardener |
| | | Mary's Lamb | | | Bed in Summer |
| | | Humpty Dumpty | | | Kidnapped (excerpt) |
| **P** | Pioneer Life | Oregon Fever (excerpt from a pioneer's diary) | | Swift, Jonathan | Gulliver's Travels (excerpt) |
| | Poe, Edgar Allan | Eldorado | **T** | Tennyson, Alfred, Lord | Crossing the Bar (from The Lady of Shalott) |
| | Poetry | Daffodils (excerpt, Wordsworth) | | Thackeray, William Makepeace | Vanity Fair (excerpt) |
| | | Ode to the West Wind (excerpt, Shelley) | | Thoreau, Henry David | Walden (excerpt) |
| | | Sonnet 18 (Shakespeare) | | Thurber, James | The Great Quillow (excerpt) |
| | | When Lilacs Last in the Dooryard Bloom'd (excerpt, Whitman) | | Tolkien, J. R. R. | The Hobbit (excerpt) |
| | Potter, Beatrix | The Tale of Jemima Puddle-Duck (excerpt) | | Twain, Mark | The Adventures of Tom Sawyer (excerpt) |
| **Q-R** | Revere, Paul | Paul Revere's Ride (excerpts, Longfellow) | | | The Celebrated Jumping Frog of Calaveras County (excerpt) |
| | Rossetti Family | Who Has Seen the Wind? | **W-X-Y-Z** | White, E. B. | Charlotte's Web (excerpt) |
| **S** | Sandburg, Carl | Fog | | Whitman, Walt | When Lilacs Last in the Dooryard Bloom'd |
| | | The Skyscraper to the Moon and How the Green Rat with the Rheumatism Ran a Thousand Miles Twice (Rootabaga Stories) | | Wilder, Laura Ingalls | Little House on the Prairie (excerpt) |
| | | | | Williams, William Carlos | The Red Wheelbarrow |
| | Shelley, Percy Bysshe | To Night | | Wordsworth, William | Daffodils |
| | | Ozymandias | | | My Heart Leaps up When I Behold |
| | Short Stories | The Tell-Tale Heart (excerpt, Poe) | | World War I | In Flanders Fields (McCrae) |
| | | The Gift of the Magi (excerpt, Henry) | **W-X-Y-Z** | Yeats, William Butler | Under Ben Bulben (excerpt) |
| | | Two Soldiers (excerpt, Faulkner) | | | The Lake Isle of Innisfree |
| | Stevenson, Robert Louis | Requiem | | | |

# PROJECTS AND EXPERIMENTS

Many articles in THE NEW BOOK OF KNOWLEDGE include useful and enjoyable projects or experiments. These excellent activities help students improve their understanding of basic concepts by giving them hands-on experiences with ideas or processes they have just read about. In addition, these activities provide many choices and ideas students can use for school projects and fairs in science, mathematics, language and literature, art, music, home economics, and personal hobbies and crafts.

| Vol. | Article | Projects and Experiments |
|------|---------|--------------------------|
| A | Abacus | The Chinese abacus |
|   | Antibiotics | How to grow a *penicillium* mold |
|   | Apple | How to sprout apple seeds |
|   | Arithmetic | Using an addition table |
|   |  | Using a multiplication table |
|   |  | Using estimation strategies |
| B | Balloons and Ballooning | What makes a balloon rise? |
|   | Biology | How a biologist explores nature |
|   | Birds | Bird-watching |
|   | Birds as Pets | Choosing a bird |
|   | Book Reports and Reviews | Choosing a book |
|   |  | How to write a book report |
|   | Bread and Baking | Making yeast bread |
|   | Bulletin Boards | How to make a bulletin board |
| C | Clowns | Suggested ways to apply clown makeup |
|   | Codes and Ciphers | Scytale |
|   |  | Rail fence cipher |
|   |  | Pigpen cipher |
|   |  | Grille |
|   | Coins and Coin Collecting | Coin collecting |
|   | Compositions | How to prepare a composition |
|   | Constellations | Creating new constellations |
|   | Crystals | Growing your own crystals |
| D | Diaries and Journals | How to start your own journal |
|   | Dogs | Choosing a dog |

| Vol. | Article | Projects and Experiments |
|------|---------|--------------------------|
| E | Eclipses | How to watch a solar eclipse |
|   | Experiments and Other Science Activities | Sample report of an experiment: |
|   |  | Controlled experiment with plant fertilizer |
|   |  | How cold temperatures affect seed germination |
|   |  | How fast your reaction time is |
|   |  | How the length of a shadow changes with the seasons |
|   |  | How to build an electric motor |
|   |  | How to create layers of liquids |
|   |  | How to identify acids and bases |
|   |  | How to make a pinhole camera |
|   |  | How to make polymer "slime" |
|   |  | How to observe the Greenhouse Effect |
|   |  | How to use chromatography to separate the components of a dye |
|   |  | How your sense of smell affects your sense of taste |
|   |  | Paper chromotography in color separation of an ink mixture |
| F | Falling Bodies | Demonstration: Air Resistance |
|   | Fiction | How to write fiction |
|   | Fish | How to determine the age of a fish |
|   | Floating and Buoyancy | Demonstration: Archimedes' principle |

| Vol. | Article | Projects and Experiments | Vol. | Article | Projects and Experiments |
|------|---------|--------------------------|------|---------|--------------------------|
| | | How an object's buoyancy can be controlled in a fluid or in the air | J-K | Jewelry | How to make your own jewelry |
| | | How shape can change an object's buoyancy | J-K | Kaleidoscope | How to build a kaleidoscope |
| | Flowers | Flowers and their animal pollinators | | Kites | How to fly your kite |
| | Forces | Demonstrations: | | | How to make a flat kite |
| | | How to find the sum of different forces on an object | | Knitting | Knitting project: squared off sweater |
| | | How the sum of three forces can be represented by vectors | | Knots | How to tie knots |
| | | | L | Leaves | Seeing if leaves need sunlight to survive |
| | Fractions | Comparing fractions | | | Preserving leaves |
| | Fungi | How to make a spore print | | Letter Writing | How to write letters |
| G | Gardens and Gardening | Gardening | | Libraries | How to use your library's reference collection |
| | Gases | Demonstrations: | | Light | How to produce a real image |
| | | How air pressure can support a volume of water | | | How light travels in straight lines |
| | | How increasing the pressure on a gas reduces its volume | | Liquids | Demonstrations: Capillarity— |
| | | | | | The surface tension of liquids |
| | Genealogy | Tracing your family tree | | | The effect of gravity on a drop of liquid |
| | Genetics | See for yourself how traits are inherited | | | The cohesive forces of water |
| | Geometry | How to construct a polyhedron | M | Macramé | How to do macramé |
| | Gift wrapping | Wrapping a gift | | Magnets and Magnetism | How to make an electromagnet |
| | Graphs | How to draw a bar graph | | Maple Syrup and Maple Sugar | Sugar-on-snow parties |
| | Gravity and Gravitation | The Earth's gravity | | Maps and Globes | Be your own map maker |
| | Greeting Cards | How to make a pop-up greeting card | | Matter | Study the forms of matter |
| | Gyroscope | Properties of the gyroscope | | Microscopes | How to build Van Leeuwenhoek's microscope |
| H | Hair and Hairstyling | How to braid hair | | | How to care for your microscope |
| | Heat | Locke's experiment | | | Some things to see with your microscope |
| | Hieroglyphic Writing Systems | How to make your own hieroglyphs | N | Number Patterns | Finding patterns in Fibonacci numbers |
| | Houseplants | How to grow houseplants | | | Demonstrations: |
| I | Ink | Secret messages | | | Finding patterns in lattices |
| | Interior Decorating | Decorating your room | | | Finding patterns in Pascal's triangle |
| | Inuit | How to build a snow house | | | Finding patterns in polygonal numbers |
| | | | | Number Puzzles and Games | Cats and mice |
| | | | | | Sisters, sisters, sisters |
| | | | | | Tower of Hanoi |

| Vol. | Article | Projects and Experiments |
|---|---|---|
| | | Numbers in boxes |
| | | Cards in order |
| | | Pennies at home |
| | | How tall will you grow? |
| | | Another weigh |
| | | Letter play |
| | | Number play |
| | | A corn-y story |
| | | Clockworks |
| | | I know your number |
| | | A dice trick |
| | | Which door? |
| | | Which pill? |
| | | Where are those signs? |
| | | Digits everywhere |
| | | Number pyramids |
| | | Pig |
| | | A number board |
| | Numbers and Number Systems | Recognizing numbers in everyday situations |
| | Numerals and Numeration Systems | Can you read and write Egyptian numerals? |
| O | Optical Illusions | Making a miniature "movie" |
| | Osmosis | Showing osmosis |
| | Outlines | Preparing an outline for a talk or composition |
| P | Papier-Mâché | How to make a papier-mâché piggy bank |
| | Parties | Planning a party |
| | Peanuts and Peanut Products | How to make your own peanut butter |
| | Pets | How to care for pets |
| | Photography | Developing the film |
| | | Printing the photographs |
| | Plant Pests | The gall maker and its home |
| | Plants | How propagation works |
| | | How plants move |
| | Plays | How to play the blocking game |
| | | How to play hot seat |
| | | How to play the scarf game |
| | | How to use makeup |
| | Poetry | How to write poetry |
| | Public Speaking | Preparing a speech |
| | Puppets and Marionettes | How to make a hand puppet |
| | | How to make a simple stage |

| Vol. | Article | Projects and Experiments |
|---|---|---|
| | | How to make a marionette |
| Q-R | Radio, Amateur | How to become a ham radio operator |
| | Recipes | Dinner for four; sweets and snacks |
| | Recorder | How to play the recorder |
| | Records and Record Collecting | Record collecting as a hobby |
| | Rubbings | The wax method |
| | | The graphite method |
| S | Shells | Collecting shells |
| | Soils | Do growing plants break up rocks? |
| | | Why should topsoil be conserved? |
| | | Observing the differences in soil particles |
| | | Testing to see if soil is acid |
| | Solar System | Creating a model of the solar system |
| | Sound and Ultrasonics | Demonstrations you can do with sound |
| | Stamps and Stamp Collecting | Collecting stamps |
| | Sun | Observing sunspots |
| T | Telegraph | Make your own telegraph set |
| | Terrariums | How to make a terrarium |
| | Tests and Test Taking | General strategies |
| | Ticks | How to safely remove a tick |
| | Tongue Twisters | Five tough tongue twisters |
| | Topology | Problems in topology |
| U-V | Valentines | How to make valentine cards and crafts |
| W-X-Y-Z | Water | Conserving water at home |
| | | Purifying dirty water |
| | Weather | How to make a dew point apparatus |
| | | How to estimate wind speed |
| | | How to make a barometer |
| | | How to make a rain gauge |
| | Weaving | Learning to weave |

| Vol. | Article | Projects and Experiments | Vol. | Article | Projects and Experiments |
|------|---------|--------------------------|------|---------|--------------------------|
| | Woodworking | How to make a CD rack | | Worms | Examining power |
| | Work, Power, and Machines | Reducing friction | | | How to make an earth-worm farm |
| | | The effect of gravity | | | |

# WONDER QUESTIONS

Wonder Questions have been an integral part of the encyclopedia since the original 1911 edition of THE BOOK OF KNOWLEDGE. They have always been a source of pleasure and adventure for those of us who are in constant search of interesting bits of information about everything.

| Vol. | Article | Wonder Questions |
|------|---------|------------------|
| A | Abolition Movement | What were the Gag Rules? |
| | Aerodynamics | What keeps a plane up in the air? |
| | Africa | What and where are the Mountains of the Moon? |
| | African Americans | What is Kwanzaa? |
| | Apple | Who was Johnny Appleseed? |
| | Asia | What and where is Asia Minor? |
| | Astronauts | Why are astronauts weightless? |
| | Astronomy | How do astronomers measure distances in space? |
| | Atmosphere | Is the Earth's atmosphere warming? |
| | Automation | What is automation? What is feedback? |
| B | Badminton | What makes a champion? |
| | Balloons and Ballooning | What makes a balloon rise? |
| | Bats | How do bats find their way in the dark? |
| | Bees | Are there really "killer" bees? |
| | Bermuda | What is the Bermuda Triangle? |
| | Birds as Pets | Can people get parrot fever? |
| | Blindness | What is a talking book? |
| | Blood | What is blood made of? |
| | Body, Human | What is the largest organ of your body? |
| | Books | What information is on a copyright page? |
| | Brain | Is it true that we use only 10 percent of our brains? |

| Vol. | Article | Wonder Questions |
|------|---------|------------------|
| | Bridges | Why were some of the early bridges in America covered? |
| | Building Construction | Why is a tree or an American flag sometimes placed on the highest part of a building under construction? |
| | | Why don't tall buildings blow down in a strong wind? |
| | Bullfighting | How did bullfighting begin? |
| | Business | What are gross income and net income? |
| | Butterflies and Moths | How can you tell a butterfly from a moth? |
| C | Calendar | Why are the abbreviations B.C. and A.D. used with dates? |
| | Candles | Why do we put lighted candles on a birthday cake and then blow them out? |
| | Card Games | What is the origin of the suits in a deck of cards? |
| | | Why are there three face cards in each suit? |
| | Cats, Wild | What is a cat's best defense? |
| | Cement and Concrete | How is cement made? |
| | Census | How is the U.S. population census taken? |
| | Checkers | How old is checkers? |
| | Circus | What was the greatest feat in the history of trapeze flying? |
| | Climate | How can scientists tell what climates were like a long time ago? |
| | Clowns | Why don't most clowns speak? |

| Vol. | Article | Wonder Questions |
|---|---|---|
| | Coins and Coin Collecting | Why are some coins grooved around the edge? |
| | Colonial Life in America | What did the colonists eat? |
| | Columbus, Christopher | Where did Columbus really land on his first voyage to the New World? |
| | | What were the consequences of Columbus' voyage in 1492? |
| | Communism | What are the differences between Socialism and Communism? |
| | Computers | Will computers ever outsmart humans? |
| | Cosmic Rays | Why are cosmic rays important? |
| D | Dairying and Dairy Products | What is a dairy farm? |
| | Debates and Discussions | What is the difference between a debate and a discussion? |
| | Deserts | How did Death Valley get its name? |
| | Dinosaurs | What were dinosaurs? |
| | | What was the deadliest dinosaur that ever walked the earth? |
| | Doctors | Is the Surgeon General really a surgeon? |
| | Dogs | What are the dog days? |
| | Dollar | How can you tell if a bill is counterfeit? |
| | Dyes and Dyeing | What makes dyes fade? |
| E | Earth | How do earthquakes help scientists learn about the Earth's interior? |
| | Earth, History of | How do geologists learn about the history of the planet Earth? |
| | Economics | What is the amazing "invisible hand"? |
| | Ecuador | What were the enchanted islands? |
| | Electricity | What is static electricity? |
| | Electric Motors | What makes electric motors run? |
| | Electronics | What is nanotechnology? |
| | Elements, Chemical | What is the island of stability? |

| Vol. | Article | Wonder Questions |
|---|---|---|
| | Elevators and Escalators | How fast can the fastest elevators climb? |
| | England, History of | What happened to the princes in the Tower? |
| | Europe | Where and what are the Low Countries? |
| | Evolution | What is artificial selection? |
| | Exploration and Discovery | Why was the New World named "America"? |
| | Explosives | What is an explosive? |
| F | Fairy Tales | Where did fairy tales come from? |
| | Fallout | How soon does fallout fall? |
| | | How long does fallout last? |
| | Family | What is a first, second, and first cousin once removed? |
| | Fibers | What is a fiber? |
| | Fillmore, Millard | What was the Know-Nothing Party? |
| | First Aid | What is a "Good Samaritan"? |
| | Fish | How big do fish grow? |
| | | What fish's "mother" is really its father? |
| | | Do fish sleep? |
| | Fishing | When was the fishing reel invented? |
| | Fission | Where does fission take place? |
| | Flowers | How big do flowers grow? |
| | Fog and Smog | Why is it difficult to see through fog? |
| | Food Preservation | What makes food spoil? |
| | | Who was Clarence Birdseye? |
| | Ford, Henry | What is the Ford Foundation? |
| | Fossils | What is the most precious fossil in the world? |
| | Fountains | Why do people throw coins into fountains? |
| G | Geiger Counter | How does a Geiger (Geiger-Muller) counter work? |
| | Gemstones | Where are gemstones found? |
| | Genetics | Are genetically engineered crops safe? |
| | Geology | What is geomythology? |

| Vol. | Article | Wonder Questions | Vol. | Article | Wonder Questions |
|------|---------|------------------|------|---------|------------------|
| | Geometry | What is Pi? | | Inventions | What is the difference between an invention and a discovery? |
| | Glue and Other Adhesives | What makes adhesives stick? | J–K | Jellyfish and Other Coelenterates | What is a reef community? |
| | | What is the best adhesive? | | Jesus Christ | What does the name "Jesus Christ" mean? |
| | Gold | What is "Fool's Gold"? | | Jewelry | What is a carat? |
| | Gothic Art and Architecture | What are gargoyles? | | Journalism | What are tabloids? |
| | Grasses | Are all grasses alike? | | Jupiter | What is the Great Red Spot on Jupiter? |
| | Gravity and Gravitation | What is the center of gravity? | J-K | Karate | What is the difference between karate and judo? |
| | Guns and Ammunition | What was the Gatling gun? | | Kennedy, John F. | Who was Lee Harvey Oswald? |
| H | Hair and Hairstyling | Why doesn't it hurt to cut your hair? | | Kidneys | Can a person survive with only one kidney? |
| | | What makes hair curly? | | Kindergarten and Nursery Schools | What is Project Head Start? |
| | Heart | What is a heart murmur? | | Kingdoms of Living Things | How many kinds of living things are there? |
| | Heat | How hot is the sun? | | Kites | How does a kite fly? |
| | | What does it mean to be "red hot"? | L | Law and Law Enforcement | What does it mean to be "admitted to the bar"? |
| | Helicopters | How does a helicopter fly? | | Lead | What is the "lead" in a lead pencil? |
| | Himalayas | Is there really an Abominable Snowman? | | Learning | Did ancient Egyptians understand the importance of the brain? |
| | Holocaust | What was Kristallnacht? | | | What is an IQ test? |
| | Huguenots | Who ordered the St. Bartholomew's Day Massacre? | | Leather | How is leather made? |
| I | Ice | What started as a dirty snowball, grew to several miles wide, and can only be seen every 76 years? | | Life | Is cloning a way to create new life? |
| | | | | Light | How do polarized sunglasses work? |
| | Ice Cream | Who invented the ice cream cone? | | Lizards | Why do chameleons change color? |
| | Indians, American | Where are the Indians now? | | Louis XIV | Why was Louis XIV called the Sun King? |
| | Inflation and Deflation | What causes an inflation? | | Lungs | What is a yawn? |
| | | What causes a deflation? | M | Mammals | How big do mammals grow? |
| | | Who benefits from inflation? | | Mars | Is there life on Mars? |
| | | Who benefits from deflation? | | Mathematics, History of | Who invented mathematical signs? |
| | | How can governments control inflation and deflation? | | Medicine, Tools and Techniques of | Why must a fever thermometer be shaken? |
| | Insects | What is an insect? | | Microwaves | Why do foods cook faster in a microwave oven? |
| | | How long do insects live? | | | |
| | International Trade | What are free ports and foreign-trade zones? | | | |

| Vol. | Article | Wonder Questions | Vol. | Article | Wonder Questions |
|---|---|---|---|---|---|
| | Middle East | What is the Fertile Crescent? | | Oceanography | Is there a new source of energy in the oceans? |
| | Milky Way | How far away is the nearest galaxy? | | Old Age | What are the problems of old age? |
| | Moon | Is there water on the moon? | | Onion | Why do most people "cry" when chopping onions? |
| | Moss | When is a moss not a moss? | | Opinion Polls | How is an opinion survey done? |
| | Mountains | What is the longest mountain chain in the world? | P | Pacific Ocean and Islands | What is the Great Barrier Reef? |
| | Muscular System | What is the levator labii superioris alaeque nasi? | | Paper | How is paper recycled? |
| | | | | Peace Movements | What is a conscientious objector? |
| | Museums | Who works in a museum? | | Pearls | What makes a pearl valuable? |
| | Music | What is the origin of clef signs? | | | How are artificial pearls made? |
| | | Why are so many musical terms written in Italian? | | Perfumes | What are toilet water and cologne? |
| | Musical Instruments | How do musical instruments make sounds? | | Photosynthesis | How do plants get energy from sunlight? |
| | | | | | How can plants produce more food? |
| | Mythology | Why are similar myths found throughout the world? | | Planets | Do planets exist beyond our solar system? |
| N | National Cemeteries | Who may be buried in a U.S. National Cemetery? | | Plants | How big can a plant grow? |
| | | | | | Why do leaves change color in the autumn? |
| | National Park System | What is the largest U.S. national park? | | | Which plant has the biggest seed? |
| | Navigation | What is a ship's log? | | Plays | Where did the terms "downstage" and "upstage" come from? |
| | | How do areas qualify to become part of the U.S. National Park System? | | Pluto | Is Pluto really a planet? |
| | | | | Political Parties | Why are some political parties called "left" and others "right"? |
| | Neptune | What is the outermost planet in the solar system? | | Population | Will population growth stop? |
| | Newspapers | Is the news truth? | | Psychology | What is personality? |
| | | What is a press release? | | Public Relations | What is the difference between public relations and advertising? |
| | Noise | How does noise affect hearing? | | | |
| | Numbers and Number Systems | What is infinity? | | Pumps | How do pumps work? |
| | Numerals and Numeration Systems | Who invented zero? | Q-R | Rabbits and Hares | What is the difference between a rabbit and a hare? |
| | Nursery Rhymes | Was Mother Goose a real person? | | Radio | Why can you hear radio stations from farther away at night? |
| | Nylon and Other Synthetic Fibers | How are synthetic fibers named? | | | What is static? |
| O | Ocean Liners | What caused the *Titanic* tragedy? | | | |

| Vol. | Article | Wonder Questions |
|---|---|---|
| | Radio and Radar Astronomy | Does life as we know it on Earth exist anywhere else in the universe? |
| | Railroads | Why does the standard gauge measure 4 feet 8 12 inches (1.4 meters)? |
| | Rain, Snow, Sleet, and Hail | What is the shape of a falling raindrop? |
| | Reformation | What was the Counter-Reformation? |
| | Renaissance | What is a Renaissance Man? |
| | Revolutionary War | Who was Molly Pitcher? |
| | Roman Catholic Church | What are holy days? |
| | | Why is it called the Roman Catholic Church? |
| | | What are sacramentals? |
| S | Salt | How do we get salt? |
| | Saturn | Where did Saturn's rings come from? |
| | Science | What is pseudoscience? |
| | Seasons | Why is it hotter in summer than it is in winter? |
| | Sharks, Skates, and Rays | How do sharks find their prey? |
| | Ships and Shipping | Why are the left and right sides of a ship called port and starboard? |
| | | Why are ships christened with champagne? |
| | Silver | Why the name "sterling"? |
| | Sleep | What happens during sleep? |
| | Soils | Can changes in temperature break up rocks? |
| | | Do growing plants break up rocks? |
| | | Why should topsoil be conserved? |
| | Sound and Ultrasonics | Why do you hear a roaring sound, like the sound of the sea, when you hold a large snail or conch shell over your ear? |

| Vol. | Article | Wonder Questions |
|---|---|---|
| | | Suppose a tree crashes to the ground in a forest where there is no one to hear it. Does the sound exist? |
| | Space Exploration and Travel | What kinds of animals have traveled in space? |
| | Spiders | What is the largest spider? |
| | Spies | What are some types of espionage agents? |
| | Stars | What are stars made of? Why do stars twinkle? |
| | Stocks and Bonds | What are blue chip stocks? |
| | | What is "cornering the market"? |
| | Stomach | What makes a stomach growl? |
| | Stonehenge | Who built Stonehenge? |
| | Submarines | How is a submarine navigated underwater? |
| | Sun | Does sunspot activity affect the Earth's climate? |
| | Supersonic Flight | Is it possible to be a passenger in a supersonic airplane? |
| T | Taxonomy | Why are the scientific names of plants and animals in Latin? |
| | Tea | How is tea made? |
| | Technology | What is high technology? |
| | Television | What are television ratings? |
| | Thunder and Lightning | What is thunder? |
| | | How can you tell how close a thunderstorm is to you? |
| | Tides | What are ocean tides? |
| U-V | Un-American Activities Committee, House | Who were the Hollywood Ten? |
| | Underground Railroad | What were the fugitive slave laws? |
| | Union of Soviet Socialist Republics | What was the Warsaw Pact? |
| | United Kingdom | What's in a name? |
| | United States, Armed Forces of the | What are special forces? |

| Vol. | Article | Wonder Questions | Vol. | Article | Wonder Questions |
|------|---------|------------------|------|---------|------------------|
| | | What does "GI" stand for? | | Vitamins and Minerals | Are natural vitamin or mineral supplements better than synthetic supplements? |
| | United States, Congress of the | What is the Congressional Record? | W-X-Y-Z | Waterpower | Why don't we get all our electric power from water? |
| | Universe | Does the universe have a center? | | | |
| | Universities and Colleges | What is the Ivy League? | | Waxes | Who invented wax paper? |
| | | Why are caps and gowns worn at graduation? | | Weather | What is El Niño? |
| | | | | Weights and Measures | How long is a meter? |
| | Uranus | Which planet has the strangest moon in the solar system? | | Westward Movement | What was the Northwest Ordinance? |
| U-V | Van Buren, Martin | Who were the Barnburners? | | Whales | Where did whales come from? |
| | Venus | Why are Venus and Earth so different from one another? | | Wonders of the World | What are the wonders of our world? |
| | Video Recording | What is instant replay? | | Wood and Wood Products | What is wood? |
| | | What is the difference between VHS and Beta? | | Wool | How is wool obtained? |
| | Viruses | Can just one virus make you sick? | | World War II | Who were the Sullivan Brothers? |
| | | | | | What does D day mean? |

# "DID YOU KNOW THAT . . . " Features

A younger relation of THE NEW BOOK OF KNOWLEDGE's well-known Wonder Questions, these features provide fascinating information on a wide range of topics.

| Vol. | Article | Did you know that... |
|------|---------|----------------------|
| A | Animals | tiny invertebrates, called leaf-cutter ants, can carry cut up leaves and flowers more than twice their own size? |
| | | the bird called an oxpecker spends almost its entire life clinging to the back of a hoofed animal such as the impala? |
| | | the bee hummingbird is the smallest living bird? |
| | | the largest structures ever built by living creatures are coral reefs? |
| | Antibiotics | our current antibiotics are focused on stopping only bacteria? |
| | Ants | ants were used as the first method of biological pest control? |
| | Atoms | it was not until the late 1890's that scientists began to understand the internal structure of the atom? |
| B | Blood | the first successful blood transfusion was performed more than 500 years ago by the Incas of South America? |
| | Body, Human | some 650 muscles cover the body's skeleton? |
| | | there are more red blood cells in the body than any other kind of cell? |
| | Boys & Girls Clubs | many famous personalities are former Boys & Girls Club members? |

| Vol. | Article | Did you know that... |
|------|---------|----------------------|
| | Brain | as many as 250,000 new brain cells are formed at times during a baby's development inside its mother? |
| C | Camping | the longest camping journey took just under two years? |
| | Cats, Wild | the sand cat can live without ever drinking water? |
| | | some cats fish for their dinner? |
| D | Dinosaurs | dinosaurs were watchful parents that carefully tended their young? |
| | Dogs | there is one person who is credited with being the most fanatical dog lover of all time? |
| | Dollar | on average, a $1 bill lasts only 18 months before it is too worn to continue circulating? |
| E | Emancipation Proclamation | the Emancipation Proclamation directly led to the adoption of the 13th Amendment to the U.S. Constitution? |
| | Emotions | a lie detector tries to take advantage of the body's response to feelings? |
| F | Fairies | very few fairy tales actually feature fairies? |
| | Field Hockey | field hockey is one of the only sports whose rules are frequently examined and modified? |
| | Fire | the first matches were invented in China in the year 577? |

| Vol. | Article | Did you know that... | Vol. | Article | Did you know that... |
|------|---------|---------------------|------|---------|---------------------|
|  | Fish | Aristotle, one of the world's most influential philosophers, was the first ichthyologist? piranhas are the most ferocious freshwater fish in the world? | J-K | Jellyfish and Other Coelenterates | the clownfish can swim and rest among the sea anemone's deadly tentacles without getting stung? |
|  | Flowers | the first plants had no flowers? |  | Jupiter | that Jupiter was the first outer planet to be explored simultaneously by two spacecraft at close range? |
|  | Folk Dance | square dancing with a caller is a uniquely American tradition? | J-K | Kingdoms of Living Things | binominal nomenclature—the method of naming living things—was introduced in 1735 and is still used today? |
|  | Folklore | singers of epic poems can spontaneously compose works that go on for hours at a time? |  |  |  |
|  | Founders of the United States | six men signed both the Declaration of Independence and the Constitution of the United States? | L | Light | you see scattered light every time you look at the sky? |
|  |  |  |  | Liver | the liver is one of the few parts of the body that can regenerate? |
|  | Fungi | a fungus disease was responsible for causing a famine that resulted in the starvation and death of more than 1 million people? |  | Lobsters | an American lobster was recorded as the heaviest crustacean ever caught? |
|  |  |  |  | Locomotives | steam locomotives are often classified according to their wheel arrangement? |
| G | Gases | every time you turn on your television set you have "tuned into" a series of products that were produced with gases? | M | Magnets and Magnetism | some creatures can detect and use Earth's magnetic field to survive? |
|  | Genetics | scientists have made mice glow green using DNA from jellyfish? |  | Microbiology | pizza is a tasty meal because of microbes? |
| H | Hawks | hawks can fly hundreds of miles without getting tired? |  | Mollusks | the largest of all invertebrates (animals without a backbone) is a mollusk? |
|  | Hibernation | that the study of animal hibernation may one day lead to treatments for a number of medical problems in humans? |  | Monkeys | the only monkeys in Europe are called apes? |
|  |  |  | N | National Forest System | some forests actually need fire? |
|  |  |  |  | Newspapers | the headline to a story is almost never written by the reporter who writes the story, but by an editor? |
|  | Hoofed Mammals | the ability of deer to regrow large, bony antlers each year is somewhat of a biological marvel? |  | Norse Mythology | some of our modern English names for the days of the week come from Norse mythology? |

| Vol. | Article | Did you know that... | Vol. | Article | Did you know that... |
|------|---------|----------------------|------|---------|----------------------|
| | Number Patterns | it is possible to add all the counting numbers from 1 through 100 in a minute or two—without using a calculator? | Q-R | Railroads | railroads opened vast regions to farming, mining, lumbering, and manufacturing? |
| O | Olympic Games | some sports and events at the Olympic Games have been discontinued over the years? | | Rocks | the oldest known rock ever found is almost 4 billion years old? |
| P | Percentage | there are laws regulating whether a discount or the sales tax is calculated first on a purchase? | S | Science Fiction | for a brief, terrifying time on October 30, 1938, thousands of people across the United States were convinced that science fiction had become science fact? |
| | Photoelectricity | the photovoltaic effect was discovered in 1839 by French physicist Antoine-César Becquerel? | | Skeletal System | a baby has about 275 bones, while a full-grown adult has only 206 bones? |
| | Plankton | the largest animal on Earth depends on some of the smallest living things for its survival? | | Space Exploration and Travel | the "space race" began on October 4, 1957, with the launch of the Soviet Union's *Sputnik 1* satellite? |
| | Plants | a plant was responsible for causing the famous mutiny aboard the British ship H.M.S. *Bounty*? | | | astronaut and geologist Harrison H. Schmitt was the first scientist to explore the moon and also the last person to set foot on the moon? |
| | | the mostly widely used pain reliever, aspirin, was named after Spiraea, a genus of flowering shrubs in the rose family? | | | some humans have spent many months living in space? |
| | | some plants can grow several inches in a matter of hours? | | | temperatures in space can be twice as high or twice as low as those in the hottest or coldest places on Earth? |
| | Plastics | some plastics are stronger than steel? | | Spiders | the class Arachnida takes its name from the mythological character Arachne? |
| | Plays | it is all right to "cheat" when you are acting? | U-V | Vegetables | many vegetables are related? |
| | Pottery | there are small studios in many communities where you can paint your own pottery? | | Volcanoes | volcanoes are found not only on Earth but on other planets and satellites in our solar system? |
| | Prehistoric People | scientists discovered an important message contained in the bones of a Neanderthal who lived more than 30,000 years ago? | W-X-Y-Z | Weather | the United States experiences more severe storms and flooding than any other country in the world? |

# FUN WITH WONDER QUESTIONS

The following pages contain a selection of Wonder Questions from THE NEW BOOK OF KNOWLEDGE. These pages can be photocopied, and the Wonder Questions can be cut apart and handed out for use in home and classroom activities. The volume and article in which each Wonder Question and its answer appear are also given. Students can try to guess the answers to the questions and then consult the encyclopedia to find the correct answers.

A complete listing of all the Wonder Questions in the encyclopedia begins on page 254. It can be used to create more Wonder Question activities.

## What were the Gag Rules?

**Volume A**

Abolition Movement

THE NEW BOOK OF KNOWLEDGE

## What and where are the Mountains of the Moon?

**Volume A**

Africa

THE NEW BOOK OF KNOWLEDGE

## What is Kwanzaa?

**Volume A**

African Americans

THE NEW BOOK OF KNOWLEDGE

## Why are astronauts weightless?

**Volume A**

Astronauts

THE NEW BOOK OF KNOWLEDGE

## What makes a balloon rise?

**Volume B**

Balloons and Ballooning

THE NEW BOOK OF KNOWLEDGE

## What is the Bermuda Triangle?

**Volume B**

Bermuda

THE NEW BOOK OF KNOWLEDGE

**WONDER QUESTION**

## What is a talking book?

**Volume B**

Blindness

THE NEW BOOK OF KNOWLEDGE

---

**WONDER QUESTION**

## What is the largest organ of your body?

**Volume B**

Body, Human

THE NEW BOOK OF KNOWLEDGE

---

**WONDER QUESTION**

## Why were some of the early bridges in America covered?

**Volume B**

Bridges

THE NEW BOOK OF KNOWLEDGE

---

**WONDER QUESTION**

## What are gross income and net income?

**Volume B**

Business

THE NEW BOOK OF KNOWLEDGE

---

**WONDER QUESTION**

## Why are the abbreviations "B.C." and "A.D." used with dates?

**Volume C**

Calendar

THE NEW BOOK OF KNOWLEDGE

---

**WONDER QUESTION**

## Why do we put lighted candles on a birthday cake and then blow them out?

**Volume C**

Candles

THE NEW BOOK OF KNOWLEDGE

WONDER QUESTION

# What did the colonists eat?

**Volume C**

Colonial Life in America

THE NEW BOOK OF KNOWLEDGE

WONDER QUESTION

# What was the deadliest dinosaur that ever walked the earth?

**Volume D**

Dinosaurs

THE NEW BOOK OF KNOWLEDGE

WONDER QUESTION

# Where and what are the Low Countries?

**Volume E**

Europe

THE NEW BOOK OF KNOWLEDGE

WONDER QUESTION

# Why was the New World named "America"?

**Volume E**

Exploration and Discovery

THE NEW BOOK OF KNOWLEDGE

WONDER QUESTION

# What is a "Good Samaritan"?

**Volume F**

First Aid

THE NEW BOOK OF KNOWLEDGE

WONDER QUESTION

# How big do fish grow?

**Volume F**

Fish

THE NEW BOOK OF KNOWLEDGE

## What is the most precious fossil in the world?

**Volume F**

Fossils

THE NEW BOOK OF KNOWLEDGE

## Why do people throw coins into fountains?

**Volume F**

Fountains

THE NEW BOOK OF KNOWLEDGE

## What is Pi?

**Volume G**

Geometry

THE NEW BOOK OF KNOWLEDGE

## What is "Fool's Gold"?

**Volume G**

Gold

THE NEW BOOK OF KNOWLEDGE

## What are gargoyles?

**Volume G**

Gothic Art and Architecture

THE NEW BOOK OF KNOWLEDGE

## Why doesn't it hurt to cut your hair?

**Volume H**

Hair and Hairstyling

THE NEW BOOK OF KNOWLEDGE

## WONDER QUESTION

### What is the Great Red Spot on Jupiter?

**Volume J**

Jupiter

THE NEW BOOK OF KNOWLEDGE

## WONDER QUESTION

### What is a yawn?

**Volume L**

Lungs

THE NEW BOOK OF KNOWLEDGE

## WONDER QUESTION

### Is there life on Mars?

**Volume M**

Mars

THE NEW BOOK OF KNOWLEDGE

## WONDER QUESTION

### What is the longest mountain chain in the world?

**Volume M**

Mountains

THE NEW BOOK OF KNOWLEDGE

## WONDER QUESTION

### Who may be buried in a U.S. national cemetery?

**Volume N**

National Cemeteries

THE NEW BOOK OF KNOWLEDGE

## WONDER QUESTION

### What is the largest U.S. national park?

**Volume N**

National Park System

THE NEW BOOK OF KNOWLEDGE

## WONDER QUESTION

### What is the outermost planet in the solar system?

**Volume N**

Neptune

THE NEW BOOK OF KNOWLEDGE

## WONDER QUESTION

### What is a press release?

**Volume N**

Newspapers

THE NEW BOOK OF KNOWLEDGE

## WONDER QUESTION

### Why do most people "cry" when chopping onions?

**Volume O**

Onion

THE NEW BOOK OF KNOWLEDGE

## WONDER QUESTION

### How is paper recycled?

**Volume P**

Paper

THE NEW BOOK OF KNOWLEDGE

## WONDER QUESTION

### Why do leaves change color in the autumn?

**Volume P**

Plants

THE NEW BOOK OF KNOWLEDGE

## WONDER QUESTION

### Who was Molly Pitcher?
**Volume Q-R**

Revolutionary War

THE NEW BOOK OF KNOWLEDGE

## WONDER QUESTION

### Why is it hotter in summer than it is in winter?

**Volume S**

Seasons

THE NEW BOOK OF KNOWLEDGE

## WONDER QUESTION

### What is the largest spider?

**Volume S**

Spiders

THE NEW BOOK OF KNOWLEDGE

## WONDER QUESTION

### Why do stars twinkle?

**Volume S**

Stars

THE NEW BOOK OF KNOWLEDGE

## WONDER QUESTION

### What makes a stomach growl?

**Volume S**

Stomach

THE NEW BOOK OF KNOWLEDGE

## WONDER QUESTION

### Who built Stonehenge?

**Volume S**

Stonehenge

THE NEW BOOK OF KNOWLEDGE

## WONDER QUESTION

### What are television ratings?

**Volume T**

Television

THE NEW BOOK OF KNOWLEDGE

## WONDER QUESTION

### How can you tell how close a thunderstorm is to you?

**Volume T**

Thunder and Lightning

THE NEW BOOK OF KNOWLEDGE

## WONDER QUESTION

### What were the fugitive slave laws?

**Volume U-V**

Underground Railroad

THE NEW BOOK OF KNOWLEDGE

## WONDER QUESTION

### What does "GI" stand for?

**Volume U-V**

United States, Armed Forces of the

THE NEW BOOK OF KNOWLEDGE

## WONDER QUESTION

### Who were the Barnburners?

**Volume U-V**

Van Buren, Martin

THE NEW BOOK OF KNOWLEDGE

## WONDER QUESTION

### What is instant replay?

**Volume U-V**

Video Recording

THE NEW BOOK OF KNOWLEDGE

## WONDER QUESTION

### What was the Northwest Ordinance?

**Volume W-X-Y-Z**

Westward Movement

THE NEW BOOK OF KNOWLEDGE